MEMOIRS

MEMOIRS

Andrei Sakharov

TRANSLATED FROM THE RUSSIAN
BY RICHARD LOURIE

HUTCHINSON
London Sydney Auckland Johannesburg

This edition first published in 1990 by Hutchinson

Random Century Group
20 Vauxhall Bridge Road, London, SW1V 2SA

Random Century Australia (Pty) Ltd,
20 Alfred Street, Milsons Point, Sydney, NSW 2061 Australia

Random Century New Zealand Ltd,
PO Box 40-086, Glenfield, Auckland 10, New Zealand

Random Century South Africa (Pty) Ltd,
PO Box 337, Bergvlei, 2012 South Africa

Owing to limitations of space, all acknowledgements of permission to reprint previously published material will be found following the index.

British Library Cataloguing in Publication Data

Sakharov, Andrei (Andrei Dimitrievich)
  Memoirs.
  1. Soviet Union. Dissidents: Sakharov, Andrei (Andrei Dimitrievich)
  I. Title
  364.131

  ISBN 0-09-174636-1

Printed in England by Clays Ltd, St Ives plc

For Lusia

CONTENTS

Contents

Contents

LIST OF ILLUSTRATIONS

Except for those starred, all photos are courtesy of Elena Bonner

FOREWORD

Other civilizations, perhaps more successful ones, may exist an infinite number of times on the preceding and following pages of the Book of the Universe. Yet we should not minimize our sacred endeavors in this world, where, like faint glimmers in the dark, we have emerged for a moment from the nothingness of unconsciousness into material existence. We must make good the demands of reason and create a life worthy of ourselves and of the goals we only dimly perceive.

From the Nobel Lecture of
Andrei Sakharov (1921–1989)

ON DECEMBER 14, 1989, the last day of his life, Andrei Sakharov addressed a contentious meeting of independent deputies in the Soviet Congress, urging them to fight for political pluralism and a market economy and to seek support from the people, "who have finally found a way to express their will." He returned home late that evening and retired to his study, telling his guests he had to prepare for the Congress, as "tomorrow there will be a battle." A short while later, his wife found his body: the heart that had kept freedom of conscience and intellect alive in the Soviet Union during long years of darkness had stopped beating.

Eulogies followed in the press and on television. The official obituary, signed by Gorbachev and other political and scientific notables, admitted that Sakharov's exile to Gorky had been "a crude injustice"; hailed him as "an outstanding scientist and civic leader, a man of honor, of candor"; and acknowledged that "everything Andrei Dmitrievich did was dictated by his conscience, by his deep-rooted humanitarian convictions."

At funeral services held on December 18, physicists who had been Sakharov's colleagues praised the genius of his scientific work, Sergei Kovalev and Tatyana Velikanova spoke of his significance for the human rights movement, and the Estonian deputy Marju Lauristin paid homage to him as "the incarnation of intellectual courage and conscience, of the true Russian spirit." World leaders, including George Bush, Margaret Thatcher, Pope John Paul II, and Lech Walesa, sent messages of condolence. But in my view the most impressive tributes to Andrei Sakharov were the red and white carnations, mingled with tears, brought by tens of thousands of ordinary Soviet citizens as they filed past his bier in the Palace of Youth, and the sentiments they inscribed in the Book of Remembrance: "Thank you for existing." "Forgive us for all the misfortune we caused you." "We are all orphans now."

ANDREI SAKHAROV first came to international attention on July 22, 1968, when *The New York Times* devoted three pages to the publication of his *Reflections on Progress, Peaceful Coexistence, and Intellectual Freedom.* This bold and prophetic essay urged an end to the cold war; stimulated Western interest in disarmament and scientific exchanges; and set forth a constructive blueprint for remaking the Soviet Union and the world. (Seemingly anticipating his own destiny, Sakharov chose for an epigraph lines from Goethe's *Faust:* "He alone is worthy of life and freedom who each day does battle for them anew.") At the time, little was known about the author. Although basic biographical data became available in 1975, when Sakharov was awarded the Nobel Peace Prize, only with the appearance of these memoirs can we reach beyond the public figure and appreciate the influences that shaped the character and sustained the spirit of this extraordinary man.

WHEN I ONCE made the mistake of referring to Sakharov as a "dissident," his wife, Elena Bonner, corrected me promptly and emphatically: "My husband is a *physicist,* not a dissident." One of the facets of his life documented in these pages is his devotion to science, from his schoolboy experiments with electricity to his fundamental work on plasma physics, cosmology, and baryon asymmetry. Readers interested in science can learn about quarks, time-reversal, and string theory; those more concerned with the formation of human personality and intellect can, if they wish, skip the technical passages without losing the thread of the narrative. But no one should slight the first substantial account of the Soviet nuclear weapons program (chapters 6–16): it will fascinate both the specialist and the general reader and provide important new information for historians and Sovietologists.

Sakharov's role as "father of the H-bomb" is confirmed in Nikita Khrushchev's memoirs, and also his use of the authority he earned to campaign against nuclear testing and ideological distortions of science:

> I used to meet frequently with Sakharov, and I considered him an extremely talented and impressive man. He was also a surprisingly young man to be involved in such important and difficult matters. He proposed that we develop a hydrogen bomb. No one else, neither the Americans nor the English, had such a bomb. We did everything in our power to assure the rapid realization of Sakharov's plans. With the help of engineers, technicians, and workers, our industry was able to develop the bomb in a remarkably short time. The hydrogen bomb represented a great contribution to the Soviet people and a great act of patriotism by Comrade Sakharov. . . .
>
> [In 1958], Sakharov called on our government to cancel a scheduled nuclear explosion and not to engage in any further testing, at least of the hydrogen bomb: "As a scientist and as the designer of the hydrogen bomb, I know what harm these explosions can bring down on the head of mankind." . . .
>
> He was devoted to the idea that science should bring peace and prosperity to the world, that it should help preserve and improve the conditions for human life. However, he went too far in thinking that he had the right to decide whether the bomb he had developed could ever be used in the future.

Although Sakharov's persistent lobbying achieved a significant success in 1963 with the conclusion of the Limited Test Ban Treaty (chapter 16), for the most part he was frustrated in his attempts to influence the Soviet establishment from within. In 1968 he decided to present his ideas to a wider audience by writing *Reflections*. Its publication abroad led to his firing from the Soviet weapons program, and he thereafter devoted more of his time to human rights issues and to developing—in *My Country and the World* and other programmatic essays—what would become the intellectual framework for the political, economic, and legal reforms that now form the basis of *perestroika*. His forceful statements criticizing human rights violations and calling for the release of individual prisoners of conscience won him international respect. But at home, in Brezhnev's constricted USSR, the authorities found him exasperating. And when he publicly opposed the Soviet military intervention in Afghanistan, he had once again gone "too far." In January 1980 he was banished to Gorky.

Sakharov was to remain outspoken and constant in his views, continuing from exile to warn against Soviet expansionism and the danger of thermonuclear war. It was the Soviet Union that began to change after the election in March 1985 of Mikhail Gorbachev as General Secretary. In December 1986, Gorbachev personally called Sakharov and invited him to return to Moscow and become, in effect, the regime's loyal opposition.

Back from Gorky, Sakharov moved to fulfill—sometimes reluctantly, sometimes awkwardly, but always with courage and integrity, discernment and compassion—his responsibilities as spokesman for the liberal intelligentsia. He was elected to the presidium of the Academy of Sciences, chosen as one of five directors of the Interregional Group of People's Deputies, appointed a member of the government commission to draft a new Soviet constitution, and made honorary chairman of "Memorial," the society founded to preserve the memory of Stalin's victims. He served as a national ombudsman, traveling around the Soviet Union to lend his support to persons suffering from official abuse. And at the June 1989 Congress of People's Deputies, with his fervent pleas for a radical reformation of the Soviet system and an end to the Communist Party's privileged position, he attempted to reinvigorate *perestroika* and to mend the uneasy collaboration between state and society inaugurated by Gorbachev's phone call. Only a few days before his death, he completed a preliminary draft of a new constitution for the "Union of Soviet Republics of Europe and Asia" and began circulating it among his associates for comment.

By his steadfast, uncompromising dedication to truth and justice, Sakharov revived the spirit of the Russian intelligentsia and quickened the conscience of mankind. And in his endeavor to "make good the demands of reason and create a life worthy of ourselves and of the goals we only dimly perceive," he revealed those rare qualities that distinguish genius from talent: the ability to identify the crucial element in complex situations, great originality, and an instinct for the currents of time.

SAKHAROV'S NARRATIVE deals primarily with the events of his life and with his ideas, but his comments on the extraordinary cast of characters he encountered during his several careers bring the human texture of Soviet society to life in a way that no foreign journalist or scholar can match. While he is reticent about personal matters, including his first marriage, the story of his second marriage is told with great feeling. He was a 49-year-old widower when he met and fell passionately in love with Elena Bonner—or Lusia, as he calls her. Indeed, the extraordinary partnership that developed between this reserved Russian intellectual and his impetuous, intensely human wife is a major theme of this book. (In *Alone Together,* Bonner has written her own moving account of the Gorky years.)

THESE MEMOIRS were written over a twelve-year period, in difficult circumstances. On four separate occasions, portions of the manuscript were stolen by the Soviet authorities; during his years in Gorky, Sakharov had little opportunity to consult reference works, his archives, or his editor; and after his return to Moscow, he was engrossed in the hectic process of *perestroika*.

The complete Russian-language text of the memoirs will be published in the United States by Chekhov Publishing Corporation. This English-language edition is slightly abridged, with some repetitions eliminated, along with a few passages of little interest to the Western reader. Mindful that these memoirs provide a unique firsthand account of historical events as well as a personal story of great interest, the editor made cuts sparingly. The result is a work of considerable length, which has been divided into two volumes. The present volume ends with Sakharov returning from Gorky; a second, shorter one, covering the years from 1987 through 1989, will follow.

Since Sakharov wrote his story in a straightforward, chronological fashion, there is a minimum of editorial apparatus. Footnotes and interpolations added by the translator are in brackets. There is a fairly complete bibliography of Sakharov's writings, and a glossary of persons named in the narrative. The translated text normally follows the Russian manuscript, which in many instances is a contemporaneous account of events. While preserving the sense of immediacy, this occasionally introduces anachronisms, so order and tense have been adjusted wherever the risk of confusion seemed large. Transliteration from Russian generally follows the Library of Congress system. Patronymics and affectionate diminutives have mostly been eliminated, since they can be perplexing for the Western reader.

Translation of these memoirs has been a formidable task, demanding expert knowledge of subjects ranging from quantum mechanics to "dissidentology." Efrem Yankelevich served as the author's representative from beginning to end. Richard Lourie translated the entire book with the exception of chapter 18 and scattered science sections that were rendered by Richard Bowers and Tony Rothman, and chapter 50, rendered by Antonina Bouis. Howard Spier took great pains to ensure that the English was faithful to the Russian original in content and tone, as did Svetlana Umricin, Antonina Bouis, and Masha Vorobiov. Andrew Blane supplied helpful advice on this foreword and other matters and Melvin Rosenthal served as a skillful and conscientious copy editor. Responsibility for the final English text rests with Ashbel Green, the editor at Alfred Knopf in charge of the whole enterprise.

December 31, 1989   EDWARD KLINE

PREFACE

IN THE SUMMER of 1978, Lusia's urging overcame my reluctance, and I began to write the first draft of these memoirs. In November of that year, even before my exile to Gorky, some chapters were stolen during a covert search of my apartment. In March 1981, the KGB walked off with a bag containing notebooks, documents and diaries, and once again parts of the memoirs were lost. In 1981 and 1982 I managed to reconstruct those parts, and continued working. Today, the book is in your hands.

WHEN I WROTE the above in September 1982, I really thought that the book would be published shortly. But a month later the KGB stole another 900 pages of the manuscript, and then additional material was confiscated from Lusia while she was traveling from Gorky to Moscow by train. She suffered a heart attack in April 1983, but the following month, ignoring medical strictures and the risk to her life, she went out at night (during the day a policeman was stationed at the door of our Moscow apartment) and passed on the pages that it had taken me six months of hard work to restore. For the next two and a half years, we were engaged in the battle to secure permission for Lusia's medical treatment abroad; after it was finally received in November 1985, she had open-heart surgery in Boston. While she was in the U.S. she wrote *Alone Together*, which was originally intended to serve as a postscript to these memoirs. In December 1986, we returned to Moscow, and now I repeat once again: Today, the book is in your hands.

Autobiographical narratives constitute an important part of mankind's memory. That is one reason why I took up the writing of this book; I suspect many others before me have been moved by similar considerations, just as others will be in the future. And because much of what has been written about my life, my circumstances, and those close to me is grossly inaccurate, I want to try to set the record straight.

I hope that my memoirs will appeal to a fairly wide audience because of the extraordinary turns my life has taken: work at a munitions factory during the war, my career in theoretical physics, twenty years developing thermonuclear weapons in a secret city ("the Installation"), research on controlled fusion, my statements on public issues, my activities in defense of human rights, the authorities' persecution of myself and my family, exile to Gorky, the years spent in isolation there, and my return to Moscow in the era of perestroika.

I have written about these events, the impressions they made on me, the persons who were involved in them, about the ideas that have influenced me, about my scientific work and my public activities. I was witness to or participant in various affairs of great moment, and I give some account of them as well. I have been free both in selection of material and in my presentation of it. This book is not a confession, nor do I lay claim to having produced a work of art. These are candid recollections of the world of science, the world of the Installation, the world of dissidents, and, simply, of my life.

Moscow
May 1989

FROM 1984 THROUGH 1986, Efrem Yankelevich, Edward Kline, Ashbel Green (editor of the American edition), and, during her stay in the U.S., Lusia, worked on the manuscript for this book, which I had sent to the West in several installments. In Gorky, where I was cut off from the outside world, the editors had no possibility of consulting me by phone or mail. Nonetheless, by the end of 1986, a Russian-language manuscript had been assembled in the West, and an English translation was more or less complete.

It was about the same time, of course, in December 1986, that Lusia and I returned to Moscow, and I could not refuse the opportunity to collaborate in the final stages of work on the book. It was the first chance I'd had to read through the proofs of the entire manuscript, making corrections and additions to take into account all that had happened since 1983.

In 1987 (in Moscow) and in 1989 (in Westwood and Newton) I added more than 200 pages of new material, describing my last three years of exile and subsequent events from January 1987 through June 1989. I have since decided to publish this material in a separate volume, under the title *Gorky-Moscow, and Beyond.* [1]

Unfortunately, the process of editing and translating these memoirs has taken much too long for a number of reasons, mainly organizational; some part of the delay must be laid at the author's door. But all things come to an end, even troublesome and tedious things. . . .

I am deeply grateful to everyone who took part in preparing this book for publication: in addition to those listed above, they include Richard Lourie and Tony Rothman, who worked on the translation; Vera Lashkova, Liza Semyonov (Alexeyeva), Marina Babyonyshev, and Ellen Gessen, who typed the manuscript; and Robert Bernstein.

My wife's editorial assistance in Gorky, Moscow, and the U.S. was invaluable. She overcame many difficulties and took many risks to send my manuscript abroad. But above all else, she has all this time been at my side.

Moscow
December 1989

ANDREI SAKHAROV

[1][The publisher felt it would be more appropriate to conclude the narrative in December 1986, and this has therefore been done, with the consent of Elena Bonner.]

I

1

MY FAMILY AND CHILDHOOD

TO MY REGRET, there is much about my family history that I don't know, but I'll put down what I do recall, even though some of the details may not be quite accurate.

My mother, Ekaterina Sofiano, was born in December 1893 in Belgorod. Her surname testifies to the presence of Russified Greeks among my ancestors. My grandfather, Alexei Sofiano, was a professional soldier, an artilleryman who earned his first officer's rank and advancement to the nobility during the Russo-Turkish War: it seems that under enemy fire near Plevna, he seized the bridle of the horse on which General Skobelev was mounted, and pulled the animal out of the mire.

My grandmother, Zinaida Mukhanova, was my grandfather's second wife. They had two children, my mother and her younger sister, Tatyana (Aunt Tusya); my grandfather also had three children from his first marriage.

Grandfather commanded an artillery unit, or perhaps it was a general army one. He spent summers with his family in a military camp near Belgorod, where Mother learned to ride and picked up a repertoire of army and Ukrainian folk songs. She was sent to a Moscow boarding school for daughters of the nobility that provided more finish than education; it was neither up-to-date nor practical, and offered no real training for a profession. After graduation, my mother taught gymnastics for a few years in a Moscow school.

Both in appearance and in personality, Mother resembled her own mother, Zinaida. Resolute and self-sacrificing, devoted to her family and always ready to help friends, she was also reserved, perhaps even somewhat dogmatic and lacking in tolerance. I inherited my physical appearance from my mother and grandmother, particularly the Mongol cast of my eyes (it's probably no coincidence that my grandmother had an Oriental maiden name, Mukhanova), and something of my character as well: a certain obstinacy, as well as an awkwardness in dealing with people that has troubled me for much of my life.

To the best of my knowledge, my mother's parents shared the prevailing outlook of the officer class to which they belonged. I remember a conversation about the Russo-Japanese War in the 1930s, after Grandfather's death; I was reading Novikov-Priboi's novel *Tsushima* at the time. Speaking with great bitterness, my grandmother insisted that Russia would never have been defeated had it not been for the antipatriotic actions of the Bolsheviks and the other revolutionaries. When she wasn't around, my father remarked that she was simply repeating her late husband's words.

After the war with Japan, Grandfather retired with the rank of major general. But he returned to active duty in 1914, at the age of sixty-nine, and demanded to be sent to the front. Instead, he was appointed to a high post in Moscow's firefighting system. He died suddenly in 1929 at the age of eighty-four, having never been sick a day in his life. This was my first experience with the death of a relative. I'd already been puzzling about death for some time—it seemed to me a monstrous injustice of nature.

My mother, like most members of my family, believed in God. My father's mother, his brother Ivan, Ivan's wife, Aunt Zhenya, and Aunt Valya, my cousin Irina's mother, were all similarly devout. I'm quite sure my father wasn't, though I don't recall his ever discussing the matter directly. My mother taught me to say my prayers at bedtime ("Our Father," "Rejoice, O Virgin Mother of God . . ."), and took me with her to confession and communion. Like many children, I was at times so literal-minded that I got comic ideas into my head. One such idea stuck with me until Lusia explained my error to me in the 1970s: I'd somehow heard the words from the church service, "Holy God, holy Mighty" (. . . *krepki*) as "Holy God, holy Greeks" (. . .*greki*)—and took the "holy Greeks" to be the Church fathers.

Moved by the spirit of the times and by my father's subtle influence, I decided at the age of thirteen that I no longer believed in God. I stopped saying my prayers and rarely attended church. My mother was very upset, but she never pressed the issue.

Today, deep in my heart, I do not know where I stand on religion. I don't believe in any dogma and I dislike official churches, especially those closely tied to the state, those of a predominantly ceremonial character, or those tainted by fanaticism and intolerance. And yet I am unable to imagine the universe and human life without some guiding principle, without a source of spiritual "warmth" that is nonmaterial and not bound by physical laws. Probably this sense of things could be called "religious."

I remember so well going to church when I was a boy—the chanting, the exaltation of worshippers at prayer, the flickering candles, the dark faces of the icons, the radiant mood of my mother and grandmother returning from church after taking communion. But neither can I forget the filthy rags of the professional church beggars, the half-crazed old women, the oppressiveness, the whole atmosphere of Byzantium, of Russia before Peter the Great—and my imagination recoils in horror at seeing the barbarism, lies, and hypocrisy of the past carried into our time.

I've encountered these two sides of religion many times, and have never failed to be struck by the contrast between them. In recent years I have witnessed stern old women singing solemnly, their eyes flashing beneath dark kerchiefs, and the ascetic faces at the graveside of my father-in-law, Alexei Vikhirev. And I recall speaking with Seventh-Day Adventists—pure, sincere, inspired folk—near the courthouse in Tashkent where their pastor, Vladimir Shelkov, was on trial. I have had many positive encounters with Russian Orthodox believers, as well as with Baptists, Catholics, and Muslims. But I have also observed among avowed believers many instances of bigotry, hypocrisy, money-grubbing, and blatant disregard for human suffering—including, at times, that of their own children. On the whole, however, I have nothing but admiration for those who are sincerely religious.

MY FATHER'S FAMILY differed from my mother's in many respects. My great-grandfather, Nikolai Sakharov, was a priest in the village of Vyezdnoe, near Arzamas. His forebears had been priests for several generations; one even became archpriest of Arzamas. My grandfather, Ivan Sakharov, was his family's tenth child, and the only one to receive a higher education. He left Arzamas for Nizhny Novgorod, sixty miles away, to attend the university there; my exile to Gorky—formerly Nizhny Novgorod—thus completed a family cycle. My grandfather became a successful lawyer and moved to Moscow. There, at the turn of the century, he rented the apartment in which I later spent my childhood. The building was owned by the Goldenveizer family; Alexander Goldenveizer, a celebrated pianist who had been a friend and follower of Tolstoy in his youth, married Anna Sofiano, my mother's sister, and later became my godfather.

My paternal grandfather was a man of liberal views for his time. The family's friends included such men of distinction as the writer Vladimir Korolenko, whom all my relatives held in high esteem (now, many years later, I too admire him greatly); Fyodor Plevako, a prominent lawyer of the day; and the novelist Pyotr Boborykin. A personal letter from Korolenko to my grandfather still survives. From an ironical and not altogether flattering reference to my grandfather in one of his articles, it seems that the writer and critic Vikenty Veresaev was also an acquaintance.

My grandfather served as defense counsel in a sensational turn-of-the-century case concerning a boat accident on the Volga. His plea at that trial, which had social implications (the defendant had ignored prescribed safety measures in an effort to satisfy the demands of the boat's owners), was published in the USSR in the 1960s in *Selected Speeches of Well-known Russian Lawyers*. Following the 1905 revolution, he edited an important collection of essays advocating the abolition of capital punishment, including Tolstoy's celebrated "I Cannot Keep Silent," whose emotional and intellectual power made it the book's focal point. I read this book as a young boy, and it made a great impression on me. The arguments it presented against capital punishment still seem to me convincing and exhaustive. My grandfather's work on this book was an act of conscience and, to an extent, civic courage.

When he was about thirty, Ivan Sakharov married a seventeen-year-old orphan, Maria Domukhovskaya (the surname suggests some Polish ancestry), who was to become my grandmother. "Babanya," as her grandchildren called her, was the daughter of an impoverished nobleman from Smolensk. I remember her lively stories about the boarding school near Smolensk where she spent her childhood. One of the stories concerned the great Russian poet Mikhail Lermontov, who was killed in a duel at the age of twenty-seven by Martynov, a fellow army officer. In the 1870s, Martynov would visit his daughter, my grandmother's classmate, at the school; the students would peer at him with awe and horror through a crack in the door. Reportedly, Martynov remained throughout his life deeply conscious of his role in the tragic (and still puzzling) story of Lermontov's death. Babanya was a person of exceptional qualities: intelligence, goodness, and compassion, an appreciation of life's complexities, and a special talent for nurturing a family and raising educated, sensitive, self-reliant children able to cope with the demands of the turbulent times. She and Grandfather had six children in all: Tatyana, Sergei, Ivan, Dmitri (my father), Nikolai, and Yuri, a large family, even for those times. Babanya was the guiding spirit of the Sakharov home, and her role (which she maintained until the day she died) was all the more pivotal because her husband's interests were for the most part centered elsewhere. Even beyond the confines of the family, there are a number of people still living who received important moral support from my grandmother and the Sakharov home.

My father, Dmitri Sakharov, was born on February 19, 1889,[1] in the village of Budaevo in Smolensk province, where my grandmother had been left a house by her parents. Mitya (as he was known in the family) spent most of his

---

[1][March 3, according to the Gregorian (New Style) calendar, adopted by the Soviet government in 1918.]

early childhood in Budaevo. One of the stories I recall hearing about those days was how Grandfather, about to leave for town, asked the children what they'd like for him to bring them. Mitya's answer: "A handkerchief." "What for?" "To wipe away my tears."

I picture the brothers as a noisy, cheerful bunch; they ran around barefoot all summer and went swimming in the pond. Mitya, though, was a quiet boy. He always loved the landscape of central Russia above all else; he never wearied of it, although as an adult he also learned to enjoy walking in the mountains. He visited the Crimea and the Caucasus several times, and the Kola Peninsula twice. In 1933, he returned from the Caucasus by plane (a Junkers), quite an adventurous undertaking in those days—indeed, he was afraid to tell Mother about his audacity. On one trip, Father made the acquaintance of the great Russian physicist Igor Tamm. This later played a part in my doing graduate work under Tamm.

At the age of six or seven, Father underwent surgery to remove an abscess, in those days a serious operation; it left a long scar down his side and back. It was about this time that the Sakharov family moved to Moscow. My father was sent to one of the best private schools in the city, somewhere near the Arbat gates (he later took me to see the building, with its soaring ceilings and beautiful windows). The headmaster warned the other boys not to be too rough with the new pupil, since his stitches might come out; they obeyed this injunction religiously, good-humoredly nicknaming my father "the glass boy." Throughout his life Father kept in touch with a few of his classmates, but the times were such that he did not see close friends for decades. (Two of them left Russia after the Revolution. Father was reunited with Leprovsky, a physician who became an Orthodox priest in France, when Leprovsky visited Moscow as a tourist just before my father's death.)

My father had begun to play the piano even before he entered school, and he practiced several hours a day. He was accepted by the famous Gnessin Conservatory, from which he graduated with a gold medal; the name "Sakharov" can still be seen on a marble plaque in the school. My father's fingers were strong and nimble, yet gentle, ideally suited for the piano. He had absolute pitch and suffered almost physically when the standard of pitch was changed. He told me that he identified tones and semitones with particular colors. He had definite and individual musical tastes: he loved Beethoven, Bach, Mozart, Chopin, Grieg, Schumann, Scriabin (whom he met shortly before Scriabin's death in 1915; he remained a friend of the composer's family and after the war spoke on several occasions about Scriabin at the composer's former home, which was preserved as a museum), and Rimsky-Korsakov, all of whom he played frequently. He held Borodin in high regard, and spoke of Wagner with respect, even awe, although the latter was not one of his favorite composers.

I remember his once praising Prokofiev highly, but I don't recall his ever mentioning Shostakovich; it was as if this great composer did not exist.

Despite his acknowledged talent, my father did not become a professional musician. But throughout his life he continued to play the piano for his own enjoyment. In his youth, and later on, after he retired, he composed music for several songs. He set to music Alexander Blok's poem "You walked away into the field . . ." He and his sister Tusya loved Blok's poetry, which somehow recaptured for them the spiritual world of their youth. Father told me he'd also written piano sonatas, and some humorous songs as well. It pains me that the music he wrote wasn't preserved; it was part of his very soul.

After completing high school, Father entered medical school, where he did well. But he soon transferred to the department of mathematics and physics at the University of Moscow, from which he graduated just before the war. Unfortunately, the standard of instruction deteriorated sharply during this period, as many distinguished professors resigned in protest against a government order that allowed police to enter the university grounds during student disturbances. (One of these professors was Lebedev, the outstanding physicist whose name was later given to the institute where I work.)

IN THE SUMMER of 1914, almost the entire Sakharov family went abroad for the first time. Only Tusya had been in Europe before, as a philosophy student in Germany. My father was on a Belgian beach when he learned that war had been declared; he immediately got on his bicycle and pedaled through the night nearly fifty miles to rejoin the family. Space was found on the deck of a coal steamer, and the family set off for home. The weather was stormy, and everyone, Grandmother in particular, suffered from seasickness. The ship sailed silently through fog without lights, for fear of German warships. And indeed, Grandmother told us, at one point a massive silhouette with gun turrets loomed up through the fog.

Nikolai was conscripted immediately into the army, and Father, too, was quickly enrolled as a medic. In later times, Father was extremely reluctant to speak about his six months at the front, somewhere near the Masurian Lakes. I remember him telling us about an incident when an officer who refused to put on the only gas mask in his platoon died alongside his men. Father kept a steel dart marked: "Invented by the French, manufactured by the Germans." Hundreds of these darts had been dropped from German aircraft during the first months of the war; they were said to be capable of running right through both horse and rider.

Between 1915 and 1918, Father taught physics in private schools as well as at the college where my mother was teaching gymnastics. It was here that they met; they married in 1918, when Father was twenty-nine and Mother twenty-five.

Shortly before the war, my paternal grandparents had bought a little house in Kislovodsk, in the Caucasus. Early in 1918, Grandfather went there, but nothing was heard from him thereafter. Worried, Grandmother suggested that my parents go to Kislovodsk—it would be something of a honeymoon, and they could find out what had happened to Grandfather. When they reached Kislovodsk, they were told that Grandfather had died, apparently from typhus. But by now the Caucasus was cut off from central Russia by civil war, and my parents found themselves stranded. They were forced to stay on for a while in a town on the Black Sea, where my father got a job playing the piano in a cinema (this was the era of silent movies).

Aunt Zhenya, the wife of my father's brother Ivan, was in Saratov with her three children: Katya, the eldest, and two boys. Uncle Yuri, Father's youngest brother, was with them. In 1920, both of Zhenya's sons died; they literally starved to death. When the second boy died, Uncle Yuri, who was himself ill with typhus, heard Aunt Zhenya weeping, got up to console her, and then lay back down and died. I heard this tragic story in my infancy; it is one of my earliest memories.

[My cousin Katya thinks Grandmother traveled with my grandfather to the Caucasus; it was on the return trip that Grandfather died of typhus, in Kharkov. Grandmother then joined Aunt Zhenya in Saratov, and returned with her to Moscow. Katya probably is right.—A.S. 1987]

That same year, my parents began the arduous trip back home. I vaguely recall their telling me about a night they spent in an enormous barn crowded with Red Army soldiers delirious from typhoid fever, about the machine-gunning of Kalmyk families, men, women, and children, trying to escape from famine, and about starving people frozen to death on the steppe.

I WAS BORN on May 21, 1921, in a maternity hospital near Moscow's Novodevichy Monastery. It was a difficult birth. I was long and skinny and could not raise my head for many months, which resulted in the flattening of the back of my skull.

For the first year or so, we lived in a basement apartment in Merzlyakov Lane. We had no baby carriage, so Father would carry me outside in a large folder meant for musical scores. I was a "good" baby and would fall asleep as soon as I was taken out of the damp cellar into the fresh air.

Grandmother continued to live in Moscow on Granatny Lane, in the Goldenveizers' former home. We moved there at the end of 1922. Besides my grandmother, the other family members living there were: Nikolai (who soon left to remarry), Nikolai's wife Valya, their daughter Irina, and Valya's mother, Sofia Bandrovskaya; Ivan, his wife, Zhenya, and their daughter Katya. Uncle Sergei and Aunt Tatyana lived elsewhere.[2]

I want to describe in more detail the house where we spent the next nineteen years. It was, in fact, a communal apartment shared by four Sakharov families, as well as two other families, in relative harmony. My immediate family was the only one lucky enough to have two rooms, covering a little over 300 square feet. There were four of us: Father, Mother, my younger brother Georgy (born in 1925 and known in the family as Yura), and myself. We used one room as a bedroom, dining room, and nursery, while the other, really more of a hallway, served as my father's study. A desk stood under the window, bookcases lined one wall, and two cupboards held linens and dishes; you could barely squeeze past them to the stove that heated our rooms. I loved to transfer decals onto the Dutch tiles covering the stove, which was fueled by wood and had to be tended daily in winter.

The house was very old, and the ceilings leaked constantly. The kitchen was used by all six families, and in that terribly cramped space six primus stoves would sometimes be roaring away at the same time. But the building still had its magnificent doors inlaid with Karelian birch, a broad staircase, and exquisite banisters. Our apartment was on the second floor, and there was a corridor wide enough for the children to ride their tricycles and play. We kept our firewood in a separate storeroom on the ground floor of the building across the courtyard. Every winter we would pack this space with ice and snow, which was always great fun for the children. We kept food in this improvised icehouse, and in summer, as the snow sank lower and lower, we had to climb down a ladder to retrieve the contents.

Our building faced an old and stately private mansion (said to have belonged to Marshal Kutuzov), surrounded by extensive grounds; it now housed the Bureau of Weights and Measures of the All-Union Institute of Standards. In those days the newspapers didn't carry obligatory Party slogans for holidays, so each establishment could choose its own. Throughout my childhood, the Bureau displayed the same banner every November 7 and May 1: "The Comintern Is the Gravedigger of Capitalism!"

Life was hard for just about everyone in the 1920s, and it got more difficult in the 1930s. My mother no longer resembled the youthful gymnast of

---

[2]Tatyana's husband, Nikolai Yakushkin, was a direct descendant of the Decembrist Ivan Yakushkin, and in the 1960s, after her husband's death, Aunt Tatyana published some of the materials he had collected about his famous ancestor. Aunt Tatyana taught English for many years. She became a vegetarian in her youth, apparently under the influence of Tolstoy, and remained true to her convictions throughout her life.

her early photographs, but to the end of her life she remained active, energetic, and selfless. And she retained the ability to admit when she was wrong—although this never came easily. My mother's life revolved around her family and her home; like most women of that time, she did not work after her marriage.

Mother did not get along very well with my grandmother, and we lived separately. But Grandmother often baby-sat for the grandchildren—my cousin Irina, my brother, and me. We felt freer and easier in Grandmother's room than anywhere else, and Irina and I took every opportunity we could to be with her. For hours on end we would go sliding down the great leather sofa, pretending it was a mountain and having ourselves a wonderful time.

When we were a bit older, Grandmother would spend hours reading to us from Pushkin's *The Captain's Daughter* and *The Tale of Tsar Saltan,* Hector Malot's *Sans Famille,* and Harriet Beecher Stowe's *Uncle Tom's Cabin,* stories I'll never forget. This was my first encounter with the miraculous world of books. Grandmother herself loved English novels, for which she had a special affinity; she'd even taught herself English in her forties. During Holy Week she would read us the Gospels; I remember her getting upset when Irina commented "How interesting" in response to Jesus' words, "Before the cock crows, you will betray me thrice." We were perfectly well aware that Grandmother wasn't reading us the Bible as entertainment.

I remember Grandmother's room clearly. The furnishings were apparently typical for her circle and era: in the corner of the room, an icon stand with a constantly burning vigil lamp; Raphael's *Madonna* and views of Venice and Rome on the walls; a portrait of Grandmother and Grandfather when they were young; a small statue of Tolstoy writing at a round table (I often attempted to sketch it); a washstand with a marble top; a coffee grinder; and heavy curtains with tasseled cords. In later years, going through some belongings, I came across a lithograph of Beethoven against a romantic landscape, but I'm not sure to which grandmother it belonged. In 1971, entering Lusia's house for the first time, I caught sight of that very same picture of Beethoven: she had inherited it from *her* grandmother. It later hung in my mother-in-law Ruth's room in Moscow.

Here's an unflattering story my grandmother told me about my early years. One day when I was two she was lying extremely sick in bed. I climbed onto her chest and asked: "Grandma, can't you do anything?" "No, not a thing." "Then I'm going to *squash* you!" And I began jumping up and down on her chest and stomach. She said she began to get really frightened, but she didn't have the strength to stop me. My mother came running; I hope she gave me what I deserved.

According to my cousin Katya, who was often asked to baby-sit for Irina and me (she called us "the little bores"), I was my mother's "little prince." I suspect "our prince" is an accurate reflection of my parents' attitude toward their first-born son. In the 1970s, I found a diary written in my father's hand but phrased as if I were the author: "Today I spent the whole morning crying, Mama was very upset, then I calmed down and looked out the window. Very interesting." The diary recorded my first words, and all the other events of my infancy. Father kept another diary when my brother Yura was born, but a less detailed one—not because he loved me more, but because the challenge wasn't the same the second time around.

One day, when I was about three, Mama was mopping up some dirty spot on the floor and complained in exasperation, "Oh, look, I've finished off the mop!" I began to bawl; through my sobs Mama managed to make out my question: "Why did you k-kill the mop?" This may not have been simple compassion for the mop (to a three-year-old, an animate being); it may also have had something to do with a certain miserliness in my character which has lasted throughout my life and has both positive and negative aspects.

Another time, my parents found me in the kitchen leaning against the back door. The expression on my face was serious and tense. Asked what I was up to, I replied, "There are burglars out there. I'm making sure they don't get in!"

My father taught physics most of his life: first, briefly, in a school; then, in the 1920s, at the Institute of Red Professors[3] and at Sverdlovsk University; and for the following twenty-five years at the Bubnov Pedagogical Institute in Moscow (renamed the Lenin Pedagogical Institute after Bubnov's arrest). For reasons unknown to me, Father left the institute in the 1950s; apparently the administration had seriously offended him in some way. Before he retired, he worked for a few years at the Moscow Regional Pedagogical Institute.

At the Lenin Institute Father conducted seminars and was in charge of the physics laboratory. He was extremely conscientious and popular with both students and colleagues, including his close friends of many years, Professors Pavsha and Bene. He was on good terms with the distinguished head of the physics department, Eduard Shpolsky, a specialist in optics and editor of the excellent journal *Achievements in the Physical Sciences.* Professor Shpolsky's successor, Professor Nikolai Malov, and my father became close friends.

After I reached the age of twelve, Father would sometimes take me to his laboratory, where he would show me experiments—dazzling "miracles," but miracles I could *understand.* I soon began performing my own experiments at home; but more about that later.

---

[3][The Institute of Red Professors was founded in 1921 for the purpose of supplying institutions of higher education with instructors in economics, sociology, and philosophy.]

In the 1920s, my father began to write popular scientific works and textbooks. His writing style was crisp, precise, and lucid, but it cost him a great deal of time and effort. He agonized over every word, and copied out sentences again and again in his elegant hand. I used to watch him, and perhaps it was this more than anything else that taught me what it is to truly work. And, indeed, the whole ethos of our home fostered the idea that one cannot live without working.

Father's first book, *The Struggle for Light,* was a popular presentation of the physics and history of lighting devices from ancient times to the present day. It took him two years to gather the material for this work, mainly from German sources. The book was one of the first of its kind to be published, and proved a great success. The Raduga Publishing House printed 25,000 copies, a huge edition for those days, which sold out quickly. Many other books followed: *The Physics of the Tramcar, Experiments with a Light Bulb,* and *Physics Workbooks* (these were in fact textbooks for adults, but the word "textbook" was not used, since in those days it was considered "bourgeois"). My father's presentation was highly original; direct current, for instance, was discussed before electrostatics. Father's later books were written in a more conventional manner.

In the 1930s, my father contributed to publications on teaching methods and to a very interesting physics textbook edited by Grigori Landsberg.[4] But Father's most important works were *Problems in Physics,* which went through thirteen editions, and his introductory physics text, which had a more complicated fate. Originally written for use in adult education classes, it was very popular, and after the reorganization of the educational system my father collaborated with Mikhail Bludov, an experienced teacher, in reworking it into a textbook for technical schools. After my father died, Bludov wrote me in the spring of 1962 and asked if I would help him update the book. I rewrote the last two chapters (and felt they turned out well), and the new edition came out in 1964. Bludov and I began to update it once more in 1970, but in 1973, after the new version had already received the Ministry of Education's seal of approval, an official campaign was launched against me and the book was banned.

My father's writing was our family's principal source of income. It enabled

---

[4]Landsberg, who later became an Academician, was a well-known scientist who (together with Leonid Mandelshtam) discovered certain alterations in the spectrum of monochromatic light passing through a transparent medium, usually called "Raman scattering."

us to enjoy a higher standard of living than the average Soviet citizen or rank-and-file member of the intelligentsia (the group to which we essentially belonged) in those difficult years. We could afford to rent one or two rooms in a country house near Moscow, and my father was able to enjoy hiking trips. All the same, it was no easy matter for him to feed the family. He could not afford any such expensive purchases as a radio or a motorcycle. Fortunately, his brother Ivan owned a motorcycle; and Father assembled a radio for himself out of spare parts—a crystal set, of course, with headphones.

The first vacuum tube radio I ever saw belonged to our neighbors, the Amdurskys. He was an engineer, she a seamstress who worked at home, an especially profitable occupation. They had no children. It was at the Amdurskys' that I heard one of Hitler's famous Nuremberg Rally speeches and the crazed, terrifying chanting of the crowd: *"Heil! Heil! Heil!"* There, too, I heard Stalin vow at the Eighth Congress of Soviets in 1936 that: "The blood our people shed so plentifully was not shed in vain." (The Stalin Constitution was adopted at that Congress; it was said to have been written by Bukharin, who was shortly to be arrested.) I listened to the splendid broadcasts of the Pushkin festivities in 1937 from beginning to end. One broadcast included a reading of *The Bronze Horseman.* [5] I remember appreciating then—and especially *then*—the tragedy and the passion of rebellion in the poem's lines:

> The piteous madman fell to prowling
> About the statue's granite berth,
> And furtively with savage scowling
> He eyed the lord of half the earth
> His breath congealed in him, he pressed
> His brow against the chilly railing,
> A blur of darkness overveiling
> His eyes; and a flame shot through his heart
> And made his blood seethe. Grimly louring,
> He faced the haughty image towering
> On high, and, fingers clawed, teeth clenched,
> As if by some black spirit wrenched,
> He hissed, spite shaking him: "Up there,
> Great wonder-worker you, beware! . . ."
> And then abruptly wheeled to race
> Away full tilt.

[5] [The "piteous madman," Evgeny, addresses the statue of Peter the Great, founder of Petersburg. Walter Arndt, ed. and tr., Alexander Pushkin, *Collected Narrative and Lyrical Poetry* (Ardis, 1984), p. 437.]

Incredibly, it was in 1937, with Stalin's dictatorship at its peak, that Pushkin was officially proclaimed a great national poet. But this was a sign of the times. The official ideology had by almost imperceptible steps come to parallel the slogan that epitomized the reign of Nicholas I: "Autocracy, Orthodoxy, Nationality"—with the Russian national spirit now personified by Pushkin, Communist orthodoxy by Lenin in his mausoleum, and Soviet autocracy by the living Stalin.

My father's literary work provided him not only with money but also with a certain degree of independence and some fame among educators. For a long time, however, he possessed neither an advanced degree nor professorial rank. Finally, during the war, the Scientific Council of the Pedagogical Institute awarded him the honorary degree of Candidate of Pedagogical Science for his book *Problems in Physics*.

A great many people loved my father. He was kind and gentle, a man of principle, wise and compassionate. It is difficult to say whether he was content with his lot. I think he knew his own worth and was aware that he had never fully realized his potential: he liked to talk to me about this. On the other hand, he possessed a humane worldly wisdom which enabled him to enjoy life to the full (a rare talent, indeed).

Father's favorite proverb was: "To live a life is not to cross a field." Those words implied a great deal: an understanding that the real world is not a simple place, a sense of life's tragedy and beauty, and forgiveness for those who stumble. Father had another favorite saying which expressed his understanding of harmony and wisdom: "A sense of moderation is the greatest gift of the gods." He applied this philosophy to all aspects of life: to art—he singled out Beethoven in particular for the simplicity with which the noble and heroic passion of his music is expressed; to teaching and science—he approved of an orderly, systematic approach, without skipping steps and without superficiality (he detested *Wunderkinder*); to politics—he would say that what the Bolsheviks lacked most of all was balance, by his lights a stern judgment; and, finally, to personal relations.

My father's views had an enormous effect on me, but I was unable to follow his example in all respects. There was a ferment inside me, an inner conflict, and moderation was something I could achieve only with great effort, if at all. This inner strain is, I suspect, a universal problem. Looking back on my life, I see not only actions which are a source of pride, but others which were false, cowardly, shameful, foolish, ill-advised, or inspired by subconscious impulses it's better not to dwell on. While admitting all this in general terms, I don't want to linger on my failings—not out of any concern for my reputation, but rather from a dislike for self-flagellation and public soul-searching. Moreover, I believe that no one really learns from other people's mistakes. It's enough to learn from your own mistakes and to emulate the virtues of others. I want these memoirs to focus less on me as a person and more on what I have seen and understood (or tried to understand) during my sixty-eight years of life. I believe that sympathetic readers will also find this approach more interesting. After all, this book is a memoir, not a confession.

My father was truly delighted with my enthusiasm for physics experiments and mathematical problems, and it was taken for granted that I would study physics at the university. Perhaps one element in this was his hope that I would achieve more than he had been able to. But far more important to him was his desire that I find satisfaction and fulfillment in my work. He was constantly warning me against any form of snobbery. He passed on to his children his own firm conviction that work done conscientiously, professionally, and with zest is work well done.

A PORTRAIT OF my childhood would not be complete without a description of our family celebrations, our vacations in the country, and the special world of our courtyard.

We had parties for the children's birthdays and name days (as did the Kudryavtsevs—more about them later), with sweets, usually homemade ice cream, games, charades, and magic tricks. It was my father who usually performed the tricks: a coin that couldn't be brushed off his hand, or matches snapped into pieces inside a handkerchief only to emerge unbroken. The adults and older children—Katya and her friends—displayed great ingenuity in charades, but the younger ones also had a chance to show what they could do in miming bandits, beggars, pirates, millionaires, even heavenly bodies. Another traditional entertainment was Father performing the shadow play "An American Reading His Newspaper," using a coat stand and a cane as props.

I've already mentioned that our family spent our summers in the country. We usually rented two rooms in the house of a large and close-knit family of Russified Germans, the Ulmers, at a place called Dunino, not far from Zvenigorod, for three or four months. (Most members of the Ulmer family—including engineers, doctors, and a lawyer—were arrested and killed in the 1930s.)

Those summers left deep impressions. We children would immediately kick off our shoes and put on our bathing trunks. After a month I would be tanned almost black. I've always loved the serene, lyrical countryside around Moscow; even now, I can think of no greater pleasure than lying on my back by the edge of the woods and looking up at the sky and trees and listening to the buzzing of insects in summer, or turning over on my stomach and watching the ants scurrying to and fro over the grass. I had no interest in fishing or hunting, and

I still don't know how to swim properly.[6] But I was never bored wandering by myself through the woods and fields sown with rye, oats, wheat, and clover.

We children would spend the whole summer with Mother at the dacha; on Sundays, Father would bring us whatever groceries he'd been able to get in town.

When the time came for his own vacation, Father preferred to travel around the country. In August 1936, when I was fifteen, he took me for a trip on the Moscow–Gorky–Yaroslavl steamer. We played chess and talked about many things, important and not so important. As far as I can recall, we didn't talk about the newspaper account I read of the Zinoviev-Kamenev trial. Vyshinsky's summation for the prosecution had been filled, as always, with cruel and affected rhetoric; I still remember Vyshinsky's concluding words at the March 1938 trial of Bukharin and his co-defendants: "The graves of the fateful traitors will grow over with weeds and thistles . . . but over us, over our happy country, our sun will shine with its luminous rays, as bright and as joyous as before."[7] The "traitors" had confessed under torture to all conceivable (and inconceivable) crimes.

In August 1939, on another of our trips, I saw the sea and the mountains for the very first time. We slept in a tent and hiked through ravines and along wonderfully fresh mountain streams, talking about Life. On the way home, we bought a newspaper and saw a report of Ribbentrop's arrival in Moscow. A week later, the Second World War broke out.

THE COURTYARD between the wings of our building—and the dozen or so boys and girls who gathered there—played a major role in my childhood. A big tree grew in the courtyard, some grass, a few stray dandelions. Now, covered over with asphalt, it seems much smaller; the house I lived in as a boy was destroyed by a German bomb in 1941, and a police station was built in its place. I went back there two or three times after the war, but I always experienced the same odd feeling of alienation. Granatny Lane has even been renamed— now it's Shchusev Street.

I have no idea whether children still play the games we used to play— Cossacks and Robbers, for example. These were exciting team games, lots of

---

[6] Lusia's son, Alexei, tried to teach me when I was fifty-two, during a vacation at the Black Sea that coincided with the beginning of the 1973 press campaign against me. For some reason, Solzhenitsyn wrote in *The Oak and the Calf* [Harper & Row, 1975] that I was anxious to return to Moscow but could not get tickets; in fact, my only ambition was to learn to swim.

[7] [For Vyshinsky's speech, see Robert Tucker and Stephen Cohen, eds., *The Great Purge Trial* (Grosset and Dunlap, 1965), pp. 514–586.]

fun, and not in the least violent. The younger children, of course, played the eternal games of hopscotch and hide-and-seek (although "Eeny meeny miny mo," for one, has changed completely). I have a scar on my foot from one game of mumbletypeg we played—it has, along with the rest of me, grown something like three times larger since I got it.

I was very close to my cousin Irina, who was my age and more vigorous and inventive in games. She persuaded me to act out scenes from literature; sometimes I would be Dubrovsky or Captain Hatteras, but usually I got the less glamorous parts, like Andrei or Yankel in Gogol's *Taras Bulba*. When the snows came, Irina and I would sled down our street. There were so few cars in those days that they weren't a problem.

My other cousin, Katya, and her friend Tasya were for many years fond of playing Chingachgook and Uncas, the Indians from James Fenimore Cooper's *Last of the Mohicans*. Playing Indians was a popular game then, although probably not so popular as with children of the previous generation. Russian children always admired the proud, brave, freedom-loving Indians. (What do children play nowadays; what do American children play?)

Any group of children is naturally a reflection of society as a whole, and the turmoil of the times penetrated our courtyard, though only in a sporadic and muted fashion. It did not prevent us from playing with one another, quarreling, fighting, and then making up again. I realize now that my parents, who could hardly be described as well-to-do by today's standards, stood then virtually at the top of the social ladder; and the children of course sensed this.

Were there ethnic problems in our courtyard? Only to a very limited extent. Grisha might be reminded that he was a Jew, but with no insult intended; it was just his distinctive feature. As for me, owing, I think, to family influence and traditions, it hardly ever occurred to me to consider whether or not somebody was Jewish. One young Polish boy, however, was treated badly at times; civil war stories of the Poles allegedly siding with the Whites, or the traditional Russian antipathy toward Poles, may have played a part in this. Our fiercest animosity, though, sometimes spilling over into fights, was reserved for students from the nearby elite "Kremlin" school. I suspect the Kremlinites' snobbery was at the root of it.

Grisha made his first appearance in our courtyard when I was six. The Umanskys, a very poor Jewish family, moved into a room on the ground floor of our building; their only window looked out over the garbage heap. The family consisted of the father, a morose, sickly-looking shoemaker; the mother, stout and loud; the elder brother, Izzy, a barber who was later run over by a bus; and my pal Grisha, with his enormous pale blue eyes, the same age as I. The first time Grisha came out into the yard to play, we had a fight; I punched him and made his nose bleed. This was practically the only fistfight I've ever had; I have no taste for physical violence or confrontations, and people don't usually try to bully me.

Grisha and I soon managed to become friends, united by a common bent for daydreaming and fantasy. It seems to me that back then I was already attracted to something I can't quite describe, something I think of as Jewish intelligence. Or perhaps "rich inner life" might be a better way of putting that quality found among even the poorest Jewish families. I don't mean to imply that other peoples lack that richness, but there is a special intensity to the Jewish spirit.

Grisha and I would walk around the courtyard for hours on end, describing our fantasies and entertaining each other with yarns that were a cross between science fiction and fairy tales. When he was ten or eleven, Grisha started to study the cello. (His parents bought him an instrument, even though it was very expensive for them.) One day, we were playing together or were absorbed as usual in some discussion, when an elderly Jew who lived in the neighborhood came up to us. Although he knew us both, he spoke to Grisha alone, ignoring my presence: "Now that you're learning the cello, you must be a well-behaved boy and not play with just anybody." Casting a stern glance in my direction, the old man hobbled away.

Grisha eventually became a dental technician, and in 1941 he was sent to the front, where his skills could be put to good use. In 1945, when the war was almost over, a truck in which he was riding was hit by a bomb and he was killed.

I still have a photograph of the children who used to play in our yard, including Grisha, Irina, my brother Yura, and myself. There are five boys of my age in the picture; to the best of my knowledge, three of them lost their lives during the war. Such was the fate of our generation. Valya (in the center of the photograph), was the eldest son of a house painter whose family occupied the basement apartment. He was a fine boy, proud, honest, and fearless, and a good brother. He went through an accelerated course for fighter pilots and was killed in 1942, on one of his first combat missions.

When I was ten, my parents gave me an imported wooden scooter. For several years I rode it up and down our street; other children also took turns riding it. These included Mishka, a boy of seventeen or eighteen, who had lost a leg hitching a ride on the back of a streetcar and who was rumored to have connections with a criminal gang; he was nicknamed "Chugalug" because he drank vodka straight from the bottle. Mishka lived at No. 6, quite close to us.

Some years later, as I was passing the market on my way home (it was quite late, since I attended the second shift of the seventh grade), I was stopped by half a dozen boys of about my age. They surrounded me and demanded that I give them five kopeks. When I ignored them and tried to push by, one did his best to trip me, while another hit me in the face, but I kept my balance and broke free.

Feeling quite pleased with myself, I slowed from a run to a walk. All of a sudden, a tall fellow of about twenty-five, with pale, mean features and a cap pulled down over his eyes, emerged from the shadows. "Got ten kopeks?" I reached into my pocket and handed him the money, but he wouldn't get out of my way. "Leave me alone. I live here." "You live here? Do you know Mishka Chugalug?" "Yes, I do." "Then tell me where he lives." "In No. 6." "Okay, now beat it while you're still in one piece!"

A few weeks later, I heard that Mishka's body had been found on the steps of St. George's, a nearby church. His eyes had been gouged out and his tongue cut off; he'd apparently been killed in reprisal for some violation of the thieves' code.

It was only years later that I put the two incidents together: the man who asked me for Mishka's address, and Mishka's murder. No doubt they would have found Mishka without my help, but his death weighs on me to this day. It never occurred to me to tell my story to the police, and I'm fairly sure I never said anything about it to my parents. And yet, who knows? Maybe my memory has played a trick on me and Mishka was killed before I ever got involved.

I GREW UP in an era marked by tragedy, cruelty, and terror, but it was more complicated than that. Many elements interacted to produce an extraordinary atmosphere: the persisting revolutionary élan; hope for the future; fanaticism; all-pervasive propaganda; enormous social and psychological changes; a mass exodus of people from the countryside; and, of course, the hunger, malice, envy, fear, ignorance, and demoralization brought about by the seemingly endless war, the brutality, murder, and violence. It was in these circumstances that there arose what official Soviet jargon euphemistically terms the "cult of personality."

By the early 1930s, I had gained some idea of current events from overhearing the conversations of grownups, who don't always realize how attentively children are listening. I remember hearing stories of teenagers fleeing from famine-stricken areas in the Ukraine, the central "black earth" region, and Belorussia. They would hide in the tool compartments under freight cars, and often were dead when finally pulled out. Starving people succumbed in railroad stations, homeless children took shelter in asphalt tanks and foundation pits. My Aunt Tusya found one such teenager and adopted him even though his parents eventually turned up alive. Egor, as the boy was called, became a highly skilled electrician, and he has worked on the assembly of all the major accelerators in the USSR. Now he has grandchildren.

I began to hear the words "arrest" and "search" more and more often. Hardly a single family remained untouched, and ours was no exception.

I've already described how Uncle Ivan's two sons died during the civil war; his own fate was tragic as well. Father often said that Ivan was a born engineer. He mastered any work he picked up and had more breadth and dash than any of the other brothers. He possessed genuine artistic talent and was a brilliant raconteur. Persuaded by Nikolai Bukharin and Valerian Osinsky (who later became prominent Bolsheviks) and other classmates from his high school that he ought to "serve the people," he abandoned engineering to enroll in law school. He rose quickly to the top of the legal profession and became a major figure in financial circles. Even then, in the 1920s, there were a great many things he didn't like about the system, and I heard him express alarm about what was going on in the country. Years later, I was told that he had drawn a caricature of Stalin with fanglike teeth and a sinister grin behind the mustache. It was a dangerous thing to do; but it wasn't this that caused his arrest.

It seems that sometime in the late 1920s, Uncle Ivan tried to help a friend leave the country by loaning him his passport. Ivan was arrested and imprisoned for about two years. His wife, Zhenya (my father's favorite sister-in-law), sought help from a former classmate of hers, Genrikh Yagoda, then deputy head of the OGPU,[8] but without success.

After his release in the early 1930s, Uncle Ivan, as an ex-convict, was unable to get his previous job back. Instead he became a draftsman, and a very good one. He started out by doing complicated designs for machine tools, and then acquired a unique specialty—drawing nomograms, sets of curves used for the graphic solution of equations. I remember his chain-smoking his way through the night's work. Aunt Zhenya, too, was working at home as a typist, and Uncle Ivan regularly cleaned and repaired her ancient typewriter. He bought himself another motorcycle and spent hours tinkering with it in the shed.

In 1935 Uncle Ivan was arrested again. This time, he was sent into internal exile. He worked for a few years as a buoy-keeper on the Volga and then became the manager (and sole employee) of a hydrological station in the same area. During the war he was arrested for a third time. He died from malnutrition in Krasnoyarsk prison hospital in 1943. A letter Aunt Zhenya had mailed to him was returned bearing the inscription: "Addressee relocated to the cemetery."

This wasn't the only misfortune to befall our family in the 1930s. Aunt Valya's second husband, a man named Belgardt, had been an officer, first in

[8][From 1923 to 1934, the state security organs were named the OGPU, the Russian acronym for Unified State Political Administration.]

the Tsar's forces and then in Admiral Kolchak's[9] army; in the mid-1930s, like most former White Guard officers, he was arrested and shot. Mother's elder brother, Vladimir, was arrested and died in a camp. Also in the mid-1930s, my cousin Evgeny was sent to a labor camp, where he drowned while rafting timber down a river. His son Yura had spent a summer with us at the dacha, and we'd all become very fond of him. In the winter of 1938, Yura contracted meningitis and died in the hospital.

In 1937, Uncle Konstantin, another of Mother's brothers, was arrested, along with his younger sister Tusya and Tusya's husband, Gennady Sarkisov. Tusya had been working as a secretary for an American correspondent. This was a very lucrative position, since part of her salary was paid in Torgsin coupons.[10] Tusya sometimes gave Mother a few coupons, and that always occasioned a family feast with butter, sugar, and other luxuries.

Konstantin had worked at a military plant—and in those days, having family links both to foreigners and to military technology was more than sufficient grounds for arrest. Konstantin was an amateur photographer and also a highly skilled radio amateur. As early as 1930, he'd built a homemade television set with a mechanical scanning system, using a Nipkow disc[11]—an absolute miracle for that time. He died during the course of the investigation. (He may have been killed while under interrogation, but we preferred not to think of that possibility.) After his death, the NKVD[12] lost interest in the case. Tusya and her husband were given what were for those days light sentences: five years for her, two years for him.

Was our family's chronicle of tragedies exceptional? Every family I know suffered casualties, and many lost more members than ours did. Different classes of society were affected to different degrees, of course, but the number of those who died was in the millions. They perished from a whole range of cataclysms: the deportation of kulaks [well-to-do peasants] to special settlements; the famine following collectivization; witch hunts for "saboteurs" and "enemies of the people" (often the more enterprising members of society); spy mania; religious persecution; ill-treatment of returning prisoners of war; campaigns against "cosmopolitans," "gleaners" [it was a crime to gather grain left behind in the fields after the harvest], and violators of work discipline; and other causes both familiar and obscure. Millions more died in the war, and the magnitude of the losses must be charged to the regime and the disorganization

9 [Admiral Alexander Kolchak commanded the anti-Bolshevik forces in Siberia (1918–1920).]
10 [Torgsin stores were the predecessors of today's Beryozka foreign-currency stores.]
11 [Early television scanner invented in 1884 by Paul Nipkow.]
12 [The state security organs were renamed the NKVD (People's Commissariat of Internal Affairs) in 1934.]

it produced. All those terrible events are now part of history, but their effects persist.

I hardly ever heard my father condemn the regime outright. But there was one occasion in 1950 when he denounced Stalin with such vehemence that Mother feared for his health. It may be that Father had refrained until then from expressing his true feelings for my sake; he may have worried that understanding too much too soon might make it difficult for me to survive in this world. This reluctance to reveal one's thoughts even to one's own son may be the most haunting sign of those times. But Father's indirect condemnation of the regime was continually surfacing in one form or another.

Uncle Ivan, on the other hand, would discuss politics and economics with far less restraint—or so I recall. (My knowledge of his views depends largely on conversations with my father late in his life, and my memory has probably been influenced by my present outlook.) Uncle Ivan regarded the socialist system as an efficient instrument for consolidating power, but one poorly geared to the satisfaction of human needs. One of his sayings sticks in my mind: Under capitalism, the seller chases after the buyer and that makes both of them work better; but under socialism, the buyer chases the seller, and neither has time to work. It's just an aphorism, of course—but one that reflects a measure of truth.

No less important are other features of the socialist system: the denial of civil liberties and of the rights of the individual, intolerance of other ideologies, and a dangerous pretension to absolute truth. But I did not become conscious of these until much later, and I don't know if my parents harbored any thoughts on these matters. I was content to absorb Communist ideology without questioning it. At the age of twelve, for example, I saw the Inca form of government as evidence of the vitality of the socialist idea; many years later, Igor Shafarevich would place the same historical facts in a completely contrary light.[13]

I remember my grandmother saying: "The Russian peasant wants to own his land—the Bolsheviks are sure to miscalculate on this!" But on another occasion she said: "Still, the Bolsheviks have managed to get things in order; they've strengthened both Russia and their own hold on power. Let's hope things will be easier for ordinary people from now on."

This seemed to me then, and still does now, evidence of Grandmother's tolerance and broad-mindedness. But there may have been something else at work as well: her apparently contradictory statements may have signaled her acceptance of the new "imperial" order that was emerging (or at least seemed to be) after many years of chaos and "experiment." Like others of her genera-

---

[13][Shafarevich, *The Socialist Phenomenon* (Harper & Row, 1980), pp. 132–142.]

tion, my grandmother used the expression "peacetime" for the era prior to 1914; true peace had not returned since, and there was a widespread yearning for stability. In our day, too, there is nostalgia for stability and order; ironically, it looks back to the Stalin era described so aptly by Anna Akhmatova, in her poem "Requiem," as "a time when only the dead smiled, glad to be at rest." In assessing my grandmother's attitude, however, it is important to understand that she anticipated and hoped for a progressive improvement in conditions.

I should say a few words about my parents' views on nationalism. It's difficult now to imagine the prevailing atmosphere of the 1920s and 1930s—not just in propaganda, in the press, and in public meetings, but also in ordinary social interchange. The terms "Russia" and "Russian" then had an almost indecent ring to them, suggesting the bitter nostalgia of people "who once had been something." After the external threat to the Soviet Union became a reality in the mid-1930s, official propaganda found a use for the idea of national pride. This idea has since been increasingly exploited, not just for defense purposes, but to bolster the fading slogan of "world Communism," to justify the country's isolation, the campaign against "cosmopolitanism," and so on.

All this official vacillation had virtually no impact on our family. My parents' tastes had been formed by Russian culture; they loved Russian literature, Russian and Ukrainian song. I was raised on all this, and it all became part of my inner world—but it never shut out world culture.

Sometimes, speaking of the First World War or the more distant past, my father would express admiration for Russian soldiers and officers. But he made flattering remarks about other nationalities as well. He would talk about General Suvorov, but always in a particular context—that Suvorov had never signed a single death sentence. This, I believe, was one way Father had of obliquely suggesting his opposition to the excesses of the current regime. (My own opinion of Suvorov changed for the worse when I learned of the brutalities he permitted in Warsaw and his other military campaigns, not to mention the way he crushed the Pugachev revolt.) I also remember Father's praising the talents of Russian émigrés, citing, for example, the achievements of Vladimir Zworykin, the inventor of the cathode ray tube used in television receivers. But there was nothing chauvinistic about my family's attitude toward Russian culture, and I do not recall a single derogatory remark about other nationalities—rather, the contrary.

Now, it no longer seems impossible that the state might openly endorse Russian nationalism as its ideology. And, at the same time, Russian nationalism is becoming more intolerant, in dissident circles as well. This only serves to confirm a viewpoint whose origin lies in my youth.

* * *

LIVING IN a different era, under different circumstances, with a different philosophy and social status, I've become more cosmopolitan, more global in outlook, more involved in public affairs than my family ever were. Nevertheless, I am profoundly indebted to them for having provided me with a sound point of departure for my passage.

2

MY EDUCATION

MY FIRST BOOKS were read to me and my cousin Irina by Grandmother, but we soon began reading for ourselves. We were encouraged by the fact that every family in our house had a library, mainly of prerevolutionary editions passed from generation to generation. Our parents naturally helped guide our selections.

I began to teach myself to read at the age of four, first spelling out the words on signboards and the names of steamships. My mother helped me perfect this skill. It gives me pleasure to list at random some of the books I read as I grew older: Pushkin's *The Tale of Tsar Saltan, Dubrovsky,* and *The Captain's Daughter;* Dumas's *The Three Musketeers* (Athos's wounded shoulder, Porthos's baldric, Aramis's handkerchief); Malot's *Sans Famille;* Hugo's *Les Misérables;* and James Greenwood's *The True History of a Little Ragamuffin,* an excellent book seemingly forgotten in its native England but popular in Russia thanks to Chukovsky's translation. I especially loved Jules Verne, whose stories I found absorbing and full of humor and geographical detail, especially *Captain Grant's Children, Mysterious Island,* a tribute to human labor and the power of science and technology, and the fabulous *Twenty Thousand Leagues Under the Sea.* I also enjoyed Dickens's *David Copperfield, Dombey and Son* (surely his best and most moving novel), and *Oliver Twist;* Gogol's early works (Uncle Ivan would read these stories aloud, brilliantly capturing the intonations and mimicking the gestures of characters in *The Gamblers, The Marriage,* and the Ukrainian tales); Harriet Beecher Stowe's *Uncle Tom's Cabin;* Mark Twain's *Tom Sawyer, Huckleberry Finn,* and *The Prince and the Pauper;* Andersen's "Thumbelina," "The Snow Queen," "The Little Match Girl," "The Steadfast Tin Soldier," and "The Tinder Box" ("Grandpa Adya, do you like 'The Tinder Box'?" my little granddaughter would ask me from faraway

Newton, fifty years later. "Yes, I do, very much!"); Mayne Reid's *The Cliff
Climbers* and *Osceola the Seminole;* Swift's splenetic, impassioned *Gulliver's
Travels;* Jack London's *Martin Eden, The Star Wanderer,* and the dog stories;
Ernest Thompson Seton; H. G. Wells's *Time Machine, Men like Gods,* and
War of the Worlds; and, a little later, of course, virtually everything by Pushkin
and Gogol. I was able to memorize Pushkin's poetry with ease. At the suggestion of my friend Oleg Kudryavtsev, I read Goethe's *Faust* and Shakespeare's
Hamlet and *Othello*. I remember discussing with Grandmother almost every
page of Tolstoy's *Childhood, Boyhood, Youth* (the memorable episode with
the green stick) and *War and Peace*—a whole world of people whom "we know
better than our own friends and neighbors." I entered adolescence enriched
by my acquaintance with these books and, of course, with many others I
haven't listed here.

IN THE FALL of 1927, I began lessons in reading, writing, and arithmetic with
a private tutor named Zinaida. When our lessons were over, she would walk
with me to the Cathedral of Christ-the-Savior, where I would run up and down
the stairway's wide balustrade, along the way telling me stories from history
and from the Bible. What she told me may not always have been accurate, but
it was extremely interesting. Zinaida was very young, unsettled, and a religious
believer. She tutored me only until the following spring, but for some time
afterward she would come to see my mother, looking more frightened and
miserable each time. Mother would give her a little money or food.

Zinaida met a tragic end. Mainly for religious reasons, she decided to leave
the USSR and tried to cross the border. But the border was, as the boast had
it, "under lock and key," and most would-be emigrants—there were thousands,
some fleeing from the campaign against kulaks, others from famine or imminent arrest—ended up in labor camps. Zinaida got ten years; we learned this
from a brief note that she managed to smuggle out. It was the last we heard
of her.

In the fall of 1928, my parents arranged for me to study at home, together
with Irina and Oleg Kudryavtsev. After four years Oleg and Irina entered
school, but I continued private lessons for another year. My brother Yura was
also taught privately for three years and my cousin Katya never attended school
at all, studying instead in a group of a dozen or so children that included Sergei
Mikhalkov, the future secretary of the Writers' Union. I sat in on some of their
drawing lessons.

I have little doubt that the home study program was Uncle Ivan's idea; my
parents and Aunt Valya simply followed his lead. They must have had serious doubts about the education provided by Soviet schools or they wouldn't

have gone to the trouble of arranging such a complicated and expensive undertaking. In theory, of course, individual tutoring fosters self-reliance and good work habits, and it may well accelerate learning and intellectual development. Perhaps I am not the best one to judge, but it seems that in our case the advantages were not fully realized. Moreover, home study impeded our psychological and social development, and for myself, this kind of education reinforced the innate lack of ability to communicate with people that has troubled me for much of my life.

Irina, Oleg, and I had two tutors—Anna Bekker, a primary school teacher, and Faina Kalugina, a German-language instructor. Our daily lessons lasted for about three hours, and we alternated between Oleg's house and ours. I studied German in later years as well, but without great success; foreign languages have never been my strong suit. All the same, I can still recite by heart a few dozen lines of classical German poetry—and, more important, I managed to get through several splendid books indispensable for my professional development.

I think the main advantages I derived from private lessons were the convenience and the opportunity for daily contact with Oleg, a truly exceptional individual. Oleg's father, a kind, rather absentminded man, taught mathematics for non-mathematicians at Moscow University and had written a textbook for his course. Oleg's mother was a thin, nervous woman who often suffered from migraines, but still managed to keep house through some difficult times. Like us, the Kudryavtsevs occupied two rooms in a communal apartment, but their study was bigger than ours, and the walls were lined with bookcases. Portraits of Descartes, Newton, Gauss, Euler, Ampère, and other famous people hung over the shelves. Their library was magnificent, and included a complete set of the Brockhaus and Efron encyclopedia, which I loved to read for hours on end.

Christmas was always a memorable holiday both in the Kudryavtsevs' household and in ours. Preparations started early, and our families designed imaginative decorations and costumes. A great many children and their parents would gather at these celebrations.

Oleg's cousins Gleb and Kirill were often at the Kudryavtsevs'. Gleb was a strong, strapping, good-looking boy, though somewhat coarse-featured; he had a loud voice and was full of self-confidence. Kirill, on the other hand, was quiet and rather shy. He was an orphan, and when Easter came round he would paint the eggs with graves and crosses—he associated Easter with visits to his mother's grave. Oleg's mother was a bit of a snob. I remember how disgusted she was that Gleb married the nurse who had tended him in the hospital after he was wounded during the war.

As for Kirill, he suffered serious burns in a tank fire. When he was discharged from the hospital, he refused to return to a tank platoon; he was sent to a punishment battalion and was killed. Okudzhava's words "There's no sense in sad soldiers staying alive" could have been written about him.

My friend Oleg decided at an early age to become a historian, and he read and learned by heart everything he could get his hands on. He was especially interested in ancient mythology, history, and culture, though he was equally enthusiastic about the works of Jules Verne: half-jokingly he called himself "the scientific secretary of the Society of Scholars" in honor of Jacques Paganelle in *Captain Grant's Children.*

Oleg was also very fond of poetry, and here again I fell under his influence. He could recite by heart page after page of *The Iliad* and *The Odyssey,* first in Russian translation and later in the original; the opening of *Faust;* and Pushkin's *Poltava* and *Boris Godunov.* Because of rheumatic fever Oleg missed several years of school, and never served in the army; he earned a history degree during the war. He was good-natured and slightly absentminded like his father. There was something courtly and old-fashioned, even comical, in his manner that was distinctly attractive. He specialized in ancient history and wrote an enormous dissertation—six hundred typescript pages—on Roman foreign policy of the second century A.D.

I owe a great deal to Oleg for opening up to me whole new vistas of knowledge and art, the entire field of the "humanities." He was one of the few close friends I've ever had, and I've always regretted that I didn't see more of him after the war. The fault was mine; it shows just how wrapped up I was in my own affairs. I visited Oleg a couple of times at his apartment, and once he visited my wife, Klava, and me. He died in 1956 at the age of thirty-five from cancer of the esophagus.

In the winter of 1932–33, after our group split up, I was given lessons by a couple of elderly sisters who lived in the same building as my godfather, Alexander Goldenveizer, on Skatertny Lane, and I often stopped in to see him. On the staircase, I would be bullied by a boy named Rostik, son of a Red Army commander, who considered himself a superior breed to the likes of me. I shudder to think what may have awaited this family in 1937.

IN THE FALL of 1933, I entered the fifth grade[1] at School No. 110, but it was a complete waste of time after my five years of education at home. It was not just an ordinary school; many of the pupils were children of Soviet officials—the daughter of Karl Radek was among them. The school emphasized chemistry and

---

[1][Soviet children generally begin school when they are seven years old and attend ten grades of primary and secondary school.]

had an excellent laboratory. The principal, Ivan Novikov, enjoyed a certain independence, and on one of my first days there I heard him speak about love and friendship—not a trivial discussion of this subject, at least for those times.

Once a week Novikov conducted a special class called "The Newspaper" in which we would take turns talking about current events. I remember speaking about the Moscow–Kara Kum–Moscow automobile endurance race (I had no way of knowing then that the entire route was guarded by troops!) and a high-altitude balloon flight. These sensational exploits functioned as a new-style "opium of the people," dulling and distracting their thoughts.

Later on, there were other spectacles—the *Cheluskin* expedition, flights to the North Pole, and so on. But there was so much we didn't know at the time: it was only forty years afterward, for example, that I found out from Robert Conquest's excellent book *The Great Terror* that the USSR may have rejected an offer of American assistance in rescuing the *Cheluskin*'s crew for fear the Americans might discover a Soviet transport ship trapped in the ice nearby with thousands of dying prisoners aboard.[2]

The paramount issue of the late 1930s was the Spanish Civil War. That tragic conflict was treated by the Soviet media as yet another diversion. How strange it is that fifty years later, the anxieties and bitterness of the Spanish war are still alive in people of my generation. There was some spellbinding force at work, a sense of romance, heroism, challenge—and, possibly, a premonition of the evil fascism would bring. At the time we were incensed by the Western powers' policy of "nonintervention"; today, we know that the role played by the USSR and its secret services was also far from straightforward. Not until the 1970s did I read Hemingway's *For Whom the Bell Tolls*, Orwell's *Homage to Catalonia*, and the work of Kirill Khenkin.[3]

I had no problems with my work at school, but I made no friends there; nor, for that matter, enemies. I do recall having some trouble in carpentry class— I've never been good with my hands. During one of my first shop lessons, a couple of older boys decided to see whether I was a crybaby and jammed my fingers in a vise. Somehow or other, I managed to hold back the tears, and the next time, one of the bullies offered to help me with my carpentry: I was having a terrible time constructing a stool.

Early in 1934, my parents decided I had wasted enough time and took me out of school. They arranged a crash course covering the fifth and sixth grades so I could pass the examinations and be accepted into the seventh grade. This period of intensive study was of great importance in my intellectual development.

---

[2] [The *Cheluskin* was caught and crushed by ice in February 1934 while attempting to navigate the Arctic Ocean from Murmansk to Vladivostok. The crew were rescued by Soviet pilots who became national heroes. See Robert Conquest, *The Great Terror* (Macmillan, 1968), p. 475.]

[3] [Russian-born journalist who fought in Spain in the 13th International Brigade.]

Father gave me lessons in physics and mathematics, and we did simple experiments which he made me write up and illustrate in my notebook. (It's hard to believe now, but I once kept neat exercise books, and in good handwriting, like my father's!) I grasped ideas quickly, with little need for explanation, and was fascinated by the possibility of being able to reduce the whole gamut of natural phenomena to the comparatively simple laws of interactions between atoms, as expressed by mathematical formulas.

I did not yet fully appreciate all the subtleties of differential equations, but I sensed and delighted in their power. It may have been this more than anything else that kindled my desire to become a physicist. Needless to say, I was incredibly fortunate to have a teacher like my father.

Tutors came to our house to teach me geography, history, biology, and chemistry. Apart from physics and mathematics, the subjects I liked best and found easiest were biology and chemistry. I was beginning to understand the theory behind chemical experiments, which added to my enjoyment of their spectacular effects. For lessons in Russian language and literature, my mother took me to Alexander Malinovsky, whose study, piled high with books, excited my envy and commanded my respect. In late spring 1934, I took the sixth-grade examinations, which I found quite simple, although the teachers told my parents that they were more impressed by my free and confident manner than by my knowledge. In the fall of 1934, I entered seventh grade at the Third Model School, which a year later was renamed School No. 113. I joined the school's literary society, but attended only one meeting before concluding that I was not cut out to be a writer or journalist. Other than that, things went smoothly in the seventh grade.

Father wanted me to spend a year (since I was a grade ahead of my age group in school) working as a laboratory assistant after my graduation from high school, but this idea fell by the wayside when the draft age was lowered in 1938 and college admission became more difficult.

On December 1, 1934, Sergei Kirov was assassinated. The whole school gathered in the auditorium, and the principal, an Old Bolshevik, told us what had happened, fighting back her tears. My father, while riding a tram, caught a glimpse of a black-bordered portrait in someone's newspaper and, thinking it was Voroshilov who had died, he rushed home in a panic, anticipating a revival of the Red Terror of 1918.[4] He calmed down when he learned that it was Kirov instead. The name meant nothing to him, which shows just how

[4] [A hero of the October Revolution and the Civil War, Kliment Voroshilov became minister of defense in 1934 and a prominent Bolshevik leader.]

remote our family was from Party affairs—Kirov had been number two in the
Party after Stalin.

Next day, the newspapers featured a decree introducing special measures for
combating terrorism, and a large photograph of Stalin standing beside Kirov's
coffin. A wave of terror was about to overwhelm a country which had just been
battered by the struggle against the kulaks and by a major famine.

For the masses who were herded by the millions into the Gulag during the
Stalin era, the infamous "1937" (shorthand for the whole 1935–1938 period)
was not necessarily the worst time; but for those who lived in the large cities,
for the intelligentsia, for government, Party, and military officials, and for
skilled workers, this was the peak of the repressions. It was also the time when
those arrested had the least chance of surviving in the camps and prisons. The
postwar camps were sinister enough, but they served an essentially different
purpose, an economic one (the exploitation of slave labor), and the mortality
rate (with the exception of certain special camps) was significantly lower than
it had been between 1936 and 1944. The same is true of our current labor
camps, for all their inhumanity.

The spiritual atmosphere of the USSR cannot be explained without harking
back to this era, to the crippling fear that first gripped the big cities and then
spread to the population at large, and which has left its mark on us even today,
two generations later. The repressions caused panic because of their pervasive-
ness and cruelty, and perhaps still more because of their irrationality; it was
simply impossible to fathom how or why their victims were chosen.

What was life like for children growing up at the time? Despite all that was
happening, many of the younger generation were able to retain the idealism
that had once inspired their elders. I do not count myself among their number,
as I was painfully introverted and totally immersed in my own affairs. Thus,
there is little I can say about my classmates. In the eighth grade I sat next to
a boy called Misha Shveitser who had a passionate love of anything to do with
literature or art and is now a prominent film director. Yet during the year and
a half we shared a desk we never once had a heart-to-heart talk, and the only
ten-minute conversation we had on a street corner seemed a major event to
me. He never visited my home, nor I his. To our right sat a row of girls, and
their life was even more of a mystery to me. I would steal a timid glance in
their direction, but never spoke a word to any of them. When the year came
to an end, Misha moved and sat next to the girl whom I found most intriguing.
I was far too bashful to give her the slightest hint of my interest.

Nor was I particularly friendly with any of the other boys in my class. One,
named Yura Orlov, wrote what seemed to me pretty good poems. His mother,
a single parent, loved her only son (slim and swarthy, he looked somehow
Greek) with an unhealthy intensity. Yura guarded his independence fiercely,
and was none too popular with the teachers. He would come out with the most

unexpected things, for example: "It's not true that Lenin was a nice fellow—his favorite expression was: *'R-r-rastr-r-relyat!* (Shoot him!).'" (Yura mimicked Lenin's uvular *r*'s.)

It was one of the first remarks I heard that cut through the cant usually surrounding Lenin's name. As for my present view of him, however, it is impossible not to appreciate the significance of Lenin's personality and the tragedy of his fate (a reflection of the fate of our country), and the great influence he had on the course of world events. I agree with Berdyaev that Lenin's initial impulse, and that of most of the other revolutionaries, was in essence humanitarian and moral; it was the logic of their struggle and the tragic twists of history that turned them into what they later became and dictated their course of action. But not only that. There was something inherently false in their basic political and philosophical premises. That is why objectivity so often was supplanted by pragmatic considerations and humanism by fanaticism, and why the Party line and Party struggle triumphed over moral principles.

Yura, who was older than I, entered the army after graduation and was killed in an ambush when Soviet troops marched into Iran in 1941.

Toward the end of eighth grade, Tolya Bashun, another classmate, suggested we join the mathematics club at the university (I was already a member of the school math club). It inspired me to hear people close to my own age discussing combinatorial analysis, number theory, non-Euclidean geometry, and the like. The twin brothers Akiva and Isaak Yaglom impressed me more than anyone else there. Later, Akiva studied physics in my class at Moscow University, and Isaak studied mathematics. We all attended the general physics course together, and our paths have crossed many times since university days.

I tried competing in the nationwide math and physics "Olympiad" more than once, but I could never manage to concentrate against a clock. I was able to solve some of the problems later at home, but the lengthier calculations tended to intimidate me.

While still in the seventh grade, I had started doing physics experiments at home. At first I used Father's book *Experiments with a Light Bulb,* then I managed with a few hints from him, and finally on my own. I compensated for my lack of manual dexterity with my ability to improvise. For instance, I constructed a fairly decent potentiometer out of a bar of ordinary soap. A light bulb served the role of an additional resistor. The device allowed me to regulate precisely the voltage applied to a neon bulb used in an experiment suggested by my father to illustrate the photoelectric effect; the strike of a match ignites the neon bulb. When I needed direct current for this and other experiments, I made a rectifier by filling a glass with a solution of baking soda and using an aluminum teaspoon and a piece of lead-covered cable as electrodes.

On one occasion, I connected the leads from a battery to the terminals of a small motor and then disconnected them carelessly, leaving my fingers on the terminals; the electric shock I received was a memorable lesson in induction. I conducted lots of experiments in electrostatics. I took up photography, and built a crystal radio receiver using my father's design. My favorite experiment was with Liesegang rings—I still like it best, even now. In optics, I experimented with polarized light, with fluorescent solutions, and with Newton's rings, and I built a Maxwell's color wheel. I observed double stars and the satellites of Jupiter through binoculars, and spent many happy hours in the planetarium, where I met Boris Samoilov, who was working there two days a week.

The popular-science and science fiction books I read were of even greater importance than the experiments. In the ninth grade, I started on more serious scientific works. Time and again, I read *Physics for Fun* and everything else by Yakov Perelman I could get my hands on. Perelman's writings on science and space travel were very popular in my day, and I only hope that today's youngsters, living in an era when they are flooded with scientific information, still enjoy these books. Perelman himself was a true champion of popular science, who in addition to his books founded the Science Club for children in Leningrad. He died during the blockade of Leningrad.

I read books by Lézan and Ignatiev; a bit later, Rademacher and Toeplitz's *Numbers and Figures*, Sir James Jeans's *The Universe Around Us*, which influenced me enormously, and Max Valier's *Space Travel as a Technical Possibility*. In tenth grade, I read Richard Courant's *Calculus*, with its original method of teaching integrals before differentials; and much, much more.

I also did some reading in biology. I was captivated by Paul de Kruif's *Microbe Hunters*, and even considered a career in microbiology. It was at that time that I learned about the genetic theory of heredity, and was then shocked and puzzled by the article in *Pravda* by Academician Mark Mitin attacking Mendel's genetics. This was my first encounter with Lysenkoist pseudo-science.[5] I read a book on paleontology and spent the next summer earnestly collecting fossils. Another book I read was *Botany for Fun* by Tsinger, an acquaintance of my father, and the author of a well-known physics manual, who took an amateur's delight in botany.

I had time for experiments and reading because I found school fairly easy, especially the exact sciences. In the seventh grade I got an "unsatisfactory" for singing, but this was never entered in my school record. I had problems with drawing, but, thanks to coaching by Katya, who was a student for a time at an architectural institute, my sketches began receiving A's. I was never out-

[5][On Lysenko, see pp. 199ff.]

standing in the humanities, but my general intelligence pulled me through. Aunt Zhenya worked on my grammar, and I was tutored at home in German when I was in the ninth grade.

I GRADUATED from high school as one of two honors students in my class. This enabled me to matriculate at the university without taking entrance examinations, and in the fall of 1938 I enrolled in the physics department of Moscow University, possibly the best department of its kind in the country.

Later I heard about the fierce competition for places and the terror of the exams, and I don't think I would have gotten through this cruel and often unfair selection process. Among those who succeeded in winning a place in our class was Evgeny Zababakhin, who some years later would become a colleague of mine. He had worked for a couple of years in an automobile plant before entering the university, which gave him a preferential right of enrollment, but he was in any case a capable and hardworking person.

The time I spent at the university can be divided into two sharply defined periods: my three years in Moscow before war broke out, and my senior year, when we were evacuated to Ashkhabad. During my first three years, I devoted all my energy to physics and mathematics. I owe a debt of gratitude to my teachers at Moscow University: Arnold, Rabinovich, Norden, Mlodzeyevsky (junior), Lavrentiev (senior), Moiseyev, Vlasov, Tikhonov, Kletennik, Elsgolts, and Shaskolsky, among others. I will never forget Professor Bavli, a punctilious and rather eccentric man who was killed by a German bomb in the first weeks of the war.

We were given lots of extra reading to do, and after lectures I would dash home for lunch or eat in the university cafeteria and then sit and study in the library until late in the evening. I soon began skipping the boring classes and spending more and more time in the reading room.

An informal student club met outside the library; some students would emerge for a cigarette, others to stretch their legs and chat. I can't recall ever talking about anything except science during these breaks.

One popular prank was for two students to steal up behind someone and flip him over in the air. Several times I was the victim. On one occasion, the joke backfired when a student accidentally smashed a bust of Molotov, touching off a "political" incident of sorts, complete with cross-examinations; only the fact that the culprit had influential connections saved him from serious trouble.

The teacher who conducted the seminar in Marxism-Leninism had various stock questions. For example: "Do the treaty and the rapprochement between the USSR and Germany demonstrate opportunism or principle?" The expected answer, of course, was: "Principle. They reflect the congruity of our positions." The press was full of this kind of thing; it wasn't till later that we found out about the secret clauses in the Soviet-German pact and the swap of prisoners between the Gestapo and the NKVD.[6] I don't think the West even now has a full appreciation of these matters.

I entered the physics department almost automatically, motivated by my father and my own deep-seated desire (my earlier dream of becoming a microbiologist had simply faded away). Even if I'd given it more thought, my choice would have been the same. The first year, I liked mathematics the most. The general physics course troubled me by a lack of clarity on certain points, an opinion shared by my classmates. Complicated matters that should never have been part of an introductory course were oversimplified and treated in a misleading and superficial manner. However, the historical method of presentation had the merit of providing a base from which it was easy and safe to move on to more sophisticated and logically consistent treatments of particular topics. Landau and Lifshitz's multivolume encyclopedia of theoretical physics is a wonderful course of this type.[7] But even at this level one still needs courses that are structured around the historical development of physics, and I was fortunate enough to read the magnificent works of Pauli at the right moment, just after the war.

The only subject that gave me trouble was Marxism-Leninism. It wasn't an ideological problem: at the time, it never entered my head to question Marxism as the ideology best suited to liberate mankind, and materialism too seemed a reasonable enough philosophy. What I didn't like was the attempt to carry over the outmoded concepts of natural philosophy into the twentieth century (the age of exact science) without amendment: for example, Engels with his Lamarckian theory of the role played by labor in turning apes into men (which conflicts with the modern theory of genetics) and the primitive, naïve use of formulas in *Das Kapital*. The very size of that book, so typical of nineteenth-century German pedantry, put me off. I have no patience with books so thick they can serve as doorstops; such excessive bulk, I feel, can only result from a lack of clear thinking. Lenin's *Materialism and Empirio-Criticism* seemed superficial, written on the level of journalistic polemic. But the absolute bane of my existence was the necessity of memorizing definitions: I was unable to absorb words devoid of meaning.

6[For the text of the Non-aggression Pact signed by Molotov and Ribbentrop on August 23, 1939, the secret additional protocols, and other relevant documents from the archives of the German Foreign Office, see *Nazi-Soviet Relations, 1939–1941*, Department of State, Washington, 1948. See Alexander Weissberg's *The Accused* (Simon & Schuster, 1951) for a victim's account of the prisoner exchange.]

7[Six volumes of the Landau-Lifshitz work were published in the United States by Addison-Wesley, 1958–1960.]

In my second year, I tried my hand at independent research. The topic assigned to me by Professor Mikhail Leontovich—the weak nonlinearity of waves in water—was too difficult and ill defined for me, and my work got nowhere. (My father had worked with Leontovich on a textbook and had sent me to him.) Now I realize that the subject did have possibilities: since that time, many people have made studies of weak nonlinearity as it relates to turbulence in plasma as well as to waves in water. The nonlinear theory of "shallow water" is of particular interest. I probably could have done something with the topic after a few years of experience, but at that time, even after reading Sretensky's book, which was recommended by Leontovich, I still didn't really understand what he expected of me. The fact of the matter is that I simply wasn't ready for original research. (Nevertheless, I feel that this purposeful effort, the hours spent in a library with a serious science book, was an important experience.) Fortunately, my failure didn't lead to any crisis of self-confidence, although it wasn't until 1943 that I managed to do independent scientific work (and then just for my own edification).

In my third year (1940–41), I diligently attended courses on the theory of probability, the calculus of variations, group theory, and topology. Unfortunately, these subjects, which should have been an integral part of the curriculum, were optional and were taught in a cursory manner, and to this day I remain conscious of my inadequate grounding in them.

I didn't make a single close friend during my first three years at the university. Although I paid an occasional visit to the home of Pyotr Kunin, a classmate, it was only after our evacuation to Ashkhabad that he and I became chums.

As 1940 DREW to a close, my grandmother had a stroke and lost her ability to speak. Father moved into her room so he could be available to assist her at a moment's notice. Mother asked me not to go and see her; even now I can't quite understand why she made that request—or, for that matter, why I agreed so meekly. After all, my relationship with Grandmother should have taken priority over my mother's desire to shield me from unpleasantness, especially since I was then already grown (a fact that my mother probably failed to notice). In any case, I disobeyed Mother on at least two occasions. I remember Grandmother indicating with her eyes that she wanted a glass of rose hip tea brought to her lips; she took a sip or two, and that was the last she ever drank or ate. She never lost her temper or gave a sign of complaint, although I know that the last weeks were very difficult for her.

On March 26, 1941, I stayed late at the university for a reading by Irakli Andronnikov, a master storyteller. When I got home, Grandmother was in her death throes, and she passed away early the next morning. Uncle Ivan, then in exile, made an illegal visit to Moscow to attend the funeral—it was the last time I saw him, and I remember his face contorted with grief. Grandmother was laid to rest in accordance with church ritual. Later, Father used to repeat that it was better that Grandmother had not lived to see the horrors of the war.

With her death, the soul seemed to depart from the house on Granatny Lane.

3

THE FIRST YEAR OF THE
WAR: ASHKHABAD

ON JUNE 22, 1941, I went to the university for a review session before the last exam of my third year. Suddenly, we were summoned to an auditorium, where, at noon, we heard Foreign Minister Vyacheslav Molotov's broadcast announcing the German invasion. He concluded his speech with a solemn vow: "Our cause is just. The enemy will be defeated. Victory will be ours!" Stalin repeated the very same words in a speech on July 3. (Marshal Kim Il Sung, the ruler of North Korea, would repeat those words once again in 1950.)

The outbreak of war is a traumatic event at any time, but there was also a strange feeling of returning to normalcy. Our people had been psychologically geared up year after year for what seemed an inevitable war with fascism; indeed, the Spanish Civil War was seen as prelude to that war. That, at least, was the thinking that prevailed until 1939. But then the puzzling alliance with Hitler intervened, ushering in a bizarre interlude of friendly relations with the fascist powers. Now that period too had ended abruptly, and the new turn of events put things back in their place, which somehow sharpened the sense of tragedy.

What did we think about the war and our country? There's no simple answer. Today only the blind and deaf do not know (or pretend not to know) that Stalin and his henchmen were responsible for atrocities unparalleled in history: the torture and deaths of millions of citizens; the devastation of the countryside and the famine which followed; the obliteration of the prewar officer corps; the disarray of the country's defenses; and—last but not least—the risky flirtation with Hitler, which Stalin initiated in hopes of reshaping the world's spheres of influence, not just of gaining time, as Soviet propaganda claimed. (In any event, in the months preceding Hitler's attack on the Soviet Union, Stalin failed to strengthen our defenses effectively.) The Molotov-

Ribbentrop Pact directly triggered the outbreak of war in September 1939. Of course, the 1938 Munich agreement played its role, but it was motivated at least in part by the West's mistrust of Stalin, and even Hitler's rise to power was abetted by Stalin's campaign to destroy Social Democracy and the destabilizing influence of our foreign policy.

It would be quite a few years before we found out about the secret clauses in the Molotov-Ribbentrop Pact, but we witnessed the partition of Poland by Germany and the USSR, the Soviet assault on Finland, and the annexation of the Baltic states and Bessarabia, all of which were made possible by the special relationship with Hitler of 1939–1941. We read Molotov's speeches in the newspapers, and they seemed exercises in cynicism (and still seem so today). Now it has become clear that in 1939 Stalin "put his money" on Hitler, and clung to belief in Hitler's reciprocal "good faith" as long as he could. Any alternative strategies Stalin may have been pursuing never amounted to anything. He miscalculated, and the nation paid for his blunder with millions of lives.

At the time, very few of us understood all that was going on, and I was not among them. Now I see many things differently, not as I did in those days, but I remain convinced that defeat at the hands of Nazi Germany would have been a far greater catastrophe than anything we suffered under our own hangmen. We had to fight to win. I always believed that our country, assisted by our allies, would emerge victorious—there was simply no alternative, and I have no doubt whatsoever that the overwhelming majority of my countrymen felt the same way. The slogan "Our cause is just" was not simply humbug—no matter who said it. I find it odd to hear anyone argue the contrary. In June 1941 the situation was tragic, but clear. Once, during a bombing raid, I met Aunt Valya (whose husband had been executed in the 1930s) in the lobby. "For the first time in years," she said, "I feel that I am Russian!"

The above does not apply to those who collaborated with the enemy; although something should be said about them, too. No other nation in World War II had as many soldiers go over to the enemy as we did.[1] What must at once be added, however, is that this fact is a condemnation of the regime, not of the nation. We should not be too quick to judge those who made that difficult choice, often under extreme duress—instant death was sometimes the only alternative to collaboration. Many hoped that they might somehow redeem themselves one day; some actually did so in the liberation of Prague and

---

[1] [George Fisher, in *Soviet Opposition to Stalin* (Harvard, 1952), has estimated that a million or more Soviet citizens fought on the German side, some because of coercion, but others because of their wish to overthrow the Stalin regime.]

in other battles.[2] For the overwhelming majority of collaborators, however, this remained a forlorn hope, and they paid in full, by suffering and death, for their choice.

The war was a terrible trial for the nation. Even now, more than forty years later, its wounds have not completely healed. Those who were children then still remember their mothers' tears over the official notifications of their husbands' deaths. Surely the desire for peace is overriding in the minds of people everywhere. "Anything but not another war!" is the general cry—and yet for many survivors the war has remained the paramount experience of their lives, an experience that restored the pride and dignity which the daily grind of a totalitarian, bureaucratic society had all but chipped away. The war made us a *nation* once again.

We all believed—or at least hoped—that the postwar world would be decent and humane. How could it be otherwise? But instead Soviet victory seemed only to intensify the regime's severity: soldiers returning from German POW camps were the first to feel the tightening of the screws.[3] As the illusions faded, the nation disintegrated into separate atoms and melted away. Today, our people's hatred of war and pride in their wartime achievements are frequently exploited by official propaganda—for the simple reason that there is nothing else left to exploit. The events connected with the war, as reflected in art, in our lives, and in our memories, still evoke powerful feelings in my generation. But alongside the genuine emotions there is the cult of the Great Patriotic War, and its *manipulation* in the service of current political interests—and that is repugnant and dangerous.

AT THE BEGINNING of July 1941, Komsomol[4] members in my class were sent to perform "special tasks." Since I'd never joined the Komsomol (for reasons of inertia, not ideology), nobody bothered to tell me what was going on. When the girls got back, I learned that they'd been digging antitank ditches for a projected line of defense. The boys had been enlisted straight into the militia. A few weeks later, many of them were surrounded by enemy troops; some were killed, others were taken prisoner, and one apparently was executed for failing to obey an order.

Many young men and women of my age joined the armed services. No one

---

[2][In May 1945, units of General Vlasov's Russian Liberation Army fought SS troops and assisted the Czech resistance in liberating Prague from the Germans.]

[3][Alexander Solzhenitsyn describes in *The Gulag Archipelago I* (Harper & Row, 1974), pp. 237–251, the filling up of labor camps with returning prisoners of war.]

[4][Youth organization of the Communist Party.]

in my course was drafted directly into the army, although quite a few enrolled in militia units were later transferred to regular units. (A number of them were demobilized after their records were examined.) Others who were not called up—young women, in particular, like my future wife, Lusia Bonner—enlisted as volunteers.

As for myself, I had doubts about my physical fitness for the front because of a chronic heart condition, but it was not the main consideration. I also knew how much grief my death would cause my parents—though who could not say the same? The fact is, I simply had no desire to rush my fate, and preferred to let events take their course. This seemed a proper attitude at the time, and it still does. I can say in all honesty that I've never wished or tried to duck responsibilities—with respect to army service or anything else. As things turned out, I never joined the army, as most of my generation did, and I stayed alive while many others were killed.

Early in July, all male students with good grades were summoned to the Air Force Academy and given a very tough medical examination, which I failed. (Among those accepted was Evgeny Zababakhin.) I was upset, since the Academy seemed a step toward direct participation in the war effort. Later on, however, I realized how lucky I had been: the cadets spent most of the war doing nothing but studying, while I was able to make a modest but real contribution during the two and a half years I spent working in a cartridge plant.

Soon after war broke out, I began repairing radio equipment for the army in a university workshop organized by Professor Pumper—I tried to compensate for my lack of experience with extra effort. I soon switched to Professor Dekhtyar's research and development group, where I was asked to devise a magnetic probe for locating shrapnel in wounded horses. I spent a lot of time making the main element of the device (an assembly of H-shaped sheets of transformer iron with the meter coil on the cross-bar), which needed to be assembled with precision. However, my design wasn't sensitive enough for its intended purpose and was never put into production. All the same, the practical knowledge I gained of magnetic measuring devices and magnetic phenomena proved extremely useful for my work at the cartridge plant, and this taste of independent scientific work gave me a psychological boost.

I also joined the volunteer air defense units at the university and at our apartment house, helping to extinguish incendiary bombs when the air raids on Moscow began. (One of these bombs, half-burned-up, I kept on my table.) Almost every night from the end of July onwards, I stood on the roof watching as searchlights, tracer bullets, and Junkers bombers crisscrossed the uneasy skies over Moscow. Once, the air raid siren caught me in a public bathhouse. I decided to ignore regulations and walked home through the deserted streets, with the glare from burning buildings lighting my way. Suddenly, a fragment from an antiaircraft shell ricocheted off a wall and struck my foot, but a slight scratch on one boot was all I had to show for the experience.

In the summer and fall of 1941, I worked with other students on Sundays and holidays unloading military equipment from freight trains (for days a bitter aftertaste lingered in my mouth after handling some components of explosives) and digging trenches and antitank ditches. I remember a girl named Irina Rakobolskaya exhorting us one evening to finish unloading the cars, in spite of our exhaustion. She went on to join the famous women's air force regiment, married one of our fellow students, and is the mother of Andrei Linde, now my colleague at FIAN [the Physics Institute of the Academy of Sciences].

On October 16, I was one of those who witnessed the notorious Moscow panic. As office after office set fire to their files, clouds of soot swirled through streets clogged with trucks, carts, and people on foot carrying household possessions, baggage, and young children. Somehow or other I made my way to the university, where a crowd of students had gathered, eager to make themselves useful, but nobody said a word to us. I went with a few others to the Party committee office, where we found the Party secretary at his desk; when we asked whether there was anything useful we could do, he stared at us wildly and blurted out: "It's every man for himself!"

After a week of indescribable chaos, the government decided to evacuate the university. Mother and Father saw me off at the railroad station on October 23.

(I learned a month later that on the day I left Moscow, our home in Granatny Lane was destroyed by a German bomb. Several people were killed, but no one in my family was hurt. My parents moved with the other survivors and their salvaged belongings into an abandoned nursery school in the next street.)

After changing trains several times, our company of students and teachers finally reached Murom, a town 175 miles east of Moscow. For part of the journey I traveled on a platform car carrying tanks to a repair shop, and heard for the first time about the real situation at the front from the tank crews: unlike the stories in the newspapers, they told of retreat and encirclement and a struggle for survival that required resilience and resourcefulness and the ability to defend yourself against your own superiors.

We spent ten days in Murom waiting for the next train. Somehow those days turned out to be very profitable ones for my scientific education: reading Yakov Frenkel's books on quantum mechanics and relativity, I suddenly achieved new insights into those subjects. We were billeted with a woman who was pilfering food from the dwindling stocks in the grocery store where she worked—from time to time her daughter would scoop up a handful of sugar she kept in a drawer and stuff it into her mouth. There was a saying in those days: "For some, war spells loss—but for others it means profits." At night, the mother was visited by a succession of soldiers.

Trying to appease our hunger somehow, we would go in the evening to the railroad canteen, where one could get mashed potatoes without a ration card. Around two o'clock in the morning, trains carrying wounded soldiers used to pull into the station. The men were removed from the train and left on stretchers in the open air, waiting for their next connection. Those still able to walk thronged the station. Women from the town and the surrounding villages brought gifts of food and tobacco, inquired about loved ones, and searched for them among the wounded.

On November 7, the anniversary of the Revolution, I listened to a broadcast of Stalin's speech and a description of the parade in Red Square. I realized that it was all carefully staged; nevertheless, it had a powerful impact on me.

At last, we set off for Ashkhabad, capital of the Turkmen Republic, where the university was to be reconstituted. Forty of us were crowded into each railway car, equipped with double bunks and a stove. During the month-long journey, the cars became separate communities, as it were, with their own leaders, their talkative and silent types, their panic-mongers, go-getters, big eaters, the slothful and the hardworking. I suppose I fitted into the silent category; I continued reading Frenkel, but I still managed to watch everything going on around me inside the car and beyond its confines. I saw a country wounded by war. The trains moving east with us carried evacuees, damaged equipment, and wounded men; those racing past us toward the west carried combat troops: their faces were tense as they peered out from the train windows, and they all looked somehow alike.

When we reached the Urals, the temperature dropped to twenty degrees below zero and even lower; every day we stole bits of coal for our stove from the piles kept at the stations to supply the locomotives. Once, I spotted a piece of gingerbread (a relic from a different world) in the snow near a water tower and swallowed it on the spot. We ran into a blizzard on the Kazakh steppe, and the chimney pipe for our stove blew off; while the train was still in motion, a first-year student named Markov, wearing a T-shirt, climbed up onto the roof and repaired the damage. In the spring, he was drafted into the army, as were all the freshmen.

Some of the students were more than happy to exchange clothing for food brought to the train by peasants along the way, but I had nothing to trade. To while away the time, we played a trivia quiz game based on Ilf and Petrov's *The Twelve Chairs* and *The Golden Calf*. The champion was Iosif Shklovsky, who was later to become a distinguished astrophysicist. In the 1970s, Shklovsky warned me not to get involved with my wife-to-be, Lusia, arguing that her dangerous dissident activities could get me into trouble! (In his unpublished memoirs, Shklovsky writes that I borrowed Heitler's *Quantum Mechanics* from him on this journey, and easily mastered it. Unfortunately, this story seems to me simply a product of his overactive imagination, as I read Heitler only in 1945 or 1946, as a graduate student.)

Once I missed the train and had to make part of the journey on an open coal car; I lay flat on my stomach to avoid the bridges, before transferring to the vestibule of the parlor car carrying Sergei Kaftanov, the Minister of Higher Education. I never saw Kaftanov himself, but recognized one of his companions, who came out for a smoke, as a distant acquaintance of my father. He was the one who told me of the destruction of our Moscow home.

We did quite a bit of socializing with the female students on our train. One of them took an interest in me, and some of my fellow travelers enjoyed a few jokes at my expense when they saw I wasn't completely indifferent to her charms. Strange as it may seem, that train ride was my first real adventure beyond the confines of my family circle and almost the first social contact I had with companions of my own age, especially girls. When we got to Ashkhabad, the girls were separated from us, and we saw very little of them.

We arrived in Ashkhabad on December 6, the same day that our forces went over to the attack on the Moscow front. The news of our counteroffensive made me realize as never before the anxieties of the recent months, and as I listened to the solemn enumeration of armies, divisions, and generals participating in the battles, I shuddered at the thought of the countless persons, dead and alive, who had been engaged in the defense of Moscow.

THE CASUAL EXISTENCE of these few weeks came to an end as we returned to our studies and to reality. In retrospect, this was a difficult time, shadowed by concern for our families and for the course of the war. Yet it was also a time to enjoy our freedom and to be happy, for we were young.

We were expected to finish our studies in four years, as opposed to the usual five, and our curriculum, already out of date, had also been curtailed. This was one reason for the major gaps in my training in theoretical physics which I have never completely overcome. All the same, four years of serious study followed directly by independent work is, in my view, preferable to stretching out the academic program to seven or eight years, in which case momentum is lost, as well as time. In our case, of course, the overriding factor was the war, which increased the need for graduates in industry and research; plainly, however, there were not enough instructors to teach the full five-year course.

The teaching of physics in the USSR during this period was affected by other events as well. Mikhail Leontovich, Igor Tamm, and Leonid Mandelshtam had been forced to quit the university after becoming the targets of vicious attacks in the slanderous, ugly, and destructive campaigns that had shaken scientific and academic institutions from one end of the country to the other in the late 1930s. Even so, the physicists didn't have as hard a time of it as the biologists or philosophers, since their assailants were less aggressive than Lysenko and company. Besides, physics was not yet a matter of great interest to the powers-that-be. (Later, when it did enter the spotlight, Igor Kurchatov knew how to keep the lid on this sort of slime.) The particular offense of Mandelshtam and his associates was their attachment to the "anti-materialist" theory of relativity. (Perhaps we should be grateful that in those days the Soviet Union did not go to the lengths of labeling relativity theory "a Jewish fabrication.")

Professor Arkady Timiryazev, whose lectures to third-year students on the molecular theory of gases were competent enough, though a bit dull and old-fashioned, played a prominent part in the attacks on the theory of relativity. Timiryazev—who bore a striking resemblance to the statue (located just off the Nikitsky Gates Square in Moscow) of his father, Kliment, a prominent biologist—was backed by the dean, Alexander Predvoditelev, the majority of the senior teaching staff, and some younger instructors who hoped to advance their careers in this way. A certain Professor Mitskevich from some technical school was active in the campaign as well. In a debate, Tamm once said of a badly phrased question that it was as meaningless as asking whether a meridian was red or green. Mitskevich jumped to his feet and declared: "I don't know about Professor Tamm, but for a true Soviet citizen a meridian is always red!" Mitskevich's insinuation was not to be dismissed lightly. Alexander Vitt, one of Mandelshtam's most capable students, was arrested and died in detention in 1937; a number of other physicists were also imprisoned. Needless to say, the removal of the "Mandelshtam group" dealt a blow to the university's standard of physics instruction.

The basic course in quantum mechanics (crucial in my case) was taught at Ashkhabad by Professor Anatoly Vlasov, a pupil of Tamm and an able theoretical physicist. As a teacher, he varied from brilliant to incomprehensible. He had a very odd manner of lecturing—covering his face with his hands and droning on in a monotone without looking at anyone. I did not realize at the time that this was a symptom of mental illness. (After the war, I heard that Leontovich, when discussing Vlasov, once said: "Earlier, when I saw that he was starting to fall apart at the seams, I would slap him, and he would come around. But without me, he's going completely mad." Of course, it wasn't only the slap that helped; I think that Leontovich's friendship and that of other people like him mattered a great deal to Vlasov.)

Vlasov's most important scientific contribution was to plasma theory, and one of its significant equations rightfully bears his name. Later, after the war, he wrote a paper applying thermodynamic concepts to systems with a small number of degrees of freedom. There were many physicists who saw this work as evidence of Vlasov's decline, but he may not have been entirely wrong. Aside from my father, Vlasov was the first person to see the makings of a theoretical physicist in me.

About the only other lecturers in Ashkhabad in 1942 were Professors Spivak and Furtsev, who had already been discharged from the military after serving at the front. But we learned to compensate for the dearth of instructors by making better use of our books—which is, after all is said and done, the most important thing—and by exchanging ideas. It's not by chance that first-class scientists tend to emerge in "batches" and, the war notwithstanding, our year furnished a bumper crop.

Classes were held in the Ashkhabad suburb of Kishi, where the university administration was located—the "Kishi government" as we nicknamed it (a pun on the Vichy government). We lived in the center of Ashkhabad; at first we were housed in a school building, and then were moved into squat, single-story dormitories. Public transportation was very poor, and we usually had to walk to class. But the worst thing was the continual hunger, though I could cope with it better than others because of my physical and psychological makeup.

In Ashkhabad, I became friendly with Pyotr Kunin, who was in my year, and Yasha Tseitlin, who was a class behind us. Kunin and I both worked for some time after the war at FIAN, and in the 1970s we started to see each other again before he died (of a heart attack) in 1976. By that time, through Lusia's influence, I had become a different and more sociable person, better able to appreciate Kunin's generosity, intelligence, and readiness to help others.

Tseitlin, for his part, had a distinctive personality; he was very conscious of his own dignity, capable of being a devoted friend, but was sensitive and easily offended. Sometimes, I would catch a glimpse of the poverty-stricken, parochial world of his childhood. What attracted me to Tseitlin were probably the same qualities that had attracted me to Grisha Umansky: his inner purity, his contemplative nature, and a melancholy empathy that seems to be an innate Jewish characteristic. He was originally from the Ukraine, which had been occupied by the Germans, and he was terribly worried about his family. At that time we did not yet know any details, but we had some inklings that a tragedy was in the making for the Jews.

After graduation, Tseitlin vanished completely, and I never found out what became of him.

* * *

I STILL RETAIN some vivid impressions of life in Ashkhabad. As spring approached, I abandoned my stuffy bedroom for the flat, clay-covered roof of our dormitory. At night I gazed up at the star-filled southern sky, and at dawn I watched the sun's first rays light up the Kopet Dagh mountains. The red-tinted peaks seemed to be transparent. Mulberry trees grew in profusion along the streets of Ashkhabad, and we picked their succulent berries to supplement our vitamin-deficient diet. The locals, who never touched the berries, looked on us with horror.

It was there that I first experienced the hostility felt by some members of the Russian working class towards intellectuals, overhearing comments like "They want the easy life. They should try really working!" (I suspect that our national minorities, on the other hand, appreciate their intellectuals, as most non-imperial peoples do.) I also encountered instances of anti-Semitism, which became more blatant and virulent during the war and persisted afterwards. Throughout my life, I've been taken often enough for a Jew, possibly owing to our family's uvular r's. "It's quarter to two. Here comes a Jew!" youngsters taunted me and Boris Samoilov, a fellow student who was no more Jewish than I.

In 1942, we graduated as specialists in "defense metallurgy," whatever that was supposed to mean—we knew little about metallurgy and still less about its military applications. Professor Dekhtyar did deliver a couple of lectures on the subject, from which I picked up a few terms like "austenite," "grain orientation," and "dislocation," so later I was not bewildered when I came across them in books.

For my senior research topic, I was assigned the problem of finding a substitute for silver in contacts of protective relays. This was a contrived topic, since even our wartime shortages did not justify shortcuts where valuable equipment was at risk. But my task was to meet the requirements for a diploma, not to argue. I decided that stainless steel could replace the silver in the relays, so I went to the market, bought a stainless steel fork, sawed off the tines (this was the most difficult part of the job), and hammered them into a socket from which I'd removed the silver. I then presented this miracle of technology to the departmental committee, along with several pages of theoretical substantiation.

In July, Professor Vlasov conducted the final examinations in theoretical physics outdoors in a public garden because of the heat. Having asked me a few questions for the sake of appearances, he entered an "A" in the register, and then inquired if I would like to stay on as a graduate student in theoretical physics.

I had been expecting this offer, and turned it down politely. I felt it would be wrong to continue studying when I could be making a contribution to the war effort, although I had no clear idea what that might be. I told Vlasov I was slated to go to a munitions factory in Kovrov, which was true—the committee had already decided our assignments, but if I had agreed to Vlasov's suggestion, a change would have been possible. Not long afterwards, I was awarded an honors degree by Moscow University—with my specialty listed as "defense metallurgy." I was also now qualified to teach physics in secondary schools.

The six months or so we spent in Ashkhabad left an indelible impression on our lives. In 1948 a terrible earthquake destroyed a large part of the city, including the neighborhoods where we had lived and studied. Witnesses who had been through the war said they had never seen a more terrible sight. The death toll may well have exceeded 80,000, although the exact number of casualties has never been disclosed. In 1973, I made a return visit to Ashkhabad with Lusia and Alexei. In one of the central squares, we saw what from a distance looked like a dry river canyon—part of the rift driven through the city by the earthquake. But Ashkhabad's residents drove and walked in the bottom of this chasm on their everyday business, oblivious to this phenomenon of nature.

4

AT THE MUNITIONS FACTORY
DURING THE WAR YEARS

ANOTHER TRAIN JOURNEY across war-torn Soviet territory, alone this time, without a single familiar face among the crowds. The stations and trains were filled to overflowing. I slept on my suitcase, on the floor, between the crowded benches. Among other features of wartime travels: the succession of delousing stations, processing passengers at night. (In one of those my boots were stolen, and I was left with an old pair of summer shoes.) Everywhere people seemed worn out, burdened by worry and confusion, and everywhere they talked endlessly, as if compelled to share the horrors that were haunting them.

We reached Kovrov late one night at the end of July 1942. As I stepped from the train, I was greeted by distant sounds of artillery fire and flashes of light on the horizon. I later learned that this was the testing of the guns produced in Kovrov. When I reported the following morning to the personnel department, I was assigned quarters with the family of a woman who worked at the factory, and told to come back a few days later.

I spent ten days in Kovrov and learned something about the kind of life people there were leading—tense, anxious, difficult, and hungry. I also witnessed what Soviet newspapers call "workers' pride"—but there it was for real: the dedication and sense of personal responsibility.

After a few days, I was summoned by the general in charge of personnel matters. The conversation began with some courteous small talk. He then offered me work in a laboratory but with no guarantee of exemption from military service. I said that wouldn't bother me; as I've mentioned, I'm a great believer in letting things take their course. It was evident that the general had expected me to refuse; he asked me to come back the next day for a final decision. I did, and was given an order stating that the Kovrov factory was unable to offer me work in my specialty. I was directed to report to the Ministry of Armaments in Moscow.

BACK IN MOSCOW, I saw my family for the first time in ten months. My father was still teaching, although there weren't many students around and some of the staff had been evacuated. My parents looked exhausted, and the hardship and scarcity were in evidence everywhere. As for me, after Ashkhabad, Moscow's blackout—dark streets, darkened windows, blue lights in the lobbies—took some getting used to, and it was cold inside the former nursery school that had become my parents' home. My brother Yura had spent the previous winter in the third shift of the tenth grade (classrooms were becoming overcrowded as school buildings were turned into hospitals). He had graduated and expected to be drafted.

Without further ado, the Ministry of Armaments assigned me to a cartridge factory in Ulyanovsk. It would be two and a half years before I saw Moscow or my parents again.

ON SEPTEMBER 2, my train arrived shortly after daybreak at Ulyanovsk Station, across the Volga from the plant. The "labor" train shuttling workers' shifts had just left, and I decided to take a ferry. On the way, I stopped by the station library, where I took out Steinbeck's *The Grapes of Wrath*—my first novel in some time and, as it turned out, a good one. (Unfortunately, I later lost the book and had a difficult time squaring accounts with the librarian.) Then, with my baggage slung over my shoulder, I walked slowly along the railroad tracks toward the ferry. Across the river I could see the vast industrial complex stretching for miles, the smoke billowing from the power plant chimney, the gray barracks where the workers lived (and where I'd be living, too), a small cluster of multistory apartment houses, and several old villages, occupied by workers—in one of which my wife-to-be lived with her parents.

I was assigned to the chief mechanic's department. This struck me as a thoroughly absurd posting, as I had no idea at all what manufacturing cartridges entailed. I had never seen the machines that stamped them out, and in any case had no aptitude for that sort of engineering work. It took time for me to find something useful to do in Ulyanovsk. The chief mechanic had no illusions about my value to him, and without so much as a glance in my direction sent me to fell trees in the countryside. It was a strenuous task, and one I was not accustomed to, but my partner, who was younger and, to his surprise, far stronger, suffered more from hunger than I did. We got on well enough, each doing his fair share of work. By the end of the day we were so exhausted we could hardly stand. The more robust men would go out to the kolkhoz fields to gather potatoes left over after the harvest; these were to provide a reserve for the winter. We weaker members of the crew were able to carry only as many potatoes as we needed for our supper. At our campfire, for the first time in my life, I heard Stalin criticized openly. "If he were a Russian, he'd feel more pity for the people": that from a worker who'd just been notified that his son had been killed at the front.

I'll never forget the little village deep in the forest where we were billeted, or the atmosphere of tragedy and anxiety that permeated every word spoken, weighed upon the women drawing water at the well, and made even the children unusually reticent. Only women, old people, and children remained in the village, where they all seemed to merge into one extended family.

At daybreak my landlady would be wakened by neighbors begging milk for their children or a handful of flour. The villagers were careful with their kerosene, lighting a lamp only during dinner and sitting for the rest of the evening in darkness. Hard as life was, there was a foreboding that things would get even worse before they got better, and the horror of the war was always uppermost in people's minds.

A couple of weeks after starting work on the timber crew, I injured my hand, and it became infected. I had to return to Ulyanovsk, walking the ten or more miles to the railroad tracks and then hopping a freight train. The personnel office had a new assignment waiting for me: junior engineer in the blanking shop. This wasn't exactly the right job for me, either, but with the help of a sympathetic senior engineer and what I could remember from my drafting classes, my work wasn't a complete waste of time. I visited almost every department in the plant and became increasingly familiar with the production process, working conditions, and the workers' lives. It all made a very strong impression on me.

Our plant followed the uniform national schedule: two shifts of eleven hours each, seven days a week. Theoretically, workers got a day off when they switched from the night to the day shift, and vice versa. In practice, however, under the pressure of our quotas, shifts were rotated only a few times a year. I worked an eleven-hour shift, almost always days. When I did work nights, I found it utterly exhausting.

The big punch presses were operated by women, recruited mainly from the surrounding villages. They sat at the deafening machines, hour after hour, in huge, dimly lit rooms, hunched over and perched cross-legged on their stools to keep their wooden shoes off the cold floor, which was flooded with water and lubricants. Their faces were hidden by kerchiefs, but when I caught a glimpse of them, I could see that they were lifeless, drained by fatigue. Now and then a machine would stop, and a woman would rush to pull from under it the box with bellcaps, to refill the feeding container, to replace the wornout die, or to cry out for the repairman. Conditions were even worse in the workshops where the furnaces were located and where strong chemicals were used.

During the lunch break, every worker received a few spoonfuls of millet porridge mixed with American powdered eggs. Often there were no utensils to eat with, although our shop eventually managed to stamp out spoons for the whole factory. The porridge was then served on sheets of paper and eaten on the spot, washed down with ersatz tea from a tin cup.

Many women from rural areas had left children behind, and they worried constantly. But getting leave was next to impossible, and being absent without leave could mean a five-year stretch in a labor camp. The only escape was to get pregnant, and so each morning a line of women big with child could be seen outside the office of the deputy personnel director. They would wait in line all night, hoping for leave so they could return to their children. But most got nowhere, because after twenty minutes or so the official would close up shop, supposedly to attend a meeting of the district Party committee. A horse-drawn carriage would come to pick him up, and the women would disperse until the next reception day and the next sleepless night.

The metal strips were pickled in acid in our shop before stamping. This was done by men whose sole protective equipment was elbow-length rubber gloves. Whenever I passed them coming off the night shift, I couldn't bear to look at their pale, bluish-yellow faces. The quality inspections were performed by very young girls; they were the only workers whose sight was equal to the task, although even their eyes suffered from the strain.

One of the major problems workers faced was how to "cash in" their ration cards. Coupons for groats, butter, and sugar were often wasted, having expired by the end of the month, unless they were traded for bread coupons or were spent in the canteen, since most of the time nothing of the kind could be found in the stores. (The canteen gave a very bad deal on these coupons, so just a few people, all singles, myself included, ate there. Moreover, to continue using the canteen I had to trade my bread coupons for groats coupons, something I was reluctant to do.) The only coupons worth their nominal value were the ones for bread, but even bread deliveries were irregular. A worker from the night shift might have to stand in line from eight A.M. till the middle of the afternoon before getting his ration. Since he had to be back at work by eight P.M., he had practically no time to sleep. And you couldn't leave the line for a moment—try it, and you'd never get your place back in the silent, unyielding queue. Of course, shopping for food was easier for families and single people who banded together—and easier still if you knew the sales clerks, as almost all the locals did.

Single workers coming from outside Ulyanovsk were assigned to dormitories. I lived in one from September 1942 until July 1943. Each room in the one-story barracks could accommodate six to twelve people sleeping in three-tiered plank bunks. People were too exhausted to make any noise, so it was usually pretty quiet, but occasionally one of my roommates would be a talkative type, and the conversations could be quite informative. The toilet was in the courtyard, about seventy-five feet away. Since many people didn't feel like walking that distance at night, there were always frozen puddles of urine outside the door. Lice were common. But there was always cold water for washing, and hot boiled water for tea from a "titan" [a wood- or coal-heated water tank]. Every morning, women from the surrounding villages brought oven-heated milk (I always bought a half pint for breakfast), carrots, and cucumbers.

I still recall with horror the day a roommate of mine came back from his shift after drinking a cupful of the methyl alcohol used in the plant. He became delirious and went berserk. Half an hour later, he was taken away in an ambulance, and we never saw him again. He was a giant of a man, exceptionally strong, with fair hair and the light blue eyes of a child.

As I learned later, conditions were better in some places and worse in others: life at plants in the Urals was harder and hungrier. And Leningrad—under siege—was unspeakably worse. Everywhere, life was hardest for "outsiders"— among them young evacuees from western parts of Russia, and especially for young apprentices (students from trade schools) working alongside adults.

In November I changed jobs after an unpleasant incident. One day, when the senior engineer was absent, the head of the department told me to start processing a new batch of metal. Everyone could see it was rusty and unsuitable for shell casings, but no one wanted to accept responsibility for rejecting it.

I took several strips of the metal to a press operator, who looked at me in disgust before stamping out a box of "caps," the first stage in producing shell casings. I hoisted the box onto my shoulder and carried it to the next shop. After the second stamping, the metal looked like a sieve and was scratching the die. Someone had to put a stop to this farce. I took the box to the foreman, told him to save the caps and not to process them any further, and put into the box a signed note repeating my instructions. It was after eight o'clock by this time, so I went home.

The storm burst the next morning. A special meeting was convened and the foreman, a man named Vrublevsky, spoke in the following vein: "Comrade Stalin has issued an order—not one step back! Soviet soldiers are fulfilling that order and fighting the enemy at the cost of their lives, but Engineer Sakharov abandoned his battle station without having completed a vital task. At the front, deserters are shot on the spot. We cannot tolerate such behavior in our plant!"

No one objected to Vrublevsky's speech—and no one supported it. Everyone was silent: no one asked any questions, and I said nothing. That was the last I heard of the matter. The rusty stampings were probably turned over to military inspectors, and somebody must have been raked over the coals for the whole business. For me, this incident was the last straw. I decided to look for a job where I could be more useful.

I applied to the central laboratory, whose head, Boris Vishnevsky, welcomed me. The chief engineer had suggested the need for an instrument that could check whether the cores of armor-piercing bullets had been sufficiently hardened. Vishnevsky asked me if I was interested in following up on that idea, and I said yes. On November 10, I started work.

My job was as follows. The armor-piercing steel cores of the 14.5-mm bullet (for antitank guns) were being hardened in salt baths. At times (mainly due to production errors), the process didn't work, and the center of the core remained too soft to pierce armor. Defective batches were identified by taking a random sample of five cores from each box and breaking them open. The quality controllers, young women, would insert the sample core halfway through a hole in a steel plate; then a steel pipe was placed over it, and the core was broken—not the lightest of work. One and a half percent of the cores were scrapped. My task was to find a nondestructive method of testing the cores. Within a month I had a promising solution and began trial experiments on a working model I had built with the help of a laboratory mechanic. (See Fig. 1.) The core is inserted by hand at point A and slides, with a bit of friction, down the inclined copper pipe through magnetizing coil K_1 and demagnetizing coil K_2. The core stops at point B opposite magnet M, which is secured to the indicator needle and spring-balanced. The number of coil turns is such that a thoroughly tempered core will be demagnetized by the second coil, and no forces will act on the magnet. On the other hand, if the core has an insufficiently hardened center, demagnetization will require a less coercive force,[1] and the demagnetizing coil will *reverse* the magnetization of the core, creating a magnetic moment of opposite sign to that created in coil K_1. The two coils are connected in series with the windings in opposite directions, and are fed from a direct current source (I used a copper-oxide rectifier). This arrangement ensures that minor current fluctuations do not affect performance. (Variations in the magnetic fields of magnetizing and demagnetizing coils compensate each other.) The magnetic field from the remagnetized core is directed along its axis and sets up a torque that acts on the indicator magnet. It was found possible to calibrate the indicator scale to show the diameter of the unhardened portion of the core. After testing, the core is removed by hand through slot C.

In December and early January I tested the device myself, spending long hours in the shop where the cores were hardened and inspected. Then the designer who had been assigned to work with me produced a drawing of an "industrial model" which was tested by a commission of experts. This indus-

---

[1][Coercive force is the demagnetizing force necessary to remove the residual magnetism of a magnet.]

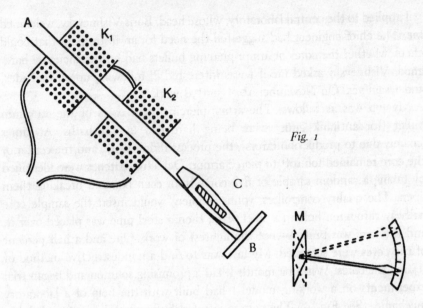

Fig. 1

trial model resembled my primitive prototype, right down to the tubing I'd found in a dump.

The machine was approved by the commission and was used for many years; it may even still be in service. I received a cash award of three thousand rubles; not very much, but nice to have. (In comparison, my pay was eight hundred rubles per month.[2]) The recognition I received also resulted in greater freedom for me at work. In 1945 I obtained a patent for my invention, and some years later I came across a description of it in the textbook *Cartridge Production*, written by the former chief engineer, Nikolai Malov.

On November 10, 1942, the same day I began work at the laboratory, I met my wife-to-be, Klavdia Vikhireva—Klava. (Twenty-five years later, we celebrated our silver anniversary on that date, instead of on July 10 of the next year, the date of our official wedding ceremony. This was Klava's idea, and I think a very good one. Unfortunately, we had never got into the habit of giving parties, so we observed the occasion by ourselves.)

I was assigned along with several other young specialists (all but me trained in cartridge production) to the laboratory's metallurgical department. Klava was employed as a laboratory assistant in the chemical department, together

[2]["Old" rubles; in January 1961, ten "old rubles" were exchanged for one "new ruble." Rubles are not freely convertible into hard currency, but Western economists estimate that a realistic exchange rate would be about ten new rubles for one dollar.]

with other young women from the Ulyanovsk region. One, Dusya Zaitseva, who was a little older, came from Leningrad, and she and Klava, who had been a student in Leningrad, enjoyed swapping stories about their time there. I remember how overjoyed they were in January 1944, when the siege of Leningrad was finally broken.

The young men paid regular visits to the chemical laboratory, and the girls, being "locals," looked after us "newcomers," and would treat us to homegrown potatoes baked right on the spot. We became more and more friendly. I remember Dusya holding me up as an example of great perseverance (despite the fact that this was the time when I started and then dropped learning English, not taking it up again until I began my graduate work). When winter came, Klava and I went to the theatre a few times (once we saw a Moscow operetta company that was visiting Ulyanovsk) and to the cinema (along with the usual fare of war films, we saw a very good English film, *That Hamilton Woman*). In the spring of 1943, our relationship unexpectedly entered a new stage.

That May, I went to Klava's home and offered my help in digging up the family garden for potatoes. I also bought seed potatoes at the market and planted a small plot for myself on virgin soil outside the factory wall. By the time Klava and I harvested those potatoes—only a couple of sacksful—we were man and wife. As late as 1971, Alexei Vikhirev, Klava's father, had fond memories of "Andryusha's potatoes." Fortunately, when recalling those days, he'd conveniently forget that in the spring of 1943, the family was left without potatoes (my extra mouth to feed had played a part in this), and we had to dig up frozen, half-rotten tubers to make pancakes by using the rather complicated "technology" developed by generations of starving peasants.

Klava and I also went rowing on the Volga two or three times; I was clumsy and dropped her shoe in the water, but I think we managed to rescue it. She found some shoes for me that had belonged to her godmother's late husband to replace the pair that had been stolen from me at the bathhouse in October. (I remember running back to the dormitory across the newly formed ice in my stocking feet, and then having to wear thin summer shoes for the rest of the winter.)

Gradually life began to taken on a new pattern. On July 10 we registered our marriage. Klava's father blessed us with an icon and made the sign of the cross over us, pronouncing some words of guidance. Then, holding hands, the two of us ran across a field to the nearest registry office. We were to live together almost twenty-six years, until Klava's death on March 8, 1969. We had three children: our elder daughter, Tanya, born February 7, 1945; Lyuba, born July 28, 1949; and Dmitri, born August 14, 1957. Our children brought us a great deal of happiness; and, of course, like all children, problems, too.

There were happy periods in our life that sometimes lasted for years, and I am grateful to Klava for them.

Klava had spent four years in the department of glass production at the Institute of Local and Cooperative Industry in Leningrad. She liked her specialty, but more important was the ambiance of student life: the freer atmosphere and the opening of new intellectual horizons. Those were happy and unforgettable years for her, but she didn't finish the institute before the war, and afterwards she simply didn't have the emotional strength to resume her studies; it would have meant losing a year and sending our daughter Tanya to nursery school. (Tanya got sick on occasion, as all children do, and we overreacted to this in the usual manner of young parents.) Generally, Klava seemed to lack the stamina needed for the demands of life (which wasn't easy for us, or for most people). We also feared—wrongly, as it turned out—that she wouldn't be able to find work in her field of glass manufacturing in Moscow, where I felt my roots to be.

Let me jump forward in time. Klava never worked after 1945. My mother didn't work, but this was commonly accepted in her generation; she looked after the family, while my father was the head of the household and its breadwinner. In our day, however, almost all my colleagues' wives worked, studied, and had a profession. Klava's lack of occupation aggravated her psychological problems. I am to blame (if any blame attaches) for not insisting that she study or find a job and for not fully appreciating how important this was; I also regret not having created a happier psychological atmosphere in the family, which might have given Klava a greater zest for life. Had we stayed in Ulyanovsk, of course, Klava would have continued working, and things might have been easier for her; our move to the Installation, to a secret, closed town, only made matters worse. We had a relatively brief period of material hardship for a couple of years immediately following the war, but most families had to live in straitened circumstances far longer, sometimes for their whole lives. In our case, later affluence never brought us much happiness, and we never learned to use it to brighten our life together. To some extent this was due to our situation, but in the main our problems were subjective ones. Life was somehow empty, and it's particularly sad that our children had too little joy in their lives. Still, we did have some good times, and we always did our best to make the children as happy as possible.

In my private life, in my relations with Klava and with the children after she died, I always tended to avoid confrontations, feeling myself psychologically unable to cope with them, and, as if in self-protection, chose the line of least resistance. But in all honesty, I never spared my time or my physical strength. Afterwards, I suffered, felt guilty, and then made new mistakes, since guilt hardly improves one's judgment. On the other hand, it has to be said that the less I concerned myself with these seemingly insoluble personal matters, the more capable I was of leading an active and productive life outside the home.

Now, BACK to 1943. Klava lived with her parents and her sister Zina in a large house in a workers' settlement not far from the Volga. I moved in with them in July. Each resident of the settlement had a large plot of land that served as potato field, kitchen garden, and orchard, and also provided cash income from produce sold at the market. I tried to help out as much as I could on the Vikhirevs' plot, and Klava's parents, especially her father, appreciated it. In the spring of 1944, I helped Alexei Ivanovich plow a piece of virgin land about a dozen miles from our house, where we planted some millet. In the fall, he harvested the millet, but it was difficult to get it home, so the two of us hitched ourselves up to a cart and pulled it after us through the night, until we finally reached the house just before daybreak.

Alexei Ivanovich always called me "Andryusha" and followed my work at the plant with interest and respect; to the last years of his life, he never failed to recollect details I'd long since forgotten, and he always felt I wasn't appreciated enough at work.

This seems the appropriate place to tell something of Vikhirev's life. He was born in 1890 in the same settlement where I met him fifty-three years later, and he grew up in this semirural environment with a minimum of formal education. In the 1930s, he began taking courses at a technical school, but he never completed them. He had a number of versions of why this happened, but the simple fact is that it's difficult for a man over forty to begin assimilating academic "wisdom."

Alexei Ivanovich apparently had worked out guidelines for his life and conduct at an early age. In some respects these principles were fairly liberal, but he followed them rigidly. He was a sociable and cheerful man throughout his life; in his youth, he liked to dress up in his finest and drive his horse and carriage with a flourish past those whom he wanted to impress. He composed songs, both words and music: they may have been somewhat primitive, naïve, and inadvertently derivative, but they were important to *him,* and they showed some spark of talent. He'd break into tears, singing a lament he composed in the 1950s for his native soil, which was flooded after the construction of the giant Kuibyshev dam and reservoir. He was a genial man, particularly to those whom he deemed worthy of respect and who belonged to his circle, and some distant acquaintance or other, mostly from the country, was always spending the night at his house.

Alexei Ivanovich had successfully tried his hand at a number of occupations, from farming to shoemaking. He prided himself on his versatility and on his reputation at the plant where he was an inspector in the instrument shop. His greatest satisfaction, however, was to recall that before the Revolution the wealthy merchants of Simbirsk (the prerevolutionary name of Ulyanovsk) had entrusted him, a mere drayman, with their storehouse keys. In the First World War he served as an infantryman.

Klava's father had no great love for authority. He'd often remark that in the Tsar's day the village policeman might have taken more than was coming to him—but at least then there was only *one* official to worry about. He talked a good deal about the savagery with which the countryside had been stripped of grain during the early years of Soviet rule under the "surplus appropriation" system, and about the slopes of the high bank of the Volga that prior to collectivization had supported the famous orchards described by Goncharov[3] and that now were denuded and scarred by landslides. Klava told me that the kolkhoz had once taken a handsome colt named Boy from her father, who was then earning extra money as a hauler for the plant. Boy died soon after; Alexei Ivanovich wept bitterly, and later disliked recalling that incident.

"The loudmouths are bragging again!" was his standard response to radio and press reports of labor achievements. He repeated rumors about Stalin's alleged murder of his wife, about daily banquets in the Kremlin, and about the millions of rubles spent on Trotsky's assassination. On the other hand, he became incensed when I once made an unkind remark about Marshal Voroshilov (this was sometime in the late 1960s), and I couldn't convince him I was right. He read practically nothing except the Gospels, which he interpreted rather freely.

Klava's mother, Matryona Andreyevna (née Snezhkina) was eight years younger than Alexei Ivanovich, reserved by nature and less outgoing than her husband. While Alexei Ivanovich was at the plant, the household chores, including selling their garden produce at the market, fell to her. She was fond of recalling that she too had worked in the plant in the 1930s, and had once met the director, who was related to Beria and had enormous power. This seems to have been the high point of her life; her job had given her not only independence but a wide circle of acquaintances.

She also liked to talk about a young man who had courted her before her marriage to Alexei Ivanovich, which may have taken place at her parents' urging. I knew from Klava that her mother and father had had their differences in the past, but I thought their marriage had attained a degree of stability. I

---

[3][Ivan Goncharov, nineteenth-century writer, native of Simbirsk (Ulyanovsk), in *The Precipice*.]

was mistaken; in the 1960s, after forty-five years of marriage, Klava's parents divorced. After that, until her death in 1987, Klava's mother lived in Leningrad with her younger daughter, a doctor, and Klava never saw her again.

Alexei Ivanovich remained in his house in Ulyanovsk (it had been moved after the Kuibyshev dam was built and its original site flooded). He died alone in 1975, and was found lying on the porch by a neighbor. The service at his funeral was read by devout old men and women with whom he had associated in his last years. Some money folded in a piece of paper and marked "For my funeral" was found in his house.

HAVING SUCCESSFULLY produced a device to test for defects in core temper, I was now recognized as an "expert" on magnetic quality-control methods. In mid-1943, I began to explore the possibility of using a similar method to check the thickness of the brass coating on the jacket of the TT (Tula Tokarev automatic pistol) bullet. This would avoid etching, which wasted bullets and large amounts of silver, then in critically short supply. I settled on a dynamic method that involved measuring the external force needed to pull a magnetized rod away from the bullet jacket; the force required depends on the thickness of the nonmagnetic coating. (See Fig. 2.)

It seemed to me that it would be difficult to construct a mechanical device to measure the force needed for separation (I may have been wrong in this). Instead, I worked out a comparison method in which the jacket to be inspected and a standard jacket were placed on opposite sides of a steel rod that had been magnetized with a coil. When the jackets were moved apart, one to the right and one to the left, the magnetized rod stuck to the jacket with the thinner nonmagnetic (brass) coating. The device was built, tested, and put into use. Needless to say, it was not exactly a triumph of design, and I think it was soon replaced by something else.

While I was working on this device, I became interested in the electrostatic analog of the magnetostatic effect on which it was based. Figure 3 represents

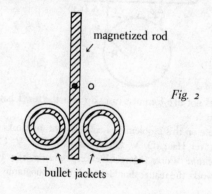

magnetized rod

Fig. 2

bullet jackets

two conducting cylinders set with their axes perpendicular to each other and a gap Δ between them. A potential difference V is applied to the cylinders. The problem of finding the force of electrostatic attraction between them is easily solved if the gap is much smaller than the cylinder radii R. In this case, the curvature of the field lines can be neglected for practical purposes when calculating the force, and the electric field can be calculated using the elementary formula[4]

$$E = \frac{V}{\Delta(x,y)}, \text{ where } \Delta(x,y) \approx \Delta_g + \frac{x^2+y^2}{2R} \text{ when } \Delta(x,y) << R$$

(here $\Delta(x,y)$ is the "local" width of the gap and x and y are Cartesian coordinates chosen in a natural fashion). According to the formula of electrodynamics, the surface force density is given by

$$f = \frac{E^2}{8\pi}$$

and the total force can be found by elementary integration. This was actually one of my first studies in theoretical physics—in this case, mathematical physics. The essential point of the exercise lay in my discovery of an ideal case $(x << R)$ in which the problem was simplified in the extreme and the calculations were easily completed.

The problem can easily be generalized to any case of finding the force of electrostatic attraction between two convex conducting bodies when the minimal distance between them is much less than the radius of curvature, and specifically to cylinders whose axes form an angle.[5]

I solved several more problems in 1943–44. I did not publish any of my results, but I was gaining confidence in my ability as a theoretical physicist,

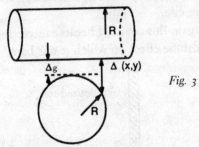

Fig. 3

[4]The reader who does not like formulas can skip over the few I have included in this book without missing very much.

[5]I included a brief note on this problem in a collection of my works published in the United States in 1982. [See D. ter Haar, D. V. Chudnovsky, and G. V. Chudnovsky, eds., *A. D. Sakharov: Collected Scientific Works* (Marcel Dekker, 1982), p. 284. Henceforth, for information on Sakharov's own works the reader should consult the bibliography beginning on page 707.]

something vital for any beginner. I have no intention of resurrecting all of my old work (the original papers have been lost), but I shall list a few of the topics studied:

1. A variational principle for the determination of the steady state of dynamical systems taking into account dissipative effects.

2. A new method of evaluating improper integrals with oscillating integrands, which is applicable to a very broad class of functions.

(I sent these two papers to Igor Tamm, but I apparently made a poor choice, since he did not find them interesting. Many years later, Tamm explained tactfully that he had sensed the high promise of my work from the papers, but he couldn't quite figure out what I was trying to say. Conceivably, my ideas may have had some merit, but simply lay outside the interests of Tamm and the other physicists at FIAN.)

3. The problem of the skin effect for an infinite conducting cylinder that is fitted with a coil of finite length. (This problem arose in connection with the development of a device to be used in testing cores for cracks, to which I shall return below.)

4. Calculation of a stochastic process that simulates recrystallization. A similar problem was solved and published by Kolmogorov a year or two later; I don't recall being at all upset. This problem and the next one are simplified versions of problems encountered in metallurgy.

5. Calculation of the growth of a flat slab of ice (at less than $0°$ C) in water of $0°$ C.

IN 1944, I began an intensive study of theoretical physics. I would sit in the Party Educational Center, where it was warm and well lit, and I was the sole visitor during working hours, and read the textbooks I brought to Ulyanovsk. The woman who ran the center eventually noticed that I was not reading Lenin or Stalin or even Marx or Engels, but some completely mysterious books. Vishnevsky, the head of the laboratory, was obliged to "reprimand" me, but he did it so politely it hardly sounded like a reproach.

I should backtrack a bit here. At the beginning of 1943, the laboratory had acquired a costly optical device, a spectroscope designed for the semiquantitative analysis of steel and other metal alloys. Since I was the only person in the laboratory (indeed, in the entire factory) who knew anything at all about optics (and my knowledge was limited to theory only), I was asked to figure out how the device worked. I managed to do this quite rapidly, learning to identify the various grades of steel. They were constantly being mixed up in the storerooms, and the idea was to use "the miracle of technology" to straighten out the situation. In order to check my results I sent some samples to the chemical laboratory, where Klava was assigned to analyze a few of them. Either from carelessness or because the exhaust hood was defective, she came down with hydrogen sulfide poisoning. This incident was one of the things that brought us closer together.

I decided to try to develop a method based on the thermoelectric effect that would distinguish different steel alloys faster than the spectroscope. I returned to the principle of comparison with a standard (Fig. 4): An aluminum plate was warmed by a specially designed heating element; then two steel rods, the one to be analyzed and another of known composition, were brought simultaneously into contact with the plate and the circuit was closed across galvanometer g. If the alloy composition of the two rods was different, the galvanometer needle was deflected when the circuit was closed. If the difference in composition was confined to a single element (e.g., chromium), that difference could be estimated quantitatively. As I recall, I carelessly violated fire-safety rules by using makeshift wiring in experimenting with this device. I narrowly avoided real trouble with the fire authorities; the matter instead was hushed up, as is usually the case with serious violations. Unfortunately, the device never reached the production stage. I later read of similar instruments developed by scientific research institutes.

One day Vishnevsky called me in for consultation on a serious production problem. At the punching stage, bellcaps (blanks for cartridge cases) were being formed with wavy upper rims ("ears"), which made it impossible to stamp 7.62-mm cartridge cases from them. I immediately recalled university lectures on texture (the orientation of the microgranules can be affected by the rolling process). To test my hypothesis, I took several steel strips from a batch that had produced "ears," scored them longitudinally, carried them back to my old shop, and asked that bellcaps be punched out of them. All came out with "ears," all at a 45-degree angle to my score marks! I sent them to Malov, who immediately flew with them to Magnitogorsk, the source of the defective strips. The rolling process was modified, and the bellcaps again came out

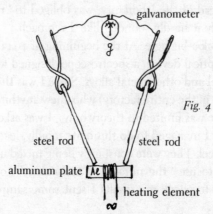

Fig. 4

smooth. Even without me, of course, somebody soon would have guessed that texture was the problem, but my experiment provided visible evidence.

Most of the work I did in 1944 involved development of a device to test 14.5-mm armor-piercing cores for longitudinal cracks. Rounds with cracked cores were exploding in the bores of antitank guns, so it was important to weed out all defective ones.

At first, I worked independently. My idea was to use the classical magnetic flaw-detection technique in which the magnetic field would be deformed by any cracks. I assumed that the cores would be magnetized by a current flowing along their length in a special machine. (For the time being, however, I performed the operation manually.) The cores were then transported into the inspection section of the machine (I was very proud of its design) in which they were rotated one by one in front of a magnetic needle. (See Fig. 5.) If the needle vibrated, the core was automatically shunted into the reject box. Unfortunately, the contraption worked poorly. Only very large cracks were registered, while smaller but still dangerous ones escaped detection. I tried to measure the field deviation with a bismuth spiral, again without success.

I knew that the same problem was being worked on by Alexei Protopopov, a staff member of a Leningrad scientific research institute who had been assigned temporarily to our plant. He was making use of the skin effect at ultrasonic frequencies, an approach I liked very much. Each core was placed for a second in an induction coil that formed an arm of an induction bridge. If a crack was present, the induction and dissipative losses rose (owing to the larger "magnetized" area), the bridge was thrown out of balance, a relay tripped, and the core was rejected.

I offered Protopopov my services as an assistant, cautioning him at the same time that I was more of a theoretician than an engineer or experimenter. He smiled somewhat sardonically, but nevertheless agreed to the arrangement. I moved from the central laboratory to the shop where Protopopov was working and subsequently received a great deal of help in my work not only from him, but also from Fyodor Balashov, an older engineer who was the hardworking and capable shop foreman.

Over the course of several months, we built a working model of the device.

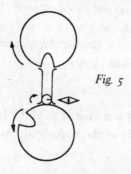

Fig. 5

The range of parameters that gave acceptable values for the impedance of the induction coil with the core inside were determined in the laboratory. It was possible to adjust them in such a way that cores without cracks were passed, while cores with minute cracks, even ones that presented no great threat, were rejected. The device was stabilized in operation with special automatic self-testing cycles. We still had to try it out in assembly line conditions—on many tens of thousands of cores, instead of the one or two hundred that we had used in the laboratory.

It was then that Protopopov was called back to his institute. He was torn: on the one hand, he really wanted to complete the device to which he had devoted over a year's work, and which was unquestionably needed; on the other hand, he was sick and tired of life as an evacuee. Apparently, there were personal considerations, too—his wife, as I learned only many years later, was seriously ill. He decided to go. That left Balashov and me.

The device was loaded onto a wagon and moved to the shop. We began our tests, using the visual inspection system as a control. The hardened cores were brought from the heat-treating department and placed on iron-clad examination tables. The inspectors, all young women, wiped the cores with kerosene-soaked rags and then inspected each one under bright lights, straining their eyes to the utmost. Officially, the girls worked eleven-hour shifts like everyone else, but in fact, they were required to continue working until they met their quotas, which might take as long as sixteen hours. The youngest inspector was fourteen, the oldest twenty.

Despite the precautions, a defective core would occasionally slip through the examination and shatter in a gun bore during test firing. Whenever that happened, the whole batch of armor-piercing shells was scrapped—all fifty thousand of them!

Our device was intended to replace this hellish and unreliable procedure. During the trial period, when I spent about a month in the shop, each core was checked both by our device and by a visual inspection. The device made a good showing. Defective cores did slip through, but no more often than with visual inspection. A special commission accepted our device, and it was put into operation. Alexei Ivanovich told me that it was used until mid- or late 1945, when it broke down and no one could repair it. That's the usual story with new technology, the result of our system of management. In this case, I found consolation in the fact that production of armor-piercing shells had almost ceased by late 1945 or mid-1946.

IN DECEMBER 1944, I was invited to visit FIAN. My father had asked Igor Tamm, who knew him from the 1930s and respected him greatly, to consider me for graduate work under his supervision (I had already, as noted, sent him a couple of my articles). Father had run into Pyotr Kunin, who was doing graduate work with Tamm, and Kunin had reinforced my father's opinion that I too should work with Tamm. Father had believed in my abilities ever since my childhood and had dreamed that I would one day become a scientist. For my part, I had been ready to shift to pure science for some time. I was sorry to abandon my work as an inventor just when I was starting to have some success, but my craving for science outweighed all other considerations.

Klava and her father were convinced that I ought to go. I asked to be released from my job and left for Moscow in mid-January to begin my graduate work. Klava was then in her final month of pregnancy. We hoped that she and the baby would be able to join me soon, but we hadn't the faintest idea where we would live or what we would live on.

Klava and her father came to see me off. My train was to leave late in the evening. It was a dark, windy, and snowy night. They said farewell to me and walked through the sleeping town to another station to catch the six A.M. "labor" train to take them home.

Tanya was born in Ulyanovsk on February 7, 1945. It was cold in the maternity hospital, and there was only paper to burn in the stoves. As is often the case with a first child, the labor was difficult.

5

GRADUATE WORK AT FIAN

My parents met me at the station. The last two and a half years had wrought striking changes in them. We had a chance to talk a little as we waited for the end of curfew, when we would be allowed to leave the station. They were still living on Spiridonevskaya Street near Granatny Lane, but had moved out of the nursery school into a two-room apartment. Now, the apartment's former tenants had returned from evacuation and brought legal action against my parents. This was an absurdity; it would have been far more logical for them to sue the Moscow City Council which had sanctioned my parents' move to new housing. But that's not how things work in Moscow. The court ruled that one of the two rooms should revert to the old tenants, and my parents kept the other. They had been living alone since Yura's army call-up; now we'd live as a threesome until Klava arrived.

I went the next day to visit Igor Tamm in his apartment on Sadovaya Street. Tamm rose to greet me as I entered his study, the room I would come to know so well in the years that followed. It was dominated by his desk, which was strewn with dozens of numbered sheets of paper covered with calculations that meant nothing to me. Above the desk was a large photograph of Leonid Mandelshtam, a leading physicist who had died in 1944, and who had been, according to Tamm, his mentor both in life and in science. I came to see for myself that this was no mere figure of speech, but something of deep significance to Tamm. Bookcases along every wall held books in Russian, English, and German, science and reference works, and a few novels. There was a long green row of copies of the *Physical Review*. And, unfortunately for me (since I'm anti-smoking), a thick cloud of light blue smoke hung above his desk, for despite the fact that cigarettes sent him into bouts of coughing, Tamm couldn't work without them. A map depicting the military situation hung on one wall. As I came in, the radio had just broadcast the latest communiqué, and Tamm was repositioning his little markers with the same surprising liveliness and ease that marked all his actions. We were in the midst of the January offensive, probably the greatest of the entire war. Tamm asked after my father, and then almost immediately launched into questions on science. He conducted this examination calmly and tactfully, but he quickly penetrated to the bottom of my rather modest, though solid and, I think, not superficial knowledge of science. (My own self-appraisal could be summed up without false modesty by the military classification: *Fit, but untrained.*) As our conversation wound to an end, Tamm became more exacting, which I took as evidence that he'd begun to take me seriously. He said he would accept me as a graduate student; formalities would take a few days. "What languages do you know?" I told him I could read German, but didn't know any English. The latter appalled Tamm. "You've got to learn English right away. First, get to the level where you can read the *Physical Review* with a dictionary; you'll have to do this very quickly, on your own, regardless of any graduate requirements. Without English you can't even get started, and you'll never get anywhere. But your principal effort should be devoted to acquiring an in-depth understanding of the books I'm going to give you. They're excellent, and fortunately they're in German, which you know."

These were Pauli's *Theory of Relativity*, a remarkable and profound survey of the subject, with a superbly detailed historical and experimental section (truly the best book on relativity, written by Pauli at the age of twenty-one!), and his *Quantum Mechanics*, also excellent. To supplement the latter, Tamm gave me a manuscript copy of Mandelshtam's article "Toward a Theory of Indirect Measurements," at that time still unpublished (and now available in a collection of Mandelshtam's selected works on optics, the theory of relativity, quantum mechanics, and electrodynamics). The article had interesting things to say on the interpretation of quantum mechanics, and was written with great depth and brilliance. Many people today consider quantum mechanics to have been thoroughly explored, but many others are still searching for "hidden parameters" or even more fantastic things; like the great Einstein, they believe that "God does not play dice." The first position is probably closer to the truth, but it does seem to me that the interpretation of quantum mechanics has not yet attained the comprehensiveness and lucidity we have in classical physics, including relativity theory (itself the main target of attacks by a whole army of would-be debunkers). Mandelshtam believed that quantum mechanics should be interpreted as a description of experiments with free particles—their masses and lifetimes, total and differential cross sections, etc. Everything else should be regarded as just "mathematical apparatus" or a system of secondary concepts not open to direct interpretation. I find this viewpoint tenable; or at least a nice reflection of the crucial epistemological notion of the relation between a mathematical formalism and its operational interpretation, primary and secondary concepts, etc. But this interpretation does not seem to me to be complete. Is it really possible, for example, that the equation of state of a cold Fermi gas or the properties of superfluid helium must be reduced to free-particle experiments? Landau and Lifshitz's textbook speaks of interpretation in terms of semiclassical processes, and this is probably closer to the truth. Final clarification would be welcome.

The notion that the theory can be applied directly only to free particles gained popularity due to the difficulties encountered in elementary-particle theory. But nonrelativistic quantum theory is completely closed; it describes a whole realm of facts and should have an interpretation independent of what will transpire in elementary-particle theory. In addition, elementary-particle theory has now been developing for more than fifteen years under the banner of rehabilitation of local quantum field theory; and it has been found that apparently insurmountable difficulties vanish in the so-called gauge theories, especially their supersymmetric variants. [Particular hopes are now vested in so-called superstring theory, a nontrivial development of the ideas of quantum field theory that requires no revision of the principles of quantum mechanics.—A.S. 1987] Actually, one is now astonished not by the difficulties, but by the progress made within the so-called standard model. But I've digressed some four decades ahead here.

IT TOOK ME a little more than three months to read Pauli's book and Mandelshtam's article. In retrospect Tamm's choice of this particular reading appears strikingly apt, for it immediately pointed my study and research in a direction that would be productive for many years to come.

I also began turning up regularly at the theoretical seminars conducted by Tamm: on Tuesdays in the conference hall and open to all physicists in Moscow; on Fridays a departmental "bull session" that met in Tamm's office to discuss topics he had selected. The department was also working as a team on a monograph survey of experimental and theoretical work on the meson (what we now call the mu-meson). Unfortunately, the survey was obsolete by the time it appeared; Powell, Lattes, and Occhialini had by then discovered the pi-meson, but even prior to that it turned out that the mu-meson interacts weakly with nuclei and is captured by them very slowly, and, therefore, has no relation to nuclear forces.

I renewed my friendship with Pyotr Kunin, and also became friendly with other graduate students within and outside the theoretical department, including a new friend of Pyotr's from the Baltic, Shura Taksar. When Klava arrived, she too became a part of this group. We often visited Shura and his wife, Tamara, at their dormitory home; Shura for some reason reminded me of my lost friend Yasha Tseitlin, although physically there was no resemblance. FIAN was still quite small in those days, and it was natural for my circle to include my contemporaries from other departments. One, Matvei Rabinovich, I'd known at the university, where he'd been a year or two ahead of me. "Musya," as he was known to everyone, was specializing in accelerators, at that time an entirely new field. His work was being directed by Vladimir Veksler, who had devised new principles for accelerating elementary particles. Musya quickly achieved major success in this field; he later switched to plasma physics and thermonuclear topics. In June 1982, I learned of Rabinovich's death, which followed a year of grave and painful illness.

After 1968, when I found myself functioning in a "new capacity," all but Pyotr Kunin disappeared from my view (some may have done so even earlier, for which I bear some blame). I learned from Kunin that in the mid-1970s Taksar was given permission to emigrate, and now lives in West Germany.

The other graduate students in the theoretical department were: Gurgen Saakian (now working in astrophysics in Erevan, in particular on the theory of stellar structure); Vladimir Chavchanidze, who became director of the Cybernetics Institute in Tbilisi; Dzhabaga Takibaev, a member of the Kazakh Academy of Sciences who works on the super-high energy processes that take place in cosmic rays; Arsatyants (unfortunately I don't recall his first name or field); and Pavel Nemirovsky. After finishing his graduate work, "Pavochka" was offered a position to continue his research at the Atomic Energy Institute (I was offered a similar position, but refused it). Nemirovsky accepted; he still works there, and he has had considerable achievements in the theory of the atomic nucleus. We later became neighbors, and Klava was on friendly terms with his wife, Shurochka.

Efim Fradkin ("Fima" to us) joined the theoretical department in 1945 after being released from the army. His entire family had been wiped out by the Germans, and he was alone in the world.

Fradkin had been drafted into the army at the age of seventeen and had fought on the western front; he'd been seriously wounded at Stalingrad, his teeth and jaw smashed and his tongue pierced by a shell fragment that entered his right cheek and exited through his left. His soldier's reflexes remained intact: as Fima told us, every time General Malyshev (a KGB general who represented the Central Committee and Council of Ministers) was seen entering the room where the theoreticians worked, he would feel an irresistible urge to leap up to stand at attention. Of all the members of our group, Fradkin came closest to earning our dreamt-of mantle of the first-rank, "cutting edge" theoretical physicist. His achievements encompassed virtually every basic area of quantum field theory (the Green's function method in renormalization theory, functional integration, gauge fields, unified theories of the strong, weak, and electromagnetic interactions, the general theory of quantization of coupled systems, supergravity, string theory, etc.). Fradkin is credited with the original discovery, independently of Landau and Pomeranchuk, of the "Moscow zero" [see p. 84]. Many of his achievements are now seen as classical, and in questions of methodology he is unsurpassed. Fradkin was elected a corresponding member of the Academy in the 1960s, and he has continued to enjoy great and well-deserved recognition.

The difficulties of quantum field theory (in particular those manifested in the "Moscow zero") had earned it a number of skeptics by the late 1950s and early 1960s, and this skepticism unfortunately affected Fradkin's work, the result being that some of his significant results were overlooked at the time only to be rediscovered later by others. Fradkin himself was less insistent than he might have been on some important points; most dramatically, perhaps, in the investigation of the Gell-Mann/Low beta function in non-Abelian gauge theories, an important mathematical device used in quantum theory. (I shall not explain these specialized terms here, noting only that, depending on the sign of the beta functions, one encounters either the "Moscow zero," a situation in which the effective charge of the electron goes to zero owing to a divergent integral in the denominator—this had been the case in all of the theories investigated up to that time—or a much more favorable case we might call "asymptotic freedom.") Fradkin and his co-author, Igor Tyutin, had everything "in the palm of their hands," but failed to draw attention to the sign of the beta function (or were too absorbed in overcoming computational difficulties to give it the attention it merited). If I recall correctly, the same misfortune had earlier befallen Terenin, an associate of the Institute of Experimental and Theoretical Physics, and Igor Khriplovich, a physicist from Novosibirsk. Terenin lacked the support of Pomeranchuk, who'd been carried away by the "funeral of the Lagrangian," i.e., of quantum field theory. The asymptotic freedom of gauge fields was later discovered by Wilczek and Gross, and simultaneously by Politzer—a landmark discovery in elementary-particle theory.

Between February and April 1945, I spent nearly every minute studying Pauli's two books. They were changing my world. Still, I did manage to produce a short paper with which I was rather pleased (although it later proved to duplicate the published work of other scientists). Dmitri Blokhintsev, who was officially a member of the theoretical department (owing to difficult relations with Tamm and the others, he often worked on his own), attended one Friday seminar. He held up a measuring glass containing water and flicked it with his finger, and we all heard a thin, clear sound. Then he shook the measuring glass, covering it with the palm of his hand. Before the bubbles had a chance to rise to the surface, he tapped the glass again—this time, the sound was muffled. Blokhintsev said this was a problem of genuine interest: "After a storm, a great many bubbles appear in sea water; this results in a sharp reduction in underwater audibility, of critical importance to submarines."

Beginning that very evening, I spent several days working out a theory of this phenomenon. When sound travels through water, the changing pressure causes bubbles to expand and contract, and, under certain conditions, the bubbles resonate, i.e., they experience large-amplitude vibrations. The presence of these oscillating bubbles changes the macroscopic speed of sound and causes acoustic "turbidity." I also found the mechanism for the damping of sound: as the air in the bubbles expands and contracts, adiabatic heating and cooling of the air takes place, while the water temperature remains practically constant. At the boundary between the air and the water, heat waves originate, leading to energy dissipation; thus, shaking the glass caused sound to be muffled.

Tamm suggested that I take my calculations to the Academy of Sciences Acoustics Institute. The people with whom I spoke (unfortunately, I don't remember any names; they may have included a future academician, Leonid Brekhovskikh) let me know right away that the ubiquitous Germans were ahead of me.

The story didn't end quite there, however. Thirty years later, my son-in-law, Efrem Yankelevich, was working at a fisheries science station, and was asked to study underwater sounds emitted by fish (they do so by setting their swim bladders into vibration). My project of thirty years earlier immediately came to mind. (The fact that the vibrations are of "quadrupole" rather than radial nature presents no difficulties.) Unfortunately, the study went nowhere, since Efrem lost his job shortly afterward.

To the physicist Isaak Pomeranchuk, everything but fundamental science was "bubbles" (not the real bubbles of the story just told, of course). I had quite a bit to do with such lightweight things; my work from 1948 to 1968 was essentially a single enormous "bubble."

At the seminars, Tamm's colleagues were required to take turns reviewing newly published scientific literature (especially articles in the *Physical Review*). This practice was also extended to the fledgling scientists who were just beginning to strike out on their own, and this made them really try their best. The implication was that this obligation was both an honor and a privilege. It was also, of course, incredibly difficult at first. But, in compensation, when I reported on Schwinger's work on the anomalous magnetic moment of the electron, I felt like the messenger of the gods. To this day I recall how

Pomeranchuk sprang to the blackboard after I had finished my report, and in a state of high excitement, tugging at his hair, said something to the effect of: "If this is true, it's exceptionally important; if it isn't true, that, too, is exceptionally important." (By then, it was already 1948, I believe.) I certainly did not easily achieve the level of breadth and understanding required to review scientific literature. And later on, after I had been drawn into military research, I almost instantly lost the heights I had taken such pains to acquire. I was never able to return to it again, which is a great pity. In my later work, however, I did rely to a considerable extent on knowledge acquired under Tamm's guidance during my first years at FIAN.

Another requirement, equally wise, was that all students do some teaching. I lectured for three semesters at the Moscow Energetics Institute, and then for half a year at the Kurchatov Institute's workers' night school. I'm afraid I wasn't much of a teacher, although I did learn fast from my own mistakes. Night school, with its different contingent of students, required me to think up a new approach, and had I gone on teaching (as I would have liked), I might in time have become fairly good at it.

The chairman of the physics department at the Moscow Energetics Institute, Professor V. Fabrikant, had great misgivings about my lack of teaching experience, and he gave me various useful tips. His fate as a scientist took a dramatic turn. It was roughly during this time period that he and his coworker Butayeva put forth the idea of the laser and the maser (which operates with microwaves instead of light), both of which make use of the effect of stimulated emission, first described in 1919 by Albert Einstein. The joy—and the fame—of realizing this remarkable idea went to others, however; some have said that this was due in part to the difficulties experienced by many Jews during those years of struggle against "cosmopolitanism," but I have no direct knowledge of this. Conditions at the university that militated against serious scientific work may have played a role: teaching overload, administrative work, a shortage of funds, poor equipment. Twenty years later I was on the committee that awarded Fabrikant the Vavilov Prize. One can only wonder whether that belated prize was any consolation to this man, then already old and ill, who had been at the very heart of one of the most astounding discoveries of our time.

I taught three courses at the Energetics Institute: nuclear physics, relativity theory, and electricity. Later on, I had to leave due to some departmental personnel problems probably also connected with the "struggle against cosmopolitanism." It took me a full day or more to prepare each of my weekly two-hour lectures, which I did not write out, merely outlined. I'd be so exhausted after each lecture that I couldn't even work.

Administering exams was always a trial for me, and I remember the first exam I gave as well as I remember the first I ever took. I started out unable to "get" my students on anything and I was giving everyone A's. I became somewhat more rigorous with the last student—when he was unable to answer a question that in truth went beyond the knowledge required, I gave him a B. Not only was this unfair; worse, we both knew it. I still feel guilty toward that young man, Markov, who was one of the best students in the group.

In the process of lecturing I was also teaching myself nuclear physics (to the level attained at that time, roughly within the bounds of Hans Bethe's survey in *Review of Modern Physics*; with electrodynamics and the theory of relativity as treated in Landau and Lifshitz's textbooks and in Pauli's monograph). I often think how wonderful it would have been if I'd had the time to go through all the disciplines of theoretical physics that way. If in the 1950s and 1960s I'd taught courses in quantum mechanics and quantum field theory, elementary particles including the theory of symmetry, and courses in statistical physics (with those new methods borrowed from field theory), gas dynamics, hydrodynamics, and astrophysics, the gaping holes in my education that for decades hindered my work might not have existed. But my life shaped up differently.

Teaching at the evening school may not have added to my expert knowledge, but the experience was very useful, as was the money. Whenever I ran into my former students in later years, I sensed a respect which I found flattering and pleasant.

My growth as a scientist came principally through the scientific work I did on my own and brought to a publishable stage. (Bohr's famous triad: *Work! Finish! Publish!*) Tamm was quite relaxed about the graduate examinations, to which some attach such great significance, and they became something of a formality.

Teaching was of great importance as a source of additional income, given my small stipend as a graduate student. I also earned some money by reviewing for *Collected Reviews* and *Progress in the Physical Sciences*. I did a good job, I think, but this was of less scientific value to me than teaching; it lacked the sort of systematic structure that helps create a firm and lasting foundation.

But I needed the money badly, and not only for food. Not that the food situation was very good—though that was true for the majority of people at that time, and for many it was much worse. After all, we had three ration cards for three people: mine as a graduate student, Klava's as a dependent, and Tanya's as a child. I don't want to give a misleading impression here; let me emphasize that there was nothing exceptional about our hardships, at the time. Nearly everyone's life was difficult in the first postwar years; ours, in fact, was rather easier financially than most people's. And, most important, everyone in our family had survived.

After I defended my dissertation I received a much better allowance, but then the ration card system was revoked and at the same time a currency reform was instituted that was ruinous for many people. The principal problem was housing. We were never able to remain anywhere longer than two months, and for reasons beyond our control, kept having to rent new rooms. These rooms were usually bad and sometimes unbearably cold; our little daughter was always catching cold, and once developed inflammation of the kidneys. During one period we lived in the front room of a basement apartment; it was very damp, and the landlords were constantly passing through our room to get to theirs. Another time the room was warm and dry, but the landlady, who demanded the rent a month in advance, was in the habit of squeezing out her tenants ahead of time through outrageous ploys in order to "harvest the same field twice." She'd always manage to use her mental-disability certification to get off scot-free. Her ruses didn't budge us; we'd just lean a sack of potatoes against the front door as we slept. But when the month was out, she turned up with a policeman (obviously an acquaintance of hers) to evict us; and so we had to go, after all. Each time we were turned out of a room, we'd have to go back to live with my parents, and relations between Klava and my mother, bad enough to begin with, would deteriorate further. Klava, my mother, and I were all to blame in aggravating the situation; only my father took a more reasonable attitude.

In 1947, despairing of finding a room in Moscow (few people wanted to rent to a family with a child), we rented two rooms in a private home in Pushkino, outside Moscow, and twice a week I'd take the local train in to FIAN. In the colder of our two rooms I set up my first study, and there, with a fur coat draped over my shoulders, I worked away at my dissertation. Every so often, Klava would have Tanya go in to check whether I'd frozen solid. Tanya would peep through a crack and report back: "Papa's laughing." The owner of the house, a former shoemaker, was bedridden and seriously ill, and the family existed on whatever his wife was able to resell at the market. (Such "speculation" is considered a punishable crime in the USSR, but a great many people live by just these means, greasing the palms of the police and others in authority and swelling the ranks of prisoners when that approach fails, as it does on occasion. This black market flourished in the first postwar years.) Our landlady was well disposed to us, and she enjoyed engaging us in friendly—and colorful—chats. Her tales of various "lucky dames" frequently contained the comic refrain: "She had boobs out to here, and he" (i.e., the husband, or "her man") "made her life a fairy tale."

I was often to recall that refrain in later years. (Lusia and I would sometimes add that phrase to our conversation, ironically saying "and he made her life a fairy tale . . . but a grim one.")

In the fall of 1947, through intermediaries, we rented a small house (rumored to belong to a KGB colonel) near the Dynamo metro station. We were just settling in when a representative of the KGB came to see Klava while I was away from home, and proposed that she "cooperate" by reporting all my meetings to him (without telling me); in return, he promised help with our household difficulties. Klava refused, and two days later we were kicked out of the house, ostensibly because of "operational necessities." I must note that I had no connection with secret work at the time; it was just an ordinary link in the network of surveillance that enveloped the whole country.

My father helped us with money for our housing, but we were still short, and in the spring of 1947 Tamm loaned me a thousand rubles which I was able to repay only after I'd defended my dissertation. At one point we found ourselves without money even to buy milk, and Klava attempted to sell the candy she'd received on her ration card; the police immediately picked her up for "speculation," and she was lucky to get off.

In January 1948, through the Institute's intercession, we were allotted a room in the Academy of Science hotel (this was officially the "Home for Visiting Scientists," but the majority of its residents were in our situation, and, what's more, had no relationship whatsoever with the Academy). I no longer recall whether FIAN paid for my room entirely or in part. In connection with housing, I used to see the director of FIAN, Sergei Vavilov, an academician and a well-known specialist in optics; he was the brother of another, even better-known academician: Nikolai Vavilov, a biologist who a few years earlier, in one of the most terrible pages in the protracted tragedy of Soviet biology, had been arrested and had perished in prison. Sergei Vavilov shortly thereafter became (or perhaps already was) the president of the Academy of Sciences, in which capacity he met regularly—at least once a week—with T. D. Lysenko, a member of the Academy of Science's presidium, who had borne the major responsibility for his brother's death. Those meetings are difficult for me to imagine. [Recently, Yakov Alpert, one of the more senior people at FIAN, told me the following story (which he had heard from Leontovich, who supposedly heard it directly from Vavilov). Vavilov had been informed (possibly by Stalin himself or one of his confidants) that there were two acceptable candidates for the post of president of the Academy: Vavilov was the first choice; if he didn't accept, it would be Lysenko. Vavilov sat up the entire night pondering his reply, smoking through several packs of cigarettes, and decided to accept the post—thereby saving the Academy and Soviet science from the devastation Lysenko's election would inevitably have caused. This story, if it is true, reveals a new and tragic aspect of Vavilov's fate, and of the fate of Soviet science in general.—A.S. 1987][1]

Vavilov was a benevolent man, kind and gentle in his personal contacts. As a deputy to the Supreme Soviet, he had many dealings with constituents who

---

[1] [According to Evgeny Feinberg, the other candidate was not Lysenko but Andrei Vyshinsky, the former Procurator General—which sounds somehow more likely, and even more frightening.]

came to him with complaints and requests. I can easily imagine what that was like on the basis of my own experience on the Human Rights Committee during the 1970s. In his desk, Vavilov kept a store of envelopes, stuffed with money from his own pocket: there being no other way for him to help most of the unfortunate petitioners, he'd often simply give them money. Word of this leaked out, and the authorities tried to put a stop to it. Vavilov directed another institute in addition to FIAN, and he was extraordinarily zealous and unsparing of himself in all his duties (in this respect, I can compare him only with a very different sort of man—Yuli Khariton, the scientific director of the enterprise where I was to work for many years). Vavilov was always considerate of his colleagues' personal lives. He had a profound and sincere love for science, did excellent work in optics, and was active in popularizing scientific material. In one of the many official speeches his position as president required him to deliver, he referred to Stalin as the "Coryphaeus of science," and this epithet became almost an official honorific (apparently, Stalin was pleased with it).

The respective fates of the two brothers—one dying of hunger and cleaning slop pails in Saratov prison; the other, president of the Academy and heaped with honors—was a paradox extreme even for those times; and yet, in a way, it summed up the whole era.

Vavilov, who had been considerate to me even before then, was well aware of my housing problems, and Tamm later told me that this played a part in my subsequent fate.

BETWEEN 1945 and 1947, Tamm developed a hypothesis he had advanced on the nature of nuclear forces (strong interactions, to use a more contemporary term; this force is the very glue that holds the atomic nucleus together). It is obvious now that this was a premature attempt which had no chance of succeeding. After all, even the pi-meson, the lightest of the mesons and the one that is largely responsible for nuclear forces at lower energies, was discovered only toward the end of this period, and its quantum numbers and other important characteristics were unknown. (I hope that the nonphysicist reader will forgive me for leaving certain terms unexplained in this book and will pass them off as vague and pretty figures of speech.) The ingenious mechanics of the strong nuclear interactions has not to this day been completely clarified, although each of the following decades has brought surprising experimental discoveries and profound theoretical insights.

A special hypothesis of Igor Tamm's attempted to explain the nuclear force by positing the existence of two kinds of mesons: a charged pseudoscalar meson and a neutral scalar meson. He suggested that Pyotr Kunin make relativistic—and very difficult—calculations of the nuclear interactions of two nucleons (this is a collective term for a proton and neutron) and to me he gave the topic of how mesons might be produced. Since the model had very little in common with reality, very little remained of our efforts, except that Kunin benefited from overcoming methodological difficulties. As for me, the main benefit was that I mastered calculations in a technique called noncovariant perturbation theory (from Heitler's *Quantum Mechanics*), at that time (before Richard Feynman's work) the acme of the science. These skills served me very well later on. Certain points in my paper remained valuable regardless of the particular form of Tamm's model. It may be scientifically trivial, but it is still worth noting, that I calculated (probably many others had already done so) particle-production thresholds in the laboratory system of reference (i.e., a system in which the target nucleon is at rest). I also showed that the thresholds shift toward lower energies when one takes into account the fact that the nucleons are bound in the nucleus, and I offered estimates of the cross sections in this broadened range of incident-particle energies. I also studied particle production and light scattering in strong fields. At the time this was of no immediate practical importance, but it was theoretically instructive. Nonlinear light scattering is now observed in laser beams and constitutes a branch of science in itself. Then, I regarded it as being more of an illustrative nature. The paper gave a particularly clear example: the case of scattering of circularly polarized light by a free electron, with frequency doubling. Classically, the electron would move on a circle; the doubled frequency, as well as other harmonics, are due to the fact that given the finite radius of the orbit, radiation's delay causes distortion of the sine wave. (This is the so-called theory of synchrotron radiation.) In quantum language, the electron absorbs two photons and emits one.

I worked on the problem under discussion for a few months in 1946, and my work was published in 1947 in one of the most important Soviet physical science journals, *Journal of Experimental and Theoretical Physics*. (My happiness at this first publication was marred by the fact that I already realized that Tamm's theory was wrong.) Not long before this, there'd been a scandal regarding an alleged leak of classified information about cancer treatment, and publishers were nervous (although the allegations later turned out to be without substance, Stalin had been enraged; in a normal society the fuss would seem absurd—but ours wasn't a normal one). The editors changed the title of my article from "Meson Generation" to the less specific "Generation of the Hard Components of Cosmic Rays." Tamm explained the change to me: "Even Lavrenty Pavlovich [Beria] knows what mesons are."

I don't think there was any possibility of Beria himself interfering; Tamm was just using him as a "worst case" example. What he really feared was an attack on the author and editor by "vigilant" members of the lower ranks. The situation in the publishing world became increasingly strained. Appalling restrictions on the publication of scientific and technical articles soon were instituted. These survived every subsequent change in leadership, and remain in effect even today. Every article had to pass through a complex bureaucratic process: references had to be submitted, long questionnaires filled out, and a recommendation procured from a special permanent commission at the institution where the author worked (if the author for one reason or another did not work in a scientific institution, he was absolutely unable to publish). The commission's recommendation had to certify that the article contained no secret information, patented ideas, or ideas and proposals with significant practical applications. These documents were then sent to Glavlit (the department of censorship, whose activity is shrouded in secrecy: no common mortal should ever know who works there!). Glavlit had its own interminable list of subjects forbidden not only in the interests of secrecy, but, in the main, out of political considerations. (For example, it was forbidden to publish information about crimes, alcoholism, health conditions, education, the water supply, suicides, the existing supply and the production of nonferrous metals, precise data on the population's nutrition and income, and movie and theatre attendance figures.) Demographic data and information on environmental problems, natural disasters and accidents, and an endless series of other matters could not be published without special permission. Glavlit's imprimatur was also required for the publication of all literary works (and to just about everything published in the country, right down to advertisements and the labels on matchboxes). Only after receiving Glavlit's approval did the scientific or technical article reach a journal's editors.

It is easy to imagine the resulting delays in publication, to which even such abstract subjects as number theory and astrophysics are not exempt. [I wrote the above lines in 1982; today, in the era of glasnost, much has changed, but the system by which scientific articles are published remains cumbersome.— A.S. 1989]

My first paper was not suitable as a dissertation. My dissertation topic was my own idea; in preparing for my lectures I'd read about two nuclear transitions in RaC' (read: radium "C" prime, a member of the radium family) and oxygen nuclei which were notable for the fact that they were not accompanied by the usual emission of gamma rays. It occurred to me that the reason for this phenomenon might be that these transitions correspond to spherically symmetric nuclear vibrations in the case when the initial and final angular momenta are equal to zero. It is obvious by virtue of symmetry that such vibrations are not accompanied by emission. I made the pertinent calculations, Tamm approved the topic, and I wrote the dissertation. In addition to the main thesis, there were some digressions and embellishments: a new charge-parity selection rule and allowance for the electron-positron interaction in pair production (the probability of pair production increases at those momentum values at which the relative velocity of the electron and positron is very low). It became apparent that the article's basic idea was not original—nonradiative transitions had been investigated long before me by the Japanese physicists Yukawa and Sakata. I was upset, but Tamm decided that my subject need not be changed; there was sufficient substance for a dissertation, especially when the "embellishments" were taken into account. Tamm wanted Landau to be one of the questioners at my defense, but Landau declined—fortunately; I would have been very uncomfortable, knowing my dissertation's shortcomings.

Two excellent physicists, Arkady Migdal and Isaak Pomeranchuk, both future academicians, served as the questioners. It took a long time to get hold of Migdal; he'd just bought a car, and was spending days on end practicing his driving on the grounds of LIPAN (as the Kurchatov Institute was then known). Migdal was a generally enthusiastic individual whose chief passion was science, in which he had substantial accomplishments. Eventually, he did write a very favorable review of my work. Pomeranchuk was more of a problem. The day of my defense approached, and his review still had not arrived; and then I did some real harm to myself with regard to the graduate exam in philosophy (Marxist, of course). These examinations were given at the Academy graduate school's philosophy department by special examiners who tested students from all the various faculties. My exam took place a week before my scheduled defense; at it, I was asked if I had read certain of Chernyshevsky's philosophical works (the fashion for "pure Russian" scientists and philosophers, free of any Western taint, had already begun). Excessively truthful, I replied that I hadn't read them, but knew what they concerned. I received a D. I completed all the required reading within a week and received an A when I retook the test, but by then everyone had left on vacation, and my defense had to be rescheduled for the fall—a financial blow, given the difficulty of living on a graduate student's stipend and rations. But even with this delay, I finished my graduate work a few months ahead of schedule.

I didn't manage to get hold of Pomeranchuk until the day that fall on which my defense was scheduled. At seven o'clock that morning, I went to Pomeranchuk's and he, clad only in his undershorts, sat down and wrote a very favorable review. An hour later, I handed it to the secretary of the Science Board. Later that day, Vavilov congratulated me: I'd been awarded my candidate's degree. I was appointed a junior researcher in FIAN's theoretical department.

Klava, Tanya, and I continued to live in Pushkino through the summer of 1947, and I commuted frequently to FIAN. With my dissertation completed, I began to think about further scientific work. I will describe two of my forays, which may be of interest and possibly useful to young scientists reading this book.

In the context of the dissertation, I pondered alternative possible explanations for the nonradiative nuclear transitions (i.e., not the spherically symmetric transitions proposed by Yukawa and Sakata and myself, but rather, hypothetical interactions that would not involve an electromagnetic field). In this connection I recalled that the literature had discussed the presence of a certain anomaly in the optical spectrum of the hydrogen atom [the so-called Balmer series] that diverged from the formula derived from theory. That is to say, there were indications (not absolutely definite, since the effect was extremely small, at the accuracy limit of optical methods for the observation of spectral levels) that two spectral lines of the hydrogen atom that, according to theory, should coincide, diverged slightly.

After some reflection, I decided that nonelectromagnetic effects have nothing to do with the nonradiative transitions nor with the hydrogen atom.

It is, unquestionably, possible to explain the nonradiative transitions trivially, as did Yukawa and Sakata. But I'd "latched onto" the anomaly in the hydrogen atom to the point of obsession. I had the idea (to describe it in somewhat simplified terms) that it was a manifestation of what are now known as radiative corrections: an effect of the interaction of the electron with quantum-mechanical vibrations of its own electromagnetic field, or, more precisely, the difference of such effects for the bound and the free electron.

In quantum mechanics there is no such thing as "rest" in the same sense as in the classical, nonquantum theory. Any mechanical system at equilibrium oscillates, so to speak, about the point of equilibrium—a consequence of the so-called Heisenberg uncertainty principle. This property is likewise extended to a vacuum, which is also regarded as a kind of mechanical system with an infinite number of degrees of freedom experiencing so-called zero-point fluctuations. Later in this book I shall discuss ideas that relate the energy of zero-point fluctuations to gravitation theory. In the 1930s and 1940s, attention was being focused on the interaction of vacuum zero-point electromagnetic field fluctuations with electrons and other charged particles. On calculation, the energy of this interaction was found to be infinite. To be more specific, the infinite energy appeared because of the contribution of high-frequency oscillation; i.e., introduction of an artificial "cutoff" frequency made the energy finite again. These infinities were a major theoretical difficulty that overshadowed development of quantum field theory for many decades. I concluded that to confront the problem of theoretically infinite quantities, it would be necessary to consider the difference between the effects for free electrons and electrons bound by a nucleus. Since (as I correctly assumed) the binding effect asserts itself only at lower frequencies, there was hope that the difference would be finite. To obtain correct results when subtracting two infinite quantities, the calculations can at first be confined to oscillations of a frequency less than a certain limiting "cutoff" frequency but high enough so that the binding effect can be ignored. This mathematical manipulation would be followed by a formal transition to the infinitely large "cutoff" frequency. I understood that the importance of this idea extended far beyond the particular problem of the hydrogen-atom anomaly, and should, among other things, be extended to scattering.

I was very excited, and in the summer or fall of 1947 I brought all this to Tamm. Unfortunately, he gave me neither support nor approval. Instead, he said these ideas were not original and had already been expressed in various forms several times in the past. That was true; but it wouldn't have been enough to stop me—I was already so interested and involved that I wasn't overly concerned with who'd been first with the idea. It was the subject itself that counted. Then Tamm told me the idea "wouldn't work" since it did not, after all, yield a finite solution. He referred me to a recently published article by the American theoretician Sidney Dancoff, who calculated the radiative corrections (renormalization) for the scattering process using a method in principle very close to the one I proposed to use for the level divergences in the hydrogen atom spectrum. I searched out Dancoff's article in the library. It was true that his calculations had not yielded a finite solution (i.e., one approaching a constant value as the "cutoff" energy approached infinity). Dancoff's calculations were very complex and intricate; this was before Feynman invented his much more compact and visual method of calculation (Feynman diagrams). Dancoff was quite simply wrong; but neither Tamm nor I was able to detect that from a casual glance. If our intuition hadn't failed us, we would have questioned Dancoff's work as many times as it took to uncover his error; or, more wisely, we'd have temporarily ignored the contradictions which arose and searched for problems simpler to calculate, whose results could have been compared to the experiment. This was the approach chosen by bolder people with more insight—and more success. But we did not, and so I lost a chance at the most important scientific work of that era, and many years would pass before I had a chance to try my hand on a problem of comparable importance. But, to paraphrase the well-known saying: Everyone gets the challenges he deserves.

What happened subsequently in this area is also well known to physicists. Lamb and Retherford (and later others) used radiospectroscopic techniques to measure the level difference between the two lines in the spectrum of the hydrogen atom [the Lamb shift]. They not only confirmed the actual existence of the level divergence (which optical methods had left in doubt), but also measured it with uncanny accuracy. Hendrik Kramers appeared at one of the scientific conferences held in 1947 (perhaps the one at Rochester)[2] with a program for calculation of *finite* radiative corrections for the measured quanti-

---

[2][It was in fact Shelter Island.]

ties—what became known as renormalization. At the same time or a bit later, Hans Bethe reported on his calculation of level divergence. Indeed, the points of departure of both papers were essentially very similar to those that I describe above. In a deliberate simplification, Bethe's calculations ignored the effects of relativity. He therefore obtained not a finite result, but one that increased logarithmically as the "cutoff" energy tended to infinity. But, as Landau liked to say: *A chicken is not a bird, and a logarithm is not infinity.*

Bethe's result signaled a breakthrough into a new domain, and indicated that it was probable that entirely finite results could be obtained in this and other electrodynamic phenomena. The rest was a matter of technique (albeit very difficult). There were titans who overcame all of these difficulties—Tomonaga, Schwinger, Feynman, Dyson, Wick, Ward, and many others. The first consistent calculation of the level divergence (which gave a finite result in agreement with the Lamb-Retherford experiment) was made in a 1949 *Physical Review* paper by Weisskopf and French.

I cannot resist telling a brief story of subsequent events in which I myself was not involved.

In 1948, Schwinger found the radiative correction for the magnetic moment of the electron. His value was soon confirmed by experiment (both for the electron and for the mu-meson; I don't recall precisely whether the first data for the electron antedated Schwinger's paper). The experimental and theoretical values were then repeatedly refined, and we now have agreement to the ninth or tenth decimal place. In no other field of science do theory and experiment agree so closely as in quantum electrodynamics. It's interesting to note that the analytic calculations were so cumbersome that it was necessary to run them on a machine with a special program (to clarify: analytic calculations involve manipulations of formulas rather than simply operations on numbers, which were initially the sole specialty of the computer).

But magnificent agreement between calculations and experiment did not guarantee that all was fundamentally well with the theory. In 1955, Fradkin, Landau, and Pomeranchuk found independently that iterative application of renormalization procedure had a monstrous consequence: total vanishing of the observable electromagnetic interactions. This celebrated absurdity became known as the "Moscow zero."

That year I ran into Landau at a New Year's banquet at the Kremlin. He looked anxious, even dejected, and told me: "We're all at our wits' end. No one has any idea what to do."

Another statement by Landau during this period applies here: "The Lagrangian is dead. It should be buried, of course, with all due honors."

The Lagrangian is the quantum analog of the Lagrange function, a fundamental concept of quantum field theory. But Landau was wrong; the Lagrangian was not dead. For many years, the "Moscow zero" difficulty was seen as indicating the need to abandon quantum field theory in high-energy physics and to look for other ways to rebuild elementary-particle theory—none of which proved effective. Not until 1974 did a new ray of hope appear, when it was shown that there is no "Moscow zero" in the non-Abelian gauge theories. (It was still necessary to manipulate infinite quantities.) And a few years later, nontrivial examples (but not yet realistic; incapable of describing the real universe) in which there are no infinities at all were found among the supersymmetry theories. The heroic effort continues in the hands of a whole army of scientists, both theoreticians and experimenters: perhaps the most daring hopes are connected with string theory, in which particles are thought not to be dimensionless points but tiny cords and rings of unimaginably small size.

Recalling that summer of 1947, I feel that never before or since have I been so close to the highest level of science—its cutting edge. I am, of course, somewhat irked that I did not prove equal to the task (circumstances are no excuse here). But, taking a broader view, I cannot help but exult in the great advances of science—and had I not once been a part of it, I would not feel this so keenly!

MY OTHER unsuccessful attempt of those months concerned an altogether minor problem, which I will nonetheless mention here. I asked myself whether the possibility that electrons and positrons forming an atomlike system (positronium) will annihilate each other depends on the angular momentum (spin) of the positronium. I began calculating the annihilation probabilities of free colliding electrons and positrons with both parallel and antiparallel spins (the former case would correspond to a positronium spin of 1 in units of Planck's constant, and the latter to 0). However, somewhere along the way I got the sign of one of the terms wrong. I had made these calculations while riding the Pushkino–Moscow train, and later consoled myself with the joke that the car had been jolted at the instant when I was writing the minus sign, so that it came out a plus sign. Pomeranchuk obtained the correct result (using the same crude method as myself). Spin 1 positronium (orthopositronium) does not annihilate into two photons, but only into three. When Landau learned of this result, he reproduced it by a much more elegant and productive method based on symmetry considerations (i.e., practically without benefit of calculations). Landau's result covered all spin 1 particles. Therefore when the decay of the pi-zero meson into two photons was detected soon thereafter, this made it totally impossible for the spin of the pi-meson to be equal to 1 (a result of enormous importance). One might formulate the system of inequalities L > P > S (L for Landau, P for Pomeranchuk, and S for Sakharov).

All of these events took place before my dissertation defense, in the summer and fall of 1947. After the defense, I confronted the problem of choosing some "solid" subject matter (I did not know that this problem would soon be solved for me). I made an attempt at doing something in plasma theory. The kinetic equation with a logarithmic "order of magnitude" cutoff struck me as kind of a monstrosity, and I wanted to come up with something more elegant and more exact. The task was beyond me, but, like the next one, to which I now turn, it helped prepare me scientifically for the problems that I would have to deal with later, in the "special subject," i.e., military, research.

I read a paper by F. C. Frank in the British journal *Nature* in the fall or winter of 1948; in it, the author discussed the historic experiments of Powell, Lattes, and Occhialini in which the pi-meson had been discovered. The experimenters used the then new technique of irradiating thick-emulsion photographic plates with cosmic rays, and found interesting decay tracks of some particle caught in the emulsion—a particle lighter than the proton which clearly produced a mu-meson on decay. Powell, Lattes, and Occhialini concluded that this particle was heavier than the mu-meson, since otherwise it could not have decayed with release of appreciable energy. The particle was later given the name pi-meson. The fundamentally important conclusion that a new kind of particle had been discovered made it necessary to analyze all possible alternative explanations. Frank included the idea that the primary particle might actually be an ordinary mu-meson that had been captured by a hydrogen nucleus, forming an atomlike particle (now referred to as a "mesoatom"). The mesoatom then combines with another hydrogen nucleus to form a "molecular mesoion." If one of the hydrogen nuclei (which normally consists of a proton) is a heavy isotope (a deuteron, or neutron and proton), a nuclear reaction may occur in the "mesoion" between the deuteron and the proton, with formation of helium-three and a photon. When this happens, the excess energy is imparted to the mu-meson and it escapes, forming a track.

The nuclear reaction in the mesoion takes place between two charged particles—a deuteron and a proton. Such reactions usually occur with some probability only if the energy of the colliding particles is high enough to overcome the electrostatic repulsion of the positively charged nuclei (as we learned in school, bodies carrying like charges repel one another; the outstretched leaves of the electroscope come straight to mind). One of the possibilities is a thermonuclear (now the word that would become central to this author's fate has been uttered) reaction. Here, the nuclear reaction takes place at a temperature at which the energy of thermal motion is high enough to overcome the repulsion of the nuclei. In the case of the hydrogen isotopes, which include deuterium, consisting of deuterons and tritium, consisting of tritons (nuclei with a proton and two neutrons), this temperature is of the order of a few kiloelectron volts (KeV) or more; for the multiply charged nuclei of all of the other elements, the "threshold" is many times higher (one reason that only thermonuclear reactions between hydrogen isotopes are used in thermonuclear weapons). One kiloelectron volt (KeV), the unit of temperature used in astrophysics and nuclear weapons theory, corresponds to approximately ten million degrees Kelvin. The temperature at the center of the sun is about 1.5 KeV, i.e., fifteen million degrees.

In laboratory studies of nuclear reactions between charged nuclei, one of the colliding particles is accelerated by an electric field, while the other is situated in a solid or gaseous "target." This is the second way of generating nuclear reactions between charged particles. Frank indicated a third way, which involved far less energy. A molecular mesoion consisting of a proton, a deuteron, and a negatively charged mu-meson is similar in structure to the ordinary molecular ion (proton + deuteron + electron). The negatively charged mu-meson or electron binds the three-body system together by attracting the positively charged nuclei. But since the mass of the mu-meson is 209 times larger than the mass of the electron, the mesoion is smaller by the same factor. Thus, the nuclei have already traveled much of the distance across which they must overcome mutual repulsion, and the rest of the path is easily covered owing to a phenomenon called quantum tunneling. Quantum tunneling, one of the most important qualitative effects in quantum physics, was discovered theoretically and studied by Robert Oppenheimer in the late 1920s; it underlies the effect of alpha decay, many effects in solid state physics, the spontaneous fission of uranium nuclei, etc.

Frank's idea was ingenious but his estimates demonstrated that the results of the experiments by Powell, Lattes, and Occhialini could not be explained in this way. The primary particle is not the mu-meson, but something new: the pi-meson. But Frank's work interested me from another point of view; in the mechanism Frank proposed, the mu-meson acts as a catalyst for nuclear reactions, facilitating their flow without expending itself in a manner entirely analogous to the catalytic reactions known from chemistry. I asked myself whether conditions could be created under which each ("accelerator-made") mu-meson would draw a larger number of deuterons into the nuclear reaction. To put it simply: what would happen if a bunch of mu-mesons were admitted into a large vessel containing deuterium? Would a nuclear reaction ensue? I thought up a name for this venture—"mu-meson catalysis"—and made several estimates (which were not very promising and which didn't come close to exhausting the complex phenomena occurring within the system), and wrote it up. That paper was classified as secret (the first work of mine to be classified, apparently done on Vavilov's initiative), but quite a good many people both within and outside FIAN became familiar with it. Although it evoked great interest, it produced no practical results. I contributed relatively little to the subsequent developments in this area, but I will outline them here.

In 1956, using a beam of mu-mesons from an accelerator, the noted American physicist Luis Alvarez observed the reaction that Frank had predicted taking place in mixtures containing small amounts of deuterium. The probability of the primary product, the protonic mesoatom, reacting with deuterium was found to be unexpectedly high: here, a deuteron "entices" a mu-meson, and a mesoatom is formed from the deuteron and the mu-meson. This mesoatom then reacts with a proton, forming a mesoion. I discussed this experiment with Yakov Zeldovich, who came up with many valuable ideas; for my part, I contributed a rough estimate of the enticement effect. The result was a joint paper that also made reference to my report, which by then had been declassified.

The following factors must be taken into account in calculating the yield of the catalytic reaction per mu-meson: the mu-meson is an unstable particle that decays in a relatively short period (two millionths of a second). Furthermore, molecular-ion formation and the subsequent nuclear reaction are not instantaneous, but require a finite amount of time. The catalyst can rapidly become "poisoned"—a term from ordinary chemistry that refers in this case to the formation of a mesoion with a helium nucleus. It is obvious that if we are looking for an appreciable nuclear-reaction yield, the time taken to form the molecular ion and the nuclear-reaction time must be much smaller than the lifetime of the mu-meson, and poisoning must be infrequent.

These factors were all analyzed thoroughly. USSR investigators working in this area included S. Gershtein, L. Ponomarev, and their co-workers. Their principal conclusions:

1. In pure deuterium, there is no reason to hope for a reaction yield sufficient to return the energy expended on production of the mu-mesons.

2. The situation in a deuterium-tritium mixture is more encouraging.

[Some theoretical and preliminary experimental results now give grounds for the hope that mu-meson catalysis could (at least in principle) provide a solution to the problems of controlled fusion. (In particular, when fusion is used for "breeding" of fissionable material, as discussed in Chapter 9 in connection with the magnetic thermonuclear reactor.) The reaction should take place not in a liquid, as I thought in 1948, but in a huge volume of compressed gas. Mu-meson catalysis was studied experimentally in the USSR by V. Dzhelepov and others (the Dubna synchrocyclotron was used as the mu-meson source). Overall, mu-meson catalysis is a broad area of research in which many people are at present involved—A.S. 1987]

In early 1948, a member of FIAN, Sergei Mandelshtam (a specialist in optics and the son of Leonid Mandelshtam), asked me to calculate certain nonequilibrium processes in a gas-discharge plasma. I don't recall the details, but I did make the calculations; in fact, they were later published. This work led to my attending a spectroscopic conference in Kiev, a very pleasant experience. I arrived by airplane—my first flight—and then had a chance to enjoy that beautiful city, with its fascinating architecture and history. I felt disengaged from all my Moscow concerns. I did attend some of the sessions, more out of general curiosity than out of any field-related interest. A sharp clash took place at the conference that echoed debates then taking place on the subject of "idealistic" quantum chemistry. The critics of quantum chemistry claimed that this science's notion of the superposition of orbits was "idealistic" and a physical impossibility. In point of fact, apart from some chemistry jargon and simplifications then in use, this was no more than the transfer of the fundamental quantum mechanic principle of the superposition of states from physics (where it was universally accepted) to chemistry. Do our chemists' Western colleagues even recall those discussions today? Fortunately, as I noted earlier, the scientific attacks in chemistry and physics were less powerful and effective than in biology.

I stayed at the Ukraina Hotel on the corner of Kreshchatik, where in the mornings nightingales could be heard singing outside. My childhood friend Boris Samoilov was my roommate. At that time, Samoilov was working at the Institute of Physics, and had brought a very interesting experimental paper to present at the conference (unlike myself, for whom spectroscopy was only a casual involvement). Boris was as boisterous, restless, and lighthearted as ever, and very good company for me. We never saw each other again, but I know he became a capable experimentalist who gained a name for himself among specialists in optics. He died recently.

That trip to Kiev proved to be a breath of freedom for me, the final interlude before my twenty years behind the curtain of secrecy. Later, accompanied by Lusia, I returned to Kiev in December 1971 and January 1972—in completely different circumstances, living a completely different life.

6

THE TAMM GROUP

I FIRST HEARD of the splitting of uranium nuclei just before the war, from my father, who had attended a lecture on the subject. A short while later, I read an article on nuclear fission in the journal *Achievements of the Physical Sciences*. I'm ashamed to admit that I did not fully grasp the importance of this discovery—this despite the fact that both my father and the article made mention of the theoretical possibility of a chain reaction (although I don't recall any clear distinction being made between a *controlled* chain reaction such as takes place in a nuclear reactor and an *explosive* chain reaction of the sort that occurs when an atom bomb is detonated).

By now, the basic principles of a controlled chain reaction have been treated throughly in the non-classified literature, and the physics of nuclear explosions has also been discussed, albeit with some deliberate inaccuracies inserted and details withheld.

In both the controlled and the explosive chain reaction a free neutron is captured by the nucleus of a fissionable isotope, whereupon the nucleus splits in two. This process releases energy, as well as two or three free neutrons; these may, in turn, cause more nuclei to split. This process is termed a chain reaction. It can proceed even at room temperature, since neutrons, being electrically neutral, are not repelled by atomic nuclei.

Of greatest importance are the chain reactions that take place in the rare uranium-235 isotope and in plutonium-239. Let us recall that atomic nuclei consist of protons, which carry a positive charge, and neutrons, which carry no electrical charge. The number of protons in the nucleus—equal to the number of the shell's electrons—determines the atom's chemical properties, as well as its size, optical properties, and so forth. Nuclei with the same number of protons but different numbers of neutrons are known as "isotopes" of a chemical element. The number of neutrons determines the atomic weight (or, to be more precise, the mass number) and the atom's behavior in nuclear reactions. For example, natural uranium contains 99.3 percent nuclei of uranium-238 (92 protons and 146 neutrons in the nucleus) and 0.7 percent nuclei of uranium-235 (92 protons and 143 neutrons). The mass number of the isotope is the sum of the protons and neutrons combined ($238 = 92 + 146$, $235 = 92 + 143$).

At low neutron energies, below one MeV (one million electron-volts), a fission reaction occurs only in uranium-235 and plutonium-239—so-called fissionable isotopes. Uranium-238 nuclei will split if struck by high-energy neutrons, but the reaction is not self-sustaining, since fission does not produce "fast" (high-energy) neutrons. A "forced" fission reaction using U-238 is possible, however, if fast neutrons are delivered from an external source such as a thermonuclear reaction (the fusion of two deuterium nuclei produces free neutrons with energies of 2.5 MeV; the fusion of one deuterium nucleus and one tritium nucleus produces free neutrons with energies of 14 MeV). [Deuterium and tritium are isotopes of hydrogen.] Inside a nuclear reactor, a chain reaction can be maintained using the mixture of uranium isotopes that occur in nature. This reaction can be controlled quite easily, since some of the neutrons are released after a delay and not at the moment when the uranium atom splits.

In 1939–1940, much of this was still unknown. The last prewar discussion of chain reactions was contained in a paper by Zeldovich and Khariton.[1] Foreign journals stopped publishing papers on the subject, although, as we know, intensive nuclear research continued in secret throughout the war. As for myself, I simply forgot about the subject until February 1945, when I read (in *The British Ally,* a magazine for Soviet citizens published by the British embassy in Moscow) a description of a heroic British-Norwegian commando raid on a cache of heavy water in Norway that the Germans had intended to use in an "atomic bomb"—an explosive device of fantastic power utilizing nuclear fission. I believe this was the first mention of an atomic bomb in the press, and the "leak" may well have been intentional, perhaps designed to discourage the German program. The psychological warfare conducted by many countries at that time was far too complex for ordinary mortals to fathom.

I immediately recalled everything I'd ever heard about fission and chain reactions. Then, during the next few months, I began to hear occasional

---

[1][An important paper by Zeldovich and Khariton was delivered at the Conference on Questions of the Physics of the Atomic Nucleus held in Kharkov, November 15–20, 1939, and published later that year. For the early history of atomic physics in the USSR, see Arnold Kramish, *Atomic Energy in the Soviet Union* (Stanford University Press, 1959).]

references to a "Laboratory No. 2," but paid little attention. Later I was to learn that "Laboratory No. 2" was a major scientific research institute headed by Igor Kurchatov—the establishment now known as the Kurchatov Institute of Atomic Energy.

As I became absorbed in the wider world of theoretical physics, my interest in atomic matters again ebbed. May 1945 was marked by an unforgettable event—V-E Day. In Europe, fascism had been defeated; the war was over. But in the Pacific it was still going on.

On my way to the bakery on the morning of August 7, 1945, I stopped to glance at a newspaper and discovered President Truman's announcement that at eight A.M. the previous day, August 6, an atom bomb of enormous destructive power had been dropped on Hiroshima. I was so stunned that my legs practically gave way. There could be no doubt that my fate and the fate of many others, perhaps of the entire world, had changed overnight. Something new and awesome had entered our lives, a product of the greatest of the sciences, of the discipline I revered.

The British Ally began serial publication of the Smyth Report, an account of the development of the atom bomb that contained an abundance of declassified information on isotope separation, nuclear reactors, plutonium, and uranium-235, and a general description of the structure of the atom bomb.[2] I would snatch up each new issue of the *Ally* and scrutinize it minutely with an interest that was purely scientific: But I was also eager to put my talents as an inventor to the test. But everything I dreamed up was either old hat (the lattice effect for reactors, which had been known for three years) or impractical (the method of isotope separation based on Knudsen flow[3] into the mouths of configured rotors). My old school friend Akiva Yaglom said, "Andrei proposes at least two new methods of isotope separation a week." After the final installment of the Smyth Report appeared, however, I gave little thought to the atom bomb for the next two and a half years.

FATE CONTINUED to weave its web around me (I recall the holiday scene from *Faust* which Oleg had read aloud to me).[4]

---

[2][The formal title of this report was "Atomic Energy for Military Purposes. The Official Report on the Development of the Atomic Bomb Under the Auspices of the United States Government, 1940–1945." It was written by the physicist Henry Smyth and released by President Truman on August 11, 1945.]

[3][Knudsen flow takes place when the mean free path of a particle is longer than the length of the chamber.]

[4][In this scene Mephistopheles, in the guise of a black poodle, circles around Dr. Faust.]

Toward the end of 1946, I received a mysterious letter requesting me to come to Room 9 of the Peking Hotel at a designated time. Some implausible pretext was provided, although I can't remember what. The Peking Hotel was on Mayakovsky Square, not far from my parents' house. Room 9 was furnished like a typical government office—the T-shaped table, the portrait of Stalin, and so on. The man at the table rose to greet me, invited me to be seated, introduced himself as General Zverev, and then outlined the true reason for the meeting: "We [he never explained whom he meant by "we"] have been following your progress in science for quite a while. We'd like you to work with us on state projects of the greatest importance after you complete your graduate studies. You'll have the best of everything for your work—libraries with scientific literature from all over the world, big accelerators, the best pay and living conditions. We know you have a housing problem; if you agree to work for us, you'll be given an apartment in Moscow that will be reserved for you even if you're assigned elsewhere for a while."

I turned the offer down: I hadn't left the munitions plant for FIAN and the frontiers of physics, only to abandon everything now. I told General Zverev that for the time being I wished to continue doing theoretical research with Tamm. Zverev said he hoped my decision was not final.

What if I *had* agreed? Several years later, at the Installation, I met Dmitri Zubarev, a theoretical physicist, who told me that he, too, had been summoned to Zverev's room, and had accepted the offer (he too had a housing problem). Zubarev ended up working near the Black Sea with scientists brought from Germany. The project's director, Avraami Zavenyagin, had pinned great hopes on the German scientists, but they weren't trusted and little serious work was done. Zubarev got bored and used his connection with Nikolai Bogolyubov to get transferred to the Installation, where he remained until 1953.

IN 1947, after completing my thesis, I was invited to discuss it at "Kurchatov's place"—Laboratory No. 2, by then renamed the "Laboratory for Measuring Instruments" (LIPAN). I spoke in a small auditorium, after which I was asked many questions by the physicists present, Kurchatov among them. Afterward, he took me to his spacious office, where he seated himself behind a large desk piled high with scientific journals and equipped with telephones of every color. As we talked, Kurchatov stroked his bushy black beard, his expressive brown eyes gleaming. On the wall facing me hung a larger-than-life oil portrait of Stalin with his pipe and the Kremlin in the background. The painting, clearly an original by one of the "court" artists, symbolized Kurchatov's high standing in the state hierarchy; it remained in place for some time even after the Twentieth Party Congress.

Kurchatov suggested that I switch to his institute and work in theoretical nuclear physics after finishing my graduate studies. I knew that Arkady Migdal and Isaak Pomeranchuk (the questioners at my dissertation defense) had accepted similar offers: Migdal worked at LIPAN, Pomeranchuk at the Institute of Experimental and Theoretical Physics, which was headed by Abram Alikhanov. Kurchatov supported basic scientific research of every type, but when the occasion demanded, he would also devote his facilities—and the brains of his scientists—to solving practical problems. He always managed this with such tact that no one felt coerced or offended. It was on Kurchatov's initiative that the science city of Dubna was built and two giant accelerators constructed there.

Kurchatov evidently had liked my talk, or me, or else Migdal had put my name forward. In any event, I turned down the offer, again citing my desire to work with Tamm. Thus, in 1946 and 1947, I twice rejected attempts to entice me away from FIAN and the frontiers of theoretical physics. But the third time, in 1948, nobody bothered to ask my consent.

TOWARD THE END of June 1948, Tamm, in a rather furtive manner, asked me, along with another of his charges, Semyon Belenky, to remain behind after his Friday in-house seminar. As soon as we were alone, Tamm shut his office door and announced his startling news: by decision of the Council of Ministers and the Party Central Committee, a special research group had been created at FIAN. Tamm had been appointed to lead the group, and Belenky and I were to be among its members. Our task would be to investigate the possibility of building a hydrogen bomb and, specifically, to verify and refine the calculations produced by Yakov Zeldovich's group at the Institute of Chemical Physics. (I gave it no thought at the time, but I now believe that the design developed by the Zeldovich group for a hydrogen bomb was directly inspired by information acquired through espionage. However, I have no proof of this.[5])

A few days later, after recovering from shock, Belenky remarked lugubriously that: "Our job is to kiss Zeldovich's ass!" Belenky's recent dissertation had been on electromagnetic shower processes in cosmic rays, but during the war he had worked at the Zhukovsky Aerohydrodynamic Institute, involved in research on supersonic flow and jet flight. That was probably why he had been

[5]David Holloway writes in "Soviet Thermonuclear Development," *International Security* 4:3 (1979/80), p. 193: "The Soviet Union had been informed by Klaus Fuchs of the studies of thermonuclear weapons at Los Alamos up to 1946. . . . It is true that Fuchs's account of these early discussions of the superbomb would have been misleading rather than helpful to Soviet scientists in a scientific sense, because the early ideas were later shown not to work." This provides some evidence for my conjecture.—A.S. July 1987

included in our group—no one else at FIAN had experience in the field of gas dynamics.

As to why *I* had been selected, I was told that the director of FIAN, Academician Sergei Vavilov, had said: "Sakharov's got a housing problem; we'll be able to help him if he's included in the group." The fact that I was working on nuclear physics and plasma theory and had some ideas about mu-meson catalysis no doubt also played a role. Vavilov may have known about the interest I'd shown in isotope separation three years before. All in all, I imagine the chief reason for my inclusion in the special group was Tamm's strong recommendation.

Vavilov was true to his word. In May 1948, I was assigned two rooms on Twenty-fifth of October Street, in the very heart of Moscow. It was not a "posh" place, despite its location: the rooms were off a long common corridor, and wood was still used for heating. At the last moment, a deputy director of FIAN appropriated one of our two rooms for his mother (a very old and quite amiable woman—she and Klava got along wonderfully). Our remaining room measured only 150 square feet, so we had no place for a dining table, and ate off stools or the windowsill. The ten families living on our corridor were served by a single small kitchen, and the toilet, which was located off the staircase landing, served two communal apartments. There was neither bath nor shower. But we were delighted. We had our own place—no more noisy hotels or capricious landlords who could kick us out whenever they pleased! And so began four of the happiest years in our family life, the source of some wonderful memories.

Klava's difficult relationship with my mother, which had upset me a great deal, improved considerably. Tanya was developing into a good, cheerful little girl who didn't lack for admirers among the boys in the building. We became friendly with our neighbors in the apartment and at the dacha (we had rented a room in a cottage in the village of Troitskoe on the Moscow–Volga Canal). Klava and Tanya spent the summer of 1948 there. Each Sunday I would bring out provisions from the city, and would stay for a day or two. I remember the sparkling water, the sun, the lush greenery, the boats gliding over the reservoir (I was, however, banished from the sailboats because of my ineptitude), and the warmth of our friendship with our neighbors, the Obukhovs, the Rabinoviches, and the Shabats. A colleague from FIAN, Moisei Markov, had rented a place close by, and I had a gentle, teasing relationship with his wife, Lyuba.[6]

I spent at least five days a week at FIAN in the room assigned to our special group. There were two more members of our team—Vitaly Ginzburg, ex-

---

[6]Obukhov, a future academician, was specializing in the physics of the atmosphere and turbulence; Rabinovich was a fellow graduate student; Shabat a mathematician; Markov, another future academician, was a theoretical physicist.

tremely talented and one of Tamm's favorite students, and Yuri Romanov, a young researcher who had recently joined the department. Ginzburg apparently was included on a part-time basis, and dropped out when the group was transferred to the Installation.

Despite summer's distractions, we worked with a fierce intensity. Our world was bizarre and fantastic, a striking contrast to everyday city and family life, and to normal scientific pursuits.

THIS SEEMS a good time to describe our approach to the ethical and human aspects of our work. My own attitude, which was initially influenced by Tamm and others around me, has continued to evolve over the years; but in this chapter I shall confine myself to the period prior to the 1955 thermonuclear test.

In 1948, no one asked whether or not I *wanted* to take part in such work. I had no real choice in the matter, but the concentration, total absorption, and energy that I brought to the task were my own. Now that so many years have passed, I would like to explain my dedication—not least to myself. One reason for it (though not the main one) was the opportunity to do "superb physics" (Fermi's comment on the atom bomb program). Many people thought his remark cynical, but cynicism ordinarily presupposes duplicity, whereas I believe Fermi was quite sincere, although he may have been begging the real question. It should not be forgotten that Fermi's complete sentence—"*After all,* it's superb physics"—implies the existence of another side to the matter.

The physics of atomic and thermonuclear explosions is a genuine theoretician's paradise. The equation of state of matter at moderate pressures and temperatures cannot be calculated without introducing simplifying assumptions into the theoretical equations (otherwise the computations involved exceed the capabilities of the most advanced computers), but it is possible, using relatively straightforward calculations, to describe what happens at temperatures of millions of degrees centigrade, under conditions resembling those at the center of a star. The equation of state can be expressed by the formula $p = aDT + bT^4$, where p is the pressure, D the density, and T absolute temperature, and a and b are easily calculated coefficients. The first term (aDT) is the pressure of the ideal, completely ionized gas, and the second (bT^4) is the radiation pressure. In old days, Lebedev had to use refined techniques to measure it, but here the radiation pressure is enormous and pivotal for the process. The calculation of the pressure of the gas is also simplified at very high temperatures: ionization is complete, and the interactions of the particles can be neglected.

Similarly, formulas to determine the thermonuclear reaction rate become straightforward. Its value is easily calculated by elementary integration if the reaction cross section is known from experiment as a function of the energies of the colliding particles. I began my work with the Tamm group by calculating these integrals, using the saddle-point method known to every student of physics and mathematics. A few days later I submitted my first secret report, which was labeled S-1 (Sakharov 1).

A thermonuclear reaction—the mysterious source of the energy of sun and stars, the sustenance of life on Earth but also the potential instrument of its destruction—was within my grasp. It was taking shape at my very desk. But I feel confident in saying that infatuation with a spectacular new physics was not my primary motivation; I could easily have found another problem in theoretical physics to keep me amused—as Fermi did, if you will pardon this immodest comparison. What was most important for me at the time, and also, I believe, for Tamm and the other members of the group, was the conviction that our work was *essential*.

I understood, of course, the terrifying, inhuman nature of the weapons we were building. But the recent war had also been an exercise in barbarity; and although I hadn't fought in that conflict, I regarded myself as a soldier in this new scientific war. (Kurchatov himself said we were "soldiers," and this was no idle remark.)

Over the course of time we devised or borrowed a number of principles, including strategic parity and nuclear deterrence, which even now seem to justify intellectually, at least to some extent, the creation of thermonuclear weapons and our role in the process. Our initial zeal, however, was inspired more by emotion than by intellect. The monstrous destructive force, the scale of our enterprise and the price paid for it by our poor, hungry, war-torn country, the casualties resulting from the neglect of safety standards and the use of forced labor in our mining and manufacturing activities, all these things inflamed our sense of drama and inspired us to make a maximum effort so that the sacrifices—which we accepted as inevitable—would not be in vain. We were possessed by a true war psychology, which became still more overpowering after our transfer to the Installation.

I have read that on August 6, 1945, Robert Oppenheimer locked himself in his office while his younger colleagues ran around the Los Alamos laboratory shouting Indian war whoops, and that he also wept at his meeting with President Truman. Oppenheimer's personal tragedy disturbs me deeply, all the more so because I believe he was acting in good faith, for reasons of principle. Of course, the whole sad story of Hiroshima and Nagasaki which so affected his soul was even more troubling. Nuclear weapons have never again been employed in battle, and my fervent and paramount dream continues to be that they will be used only to deter war, never to wage war.

Have Soviet and American atomic scientists helped to keep the peace? After more than forty years, we have had no third world war, and the balance of nuclear terror—the threat of MAD (mutual assured destruction)—may have helped to prevent one. But I am not at all sure of this; back then, in those long-gone years, the question didn't even arise.

What most troubles me now is the instability of the balance, the extreme peril of the current situation, the appalling waste of the arms race. Thermonuclear weapons could end human civilization; they have become so frightening that the very thought of using them seems unreal. Their credibility as a deterrent has thus decreased, while their threat has increased enormously.

Is there a way out? That question will soon be answered. Each of us has a responsibility to think about this in global terms, with tolerance, trust, and candor, free from ideological dogmatism, parochial interests, or national egotism. I believe the time has come for nuclear deterrence to be replaced first by parity in conventional weapons, which, in the ideal case, will in its turn be succeeded by an equilibrium reached through farsighted statesmanship and compromise. I know I'm not alone in this conviction; I was pleased to find similar ideas in an article by Dr. Wolfgang Panofsky. One word of caution: I am convinced that the transition from nuclear deterrence to parity in conventional weapons must be managed with care and executed in stages. (This view is, of course, based on my assesssment of the present-day situation.)

AT ABOUT the same time that we Soviet scientists were beginning our calculations, Robert Oppenheimer, then chairman of the General Advisory Committee of the Atomic Energy Commission, was trying to apply the brakes to the American hydrogen bomb program in the expectation that the USSR would then refrain from developing thermonuclear superweapons of its own.

Oppenheimer's judgment was challenged by Edward Teller. Teller had experienced firsthand the 1919 Communist revolution in his native Hungary, and he had a deep-seated mistrust for the socialist system. He insisted that only American military strength could restrain the socialist camp from an expansion that would threaten civilization and democracy and might trigger a third world war. That is why Teller believed it necessary to speed development of an American H-bomb and continue nuclear testing despite the genetic damage and other nonthreshold biological effects that implied. (Later on, I was to object to his position on testing.) And that is why he testified against Oppenheimer. Teller has been ostracized ever since by many American scientists, who consider his testimony and his overall position to have violated ethical norms binding on the scientific community, as Freeman Dyson, for one, makes clear in his memoirs.[7]

7[*Disturbing the Universe* (Harper & Row, 1979), p. 90.]

What are we to make of the tragic conflict between these two extraordinary individuals, now that we can view it through the prism of time? In my opinion, both men deserve respect. Each was certain that truth was on his side and that he was morally obligated to see the matter through to the end—Oppenheimer by behaving in a way that was later construed as a breach of his official duties, and Teller by disregarding the tradition of "good form" in the scientific community. Issues of principle were further complicated by technical and policy questions. Oppenheimer apparently believed (and had impressive evidence to back his view) that the designs that had been concocted for a hydrogen bomb were not very promising. Teller believed that a practical solution would be found sooner or later; he may already have had some idea of the eventual design; and he was, of course, right in this respect.

The dispute over their opposing stands continues to this day, but the facts that have come to light about the state of affairs in the late 1940s support Teller's point of view. The Soviet government (or, more properly, those in power: Stalin, Beria, and company) already understood the potential of the new weapon, and nothing could have dissuaded them from going forward with its development. Any U.S. move toward abandoning or suspending work on a thermonuclear weapon would have been perceived either as a cunning, deceitful maneuver or as evidence of stupidity or weakness. In any case, the Soviet reaction would have been the same: to avoid a possible trap, and to exploit the adversary's folly at the earliest opportunity.

Still, Oppenheimer's position was not without merit. His assumption was that it would be exceedingly difficult to build a hydrogen bomb, and he hoped an American moratorium would lead the USSR to abandon further research on the grounds that: "The Americans have failed, so let's not waste our time. Even if we succeed, they'll catch up and pass us before we know it, and we'll end up losers again." Oppenheimer surely realized that for his plan to work, several conditions had to be met: consensus within the American administration; skillful American diplomacy; Soviet H-bomb research had to be at a point where the USSR would be ready to call it quits (and this was probably not the case); and the United States had to be willing to accept some risk. All this must be judged in the context of the times: it was the period of maximum mutual distrust—the Cold War, the Berlin blockade, soon the Korean War—and Moscow enjoyed superiority in conventional arms, just as it does now.

Oppenheimer felt he had little hope of convincing his opponents that he was right, and so he acted in a roundabout manner. He must have realized that more conventional, seemingly safer policies were likely to prevail; and in that case he was prepared to quit the game. He had every moral right to do so, and this is indeed what happened.

I cannot help but feel deeply for and empathize with Oppenheimer, whose personal tragedy has become a universal one. Some striking parallels between his fate and mine arose in the 1960s, and later I was to go even further than Oppenheimer had. But in the 1940s and 1950s my position was much closer to Teller's, practically a mirror image (one had only to substitute "USSR" for "USA," "peace and national security" for "defense against the communist menace," etc.)—so that in defending his actions, I am also defending what I and my colleagues did at the time. Unlike Teller, I did not have to go against the current in those years, nor was I threatened with ostracism by my colleagues. I had to overcome some resistance on technical questions, but I was not without support; the struggle for the "Third Idea" [see Chapter 12] arose for different reasons and was conducted in different circumstances than in Teller's case.

How did these directions find expression in my life? This book is my answer to that question.

If I am right in believing that the thermonuclear weapon model on which Zeldovich, Kompaneyets, and their team were working in the 1940s and early 1950s was the fruit of espionage, then Oppenheimer's case is strengthened, at least in theory. It would then be plausible that if the Americans had not initiated the whole chain of events, the USSR would have pursued the development of a thermonuclear bomb only at a much later date, if at all. A similar scenario has been repeated with other weapons systems, including nuclear-powered submarines and MIRVs [missiles carrying several warheads which can be independently targeted]. Now isn't it once again time to stop and think before it's too late? I have in mind SDI, the Strategic Defense Initiative.

However, it is clear now that the situation was already out of control by the time the Teller-Oppenheimer dispute erupted, and neither the USSR nor the United States could then have pulled back. We have been building thermonuclear weapons ever since; but so far, at least, we have avoided the abyss of a third world war.

Before moving on to another subject, I would like to note that Teller's colleagues seem quite unfair (and rather mean-spirited) in their condemnation: Teller was, after all, taking a stand based on principle. The very fact that he was willing to maintain a minority stance on an issue of such critical importance should be viewed as evidence in his favor. It is surely ironic that in 1945 Teller and Leo Szilard strongly favored exploding an atom bomb at some uninhabited site in hopes that a demonstration of its power might end the war without use of the new weapon against a Japanese city, while Oppenheimer persuaded them (Teller himself says in retrospect, too easily) that the decision should be left to soldiers and politicians.

After this lengthy but vital digression, I want to return to my starting point—"superb physics." Research on the atomic bomb no doubt involves "superb physics," but it is essentially "consumer-oriented." Exploring elementary particles and other phenomena through fission and fusion explosions is a very different matter from working in laboratory conditions, although from the point of view of elementary processes there is little difference. These processes involve atomic nuclei and electrons and photons with energies in the 20 KeV range, easily attainable in laboratory conditions, and the behavior of elementary particles at that energy level has been thoroughly investigated. To learn something new, one needs high-energy levels at each elementary interaction, and not massive explosions consuming immense resources and producing great destruction. These high-energy levels are sought in cosmic rays or through the use of particle accelerators. Physicists have also turned to cosmology in their study of high-energy processes; and it is from these sources, and not from nuclear explosions, that new discoveries in fundamental science will come.

Perhaps the sole contribution of nuclear explosions to fundamental science has been the opportunity they provide to study the properties of the transuranic elements. The hypothesis is now generally accepted that all elements with atomic numbers greater than that of iron are products of thermonuclear reactions in supernovas and other stars. Similar processes could be initiated in specially designed thermonuclear charges. I don't know whether such "scientific" explosions have been conducted in the USSR or the United States, but I remember reading somewhere that the element californium (atomic number 98) was discovered in the course of testing a certain type of American thermonuclear weapon. Research into the transuranic elements is a rather narrow specialty, however, and has had little impact on physics as a whole: in this sense, the mountain has brought forth only a mouse. In the future, it may be possible to use nuclear explosions to accelerate elementary particles, but that is only a dream so far, and perhaps not a very practical one.

I WAS INVOLVED in top-secret work on thermonuclear weapons and related research for some twenty years. I was a member of Tamm's special group at FIAN from June 1948 until March 1950, when I was assigned to the Installation [obyekt]—the secret city where those developing atomic and thermonuclear weapons lived and worked. I was employed there until my clearance was revoked in July 1968.

I shall remain silent about some aspects of my life and work in the period between 1948 and 1968. No matter what fate may have in store for me, I consider myself bound for life by a pledge not to divulge state and military secrets, a commitment I undertook of my own free will in 1948.

The task of Tamm's special group, as he himself formulated it, was to analyze, refine, correct, and extend the calculations of Zeldovich and his team, and to assess the whole project of building a thermonuclear weapon (i.e., just what Belenky had said so colorfully). I spent two months studying Zeldovich's reports and improving my meager knowledge of gas dynamics—we were all using Landau and Lifshitz's volume on this subject—and of astrophysics (the physics of stars and the physics of a nuclear explosion have much in common). Once, as I was standing in line for the cashier at the public baths, mulling over certain questions in gas dynamics (I couldn't stop thinking about them), I realized that an explosion in an ideal, cold gas can be described hydrodynamically by a function with a single variable if certain simplifying assumptions are made. I later discovered that my solution had been anticipated by Leonid Sedov, and still earlier by Theodore Taylor, but I went on to work out other self-similar solutions that were useful for the qualitative and semi-quantitative description of processes that interested us.

Two months later, I radically changed the direction of our research by proposing an alternative design for a thermonuclear charge that differed from the one pursued by Yakov Zeldovich's group in both the explosion's physical processes and the basic source of the energy released. I will call this the "First Idea."

Vitaly Ginzburg soon suggested a "Second Idea" which constituted an important addition to my proposal. The main feature of our design, as compared to the Zeldovich team's, was that the question of theoretical feasibility did not arise; there were also some essential engineering and technological differences. (After the 1953 thermonuclear test, the new design was further improved by the "Third Idea," of which I was one of the chief authors.)

Tamm supported the First Idea from the moment I told him about it in 1948; he'd been skeptical from the start about the earlier approach. At Tamm's suggestion, I paid a visit to the Institute of Chemical Physics, where I met with Zeldovich's deputy, Alexander Kompaneyets. Zeldovich, in addition to his duties at the Institute, had been associated with the Installation since its founding. He was spending much of his time there with the top-secret atom bomb group which he headed, since our first test of a fission device was in the offing.[9] Kompaneyets did not accept my ideas immediately, in part because he mistrusted my calculations. A week later I spoke directly with Zeldovich, who at once saw the merit of my proposal. It was our second encounter; we'd first met at a seminar where the discovery of a whole new family of elementary particles had been announced. Professor Alexander Shalnikov from the Institute of Physical Problems had asked sarcastically: "How much will each particle cost?" The speaker replied gloomily: "A lot." What he should have answered

9[The first Soviet atomic explosion detected by the United States occurred on August 29, 1949.]

was "An infinite amount": all the particles were the product of experimental error, and so the divisor in the true cost equation would be zero.

After our second meeting, Zeldovich invited me back to his home, which wasn't far from the Institute of Chemical Physics. He introduced me to his family, light-heartedly remarking that the greatest blessing in life is a good-natured wife. His wife's smile seemed to me rather tense. We discussed both our projects at length and agreed that Tamm's group would concentrate on the new proposal, while his team would continue work on the earlier design, at the same time providing any help we might need, since there were still many gaps in our knowledge. Though he did not say so, I think Zeldovich decided then to ask for my transfer to the Installation, a request which had to be referred to the highest level. At one of our follow-up meetings, he questioned me about my family and my medical history. I was taken by surprise, but I guessed what was afoot. I told him that for all practical purposes I enjoyed good health, which was essentially true.

From the beginning, the Tamm group operated under conditions of strict secrecy, something we weren't accustomed to. Only members of the group could enter the room assigned to us, and the key was kept in the security office. All notes had to be made in special tablets with numbered pages. At the end of the working day, they were placed in a suitcase, sealed, and handed in for safekeeping. I suppose we were flattered at first by all the rigmarole, but it soon became routine—although it could, on occasion, become the cause of tragedy.

Once, some years later at the Installation, one of my colleagues sent a note with a problem to be solved to the Institute of Applied Mathematics, which performed numerical computations for us. A typist at the Institute apparently burned the sheet of paper when it was no longer needed, but she neglected to record its destruction. That prompted a visit from our Ministry's head of security to investigate the "extraordinary incident." The man's appearance alone, his fixed gaze from under drooping eyelids, evoked a physical dread in me. He had been chief of state security in Leningrad when some 700 ranking officials were executed there during the "Leningrad Affair" [the purge of the Party organization there in 1949]. He talked for an hour with the head of the Institute's security department, who spent the next day, Sunday, with his family, by all accounts cheerful and affectionate with his children. On Monday morning he arrived at work fifteen minutes early and shot himself before anyone else arrived. The typist was arrested and spent more than a year in prison.

In the fall of 1948, my salary was increased, and if memory serves me right, my status as a senior scientist was approved. Two months after the First Idea was accepted as the basis for our group's research, I was invited to meet with General Fyodor Malyshev, a state security official, who was the authorized representative of the Council of Ministers and Party Central Committee at FIAN. In point of fact, Malyshev represented the Beria machine: similar posts had been created in all scientific institutions conducting significant secret work, as well as in many other projects and enterprises; this was Beria's means of exercising direct control over all military research and development. Malyshev's small but impressive office was next to the security department. It contained a safe and the requisite number of telephones.

Malyshev complimented me on my work and then urged me to join the Party, saying that a Party member could do more for our people and for mankind in its progress toward a radiant future in which there would be no room for war; Party membership is not a privilege, not a guarantee of an easy life, but rather a great responsibility before the people and a readiness to serve the Party whenever and wherever needed; the compensation you receive is the feeling that you are part of a great cause. Malyshev offered to recommend me for membership.

I replied that I would continue to do everything in my power to ensure the success of our work, but I could not join the Party, because a number of its past actions seemed wrong to me and I feared that I might have additional misgivings at some future time. Malyshev asked me which actions I thought mistaken. "The arrest of innocent people and the excesses of the collectivization campaign," I replied. Malyshev argued: "The Party has severely condemned the mistakes committed during Yezhov's purges [in 1937–1938], and they have all been rectified. As for the kulaks, what were we supposed to do when they came at us with shotguns?"

Malyshev asked me to give very serious consideration to his suggestion. Had I agreed to join the Party, I imagine I would have been appointed to a major administrative post in the atomic research program, that of scientific director at the Installation, say, or something similar, and that wouldn't have done the program much good! What kind of an administrator would I have made?

Early in 1949, Tamm and I were summoned to the office of Boris Vannikov, head of the First Main Directorate of the Soviet Council of Ministers. (This was the provisional designation given the agency responsible for the entire atomic program; it had for some time exceeded a normal ministry in size. It was subsequently renamed the Ministry of Medium Machine Building, and the Committee on the Peaceful Uses of Atomic Energy was carved out of it.) Vannikov (not his original name, which was identifiably Jewish) was a very colorful personality. When I met him, he was no longer young; he had joined the Party in the early years and served it with distinction during the Revolution. Then, during the 1930s, when any slip could mean destruction, he gained considerable experience managing industrial and scientific projects for the military. With this background, it is no wonder that he was cautious, clever—

and cynical. He had been arrested during the war, but released after a week or so and appointed to a top post in the defense industry.

Vannikov received Tamm and myself in his spacious office. A man by the name of Nikolsky—presumably Beria's representative—was also present. After cracking a few jokes, Vannikov came to the point: "Sakharov should be transferred to work on a permanent basis with Yuli Khariton [meaning to the Installation, where Khariton was the scientific director]. It's necessary for the project."

Tamm became agitated and said I was a very talented theoretical physicist who could accomplish a great deal in key fields of science (he was so excited he forgot to say *"Soviet* science"); to limit me to applied research would be a great mistake, and not in our country's best interest. Vannikov seemed to be listening closely, a somewhat forced smile on his face. The direct Kremlin line rang. Vannikov answered and then tensed up. "Yes, they're here with me now," he said. "What are they doing? Talking, arguing." There was a pause. "Yes, I understand." Another pause. "Yes sir, I'll tell them." Vannikov hung up and said: "I have just been talking with Lavrenti Pavlovich [Beria]. He is *asking* you to accept our request."

There was nothing left to say. As soon as we left Vannikov's office, Tamm commented: "Things seem to have taken a serious turn." In reality, the serious turn had occurred a lot earlier.

7

THE INSTALLATION

FOR THE SUMMER of 1949, we rented a dacha not far from Moscow, on the October railway line. We shared the cottage with a nice old Jewish grandmother, who was forever grumbling about her grandchildren: "Are these kids? Devils, that's what they are!" One day, toward the end of June, an M-1 car stopped at the dacha, and a smart-looking officer got out. He asked me to accompany him at once to a meeting with Vannikov.

My conversation with Vannikov couldn't have been briefer.

"Do you fly?" he asked.

"Yes."

"I don't like planes. We have to leave for Khariton's place right away." He gave me an address and said: "They'll explain everything there."

When I arrived at the designated address, I saw a sign reading "Vegetable and Fruit Warehouse." I descended a flight of stairs and walked past several people who looked like forwarding agents or *tolkachi* [semi-official expediters]. One man was dozing in a chair, two others were playing dominoes. Hearing that I was going to "Khariton's place" for the first time, a pale, nervous man at a desk in the next room handed me a pass and told me which train and precisely which railway car to take. For several years thereafter, I obtained my pass for each trip to the Installation in the same fashion, by reporting in person to that unforgettable "warehouse." Later I was given the right to make my arrangements by phone, something my colleagues were never permitted to do. (The authorities evidently were worried that a spy might use the telephone to gain entry into the Installation.)

That same evening I went to the railroad station, passed through a cordon of people, some in uniform, some in civilian clothes, and boarded what turned out to be Vannikov's personal car. We were joined by Mikhail Meshcheryakov, scientific director of the accelerator under construction at Dubna [then Ivan-kovo]; he had been a student of Kurchatov's, and was a favorite of the government brass. A few minutes after the train pulled out of the station, Vannikov invited us to join him at dinner. I listened closely to the conversation between Meshcheryakov and Vannikov, who referred to institutions, projects, and personal names that were completely unknown to me. (They finally deigned to explain that "Borodin" was the code name for Kurchatov.)

That night in my stuffy compartment, I couldn't sleep. It was not that I was mulling over distressing events or my own mistakes, as is often the case now when I suffer from insomnia; what kept me awake was a new and challenging idea, the possibility of a controlled thermonuclear reaction. But it would take me another year to find the key to a promising approach: magnetic confinement. (Tamm backed this idea and played a role in its development.)

Apparently we were supposed to make at least part of the journey by air—which is why Vannikov had asked whether I minded flying—but no aircraft was available. As soon as the train reached its destination, we piled into waiting automobiles and set off for the Installation. We drove at breakneck speed, bouncing from one bump to another on country roads and scarcely slowing as we passed through villages just coming to life. The pale light of dawn illuminated tumble-down peasant huts, their roofs of old straw or half-rotted shingles, torn rags hanging on clothesline, and kolkhoz cattle—dirty and scrawny even in summer. The car ahead of us ran over a hen as we raced on through fields and stunted groves. Suddenly the driver slammed on the brakes: we had reached the "zone"—two rows of barbed wire strung on tall posts and separated by a strip of ploughed land ("our barbed-wire home," as we came to call it).

Our cars had stopped in front of a locked gate, and two officers emerged from the guard post. They checked identification papers in the car ahead of us, then saluted, and the car passed through the barrier. When the officers walked over to our car, Vannikov, in a foul mood from the journey, cursed obscenely and ordered our driver to "step on it!" The officers leaped back as the car accelerated past them.

I checked into the hotel for VIPs without wasting any time. The downstairs dining room in the hotel was reserved for the top brass (we called it "the generals' mess"); stars had been painted on the walls (I learned later that this was the work of a woman prisoner). I managed to nick myself badly, since I wasn't used to shaving with a straight razor. I was just going downstairs when a door across the hall opened and Igor Kurchatov stepped out, accompanied by his "secretaries" (as bodyguards were called). Both Kurchatov and Khariton had "secretaries"; I had them myself from 1954 until 1957, and Zeldovich had them too for a short time. The bodyguards were relatively high-ranking officers in a special section of the KGB. Kurchatov was on close terms with his "secretaries" and often had them run errands for him. They respected him greatly, perhaps even loved him.

Kurchatov greeted me loudly: "So, the man from Moscow's here. Welcome!" Without breaking stride, he continued on with his entourage to the limousine that awaited him.

In a short while, Zeldovich came by to drive me over to meet my new colleagues in the theoretical department and be briefed on its work. But first he drew me aside to where we wouldn't be overheard and told me Kurchatov and some other bigwigs were visiting because of the forthcoming test of an atomic "device" [izdelie] (as we called all atomic and thermonuclear charges [zaryady], whether experimental or production models). "The 'chiefs' are holding some important conferences. Don't get offended if you're not invited. They don't invite me very often—only when they want my opinion. Try to understand: there are secrets everywhere, and the less you know that doesn't concern you, the better off you'll be. Khariton has taken on the burden of knowing it all, but he's different. There's quite enough for us to do for now in the theoretical department."

After Zeldovich's remarks about the forthcoming test, I could appreciate the significance of a tense exchange I'd overheard between Vannikov and the Installation director on our arrival. "Is it here?" Vannikov had wanted to know.

"Yes."

"Where?"

"In the storehouse." (The place had another, more colorful name, which I won't divulge.) What they were talking about was a sample of fissionable metal (plutonium or uranium-235) recently received from the factory. Zeldovich later told me that when he saw those ordinary-looking pieces of metal, he couldn't help feeling that a multitude of human lives had been compressed into each gram: he had in mind not only the prisoners who worked in the uranium mines and at the nuclear installations, but also the potential victims of atomic war.

MY NEW COLLEAGUES gathered around, eyeing me with open curiosity. Zeldovich introduced me to each in turn: David Frank-Kamenetsky, Viktor Gavrilov, Nikolai Dmitriev, and Revekka Izraileva.

"And those are our captains!" Zeldovich said, indicating two young men sharing a desk and drawing in a large sketchbook. To my surprise, I recognized one of them as my former classmate Evgeny Zababakhin, whom I had last seen in July 1941 at the Air Force Academy's recruiting commission. He had graduated from the Academy with the rank of captain and, in a stroke of good fortune, his dissertation had been given to Zeldovich to review. Zababakhin ended up at the Installation, where he could put his knowledge of gas dynamics to good use. The other captain was named Evgeny Negin.

The oldest scientist, and the most enthusiastic, was Frank-Kamenetsky. His ideas were often very valuable and to the point, if occasionally mistaken. Frank-Kamenetsky readily accepted criticism and would respond by suggesting fresh ideas. It was he who, perhaps more than anyone else, introduced a spirit of friendliness into our life. He also had a tendency to cross the t's and dot the i's in his work and in his personal relationships. When the Installation's "heroic" period came to an end, his enthusiasm waned and he returned to his earlier passion, astrophysics (I borrowed something from him in that regard). After his health deteriorated, he moved to Moscow, where he worked on controlled thermonuclear reactions and also translated several books from English. In his last years he had difficulty walking up to the fourth floor of the building in which we both lived (I was on the third floor), and he asked me to petition the Moscow city council to have an elevator installed. Unfortunately, I delayed doing so, and Frank-Kamenetsky died almost immediately afterwards.

Kolya Dmitriev was the youngest of my new colleagues. He was a gifted mathematician who went from one brilliant piece of work to the next. Zeldovich said of him that he was possibly "the only one of us with a divine spark in him. You might think Dmitriev is only a quiet, modest boy, but in fact we all tremble before his judgments."

Dmitriev had been a child prodigy. With Andrei Kolmogorov's backing, he had attended classes at the university from the age of fifteen, passed all his university exams in mathematics while still in high school, and then started working on the theory of probability.

In 1950, when I was living at the Installation, I dropped by to see Dmitriev on my birthday. I wasn't allowed to go to Moscow and didn't know what else to do to mark the occasion. He had just married a girl named Tamara, and the two of them began giving me a lesson in how to drink pure alcohol: I'd never touched anything stronger than vodka before, and then only a drop on rare occasions. We listened to music and had a wonderful conversation about the meaning of life and the future of mankind. They gave me a marvelous birthday present—Shteingauz's *Mathematical Kaleidoscope*.

Zeldovich disliked Tamara intensely and seemed jealous of her relationship with Dmitriev. He complained that she was taking up Dmitriev's time with domestic matters—teething rings, diapers, and the like—and keeping him in bed too long: she would ruin his scientific career. In 1955, Tamara jumped from a fifth-floor window a few days after having a thyroidectomy, leaving Dmitriev alone with two children. A few years later, he married a woman from our math department. He was a member of the auxiliary police, and would go around town hauling in drunks.

Dmitriev's fate as a scientist was complicated. I don't think it was domestic or personal problems that caused his brilliant promise to fade, but other, deeper reasons. Mathematical work at the Installation was becoming increasingly routine. Dmitriev could still rise to the occasion when something "elegant" was needed, but these sporadic bursts of creativity were less satisfying than the sustained demand for his talents in earlier years. The Installation was turning into a factory. A sense of duty kept Dmitriev at his station, but he was by nature a master jeweler, not an assembly-line worker. Zeldovich tried to draw him into "big" physics, but nothing came of it, since Dmitriev couldn't serve two masters at one time. In his last years at the Installation, he continued to be far more productive than most of his colleagues in the mathematics section, but there was the feeling that in another field he could have accomplished something quite exceptional.

Dmitriev was always interested in philosophical, social, and political questions, which he attacked with his absolute intellectual integrity, his sharp mind, and a paradoxical wit. After Stalin's death he did not exchange his Stalin Prize medal for a State Prize medal, as almost everyone else did; this was a token of his respect for historical authenticity.

Dmitriev was a nonconformist who resisted official ideology and my views in equal measure. He was the only one from the Installation to visit me openly after my books *Reflections on Progress, Peaceful Coexistence, and Intellectual Freedom* and *My Country and the World* appeared. He asked for copies so that he could read them and then discuss them with me. He disagreed completely with my ideas, but his arguments were rational and to the point.

I was also very fond of Viktor Gavrilov (who, incidentally, adored Dmitriev). Gavrilov's life was not a simple one. I was given to understand that he was the son of a German industrialist or professor who had come to Russia during the Civil War and a Russian woman who worked in a hotel. His mother raised him alone under difficult conditions. She was deeply religious, and Gavrilov's own attitude toward religion was somewhat ambivalent. He was working with the astrophysicist Alexander Lebedinsky in Leningrad when Zeldovich recruited him for the Installation.

Gavrilov brought a Teutonic precision to his work but, like so many of us, he enjoyed philosophizing. He and Zeldovich did not get on well, despite the fact that it was Zeldovich who had brought him to the Installation; soon after I arrived, Gavrilov switched to experimental work and was put in charge of a small department.

A few years later there was an accident in Gavrilov's laboratory involving a contraption with the strange-sounding name of FIKOBIN (Physics Boiler for Fast Neutrons). This was a rather peculiar apparatus, consisting basically of the two halves of an atomic charge, held apart by separators or spacers (resembling large washers). It was used to measure the nuclear properties of various materials. These materials were placed in the center of the charge, where there was a special cavity containing the neutron source and the substance under investigation. By regulating the thickness of the spacers, it was possible to achieve a significant amplification—the result of chain reaction—of the emerging neutron stream. I recount this here because I don't see anything secret in the details, while they give a vivid picture of our working conditions.

In the first, "heroic" period of our labors, all manipulations of the separators were performed by a middle-aged man by the name of Shirshov, using a manual winch. It all ran smoothly, without mishaps. But Shirshov had a weakness for the bottle, and one day the boss (Vannikov, it seems) caught him at this occupation near the apparatus and immediately expelled him from the division. With time, FIKOBIN became overgrown with regulations and automatic emergency systems. In this state it fell into the hands of Gavrilov.

To measure how far the system was from criticality (the point at which a chain reaction would become, with the aid of the delayed neutrons, self-sustaining), a certain unit was introduced that is inversely proportional to the coefficient of multiplication of the number of neutrons. In honor of Shirshov, Frank-Kamenetsky, who first developed the theory of FIKOBIN, dubbed this unit the "Shirshi." Gavrilov, who also took part in these theoretical calculations, now dealt with Shirshi in practice ("Give me a 5-Shirshi spacer").

A worker once made a mistake when changing the separators, resulting in an accident. The system crossed the lower critical threshold. (If it had crossed the "higher" critical threshold [a self-sustaining chain reaction without the aid of the delayed neutrons], it would have been a lot worse; the risk of this happening, however, is practically nonexistent.) An analogous accident is described in Dexter Masters' novel *The Accident,* [1] in which he tells of the death of a young scientist by neutron irradiation at Los Alamos in 1945. The accident occurred during the checking of subcriticality of one of the first American atomic charges. (Judging from the story, the Americans took even more chances than we did at the time of Shirshov.)

In our case, no one was injured, but a lot of equipment was destroyed and panic ensued. Gavrilov was obliged to quit the Installation, but he found a job in the Ministry. In the late 1950s he again made a radical switch, this time to molecular biology. Kurchatov was organizing a genetics laboratory to counteract Lysenkoism—something his privileged status allowed him to do under

---

[1][Alfred A. Knopf, 1955. Clifford Honicker described a similar accident which led to the death of a young physicist, Louis Slotin, in May 1946, in "The Hidden Files," *The New York Times Magazine*, November 19, 1989.]

the umbrella of his Institute of Atomic Energy. Gavrilov's work in this new field and his relations with the biologists who became his colleagues were beset by difficulties. He and I became close again around this time, and we met frequently when I came to Moscow. We particularly enjoyed discussing the future of mankind—Gavrilov told me how grateful he was that he hadn't been born in the twenty-first century! Our conversations helped educate me about ecological, demographic, and other global issues.

He and his wife were childless; in the late 1950s they adopted a ten-year-old boy, Vanya. During the difficult period of Klava's illness and eventual death, Gavrilov was exceptionally kind and considerate. He died of heart disease in the early 1970s. I regret to this day that I only learned of his death several months after it occurred, and too late to pay my final respects at his funeral.

Revekka Izraileva was the sole woman in our department. In addition to her regular work, she would copy out the "boys'" scribbled calculations in a clean hand—use of a typewriter to make copies was forbidden, and not even the girls who did the security department's typing were allowed to see our top-secret reports.

Mattes Agrest headed the theoretical department's mathematics group. He'd been partially disabled in the war, and was a businesslike, if rather eccentric, individual. I was a regular visitor at the cottage his large family occupied. Agrest's father, a tall, striking old man, reminded me of the Jews in Rembrandt's paintings. Both he and his son were deeply religious. I heard that Zeldovich (although he denied this) had upset Agrest greatly by making him work on the Sabbath. Agrest was before long forced to quit the Installation, because he allegedly had relatives living in Israel. At the time, we all, including myself, saw this as valid grounds for dismissal. All I could do for him was to let him and his family use my empty apartment until he found other employment. In later years, Agrest discovered a new passion: scrutinizing the Bible and other scriptures for evidence that the earth has been visited by extraterrestrials. To say I am skeptical about this activity would be putting it mildly.

Zeldovich introduced me around and then briefed me on the basic work that had been done on atomic charges. (Later on, when I became the leader of a group myself, I enjoyed repeating the same information, along with something about thermonuclear charges, to newly arrived researchers, and watching the astonishment on their faces.) I, in turn, gave Zeldovich a rundown on the Tamm group's work and proposed specifications for a device based on the First and Second ideas. Of course, it was all a bit tentative, and there were still many flaws in our proposals.

My first visit to the Installation lasted about a week. I learned a great deal about atomic charges, some of it quite unexpected, that was of enormous importance for our work. (Nothing of this was to be mentioned outside the

Installation, even to persons with top-secret clearance, and no copies were made of reports, not even for Moscow.)

MY CONVERSATIONS with Zeldovich and his colleagues outside working hours gave me a vivid taste of the distinctive atmosphere that prevailed among the scientists at the Installation—professional and friendly, yet extraordinarily intense: work went on around the clock when necessary. I also learned about the specific regulations in force at the Installation, and about the prisoners who worked there—I had already had a glimpse of them, of course.

In 1950, I was transferred to the Installation, where I lived for eighteen years, sometimes with my family, sometimes alone.

The town where we lived and worked was a curious artifact of our time. The peasants in the poverty-stricken villages nearby could see nothing but a barbed-wire fence enclosing a vast expanse, and I was told that they had invented a highly original explanation for what was going on beyond this fence: a "test model of Communism" was under construction. The "test model" (the Installation) in fact embodied a curious symbiosis between an ultra-modern scientific research institute, with its experimental workshops and proving grounds—and a large labor camp.

In 1949, I still heard stories about the time when the place had been simply a camp, with a mixed prisoner population, including long-term convicts—probably much like the "typical" camp described in Solzhenitsyn's *One Day in the Life of Ivan Denisovich*. The workshops, the proving grounds, the roads, and even the housing for the Installation's employees had been built by prisoners. They themselves lived in barracks and were escorted to work by guard dogs. On my first visit to the Installation, Gavrilov told me about a mutiny that had occurred a couple of years earlier.

A small group of prisoners, including an ex-colonel (possibly from the Russian Liberation Army), had been digging a foundation pit. One of the zeks [prisoners] bent down by the wheel of their truck as if to check a tire; there was only one guard around and he instinctively bent down, too. A zek hit him over the head with a shovel while the colonel grabbed his submachine gun, shouting, "Follow me, men!"

They threw the driver out of the truck, and one of the zeks took the wheel. The colonel, standing at the back, shot up a passing vehicle carrying officers and obtained all the weapons the mutineers needed. Bursting through the camp gates, they shot several guards and disarmed others. At this point, the colonel and his followers (there were fifty or more of them) fled the camp. They probably hoped to scatter and hide in the forests and villages nearby, but three divisions of NKVD troops (so I was told, but I doubt whether anyone knew the precise number) had already answered the alert. They cordoned off a large area and began to tighten the ring. The final act in the tragedy came when the fugitives' defensive position, organized with great tactical skill, fell under mass artillery and mortar fire. I think the besiegers even used aircraft. Every last escapee was slaughtered. Probably many who did not join the fugitives were executed as well. (That was the outcome of another zek rebellion in the 1950s, which took place on the site where a hospital was being built for the Ministry, not far from our Moscow apartment.)

After the uprising, the convict population was radically altered. Those with long sentences and nothing to lose were replaced by short-term prisoners, typically those serving one to five years for petty theft, gleaning grain from a kolkhoz field after the harvest, disorderly conduct, leaving a job without official permission, unauthorized halting of a train with an emergency brake, and so on.

There were no more mutinies. But the authorities were faced with another awkward problem: what to do with prisoners when their terms were up. They might reveal the location of the Installation, still regarded as top secret even though foreign intelligence services doubtless knew it. The authorities found a solution to their problem that was simple, ruthless, and absolutely illegal: released prisoners were permanently exiled to Magadan and other places where they couldn't tell any tales. There were two or three such deportations, one in the summer of 1950.

We lived in close proximity to that labor camp from 1950 to 1953. Every morning long gray lines of men in quilted jackets, guard dogs at their heels, passed by our curtained windows. It was some consolation, of course, that the zeks were not dying of hunger, that lumber camps and uranium mines were far worse. We could help the prisoners (at least the trusties) in small ways, with old clothes, a little money, something to eat. Our neighbors the Zysins raised chickens, and their housekeeper, Raya, once boiled a dozen for prisoners working nearby. After the 1953 amnesty that followed Stalin's death, the zeks were replaced by army construction battalions (another form of conscript labor, but at least they weren't prisoners).

The lives of the "free" people were also subject to strict regulation. Those of us connected with the Installation were better off than the natives of the little town on whose territory the Installation had been built. When I was in the hospital in 1952, the nurse distributed food along with the instructions: "Butter, Kasha, and Kisel [fruit soup]—for Installation people; Kasha and tea—for townspeople."

No one was permitted to go on vacation, visit a relative (even one who was critically ill), attend a funeral, or travel on business without permission from the administration department. Such permission was granted to the townspeople only in exceptional circumstances. Young specialists were not allowed to leave at all during their first year of work, and had to spend their first vacation in the "nurturing production setting." Even after the first year, permission to travel for personal reasons was doled out sparingly, and only to those who had already been away on official business.

Getting permission to travel was a time-consuming business, and delay often defeated the purpose—as in the case of a funeral. It was useless to argue with the official with whom we communicated through a small window. He couldn't decide anything on his own; decisions were made behind the scenes by a representative of the Central Committee and the Council of Ministers, someone we never met in person. Thirty years later, my exposure to OVIR [the agency which issues emigration and travel visas] reminded me very much of the administration department of the Installation.

SECURITY WAS carried to ridiculous extremes. There was the case of Boris Smagin, a scientist whom I met for the first time in Ashkhabad—he'd been two years behind me at the university, and graduated after returning from the war. (I still remember Smagin's telling about a hanging he'd witnessed of a Ukrainian nationalist partisan who with her dying breath cried out: "Freedom for the Ukraine!") He was sent to the Installation as a physicist and, not long before my arrival, was put in charge of some small department (responsible for monitoring radiation, I believe). He was extremely proud of his appointment, and a mutual acquaintance told me with a laugh that Smagin was much given to saying, "Kirill and I have decided . . ."—Kirill being Kirill Shchelkin, then Khariton's deputy.

One day, Smagin lost a secret part from a nuclear device (I won't be any more specific), and he was arrested. Using all his powers of persuasion, he begged his interrogators to search the sewer pipes, hoping that the part had fallen from his pocket into the toilet. KGB officers cordoned off the spot where the sewer pipes emptied into the river, and then spent three days chopping through frozen excrement, layer by layer. Fortunately, they found the missing part. So Smagin stood convicted only of having a hole in his pocket. He was released from custody, but fired from his job. As someone possessing both state secrets *and* holes in his pockets, he was not allowed to leave the Installation. For more than six months he couldn't let anyone outside know of his plight, and he had no means of earning money. (I was "guilty" during that period of delivering a letter to his wife in Moscow.) Only one of his former friends dared to associate with him: Vitaly Alexandrovich, a unique individual who, during the war, had concealed Jews and partisans from the Germans while he was managing a gas station in the Crimea. Smagin finally got a job teaching at our high school, and some years later succeeded in leaving the Installation. He now works for a popular science magazine, writing science fiction.

AN ACCIDENT that occurred outside the Installation, at the site of plutonium production reactors, illustrates the temper of the world we lived in. A trolley carrying "hot" uranium slugs derailed in the water-filled pool under the reactor. (Uranium slugs left in the reactor's core long enough for most of the U-235 nuclei to split, resulting in the accumulation of plutonium and other fission products, become a source of intense gamma radiation.) Robots that could return the trolley to its tracks did not yet exist. Shutting down the reactor would have meant a long interruption in the production of plutonium and a shortfall of perhaps ten, perhaps twenty, or even more atomic charges. A decision was made at some administrative level, unknown to me, to send a diver into the pool. He managed to repair the damage, but received a fatal dose of radiation while doing so. The diver was buried in the Installation cemetery, and, in accordance with nautical tradition, a bronze anchor was erected over his grave. This was a real-life version of Pushkin's poem "The Upas Tree" in modern dress![2]

We were encouraged to throw ourselves into our work by the fierce concentration on a single goal, and perhaps also by the proximity of the labor camp and the strict regimentation. We saw ourselves at the center of a great enterprise on which colossal resources were being expended. We shared a general determination that the sacrifices made by our country and people should not be in vain; I certainly felt that way myself. We never questioned the vital importance of the work. And there were no distractions: the rest of the world was far, far away, somewhere beyond the two barbed wire fences. High salaries, government awards, and other privileges and marks of distinction contributed to the psychological atmosphere in which we lived. It would require the passage of many years and radical upheavals for new currents to effect a shift in our view of the world.

I ENDED my first visit to the Installation in 1949 with a talk on quantum field theory, delivered at Zeldovich's request. I knew nothing of the important results achieved by Schwinger, Feynman, and Dyson during the two years since

---

[2]["The Upas Tree" tells of a slave who died after collecting and bringing back to his master the sap of the Upas tree, a potent drug used for arrow poison. For an English translation, see Walter Arndt, *Pushkin Threefold* (Dutton, 1972).]

I had studied the subject, so my lecture was based on the rather dated books of Walter Heitler and Gregor Wentzel.[3] After this, I took off for Moscow, where Tamm, my other colleagues, and Klava—who was in her ninth month of pregnancy—were impatiently awaiting my return.

Now, a brief digression about where I stood with "grand" science during this period. A couple of years later, probably on a visit to Moscow sometime in 1951, I mentioned to Vitaly Ginzburg an idea of mine in electrodynamics (which turned out to be trivial or mistaken, as I recall). He was amused, and said, "So you want to do real physics and not just be a bombmaker anymore." In fact, it was virtually impossible to combine such basically incompatible occupations. (Zeldovich succeeded to some extent, but his was a special case.) Everything became still more complicated for me in 1968, when I was drawn into public affairs after writing *Reflections on Progress, Peaceful Coexistence, and Intellectual Freedom*—but I'll leave that story for later.

Soon after my return from the Installation, Klava and I celebrated a happy event—the birth of our second child. On the morning of July 28, 1949, Klava was still able to do the wash at the dacha. After she finished, we went by train to Moscow, and that same evening, I took her in a taxi to the nearest maternity clinic. Two hours later, our daughter Lyuba was born. (Tanya, four and a half at the time, chose the name.) While Klava was in the clinic, Tanya and I stayed with my parents.

In the fall, following Zeldovich's advice, I phoned Kurchatov to ask his help in finding an alternative to our cramped room in a communal apartment. Kurchatov promised to take care of our problem, and we soon moved into an enormous (by our standards) three-room apartment on the outskirts of Moscow. The apartment faced onto a park. (Unfortunately, the park was littered with trash, but once a hare came running out of it, delighting the children— and me.) Zeldovich joked that my getting this apartment was the first use of thermonuclear energy for peaceful purposes.

In November 1949, I made a second trip to the Installation, but my memory of this visit is hazy. At the beginning of March 1950, Yuri Romanov and I were ordered to move to the Installation without delay. Our appointments were permanent ones, but our absence from FIAN was listed formally as a "prolonged assignment"—which in my case lasted until July 1968!

Our salaries at our new place of work were huge; I was paid 20,000 old rubles per month (the equivalent of 2,000 "new" rubles). Although pay scales were reduced a bit when more scientists joined the project, our salaries remained very high.

[3][Walter Heitler, *The Quantum Theory of Radiation* (Clarendon Press, 1936), and Gregor Wentzel, *Quantum Theory of Fields* (Interscience, 1948) (original German edition 1943).]

Romanov and I were assigned a small office next to Zeldovich's department, and we set to work at once. We shared a room in the hotel located in the neighborhood and set aside for engineering and technical personnel. (The hotel was only fifty yards from the cottage that was to become my family's home; as chance would have it, it was then occupied by the same Protopopov with whom I had worked at the munitions plant six years earlier. Protopopov, who had become a radiochemist, soon returned to his beloved Leningrad.)

I immediately took the official steps necessary to have Klava join me, but the process dragged on for six months. Afterward, Klava's father told me that the Ulyanovsk security organs studied his family tree carefully that summer—nothing stays a secret in the provinces.

I lived in the hotel until November. Yuri Romanov and I were inseparable during that time. We worked together in the daytime, relaxed together in the evening, and slept in the same room at night. I was very fond of him then, as was Tamm, who called Yuri a "child of nature." Five or six years younger than I, lively, direct, and almost childishly impressionable, Yuri was hardworking and capable. In fact, everyone was fond of him. Two young women lived in the room beneath ours—Revekka Izraileva, who worked in Zeldovich's department, and Lena Malinovskaya, who moved to the Installation at the same time we did and worked in the mathematical department. (Her chief, Mattes Agrest, was wont to observe: "Lena's a nice girl, but she needs a bit of a push from time to time.") In the evenings Yuri and I usually visited the girls. He would dance somewhat awkwardly with each of them in turn, while I would sit and relax; I didn't know how to dance. Sometimes Lena would sing for us. Smagin soon joined our group.

At the beginning of April, Tamm himself moved to the Installation. (Semyon Belenky, who had a serious heart condition, was left behind in Moscow at Tamm's request; there he completed some research in hydrodynamics, important for understanding the physics of explosion in our devices. He died in 1960 or 1961.) When we went to pick up Tamm at the airfield, he emerged from the plane with a knapsack on his back and a pair of skis (they would come in handy), squinting in the bright April sun. Both our work and our free time grew much livelier after his arrival.

A couple of months later, two more outstanding scientists arrived at the Installation—Isaak Pomeranchuk, who had been on the panel at my dissertation defense, and Nikolai Bogolyubov, already widely known in scientific circles despite his youth. Pomeranchuk, who worked for our Directorate, had come on instructions from Vannikov, but Bogolyubov's transfer, according to Tamm, was sanctioned personally by Stalin. Tamm added that Bogolyubov seemed to take pride in that fact. Bogolyubov was preceded by three of his students: Valentin Klimov, Dmitri Shirkov, and Dmitri Zubarev. They joined our little company right away, and Klimov became the leader in our walks, our swimming, our running at the stadium, and our other athletic activities.

Even an innocent pastime had its risks at the Installation. During the May holidays we went hiking in the woods that surrounded us on all sides. Absorbed in conversation, we didn't realize that we had entered the boundary zone. We must have been spotted from a guard tower; all of a sudden someone behind us shouted: "Stop, don't move!" We turned around and saw a squad of soldiers and an officer of the Border Guards pointing their submachine guns directly at us: they meant business.

We were taken to a truck and ordered to sit on the floor with our legs stretched out in front of us. Four soldiers sat on a bench across from us brandishing their submachine guns. We were told that if anyone tried to escape or pulled up his legs, they would shoot without warning. Somehow or other, bouncing over roots and bumps, suppressing the desire to bend our knees and soften the jolts, we reached the army camp. Our guards lined us up with our faces to the wall while they went off to report to their superiors. Half an hour later, having satisfied themselves that we were not prisoners on the run, they graciously let us go.

During the May holidays, Tamm was permitted to visit his family in Moscow, and he made another trip home during the summer. I didn't receive permission to visit Moscow until late October. In the meantime, I was not allowed to call home or send letters or telegrams. These restrictions were later eased somewhat.

KLAVA RECEIVED permission to go with me to the Installation, and so on November 9 we packed our suitcases, tied our bedding into bundles, and took a taxi to the airport. Klava clutched six-month-old Lyuba in one hand and a bundle in the other, while five-year-old Tanya, dragging a bag, followed her. I carried the rest of our baggage—there were no porters. I saw the familiar face of the forwarding agent in one corner of the departure lounge. He checked us off on his list and disappeared. An hour later he reappeared and ordered us to board the plane.

Carrying our things, we set off at a run for the far end of the field. The procedure never varied. Once on board the plane, we sat down on folding metal chairs. We took off and after some time (even children were trained not to tell anyone in Moscow how long we were in the air) began our descent. The Installation's two barbed-wire fences and the guard towers flashed past under the wings. We were home. We still had to have our passes checked, but within the hour we were unpacking in the two rooms assigned to us until the cottage became available.

At first, like everyone else, we found it difficult to settle into a daily routine. It was a particular problem to find milk for the children. But things gradually fell into place.

8

FOUR SCIENTISTS
Tamm, Pomeranchuk, Bogolyubov, Zeldovich

It was my destiny to meet four great theoretical physicists who would in their own ways and in different degrees influence my views and my work as a scientist and inventor. As is customary in memoirs, I will not essay detailed portraits, but will limit myself to the broad brushstrokes.

Igor Tamm played the largest role in my life, and was the only one of the four to influence my opinions on—or, more precisely, my fundamental approach to—social questions.

Tamm worked at the Installation from April 1950 until August 1953. This was the period of our closest collaboration, and I grew to know him in ways that would have been impossible in Moscow. We worked together uninterruptedly throughout the day, had breakfast and lunch together in the canteen, and ate supper and relaxed together in the evenings and on Sundays.

When Tamm moved to the Installation he was already fifty-five, and had many brilliant scientific achievements to his credit. (He was to make a further significant contribution with his work on isobaric resonances [or isospin], and after this came his heroic attempt to develop a nonlocal theory—his approach *seems* incorrect now, but who can be certain?)

Tamm came late to his scientific career; earlier, his activist bent and his socialist convictions had led him to concentrate on politics. At one 1917 congress, Tamm, then a member of the Mensheviks, had been the sole member of his party to vote in favor of immediate peace ("Bravo, Tamm!" Lenin thereupon exclaimed). During the civil war, Tamm had some narrow escapes, crossing the front several times on dangerous assignments. Only after these adventures did he begin to study science, influenced and greatly aided by Leonid Mandelshtam, whom he met in Odessa during the final phase of the civil war. Tamm talked about his life and many other things during evenings we spent in his hotel room or wandering along the deserted forest paths of the Installation (one of them was the local "Lover's Lane"). We would discuss the most sensitive questions: the repressions, the camps, anti-Semitism, collectivization, the ideal and real faces of communism.

Above, I emphasized that Tamm influenced primarily my *approach* to social questions: many of my specific opinions, especially now, differ markedly from his. I once heard Mikhail Leontovich remark with affectionate irony: "Despite everything, the member of the Elizavetgrad Soviet Executive Committee lives on in Tamm." That, of course, was only part of the truth. Tamm was capable of a critical self-analysis, and he frequently cursed his past follies. (Evgeny Feinberg, in his wonderful memoir of Tamm, relates one such incident concerning the Comintern's dogmatic position on the social democrats, which Tamm debated with Bohr in the 1930s.) What remains significant for me are the underlying principles by which Tamm was guided: absolute intellectual integrity and courage, willingness to reexamine his ideas for the sake of truth, and readiness to take action. Instead of brooding about the state of affairs within the confines of his own circle, he would relentlessly pursue his goals. In those early years, Tamm's every word seemed a revelation to me—he already understood so many things I was just beginning to notice, and he was more knowledgeable and astute about them than almost anyone else with whom I could talk freely.

Tamm had been imprisoned by both Denikin's counterintelligence and the Cheka.[1] (One of Tamm's fellow prisoners had a habit of reciting the pornographic verse of Ivan Barkov, which reinforced Tamm's existing aversion to that sort of literature.) His survival was apparently due to chance. The Chekists were executing half a dozen prisoners every morning, but Tamm's number never came up; he was freed on Felix Dzerzhinsky's orders. The Chekist commander who personally released him remarked in evident frustration: "But all the same you're a White Army spy!" When asked what basis he had for this accusation, he showed Tamm a school photograph of Tamm's wife-to-be which had been confiscated during a search. The photograph was inscribed: "We're all your agents." In the 1930s, Tamm was saved once more by a stroke of luck, and by the fact that after quitting the Mensheviks he had not joined any other party, not even the Bolsheviks. By then, he had established a scientific reputation in the USSR and abroad, and that may also have been a helpful factor.

[1][General Anton Denikin commanded the anti-Bolshevik forces from 1918 to 1920. Cheka is the Russian acronym for the Extraordinary Commission for Fighting Counterrevolution and Sabotage, established by the Bolsheviks on December 7, 1917, and first headed by Felix Dzerzhinsky. Members of the KGB—the Cheka's present-day successor—are often called *chekisty*.]

We talked a great deal about the repressions of the 1930s. Tamm recalled how one of his favorite students, Semyon Shubin, would repeat the stock line: The NKVD doesn't arrest people for no reason; I've done nothing anti-Soviet, so they won't touch me. (Such words were spoken by so many people at the time. What lay behind them? Blindness? Hypocrisy? Self-deception as a means of surviving psychologically in an environment of universal terror? The sincere delusions of doomed fanatics?) Tamm and Shubin's final argument began one evening in 1937, and it lasted almost until dawn. The next day Shubin was arrested, and he died not long afterward in a camp. Inquiries as to the cause of his death elicited the answer (any response at all was a rare concession) that Shubin had died from a "chilling of the epidermal integument." Many other physicists, including Alexander Vitt and the brilliant young theoretical physicist Matvei Bronshtein,[2] were arrested and perished in the 1930s.

JUST ABOUT the time we moved to the Installation, a campaign against "kowtowing to the West" was unleashed from above and roared through the press, scientific and cultural institutions, and the academic world. Russians were advertised as the first to have discovered or invented anything and everything. "Russia, homeland of the elephant," ran the stock joke. But the campaign didn't always run smoothly. In one instance, a biography of Admiral Alexander Mozhaisky, who was supposed to supplant the Wright brothers as the inventor of powered flight, was rushed into print so fast that his portrait and his achievements were confused with those of his brother.

The battle against "kowtowing" fused with an anti-Semitic campaign, thinly veiled as "anti-cosmopolitanism." Vannikov, a Jew himself, entertained his high-ranking colleagues with anti-Semitic jokes. "If you don't want to be known as an anti-Semite," he remarked, "say 'cosmopolitan' when you mean 'kike.'"

Tamm's opinion on this subject was categorical; he voiced it often and with passion. For him there was no "Russian"—let alone "Soviet"—science any more than there was "American" or "French" science: science is universal. It is a vital part of the world's cultural heritage, worth pursuing as an end in itself, but it also offers mankind hope for a better future. As for anti-Semitism, Tamm declared that there was "one foolproof way of telling if someone belongs to the

---

[2]Bronshtein's work on the quantization of weak gravitational waves and on the stability of photons remains significant. In his last paper he argued that the "tired light" hypothesis [a now discredited theory which asserted that photons lose energy because of their interaction with intergalactic matter en route to earth] was not the correct explanation for the red shift phenomenon observed in cosmology.

Russian intelligentsia. A true Russian *intelligent* is never an anti-Semite. If he's infected with that virus, then he's something else, something terrible and dangerous."

In the fall of 1956, I asked Tamm what he thought of Khrushchev (adding that I admired him very much since he was so different from Stalin—our conversation took place some months after the 20th Party Congress). With no hint of amusement at my enthusiasm, Tamm replied, Yes, he liked Khrushchev, and of course he was no Stalin—but it would be better if he were even *less* like Stalin! The uprising in Hungary took place that October, but I don't recall discussing it with Tamm; our meetings were becoming less frequent.

In 1968, I published *Reflections on Progress, Peaceful Coexistence, and Intellectual Freedom.* Tamm, by then seriously ill, was skeptical about my ideas, and especially that of "convergence." He remained faithful to the ideals of his youth, to a belief in a pure, undistorted socialism as the only means of resolving mankind's problems and ensuring general happiness. He held back from any discussion of ways to prevent a nuclear or ecological catastrophe in a divided world, but he did acknowledge that I'd posed some critical questions.

Whatever our differences, they never altered the respect and deep affection, even love, that Tamm and I felt for each other. I recall with pride that he asked me to stand in for him in 1968, when he received (along with Powell of Great Britain, discoverer, with Lattes and Occhialini, of the pi-meson) the Academy's highest scientific award, the Lomonosov medal. A recipient traditionally delivers a lecture after the award ceremony, but Tamm, by then kept alive only with the aid of a respirator, was unable to attend. He did write out his Lomonosov lecture and discuss it with his students, myself included. Typically, it was devoted not to his past achievements, but to new scientific ideas that excited him. It was with great emotion that I read his lecture from the podium at the Academy's General Assembly.

IN AUGUST 1968, Soviet tanks rolled into Prague, shocking many in the USSR and abroad. I can't recall now who proposed to Tamm that he add his name to a collective letter of protest. He did sign, but later withdrew his endorsement at the urging of a colleague and favorite student, who argued that this was necessary to protect the theoretical department at FIAN, to which Tamm had devoted his life. I was sorry to see this happen, for I believe that Tamm's signature would have been of enormous significance and would also have given him the satisfaction of adding another valiant deed to a glorious life. The concern for the future of FIAN's theoretical department seemed grossly exaggerated, but people continually justify their failure to act in times of crisis by arguments of this sort.

I HAVE DESCRIBED my feelings about working on nuclear weapons during the period 1948–1956, but I can't speak with the same degree of certainty about Tamm's attitude. I don't recall any conversation with him that really got to the bottom of the issue; I simply assumed that his views on the matter were similar to mine. Tamm once told me about Pyotr Kapitsa's refusal to participate in the development of nuclear weapons. [See p. 302 for Sakharov's conversation with Kapitsa on this subject.] When Kapitsa was called to come to Beria's office, he replied that he was extremely busy with scientific work, but if Beria needed to speak with him, he was welcome to visit the institute. In telling me this, Tamm didn't seem to be praising Kapitsa for his courage; on the contrary, he said something to the effect that "Of course, Beria was a far busier man than Kapitsa." I took this remark at face value as a criticism of Kapitsa, since I then saw Beria as no more than a part of the state machine, engaged like the rest of us in "a project of the utmost importance." And it seemed to me that Tamm shared my opinion. Now I am almost certain that Tamm was being ironic; he may have overestimated my ability to catch his drift.

Around that time, Zeldovich asked me: "Do you know why it was Tamm and not Dau [Lev Landau] who proved so useful to the project?" Zeldovich answered his own question: "Because Tamm has higher moral standards!" (meaning a readiness to devote himself singlemindedly to "the cause"—to my mind, neither the whole story, when it came to Tamm's stance, nor a completely sincere statement on Zeldovich's part).

I know little about Landau's own thoughts on the subject. Once, in the mid-1950s, I paid a visit to the Institute for Physical Problems, where Landau headed the theoretical department and also a separate team performing calculations for nuclear weapons. After we'd finished our business, he and I took a stroll in the garden. It was the only private and candid conversation we ever had. Landau said: "I don't like any of this" (meaning nuclear weapons in general, and his involvement with them in particular).

"Why not?" I asked, perhaps a little naïvely.

"Too much noise."

The toothy grin that so often lighted up Landau's face was missing on this occasion; he appeared quite grave and melancholy.

DURING THE YEARS we spent together at the Installation, Tamm and I naturally had many discussions about science. He was fond of saying that all areas of knowledge interested him—with the exception of philosophy and law.

I completely agreed with him about law; despite my later personal involvement in that murky subject, I've never really accepted it as having anything to do with the real world. As for philosophy, I suspect that Tamm had in mind dogmatists and those who, as Feynman put it, "flit around" the edges of science. He was hardly dismissing the great philosophers of the past, or the present-day contributions of sophisticated philosophical analysis.

Tamm often talked about biology in those days. I was in complete accord with his negative opinion of Lysenkoism (and of Lepeshinskaya, Boshian, and Bykov,[3] who were much in the news at the time). But I didn't share his view that a satisfactory explanation of the phenomenon of life would require entirely new principles in biology, possibly in physics as well—a break with the past comparable to the emergence of quantum mechanics. I argued that stereo-chemistry (with its "lock-key" principle), augmented by electrochemistry, was adequate to "explain" the origins of life (just as a primitive alphabet can be used to express the most complex notions). I consider that the scientific discoveries of recent decades, beginning with the breaking of the DNA code, tend to confirm my opinion. Yet the structures now being uncovered have proved infinitely more complicated, varied, and intricate than anyone could have imagined thirty years ago. So much remains unclear, so many crucial questions must still be formulated accurately, so many details will have to be resolved.

Tamm was convinced that the main thrust of science would shortly switch from physics—the cutting edge of progress in the first half of the twentieth century—to the life sciences. I agreed with him in this and, indeed, the proportion of intellectual and material resources then devoted to the life sciences was utterly inadequate and did not correspond to their practical and theoretical value. Now they have been accorded a greater priority, but the exact sciences have not surrendered their position in the front rank; interest in them has not diminished as they continue to produce unexpected discoveries of enormous significance. In choosing their specialties, young scientists should be guided by their own inclination and their instinct for what is new, something that is mysteriously reborn in every generation.

In the 1950s Tamm used to say that if he had to choose his specialty over again, he would pick biology. I never took this literally, for fundamental physics was his true passion: it both tormented him and gave his life meaning. A few years before his death, at a time when he was already seriously ill, he declared that his dream was to live to see (and to be mentally capable of understanding)

---

[3][Influential authors of sensational but scientifically unsound biological theories: Lepeshinskaya's "life substance," Boshian's "discovery" of virus-to-bacteria transformation.]

a new theory of elementary particles, one that answered all the "accursed questions." (Living to see answered such questions as the secrets of the human brain, the differentiation of embryonic cells, and the origin and evolution of life wasn't mentioned.)

Evgeny Feinberg has remarked that if Tamm hadn't concentrated on the most difficult problems on the frontiers of physics, he could have done valuable work elsewhere simply by virtue of his erudition, his professionalism, his phenomenal capacity for work, and his talent for exact mathematical calculation. This is evident from his work on magnetically confined fusion [see Chapter 9], from all his applied work, and from the papers he wrote during his rare periods of "scientific depression" when he became discouraged by his failures on the cutting edge of physics.

Indicative of Tamm's true passion was the work of his final years, in which, on the basis of Snyder's ideas, he sought to construct a theory with curved momentum space. The work demanded an immense effort on the part of Tamm, whose life by then was entirely dependent on the use of a respirator. Others in his situation might have sunk into apathy or despair and given up the ghost. The thrust behind this last undertaking was his conviction that the theory of renormalization—then regarded as the definitive solution to the problem of "ultraviolet divergences"—was in fact no more than a temporary and partial solution, or at best, a phenomenological one at low energies. Only a few people (among them Dirac) were of this opinion, especially before the discovery of the "Moscow zero." It seems to me that Tamm was correct in principle and incorrect only in expecting too much from his theory of curved momentum space. Nowadays great hopes are invested in gauge supersymmetry theories, and especially in "superstrings." But the matter remains far from resolved.

LET ME RETURN to the story of our life in the 1950s. Tamm, Romanov, and I normally ate breakfast and lunch together. Tamm would report any news (politics, sports, or odd items of interest) he had picked up from foreign radio broadcasts. He listened regularly to BBC programs in English and Russian, something very few people did at the time. It was Tamm who told us of Hilary and Tenzing's ascent of Everest in 1953. (I thought of this recently when Tamm's son, Evgeny, led a Soviet expedition to Everest. Back then, Tamm cursed himself for whetting his son's interest in mountain climbing, a dangerous passion.) But what mattered was not so much the content of Tamm's reports as his approach to the news (as to everything else): intelligent, passionate, and open-minded.

He never let us get down in the dumps. He himself was enthusiastic and sociable, and he encouraged us to have fun in our spare time. We played chess in the evening, sometimes with four players, or without looking at the opponent's pieces, or in some other variation. Tamm taught us the Chinese game Go and another game, Taking the Stones, which can be solved using an algorithm based on the "golden section" (we racked our brains over that one!).[4]

We skied and went hiking, and in the summertime we swam. (I was hopeless in the water, but Tamm tactfully spared me unnecessary embarrassment.) Pavel Guryanov, our driver, joined in these activities on an equal footing with the rest of us; in Tamm's company this seemed perfectly natural, but later I saw bosses treat subordinates in an entirely different fashion.

Guryanov once saved Tamm's life, and mine, when an army truck passing on a narrow, winding road came hurtling at us. With the split-second reactions of a former tank driver, Guryanov avoided a head-on collision by swerving onto the sidewalk, threading his way among pedestrians. Sadly, he later took to drink, and was sent to work as a railroad engineer.

Tamm had money problems for the greater part of his life. His Stalin Prize helped, but he earmarked a portion of the money for talented individuals in need. He would ask people to identify potential recipients (who were never told where the money came from). I wish this idea, or something like it, had occurred to me. I only learned of Tamm's generosity after his death.

I agree completely with what Evgeny Feinberg wrote in his memoir of Tamm:

> In late 19th century Russia there existed something of fundamental importance—a solid, middle-class, professional intelligentsia which possessed firm principles based on spiritual values. That milieu produced committed revolutionaries, poets, and engineers, convinced that the most important thing is to build something, to do something useful. That was the milieu which produced Igor Tamm, and he shared its virtues, and its shortcomings. Perhaps most important of all was his independent spirit in matters large and small, in life and in science. . . .[5]

Tamm's wife, Natalya Vasilievna, possessed similar virtues. Things were probably not always easy for her—life, after all, is a tricky thing. Once, in an attempt to allay the doubts (absolutely groundless) that tormented Klava, Natalya told her: "A man's love is often inconstant: it can fade and almost

---

[4][In Taking the Stones, there are two piles of stones. Each player in turn must take an equal number of stones from each pile or else any number of stones from one pile. The player who takes the last stone loses.]

[5][Evgeny Feinberg, ed. *Reminiscences about I. E. Tamm* (Nauka, 1987).]

vanish, but the flame returns." I have only Klava's report of this conversation and I can't be certain that Natalya was referring to her own marriage, but her words are evidence of considerable experience and a kindly wisdom. In the many years they spent together (Natalya survived Tamm by nine years), she always supported him, both in his moments of triumph and during the periods of depression to which active and sensitive individuals are prone.

Much has been written about Tamm, but I hope I have managed to add a few brushstrokes to the existing portraits of a man who played a major role in my life. Perhaps the great fortune of my early years was to have had my character molded by the Sakharov family, whose members embodied the generic virtues of the Russian intelligentsia described by Feinberg, and to have then come under the influence of Igor Tamm.

ISAAK (YUZIK on his passport) Pomeranchuk was a completely different sort from Tamm, but another uncommonly fascinating individual. He was extremely upset by his assignment to the Installation in the summer of 1950: we were tearing him away from his important work on elementary particles and field theory—and from his young wife. He had just remarried and was very much in love. His previous wife or wives (there may have been more than one) had left him in short order. This time the story was reversed: he'd stolen the wife of a general. Night after night he'd waited beneath her window, hoping for an occasional glance from behind the curtain. (Gossip based on hearsay; but it accords well with Pomeranchuk's character.)

I recall his pacing the small yard of his cottage, ruffling his black hair, and humming a song that ran something like this: "I grew up and blossomed before seventeen, then a girl in love starts wilting." (I presume he was casting himself as the "girl" in that song.) He said to me once: "You know, I guess I'm just an old-fashioned man, for whom such odd notions as love are most important."

In spite of his emotional distractions, Pomeranchuk quickly and brilliantly solved the problems in theoretical physics Tamm and I assigned him. He was a virtuoso of theoretical technique, and knew many methods that were new to me. And yet he regarded this work with utter disdain. Someone told me that he'd once grabbed the director of a large physics institute by the lapel and asked him: "Do you have a 600 MeV accelerator? . . . You don't! Then you're a building superintendent, not a director!"

This was not a pose, but an expression of Pomeranchuk's true character and his consuming passion. He believed that the fundamental laws of nature could be discovered in their "naked" undistorted form at very high energies. The problem was simply to determine the energy level necessary, and then conduct your experiments with elementary particles at those levels. The progress of science over the next thirty years confirmed his intuition, but Pomeranchuk didn't live to see these developments: he died in 1966. (And none of us is likely to live long enough to see all the important questions answered either.)

After Pomeranchuk had moped around the Installation for a few months, the administration realized it would be better to let him return to his own work and to his wife.

In the 1960s, Pomeranchuk's zeal was rewarded when he made a number of fundamental discoveries in high-energy physics. Justice triumphs—sometimes. One of his successes—the well-known "Pomeranchuk's theorem"— states that the cross sections of collisions between a particle and a target and an anti-particle and the same target become asymptotically equal at high energies. His name is also associated with the Regge trajectory with zero quantum numbers. But this, of course, is only the tip of the iceberg, a mere token of his accomplishments. He spent much time working with talented students—Vladimir Gribov, Lev Okun, Boris Ioffe, Karen Ter-Martirosian, and Igor Kobzarev among others—and enjoyed his collaboration with them.

I saw Pomeranchuk quite often during his last years, when he was trying to return to fundamental science. He was still on fire with scientific projects, and I remember his excitement and his doubts about quarks, the elementary particles posited by Gell-Mann and Zweig. Pomeranchuk's wife had died, and he himself was suffering from cancer of the esophagus. A wise and sympathetic doctor, the late Professor Kassirsky, who knew his patient well, advised Pomeranchuk to make liberal use of painkillers if he wished to live out decently what remained of his life. He heeded this advice, and as a result was able to go on working until the day he died.

Just before his death, he discussed with his students their last joint article, on scaling. Björken's well-known paper on the same subject had appeared at about the same time, followed by Feynman's work. All three articles had been born of the spectacular results obtained from the giant Stanford Linear Accelerator. Pomeranchuk was still on the cutting edge.

The last time I saw him, he was terribly ill and emaciated. With grim humor, he told me that he now confined his walks to the nighttime so people wouldn't be scared at the sight of him. Apart from that one remark, he spoke only of science. Pomeranchuk is remembered by all who knew him as the shining knight of theoretical physics.

I FIRST HEARD Nikolai Bogolyubov's name in 1946. Akiva Yaglom, a member of my school's math club and later my classmate at Moscow University, told me that an exceptionally gifted young physicist had come from Kiev, a stray pup overflowing with so many ideas that he was handing them out right and left.

Later, at FIAN, I attended a remarkable lecture by Bogolyubov on superfluidity. Of course, it was just a model theory, and, moreover, one that relied
on perturbation theory, but it was the first theoretical investigation that
derived the surprising phenomenon of superfluidity from first principles, without relying on a specially postulated spectrum of elementary excitations. Unfortunately, certain scientists did not appreciate his approach, and Bogolyubov,
to say nothing of his students and associates, engaged in some rather dubious
conduct during the squabbles that followed. Ten years later, however, when
articles on superconductivity by Bardeen, Cooper, and Schrieffer appeared,
Bogolyubov had a suitable theoretical framework ready, and he capitalized on
it brilliantly.

He strengthened the mathematics department at the Installation by finding
a new director to replace Agrest, and recruiting a large team of talented
associates. He also did some work on Installation topics that coincided with
his own interests, and on these occasions proved to be a topnotch problem-
solver. But he had no interest whatever in technical, design, or experimental
work.

Once, when Bogolyubov happened to attend a meeting on engineering
problems in Khariton's office, he left with a baffled expression on his face and
was heard to say, half in earnest and half in jest, that he had "got tangled in
the nuts and bolts." That expression became proverbial with us. Bogolyubov
made no secret of the fact that he devoted most of his time to topics that had
nothing to do with the Installation—much later I did the same thing myself—
and to writing monographs on theoretical physics. This was the principal
reason he brought Klimov, Shirkov, and Zubarev to the Installation. He
achieved his greatest success with Dmitri Shirkov, the youngest of the three;
their joint monograph on quantum field theory was universally and justly
acclaimed. Bogolyubov also produced an excellent monograph in collaboration
with Zubarev, but Klimov and Bogolyubov did not hit it off; after Bogolyubov
left the Installation, I took Klimov into my department.

Tamm and I got along well with Bogolyubov after working hours. We would
occasionally drop by his hotel room, where he welcomed us and offered us "what
God has provided" (and He provided some very tasty things). Bogolyubov would
pace the room, talking and gesticulating. I always found our conversations
interesting even though we never touched on sensitive subjects. Bogolyubov was
erudite in the most diverse fields, had an excellent command of several languages, and possessed a sharp, original mind and a sense of humor. Half-jokingly,
he predicted that in short order my chest would be so thickly covered with
medals there wouldn't be room for them all. It was he who first drew my
attention to cybernetics and the work of Norbert Wiener, Claude Shannon, and
John von Neumann (this supplied ammunition for my arguments with Tamm
about the nature of life), and to the enormous potential of computers.

Bogolyubov quit the Installation at the same time as Tamm, after the 1953 test. We met only sporadically after that, even though we lived on the same floor of a building in Moscow for a while.

It seems to me that the years Bogolyubov spent in relative isolation at the Installation laid the foundation for his outstanding work on quantum field theory and elementary particles in the 1950s and 1960s; those achievements are widely known and there's no need to discuss them here.

Bogolyubov has many disciples among physicists and mathematicians, including both genuine scientists and those he has just chosen as his sycophants. He heads the theoretical physics and mathematics departments at several institutes and has become something of a scientific "general." What he needs all that for is beyond me, but "status" is apparently an integral part of his style and his sense of well-being. I prefer to remember how his expression would light up with excitement at word of a new development in science, and the spate of ideas he would immediately generate.

MY LONGEST RELATIONSHIP—spanning four decades—was with Yakov Zeldovich. I write of him with mixed feelings. He played an important role in my work in the 1950s and an even greater one in my theoretical work of the 1960s. For many years I valued our friendship highly, regarding it as close and congenial. When Lusia and I were beginning our life together in 1971 and she asked me who my friends were, I answered: Zeldovich. Even now, I don't doubt he was sincere when he telephoned that same year on my fiftieth birthday to say that he loved me. All the same, in retrospect, I detect a touch of the "operator" in the way he behaved on certain occasions. And in the 1970s and 1980s, some of his actions (or failures to act) were not friendly at all.

Zeldovich was seven years older than I. I don't know much about his family background; I believe his father was an accountant. When we first met, Zeldovich occasionally wore a hat inherited from him: round, green-tinged, with a brim—it reminded me of turn-of-the-century photographs of Jewish life in the Pale of Settlement. It's my impression that his parents lived in straitened circumstances. He never spoke of his childhood and youth, although once he mentioned an "inferiority complex" he claimed to have overcome (but, who knows, perhaps he spent his whole life battling it). He was short in stature, but had been exceptionally strong as a youth.

Zeldovich was not a university graduate; he was, in a sense, self-educated. He worked as a laboratory assistant in several scientific institutions in Leningrad, after moving there from Belorussia around 1930, and published his first papers at the age of seventeen, highly original work, primarily in physical chemistry. His formula pertaining to surface phenomena is well known, and his work on the kinetics of chemical reactions contains the seeds of a theory for a chemical chain reaction. His reputation soon earned him a master's (*kandidat*) degree and then his doctorate (his dissertation concerned the production of nitrogen oxide from fuel gas) without his ever bothering about a bachelor's degree.

The physics of combustion, of explosions, and of other chemical phenomena continued to engage him throughout his life, but his scientific interests kept expanding, and he was invariably among the pace-setters in new fields. He worked on fission chain reactions and atomic technology, jet propulsion, and thermonuclear weapons, then made an abrupt switch to elementary particles, and finally turned his attention to cosmology and astrophysics. Few scientists are competent in such a wide range of fields. As a sideline, Zeldovich published survey articles and monographs, as well as his very interesting *Mathematics for Beginners*. Of course, he wrote most of his books with coauthors, but his hand can be felt in all of them, and they reflect his ideas. (He later found himself at odds with some of his coauthors; it's difficult to say who was to blame.)

Among Zeldovich's many published works (I shall mention only a few highlights of his distinguished and prolific career), his papers written with Khariton and published in 1939 and 1940 on the theory of fission chain reactions were landmarks. During the war Zeldovich worked on jet propulsion, and in 1945 he was sent to Peenemünde to gather information on the Germans' V-2 rocket program. He traveled in the uniform of a Soviet army captain, and was once invited to dinner by the KGB boss of the Soviet zone, who in effect exercised power over half of Germany. Zeldovich recalled their meeting with some fear, but also with a tinge of admiration, a sin of which we were all a bit guilty at that time.

In the 1950s, his best-known work on elementary particles was the article he coauthored with S. Gershtein in which they introduce charged current and formulate the law of conservation of vector current. This paper anticipated the idea of "current algebra" and provided a basis for formulating the theory of weak interactions. But Zeldovich and Gershtein failed to take the final, decisive step—the introduction of a parity-breaking operator in the interaction of currents. This was left to Marshak and Sudarshan, Gell-Mann and Feynman. But what would appear to be the final theory of weak interactions was not constructed until much later, by Glashow, Weinberg, and Salam. ["Final" is too strong a word. Much remains unknown: the masses and other properties of neutrinos, the mechanism of CP-violation, etc.—A.S. 1987] I shall deal in Chapter 18 with Zeldovich's work on cosmology and the theory of elementary particles in the 1960s, which served as a stimulus and starting point for my own research into those fields.

* * *

I GREW CLOSER to Zeldovich when I was transferred to the Installation in 1950. We worked in adjacent offices. (In the early days, all of us had to share offices; I shared mine with Tamm and Romanov.) The cottages in which we lived were always close by. In 1949–1950, Zeldovich lived with the Zababa-khins; his room, actually an enclosed terrace, was nicknamed "Storage for a Corresponding Member of the Academy of Sciences." We visited each other's offices several times a day, to share a new idea, discuss a problem, or simply joke and talk. Certainly we discussed serious scientific matters, but we also amused ourselves with "brainteasers" in mathematics and physics, competing to find the fastest and most elegant solution. It never entered my mind that we might engage in any form of rivalry other than this sort of battle of wits.

One evening in the spring of 1950 on my way home from work, I caught sight of Zeldovich. The moon was out, and the bell tower cast a long shadow on the square in front of the hotel. Zeldovich was walking deep in thought, his face somehow radiant. Catching sight of me, he exclaimed: "Who would believe how much love lies hidden in this heart?"

In many respects, the Installation was a big village in which nothing re-mained secret. I knew Zeldovich was having a love affair with Shiryaeva, one of the prisoners, an architect and artist by profession. Her husband had re-nounced her after her arrest on charges of anti-Soviet slander; such stories were common in those days. It was Shiryaeva who had painted the murals in the VIP dining room, in our theatre, and in the homes of the Installation's bosses. She had been granted trusty status, apparently as a reward for her services.

A few months after our encounter in the moonlight, Zeldovich woke me in the middle of the night. Romanov, in the other bed, looked up for a moment, but then turned over and remained silent: he never asked questions. Zeldovich was agitated. Could I lend him some money? Fortunately, I had just been paid, and I gave him everything I had. A few days later I learned that Shiryaeva's term had expired, and that she was being sent to Magadan, far to the east, for "permanent resettlement." Zeldovich managed to get the money to her, and after some months I learned from him that Shiryaeva had given birth to their daughter in a building where the floor was covered in ice an inch thick.

Zeldovich managed to obtain some improvement in Shiryaeva's situation, and twenty years later, at a conference in Kiev, he introduced me to Shurochka, the daughter born in Magadan. She looked amazingly like his other daughter— by his wife, Varvara Pavlovna. (Zeldovich had a number of other affairs—too many—most of them strictly sexual liaisons. I don't like some of the stories I've heard.) He dreamed of someday bringing all his children together. I hope he succeeded. Time is a great healer, provided there's complete honesty.

IN THE MIDDLE of 1950, a commission visited the Installation to check up on senior scientific personnel. We were all called in, one at a time. Among other questions, I was asked what I thought of the chromosome theory of heredity. (After the Academy of Agricultural Science's meeting in the summer of 1948 and Stalin's endorsement of Lysenko, belief in Mendelian genetics was regarded as an indication of disloyalty.) I replied that the theory seemed scientifically correct. The commission members exchanged glances but said nothing. Evidently, my position and reputation at the Installation disposed them to overlook my sins.

A couple of weeks later, Zeldovich came to me and said that we had to help Lev Altshuler, the head of one of the experimental departments. He was a longtime acquaintance of Zeldovich and had played a major role in the development of fission charges and in research on physical processes at high pressures. It turned out that Altshuler had been asked the same question by the commission and, with his typical forthrightness, had given the same answer I had. He, however, was threatened with dismissal.

"Zavenyagin is at the Installation," Zeldovich informed me. "Andrei Dmitrievich, if you appeal to him on Altshuler's behalf, they might leave him alone. I've just been talking with Zababakhin. It would be best if you went together with him." Within the hour, Zababakhin and I were in the director's office, where Zavenyagin received us.

At the time, Avraami Zavenyagin was nominally Vannikov's deputy, but since Vannikov spent a lot of time on matters of state outside the bailiwick of the First Chief Administration, in practice Zavenyagin decided many matters on his own. He was from "Ordzhonikidze's team,"[6] and at one time had been director of the Magnitogorsk industrial complex. He came under attack in the 1930s but was not arrested; instead, he was sent to run the Norilsk construction conglomerate in Siberia. The town and the ore-processing facilities were built from scratch in the tundra by zeks working in conditions of permafrost, blizzards, and, for most of the year, polar night. It was impossible to escape, but desperate convicts would occasionally try to do so. A pair of professional criminals would find a "pigeon" to take along with them; if their supplies ran out, they could kill and eat their companion (and I don't think this was just a tall tale). The mortality rate at Norilsk was almost as extreme as at Kolyma: the temperature in the mines was a bit higher, but still below freezing. After Zavenyagin's death in 1956, the Norilsk mining and smelting complex was named in his honor.

[6][Grigory Ordzhonikidze was Minister of Heavy Industry in the 1930s.]

Zavenyagin was a tough, decisive, exceptionally enterprising chief. He heeded the opinions of scientists and understood their role in the project. He made some attempt to study the concepts involved in our work, and from time to time would come forth with technical solutions, usually quite sensible. He was a man of great intelligence—and an uncompromising Stalinist. He had large, black, melancholy Asiatic eyes, a reminder of his Tatar ancestry. After Norilsk, he always felt cold, and he wore a fur coat draped over his shoulders even in a warm room. Surprisingly, given his background, there was a gentleness apparent in his relationships with some people— I was later to find myself included in this select group. He held the rank of lieutenant general in State Security; behind his back we called him "the General" or "Avraami."

I sometimes wonder what motivates such people. Ambition? Fear? A thirst for action and power? Conviction? I have no answers. Back in 1950, we simply accepted Zavenyagin as a top official.

He heard us through and then said: "I'm aware of Altshuler's hooligan conduct. You say he's done a lot for the Installation and he'll be useful in the future. Fine. We won't take official action now, but we'll watch how he behaves."

Then, before dismissing us, Zavenyagin asked how the work was going in our department. He was pleased that we knew all the figures by heart and remarked that Beria's favorite method for checking a person's professional competence was to ask him for facts and figures.

Things turned out well, but now, all these years later, I ask myself why Zeldovich didn't go himself to see Zavenyagin, or at least accompany us. Possibly he feared that Zavenyagin was aware of his personal relationship with Altshuler and would discount his plea, but it seems more likely that this was an example of Zeldovich's tendency to hide behind others when trouble was in the offing, even relatively insignificant trouble. The pattern was repeated later when he asked me to write a letter about literary matters, and to speak out in defense of a mutual acquaintance of ours who was under arrest, a story I'll tell later.

The fact that Zeldovich was a Jew undoubtedly had something to do with all this; perhaps he felt vulnerable and feared his interventions would be ineffective. But I know Jews and members of other nationalities who, lacking Zeldovich's standing and virtual immunity, still behave very differently, and are able to look beyond their group affiliation in matters of civic responsibility. There may not be many of them, but they do exist.

Up to a certain point, I was inclined to regard these aspects of Zeldovich's behavior as minor failings. Everyone does what he can, and Zeldovich did a great deal in his professional work and in popularizing science and introducing young people to it. He and I discussed social issues, though I don't know whether he was always candid. But since I myself was often slow to appreciate the true state of affairs, why should I assume that others understood everything and were engaged in deliberate deceit? And yet, could Zeldovich have been serious when he claimed to like *The Morning of Our Motherland,* a painting that depicts Stalin standing before a blue-green background of kolkhoz fields and construction sites? It is, of course, possible that he was sincere. . . .

Still, Zeldovich could be an interesting conversationalist who spoke with intelligence, sincerity, and emotion. It was at his home that I first saw certain samizdat publications, including Tvardovsky's *Tyorkin in the Other World* and Akhmatova's "Requiem." I often felt a certain warmth in Zeldovich's relationship to me—in both word and deed. That made all the more bitter some of his actions in the 1970s and 1980s.

In 1973, Zeldovich telephoned me after a tendentious newspaper article denounced a letter I'd written with Alexander Galich and Vladimir Maximov in defense of Pablo Neruda [see p. 389]. Lusia answered the phone and said: "We're so happy; my daughter Tanya had a little boy!" Zeldovich interrupted her: "You'd better look after your other 'little boy'!" When I came to the phone, he attacked me in such clichés that I couldn't take him seriously. Two years later, after my Nobel Peace Prize was announced, Zeldovich phoned once again and urged that I refuse the award, calling it a provocation. He sounded like the newspaper *Trud,* which had termed the award "thirty pieces of silver" (and had also made an innuendo about my wife's Jewish extraction). In both instances Zeldovich must have known that my telephone was tapped. He followed up his 1975 call with a letter, again surely aware that the KGB reads all my mail.

I don't understand why Zeldovich felt obliged to make such a display of his loyalty to the regime and to demonstrate my isolation. I thought I had the right to count on him—and other colleagues whose positions shielded them from reprisals—to defend my rights after I was illegally exiled to Gorky in 1980. In 1981, I wrote to Zeldovich and Khariton, asking them to intercede (privately, not publicly) on behalf of my stepson's fiancée, Liza Alexeyeva, who had become a hostage because of her link to me. I made plain my distress and how much I was relying on their help; Khariton did not respond at all, while Zeldovich cited the shakiness of his own situation in refusing to intervene, complaining that he wasn't allowed to travel any further than Hungary! This was the excuse offered by an academician, a three-time Hero of Socialist Labor, a man who had never made good use of the considerable power that comes with such status. And that status, I am convinced, was very secure indeed. In essence, I was asking him to do no more than what I'd done in the Altshuler affair. (Whether his intercession would have helped is another matter.)

* * *

THE PRECEDING description of my complicated, contradictory relationship
with Yakov Zeldovich was written in 1982. The bitter taste left by Zeldovich's
inaction in Liza's case and by other unpleasant incidents lingered on and
colored the tone of my account. Now, I would like to take a more tolerant view
of a complex personality. Not long ago, Zeldovich came up to me at an
Academy of Sciences meeting (in a rush, as always) and said: "A lot happened
in the past. Let's forget the bad: Life goes on!" Of course it does. . . .[—A.S.
1987]

ON DECEMBER 2, 1987, Zeldovich died of a heart attack.[7] Any chance of our
meeting and talking again was lost. The petty and superficial aspects of our
relationship have faded; what remains is his enduring, truly immense contributions to science. And all those whom he helped to enter the realm of science.

At times I still catch myself carrying on a mental dialogue with Yakov
Borisovich on scientific matters. . . .[—A.S. 1988]

[7][Sakharov was listed among the scientists and Party officials who signed Zeldovich's obituary,
which appeared in Pravda on December 5.]

9

THE MAGNETIC
THERMONUCLEAR REACTOR

My work with Igor Tamm on the problem of a controlled thermonuclear reaction belongs to the early period at the Installation, 1950–51.

Although these questions were already on my mind in 1949, as yet I had no concrete, intelligent ideas. Then, in the summer of 1950, Beria's secretariat sent us a letter from Oleg Lavrentiev, a young sailor in the Pacific Fleet, who noted the importance a controlled thermonuclear (i.e., fusion) reaction might hold for future energy production and then offered a proposal to create a high-temperature deuterium plasma by means of electrostatic confinement. Specifically, he proposed that two or three metal grids be used to surround the reactor volume. An electric charge of several dozen KeV applied to the grids would create an electrostatic field that would deflect deuterium ions and electrons and prevent them from escaping the reactor. I wrote back that Lavrentiev had raised an issue of immense significance, and had displayed initiative and creativity that merited all possible support and aid. His specific plan, however, struck me as impracticable: there was no way to ensure that the hot plasma would not come into contact with the grids, which would inevitably result in enormous heat loss and render such means incapable of attaining sufficiently high temperatures for thermonuclear reactions. I probably should have mentioned that Lavrentiev's idea might prove fruitful in conjunction with other ideas, but at the time I had nothing specific to suggest.

My first vague thoughts on magnetic rather than electrostatic confinement occurred to me as I read Lavrentiev's letter and wrote my reply. The fundamental distinction between a static magnetic field and a static electric one is that the force lines of a static magnetic field can be closed outside material bodies (or form closed "magnetic surfaces"); in this way, the "contact problem" might in principle be solved. The appearance of closed magnetic force lines is particularly evident within the interior of a toroid when the current passes through the toroidal winding situated on its surface. It was this sort of system that I decided to explore.

Tamm returned to the Installation from Moscow at the beginning of August 1950. He responded enthusiastically to my ideas, and from that time on the development of the notion of magnetic confinement was entirely the product of a joint effort. Tamm was particularly helpful in providing calculations and estimates, and in analyzing such basic physical concepts as magnetic drift, magnetic surfaces, etc. Initially, I'd suggested that our project be called TTR (for Toroidal Thermonuclear Reactor), but Tamm came up with the happier designation MTR (Magnetic Thermonuclear Reactor); this more general name stuck, and is now applied as well to other systems using magnetic confinement.

We began by turning our attention to magnetic drift, a problem, albeit not the most serious. The general picture of the motion of a charged particle (ion or electron) in a strong magnetic field is that of a spiral "wound" around a magnetic force line. The radius of the spiral's turns (known as the "Larmor radius") is inversely proportional to the strength of the magnetic field. The particle does not leave the reactor space as it moves along the line of force, nor does it contact the walls if the force lines themselves do not extend to the walls. But this ideal situation is virtually unattainable; in practice, the in-homogeneity (irregularities) of the magnetic field forces a shift in the center of the Larmor circle away from the magnetic force line—"magnetic drift." Drift may also occur as a result of electric fields ("electric drift"). It is simple to see how drift arises. In Figure 6 it has been assumed that the magnetic field is perpendicular to the picture plane and that its intensity increases along the X axis. The curvature of the charged particle's path is proportional to the strength of the magnetic field and is greater at point B than at point A; as a result, the particle's trajectory (more precisely, its projection onto the plane perpendicular to the magnetic field vector) remains open, as indicated in the figure (drift along the Y axis). An electric field directed along the X axis has a similar effect. The magnetic field created by the toroidal winding (in the absence of plasma) coincides inside the toroid with the field of the direct current flowing along the axis of rotation; its intensity is inversely proportional to the distance to the rotation axis. In either case, containment is violated. As a result, charged particles drift from their appointed trajectories and strike the wall of the toroid.

A way out of this difficulty can be found by considering systems in which a field created by the circular current flowing inside the toroidal space is superimposed on the field set up by the toroidal winding (see Figs. 7 and 8). In such systems there are no longer any closed magnetic force lines; instead,

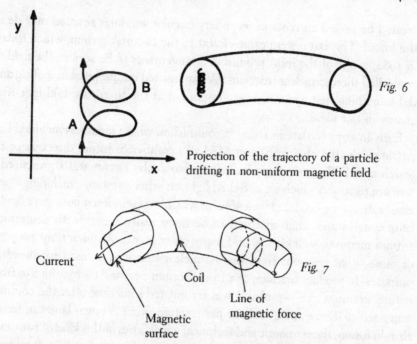

Fig. 6

Projection of the trajectory of a particle
drifting in non-uniform magnetic field

Fig. 7

Current

Coil

Line of
magnetic force

Magnetic
surface

closed magnetic force surfaces surround the circular current. The magnetic
force lines wind in spirals around these surfaces without leaving the confines
of the internal space. Magnetic surfaces were discussed long before we had
need of them for our work, in Tamm's textbook *The Theory of Electricity*.[1]
Tamm developed these ideas during 1950–1951, with Nikolai Bogolyubov also
making an important contribution at this stage. Later, other scientists continued to elaborate the mathematical problem of magnetic surfaces. As early
as 1950, we showed that although magnetic drift does occur in these systems,
it no longer drives particles out of the area of confinement. Tamm then made
an important observation that anticipated a problem that MTR researchers
were to encounter many years later. He warned of the possibility of disturbances to the structure (topology) of the magnetic surfaces occurring, in which
certain magnetic force lines would be "pulled together to a point" inside the
toroidal space. This, he said, would be extremely dangerous. Such a "banana"
structure could arise, for example, as a result of improper toroidal winding or
from plasma instabilities. The result would be a colossal increase in heat release.
In our first proposals we considered two possible ways to set up the circular
current—with the aid of a special current-carrying ring placed inside the
reactor space or an induction current flowing directly through the plasma and

[1][Tamm's text, first published in 1946, has gone through numerous editions. An English
translation published in 1979 is based on the 1976 Russian edition.]

created by pulsed currents in secondary circular windings situated outside of the toroid. This last system came closest to the tokamak system, which today, in 1982, is one of the most promising arrangements to be seen in the field of controlled thermonuclear reactions. We submitted our proposal in writing and did something that was even more important at the time—we told Igor Kurchatov of our ideas.

Early in 1951 (or late in 1950), a commission whose members included Lev Artsimovich (the chairman) and Mikhail Leontovich, future directors of research on MTRs, arrived to discuss our proposals. Tamm and I presented a series of papers in which we also shed light on other questions, including "best case" estimates of system efficiency, for which we considered both pure deuterium systems and what appeared to be more realistic ones with deuterium-tritium mixtures; wall effects; and many other points. An important proposal of mine—that neutrons from thermonuclear reactions be used for breeding purposes (to produce uranium 233 from thorium 232, and plutonium 239 from natural uranium 238)—probably was formulated sometime after the commission's arrival. Since energy release per reaction event is much larger in fission than in fusion, the economic and technical possibilities of this kind of two-stage energy production exceed those of direct production of energy in the fusion reactor. Fissionable material is produced in the MTR and then burned in nuclear reactors of comparatively simple design—simpler than fast neutron reactors, in which, moreover, the accumulation of fissionable materials is comparatively slow. If I did bring up this proposal, it attracted no attention. The discussions focused on the problems of so-called plasma instabilities, which are crucial to the question of whether the MTR is theoretically feasible. We knew something about these instabilities and of course were concerned about their effects, but we hoped that in sufficiently large systems and over periods of short

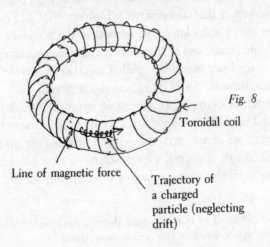

Fig. 8

Toroidal coil

Line of magnetic force

Trajectory of
a charged
particle (neglecting
drift)

duration (for example, in pulsed thermonuclear reactors) they would not assert themselves to an extent that would make the MTR impracticable. Then-current theories of turbulent diffusion of plasma in magnetic fields gave very large values for heat dissipation (though smaller than in the absence of magnetic fields). If these theories were applicable, the MTR would be a practical impossibility—or, at best, very complex, costly, and cumbersome to build. But back in the summer of 1950 we didn't know this; and the grandeur of our visions made us reluctant to surrender without a fight when Artsimovich told us of these theories. On the face of it the situation was almost precisely that of Einstein's famous description of how inventions occur. First, the experts present weighty arguments why it's impossible; then an ignoramus appears who doesn't know any of this—and goes ahead and makes the invention. This must be taken with a grain of salt: the so-called ignoramus must in fact be up to the state of the art and possess certain qualities, or he won't get anywhere. He should be aware of the difficulties but have intuition enough not to be put off by them, even if he can't yet provide a strictly logical case for his belief. Up to a point, this was exactly our situation.

But the main thread running through the history of MTR development was the great variety of types of plasma instabilities, many of which were unsuspected at the time, and the extreme hazard they presented. The simplest—and, as it turned out, the most damaging—are so-called hydrodynamic instabilities, in which the plasma can be treated macroscopically, as a continuum. An example of hydrodynamic instability is the formation of a "pinch" on the plasma column through which electric current flows. The current creates a circular magnetic field whose pressure squeezes the column it surrounds. The intensity of the magnetic field being inversely proportional to the radius, the field pressure is higher at the pinch, which therefore becomes progressively deeper. Even a slight accidental pinch will rapidly deepen to the point where the plasma column "breaks."

Experimentalists at LIPAN stumbled onto this problem under dramatic circumstances, as they were conducting experiments with a deuterium plasma, creating powerful impulse discharges. The plasma was contracted as expected by the magnetic field, and it was assumed that pressure, density, and temperature within the column would increase greatly as this occurred. According to their estimates, no fusion reaction was to be expected—but just in case, they set up a diagnostic instrument. Unexpectedly, a small quantity of neutrons was produced at the moment the impulse was registered, and there was a flash of hope that the temperature and density of the plasma were higher than calculated and a thermonuclear reaction was taking place. It really was enough to make your head spin . . . but fortunately, Artsimovich, Leontovich, and the majority of experimentalists and theorists at LIPAN were not dazzled, and

Artsimovich hypothesized (it was later confirmed) that the neutron emission was the result of a break in the plasma column. High-voltage current flowing through the column meant that an electric field would appear at the point of the break (this was essentially the same phenomenon that I "observed" with my fingers as I disconnected the battery from an electric toy motor). The field accelerated nuclei located at the break point, which then interacted with other nuclei, just as in a normal particle accelerator. A fusion reaction did indeed occur—but not a thermonuclear one. Efforts were later made to increase the effect by using stronger impulse currents, which, if we were in fact dealing with a thermonuclear reaction, might be expected to yield a sharp increase in neutron exiting. But nothing of the sort was observed; what we had was just an accelerating tube—and a poor one, at that. Still, although the excitement soon died down, the phenomenon itself was fascinating.

The tale of the "false" neutrons is reflected to some extent in Mikhail Romm's 1965 film, *Nine Days in a Year*. When the film first came out, Tamm told me a bit about its background: In planning the project, Romm had originally gone to Professor Vasily Emelyanov, then the director of the board for the peaceful uses of atomic energy, with a request for information. (Emelyanov, an Old Bolshevik and author of several volumes of memoirs, also published a stinging attack on the writer Viktor Nekrasov in *Pravda* in the 1960s, accusing him of belittling the role of the working class.) I don't know what Emelyanov, a glib and enthusiastic talker, said to Romm; in any case, the upshot was that Romm went to see Tamm, and the two had several conversations about the history of MTR. The first name and patronymic of the hero of Romm's film, Dmitri Andreyevich Gusev, are suggestive of my own; but Gusev is an experimental, not a theoretical physicist, and his father lives in the country and is the very incarnation of folk wisdom. Romm tried to give a behind-the-scenes view of a nuclear research institute, the emotional and the psychological implications of working on peaceful (and hidden military) applications of thermonuclear energy. I began by liking the film, but I now find it marred by the artificiality of its plot. For Romm himself, the film seems to have been a transition from *Lenin in October* to his marvelous and thrilling *Ordinary Fascism* [see p. 471].

The film's central episode has Gusev irradiated by neutrons from the experimental thermonuclear unit—a remote possibility, then and now.

In 1950, we hoped to have the MTR operational within ten, at most fifteen, years. (Tamm and I were among the "hotheads" of the LIPAN staff; Artsimovich and Leontovich were more cautious.) More than thirty years have passed since then, years of intensive work by hundreds of gifted researchers worldwide, conducting numerous experiments under a wide variety of conditions and carrying out copious, often extremely sophisticated and profound theoretical research. And it is only now that a reasonable claim can be made that tokamak-type systems and the behavior of plasma in inhomogeneous magnetic fields are understood to an extent that provides more than an intuitive hope that such systems will one day be practicable. Certainty, however, demands a successful experimental demonstration, and we can only hope that this will happen in the coming decade.

The commission's report prompted the Council of Ministers to pass a resolution entrusting the work on the MTR problem to LIPAN. Lev Artsimovich was made executive director; Mikhail Leontovich was in charge of theoretical work. Tamm and I, as authors of the proposal, were made standing consultants. (It was understood that our principal responsibility continued to be the development of a thermonuclear charge.) Artsimovich and Leontovich played a vital role in all the subsequent work. Artsimovich had already acquired experience with plasmas in his work on electromagnetic methods of isotope separation. Even more important were his impressive general knowledge of physics, his excellent command of experimental techniques and theory, and his sharp, skeptical, but pragmatic intellect. Artsimovich played a crucial role in pushing through the decision to use the tokamak model as the basis for our research. As for Leontovich, no better director for the theoretical work could have been found. Dubious as he was that it would ever succeed, he still did everything in his power to make it happen. He was demanding but paternal in his relationship with co-workers, and entirely selfless. The enormous accomplishments in the theoretical physics of MTR's plasma would have been impossible without him.

A few weeks after the commission met, I was summoned by Beria. I had been in No. 13, Beria's Kremlin office, once before, as part of a large group headed by "senior men" (Vannikov and Kurchatov). I'd be there again with them many more times. A typical visit might go like this. After arriving in Moscow, I would be "on call"—sometimes for as long as a week—until the signal arrived from our Directorate: "You're wanted upstairs." We would assemble and set off for the Kremlin in a group. After receiving passes, we would go through several checkpoints: as one officer scrutinized our passports and passes, another would stare watchfully at our faces for any suspicious expression. As a matter of course, they would ask if we had any weapons in our possession, but there was never any search.

This time, I went alone. In Beria's waiting room I found Oleg Lavrentiev, who had been recalled from the navy. We were invited in together to see Beria. Beria was seated as usual at the head of the conference table, wearing his pince-nez, with a light-colored raincloak draped over his shoulders. Sitting beside him was his personal aide, Makhnev, former head of a camp in Kolyma. Later, after Beria's fall, Makhnev became head of our ministry's information department, and the ministry as a whole became known as a "preserve" for Beria's former associates.

With a manner that verged on the ingratiating, Beria asked me what I thought of Lavrentiev's proposal. I restated my opinion. Beria put a few questions to Lavrentiev, whom he then dismissed. I never saw Lavrentiev again. I know that he enrolled in some physics department or radio physics institute in the Ukraine and went to work at LIPAN when he graduated. But within a month, he became embroiled in serious differences of opinion with all of his LIPAN co-workers, and he returned to the Ukraine. I received a letter from him in the 1970s in which he wrote that he was a senior staff member in an applied-science research institute and asked me to send him documentation of his 1950 proposal and my favorable evaluation of it at the time. Having nothing on hand, I wrote from memory and then had the letter officially notarized at the FIAN office. For some reason, that first letter did not arrive, and Lavrentiev asked me to send a second one, which I did. I heard no more about him. Perhaps back in the 1950s Lavrentiev should have been given his own small laboratory and a free hand—but the people at LIPAN believed that this would only lead to trouble.

After Lavrentiev left, Beria asked me how the MTR work was going at Kurchatov's institute. I answered the question. Beria rose as a sign that our conversation was over, but then suddenly asked: "Is there anything you want to ask me?"

I was absolutely unprepared for such a blanket offer. Spontaneously, without hesitating, I asked: "Why are our new projects moving so slowly? Why do we always lag behind the USA and other countries, why are we losing the technology race?"

I don't know what sort of answer I expected. Twenty years later, when Turchin, Medvedev, and I posed that same question in our Letter [see p. 300], we answered that insufficiently democratic institutions and a lack of intellectual freedom and free exchange of information were to blame. At the time, however, I wasn't thinking consciously of such matters. Beria gave a pragmatic answer:

"Because we lack R and D and a manufacturing base. Everything relies on a single supplier, 'Elektrosyla.' The Americans have hundreds of companies with large manufacturing facilities."

(This sort of answer, of course, held no interest for me.) Beria offered me his hand. It was plump, slightly moist, and deathly cold. Only then, I think, did I realize that I was face to face with a terrifying human being. It hadn't entered my mind before, and I had been completely free in my manner. At my parents' house that evening, I talked about my meeting with Beria, and their fear made me conscious—perhaps for the first time—of my own reaction.

Unfortunately, I was not to take an active part in later work on the magnetic thermonuclear reactor. The theoretical research rapidly surpassed the level of my expertise in 1950–1951, and any work I could have done would have been amateurish. As I've said, many types of plasma instability were found, a flood of unpleasant discoveries that only began to dry up toward the end of the 1960s. At the same time, there were many new inventions which gave the impression of an ever-increasing range of possibilities. The first of these apparently was the "Probkotron" ["Plugatron"] a linear system with magnetic "plugs" (a so-called mirror machine) devised by Andrei Budker. A great number of electromagnetic fusion devices were proposed in the USA and other countries; these included Lyman Spitzer Jr.'s stellarator [1951], another toroidal system. Special attention was accorded methods of suppressing instabilities. The supply of ideas and inventions here was copious—maybe even greater than the supply of instabilities. Right up until 1968, when I broke from (or was broken from) MSM (the Ministry of Medium Machine Building, as our agency was known after 1953 or 1954), I maintained very close scientific and personal contact with Artsimovich and Leontovich's group at LIPAN and, to a lesser extent, with the other groups. I was personally acquainted with nearly all the theorists working under Leontovich's tactful yet confident direction, and with a great many of the experimentalists. I valued their skill and inventiveness and the untiring enthusiasm that allowed them to persevere in that marathon scientific effort and to survive the dashing of their initial, overly optimistic hopes. Selflessly and persistently, they worked on, gradually approaching their goal, at the same time enriching the science of plasma physics. (Space programs were another important stimulus to the research in plasma physics.)

Kurchatov considered research on the MTR to be of great importance, and early on, he came to the conclusion that it was vital that it be conducted openly, with close international cooperation. He had the chance to make that dream come true in 1956, when a visit by Khrushchev and Bulganin to Great Britain was in the works (Khrushchev was traveling officially, as a member of the Presidium of the Supreme Soviet). Khrushchev proposed that Kurchatov accompany them and that he give a paper at Harwell, the British atomic center. Kurchatov chose to speak on Soviet work on fast-neutron breeder reactors and on MTR. By that time, Andrei Leipunsky had been running the work on breeder reactors for several years, and a technologically realistic solution to the breeding problem (using a basic isotope of uranium) looked promising within a few years. Though similar work was being done in a number of countries at that time, we had cause for pride in this area of such great significance for nuclear energy of the future. Kurchatov had worked with Artsimovich on his MTR paper (and perhaps with Leontovich and others as well); Tamm and I were also recruited for this task. The paper had as its formal basis the reports Tamm and I had prepared in 1951, as well as the numerous theoretical and experimental reports done at LIPAN between 1951 and 1956. These and other reports were subsequently published in *Proceedings* of the First United Nations Conference on the Peaceful Use of Atomic Energy (the First Geneva Conference).[2] Kurchatov's talk, especially the part dealing with MTR, made a great impression on the audience, and later on the international scientific community and the world as a whole. Research on controlled thermonuclear reactions apparently was already under way in some other countries, but it was all highly classified and the scope of the work and the hopes vested in it were minimal. I still don't know the details of that work; I was aware only of an article published by the Englishmen Cousins and Ware (in 1951, if I am not mistaken). In this experiment, electromagnetic impulses were used to excite a circular plasma discharge in a glass toroid. The authors wrote that similar research might make it possible to carry out a controlled thermonuclear reaction in deuterium. By the time we became aware of this article, many similar experiments had already been conducted at LIPAN. Cousins and Ware's work made no mention at all of toroidal winding. We were under the impression that this was the work of independent inventors; to us, it was already clear that MTR work required a very different approach—project-oriented collaboration by a large group of experimentalists, theorists, and engineers.

As a result of Kurchatov's initiative, work on controlled thermonuclear reactions remains open and unclassified throughout the world. Close international cooperation is the rule: there have been numerous international conferences, and exchanges have enabled scientists and engineers to visit and conduct research in laboratories in other countries. This highly successful international cooperation provided a model for the system of international scientific cooperation that took shape in the 1960s and 1970s. Science's very nature is international, and scientists readily took advantage of the opportunities afforded by this new climate. Benefits to scientific progress and to efforts to solve the problems facing humanity at this difficult and critical juncture, with the very future of civilization at stake, were obvious.

But [in the years 1975–1985] cooperation was threatened and the existing system began to unravel when the Soviet authorities sentenced Yuri Orlov to twelve years in camp and stripped him of membership in the Armenian Academy of Sciences; they arrested Anatoly Shcharansky and Sergei Kovalev; and exiled the author of these lines to Gorky.

In 1960–1961, I advanced another proposal concerning a controlled ther-

2[Geneva, 1956.]

monuclear reaction. Reports had just been received that in the United States, Theodore Maiman had created the first ruby laser. I gave a report at the Installation arguing the possibility of using a laser to ignite a thermonuclear reaction in pellets containing thermonuclear fuel. According to my report, these pellets would implode when their surface was heated by a laser impulse, due to hydrodynamic effects. My first estimates of the parameters necessary to initiate the reaction, given in this report, were refined in a series of computer calculations performed by colleagues of mine, in particular, Nikita Popov. Fields where this principle might be applied, I said, included energy generation and thermonuclear impulse-propulsion engines for spacecraft of the future. My ideas became known to laser specialists in other institutions, as well as to my co-workers at the Installation. Wide-scale research is now under way in the USSR, the USA, and other countries on methods to initiate thermonuclear reaction by compression of the fuel with laser beams or with powerful pulsed electron beams. But it still seems to me that for large-scale power generation the most promising systems are those based on magnetic confinement (of the tokamak or perhaps the stellarator type, although the latter strikes me as less likely). I feel that first will come breeder systems, with fusion used to produce fuel for the fission reaction, which will produce electrical energy. As for systems that do not use uranium or thorium (reserves of which are not unlimited, and which pose a certain ecological hazard in storage of their radioactive fission products and the release of radioactive gases), I see them being based on tritium breeding, since reactors that run on pure deuterium will always be a second choice after those that use the deuterium-tritium reaction, whose cross section [reaction probability] is nearly one hundred times larger than that of deuterium alone.

Tritium will be "bred" as the result of deuterium-deuterium reaction. It can also be produced by bombarding lithium-6 or deuterium with neutrons, perhaps in conjunction with neutron breeding, if fissionable and other elements are used in the reactor. Needless to say, the above arguments represent only the private opinions of (at this point) something of an "amateur."

In 1951–1952 I proposed two designs to produce super-strong pulse magnetic fields and electric currents by using the energy of explosion. The designs were subsequently named MK-1 and MK-2, where MK is the Russian acronym for "magnetic cumulation." Certain modifications of those designs were later proposed by other authors, but all of them use the same basic principle: the full magnetic flux of the field generated by a coil carrying current does not change if the coil is rapidly deformed. Should the deformation lead to the decrease in the coil's inductance, the energy of the magnetic field will increase.

This is possible only if the coil is deformed by external forces, in case of MK by the pressure created by the explosion. The simplest MK-1 system (depicted in Fig. 9) is a hollow metal cylinder compressed by pressure from the products of an explosion. The explosive charge is placed outside the metal cylinder; the initial magnetic field in the hollow interior is directed along the axis of the cylinder. The action of the device can be visualized as the compression (the gathering or "cumulation") of a bunch of magnetic force lines by the moving metal walls of the cylinder (hence, "magnetic cumulation").

In an ideal case, disregarding the finite electric resistance of the cylinder and the losses of magnetic flux, the magnetic field and its energy grow as the cylinder's interior radius decreases at a rate inversely proportional to the square of the radius. An experimental group formed at the Installation to verify these ideas conducted the first MK-1 experiment in May 1952, while the more complex MK-2 (see Fig. 10) system was tested toward the end of the year. The group was headed by Ekaterina Feoktistova, an experienced and innovative specialist in "gas dynamics," as we called work with explosions. For some reason she dubbed me "the Martian"—an "exotic" and to my mind rather flattering nickname. (In 1983, when *Izvestia* published an article attacking me signed by four academicians [see p. 584], Feoktistova wrote me an abusive letter.) Among the younger workers, I had an especially close and friendly relationship with Robert Lyudaev and Yuri Plyushchev, a former member of the theoretical department. Georgy Tsirkov, Alexandra Chivileva, and Evgeny Zharinov also took part in these first experiments. (Lyudaev and Plyushchev continued to work on MK at least until 1968, and probably beyond then.) I remember my first visit to the test area in May 1952. The explosions were detonated in a clearing surrounded by young birches and aspens with tender young leaves. Shell fragments tore the bark off many trees, leaving a wartime

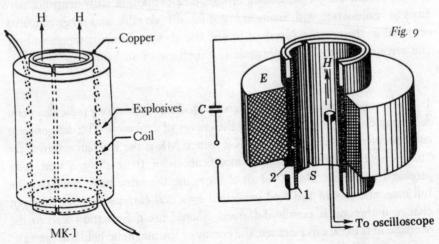

Fig. 9

MK-1

picture of a battlefield forest. I went down into the bunker, which served to protect people and the recording equipment from the explosion. There I saw Robert Lyudaev, Yuri Plyushchev and Evgeny Zharinov (possibly only one of the latter two) squatting around a small stove on which a teapot was being heated. They didn't offer me tea—they were using the teapot to melt the explosive, which they then poured into waiting molds. Their treatment of the substance, a tiny amount of which could blow off a hand, or do even worse damage, seemed rather cavalier, but they knew what they were doing, and the operation was basically safe. Lyudaev told me right away about an improvement they had made in the design of MK-1 (his idea, I think): a slanted cut made in the wall of the metal cylinder to allow the magnetic field to enter the cylinder. Without that cut, the initial magnetic field created by the outer windings would be too slow in penetrating the cylinder's conductive walls. During the explosion, the cut would slam shut, leaving no trace. This simple idea contributed considerably to the success of all the experiments.

Twilight was already falling when I left the bunker. Delighting in the forest's moist spring air, I walked along the narrow path to the road where the car was waiting. I probably didn't go home since we were very busy preparing for the test scheduled for the following year.

THE FIRST TEST of the MK-1 in May had already produced a record magnetic field: 1.5 million Gauss. In 1964, using MK-2 to feed the MK-1's winding, a field of 25 million Gauss was achieved, the pressure of this field being equal to 25 million kilograms per square centimeter. Magnetic cumulation offers a broad range of possibilities for research on the properties of matter in super-strong magnetic fields and/or under super-high pressures (without heating the matter with shock waves, crucial in the evaluation of these experiments). Published results are still few, apparently due to the difficulties that experiments with explosives entail. Recently it has been reported that American researchers had used this method to successfully carry out a phase transition of hydrogen to a metallic form. (So far, it seems this report has not been corroborated.) The MK-2 system is an impulse source of a very strong current (in relatively small devices, the energy of 1 kg of explosives can be turned into the energy of a magnetic field, with the current reaching 100 to 200 million amperes). It has applications in many technical problems. One of my own publications describes an electrocannon which fires an aluminum ring at a speed of 100 km per second.

In those years, the MK's most important scientific application seemed to me the creation of impulse accelerators for elementary particles with high energies and beam intensities. I proposed a two-stage system. At the first stage the

Fig. 10

windings of an iron-free inductive accelerator (of the betatron type) are fed by the impulse current generated by MK-2. At the second stage the windings of the accelerator are compressed by an explosion, which further increases the energy of accelerated particles. For an accelerator with even higher performance the energy has to be supplied by either nuclear or thermonuclear explosion (of course, the entire experiment must take place underground). This grandiose project was not realized. The main objection was that it was not cost-effective to create such expensive devices for one-time use. Experimentation traditionally requires a number of adjustments or variations of experimental conditions before worthwhile results are obtained. The entire experimental program often ends up being rearranged. It seemed to me, however, that one-time systems with record characteristics might also provide very valuable scientific information; in fact, I still wouldn't rule out the possibility that at some point it might become necessary to return to the impulse MK accelerator.

The first purely theoretical publication on MK, by Professor Yakov Terletsky, appeared in the Soviet press in 1957, and contained a proposal for a system very like MK-1. I later learned that the idea of using the energy of an explosion to obtain superstrong magnetic fields had been suggested earlier by Academician Vladimir Arkadiev, a professor at Moscow University. Others may well have expressed these ideas independently. MK only became practicable after experience had been acquired during World War II of dealing with cumulative explosive charges and explosive "lenses," and then with implosive charges (i.e., charges where the movement is directed toward the axis or center of symmetry). The Installation, and institutions like it, were the best place for this kind of project, since here 99 percent of the work is in implementation of the idea.

In contrast to our work on MTR, all MK work remained classified until the mid-1960s. The first foreign publications (with a description of an MK-1-type system) appeared in 1964. It was only with great effort that we managed to secure permission to publish an article containing descriptions of our initial ideas and basic experimental results; signed by the chief contributors to the work in the years between 1952 and 1965, this appeared in 1965 in *Reports of the Academy of Science*.[3] The Institute of Atomic Energy, which was identified as the authors' workplace, soon received an invitation from Professor Knoepfel in Italy for a conference to be held in September 1965 on superstrong magnetic fields generated by explosions.

We decided to seek permission to attend and deliver a paper. This simple request caused great complications. In the summer of 1965, I attended a session at the Ministry at which there was discussion of our draft report which contained certain insignificant additions to our note in the *Reports of the Academy of Science*, that had all been carefully considered from the viewpoint of secrecy. The session was chaired by Deputy Minister Alferov, who announced that the Ministry objected to sending a paper which exceeded the boundaries of the published text. Khariton, the Installation's scientific director, rose and replied that a committee under his chairmanship had come to the conclusion that the paper revealed no state secrets and should be cleared; it would enhance the prestige of Soviet science. Alferov responded with a smirk: "Not that we'd support any opinion Comrade Khariton might espouse . . ."

[3] A. D. Sakharov, R. Z. Lyudaev, E. N. Smirnov, Yu. N. Plyushchev, A. I. Pavlovsky, V. K. Chernyshev, E. A. Feoktistova, E. I. Zharinov, Yu. A. Zysin, "Magnetic Cumulation," *Doklady AN SSSR*, 165, 1 (1965).

Khariton flushed—Alferov's words were a public slap in the face—but held his tongue.

A few years earlier, I'd had occasion to speak with Alferov, who was then working at the Installation: "It's a good thing to show strength [or to be strong, I don't remember]," he'd told me. "I recall that just before our troops entered Vyborg, the newspapers were writing all kinds of goddamned nonsense about us; Russians couldn't go outside without being insulted and beaten up. But as soon as the Red Army entered Vyborg, everything changed. Those same newspapers started writing about cooperation, and the Finns started doffing their caps."

We had initially proposed that Alexander Pavlovsky, Vladimir Chernyshev, and I attend the conference, but I decided to withdraw; I felt that with my level of clearance, significantly higher than that of my younger colleagues, I had no hope whatsoever of receiving permission for the trip. In retrospect, this seems an error. But I had no desire to go through all the wearisome and time-consuming stages of seeking permission (the forms, references, medical examinations, etc.), all to no avail. Moreover, and this is the main reason, I was depressed because I would only be allowed to speak about matters covered in the published article, which would make me feel like an idiot. Politburo members were polled by telephone on the issue of granting permission to Pavlovsky and Chernyshev. A memorandum had been submitted by KGB head Semichastny, who objected strongly to the trip, and permission was denied. If I had headed the group, it might have been granted permission, so long as the requisite number of KGB officers accompanied us. Who knows? In the period before I withdrew, the overt KGB tail on me was beefed up considerably. (A funny incident: I'd stuffed some papers with unimportant, innocent formulas into my galoshes to make them fit; these were removed and confiscated. I was obviously being pushed to give up the trip.)

Moscow physicists who attended the conference (which took place in Frascatti, near Rome) later told me that the American scientist Willy Fowler had come from Los Alamos; he'd received permission to attend when Knoepfel told him that I'd probably be there. Fowler arrived with his two daughters—and, I believe, some FBI agents.

Late in 1965, I was given permission to publish a review article on MK in the journal *Progress in the Physical Sciences*. It appeared in April 1966,[4] along with a reprint of a *Scientific American* article by Francis Bitter describing American achievements. Vladimir Orlov, a well-known author of many popular-science books, came to see me that same year (1966), after which he

---

[4]["Magnetoplosive Generators," *Usp. Fiz. Nauk.* 88, No. 4 (1966).]

published a long article in *Pravda* on magnetic cumulation and its prospects.

Magnetic cumulation undoubtedly has important scientific and practical possibilities. I continued taking an active part in MK work until 1968. After being removed from secret work, however, I lost contact with the MK group, and have absolutely no idea what has been going on in that area.

I recently learned indirectly that a grave illness had befallen one of my young colleagues in that work, Robert Lyudaev. I still see him as he was that day thirty years ago on the test site, vigorous and healthy and filled with hope.

10

BEFORE THE TEST

BETWEEN 1950 and 1953, the Installation and many associated organizations and enterprises committed a significant part of their resources to preparations for testing our first thermonuclear charge. The work included experimental and theoretical research into the gas dynamics of explosions, research in nuclear physics, design engineering, the development of control and electrical systems for the device, and the development of special instruments and new techniques for monitoring the physical processes taking place during an explosion and determining its power. The manufacture of the substances needed for the device and all the other production and technical work required an enormous expenditure of manpower and resources.

The theoretical groups played a key role in the first thermonuclear test (as also in later tests). They established the main directions of research, studied the explosion process, investigated possible variants of the devices, and supervised detailed calculations of the explosion parameters for selected models. The actual numerical calculations were performed by secret mathematical teams in several scientific research institutes in Moscow.

It was necessary first of all to develop calculation methods that would not be nullified by the small errors that were bound to occur, and that would still, without an inordinate amount of work, yield sufficiently precise results. The computations themselves were straightforward, almost mechanical, but extremely time-consuming. At first, they were performed by brigades of human operators using electric calculators; later by computers. The vacuum tubes of the first Soviet computer models were replaced by transistors as the demands of a rich and powerful customer (our use of computers accelerated after 1953) stimulated the development of new generations of computers with superior speed, memory, logical capacity, and peripherals. (Rocket and space research provided other "wealthy" customers for computers.)

The theoretical groups were also responsible in most instances for assigning tasks to other departments at the Installation and affiliated organizations, coordinating their work, and analyzing their results.

The functioning of the theoretical groups can be illustrated by a brief description of our nuclear physics program. Research was pursued along two separate tracks. On one, a number of groups at the Installation and elsewhere measured the probabilities (cross sections) of elementary nuclear processes; these were subjected to theoretical manipulation and then employed in calculations. For example, the cross section for the deuterium-deuterium or deuterium-tritium fusion was used to calculate the rates for thermonuclear reactions at various temperatures.

On the second track, in the Installation's experimental groups, researchers tried to simulate nuclear processes in geometric configurations similar to those of the actual devices. (FIKOBIN was an example of such a working model.) I developed a close working relationship with Yuri Zysin, the director of one of these groups; I would visit his laboratory at least once a month. It was a world apart—high-voltage equipment, flickering lights on the decoders, and metal gleaming mysteriously with a play of violet color. (In documents of the period, that metal—uranium—is designated by an arcane combination of letters and numbers.) Zysin's colleagues worked in shifts, but they would all turn up when they knew I was coming, and we would discuss the results of their experiments in a calm, friendly, unhurried manner until nine or so in the evening. (In the 1980s, after I was exiled to Gorky, Alexander Lbov, one of the young scientists in Zysin's group, resurfaced in my life by sending an abusive letter condemning my appeal to the Pugwash Conference.)

Zysin and I saw each other socially as well as during business hours. We were next-door neighbors, and Zysin's older son was the same age as my second daughter, Lyuba. The friendship was especially important to Klava, who felt quite isolated at the Installation. Often we all went skiing together. In March and April Yuri would strip to the waist during our excursions and acquire a deep tan. (I have kept a photo of our two families emerging from the forest: Klava and Irina, Yuri's wife, are laughing as they pack snowballs.)

Sometimes Zysin would tell stories about his life before the war, his military service, and the first postwar years at LIPAN. At a seminar there, he had outlined the principle of "hard focus" in accelerator design, but at that time the specialists in the field did not appreciate his idea and "proved" that such a thing could not exist. Today, no one would think of building a large accelerator without applying the hard-focus principle, which allows for dramatic reduction in the size of the vacuum chamber and, therefore, in the weight of the magnet, with savings of tens of millions of rubles, if not more.

I had frequent dealings with the gas dynamics researchers, and also, to a lesser degree, with the design groups. My relations with them became much closer later on, when we were working on the Third Idea.

IN THE FALL of 1952, Viktor Davidenko, director of one of the sectors at the Installation, Zysin, and I were sent to a Leningrad research institute where extensive preparatory work was underway for radiochemical monitoring of the forthcoming thermonuclear test. I had a vision of Leningrad, inspired by all I'd read and heard, and my first visit more than lived up to it. I did not see Leningrad again until 1971, when I went there with Lusia. On my 1952 trip, I had a chance to see Protopopov, whom I'd known since Ulyanovsk. He was working at the institute we visited, but he was very ill and died soon afterward.

In November 1952, the U.S. detonated a powerful device at Eniwetok. A few days later, just about the time the radioactive debris from the test, carried by high-altitude winds, was likely to reach our longitudes, there was a heavy snowfall at the Installation, the first of the year. Either Davidenko or I suggested that we take advantage of this opportunity to learn something about American thermonuclear explosives. We drove out of town and brought back several large cardboard cartons full of wet, newly fallen snow, and then began procedures to concentrate any radioactive fallout. We expected to find elements specific to one type or another of thermonuclear charge (beryllium-7, uranium-237, etc.). Unfortunately, one of the chemists who was apparently emotionally upset over some personal matter absentmindedly poured our concentrate down the drain. The whole affair appeared to escape the notice of the administration.

Thirty years have passed since that incident. I am sitting in Gorky, writing my memoirs—or, rather, reconstructing them after their theft. It is again the beginning of November [1982] and the first damp snow has fallen. That's one thing that hasn't changed.

TENSION INCREASED at the Installation as the test date approached. In the summer of 1952, if memory does not fail, we were having trouble producing a particular material needed for the device. Nikolai Pavlov, a colonel (or possibly by then a general) in the KGB and an official in the First Main Directorate, was responsible for its production. A choice had to be made: the old method made use of a plant that had been built for another purpose, while the alternative required a specially designed facility to take advantage of a new, much more promising technology. Pavlov, in an attempt either to play it safe or to economize by using the existing plant, decided to combine both methods, and failed to meet the planned output.

Someone raised this matter at a conference which I attended. Beria, apparently briefed in advance, rose and said something like this: "When we Bolsheviks want to get something done, we close our eyes to everything else [here Beria screwed his eyes shut, so that his face seemed even more frightening]. Pavlov, you've lost your Bolshevik edge. We won't punish you now, and I hope you'll correct the error. But don't forget—we have plenty of room in our prisons."

Beria growled the word "prisons" threateningly, and his use of the formal style of address had a sinister ring. Pavlov sat in silence, his head bowed (as did everyone else). He did not show up at work that afternoon, which surprised no one. Needless to say, Pavlov completely revised his ideas and gave up the old method.

Pavlov was one of the more important officials in the second echelon of the First Main Directorate. In 1937 or 1938, he had been recalled from his final year at the university (I believe he was studying chemistry) and put to work as an investigator in state security. At that time, Beria was totally overhauling the security organs. He had most of the staff he had inherited from Ezhov arrested, and many NKVD officers perished in the camps together with their own victims. Pavlov proved suited to his new work, and quickly rose to the top. I won't hazard a guess about his methods: he used to say that he never resorted to physical violence; the fierce gaze of his dark eyes alone sufficed to make enemies of the state confess to all their crimes. He was chief of state security for the Saratov region in 1942, at the time when the internationally known geneticist Nikolai Vavilov was starving to death in Saratov Prison. (Leontovich noted this coincidence with a bit of black humor: "Pavlov's connection to science is longstanding.") That fall, he was promoted and became head of counterintelligence on the Stalingrad front, a crucial post.

Twenty years later, David Fishman, an acquaintance of mine, was traveling with Pavlov through the region where the latter had served during the war. They were standing on the platform of the railway car, smoking. Pavlov stared at the endless, dismal salt-marsh steppe, sparsely dotted with stunted bushes, and then all of a sudden, apparently overcome by memories, broke his silence and began to speak of the past. Fishman refused to tell me exactly what Pavlov said—he let slip only that it was terrifying beyond belief.

At the beginning of 1943, on orders from Beria, Pavlov was appointed representative of the Central Committee and Council of Ministers at Laboratory No. 2 (which later became LIPAN, and then the Institute of Atomic Energy). Kurchatov was named scientific director at the same time. Pavlov became an "atomic expert," again displaying his exceptional competence, both organizational and administrative, as well as an understanding of the scientific and engineering aspects involved.

I met him after he had joined the First Main Directorate. He was a sturdy man with a ruddy complexion, slick, blue-black hair, and very dark eyes set in a bright, good-looking, energetic face. He was on the short side, but he moved briskly, spoke loudly, and laughed heartily. He possessed inexhaustible energy and a great capacity for work, never forgot a detail, and knew everyone. He was extremely well disposed and respectful toward me. Once, in my presence, he told a large company: "Sakharov is our gold reserve."

Tamm liked capable people, and he was fond of Pavlov at first. But on one occasion, when Tamm requested his help in recruiting young specialists, Pavlov asked: "How come you've got all Jews here? Why not some good Russians?" After that, Tamm's admiration cooled noticeably.

Pavlov was made a general in the KGB at the age of thirty-four; not without pride, he would boast that he and Napoleon were the youngest generals in history. Beria's fall dealt a serious blow to Pavlov's career, but he managed to recover.

In the mid-1950s, when I started to worry about the biological consequences of the testing, Pavlov said to me: "The struggle between the forces of imperialism and communism is a struggle to the death. The future of mankind, the fate and happiness of tens of billions of people, alive now and yet to be born, depend on the outcome of that struggle. We must be strong in order to win. If our work and our testing are giving us strength for that battle—and they certainly are—then the victims of that testing, or any other victims, don't matter."

Was Pavlov sincere, or was he just indulging in wild rhetoric? I would say, both. But in any case, such reasoning is wrong in principle. We know too little about the laws of history. The future is unpredictable. We are not gods. We should apply ethical standards to all our actions, no matter how large or small, rather than relying on the abstract arithmetic of history. The moral imperative is categorical: "Thou shalt not kill."

The last time I saw Pavlov was at the unveiling of Kurchatov's monument in 1971. He was then director of a small but important plant in the Ministry of Medium Machine Building. He walked over and said: "I wish you success in all your endeavors." He was well aware that I was no longer building bombs—I really don't know what he meant by his remark.

AT THE SAME meeting where Beria threatened Pavlov, there was a discussion about sending Academician Mikhail Lavrentiev and Alexander Ilyushin, a corresponding member of the Academy, to the Installation as "reinforcements." Beria nodded in approval when he heard Ilyushin's name, evidently one familiar to him. Kirill Shchelkin, Khariton's deputy and a man experienced in organizational matters, told me afterward that Lavrentiev and Ilyushin had been sent to the Installation as potential replacements for the current chiefs. If the test failed, they were to take over at once; if it succeeded, they would replace some of us later on.

Lavrentiev kept a low profile and soon quit the Installation. Ilyushin behaved differently. He sent for several colleagues (with the doctoral degrees that some of us lacked; a point was made of that) and set up a sort of shadow opposition. At each meeting of the scientific staff, Ilyushin would call attention to another flaw in our work that would inevitably lead to failure. Ilyushin did not lack intelligence or experience, but he tended to make mountains out of molehills and apparently wanted to be in a position to say "I told you so" if the test failed (and in that case, we might well have tripped over his molehills and broken our necks).

At a session of the Scientific Council, Ilyushin's troublemaking upset me so much that I blurted out: "Ilyushin is trying to prove something to us. But if we use our brains, things won't turn out the way he predicts." From then on, Zeldovich was fond of saying: "Let's apply the Sakharov principle—let's use our brains. . . ."

Ilyushin lived alone in one of the cottages with a huge dog, and at night they would roam the deserted streets together. His star fell after Beria's ouster. Shchelkin, and possibly Khariton as well, never forgave him for what he had put them through. He was not even permitted to observe the test—a slap in the face for someone of his rank.

11

1953

NINETEEN FIFTY-THREE will be remembered by the world at large as the year of Stalin's death and the aftershocks which followed it, but for us at the Installation it was also the year of our first thermonuclear test.

Stalin's final months were ominous. In early 1953, the Soviet press began hammering away at the "Doctors' Plot": a group of physicians in the Kremlin Hospital, nearly all Jews, had supposedly committed several well-disguised medical murders of Party and government officials, including Alexander Shcherbakov and Andrei Zhdanov, and had begun plotting the assassination of Stalin. The investigation ostensibly had been triggered by a letter from Lydia Timashuk, also a physician in the hospital (and no doubt a secret KGB collaborator). In fact, however, everyone who had lived through the campaigns of the 1930s quickly understood that the Doctors' Plot was a wide-ranging anti-Jewish provocation, an extension of the chauvinist "anti-cosmopolitan campaign" directed against Jews and foreigners, a continuation of anti-Semitic atrocities like the 1948 murder of Solomon Mikhoels and the 1952 execution of Perets Markish and other Yiddish-language writers.

After Stalin's death we heard that trains had been assembled in the beginning of March to transport Jews to Siberia and that propaganda justifying their deportation had been set in type, including a lead article for *Pravda* entitled: "The Russian People Are Rescuing the Jewish People." The article was rumored to be the work of Dmitri Chesnokov, whom Stalin in 1952 placed on the Presidium of the Central Committee (Stalin enlarged the Presidium at that time after he began to distrust its members). Meetings were held everywhere to denounce the medical murderers and their accomplices, and a number of Jewish physicians were fired. The campaign at the Installation was muted, but I know of at least one dismissal (that of the ophthalmologist Dr. Katsenelenson, husband of my university classmate Lena Feldman), and there may have been more. Passions grew more frenzied with each passing day, and people began to fear that pogroms were in the offing.

Yves Farge, a French author and politician, arrived in Moscow in early 1953 to accept a Stalin Prize. His request to see the detained physicians was granted, and during his meeting with them he inquired how they were being treated. Naturally, they answered that they were being treated very well, but one of them rolled back his sleeve and silently displayed the marks of torture. Shaken, Farge rushed off to Stalin, who may well have issued an order to prevent this overly curious man from leaving the USSR. In any event, a few weeks later, Yves Farge died in suspicious circumstances in the Caucasus. (I have never been able to confirm my suspicion of foul play, but a few years later, when I mentioned Farge's fate to Slavsky and other top officials, no one said a word.)[1]

In January or early February, I witnessed a revealing incident in the Installation's VIP dining room. I was sitting within earshot of Pavlov and Kurchatov when a report came over the radio that unidentified terrorists had thrown bombs at the Soviet mission in Tel Aviv. I glanced at Pavlov and saw his face light up. "That's what those Jews are like!" he exclaimed. "They hurt us here and abroad. But now we'll show them!" Kurchatov said nothing, and his mustache and beard masked his expression.

Some people believe that the Doctors' Plot was intended as a prelude to a wide-ranging terror like that of 1937, affecting top government and Party officials, and that Stalin's associates sensed the danger hanging over their heads. Such an assumption lends plausibility to Avtorkhanov's theory that top Party officials had a hand in Stalin's death, although the tenor of Khrushchev's account suggests that he died of natural causes.[2]

It is now widely believed that Stalin's death occurred several days before it was reported on March 5, but the announcement certainly came as a complete shock. We realized that things would change, but in what direction? People feared the situation would deteriorate—but how could it get any worse? Some, including those who harbored no illusions about Stalin and the regime, worried about a general collapse, internecine strife, another wave of mass repressions,

[1][In *The Fellow-Travellers* (Macmillan, 1973), p. 292, David Caute reports that Farge "was killed driving from Gori to Tbilisi in a chauffeur-driven car. The rumour went about that this had been no accident. But in fact the car had hit a stationary lorry and his wife, who was with him, emerged unscathed, which makes the insinuation look extremely improbable."]

[2][In his book *Zagadka smerti Stalina* (The Riddle of Stalin's Death, 1976), Abdurakhman Avtorkhanov deduces from indirect evidence that Stalin was the victim of a plot by Malenkov and Beria. For Khrushchev's account of Stalin's death, see *Khrushchev Remembers* (Little, Brown, 1970), pp. 316–320.]

even civil war. Tamm brought his wife to the Installation in the belief that at such times it was safer to be as far from Moscow as possible.

Downtown Moscow was invaded by hundreds of thousands of Soviet citizens who wanted to view Stalin's body laid out in the Hall of Columns. The authorities hadn't expected this surge of people; in the unwonted absence of orders from above, they failed to take timely security measures, and hundreds of people, possibly thousands, were killed in the crush.

A few days later, in the corridors of power things got sorted out—if only briefly—and we learned that Malenkov was the new chairman of the Council of Ministers. (I recall Zeldovich's remarking: "Decisions like that aren't made for one year; they're made for thirty. . . ." In Malenkov's case, he was wrong.)

People roamed the streets, distraught and confused, with funeral music constantly sounding in the background. I too got carried away at the time. In a letter to Klava, obviously intended for her eyes only, I wrote: "I am under the influence of a great man's death. I am thinking of his humanity."

I can't vouch for that last word; but it was something of the sort. Very soon I would be blushing every time I recalled these sentiments of mine. I can't fully explain it—after all, I knew quite enough about the horrible crimes that had been committed—the arrests of innocent people, the torture, the deliberate starvation, and all the violence—to pass judgment on those responsible. But I hadn't put the whole picture together, and in any case, there was still a lot I didn't know. Somewhere at the back of my mind the idea existed, instilled by propaganda, that suffering is inevitable during great historic upheavals: "When you chop wood, the chips fly." I was also affected by the general mourning and by a sense of death's universal dominion. I was more impressionable than I care to recall.

But above all, I felt myself committed to the goal which I assumed was Stalin's as well: after a devastating war, to make the country strong enough to ensure peace. Precisely because I had invested so much of myself in that cause and accomplished so much, I needed, as anyone might in my circumstances, to create an illusory world, to justify myself. (Of course, I am exaggerating a bit to make my point.) I soon banished Stalin from that world (it seems likely that I admitted him to it only for a limited time and to a limited extent under the influence of those disjointed, emotion-packed days following his death). But the state, the nation, and the ideals of communism remained intact for me. It was years before I fully understood the degree to which deceit, exploitation, and outright fraud were involved in those notions, and how much they deviated from reality.

In the face of all I had seen, I still believed that the Soviet state represented a breakthrough into the future, a prototype (though not as yet a fully realized one) for all other countries to imitate. That shows the hypnotic power of mass ideology.

I later came to regard our country as one much like any other. Conventional wisdom holds that all nations have their faults: bureaucracy, social inequality, secret police; crime and the retaliatory cruelty of the judges, police, and jailers; armies and military strategists, intelligence and counterintelligence; a drive to expand their spheres of influence on the pretext of national security; mistrust of the actions and intentions of other governments. This view of the world (probably the most widely held one) can be called the "theory of symmetry": all governments and regimes are (in the first approximation) bad, all nations are oppressed, all of us are threatened by common dangers.

Then, during my activist period, I came to realize that the symmetry theory needed refinement. How can one speak of symmetry between a normal cell and a cancerous one? With its messianic pretensions, its totalitarian suppression of dissent, and its authoritarian power structure, our regime resembles a cancer cell. The public in our country has had no control whatsoever over vital political decisions, foreign or domestic. We have lived in a closed society in which the government concealed matters of substance from its own citizens. We have been closed off as well from the outside world, and our citizens have been denied the right to travel abroad or exchange information. And yet I do not mean to be quite so categorical in my assessment as I may sound. Although I finally reject the theory of symmetry, it does contain a measure (a large one) of truth. The truth is never simple.

What conclusions are we to draw from all this? What should we in the USSR do? What should the West do? It's not possible to respond to such questions in a word. And I hope that no one will claim to know the final answers; no good comes from prophets. But even while acknowledging our fallibility, we must nevertheless continue to think about these matters and give the advice to others that intellect and conscience dictate. And let God be our judge, as our grandparents used to say.

ON MARCH 27, 1953, a far-reaching amnesty was proclaimed. It was unofficially called the "Voroshilov amnesty" because Marshal Voroshilov signed the decree as chairman of the Presidium of the Supreme Soviet (the decision was, of course, a collective one). One important result of the amnesty was a sharp reduction in the forced labor available for a system based on slavery. On the negative side, the release of common criminals led to a temporary increase in crime. But the amnesty's most serious failing was that it did not apply to political prisoners. Millions of innocent victims of Stalin's terror remained behind barbed wire in countless labor camps, in prisons, in exile, and in special settlements for persons "eternally banished" from their former homes. It took several more years for the survivors to regain their freedom; their release was a consequence of the country's gradual liberation from the Stalinist nightmare and the expulsion of many of Stalin's cowardly, cynical, and vicious henchmen from positions of power. Khrushchev and his advisers deserve much of the credit for these changes. I have heard that it was Alexei Snegov, a former Party official and long-term prisoner himself, who wrote a substantial portion of Khrushchev's secret speech to the Twentieth Party Congress and played an important role in the rehabilitation process.

A week after the amnesty was announced, the case against the Kremlin doctors was dropped. Tamm heard the news first on his shortwave radio. I remember his running into our department, short of breath and shouting from the doorway: "They've freed the doctors!"

A few hours later we read about it in the Soviet press: "The accused were all arrested without any legal basis. They have been completely exonerated and have been freed from imprisonment. The persons accused of improper methods of investigation have been arrested and charged with criminal responsibility."[3]

Tamm was ecstatic and kept repeating: "Have we really lived to see it? Have we really lived to see this moment?"

A new era seemed to be dawning. Of course, as is often the case, Tamm (and the rest of us) drew conclusions that were too far-reaching; some of our hopes have never materialized, and others only after long delay. All the same, the worst *was* behind us.

Besides the official communiqué on the doctors' release, we were thrilled by *Pravda*'s editorials on "The Invincible Friendship of Nations" and "Socialist Legality Is Inviolable" [April 6]. But they were the first and the last of their kind.

Zeldovich too was jubilant. He boasted: "And it was our Lavrenty Pavlovich [Beria] who brought all this to light." That jarred me a bit, but I simply replied: "Bringing it to light wasn't so hard. All it took was the will to do it."

IN THE SPRING of 1953, we were getting ready to write our final report on the test device and the results we expected to obtain. Zavenyagin asked us to draft it so that it could be read by the "architect" (Beria) and the "electrical engineer" (Malenkov), as well as by specialists. But the architect soon would be busy with other matters.

One day that summer [July 10], we noticed that the signs on Beria Street

---

[3][The announcement that the accusations against the doctors were false was carried in *Pravda* and *Izvestia* on April 4. For the full text of this announcement and other details of the Doctors' Plot, see Yehoshua Gilboa; *The Black Years of Soviet Jewry* (Little, Brown, 1971).]

had been replaced by cardboard markers reading: Kruglov Street. Sergei Kruglov had been appointed minister of internal affairs. (Subsequent events would require the street to be renamed once again.) That same day, the removal from office and arrest of Beria and his accomplices were announced over the radio.

I heard later that Beria had been arrested in the Kremlin during a session of the Presidium. On Marshal Zhukov's orders, the Kremlin guard had been replaced by regular army officers an hour before Beria's arrival. After passing Beria's limousine into the Kremlin, they barred the car carrying his bodyguards. At the same time, army units moved into Moscow and blockaded KGB headquarters and other sites where KGB and MVD troops were stationed. Beria was arrested by Zhukov and General Moskalenko, who entered the hall while the Presidium was in session and took him by surprise. He was imprisoned in the basement of the Ministry of Defense. I have heard that he appealed for mercy, promising to redeem his mistakes through honest work and reminded the Presidium of his experience as an industrial manager and of his wartime achievements. Marshal Konev presided at Beria's trial in December 1953. He was sentenced to death and executed together with his henchmen, Vsevolod Merkulov, Vladimir Dekanozov, Bogdan Kobulov, Pavel Meshik, Sergei Goglidze and Lev Vlodzimirsky.[4]

Toward the end of July, I was invited to the City Party Committee and shown a letter distributed by the Central Committee to Party organizations that explained Beria's arrest. Although I wasn't a Party member, my position warranted my inclusion among the document's readers. (In 1956, the text of Khrushchev's secret speech at the Twentieth Party Congress was shown to me in similar fashion.) The letter was bound in a blood-red cover, so I mentally dubbed it the "Red Book." It began by calling Beria a bourgeois degenerate, a Mussavat [Muslim democratic party active 1911–1918 in Azerbaijan] intelligence agent, who had abused the nation's trust and committed vile crimes. It went on to describe some of Beria's horrible deeds as Stalin's accomplice and as a key figure in the whole apparatus of repression. What any of this had to do with being a "bourgeois degenerate" remains a mystery: if that epithet has any meaning, it did not apply to Beria alone.

The letter described the actions of Beria and his accomplices in Georgia— the mass arrests, the executions, the cruel tortures. There were several pages on Nestor Lakoba, the chairman of the Abkhazian Party Central Committee. After Lakoba himself was murdered by the NKVD in 1936, his widow was arrested and tortured to get her to confess to her husband's guilt. When she refused, Beria's accomplices arrested her fourteen-year-old son and began tor-

---

[4][For Khrushchev's account of Beria's downfall, see *Khrushchev Remembers*, pp. 321–341.]

turing the mother in front of the son and the son in front of the mother. But they refused to denounce Lakoba, and they were killed.

The Red Book also gave a detailed account of the 1936 killing of Agasi Khandzhian, first secretary of the Armenian Communist Party, and of several other murders personally committed by Beria. I recall a passage on the Beria gang's Moscow activities from a letter written by Robert Eikhe, a Latvian and a candidate member of the Politburo. He had been tortured by Pavel Meshik, who later headed our security department, and greatly enjoyed playing chess with scientists at the Installation. Meshik, aware that Eikhe's vertebrae had been fractured by the Tsar's political police, had taken care to beat him with a cane on the most sensitive spots.

The Red Book revealed that shortly after war broke out in June 1941, Beria sent Stalin a lengthy list of political prisoners to be executed; it contained, if my memory doesn't deceive me, about four hundred names, including forty or so well-known Party and government officials, many of them heroes of the Revolution and Civil War. They had been sentenced to various terms of imprisonment and incarcerated in secret prisons in Kuibyshev and the outskirts of Moscow. Stalin signed the list; everyone on it was executed. A mention of Stalin in this context was shocking at that time. (I was told that a great moan ran through the hall when this part of the Red Book was read out at a Party meeting in some large factory.) Now we know that there were many such "preventive" and completely illegal mass executions before and during the war. (The murder of Polish officers at Katyn was of this nature.)

Beria's deputy, Vladimir Dekanozov, a former ambassador to Germany, liked to drive around the streets of Moscow looking for women; he would rape them in his limousine in the presence of his bodyguards and chauffeur. Beria was less crude about it. He would walk near his house in Malaya Nikitinskaya Street and point out women to his bodyguards, who would later deliver them to his apartment, where he would force the women to have sex with him. When one fourteen-year-old victim attempted suicide, Beria spent the night at her bedside, but the girl could not be saved.

Political prisoners were often interrogated in Beria's office. He would demand that everyone take turns beating the victim—the gangland practice of ensuring solidarity through complicity—and would taunt the "theoretician" (Merkulov), who refused to join in. On the other hand, it was Merkulov who formulated the basic plans for mass repression and surveillance, the "sieve-and-net" system. (I don't remember the details, but I do recall that term.) Following Beria's arrest, two truncheons were found in the desk of office 13, where I had met with him on several occasions. (In his remarkable memoirs, Evgeny Gnedin mentions being beaten by Bogdan Kobulov in Beria's presence, possibly with one of those very truncheons.)

Beria organized a "sincerity laboratory" where research was apparently done on mind-altering drugs, and perhaps on the technology of torture as well. The laboratory was run by the same physician who carried out for Beria such delicate assignments as disposing of people clandestinely, without the formality of an arrest. The intended victim would be lured to a secret apartment in Ulyanovsk, where the doctor would scratch him with a poison-tipped cane. More than thirty people were eliminated in this fashion. (I was reminded of that story when I heard a broadcast about Bulgarian political émigrés murdered with poison-tipped umbrellas.)

The Red Book reported that in order to bolster his standing, Beria had staged a sham attempt on Stalin's life. He was also blamed for several major mistakes, such as summoning all the KGB *rezidents* [station chiefs abroad] to a peace conference that exposed them and led to a whole series of disasters.

AFTER BERIA'S FALL we got a new chief—Vyacheslav Malyshev. In June 1953 he was appointed a deputy chairman of the USSR Council of Ministers and the head of the First Main Directorate, now renamed the Ministry of Medium Machine Building. Malyshev's duties included supervising missiles and other advanced military technology, as well as atomic matters.

Half of our cottage at the Installation had been used as a dormitory for young women working on calculations, but they were now hastily moved out and the premises remodeled so that Malyshev could be put up there. A wooden walkway was laid from our gate to the door of the house. Soon after, I caught sight of a short, ruddy-faced man trotting briskly down it, followed by the Installation's directors, who were straining to keep up.

Malyshev had come directly to the Installation after receiving his appointment. Within hours we were briefing him about our device and our degree of readiness for the test. Malyshev was Malenkov's man. He later confided to a select few that Malenkov had been kept in the dark about our work on thermonuclear weapons before Beria's arrest, since all information on the subject was tightly held within Beria's immediate entourage. I'd been aware that the resolutions of the Council of Ministers and Central Committee concerning our work were in fact drafted by Beria and his people, but I'd never dreamed that they were kept secret even from the chairman of the Council of Ministers.

Malyshev's background, as he related it in my presence, was extraordinary. The son of a railroad worker, he had been assigned to the Kolomna Locomotive Works after graduating from a railroad engineering school. Since all the engineers in that enormous plant had shortly before been arrested as "saboteurs," he was immediately appointed chief engineer. Surprisingly, he measured up to the job. During the war he was promoted to senior management posts in arms production. He became a close associate of Malenkov, and in 1953 his career reached its zenith. I asked Zeldovich whether Malyshev appreciated the exceptional nature of his new responsibilities, and was assured that he did.

By July 1953, we had completed our work on the device, and the time had come to leave for the test site in the Kazakhstan steppe, near Semipalatinsk. Since I was not ordinarily permitted to fly (there were several of us who were considered too valuable to risk in a plane crash), I traveled in Khariton's private railway car together with Mstislav Keldysh, Mikhail Lavrentiev, and Viktor Davidenko.

Davidenko, then the head of the Installation's nuclear research department, had lived in our house for several months. He spent the journey, which lasted five or six days, making rods and reels, more from the habit of working with his hands than from any love of fishing. He confided that he had gained the most satisfaction from his work when he was a young technician in a factory, making "real things."

During the journey, I would run into Keldysh and Lavrentiev in the lounge, but they were usually discussing Academy and organizational matters that meant nothing to me then. Their conversations about computers and missiles were much more interesting, and I could enter into the discussion.

My concerns rarely overlapped with Lavrentiev's, so I never really got to know him. But my path crossed Keldysh's quite often, and I came to appreciate his businesslike approach, lively intelligence, and ability to formulate complex scientific, engineering, and organizational problems in terms so clear that often they were revealed in a new light. I was told later that he had been impressed by me ever since our first meeting in 1952, and that he had spoken of me enthusiastically as a rising star in science. Keldysh headed the special mathematics department which performed our calculations, and he helped us a great deal.

We stopped for a few hours in Novosibirsk, which gave us time to inspect the old log houses still preserved in that Siberian city and to bathe in the warm water of the Ob River, which rises in the south and flows north to empty into the Arctic Ocean. We continued along the Turkestan–Siberian railway line, flying the last hundred miles to the test site in a small YAK-15 that had been sent to fetch us. As we skimmed the ground, rising only occasionally to avoid power lines, we got a marvelous view of the Kazakhstan steppe, dotted with herds of sheep and cows, and ducks, floating on the many ponds—they would fly off as we came near.

On arrival at the test site we were confronted by an unexpected complication. The device was to be detonated on a special tower built in the center of a field. Ground-level explosions were known to produce bands or "patterns" of radioactive fallout, but no one had appreciated the fact that an explosion of the power we anticipated would spread fallout far beyond the test site and jeopardize the health and lives of thousands of innocent people.

We had all been so busy preparing the device, organizing the test, and performing calculations that we simply lost sight of the fallout problem. Such lapses happen at least as often in important matters as they do in trivial ones. It was Viktor Gavrilov, now working for the Ministry in Moscow, who alerted us to the danger.

The chiefs were in a panic. Malyshev vented his feelings by complaining: "We were ready for the tests, everything was going beautifully, and then all of a sudden Gavrilov pops up like an evil genius, and now everything's a mess." From then on we called Gavrilov the "Evil Genius"—a nickname which suited his fiercely critical nature.

Several teams were assigned to the fallout problem. Each worked in a separate hotel room, virtually around the clock. A couple of days later, making liberal use of the Black Book (an American manual on the effects of nuclear explosions), we had estimates for the dispersion of fallout under the conditions anticipated for our test: the power of the explosion, the weather, the soil, and the height of the tower.

The Black Book—we called it that only partly because of the color of its cover—served for a long time as a valuable reference work during our tests and in discussions of nuclear warfare and defense systems. A Russian translation appeared toward the end of the 1950s, but the Black Book, like its Soviet equivalent, was classified "for official use only" and was never put on sale. One reason was the subject, but there was a second reason as well. People in our country are spared knowledge that is too shocking, and the Black Book contained horrifying details that could have alarmed the public. The suppression of unpleasant facts is one element in a general strategy of psychological mobilization. For instance, the bodies of accident and crime victims are never shown on Soviet television, although this restraint does not apply to foreign disasters. [This was written before the era of glasnost changed the habits of our press— A.S. 1988]

A fallout pattern is formed in the following manner: A ground-level explosion sucks up dust from the earth. The surfaces of the dust particles melt and in the process absorb radioactive material produced by the fission of uranium and plutonium nuclei. The atomic cloud blazes upward, mixing with the air and cooling as it is carried along by the stratospheric winds. The dust particles gradually fall to earth, the heavier ones first, while the lighter particles are carried to a greater distance. A fallout pattern is formed that grows broader as it moves out from ground zero.

Radioactive fallout could cause terrible damage in a large-scale thermonuclear war. The belligerents are likely to explode nuclear devices at or near ground level in order to destroy the enemy's underground missile silos and other hardened targets. The fallout pattern would then extend over a vast area and add its toll of death, illness, and genetic damage to the destruction caused by shock waves and heat radiation (which might well claim millions of victims). The poisoning of the earth's atmosphere would later cause long-term biological effects. These are matters to which I have given a great deal of thought since that first thermonuclear test.

At the time, we decided that it was absolutely necessary to evacuate everyone downwind from ground zero in the zone where total radiation was likely to exceed 200 roentgens. The estimates we were using predicted that 100 roentgens might cause serious injury to children and to some people in weakened condition, while 600 roentgens would kill half the healthy adults exposed. We assumed, however, that no one in the danger zone would receive the full 200 roentgens, since people would not remain continuously in the open, and they could still be evacuated after the explosion if necessary. Nonetheless, tens of thousands of people would have to be moved.

We brought our results to Kurchatov, Malyshev, and the military director of the tests, Marshal Vasilevsky, who was Marshal Zhukov's deputy. They took us very seriously and were faced with a choice: either switch to a scenario in which the device would be dropped from a plane (which would have meant an impermissible delay of six months or longer), or evacuate the danger zone we had mapped out.

The alternative of evacuation was adopted, but the chiefs wanted to double-check our recommendations. I remember one of the many discussions particularly well; it took place at night, ten to twelve days before the test. Malyshev began by reminding us in dramatic tones that we would be subjecting tens of thousands of people—including the sick, the elderly, and the young—to the difficulties and dangers of a hasty evacuation by truck in a region lacking decent roads. Casualties would be inevitable. Malyshev called on each of us by name, Kurchatov included, to stand and state his opinion. Everyone agreed that evacuation was necessary. Vasilevsky had already deployed 700 army trucks; the operation could begin at once.

Later, Vasilevsky told a few of us in private: "There's no need to torture yourselves. Army maneuvers always result in casualties—twenty or thirty deaths can be considered normal. And *your* tests are far more vital for the country, and its defense."

That was not a view we could accept. Of course, we worried about the success of the test, but for me, anxiety about potential casualties was paramount. Catching a glimpse of myself in a mirror, I was struck by the change—I looked old and gray.

I remember Zeldovich's words at the time: "Don't worry, everything will be fine. The Kazakh kids will survive. It will all turn out okay."

To skip ahead: Subsequent events did confirm that evacuation had been necessary. Radioactive fallout contaminated the settlement of Kara-aul, located within the evacuation zone. The residents had been told that they could return in a month, but in fact they were not able to go home until the spring of 1954, some eight months later.

In March 1954, a Japanese fishing boat, the *Fuku-maru*, sailed into the fallout zone of an American nuclear test. The radio operator died as a result of his exposure, and the vessel's entire tuna catch turned out to be radioactive. This incident added fuel to the international campaign to end nuclear tests. The entire population of Kara-aul might well have suffered the same fate as the crew of the *Fuku-maru*.

ON AUGUST 5, 1953—exactly one week before the test—Malenkov delivered a major report to the opening session of the Supreme Soviet, announcing significant changes in domestic and foreign policy: workers on collective farms would receive larger allocations of land for their personal use and fair compensation for their labor instead of the inadequate payments which had led to the ruin of the countryside under Stalin; capital investment in the consumer goods sector would also be increased; and a policy of détente would be pursued in international relations. Stalin was not yet denounced in public, but many of his policies were revised. I do not know the exact roles played in all this by Malenkov, Khrushchev, and Stalin's other former comrades-in-arms, but change was inevitable.

In concluding his address, Malenkov said that the USSR had everything necessary for its defense, including the hydrogen bomb. This boast was greeted with enthusiastic applause and was reported in newspapers around the world, causing an international sensation.

We listened to Malenkov's speech in the dimly lit lobby of our small hotel. The device had not yet been installed on the tower; hundreds of trucks were still carrying families and their hastily gathered belongings away from ground zero to the south, east, and west across the trackless Kazakhstan steppe. Malenkov's remarks would have raised the level of tension if we had not already been keyed up to the maximum.

In early August, an atomic (fission) device was tested; this would ordinarily have been a great event for me, but I was so completely absorbed in the forthcoming thermonuclear test that I barely noticed it. At last, our day arrived—August 12, 1953. The night before, I followed Zeldovich's advice, took a sleeping pill (something I rarely do), and retired early. All of us in the hotel were awakened at four A.M. by the alarm bells. It was still dark, but I could see the headlights of trucks sweeping across the horizon, as the observers were driven to their posts.

Two and a half hours later I reached my station twenty miles from ground zero, where I was to observe the explosion in the company of young scientists from my group and Zeldovich's group. When the test managers and the heads of operations arrived, Tamm, who was with them, was invited to the nearby bunker set aside for VIPs. I came up to him to exchange a few words of reassurance and noticed that the chiefs were just as nervous as we were.

On the first step of the bunker Malyshev turned to Vannikov and said, "Quick, Boris, tell me a joke."

Vannikov responded immediately. "Why are you so sad?" "My condoms are in bad shape." "Do they drip?" "No, they droop."

Malyshev snorted with laughter and said: "Good man, let's go."

I returned to my station. Following instructions, we all lay down on the ground, facing the tower. We listened to the countdown coming over the loudspeakers:

Ten minutes to go.

Five minutes.

Two minutes.

We put on our dark goggles.

Sixty seconds. Fifty, forty, thirty, twenty, ten, nine, eight, seven, six, five, four, three, two, one.

We saw a flash, and then a swiftly expanding white ball lit up the whole horizon. I tore off my goggles, and though I was partially blinded by the glare, I could see a stupendous cloud trailing streamers of purple dust. The cloud turned gray, quickly separated from the ground and swirled upward, shimmering with gleams of orange. The customary mushroom cloud gradually formed, but the stem connecting it to the ground was much thicker than those shown in photographs of fission explosions. More and more dust was sucked up at the base of the stem, spreading out swiftly. The shock wave blasted my ears and struck a sharp blow to my entire body; then there was a prolonged, ominous rumble that slowly died away after thirty seconds or so. Within minutes, the cloud, which now filled half the sky, turned a sinister blue-black color. The wind was pushing it in a southerly direction toward the mountains and the evacuated Kazakh settlements; half an hour later the cloud disappeared from sight, with planes of the radiation-detection service following after it.

Malyshev came out of the bunker and congratulated us on our success—we knew already that the power of the explosion had come close to our estimate. Then he declared with appropriate ceremony: "The chairman of the Council of Ministers, Georgy Malenkov, has just telephoned. He congratulates everyone who helped build the hydrogen bomb—the scientists, the engineers, the workmen—on their wonderful success. Georgy Maximilianovich [Malenkov] requested me to congratulate and embrace Sakharov in particular for his exceptional contribution to the cause of peace."

Malyshev embraced and kissed me, and invited me to join the test chiefs for a tour of the test site to see "what went on out there." We stopped at a checkpoint where we were issued dustproof jumpsuits and dosimeters. We drove in open cars past buildings destroyed by the blast, braking to a stop beside an eagle whose wings had been badly singed. It was trying to fly, but it couldn't get off the ground. One of the officers killed the eagle with a well-aimed kick, putting it out of its misery. I have been told that thousands of birds are destroyed during every test; they take wing at the flash, but then fall to earth, burned and blinded.

Our convoy drove on and stopped within two hundred feet of ground zero. Malyshev got out, and I followed him, while everyone else stayed put. We walked over a fused black crust that crunched underfoot like glass toward the concrete supports with a broken steel girder protruding from one of them—all that was left of the tower. After staring at the debris for a few moments, we returned to our car, drove back past the yellow warning flags, and handed in our jumpsuits and dosimeters (which got mixed up in the process).

That evening we met at Kurchatov's to hear a preliminary report prepared by the test range staff. Kurchatov opened the meeting by saying: "I want to congratulate everyone here. I want to congratulate Sakharov personally and thank him on behalf of the leadership for his patriotic work."

I rose from my seat and bowed, but I can't recall what I was thinking at the time.

The test on August 12 excited and interested people around the world. In the United States they named it "Joe-4"—"Joe" in honor of Stalin, and "4" because it was the fourth Soviet test. [The three earlier tests had presumably been of fission devices.]

IT TOOK two or three weeks to process and review the results. The chiefs were delighted to learn that the power of the explosion and the other test parameters had been on target. We realized what a long road still lay ahead, but even so, we underestimated the time needed to finish our task.

One evening shortly after the test, Zeldovich asked me: "What are your plans? What do you want to work on now?" Then, anticipating my reply and perhaps trying to sway me at the same time, he continued, "You'll probably concentrate on developing a magnetic thermonuclear reactor."

I replied, "No, I ought to complete our work on the device." (As I will explain in the next chapter, I botched my first attempt to fulfill this intention, but my overall contribution to the project was very substantial.)

After the test we had some free time. We went to the movies, though sometimes a film would be interrupted by a messenger summoning Zeldovich or me to report to the chiefs. I took walks with Tamm along the Irtysh River, picking the sweet and tart rose hip berries that grew in thickets along its banks. We would occasionally stop and talk with Kazakhs, and two such conversations stick in my mind. A fourteen-year-old girl named Madriza told us with pride that she wanted to become a teacher, obviously a very high ideal for her. An elderly Kazakh, tending a small herd of cows, complained that after delivering the state quotas, they did not have enough milk left, even for the children. These two incidents illustrate what Soviet rule has meant for the people—the two sides of the coin. Both must be taken into account, but reality is in fact still more complex and contradictory than that; and besides, times have changed since 1953.

Once Zavenyagin asked me to go for a walk with him. Like Pavlov, he had been one of Beria's men, and it took a while for him to regain his standing. Zavenyagin questioned me about the prospects for a magnetic thermonuclear reactor and about our plans for perfecting a thermonuclear device. Before Beria's fall, he had been one of the first to know what was going on, but now he was grateful for any scraps of information I could give him. When saying goodbye, he gave me a book by the Australian author Frank Hardy, *Power Without Glory,* adding a warm inscription. I am not sure whether he meant the title to serve as some sort of allusion.

Malyshev thought the Installation's scientists should be kept well informed on the latest in military technology generally as well as on their own specialties. This, of course, meant a break with the traditional practice of limiting a person's knowledge of secret work to the minimum needed to do his own job. In fact, however, broader horizons are a great help in creative work. And to the best of my knowledge, scientists seldom have been responsible for leaks of secret information, although Klaus Fuchs was a notable exception. Fuchs, a German émigré, worked in the theoretical physics department at Los Alamos during the war and between 1943 and 1945 passed on to the USSR, on his own initiative and for ideological reasons, exceptionally important information about the atom bomb.[5] After Malyshev left, his successors had little choice but to continue his liberal policy with respect to technical knowledge, but they tried to cut the scientists off from information on political or social matters. Of course, the times being what they were, a total blackout was impossible.

[5][See Robert Williams, *Klaus Fuchs, Atom Spy* (Harvard University Press, 1987).]

While we were still in Kazakhstan, we were shown some fascinating secret films of earlier atomic tests and of new weapons. Then, after we returned to the Installation, Malyshev organized a series of "excursions" for us, including a trip through a ballistic missile plant where I met Sergei Korolev, the chief designer, for the first time. We had always thought our own work was conducted on a grand scale, but this was something of a different order. I was struck by the level of technical culture: hundreds of highly skilled professionals coordinated their work on the fantastic objects they were producing, all in a quite matter-of-fact, efficient manner. Korolev explained things and showed us some films. Since his death [in 1966] the Soviet press has referred to him quite often and in heroic terms, but at the time of our visit, his existence was still shrouded in secrecy. Despite Korolev's posthumous fame, it is only very recently that his arrest in the 1930s and his term in a Kolyma labor camp have been mentioned in print.[6] He would have died there if Tupolev had not recruited him for his famous *sharashka*, where imprisoned scientists designed and built aircraft. Legend has it that one professor confined there was pleading his innocence of any wrongdoing, when Beria interrupted him to say: "My dear man, I know you're not guilty of anything. Get the plane in the air and you'll go free."[7]

Korolev was a brilliant engineer and organizer and a colorful personality who shared many of Kurchatov's qualities. One of Kurchatov's most pronounced traits was his fascination with "grand" science. Korolev dreamed of the cosmos, and he clung to that dream throughout his youth and his stint with the famous Jet Propulsion Research Group. He never believed, as so many did, that the rocket pioneer Konstantin Tsiolkovsky was simply an impractical dreamer. Korolev also shared Kurchatov's rather crude sense of humor. Both took good care of their subordinates and colleagues and had a sure grasp of the practical, but Korolev was possibly a bit more cunning, ruthless, and cynical than Kurchatov. Both men became key figures in the military-industrial complex, yet managed to preserve the enthusiasm of amateurs.

I recall several other trips to visit Korolev, including one in 1961, shortly after the test of an intercontinental ballistic missile and just before the launch of an artificial satellite. He showed us the satellite, which was receiving its final checks, and he joked as usual, although I sensed the enormous stress he was under. I slipped a souvenir into my pocket, a bit of fused metal that was found

[6][Sakharov himself mentioned the arrest and imprisonment of Korolev in his review (*Moscow News*, November 8, 1987) of the documentary film *Risk*.]

[7][*Sharashka* is Soviet slang for one of the special research centers established by Beria and staffed by imprisoned scientists. Solzhenitsyn's *The First Circle* describes one such establishment.]

on the spot where a rocket had fallen back to earth. (There were thousands of such fragments, so it really couldn't be considered theft.)

I last saw Korolev at a General Assembly of the Academy. I had just learned from a foreign broadcast that the Americans had used a gigantic Saturn rocket to boost a nineteen-ton space station into orbit, a long stride on their way to the moon. I couldn't resist asking Korolev if he had heard the news (knowing, of course, that we had nothing to match the American rocket). Korolev smiled, put his arm around my shoulder, and, using the familiar form of address, said to me: "Don't worry, we'll have our day yet . . ." I was surprised by his unexpected display of warmth. A few weeks after this conversation, Korolev died during surgery.

I don't think he ever forgot his time in the camps. He once tried to organize support for Yuri Rumer, a theoretical physicist who had also worked in Tupolev's *sharashka*, when Rumer became a candidate for corresponding membership in the Academy. Korolev failed to get Rumer elected, though in other instances his efforts were more successful.

Shortly before we left the test site, the chiefs had a farewell picnic. Tamm and Khariton were invited, but Zeldovich and I were still considered too junior to be included. (Tamm reported to us Vasilevsky's confession at the picnic: "Marshal Zhukov summoned me and said: 'You're going to a hydrogen bomb test.' If anyone else had said that, I would have taken it as a bad joke." In a talkative mood, Vasilevsky had gone on reminiscing about how he and Zhukov had served together at Stalingrad during the war and admitting with a wry smile: "I'm not really the same person anymore—my head worked a lot better then.")

During the picnic, Tamm asked Malyshev for permission to return to Moscow; he considered his mission at the Installation completed. Malyshev gave his consent. Tamm was soon on his way back to FIAN and the theoretical physics department he had created there. In the next few years he and his colleagues were to accomplish some important work that I have already described. In particular, it was then, soon after his return to FIAN, that he was able to show that resonance should be considered a bona fide particle.

I assumed Tamm's duties as head of the theoretical department at the Installation. Tamm rarely visited us, so we saw each other mainly in Moscow. We spent less and less time discussing Installation matters, but the idea of a magnetic thermonuclear reactor continued to intrigue him. At the 1964 celebration of Khariton's sixtieth birthday—the last time Tamm visited the Installation—he was as charming as ever, but physically weak and already displaying symptoms of the illness which was to plague him until his death in 1971.

But I have run ahead of my story and should return to the late summer of

1953, when I got back to the Installation from the test site. The experience we had acquired there opened the way to the creation of advanced weapons, but it also made me more aware of the human and moral dimensions of our work. It was, of course, just a beginning, but I have continued ever since to ponder these questions, spurred on by the pressure of events.

THE ANNUAL ELECTIONS to the Academy of Science were held in October. In the spring of 1953, following Kurchatov's request, I had completed the necessary paperwork to become a candidate for corresponding membership. In the ordinary course of events, a person first becomes a corresponding member, and only after an interval is he considered for full membership. But now, after the test's success, Kurchatov changed his mind, and I was nominated for full membership straightaway.

Nominees are supposed to have their doctorates. In the summer a special meeting of the Academic Council was convened at the Installation. I was awarded the degree of Doctor of Physical and Mathematical Sciences after presenting a brief report. (Nikolai Dmitriev received his candidate's degree at the same meeting.) Tanya, my eight-year-old daughter, was very happy that I had become a doctor—now I could treat sick children. She was upset when she learned that I was not a "real" doctor.

Late one evening, after the meeting of the Academy's physical and mathematical department, Kurchatov called me at home and told me: "Those doddering academicians have just voted for you unanimously. Congratulations. Get some rest." (A favorite expression of his.)

I do not know of anyone who has been unanimously elected to the Academy since then. I officially became an Academician on October 23, 1953, when my election was confirmed by the General Assembly. By that time I had already attended a meeting of my department,[8] where I saw for the first time many well-known physicists and mathematicians whom I greatly respected but had previously known only by reputation. It was also my first opportunity to observe from the inside the Academy's electoral process and the passions it excites.

A number of "our people" were also elected members of the Academy on October 23: Tamm, Khariton, Bogolyubov, Isaak Kikoin, Anatoly Alexandrov (later president of the Academy), Lev Artsimovich, and other scientists. Unfortunately, Zeldovich was not elected, which was absolutely unfair. (There are often problems with the election of scientists engaged in secret work whose

[8][Sakharov was initially elected to the Department of Physical and Mathematical Sciences. That department was later split, and Sakharov was assigned to the Nuclear Physics Department.]

qualifications have to be taken in some measure on faith.) This omission upset me and placed me in an awkward position.

IN NOVEMBER, Khariton and Zeldovich went on vacation. While they were gone, Malyshev summoned me to the Ministry in Moscow and asked me to submit a brief written report on my conception of a second-generation device, its principles of operation, and its approximate specifications. I should have refused, pointing out that such things could not be decided in haste by a single scientist; they require more serious deliberation. But I had an idea which at the moment seemed promising (it later turned out to be neither very original nor successful). I had no one with whom to consult. I nevertheless wrote a report on the spot and gave it to Malyshev. Several factors were at work here: my self-confidence, at a peak after the test; a certain euphoria, which passed quickly, but not quickly enough; and Malyshev's faith in me, which had been fostered by Kurchatov, Keldysh, and many others, and reinforced by the successful test and by my manner at the time—outwardly modest but actually quite the opposite.

Two weeks later, I was invited to a session of the Presidium[9] chaired by Malenkov. Malyshev assured me that there was no need to worry: "Things aren't the way they used to be; Malenkov treats people with respect." And Malyshev was right. Malenkov handled the session smoothly, never once interrupting the speakers. He sat at the head of the table, saying little, a stocky, moon-faced man in a gray tunic. (I have heard that he used to stand throughout the meetings he chaired when Stalin was in attendance.)

Malyshev did most of the talking, so all I had to do was to clear up a few points. I spoke cautiously, including as many caveats as possible. The audience evidently thought I was simply playing it safe, especially since Malyshev had already made some risky promises. Molotov was the only person who asked specific questions. I was shocked by his appearance, not at all like his portraits: his face was the color of parchment, and he had a guarded expression, as if he might fall into a deadly trap. With some difficulty, I also recognized Kaganovich, whose portraits had once hung everywhere. He kept silent, never uttering a single word. I don't recall any of the other members of the Presidium who were present.

This meeting, and a second one attended by missile experts, gave rise to two resolutions of the Council of Ministers and the Central Committee. The first

---

[9][The Politburo, the executive body of the Central Committee of the CPSU, was officially called the Presidium from 1952 to 1966.]

obliged our Ministry to develop and test by 1955 the device I had so incautiously proposed in my report to Malyshev. The second ordered the missile scientists to build an intercontinental ballistic missile to carry it.

In essence, this meant that the weight of the thermonuclear charge, as well as the dimensions of the missile, had been fixed on the basis of my report. The program for an enormous organization was set in this manner for many years to come. The rocket designed for that program launched the first artificial satellite into orbit in 1957, and also the spacecraft with Yuri Gagarin aboard in 1961. The thermonuclear charge that provided the original rationale for all this, however, fizzled out, and was replaced by something quite different.

In early November 1953, I fell seriously ill. The Academy's physicians diagnosed it as mumps and put me in the infectious ward of the Kremlin hospital, but then they decided it wasn't mumps, but most likely severe tonsillitis. I ran a fever of more than 106° F., became delirious, and suffered from severe nosebleeds and a blood disorder. As soon as my temperature dropped, I fled from the hospital, even though my blood tests were still not normal. The illness recurred a few months later, although in a milder form. It is possible that I received an overdose of radiation when I nonchalantly walked across the field with Malyshev after the test, but to this day I'm not sure what was wrong with me.

Toward the end of 1953, the Presidium of the Supreme Soviet conferred on Tamm and myself the title of Hero of Socialist Labor, while the Council of Ministers rewarded us with Stalin Prizes worth 500,000 rubles (50,000 rubles in today's currency), a colossal sum which greatly exceeded the Stalin Prizes announced publicly. (I will explain later what poor use I made of this sudden wealth.) Expensive dachas were also awarded us in Zhukovka, a Moscow suburb, although I was not informed of this at the time. Many people at the Installation and in affiliated organizations received prizes after the successful test. Kurchatov, Khariton, Zeldovich, and Khariton's deputy, Kirill Shchelkin, were each awarded their second Hero of Socialist Labor medals.

A number of us were invited (in February 1954, if I recall correctly) to a session of the Presidium of the Supreme Soviet in the Kremlin, where our awards were presented by the chairman of the Presidium, Marshal Voroshilov. By then, Voroshilov was quite old and somewhat wizened, though still vigorous. When my turn came, Voroshilov said: "I have been told that Sakharov's work was especially outstanding. Let me kiss you."

He did so, and then one of his assistants pinned the medal on me.

12

THE THIRD IDEA

WE RECOGNIZED early in 1954 that the ideas put forward in my report were not leading anywhere. I had set great store on certain "exotic" features, but projections indicated that they would at best boost the power of the device by a negligible amount, while the design would complicate its production and limit potential applications. We tried eliminating the exotic features, but it then became apparent that the device itself lacked promise: calculations performed in Moscow consistently showed that the alternatives we suggested all lacked the requisite power.

Meanwhile, however, we had come up with a new and quite original concept: the Third Idea. (The first two ideas were those proposed by Vitaly Ginzburg and myself in 1948.) Something like the Third Idea had been the subject of earlier speculation; but in 1954 our flight of fancy became a genuine option.

Several of us in the theoretical departments came up with the Third Idea at about the same time. I was one of them, and it seems to me that my early understanding of the Third Idea's basic physical and mathematical aspects, together with the authority I'd acquired, enabled me to play a decisive role in its adoption and implementation. True, Zeldovich, Yuri Trutnev, and others undoubtedly made significant contributions, and they may have grasped both the promise and the problems of the Third Idea as well as I did. At the time, in any case, we were all too busy (at least, I was) to worry about who received credit. Any assigning of honors at that time, moreover, would have been "skinning the bear before it was killed." Now it's too late to recall who said what during our discussions. And does it really matter that much?

From the spring of 1954, the two theoretical departments (Zeldovich's and my own) concentrated on the Third Idea. We devoted minimal thought and effort to the "classical" device; we recognized the risks of that neglect, but we were convinced that our strategy would pay off. Our resources were too limited to pursue both tracks aggressively. And in any case, we couldn't envision an approach that would radically improve the first device. Soon the designers, the gas dynamics team, and others started to move in this new direction. Also, Ekaterina Feoktistova and her associates did some particularly valuable work at this juncture.

Khariton was willing to accept the considerable responsibility for redirecting the Installation's work because he had confidence in the theoretical departments; he believed in the new approach himself. Kurchatov was also kept informed about the developments.

Our Ministry soon discovered what was afoot even though we didn't advertise it. Technically, we were guilty of flagrant insubordination: the resolution adopted by the government instructed us to produce a classical device, and nothing more. Malyshev flew out to the Installation. He, more than anyone else, was in a bind, since he had pushed the resolution on the basis of my report, and bore primary responsibility for implementing it and the complementary resolution on missile development. On his arrival, he hit the ground running, immediately convening a meeting of the Scientific Council and demanding a progress report on the classical device. He conceded from the start our right to explore new ideas, no matter how fantastic—but not at the expense of the classical device ("a bird in the hand . . . ," he reminded us). Malyshev looked to me for support—he considered me equally responsible for the resolution—but I agreed with Zeldovich and Khariton that only the Third Idea offered any real promise. I urged that, in spite of the risk, we investigate its potential fully, keeping the classical device as a fallback option.

Malyshev did not agree. He delivered a long, impassioned speech, which might have been called brilliant had his thesis been correct—but we all stuck to our guns. He lost his temper and began to shout that we were reckless gamblers toying with the country's fate. Malyshev was neither willing nor able to forbid all work on the Third Idea, and our lack of enthusiasm for the classical device was beyond his control. We had several more of these meetings; they became increasingly tiresome, some of them dragging on for hours.

Kurchatov was firmly on our side, which helped keep Malyshev in check. In his turn, Malyshev eventually engineered a severe Party reprimand for Kurchatov's "anti-state behavior" (or some such thing). The reprimand was expunged a year later, after Malyshev had retired and the Third Idea had proved successful.

I'd like to emphasize that Malyshev was by no means a conservative who resisted all innovation. On the contrary, he actively supported new ideas, and he deserves much of the credit for the priority given to missile technology. He was fully capable of understanding the merits of the Third Idea. But he was bound hand and foot by a state of affairs that was, in part, my doing. Probably, with time, the conflict would have been resolved, and Malyshev would have come over to our way of thinking, at least after the test of the Third Idea. But, in February 1955, Malenkov's replacement as chairman of the Council of Ministers by Marshal Bulganin automatically led to the removal of Malyshev, one of Malenkov's people.

Within a year, Malyshev was dead of acute leukemia. As with my own illness, our walk after the 1953 test cannot be blamed with certainty—but who knows? Many years after his death, I ran into Malyshev's daughter, who told me what a terrible blow retirement had been for her father, still a relatively young man, energetic and ambitious.

Avraami Zavenyagin inherited all of Malyshev's posts.

I WAS PRESENT when Zavenyagin's report prompted the Presidium to schedule a test for the fall of 1955 which would put to trial the principles of the Third Idea. A classical device would be available as a backup, to be detonated only if the result of the first test was negative.

Bulganin chaired the session. Khrushchev, his hands thrust into the pockets of his blue jeans, paced nervously back and forth by the windows. Malenkov sat on the edge of his chair. His appearance had altered greatly since 1953; his cheeks were sunken and his face dark. Malyshev, of course, was not present.

The official reason for his dismissal had been his failure to move to organize a second Installation—a parallel institution, with goals comparable to ours. The sponsors of this proposal hoped that competition between the two organizations would generate new ideas and new leaders and spur an overall expansion of research. Malyshev apparently had believed that a second Installation would only dissipate limited resources. Zavenyagin, of course, immediately set about organizing the second Installation, and Zababakhin, Zysin, Romanov, and Feoktistova were among those sent to work there.

In the years to come, difficult relations with the second Installation would affect our work significantly. I'll describe later the tragedy of the duplicate tests of 1962 and my unsuccessful attempt to prevent the second one. The Ministry overtly favored the second Installation, especially under Zavenyagin's successors. There were few Jews in its leadership (almost certainly no accident), whereas the first Installation had a large Jewish contingent, including Khariton, Zeldovich, Altshuler, and Tsukerman (and then there was yours truly: not Jewish, but perhaps something even worse . . .). In private, ministry officials nicknamed the second Installation "Egypt" (implying that ours was "Israel"), and referred to our dining room as "the Synagogue."

The setting of a test date accelerated the already feverish pace of our work. A lot of the responsibility for meshing our theoretical concepts with the actual design of the device fell to me. Relying on intuition, and without waiting for the resolution of all theoretical questions or the final calculations, I issued instructions and explained to the designers which specifications were critical, and which could be adjusted. Through frequent visits, I established close professional relations with the technical personnel employed in the design sector. I came to appreciate the difficult, painstaking nature of their work, and the specialized knowledge and talent it required.

But all the theoreticians, myself included, were mostly occupied with mathematical calculations. Soon after we began the project, I'd come up with an approximate analysis of the important processes specific to the Third Idea. Mathematically, these were the so-called self-similar solutions for certain partial differential equations. (Zeldovich did not trust my results until Kolya Dmitriev put them in final mathematical form—a point I still recall because it was something quite rare for Zeldovich: he is usually very sharp.)

Nevertheless, we needed something better than analyses of individual processes using simplified assumptions. Mathematicians at the Installation and in Moscow worked out new methods for performing complicated calculations by computer. A team headed by Izrail Gelfand, a corresponding member of the Academy of Sciences, played a critical role. I worked closely with Gelfand and his group to develop the basic programs, and we established an excellent rapport despite Gelfand's habit of flying into a rage and shouting at his colleagues (and sometimes at me as well). After a flare-up, he would stride up and down his office in silence for a few minutes. When he had regained his composure, he would return to work and even, on occasion, apologize for his outburst. Still, I got the impression that Gelfand's colleagues loved him, and that he had a paternal attitude toward them. Despite Gelfand's major contributions to modern mathematics, his promotion to full member of the Academy was delayed until the 1980s. The internal politics of the mathematics section were chiefly to blame, but part of the problem was his signing of a 1968 letter in defense of Alexander Esenin-Volpin.

Sometime in the spring or summer of 1955, we realized that we should use a new kind of material in our projected device. Normally it requires a long time to produce anything new, but I appealed for assistance to Boris Muzrukov, the Installation's new director. (Muzrukov's predecessor, General Alexander Alexandrov, had been fired, ostensibly because of an affair with a woman working in a foreign embassy. The authorities claimed she was a spy; in fact, as Alexandrov was aware, she was a double agent working for the KGB. The true cause of Alexandrov's removal was probably a conflict with his predecessor, who had been promoted and was now Alexandrov's superior. Khariton tried to save

Alexandrov, and several people, myself included, signed a letter on his behalf, but to no avail.)

Muzrukov was a colorful personality and one of the great captains of industry. Like Zavenyagin, he got his start at Magnitogorsk. During the war he went on to become director of the Ural Machinery Combine, a conglomerate in the Sverdlovsk region which included many factories relocated from the western USSR; it produced tanks and other armaments. Conditions for the starving evacuees and youngsters employed by the Combine were horrifying. Many died; and no one cared at all about the zeks working there. Managing such an operation demanded total commitment and great organizational and technical skill.

Muzrukov ended the war minus one lung; but with his first Hero of Socialist Labor award. He went on to manage our Ministry's factories, no easy task, and arrived at the Installation in 1955, probably the most dramatic year in its history.

Muzrukov received me in his office. Our conversation began in a formal vein, but as soon as I mentioned that we needed facilities to produce a new material for the device, his expression changed. The cold, almost arrogant mask dissolved into childlike excitement. He took a notebook from his safe and asked me to jot down the specifications. I filled up several pages with my entries; he read them through, and then, without another word, dialed a number on his special phone. He spoke to the director of a distant factory with whom he was obviously on close terms and asked him to retool a production line for a special assignment, which he outlined. When asked about likely difficulties with the plan, Muzrukov told the director: "Do your best. If you land in trouble, we'll help you out. We'll find some way to count the production toward your quota." The problem was solved, and I thanked Muzrukov. Other difficulties that arose in preparing for the tests were settled with equal dispatch.

THIS SEEMS as good a place as any to relate an incident that occurred in 1955, as I waited with others from the Installation and the Ministry to enter the room where the Presidium was meeting. Alexander Gorkin [secretary of the Presidium] came out (I think it was he, although I don't entirely trust my memory on this point) and asked us to excuse the delay: "We're finishing a discussion of Shepilov's report. He's just back from a trip to Egypt. It's an extremely important matter, involving a decisive shift in our Middle East policy. From now on, we'll support Arab nationalists. Our strategy is to sour Arab relations with Europe and the U.S. and to foment an oil crisis. That will complicate life for Europe and make it dependent on us."

In recalling this incident I may err in detail, but I can vouch for the gist of what I heard when I was still an "insider."

Gorkin's remarks seem to me persuasive evidence that oil lies at the root of the tragic course of events in the Middle East. No attention was paid to my earlier report of this incident,[1] but I believe it is still worth pondering; especially now, when the Europeans have financed a pipeline linking them to Soviet gas fields, and they are debating the future of nuclear energy.

[1][See *My Country and the World* (Knopf, 1983), p. 81.]

13

THE 1955 TEST

BY EARLY OCTOBER, three devices—the one based on the Third Idea, the "classical" backup device, and another—had been assembled, loaded onto a military train, and sent east. A few days later, I set out for the test site, once again in Khariton's private railway car.

I was accompanied by the bodyguards from a special KGB detachment who'd been assigned to me since the summer of 1954 (as mentioned earlier, they were known euphemistically as "secretaries"). Their job was to protect my life and—they made no secret of this—to prevent undesirable contacts. They lived next door to me, both at the Installation and in Moscow. I had to signal them whenever I went out by pressing a special buzzer, and I was supposed to summon them in the event of danger. One was a KGB colonel who had served with the border troops and, later, in Stalin's personal guard. (It was he who had arranged for the accommodations in Gorky which Stalin and his staff would have used if the planned evacuation in October 1941 had not been canceled. Again Gorky . . .) Then he had been "in arrests" (as he put it) in the Baltic states—dangerous work. He was tactful, never intrusive, always obliging. He was starting to think about retirement. My other "secretary," a lieutenant, was also diligent and obliging; he made some effort to "educate" me politically, but without great success. He was taking a correspondence course in law.

My "secretaries" carried Makarov pistols, which they kept concealed; they boasted that they were able to fire without drawing them from their pockets. Their wives lived at the Installation; Klava and I would run into them at the movies, and they would come to the station to see their husbands off when I left for Moscow. The secretaries made Klava nervous, but they didn't really bother me. Zeldovich found his secretaries terribly annoying when they were assigned to him in late 1956. He complained to Khariton, who spoke to Suslov, and Zeldovich's bodyguards (and mine) were removed in November 1957. Kurchatov's and Khariton's stayed on.

We departed for the test site from Moscow's Yaroslavl station. KGB officers, in and out of uniform, were milling about the platform, and my secretaries introduced me to their boss, the chief of the bodyguard detachment. Our car was attached to the Moscow–Peking Express, and as we entered we could hear the radio playing "Moscow to Peking," a song about Soviet-Chinese friendship with the refrain: "Stalin and Mao Zedong, Stalin and Mao Zedong."

At the test site a new complication, though not so dramatic as that of two years earlier, awaited us. Once again, it was Gavrilov who spotted it, living up to his nickname of the "Evil Genius." In order to minimize the fallout problem, the device was to be dropped from a plane and detonated at a sufficiently high altitude so that dust would not be drawn up into the radioactive cloud. Gavrilov pointed out, however, that heat radiation from the thermonuclear explosion might destroy the aircraft. Aviation experts had taken precautions to reduce this danger, coating the plane with white reflective paint and even leaving off the red stars traditional for military aircraft, lest the heat melt holes through the wings. But they hadn't realized the power of the device, and their measures were inadequate. The solution was to put more distance between the aircraft and the explosion. Specialists from the Parachute Research Institute helped us select an appropriate cargo parachute to brake the bomb's momentum, which would cause it to follow in the plane's path. (Other solutions for this problem could be used under battle conditions, but I won't go into them here.)

One night, unable to sleep, I calculated the bomb's trajectory, the airplane's exposure to heat (in calories per square centimeter), and the likely effect of the heat on the airplane's surface. Of course, there were others employed to do that work, but it's a pleasure to figure out such things for oneself.

Another day, I found myself sharing a table in the dining room with an air force general. I asked permission to ride on the plane that would drop the device. He said it was out of the question—only crew members were permitted to fly on military aircraft. Besides, on a combat mission the cabin would not be pressurized, and I was unaccustomed to wearing an oxygen mask.

The first test—unrelated to the Third Idea—of the series was conducted at the beginning of November, and made no special impression on me. What *did* impress me were the natural wonders of Siberia. The small town where we were billeted was on the Irtysh River, and in mid-November I saw the autumn ice rush; a common occurrence on Siberian rivers flowing south to north. I had spent my life in the European part of the country, so it was a new and spellbinding experience for me, a majestic, amazingly beautiful sight. The dark, turbulent waters of the Irtysh, dotted with a thousand whirlpools, bore the milky-blue ice floes northward, twisting them around and crashing them together. I could have watched for hours on end until my eyes ached and my head spun. Nature was displaying its might: compared to it, all man's handiwork seems paltry imitation.

D-Day, November 20, was approaching. On D-Day minus 2, we conducted a dress rehearsal in which a mockup identical to the device in weight, shape, and center of gravity was dropped by parachute. The automated release system performed successfully, as did the complicated mechanisms on the test field and the instruments designed to measure the explosion's power and other parameters.

On November 20, the plane took off from an airfield near Semipalatinsk with the device loaded in its bomb bay. The observers were at their stations. Suddenly, an hour before the test, the weather changed. Low clouds made it impossible to use optical sighting to aim the bomb. More important, we couldn't rely on our optical systems to monitor the explosion. The test managers decided to abort and reschedule.

Their decision raised questions about the risk of landing a plane with a nuclear device aboard close to the city of Semipalatinsk. Zeldovich and I were summoned to the command post, and we stated in writing that we saw no reason to anticipate a major problem, even in the event of a crash landing. The final decision was up to Kurchatov. ("One more test like the ones in 1953 and 1955, and I'm retiring," he remarked later.) To top things off, the airfield iced over while the plane was still in the air. Fortunately, an army unit stationed in Semipalatinsk was able to clear a runway, and the plane landed safely. So ended a very long day.

WE FINALLY TESTED the device based on the Third Idea on November 22, 1955. Visibility was good that day, and the meteorologists and explosion analysts gave the go-ahead despite the presence of a temperature inversion (that is, the temperature of the air rose with increasing altitude, rather than falling as it normally does).

Headquarters for the test was a laboratory building on the outskirts of the small town where we were working and living. The majority of the observers were stationed at a point midway between ground zero and the town, the post I was assigned to in 1953. Zeldovich and I and a few others needed for consultation were assigned places on a low platform built on the grounds of the laboratory. The steppe began immediately beyond the laboratory fence; it was covered by a thin coating of snow through which scattered plumes of feather grass protruded.

An hour before the drop, I spotted our dazzling white craft banking over the town to gain altitude after takeoff: with its sweptback wings and slender fuselage extending far forward, it looked like a sinister predator poised to strike. I recalled once reading in a splendid book on folklore by Vladimir Propp that for many peoples, the color white symbolizes death.

After an hour of tedious waiting, the controller announced over the loud-speaker in his customary sonorous tone:

"Attention! The plane is over the target. Five minutes to the drop, four, three, two, one, zero. The bomb has dropped! The parachute has opened! One minute! Thirty seconds, twenty, ten, five, four, three, two, one, zero!"

This time, having studied the Americans' Black Book, I did not put on dark goggles: if you remove them after the explosion, your eyes take time to adjust to the glare; and if you keep them on, you can't see much through the dark lenses. Instead, I stood with my back to ground zero and turned around quickly when the building and horizon were illuminated by the flash. I saw a blinding, yellow-white sphere swiftly expand, turn orange in a fraction of a second, then turn bright red and touch the horizon, flattening out at its base. Soon everything was obscured by rising dust which formed an enormous, swirling, gray-blue cloud, its surface streaked with fiery crimson flashes. Between the cloud and the swirling dust grew a mushroom stem, even thicker than the one that had formed during the first thermonuclear test. Shock waves crisscrossed the sky, emitting sporadic milky-white cones and adding to the mushroom image. I felt heat like that from an open furnace on my face—and this was in freezing weather, tens of miles from ground zero. The whole magical spectacle unfolded in complete silence. Several minutes passed, and then all of a sudden the shock wave was coming at us, approaching swiftly, flattening the feather-grass.

"Jump!" I shouted as I leaped from the platform. Everyone followed my example except for my bodyguard (the younger one was on duty that day); he evidently felt he would be abandoning his post if he jumped. The shock wave blasted our ears and battered our bodies, but all of us remained on our feet except for the bodyguard on the platform, who fell and suffered minor bruises. The wave continued on its way, and we heard the crash of broken glass. Zeldovich raced over to me, shouting: "It worked! It worked! Everything worked!" Then he threw his arms around me.

We were tremendously excited. After a few minutes, the chiefs emerged from headquarters: Marshal Mitrofan Nedelin, the military director of the test and Deputy Minister of Defense; Kurchatov; Zavenyagin; Khariton; Ivan Serbin, the head of the Central Committee department dealing with defense matters; other military, government, and Party officials; and the heads of the test services. Zavenyagin was rubbing a prominent bump on his bald head—the shock wave had cracked the ceiling and knocked loose the plaster—but he looked excited and happy, as did everyone. (Zavenyagin did not know it at the time, but this was in fact the zenith of his career. He died of a heart attack about two years later when the ambulance arrived too late to revive him; he was living alone, having divorced his wife.)

The test crowned years of effort. It opened the way for a whole range of devices with remarkable capabilities, although we still sometimes encountered unexpected difficulties in producing them.

A few hours after the test, we learned that the shock wave had caused far more serious damage than a cracked ceiling and a bumped head. Our scientists at the midway point had been lying flat on the ground according to their instructions, and none had suffered any injury, not even a man who lost control of himself and began running away from the blast—he was only knocked to the ground. But the force of the explosion had collapsed a nearby trench sheltering a platoon of soldiers, and one, a young boy in his first year of service, had been killed.

Another terrible accident occurred in a settlement that, according to our calculations, should have been well beyond the danger zone. The inhabitants had been ordered to take refuge in a primitive bomb shelter. After they saw the flash, they decided it was safe to emerge. They left behind a two-year-old girl who was playing with blocks; the shock wave demolished the shelter, and the girl was killed. (I was told that her single mother was one of the ethnic Germans deported to Kazakhstan at the outbreak of the war.) In another village, the ceiling came crashing down in the women's ward of a hospital, seriously injuring half a dozen people. When I got back to Moscow, I phoned Avetik Burnazian, the deputy minister of health, and asked him to provide special assistance for the women and to make sure they received pensions from our ministry's funds. He said he would take care of it, but unfortunately I never followed up to find out what, if anything, was done.

There were many lesser mishaps. Glass was shattered throughout the town where we were based. At a meat-packing plant in Semipalatinsk, a hundred miles from ground zero, splinters of window glass fell into ground beef. Further away, in Ust-Kamenogorsk, people became frightened when soot from their stoves was blown back into their homes.

Had we been more experienced, the temperature inversion would have caused us to delay the test. The velocity of a shock wave increases as the temperature does: if the air temperature rises with altitude, the shock wave bends back toward the ground and does not dissipate as fast as under normal conditions. This was the reason the shock wave's force exceeded our predictions. Casualties might have been avoided if the test had been conducted as scheduled on November 20, when there was no temperature inversion.

The consequences of an explosion are hard to predict. A year before the 1955 test, during army maneuvers, the shock wave from a less powerful atomic blast traveled far down a narrow ravine. Some children in a village near the end of the ravine saw the flash and rushed to their windows. The shock wave shattered the glass, and many suffered eye injuries. At the same time, the shock wave merely knocked the hats off generals, headed by Zhukov,[1] who were much closer to ground zero. Eyewitnesses told me that Malyshev burst into laughter; I doubt that Zhukov found the situation funny. (Apparently, for reasons unknown to me, Zhukov and Malyshev were bitter enemies. Gavrilov told me he was present at a meeting where they clashed publicly: cursing loudly, they threatened to shoot each other. During the exchange, their subordinates sat there petrified.)

After the 1955 test, we drove around the field just as we had in 1953, but this time with a purpose. Accompanying the crew that retrieved films and recorded instrument readings, we walked past buildings that had been specially constructed to determine the effects of the shock wave and heat radiation. Many were damaged or obliterated. Fires blazed in several places, water jets shot up through the ground from broken mains, and glass from shattered windows crunched underfoot, bringing back memories of the war. An oil tank had ruptured, and the oil, ignited by the heat radiation, burned for several days, sending thick black smoke drifting along the horizon. Special crews retrieved the experimental animals (dogs, goats, and rabbits). I found it painful to watch their suffering, even on film.

A few hours after the test, Zeldovich announced: "The device [he used the code number instead of the word] is shit!" He was referring to the news that the observed value of one parameter deviated sharply from our prediction. This might mean that we had ignored some factor that could improve performance significantly. It turned out that he was right to some extent, but at the time his words annoyed me; they seemed to be bravado, almost a blasphemy, tempting fate.

Needless to say, we all understood the military implications of the test: it had essentially solved the problem of creating high-performance thermonuclear weapons. The test device could serve as a prototype for charges of various powers, weights, and purposes.

We were stirred up, but not just with the exhilaration that comes with a job well done. For my part, I experienced a range of contradictory sentiments, perhaps chief among them a fear that this newly released force could slip out of control and lead to unimaginable disasters. The accident reports, and especially the deaths of the little girl and the soldier, heightened my sense of

---

[1][Georgy Zhukov, the Defense Minister.]

foreboding. I did not hold myself personally responsible for their deaths, but I could not escape a feeling of complicity.

AFTER THE TEST, Marshal Nedelin gave a banquet for selected personnel from both Installations, the ministry, the test range, and the armed forces.

Nedelin had served with distinction as an artillery officer during the war, and rose to become chief of artillery for the front lines. He was a thickset, stocky man who spoke softly but with a confidence that brooked no objection. He impressed me as far from stupid, as energetic and competent, and considerably more active than his predecessor, Marshal Vasilevsky. Nedelin lived with an orderly who doubled as a projectionist, and his favorite pastime was watching movies at home. After one of the many meetings he held, he invited a dozen of us to his cottage, where we watched *Thérèse Raquin,* an interesting French film, and a travelogue on Indonesia.

On the evening of November 22, a festive table was laid in one room of the marshal's cottage. While we were seating ourselves, I heard Nedelin tell the commander of the test range (General B.) that it was his duty to speak at the funeral of the soldier who had been killed, as well as to write to the soldier's parents: "Say that their son was killed on active duty, and make sure they receive a pension."

When we were all in place, the brandy was poured. The bodyguards stood along the wall. Nedelin nodded to me, inviting me to propose the first toast. Glass in hand, I rose, and said something like: "May all our devices explode as successfully as today's, but always over test sites and never over cities."

The table fell silent, as if I had said something indecent. Nedelin grinned a bit crookedly. Then he rose, glass in hand, and said: "Let me tell a parable. An old man wearing only a shirt was praying before an icon. 'Guide me, harden me. Guide me, harden me.' His wife, who was lying on the stove, said: 'Just pray to be hard, old man, I can guide it in myself.' Let's drink to getting hard."

My whole body tensed, and I think I turned pale—normally I blush. For a few seconds no one spoke, and then everyone began talking loudly. I drank my brandy in silence and didn't open my mouth again for the rest of the evening. Many years have passed, but I still feel as if I had been lashed by a whip. Not that my feelings were hurt; I am not easily offended, especially by a joke. But Nedelin's parable was not a joke. He wanted to squelch my pacifist sentiment, and to put me and anyone who might share these ideas in our place.

The point of his story (half lewd, half blasphemous, which added to its unpleasant effect) was clear enough. We, the inventors, scientists, engineers, and craftsmen, had created a terrible weapon, the most terrible weapon in human history; but its use would lie entirely outside our control. The people at the top of the Party and military hierarchy would make the decisions. Of course, I knew this already—I wasn't *that* naïve. But understanding something in an abstract way is different from feeling it with your whole being, like the reality of life and death. The ideas and emotions kindled at that moment have not diminished to this day, and they completely altered my thinking.

A YEAR AFTER the test, in October 1956, the Council of Ministers passed a resolution rewarding those of us who had taken part in the development and testing of the Third Idea. Zeldovich and Khariton received their third Hero of Socialist Labor medals. (Kurchatov had already gotten his third Hero award in 1954.) I was given my second medal, and many other theoretical physicists at the Installation were decorated as well. Several of us received Lenin Prizes. Mikhail Georgadze, secretary of the Presidium of the Supreme Soviet, presented the awards at a special meeting. Before the ceremony, he chatted with us about the recent Hungarian uprising and the war in the Middle East, saying: "Well, we're hitting them hard in Hungary. We ought to let them have it in the Middle East as well, but it's too far away. A shame!"

On December 31, Klava and I were invited to the Kremlin's New Year's Eve reception. We ran into Nedelin on the stairs, but he didn't reply to my greeting. I don't think it was an intentional slight, but it's at least possible that he was snubbing me because he no longer considered me one of "theirs."

Nedelin was killed in 1960, during preparations for an intercontinental ballistic missile (ICBM) test. The USSR already had an ICBM, but the new version possessed many military advantages, and it had been given high priority. Nedelin, then commander of Soviet strategic forces, was in charge of the test.

The missile had been set up on a launch pad, and the splashdown zone in the Pacific Ocean announced. The navy was patrolling its perimeter, and special vessels fitted with telemetry equipment had taken their stations. During the final check of the missile's systems, the control panel signaled a possible malfunction. The technicians in charge recommended that all work be halted until the problem was identified and solved. But Nedelin objected: "The government set the schedule and we've got to stick to it." He ordered them to resume preparations for a launch.

The marshal had his desk placed on the pad directly under the exhaust tubes. The technicians returned to their posts. Suddenly the main engines began firing. Jets of red-hot gas shot out of the exhaust tubes, struck the launch pad, and rebounded upward, engulfing the scaffolding and the workers on it. Nedelin was probably killed in the first seconds. The automatic cameras had been triggered along with the engines, and they recorded the scene. The men on the scaffolding dashed about in the fire and smoke; many jumped off and vanished into the flames. One man momentarily escaped from the fire, but got tangled up in the barbed wire surrounding the launch pad. The next moment he too was engulfed by the flames.

All told, some 190 people died that day.

14

NONTHRESHOLD BIOLOGICAL EFFECTS

In the years following the successful 1955 test of the Third Idea, a number of thermonuclear devices with differing specifications and configurations designed for various carriers were developed at the two Installations. These were extensions of the original design, but considerable effort and testing were necessary nonetheless.

I worried more and more about the biological effects of nuclear tests. My concern was prompted by the course of events and by my own part in the testing program. An important role was also played by my abstract intellectual bent, as well as my emotional idiosyncrasies (I'm not claiming any credit—or, for that matter, blame—in this respect, merely stating a fact). The long-term biological consequences of nuclear testing (particularly atmospheric testing, in which radioactive fallout is dispersed throughout the hemisphere) can be predicted, and the total number of casualties calculated with some accuracy. What cannot be determined is the identity of individual victims, lost as they are in the human sea. We can never establish with certainty that a *particular* cancer victim or congenitally deformed child is a casualty of nuclear testing. People differ markedly in their reactions to the fact that the consequences of nuclear testing can be described only in anonymous statistical terms. I am baffled, however, by those who simply ignore the problem.

The long-term biological consequences of nuclear explosions are generally associated with so-called nonthreshold effects (where no "threshold," or minimum dosage below which damage will never occur, exists). These include genetic damages, and this prompted a reawakening of my youthful interest in genetics. Dramatic progress had taken place in this branch of science, notably Watson and Crick's decoding of the molecular structure of the DNA molecule (the "double helix") and confirmation of its role in heredity. I read about their work in a brilliant *Scientific American* article by George Gamow in which he also expressed his own ideas on the genetic code.

Experimental work on the effects of radiation on heredity had been conducted for some time. Even the smallest dose of radiation can damage the mechanism governing heredity (which we now know involves DNA replication and transmission) and lead to disease, or to death. Genetic damage is a matter of statistical probability; to give a somewhat oversimplified example: *if* an active molecule such as hydrogen peroxide produced by ionizing radiation should attack a section of DNA, damage is certain—but *if* it does not act upon that section, there will be *no* effect. The probability of damage is directly proportionate to the radiation dose, but within certain known limits, the character of the damage is not dependent on the amount of radiation. The greater the amount of radiation, the greater the number of people it is likely to affect; but the *severity* of the damage to each victim is not altered. The probable incidence of injury can be determined by multiplying the amount of radiation by the number of people exposed to it. (If we reduce the amount of radiation by a factor of one hundred, while at the same time increasing the number of those exposed by the same factor, the number of victims will remain constant.) This is the nonthreshold situation as it pertains to genetic damage— and similarly in other areas.

Nonthreshold biological effects confront us with a serious moral dilemma. As I said above, their victims are unidentifiable—"anonymous." And while the nuclear tests of the last decades may be responsible for only a relatively small increase in the general mortality and disease rates, considering the billions of persons who will be exposed to nonthreshold effects during the radioactive decay period of the elements generated by the tests, the total number of "anonymous" victims will be staggering. (I am referring here to surface, atmospheric, and underwater testing, not to underground nuclear tests.)

We must bear in mind, however, that the biological effects of very small doses of radiation on the order of naturally occurring "background" radiation are not yet fully known. Research in this area faces serious difficulties, including the impossibility of conducting a controlled experiment, the heterogeneity of the population, and the need for a prohibitively large statistical base. It is not inconceivable that, where small doses of radiation are concerned, natural corrective mechanisms may come into play, and the effect of radiation may be nonlinear. The possibility cannot be excluded that small doses might even have some positive biological effects. For this and other reasons, the statements and calculations made in this chapter should be treated with some caution.

I HAD A THREEFOLD interest in genetics: in addition to my consciousness of the harmful genetic effects of nuclear weapons, and my intellectual curiosity, I had on my mind the ordeal that Soviet biology had suffered at the hands of the Lysenko "mafia." I had already had several brushes with Lysenkoism, and friends and acquaintances, in particular Tamm and people at the Academy of Sciences, had briefed me thoroughly on this subject.

It was in 1956, as I recall, that Zeldovich took me to see Nikolai Dubinin, one of the scientists Lysenko had denounced. We went to Dubinin's apartment, which doubled as his laboratory since genetics was banned at the institute where he was officially employed. Dubinin showed us colonies of fruit flies that he used for his experiments, and he offered a concise account of the enormous advances being made in genetics abroad. He spoke of our country's backwardness in the field, and the billions of rubles that could be saved if new techniques were applied to Soviet agriculture and medicine. Dubinin impressed me with the range of his intelligence and businesslike manner.

Our visit wasn't a pleasure trip; Kurchatov was planning to take disgraced geneticists under his wing, and to make his institute something of a haven for them, and he was anxious to get the opinions of impartial outsiders. Not long after our meeting with Dubinin, I had occasion to ask Alexander Nesmeyanov, president of the Academy, how he could tolerate the destructiveness of Lysenko and his theories; Nesmeyanov replied that he thought Lysenko was slowly but surely losing ground in a rear-guard battle. Nor were honest biologists wasting time—a letter was about to go to the Central Committee which they hoped would change the situation.

It was too bright a picture that Nesmeyanov painted. True, a letter signed by four hundred biologists was indeed sent—but it was dismissed as an unauthorized collective action, and some of its signatories found themselves in trouble. Meanwhile, Lysenko had a full-page spread in *Pravda* presenting his latest theoretical and problem-solving "insights."

There seem to be two main reasons for the ability of Lysenko and his gang to maintain their positions through the Khrushchev era, when it was no longer a simple matter of using the tactics of denunciation and pseudo-philosophy that had served them so well in the 1930s and 1940s. First, Lysenko was always ready with a new idea that promised immense payoffs for Soviet agriculture— the sort of "quick fix" that Khrushchev found irresistible. (And when it fell through, Lysenko would be ready with a new, equally "surefire" idea.) Second, and even more important: the Party agriculture bureaucracy was full of people who had long since cast their lot with the Lysenko mafia. It was too late for these people to change their colors; and so they supported every new Lysenko venture, and bitterly opposed properly conducted biological experiments which constituted a threat to their vested interests. It took the "second October

Revolution" of Khrushchev's ouster in October 1964 to get them to shift their allegiance—which they then did en masse. To my mind, the whole Lysenko saga is extremely revealing about the manner in which our country is run, and is worth the attention of foreign Sovietologists.

ZELDOVICH GOT ME involved in other public issues, but my role in these was relatively passive. One of them involved a 1954 press campaign against a play by Leonid Zorin, *The Guests*. I don't recall the precise thrust of the attacks; the play, written at the height of the post-Stalin "Thaw," contrasted the highhanded greed and selfishness of the new Soviet Party bureaucracy with the honesty of "the people" and "true Leninists" (including recently rehabilitated Old Bolsheviks). Zeldovich who himself eschewed any public role in this affair, urged me to write to Khrushchev in the play's defense. It wasn't the most propitious beginning to my letter-writing career; it was undramatic and unproductive, and done mainly in response to Zeldovich's urging. Still, one has to begin somewhere; and to come out against what Djilas called "the new class" was in itself worthwhile. It was my first letter to Khrushchev, the first step I'd taken outside my own field. I don't recall clearly how the matter ended; I think with some *pro forma* response from a Central Committee bureau.

I also spoke out in the ongoing debate about whether special high schools emphasizing physics and mathematics were necessary, and whether or not they violated certain social and pedagogical principles. Zeldovich and I wrote to *Izvestia* in the schools' defense, concentrating on the arguments in favor of the schools and for the most part avoiding a direct answer to the schools' critics. Our letter sparked a lively exchange and a witty and venomous article in the satirical magazine *Krokodil* by Nosov, the author of the popular children's book *Mr. Know-nothing*.

TO RETURN to this chapter's theme, I was becoming increasingly concerned during this period with the biological consequences of nuclear testing. Working on the article, "Radioactive Carbon from Nuclear Explosions and Nonthreshold Biological Effects" (written in 1957 and published the following year in the Soviet journal *Atomic Energy*), did much to develop my ideas on the moral issues involved in nuclear testing; I will try, therefore, to recall just how I came to write it.

Early in 1957, Kurchatov suggested (I may have initiated the idea) that I write something about the effects of radiation from the so-called clean bomb. This was prompted by foreign press reports about the development in the U.S. of a "clean" thermonuclear bomb which used no fissionable material and produced no radioactive fallout. Some people thought such weapons would be more morally and politically acceptable than conventional thermonuclear weapons and could be more widely used, since damage would be limited to the zone affected by the shock wave. I was supposed to show that this was not in fact the case, and to denounce the new American development, without implicating "conventional" thermonuclear weapons. In other words, the original aim of the article was to have been openly political, and the approach one-sided.

But after reading through the extensive humanistic, political, and scientific literature on the subject, I extended the article's scope and reached more balanced conclusions. My scientific sources included articles by Ovsei Leipunovsky (whose brother was one of the inventors of Soviet breeder reactors), Libby, Adashnikov, and Shapiro. Among the writers with a philosophical and humanist perspective, Albert Schweitzer left a lasting impression on me: eighteen years later, as I drafted my Nobel lecture, I would recall his words.

In my article, I dealt with the fact mentioned earlier in this chapter, that "the number of victims of additional radiation is determined by nonthreshold biological effects." Such effects, including carcinogenesis and genetic change, which in theory might occur at even the very lowest radiation levels, could lead to many deaths and cases of disease as huge populations—over the course of many generations—are exposed to them. "The simplest nonthreshold effect," I wrote, "is the influence on heredity. . . . A single ionization event is sufficient to cause irreversible change—a mutation—in a gene. . . . The probability of damage is in direct proportion to the radiation dose." I estimated that the probability of hereditary disease increases with radiation at the rate of 10^{-4} per roentgen. I posited that cancer and damage to the body's immune system (resulting in premature death) may also be due to nonthreshold effects. An estimate for the combined impact of damage to the immune system and the cancer-promoting effect of radiation was calculated based on data reflecting an average life span reduction of five years for X-ray technicians and radiologists whose total lifetime exposure to radiation probably does not exceed 1,000 roentgens. I also suggested that a global increase in mutations of bacteria and viruses (irrespective of the cause of the mutations) might have been an important factor in the spread of such diseases as diphtheria in the nineteenth century, or the influenza epidemic, and that low-level radiation might further increase the rate of mutations. I therefore estimated the total radiation impact to be equivalent to at least 3×10^{-4} per roentgen. Bearing in mind that an average human lifetime is 20,000 days, each roentgen of global radiation will reduce this average lifetime by one week! My overall estimate of the number of human victims of a one-megaton detonation was 10,000.[1] Two-thirds of this

---

[1][Frank von Hippel of Princeton University has used recent UN surveys of population exposures to atmospheric fallout and of the health effects of ionizing radiation to obtain an estimate

huge figure was attributed to the radioactive isotope carbon-14, which is formed during both "clean" and "normal" thermonuclear explosions.[2] Carbon-14 has a half-life of 5,000 years; its damaging effects thus continue over thousands of years. I had assumed during this period the average size of the Earth's population would be 30 billion. The radioactive products of "normal" nuclear explosions—my calculations took account of strontium-90 and cesium-137 only—would do immediate damage, affecting perhaps one-third of the estimated mid-1950s world population of two billion. The "clean" bomb does not produce strontium and cesium, but it does produce carbon-14.

By 1957, the total power of the nuclear bombs that had been tested around the world added up to nearly fifty megatons. According to my estimates, this would mean 500,000 casualties. Moreover, the figures were increasing swiftly. I concluded my article:

What sort of moral and political conclusions should be drawn from the figures cited? One argument used by those who maintain that testing is "harmless" is that cosmic rays are a source of greater doses of radiation. But this argument does not alter the fact that to the suffering and death already existing in the world there would be added hundreds of thousands of additional victims, including people living in neutral countries and yet-unborn children. The two world wars increased the mortality rate in our century by less than ten percent—but that does not make war a normal phenomenon.

Another argument frequently encountered in various countries' literature is that the progress of civilization and the development of new technology have led to human casualties in many other cases, as well. The example of automobile accidents is often cited. But the analogy is neither precise nor apt. Automobiles improve people's lives; they only cause harm in case of an accident, and careless drivers can be held criminally responsible. In contrast, each and every nuclear test does damage. And this crime is committed with complete impunity, since it is impossible to prove that a particular death was caused by radiation. Furthermore, posterity has no way to defend itself from our actions. Halting the tests will directly save the lives of hundreds of thousands of people, and it also promises even

---

of 1,000 to 25,000 cancers and genetic disorders per megaton, which is consistent with Sakharov's earlier estimate.]

[2] Carbon-14 is produced when neutrons from a thermonuclear explosion interact with atmospheric nitrogen. The numbers of neutrons produced by "clean" and "normal" charges of the same power are about equal, and so are the amounts of carbon-14.

greater indirect benefits, reducing international tension and the risk of nuclear war, the fundamental danger of our time.

The article was published in 1958, a few months after Khrushchev had become chairman of the USSR Council of Ministers and announced that the Soviet Union was unilaterally halting all nuclear tests. This was an auspicious beginning for the Khrushchev era; but seven months later, testing was resumed.

At Kurchatov's request, I also prepared a more popular version of the *Atomic Energy* article, which appeared in English, German, French, Spanish, and Japanese translation, in magazines published by Soviet embassies and propaganda agencies. The German version was published in *Die Sovietunion Heute* (*The Soviet Union Today*, distributed by the Soviet embassy in West Germany) under the title "The Radioactive Danger of Nuclear Tests"; in it, I praised the historical significance of the Supreme Soviet's decision to institute a unilateral cessation of testing, noting that this represented a serious step toward banning nuclear weapons and reducing the danger of nuclear war; and continued:

> There is good reason for the other great powers which are working on nuclear weapons to follow the USSR's example. Since the USSR and the other countries of the world socialist system are pursuing a policy of peace, the continuation of testing cannot be justified by the need to preserve military parity.

I explained the essence of the nuclear threat and offered statistics I had prepared for *Atomic Energy*, although the editors of the translations, instead of using the original article's upper *and* lower limits for the number of potential victims, used only the figures I had calculated for the upper limits. Thus, my estimates, high enough already, most likely appeared to Western readers to have been exaggerated for propaganda purposes. I concluded by criticizing some statements made by Edward Teller and Albert Latter in their book *Our Nuclear Future:*[3]

> In most instances, [Teller and Latter] do not use absolute figures, but resort instead to unsubstantiated comparisons with other causes of death that have nothing to do with the subject at hand. From this one might conclude that a package of cigarettes is more harmful than nuclear testing. . . .

[3][Criterion Books, 1958.]

"It is obvious," I said, "that we are dealing with a clear case of logical, moral, and political confusion," and I cited the following passage from the book:

It is said that not even a single human life should be put at risk. But wouldn't it be more realistic and more in keeping with humanity's ideals if we strove for a better life for all of mankind?

I remarked:

This last idea would undoubtedly be correct if the authors had in mind peaceful coexistence, disarmament, and, above all, a halt to nuclear testing, and not the dangerous idea of mutual deterrence based on military parity which is only one step away from preventive war.

The Soviet state was compelled to develop nuclear weapons and conduct tests to provide for its security in the face of American and British nuclear weapons. But the USSR's goal is not universal nuclear destruction, but peaceful coexistence, disarmament, and the banning of nuclear weapons.

Khrushchev himself authorized the publication of my articles. Kurchatov discussed the matter twice with him and then referred some minor suggested editorial changes to me. Khrushchev approved the revised versions at the end of June, and they were sent off immediately to the editors.

I have quoted at such length from both articles because of the importance of the nuclear test issue, and because the quotations accurately reflect my frame of mind at the time when I was just beginning to stray from the official position. Later recollections are no substitute for what I actually wrote all those years ago. (The fact that those articles were edited should also be taken into account.) In 1959, my article (the scholarly version, I believe) appeared in the collection Soviet Scientists Against the Nuclear Menace.

To the best of my knowledge, no notice of these publications of mine was taken in the West, probably because my name was still quite unknown—no one associated it with the author of works on controlled thermonuclear reactions published two years earlier. Although it is no longer true in my case, the poor use Western journalists make of their archives and reference works, and the lack of interest they show in new names still amazes me.

When nuclear tests were driven underground in 1963, the biological effects of nuclear radiation ceased to alarm people. I was no exception. But the 1986 disaster at Chernobyl brought the matter back to public attention in a particularly tragic manner.

LATE IN 1957, Grigory Barenblat, a young specialist in theoretical mechanics who had collaborated with Zeldovich on a number of articles, asked me to help his father, Isaak Barenblat. I had met the senior Barenblat, a well-known endocrinologist, not long before, when Klava had gone to him for an examination. He had allegedly told his patients jokes about the "intimate relationship" between Khrushchev and Ekaterina Furtseva, the first woman elected to the Presidium, and he had been arrested. (The topic was a popular one—probably less out of any interest in the putative "intimacy" between the head of state and the minister of culture, which in any case probably was just gossip, than in the sensational fact that a woman[!] had been admitted to the Presidium. Many years earlier, when the colleagues of the great German mathematician David Hilbert objected to Emmy Noether's admission to the Philosophy Faculty of Göttingen University on the grounds that she was a woman, he had exclaimed: "But gentlemen, after all, the Philosophy Faculty is not a bathhouse!" This "bathhouse" principle was extraordinarily tenacious in the Soviet Union.) Isaak Barenblat, it was later learned, had been denounced by a colleague, someone he had considered a friend. I decided to write, with Grigory's assistance, to Khrushchev himself, and sent off the letter to the Central Committee that same day. About two weeks later (I know it was in January 1958), I was summoned by the head of the Central Committee's general department. After some elaborate preliminaries, including questions about my relationship with Barenblat and heartfelt sighs—"To say such things about such respected people"—he told me Khrushchev had assigned Suslov to look into my letter.

Two days later, Suslov summoned me. It was around eight o'clock in the evening when I entered his spacious office in the Kremlin. An unusual carved wooden table by the window was set for tea. We sat facing each other; next to Suslov was a desk on which lay a dossier on Barenblat and a notebook in which he made occasional entries. He drank tea and munched pastries as we talked. I took a few sips from my glass.

"I'm very glad to meet you, Andrei Dmitrievich. You're asking me about—what was his name again?"

"Dr. Barenblat. Mikhail Andreyevich, I'm convinced that he has done nothing that merits criminal punishment. He's an honest man and a fine doctor."

"I've looked into his case. He said some inadmissible things. He's not our type of person at all, we found 300,000 rubles at his home, and yet he lives on macaroni from the student cafeteria."

I found it impossible to come up with an appropriate response to the remark about the macaroni. I'm convinced that it reflected a deeply rooted facet of

Suslov's psychology, whether it was hatred of Party enthusiasts of an earlier era, with their disdain for money, or simply a generic distaste for misers. I simply replied that a popular physician in honest practice could easily save 300,000 rubles (30,000 of today's rubles); a great state shouldn't be so concerned about jokes in any case. During the war, Barenblat had proved himself a faithful defender of our system—what were words compared to deeds?

Suslov listened to me with a slightly condescending air. He repeated several times that Barenblat had said "inadmissible things," without specifying what they were. I asked again, what were words compared to deeds? The impasse began to assume a certain ominous quality. Finally, Suslov said: "I'll take another look at the case. Let's move on to something else. Do you know anything about this decision?"

He placed before me the text of a Presidium decision to announce a unilateral halt in nuclear testing. The typewritten text had the usual red stamp on the margin, a warning that no copies should be made. A section of the page had been cut off with scissors. "We're going to announce this at the Supreme Soviet session in March," Suslov said. "What's your reaction?"

I was excited. "I knew nothing of this; I don't think anyone at our Installation knows about it, not even our director, Khariton. I believe it's very important that nuclear tests be stopped; they're responsible for significant genetic damage—but we should have been informed of such a major decision beforehand so that we could tie up loose ends at the Installation."

Suslov didn't ask what I meant by "loose ends"; that probably would have pushed our conversation into an area where he was not comfortable. He changed the subject.

"You referred to the 'genetic consequences' of testing. What are your thoughts on genetics? Kurchatov is setting up a genetics laboratory right now—do we need it, or could we do without it?"

I replied that genetics was of enormous theoretical and practical significance; our country's past rejection of it had been very damaging. In the beginning, genetic theory had been deduced from variations in inherited characteristics. Now, however, a new theoretical foundation had been provided by molecular biologists; and it was molecular biology that was to be studied in Kurchatov's new laboratory: an important and necessary beginning. A laboratory of this type could not be set up at the Lenin All-Union Academy of Agricultural Sciences so long as it was still being run by reckless opportunists and schemers, I added.

Suslov listened closely, asking questions and taking notes. I don't recall whether Lysenko was mentioned by name, but it was clear enough whom and what I meant. I have no idea whether Suslov took any steps concerning the quarrel between the Lysenkoists and the geneticists before Khrushchev's October 1964 ouster. It's possible that when the moment came, Suslov recalled the information about genetics I'd given him six years earlier, or even took another look at his notes. As for Barenblat, he was given a two- or two-and-a-half-year sentence, but was released after one year, and I'd like to think that my intercession played some part in this relatively mild treatment.

My COLLEAGUES at the Installation could not believe their ears when they learned of the forthcoming halt in testing. But it was decided not to change any of our plans, since we suspected that testing might be resumed before long—which is indeed what happened. The Americans and British were even more surprised than we were by Khrushchev's decision, which was announced at the session of the Supreme Soviet when he assumed the post of chairman of the Council of Ministers. They insisted that negotiations on verification procedures continue, to ensure that any test ban was being observed, and declared that they would in any case proceed with their own planned tests, which would take about a year to complete.

In the summer of 1958, the United States and Great Britain began a long series of tests, and a propaganda war ensued. We claimed that an unprecedented initiative on the part of the USSR had again failed to find Western support. The West claimed (mistakenly) that the USSR had prepared itself for the halt in testing while the U.S. and Britain were caught by surprise, before they'd been able to carry out the scheduled programs. Then and only then would it be possible for the U.S. to follow the USSR's example.

Meanwhile, it became apparent that the devices scheduled by the Installation for testing were extremely important, both technically and conceptually. Could devices so nearly ready for our arsenal be renounced? Could a portion of them, at least, be accepted without testing? Was it possible to design new devices, perhaps with inferior characteristics, that could become part of the arsenal without prior testing? Or was it altogether inconceivable to accept untested devices under any circumstances?

While we were heatedly engaged in discussing the new situation, orders came from Khrushchev to prepare to resume testing, because of the American and British refusal to follow our example. Thus the question was decided politically without regard to its technical aspects. At the Installation, it was "all hands on deck" as we prepared for testing in the late fall.

I found what was happening completely unacceptable, both politically and morally. I felt that such rapid changes of position would lead to a complete loss of trust in the USSR on this already exceedingly complex issue. Also, I had by this time calculated that every one-megaton atmospheric test would cost ten thousand human lives! If the USSR now resumed testing, the signing of a test ban agreement might well be delayed for several years—meaning tens, perhaps even hundreds, of megatons of atmospheric detonations, and hundreds of thousands or millions of new casualties. Even if my estimates were on the high side, the number of potential human casualties was still colossal. I proposed that the USSR should:

1) In no case begin testing within a year of Khrushchev's announcement—the Americans and British had said a year was all they needed.

2) Redesign the devices scheduled for testing, so that they could in principle be deployed without testing.

3) Renounce the doctrine that no device could be adopted without testing as being inflexible, dogmatic, and inappropriate to the coming "test-free" era.

4) Invest substantially in computers and new calculating techniques with a view to a wider use of calculations in place of tests.

5) Develop new experimental methods for modeling various functions of devices without full-scale testing.

In September 1958 I brought these proposals to Kurchatov, whom I regarded as the only person who had any chance of influencing Khrushchev, and the one official in our ministry who might be sympathetic to them. We met at his small house at his institute. We sat on a bench beneath dense, overhanging foliage—Kurchatov called his cottage a "forester's hut," I think in memory of his father's house, his childhood home. Because of an illness two years earlier, doctors had severely curtailed his working hours, and he often summoned people to the cottage instead of going to the Institute. He would take notes in a thick notebook he had camouflaged with the dust cover of Nehru's *Memoirs*.

Kurchatov listened closely to what I had to say. He was in basic agreement with me. "Khrushchev's in the Crimea now," he said, "vacationing by the sea. I'll fly to him if I can convince my doctors to let me go, and I'll present your ideas to him."

At the end of our conversation, which lasted about an hour, Kurchatov's secretary, Pereverzev, appeared with a camera and proceeded to take a series of pictures of us from a variety of angles. Kurchatov's dog, who'd been getting under his feet the whole time, also got into several of these shots. Pereverzev was putting together a photobiography of Kurchatov. He eventually produced several collections of photographs and gave me one that included the pictures he'd taken that day.

Kurchatov's trip to Yalta was unsuccessful. Khrushchev found our proposals unacceptable. I do not know the details of their conversation, but I heard that Khrushchev was extremely displeased and that from then until Kurchatov's death a year and a half later, he no longer enjoyed Khrushchev's trust.

A couple of months later new tests took place—and were indeed a great success and important from a technical point of view.

In a 1959 speech to the Twenty-first Party Congress, Kurchatov stated that the West's unwillingness to follow the USSR's "prudent example" had forced us to resume testing:

> . . . during the spring and the summer of 1958, the USA conducted more than 50 tests, which forced our country to resume tests in the fall. It should be noted that the tests proved very successful, and demonstrated the extreme effectiveness of various new design principles worked out by Soviet scientists and engineers. The Soviet Army has acquired a more powerful, reliable, and less costly nuclear and thermonuclear weaponry.

It is not surprising that Kurchatov, after failing to change the official position, now publicly supported it. He was both sincere and correct in his assessment of the test results—not that this in any way alters the fact that we could have done without atmospheric tests if we had by then concluded something on the order of the future Moscow Limited Test Ban Treaty.

At his last public appearance Kurchatov declared: "I am glad that I was born in Russia and have dedicated my life to Soviet atomic science. I deeply believe, and am firmly convinced, that our people and our government will use the achievements of that science solely for the good of mankind."

Kurchatov's sincerity in this is unquestionable; at least he certainly wanted this to be true. However, I think now that it would have been better not to have spoken of "Soviet" science, since for me science has no national boundaries, but that is what Kurchatov said, and he chose his words consciously.

I had great respect for Kurchatov, despite the differences in our position and in our whole outlook on life. In the spring of 1959, while Kurchatov was still alive (he died in February 1960), I went for a walk at the Installation with Davidenko, who had known Kurchatov well. Davidenko was not quite so enthusiastic as I. "Kurchatov is a fine person," he said, "a major scientist and an excellent organizer. He loves science and has made great contributions to it. He's a decent man, warm and caring, loyal to old friends and comrades. He has a sense of humor and he's certainly no bore. But don't overestimate his closeness to you! Kurchatov was first and foremost an 'operator,' and what's more, an operator under Stalin—and he was like a fish in water then."

Davidenko was right about some things, but I think he was underestimating Kurchatov's open-mindedness and willingness to take risks in unusual situations, as evidenced in that 1958 trip to see Khrushchev.

15

KHRUSHCHEV

Khrushchev and Brezhnev in 1959.
July 10, 1961. My note and Khrushchev's
speech. A major series of tests. My father's
death.

I HAD my first encounter with Nikita Khrushchev as head of government in 1959, when Khariton and I were invited to represent the Installation at an interdepartmental conference on a certain military issue. Khrushchev, who was chairing the meeting in the Kremlin's Oval Hall, delivered the opening address. He stressed the importance of the issue to be discussed and sharply criticized several leading officials, in particular Marshal Dmitri Ustinov [then the Council of Ministers' deputy chairman in charge of arms production, later Minister of Defense] and the aircraft designers Alexander Yakovlev and Andrei Tupolev. Khrushchev accused Yakovlev of neglecting his job in order to make his mark as a writer. (I learned later that Yakovlev had written memoirs that contained fulsome praise of Stalin; this may have been the underlying reason for Khrushchev's displeasure. The memoirs were eventually published in 1966, after Khrushchev had been ousted.) As for Tupolev, Khrushchev claimed he was being carried away by extravagant dreams and gigantomania.

Khrushchev appeared anxious to limit the resources invested in military technology and to concentrate on the most effective programs. In this, as in other of his initiatives, he seemed to meet with a sullen resistance (if not outright sabotage) from certain circles in the bureaucracy. The situation was complicated by Khrushchev's tendency to pursue his sound ideas and his unsound ones (of which he had more than enough) with equal drive and tenacity. He began by introducing sorely needed reforms, delivering his epoch-making speech against Stalinism at the Twentieth Party Congress, and releasing those political prisoners who had managed to survive in the bowels of the Gulag. But he lacked the consistency and insight needed to mobilize support in the country at large, and he was handicapped by his inability to free his thinking completely from dogmas he had espoused when he had been one of

Stalin's favorites, and an executor of Stalin's criminal will. Nonetheless, Khrushchev did renounce many of his preconceptions, and I believe that this readiness to revise his views, combined with his innate intelligence and an ambition to be worthy of his post, ensured that his accomplishments would outweigh his mistakes (and even his crimes) on the scales of history.

Khrushchev's later years in office were marred by blunders and reckless adventures. A lack of wise and well-intentioned advisers and Khrushchev's own loss of touch with reality, caused by the illusion of absolute power, took their toll. Still, the Cuban missile crisis did display his mettle—even though he was the one who forced that dangerous confrontation on the world in the first place.

But back in 1959, we had yet to witness the decisive denunciation of Stalin at the Twenty-second Party Congress, a tightening of the screws in the labor camps, disastrous agricultural and foreign policy ventures, the Berlin Wall, the assault on the Party bureaucracy's monopoly of power (a test of strength which rebounded on Khrushchev himself), his attempt to curb military expenditures and to demilitarize the economy, which provoked resistance in the armed forces, absurd clashes with the cultural intelligentsia, the resurrection of Lysenkoism, the Moscow Limited Test Ban Treaty, and, finally, the Cuban missile crisis and the 1963 food shortages. Khrushchev's ouster in October 1964 put a stop to this kaleidoscopic succession of incongruous events and cleared the way for the conservative Party bureaucracy personified by Brezhnev, and for augmented roles for the military-industrial complex and the KGB.

The 1959 meeting was my first opportunity to watch Khrushchev in action since 1955 (I had not been invited to any of the intervening Politburo sessions). His manner was much more assertive. He no longer remained in the shadows, but with evident pleasure took center stage, asking the speakers pointed questions, interrupting, and making it clear that he had the last word. He impressed me as an intelligent man and a leader of stature, though also as brash, susceptible to flattery (true, this is easier to see in hindsight) and uncultivated (this, too, I probably became conscious of only later).

USTINOV FOLLOWED Khrushchev. He briefly but competently outlined the activities and plans of the numerous scientific and industrial establishments engaged in military projects. He concluded with the admission: "I agree with you, Nikita Sergeyevich, that major errors have been committed in determining goals and priorities, and I promise you I will do all I can to correct them."

Ustinov spoke so softly I couldn't make out everything he said; he seemed to be talking directly to Khrushchev, whose expression remained inscrutable, although it was evident that he was listening with attention. Ustinov appeared to have in mind some higher purpose that transcended the conventional concerns of an official, even of one who stood at the pinnacle of the apparatus. Ustinov shunned the spotlight, leaving that to Khrushchev and others, but I knew he had a central role in the research, development, and production of armaments, and I thought to myself: "That's *our* military-industrial complex" (the term was just coming into vogue in our press, with respect to the U.S.). I had a similar reaction when I met Leonid Smirnov, another top defense industry official, who participated in the negotiations on the SALT and ABM treaties. (Kissinger speaks highly of Smirnov in his memoirs.[1] They met at the SALT negotiations.) Both Ustinov and Smirnov were professional, knowledgeable, talented, and energetic, with excellent organizational abilities, and entirely devoted to their work; it had become an end in itself, to which they subordinated all other matters. Men of this stripe are valuable—but sometimes dangerous.

Speaking next after Ustinov were the ministers responsible for military production and senior officials from R&D institutions. In contrast to Ustinov, their tendency was to blame any difficulties on circumstances beyond their control and on their suppliers.

If memory serves, my first look at Leonid Brezhnev had also come in 1959, just prior to this conference.

I MUST BACKTRACK at this point. In 1957, after Zavenyagin's death, Mikhail Pervukhin, a Presidium member, had been appointed minister of Medium Machine Building and deputy chairman of the Council of Ministers with responsibility for new military technology. Pervukhin began—as had Malyshev four years earlier—by flying to the Installation, accompanied by assistants and bodyguards. A second airplane followed with supplies, including several refrigerators with a private stock of delicacies—one of Pervukhin's "perks" as a Presidium member.

He spoke before the assembled staff, and then held a series of meetings to learn what was happening at the Installation. He did not, however, have a chance to put the knowledge to use: just a couple of months later [June 29, 1957], the "Anti-Party Group of Malenkov, Kaganovich, Molotov, and Shepilov, who joined them" (to use the standard phrasing of that time) was "unmasked." Pervukhin was soon added to this list, and he lost his post as minister of Medium Machine Building [on July 24]. The group had evidently been plotting to overthrow Khrushchev, to bolster their own shaky positions, and to

[1][Henry Kissinger, *White House Years* (Little, Brown and Co., 1979), pp. 1233–38]

put an end to the "time of troubles" the Twentieth Party Congress had triggered. (The same period was often described as "the Thaw," a term coined by Ilya Ehrenburg with reference to the cultural scene.) Today, we would simply call Khrushchev's antagonists Stalinists, but he avoided that term, which was too pointed and could cut both ways.

Khrushchev had granted the secretaries of the regional Party committees a freer hand, and they, together with several officials in the central apparatus, helped him eliminate the Anti-Party Group's threat to his position (and to the world). All those involved were dismissed from office. Some were simply pensioned off, but Pervukhin was sent into honorable exile as ambassador to East Germany, and Molotov was similarly appointed ambassador to Mongolia. Khrushchev then moved quickly to fill key slots with people he considered "reliable." Nikolai Ignatov, first secretary of the Gorky regional Party committee, and Ekaterina Furtseva, who had supported Khrushchev at the crucial Central Committee meeting which rejected the Anti-Party Group, were among those appointed full members of the Presidium. Khrushchev also reorganized the political power structure, a tactic he employed often thereafter, though with diminishing success.

Efim Slavsky was named to replace Pervukhin as minister of Medium Machine Building—and he succeeded in holding on to that post for more than a quarter of a century. Trained as a metallurgical engineer, he was a skillful organizer and a hard worker, decisive and bold, quite thoughtful, intelligent, and eager to nail down a definite opinion on every subject. He was also stubborn and often intolerant of the views of others. He could be gentle and polite; or, on occasion, extremely crude. Politically and morally a pragmatist, he seemed sincere in his approval both of Khrushchev's de-Stalinization program and of Brezhnev's stabilization; he was ready to follow every turn of the Party line. Slavsky adored technology, machinery, and construction. He was genuinely enthusiastic about both military and peaceful applications of atomic energy, and impatient with whiners, nitpickers, and doubters. He was unsentimental about such "minor matters" as the damaging effects of radiation on the health of workers at atomic plants and mines, and even less concerned about the anonymous victims of nuclear weapons testing who so worried Sakharov.

During the civil war, Slavsky had served as an officer in the First Cavalry Army, and he was fond of reminiscing about that period. His appearance matched his character: he was a tall, powerful figure with strong hands and broad, sloping shoulders, a ruddy face with prominent features, and a loud, assured voice. I met his wife once and was struck by the contrast between them: she seemed a quiet, cultivated woman, no longer young, wearing an old-fashioned hat. He paid her marked attention and was unusually gentle with her.

In one of our last meetings before I became a "renegade," Slavsky said to me: "Andrei Dmitrievich, if you're so worried about nuclear weapons, why not work on peaceful applications of nuclear explosions? What a magnificent opportunity to benefit mankind. The Udokan copper mine alone is worth any price.[2] And think of all the canals and dams to be built—they'll change the face of the Earth."

Despite his appointment as minister of Medium Machine Building, Slavsky, unlike his predecessors, did not become a deputy chairman of the Council of Ministers. Perhaps his rank in the Party hierarchy was too low, or perhaps Khrushchev was reluctant to concentrate so much power in the hands of one person; in any event, some functions previously associated with the post of deputy chairman were shifted to Leonid Brezhnev, a newcomer on the Central Committee staff whom Khrushchev had summoned from Kazakhstan. Brezhnev already had close ties to Khrushchev and enjoyed his complete confidence (this most likely was the reason he'd been chosen to implement the "virgin lands" program in 1954).

In the spring of 1958, we had learned that the Central Committee's Defense Bureau (or it may have been the Committee on Defense Technology) was in the process of drafting a resolution which affected the allocation of resources within the military sector, and which we regarded as seriously flawed. Such matters were no longer empty formalities as in Beria's time; if the Council of Ministers adopted the resolution, it would acquire the force of law and, in our opinion, lead to a diversion of intellectual and material resources from more important projects. Khariton decided to appeal to Brezhnev, whose responsibilities included oversight of military research and development, and he took me with him to Moscow for support, as a fresh face.

Brezhnev received us in the small new office he had recently been given in the same building where I'd met with Beria. As we entered, Brezhnev exclaimed, "So, the 'bomb squad' is here!" While we were making ourselves comfortable, he told us that his father, a purebred worker, regarded the creators of lethal weapons as consummate villains; he used to say that they should be taken to a high hill and hanged as a warning to others. "And now," said Brezhnev, "I'm involved in that dirty business myself, just as you are, and with the same good intentions. Right, let's hear what you have to say."

Brezhnev listened carefully, taking notes. Then he said: "I understand perfectly. I'll consult my comrades and let you know the decision." He accompanied us politely to the door, and shook our hands.

The resolution was not adopted by the Council of Ministers.

---

[2][Slavsky was referring to the proposed use of a thermonuclear explosion to exploit copper ore which had been discovered in Siberia near Udokan.]

No NUCLEAR TESTS were conducted by the USSR, the United States, or Great Britain in 1959, 1960, or the first half of 1961. [France, however, detonated its first nuclear device in March 1960.] This was a voluntary, *de facto* moratorium on testing, possibly based on some sort of informal agreement. In 1961, Khrushchev reached a decision which, as usual, came as a surprise to those most directly affected: to end the moratorium and resume testing.

In July of that year, Klava, the children, and I were staying at the Council of Ministers' Miskhor spa on the southern coast of the Crimea. This was our second holiday there, and we thoroughly enjoyed the sea, the sun, and the wonderful accommodations at that resort for the privileged. Late on July 7, I received a telephone call from the Ministry summoning me to Moscow (our vacation was in any case almost over). We left the next day.

I saw Khariton on July 9 and expressed my hope that the forthcoming meetings would result in an understanding with Khrushchev and his colleagues. Khariton smiled at my naïveté and warned me with more than a hint of sarcasm not to count on mutual understanding. He proved to be right.

At ten the next morning, I entered the same Oval Hall where I had seen Khrushchev two years earlier. This 1961 conference, referred to in official papers as "A Meeting of Party and Government Leaders with the Atomic Scientists," had been convened at Khrushchev's personal initiative.

Khrushchev announced his decision at once: nuclear tests would resume in the fall, because the international situation had deteriorated and because the USSR lagged behind the U.S. in testing (by a substantial margin, if Britain's tests were taken into account). We would have to add to our nuclear might and show the "imperialists" what we could do.

Although Khrushchev made no reference to his recent meeting with Kennedy in Vienna [June 1961] or to the imminent construction of the Berlin Wall (I had no inkling of that scheme), it was perfectly clear that the decision to resume testing was politically motivated. Technical considerations played even less of a role than they had in 1958.

As might be expected, no provision had been made for discussion of the decision. After Khrushchev's speech, the key people were supposed to talk for ten or fifteen minutes each about their work in progress. When my turn came toward the middle of the roll, I spoke quickly about our weapons research, and then volunteered the opinion that we had little to gain from a resumption of testing at this juncture in our program. My remark registered, but evoked no immediate response. I went on to describe some of my department's more exotic projects, such as the use of nuclear explosions to power spacecraft and other "science fiction" schemes. (I have since learned from Freeman Dyson's

Disturbing the Universe that in 1958 he too began studying the feasibility of a nuclear spaceship in the American Orion Project.) Returning to my seat, I borrowed some paper from Evgeny Zababakhin (who was sitting next to me), scribbled a note to Khrushchev, and passed it down the aisle.

To the best of my recollection after the lapse of more than twenty years (I did not keep a copy), my note read:

> To Comrade N. S. Khrushchev.
>
> I am convinced that a resumption of testing at this time would only favor the USA. Prompted by the success of our Sputniks, they could use tests to improve their devices. They have underestimated us in the past, whereas our program has been based on a realistic appraisal of the situation. [I have omitted a sentence for reasons of security.] Don't you think that new tests will seriously jeopardize the test ban negotiations, the cause of disarmament, and world peace?
>
> A. Sakharov

Khrushchev read the note, glanced in my direction, and shoved it into his jacket pocket after folding it into quarters. When the reports had been completed, he rose, thanked the speakers, and then added: "Let's all take a break. On behalf of the Central Committee Presidium, I invite our guests to dine with us an hour from now."

At the appointed time, we reassembled in the banquet hall, where a festive table had been set for sixty, with wine, mineral water, salads, and the freshest available caviar. The Presidium members filed in after the scientists had taken their assigned seats. Khrushchev, who remained standing, waited for quiet, and picked up a glass of wine as if to propose a toast. But instead, he set the glass back down and began to speak about my note—calmly at first, but then with growing agitation, turning red in the face and raising his voice. He talked for half an hour or more, and I will again do my best to recall the gist of his remarks from memory:

> Here's a note I've received from Academician Sakharov. [He held up the note but did not read it aloud, so my arguments weren't really clear to the audience.] Sakharov writes that we don't need tests. But I've got a briefing paper which shows how many tests we've conducted and how many more the Americans have conducted. Can Sakharov really prove that with fewer tests we've gained more valuable information than the Americans? Are they dumber than we are? There's no way I can know all the technical fine points. But the *number* of tests, that's what matters most. How can you develop new technology without testing?

But Sakharov goes further. He's moved beyond science into politics. Here he's poking his nose where it doesn't belong. You can be a good scientist without understanding a thing about politics. Politics is like the old joke about the two Jews traveling on a train. One asks the other: "So, where are you going?" "I'm going to Zhitomir." "What a sly fox," thinks the first Jew. "I know he's really going to Zhitomir, but he told me Zhitomir so I'll think he's going to Zhmerinka."

Leave politics to us—we're the specialists. You make your bombs and test them, and we won't interfere with you; we'll help you. But remember, we have to conduct our policies from a position of strength. We don't advertise it, but that's how it is! There can't be any other policy. Our opponents don't understand any other language. Look, we helped elect Kennedy last year. Then we met with him in Vienna, a meeting that could have been a turning point. But what does he say? "Don't ask for too much. Don't put me in a bind. If I make too many concessions, I'll be turned out of office." Quite a guy! He comes to a meeting, but can't perform. What the hell do we need a guy like that for? Why waste time talking to him? Sakharov, don't try to tell us what to do or how to behave. We understand politics. I'd be a jellyfish and not Chairman of the Council of Ministers if I listened to people like Sakharov!

Khrushchev broke off abruptly on this harsh note, saying: "Perhaps that's enough for today. Let's drink to our future successes. I'd also like to drink to your health, dear comrades, but my doctors won't allow me anything stronger than mineral water."

While Khrushchev was speaking, the room was still. Everyone sat frozen, some averting their gaze, others maintaining set expressions. Anastas Mikoyan bowed his head low over his plate to conceal a grin playing on his lips. Now everyone else drank, but I did not. No one looked in my direction.

After he cooled down, Khrushchev added a few more words: "I can see Sakharov's got illusions. The next time I go for talks with the capitalists, I'll take him with me. Let him see them and the world with his own eyes, and then maybe he'll understand." That was a promise Khrushchev did not keep.

The late Yuri Zysin was the only person to come over after the meeting and express support for my position.[3]

* * *

[3] [For Khrushchev's account of this incident, see *Khrushchev Remembers: The Last Testament* (Little, Brown and Co., 1974), pp. 68–71.]

I WAS TO SEE Khrushchev twice more after that memorable day. The first occasion was in mid-August 1961, after the Berlin Wall had been built, and after the flight of Vostok-2 (I remember Khrushchev's mentioning the astronaut Titov). Preparations for our tests were in full swing. Khariton delivered a brief progress report, but Khrushchev was already familiar with the test program, and in particular with our plan to explode a device of record-breaking power, the "Big Bomb." I had decided to test a "clean" version: this would reduce its force, but the Big Bomb would still greatly surpass any previously tested charge, and would be several thousand times more powerful than the bomb dropped on Hiroshima. By reducing the fission component, we would minimize the number of casualties from fallout, but radioactive carbon would still cause an enormous number of victims over the next five thousand years.

While Khariton had the floor, Khrushchev asked: "Does Sakharov realize that he was wrong?" The question was addressed more to Khariton than to me, but I was sitting near Khrushchev, so I answered him directly: "My opinion hasn't changed, but I do my work and carry out orders."

Khrushchev muttered something I couldn't quite make out and then spoke briefly. He emphasized the heightened importance of our work in light of the tense world situation. He spoke only in passing of the Berlin Wall—the chief cause of increased tension at the time. He mentioned the visit to the Soviet Union of an American senator who had seemed to be probing for possible compromise. Khrushchev had told him about the scheduled tests and the 100-megaton bomb. According to Khrushchev, this information caused the senator's grown daughter to burst into tears. [It is possible that this was John McCloy, a presidential adviser, but not a senator. Somewhere along the line confusion crept in—whether it was my mistake or Khrushchev's, I'm not sure.—A.S. 1988]

IN LATE AUGUST, Khariton went to see Brezhnev to try once again to have the tests canceled. I was delighted that the Installation's scientific director supported me in this matter, but from the little he told me, it sounded as if his arguments were too narrow and technical to make any real difference, given the political context of the decision. In any event, his efforts proved futile.

Our preparations were progressing quickly and smoothly as we drew upon the large store of ideas and preliminary research that had been amassed during the three-year moratorium.

On Khrushchev's orders, military maneuvers using nuclear weapons had been scheduled to supplement the tests, but they were apparently canceled, with a single exception. One of the wilder ideas suggested was for fifty strategic bombers to fly in battle formation across the entire country, evading defensive measures and finally dropping their bombs on an "enemy" target: forty-nine of the bombs would be dummies, but the fiftieth would be a real thermonuclear bomb. There were even more serious plans involving ballistic missiles. Khrushchev certainly was no "jellyfish."

AT THE BEGINNING of October I was in Moscow to discuss the calculations, and those relating to the Big Bomb in particular. I met with Izrail Gelfand at his home and saw his wife for the first time since my student years (she had been the instructor in charge of our seminars). Their son had died of leukemia not long before, and although we never talked about this, I wonder if his long years of work in mathematical biology may not have been motivated by that tragedy.

The next day I visited my parents at their dacha. My father had retired several years earlier, but he continued to devise physics experiments. A year earlier, he had published an article on polarized light in *Achievements of the Physical Sciences*. He had taken up his music again, and now—after a thirty-year hiatus—was composing short pieces, and spending hours at the piano. It's a pity none of his compositions was preserved.

I showed up unannounced: my mother, who was on the terrace making apple jam, dashed off to make tea. The apples were from their own trees; my father was an enthusiastic gardener, and his labor of love yielded a fine harvest every autumn.

After we finished our tea, he showed me a new experiment to investigate the mechanism that transports water from the roots to the leaves of trees. (The theoretical literature on the subject was contradictory at that time, and I'm not certain that the questions involved have ever been resolved.) Father cut a branch from a tree, and then, after bending it into an arc, he used it to connect glasses with equal water levels. Water would flow through the branch in the direction that corresponded to a path from roots to leaves before the branch was cut, and in a few hours the water level in one of the glasses would be higher than in the other. This experiment struck me as elegant and informative, and as far as I know, my father was the first person to try it.

I traveled back to Moscow with my father. He told me he had experienced a sharp pain in his chest during a recent walk, but had said nothing about it to Mother. He added that he was feeling fine now and that his mind seemed to function as well as ever. I returned to the Installation the next day.

BY NOW, the Big Bomb was almost ready for shipment. It was being assembled in a special workshop atop a platform car. A few days later, when everything was ready, the superstructure would be dismantled and, under cover of darkness, the platform would be coupled to a special train that would transport the device along an open track all the way to the airfield where it would be loaded into the bomb bay of a waiting plane.

Evsei Rabinovich, one of my colleagues, dropped by my office. With an embarrassed smile, he asked me to accompany him to his work room. The whole department was assembled there, including Adamsky and Feodoritov, who were in charge of the Big Bomb. Rabinovich explained why, in his opinion, the device would not work. He had come to that conclusion a few days earlier and had told everyone in the department except me; most now shared his doubts. I had worked closely with Rabinovich for more than seven years and thought very highly of his keen, analytical mind, his knowledge, experience, and intuition. He outlined his misgivings in a clear and emphatic fashion, and they had a plausible basis, even though I believed his conclusion to be incorrect. Unfortunately, we lacked the mathematical tools I needed to prove this (partly because we had departed from precedent in our drive for a more powerful device). So Adamsky, Feodoritov, and I had to rely on estimated figures to refute Rabinovich. He, too, of necessity had relied on approximations. We knew from experience that, while estimates are useful, they can be influenced by subjective opinions and emotions.

I decided to introduce some changes into the design of the Big Bomb, trying to minimize the margin of error in calculating the subtle processes which worried Rabinovich. I hurried off to David Fishman, the head of the design department, who did not even bother to complain—the matter was too serious. The designers did not go home that night until they handed in revised blueprints; the actual physical changes were made the following day.

I wrote a carefully phrased report to the Ministry, describing the situation without extraneous comment. Two days later, Slavsky called me in a rage. He said: "Tomorrow Malinovsky [minister of defense from 1957 to 1967] and I are supposed to fly out to the test site. What am I supposed to do? Call it off?"

I replied: "You don't need to do that. I didn't recommend cancellation. I wanted to let you know that the device has some risky new features, and the theoretical physicists don't agree on its reliability."

Slavsky grumbled his displeasure, but he calmed down a bit and hung up. The test of the Big Bomb was scheduled to coincide with the final sessions of the Twenty-second Party Congress. This was no accident; Khrushchev was counting on its psychological effect. Many devices of various sorts had already been detonated at the Kazakhstan and Novaya Zemlya sites; in fact, their number almost equaled the cumulative total of all our preceding tests. Furthermore, I heard that a purely military test had been conducted at another location.

On the day the Big Bomb was to be tested, I sat by the phone waiting for news. Early that morning, Pavlov called me to let me know that the carrier plane was flying over the Barents Sea headed for the drop zone. We just couldn't keep our minds on our work. My colleagues were hanging around in the corridor, continually dropping in and out of my office. At noon, Pavlov called again. This time he announced triumphantly: "There's been no communication with the test site or the plane for over an hour. Congratulations on your victory!"

The reason for his jubilation was that the ionized particles released by a powerful explosion interfere with radio transmissions; the more powerful the explosion, the longer the communications blackout. Half an hour later, Pavlov called a third time, and informed me that the cloud had reached a height of forty miles or more (after so many years, I cannot recall the exact figure, but it was extraordinary).

IN ORDER to finish off the subject of the Big Bomb, I shall tell a story that properly belongs to a later time. It illustrates my state of mind during this period, which motivated me to do more than was required of me, to take initiatives, and generally to do the best I could. This predilection persisted even as I drifted further and further away from orthodox views. Of course, this state of mind was rooted in the conviction that our work was crucial in preserving the parity necessary for mutual deterrence (or, as it later became known: "mutual assured destruction"—MAD).

After the test of the Big Bomb, I was concerned that the military couldn't use it without an effective carrier (a bomber would be too easy to shoot down). I dreamed up the idea of a giant torpedo, launched from a submarine and fitted with an atomic-powered jet engine that would convert water to steam. The targets would be enemy ports several hundred miles away. Naval experts assured us that the war at sea would be won if we could destroy the enemy's harbors. The torpedoes' bodies would be made sturdy enough to withstand exploding mines and to pierce anti-torpedo nets. When they reached their targets, the 100-megaton charges would explode both underwater and in the air, causing heavy casualties.

I consulted with Rear Admiral Fomin at an early stage of the torpedo project. He was shocked and disgusted by the idea of merciless mass slaughter, and remarked that the officers and sailors of the fleet were accustomed to fighting only armed adversaries, in open battle. I was utterly abashed, and never discussed the subject with anyone else. I'm no longer worried that someone may pick up on the idea; it doesn't fit in with current military doctrines, and it would be foolish to spend the extravagant sums required; in addition, research and development work on such torpedoes couldn't be kept secret (among other reasons, because radioactive contamination of the ocean would be inevitable), and countermeasures (nuclear mines, for instance) could easily be devised to detect and destroy the torpedoes en route to their targets.

ON THE EVE of the test of the Big Bomb, I had received an alarming letter from Mother: Father had suffered a severe heart attack and had been taken to the hospital. I was unable to leave the Installation or even call from home (the telephone was disconnected while tests were in progress), but I managed to get through on my office phone to the Ministry's duty officer, who patched me through to my mother. Father was still in the hospital, but the doctors had assured Mother that his life was not in immediate danger.

While we were developing the Big Bomb, I had also been working hard on another device I had nicknamed the "Extra." I was trying to squeeze all I could out of this series of tests, hoping that there would be no more. I had not received a request for a device with the Extra's characteristics (the value of one parameter was absolutely unprecedented), but I assumed that sooner or later the military would order one, and then most likely on a rush basis. That could lead to another round of tests (something of the sort had happened in 1958), and I desperately wanted to avoid that.

Slavsky did not approve of such tactics, and at one meeting he alluded to "theoreticians who think up new devices while sitting on the toilet and propose them for testing before they've buttoned up their pants." He probably assumed there would be plenty of tests in the future, so why rush things?

No atomic charge was available for the Extra, since it had not been mentioned in an official resolution, and Slavsky refused to requisition one from the production line. For the first and only time in my life, I performed miracles of string-pulling, making parts of plutonium and uranium-235 borrowed from FIKOBIN and gluing them together with epoxy. Fortunately, the primitive techniques worked satisfactorily. Eventually Pavlov lent his support to the Extra, not because he agreed that testing should be ended, but because he wanted to "go all out" and start the next series of tests from the most advanced point possible. And I was "going all out."

ON NOVEMBER 4, the day the Extra was to be tested, I was finally able to leave for Moscow. I called my mother from the airport, and then went straight to the hospital near Izmailovo Park where Father was a patient. I took the time, however, to phone Pavlov, and I learned that the test of the Extra had been successful.

Although he had been in the hospital for a month and a half, my father did not complain. He kept busy observing the people around him: the patients, doctors and nurses, and their touching, sometimes humorous foibles. But he was worried about my mother and my brother in the event of his death. He also spoke of me: "When you were at the university, you said that uncovering the secrets of nature could make you happy. We don't choose our fate, but I'm sorry that yours took a different turn; I imagine you could have been happier."

I don't remember my reply. I think I agreed that we don't choose our fate. What more could I have said to him on that November day in 1961? The twists and turns in my life that might have cheered him—or pained him—still lay in the future. I couldn't tell him about the latest test, nor would it have been to the point. I couldn't even share my concern about the dangers of testing. He knew my papers on the peaceful use of thermonuclear energy, and he was proud of them. But they weren't enough to allay his misgivings. The one thing I might have said to cheer him up was that I intended to work seriously on theoretical physics and cosmology, but that wasn't yet clear in my own mind. And I didn't want to believe that these conversations would be our last ones. I was wrong, although my mistake was a common one.

At the time I had no idea that I would become involved in public affairs. Ten years later, speaking of my book *Reflections on Progress, Peaceful Coexistence, and Intellectual Freedom*, Aunt Tusya said to me: "Your father would have been proud of you." (Tusya survived my father by many years, although she was the eldest of his siblings.)

On December 10, I visited my father in the hospital. He told me he'd suffered a second heart attack the day before, but he'd concealed it from the doctors, fearing they might not discharge him. I promised not to betray his secret. I had to leave for the Installation the next day, but Mother and I agreed that four men would carry Father up to the fourth-floor apartment in a chair; in no event was he to climb the stairs himself. Father, however, countermanded this "unnecessary" precaution, and Mother found out too late to do anything about it. The men carried the chair, while Father climbed up to the apartment, sitting down to rest several times on the way. I don't know what I could have done if I had been there, but the thought continues to torment me. My mother told me that Father was very happy to be at home, but he spent only two days there. He died suddenly on the night of December 15. His last words were: "You don't have to call Adya [his nickname for me] yet." He thought I was still at the Installation, but I'd arrived in Moscow that evening, intending to see him in the morning.

On December 17, Father was buried at Moscow's Vvedensky cemetery alongside his mother, my grandmother.

16

THE DUPLICATE TESTS

My opposition to the duplicate tests.
My mother's death. The Moscow Treaty.

IN FEBRUARY or March 1962, the Presidium of the Supreme Soviet issued a decree decorating many persons from the two Installations and other organizations involved in the 1961 tests. I received my third Hero of Socialist Labor medal, and Slavsky sent me an unusually warm letter of congratulations, signed as well by his deputies and department heads. Khariton, Zeldovich, and Shchelkin, each of whom had already received three Hero medals, were given other awards. Khrushchev made the presentations in the Kremlin with great ceremony and with the Politburo and the Presidium of the Supreme Soviet in attendance. As I was walking toward the main hall, Brezhnev darted out of a side corridor and greeted me effusively, taking both my hands in his and shaking them without letting go for several seconds.

Khrushchev pinned my third star next to the two I already had and embraced me. After the ceremony, he invited us to the banquet hall, where I was given the place of honor between him and Brezhnev. Khariton was seated on Khrushchev's right. Khrushchev's speech on this occasion was in quite a different vein from the one he had given at the 1961 meeting with atomic scientists. He spoke of the war and of Stalingrad, calling on the marshals seated at the table as witnesses. He thanked us for our work, which, he said, was helping to prevent a new war, although the danger was not yet over.

In closing, Khrushchev made a casual reference to the note I had sent up to him in July 1961, but then went on to say that Khariton and Sakharov had been doing excellent work and kissed each of us in turn. Brezhnev spoke next, and he also embraced us. Marshal Malinovsky, the defense minister and the third speaker, toasted me by name. Khariton and Anatoly Alexandrov, who had succeeded Kurchatov as director of the Institute of Atomic Energy, offered toasts in response. Alexandrov praised "dear Nikita Sergeyevich [Khrushchev], who is ridding us of all that poisoned our life in the past and held us back," and concluded his remarks by asserting that "Nikita Sergeyevich's achievements in Marxism are so great that he before anyone else deserves election to the Academy of Sciences." It was not altogether clear whether Alexandrov was joking or serious, and Khrushchev assumed the same half-jocular tone in replying that he made no claim to being on the level of an academician.

Now it was my turn to speak. I decided to escape my predicament by replying to the third toast only, and proposed that we drink to Marshal Malinovsky, the representative of our glorious armed forces.

Leaving the Kremlin, I went directly to Alexei Tolstoy Street, where my mother had been living with my brother Yura since my father's death. She gasped at the sight of me decked out in my fancy regalia.

BUT THE YEAR 1962 did not end with the same pomp and ceremony with which it began. It turned out to be one of the more difficult years of my life.

During the 1950s, I had come to regard testing in the atmosphere as a crime against humanity, no different from secretly pouring disease-producing microbes into a city's water supply. But my views were not shared by my associates, and I saw how easy it is for people to adapt their thinking to what they regard as their own best interest. Even well-disposed individuals would argue that if I were right, diagnostic X-ray examinations should be banned first. "After all, the patient receives a larger dose of radiation than he does from your tests." Whenever I tried to explain that the issue is the total, cumulative dose for the whole of mankind—since this factor determines the overall number of victims of nonthreshold biological effects—people either failed to understand or scolded me for being too "abstract." (What to do about diagnostic X-rays is a separate question; probably, we should make more use of scanning devices which entail much lower doses of radiation.)

In 1962, these abstract arguments suddenly assumed a very concrete form. Needless to say, my hopes that it might be possible to halt testing with the 1961 "demonstration" series turned out to be naïve in the extreme: further tests were already in the works.

The United States and Great Britain resumed testing in 1962, and we spared no effort trying to find out what they were up to. I attended several meetings on that subject. An episode related to those meetings comes to mind (when it occurred, I would rather not say): Once we were shown photographs of some documents, but many were out of focus, as if the photographer had been rushed. Mixed in with the photocopies was a single, terribly crumpled original. I innocently asked why, and was told that it had been concealed in panties. Another time (again, I will not specify the date) I was summoned by my chiefs and asked to supply some answers for our intelligence people. A couple of the questions were along the following lines: What data about American weapons would be most useful for your work and for planning military technology in general? What should Soviet scientists look for on exchange visits to American laboratories? I answered these ticklish questions as best I could.

I was especially disturbed by the plans for our important fall 1962 series because the most powerful and potentially most lethal device was to be tested in two variants. One had been proposed by Boris Kozlov, of our Installation, and the other, differing only slightly in tactical and technical features (power, weight, and cost), by the second Installation. Each explosion could cause cumulative long-term casualties running into six figures. I did not question the need for one test: the device, developed for a promising new carrier, would be mass-produced and become a key element in our strategic armory once it was proven. But there was no justification at all for a second test; it could—and should—be cancelled, since it would not add anything to our military capability. For the next several months, I gave top priority to trying to avert this duplication. But in the process I found myself encroaching on powerful bureaucratic interests, and quickly realized that they held many of the cards.

I began by approaching Khariton for support. He had come to our department on business, and I spent half an hour arguing my case as we paced back and forth along the asphalt driveway, while his driver and secretary waited in the car.

"I can't interfere in this matter," Khariton decided. "You know how difficult relations with the other Installation have been. My intervention would give people the wrong idea. Their design differs from ours, and from their point of view, and the Ministry's point of view, that justifies testing both devices."

I did all I could to convince Khariton that "giving people the wrong idea" and similar worries should be set aside in this case, but I could see that it was no use. Khariton, who had backed me in 1961 (albeit indecisively), was unwilling to take any initiative. I got the impression, however, that he would allow me freedom of action. I made a point of telling him that I wanted to discuss the issue with Zababakhin and Slavsky.

A few days later I went to see Slavsky in Moscow. He agreed that there was no need for two tests, and that the second could be cancelled if the first was successful, but he wanted both devices made ready and asked me which should be tested first. I replied that this wasn't a major issue, but that it would make sense to test ours first since it was simpler and more reliable. We parted on that note.

I flew out to the second Installation, hoping that Zababakhin would accept my proposal. Aware of the purpose of my mission, he convened five or six people, the "brain trust" of his Installation. Though tired from my journey of two hours in the air and sixty miles by car, I think I was persuasive and logical.

To clinch my case, I was counting on colored drawings, which I hung over the blackboard: the two devices looked like twin brothers, but with one normal and robust and the other battered and worn out.

Finally, after an awkward silence, Zababakhin spoke without looking me in the eye: "You can do whatever you want so long as our device is tested first. But if yours is first, we'll insist that our device be tested, too. Its design may make it significantly more powerful."

"How great a difference could there be?" I asked. "Ten percent?"

"I can't say right now."

"Zhenya, what are you doing?" I demanded, beginning to shout. "This is tantamount to murder!"

Zababakhin remained silent. The others backed their chief, and I could think of nothing more to say. At the very least, however, I should have demanded that they refrain from modifying their design in any way prior to the tests, but the thought that they might do such a thing never entered my mind.

I had to return to Moscow the following day, but I nearly got stranded at Koltsovo airport, near Sverdlovsk. All passenger flights throughout the USSR had been cancelled because of an air disaster near Sukhumi (Yavlinsky, a colleague from LIPAN and my neighbor, was among those killed, together with his wife and child), but since I was a three-time Hero of Socialist Labor, the airport manager found me a seat on a special flight.

In Moscow, I told Slavsky that the other Installation's device would be tested first since they insisted on it, but the principle of no duplication should be respected. "I've already agreed to that," Slavsky confirmed.

But Slavsky broke his word. To be fair, I should acknowledge that the situation had changed. A few weeks before the test, the second Installation sought to make their rather puny and somewhat peculiar device more reliable by increasing its weight approximately ten percent. If they had succeeded in increasing its power by some twenty percent, as they hoped, the Ministry no doubt would have forgiven the additional weight, and Kozlov's device would have been safely forgotten. He would have been disappointed, and I would have breathed easier. But the second Installation's device turned out to be no more powerful than ours. So the increase in weight turned out to have been unjustified.

The heavier device should have been held in reserve as a backup. The tests would have been conducted in the proper sequence had a single executive controlled both devices—or if Slavsky had ordered that ours be tested first. As a professional engineer, he must have preferred our device from the beginning, but he didn't want to sour his relations with the second Installation, and he kept hoping that they might produce a "miracle." No miracle occurred.

It was in these circumstances that Slavsky broke our agreement and tested

Kozlov's device seven days after its rival. His principal argument was that the lesser weight of our device increased its utility as a warhead for the designated missile. In practical terms, the lighter device would slightly increase the weapon's range, but pairing targets and launch sites to minimize the distance between them could largely compensate for this.

I learned of Slavsky's decision only on September 25, when I flew back to the Installation and discovered that Kozlov's device was to be tested the next day. I went straight to Khariton, but he refused to intervene, despite his annoyance over the second Installation's having tampered with the weight of their device. I spent the next two or three hours using the high-frequency phone[1] in his office—I didn't want to waste time returning to my office and, besides, Khariton might still prove useful. The whole time I was on the phone, he remained at his desk working on some papers; naturally, he heard everything I said, but he didn't interrupt.

I called Slavsky and told him he had broken our agreement. "If you don't call off the test," I said, "a lot of people [I specified a six-figure number] are going to die for no reason."

Slavsky cited the difference in weight of the two devices.

"But you know that's a minor detail," I insisted. "We've never tested devices with such similar parameters. It's pointless, and in this case, criminal."

"The decision is final," he said.

"If you won't call it off, I can't work with you anymore. You've double-crossed me."

In a rage, Slavsky shouted: "You can go to hell if you want. I don't have you on a leash!" And he hung up.

I decided to call Khrushchev, but he wasn't at his Kremlin number. His assistant told me that Khrushchev had gone to Ashkhabad to present an Order of Lenin to the Turkmen Republic and gave me a number there. I reached it, but was told that Khrushchev was at the theatre for the ceremony.

An hour later, I placed the call again, and Khrushchev came to the phone. "I'm listening, Comrade Sakharov."

I had rehearsed what I was going to say, but it still sounded unconvincing and muddled. On top of that, the connection was poor.

"I don't quite understand," Khrushchev complained. "What do you want from me?"

"I believe the test is pointless, and it will kill people for no reason. Slavsky and I disagree. I'm asking you to postpone tomorrow's test and to appoint a commission from the Central Committee to look into our dispute."

---

[1][The high frequency network links a number of top officials and major enterprises in the USSR. The telephone instruments bear the legend "HF Communication—KGB USSR."]

"I don't feel well today," Khrushchev said. "I even had to leave the concert. I'll call Comrade Kozlov right away and ask him to look into it." (Frol Kozlov was then one of the most influential members of the Politburo.)

"Thank you very much, Nikita Sergeyevich," I replied.

I USUALLY ARRIVED at work by nine A.M., but the next day the secretary phoned me in a panic at eight-thirty to tell me "someone named Kozlov" had called.

Fifteen minutes later I was on the high-frequency phone, but it took almost half an hour to reach Kozlov. Our conversation got off to a poor start. I said that the test had to be postponed until my dispute with Slavsky was resolved. Kozlov didn't respond directly; instead he argued that my approach was mistaken; the more often we conducted powerful tests, the sooner the imperialists would agree to a ban and the fewer overall casualties there would be. The conversation was pointless. There was no way I could convince him to call off the test, and he was saying things he probably didn't believe himself. He simply didn't want to get into an argument with Slavsky, the influential Minister of Medium Machine Building. I repeated my request that the test be postponed until the Central Committee appointed a commission of inquiry.

Next, I called Pavlov, my last hope. There was always a chance that weather conditions might force a postponement, or perhaps I could convince Pavlov to delay the test for one day, but he told me that it had been moved up four hours on Slavsky's orders. The aircraft had taken off from the field where Pavlov was stationed, had crossed the Barents Sea, and would soon be over the test range. Evidently, Slavsky had feared that I might sway Khrushchev (whose actions were often unpredictable), or find some other way to delay the test, and he had taken no chances.

It was the ultimate defeat for me. A terrible crime was about to be committed, and I could do nothing to prevent it. I was overcome by my impotence, unbearable bitterness, shame, and humiliation. I put my face down on my desk and wept.

That was probably the most terrible lesson of my life: you can't sit on two chairs at once. I decided that I would devote myself to ending biologically harmful tests. That was the main reason I didn't carry out my threat to quit the Installation. Later, after the Moscow Limited Test Ban Treaty was signed, I found other grounds for postponing my resignation.

An hour after my call to Pavlov, I learned that the test had been a complete success. I congratulated Boris Kozlov on his magnificent achievement.

*   *   *

I'LL NOW SAY something about my role in the Moscow Limited Test Ban Treaty. Negotiations to ban testing had been in progress for several years, but the problem of monitoring underground explosions had blocked agreement. By collecting air and dust samples on a regular basis, the U.S., or any other country, can detect testing in the atmosphere or at ground level; it takes only a week or two for the winds to carry material from a nuclear explosion throughout the hemisphere. Nuclear explosions under water or in space can also be monitored without difficulty, but underground tests are a different matter. How can their seismic shock waves be distinguished from the natural tremors which occur continually? After years of intensive research, scientists have learned to tell them apart, but mistakes can still be made when the explosions are relatively small. Furthermore, if a country is intent on deception, it can conduct its tests in a large underground chamber with little fear of detection. Mutual distrust, sometimes fading but then flaring up again, compounds the technical difficulties.

Tamm, Lev Artsimovich, and some other acquaintances of mine were members of a technical group working in Geneva on verification. Evgeny Fedorov, as chairman, ensured strict Party control. They met with Hans Bethe and other outstanding scientists, and took walks along the shores of Lake Léman, but they couldn't find a way out of the impasse.

A solution did exist, however. In the late 1950s, several journalists and politicians, including President Eisenhower, suggested a treaty banning all nuclear tests except for those conducted underground, but the Soviet side had declined to discuss this idea on some pretext or other. In the summer of 1962, Viktor Adamsky reminded me of Eisenhower's proposal and observed that the time might be ripe to float the idea again. I agreed and decided to see Slavsky at once.

Adamsky was a senior member of the theoretical physics department. He'd begun working at the Installation in 1950 or thereabouts (first in Zeldovich's department, later directly with me) and he'd participated in all our basic research. Like most of the younger theoreticians, he took an interest in political matters, and I enjoyed visiting him in his cubbyhole near the stairs for chats about politics, science, literature, and life. I found him sympathetic to my views about the harmful effects of testing, a welcome relief from the cynicism and lack of understanding I usually encountered. (The last time I saw him was on my fiftieth birthday in 1971, when he stopped by to congratulate me, but left quickly.)

Slavsky was then staying in a government spa in Barvikha. I had a Ministry car take me to the entrance of the resort, dismissed the driver, and walked through a splendid flower garden to Slavsky's cottage. He was delighted to see me (this was before our quarrel over the duplicate tests). He was recuperating from a stomach operation, which, he proudly informed me, had been performed by none other than his friend Boris Petrovsky, later an Academician and Minister of Health. I outlined the idea of a partial test ban, but without mentioning either Eisenhower or Adamsky; I said that it might resolve the Geneva deadlock and be timely from a political standpoint. Were we to make such a proposal, the United States would almost certainly accept.

Slavsky heard me out and seemed sympathetic. At the end of our conversation, he promised: "Yakov Malik [Deputy Minister of Foreign Affairs] is here. I'll speak with him today and pass on your idea. Of course, the boss himself [i.e., Khrushchev] will have to decide." Slavsky then escorted me to the door.

A FEW MONTHS LATER, not long after our quarrel over the duplicate tests, Slavsky called me at work and said in a most conciliatory tone: "No matter what happened between us in the past, life goes on and somehow or other we've got to get back on good terms. I'm calling to let you know that there's a great deal of interest at the top in your proposal, and in all probability some steps will shortly be taken by our side." I told him this was important news for me.

A few more months passed, and then the USSR proposed a treaty banning tests in three environments: in the atmosphere, under water, and in outer space. Kennedy welcomed Khrushchev's initiative, and what became known as the Moscow Treaty was concluded in short order.[2] It is open for signature by other countries, but France and the People's Republic of China have to this day not acceded to the treaty. The atmospheric nuclear tests conducted by those two countries since the Moscow Treaty was signed will result in hundreds of thousands of victims. (At present, France is not carrying out atmospheric tests.) China launched a campaign attacking the Moscow Treaty, which aggravated Sino-Soviet differences—that may have been one of the treaty's unstated strategic aims.

I consider the Moscow Treaty of historic significance. It has saved the lives of hundreds of thousands, possibly millions, of people who would have perished had testing continued in the atmosphere, under water, and in space. And perhaps even more important, the treaty was a step toward reducing the risk of thermonuclear war. I am proud of my contribution to the Moscow Treaty.

As things worked out, no effort was necessary on my part after the conversa-

[2][Khrushchev made his proposal in a speech delivered in East Berlin on July 2, 1963. The Treaty Banning Nuclear Weapon Tests in the Atmosphere, in Outer Space and Under Water was signed in Moscow on August 5, 1963, and entered into force on October 10, 1963. See Glenn Seaborg's *Kennedy, Khrushchev, and the Test Ban* (University of California Press, 1981).]

tion with Slavsky in the summer of 1962; things moved ahead on their own. But I still believed that my presence at the Installation might prove decisive at some critical moment, and this was one of the reasons I didn't leave to "do science" like Zeldovich. I should add, however, that I continued to work energetically and conscientiously to exploit our earlier successes, and also made attempts to break new ground, though these rarely got beyond the discussion stage. My professional labors in weapons research continued until 1968, when I was dismissed, but from the fall of 1963, I began to work seriously on "grand science" as well.

One incident, an echo of earlier events, seems worth recording for the light it casts on Brezhnev's character. In 1965, Khariton and I briefed a regional Party secretary on the theoretical department's research program (the secretary was inspecting the Installation). Afterward, speaking with me one-on-one, he said that he had recently talked with Brezhnev, who asked how I was getting on. Then, without further reference to Brezhnev, he suggested that I join the Communist Party. I replied that I could be of greater use to the country if I remained outside Party ranks. I later learned that Brezhnev had told the Party secretary: "Sakharov has some doubts and inner conflicts. We ought to try to understand and do all we can to help him."

MOTHER'S HEALTH deteriorated after my father died. She developed emphysema. I managed once, in the spring of 1962, to take her to visit Father's grave; after that, the trip was too much for her. She spent the summer of 1962 at the dacha with her niece Marina, never leaving it. Whenever I visited her there, she spoke about the past and about people she had known, often with a new tolerance.

By the end of March 1963, she had become so weak that I had her admitted to the ministry hospital, which was close to our home. I spent April 14, Easter Sunday, with her. Early the next morning, I was called to the hospital. I rushed there with Aunt Tusya and my brother Yura, but Mother was unconscious by the time we arrived.

She was buried with religious rites in Vagankov cemetery, alongside my grandmother and near several other members of the Sofiano and Goldenveizer families.

Mother survived my father by one year and four months.

17

THE 1964 ACADEMY
ELECTIONS

IN [JUNE] 1964, regular elections for membership in the Academy of Sciences were held. In the first round, each department of the Academy nominates by secret ballot its quota of candidates for full and corresponding membership, respectively. (The quotas are set, I believe, by decision of the Council of Ministers.) Then the Academy's General Assembly must approve each candidate by a two-thirds majority. Attendance at the Assembly is mandatory except for members specifically excused by the Academy's presidium on account of illness, travel abroad, or other weighty reasons. (I wonder what category they put me in during my Gorky years!) In the vast majority of cases, the Assembly confirms the nominees automatically; the few negative votes are usually cast by academicians who also opposed the given candidate's nomination at the department level, since members from other disciplines customarily defer to the recommendation of the nominee's colleagues.

I heard during a meeting of our department that the biologists had voted to elevate Nikolai Nuzhdin from corresponding member to full member. Nuzhdin was one of Lysenko's closest associates, an accomplice in his pseudo-scientific schemes and in his persecution of genuine scientists. As I recalled the tragedy of Soviet genetics and its martyrs, my indignation toward Lysenko boiled up once again, and I decided that Nuzhdin's candidacy must be defeated. The idea of speaking out at the General Assembly began to germinate in my mind.

During a break in our department's voting, I walked over to Academician Lev Artsimovich and told him what I thought of Nuzhdin's nomination. Perched on the arm of his chair, Artsimovich was taking a break from the electoral squabbling. He readily agreed: "Yes, I know he ought to be blackballed. But you wouldn't really dare speak out at the General Assembly, would you?"

"Why not?" I retorted, and moved on.

The Assembly was scheduled for the following day. Unbeknownst to me, other scientists, both physicists and biologists, were also preparing for action. That evening, there was a discreet gathering in the apartment of Academician Vladimir Engelgardt, a distinguished biochemist and long-time enemy of Lysenko. Tamm and Leontovich attended, and it was decided that they and Engelgardt would make a concerted attack on Nuzhdin the next day. I repeat: I knew nothing of their plans.

The Assembly opened as usual. The secretaries of the respective departments reported on the nominations and briefly described their candidates' scientific accomplishments. No one asked questions or requested the floor. The election commission prepared ballots for voting. At last, it was the turn of the biology department. I believe that it was Academician Alexander Oparin, a Lysenko supporter, who announced that the biology department had nominated Nuzhdin, whom he described as an eminent scientist. I had made up my mind to speak and outlined key points on the cover of my program (which, unfortunately, I did not keep).

Unintentionally forestalling Tamm, Engelgardt, and Leontovich, I raised my hand, and Keldysh called me to the rostrum at once. So far as I can recall, I said more or less the following:

> The Academy's Charter sets very high standards for its members with respect to both scientific merit and civic responsibility. Corresponding member Nikolai Nuzhdin, who has been nominated by the biology department for elevation to full member, does not satisfy the criteria. Together with Academician Lysenko, he is responsible for the shameful backwardness of Soviet biology and of genetics in particular, for the dissemination of pseudoscientific views, for adventurism, for the degradation of learning, and for the defamation, firing, arrest, even death, of many genuine scientists.
>
> I urge you to vote against Nuzhdin.

There was a deafening silence, followed by cries of "Shame!"—but also by applause in the greater part of the hall, especially from the back rows where guests and corresponding members were seated. As I walked to center stage and down a flight of carpeted stairs to return to my place, the uproar and applause grew louder, continuing for several minutes. Lysenko, who was seated near me, exclaimed in fury: "People like Sakharov should be locked up and put on trial!"

Even as I was speaking, Tamm, Engelgardt, and Leontovich had requested the floor. Terribly excited, Lysenko jumped up from his seat and demanded the right to reply, but Keldysh let Tamm, Leontovich, and Engelgardt go first. They all spoke well and to good effect. When Lysenko's turn came, he said, as might have been expected, that we had slandered Nuzhdin outrageously, and that his contributions to science were substantial.

Keldysh himself spoke next. He began by reprimanding Academician Sakharov for using impermissible language, added that Sakharov was mistaken in his opinion, and then urged the Assembly to consider Nuzhdin's candidacy calmly, impartially, and fairly, taking the biology department's recommendation into account. Addressing Lysenko, he added: "I do not agree with Sakharov, but, Trofim Denisovich, every Academician is entitled to speak in accordance with our regulations and is free to defend his point of view."

Long after this meeting, Pyotr Kapitsa told me that Leonid Ilyichev, the head oɹ the Central Committee's agitation and propaganda department and a member of the Assembly's presidium, had been upset by my speech and wished to take the floor. He turned to Kapitsa, who was seated next to him, and asked, "Who's that speaking?" "That's the father of the hydrogen bomb," Kapitsa replied. Whereupon Ilyichev apparently decided it would be more politic to remain silent.

An hour or so after the debate on Nuzhdin, we filed out of the hall into the lobby, where the ballot boxes had been placed. Many complete strangers shook my hand and thanked me for my speech. Katya Skubur, my Moscow University classmate who had become Artsimovich's secretary, assured me: "Our fellow students will hear about your speech!"

Nuzhdin's bid to become a full member of the Academy was defeated.

Like my struggle against atmospheric testing, the Nuzhdin affair was another landmark (albeit a less fateful one) on my way to becoming active in civic affairs. Why did I take the uncharacteristic step of speaking out publicly against someone I didn't even know? Probably the main reason was the premium I place on the freedom and integrity of science; after all, science remains a keystone of civilization, and any unwarranted encroachment on its domain is impermissible. Chance, too, played its part—no one had told me about the meeting at Engelgardt's apartment. In the event, destiny may have tipped the balance in my impulsive but fateful decision to speak out.

A FEW DAYS LATER I received a visit at home from Zhores Medvedev, a young biologist. Although I hadn't met him previously, his name was known to me. He told me he was working in a research institute on the genetic problems of aging, and for six or seven years had been using his access to the archives to collect material on the history of Lysenkoism. He'd been impressed by my speech, and he asked me to go over in as much detail as possible exactly what

I'd said and the circumstances in which I'd said it. He took careful notes for the book he was writing (he left me a draft of it, which I found fascinating).[1]

I spent July and August, as usual, at the Miskhor spa with my family. On the return journey, I bought a copy of *Selskaya zhizn* [Rural Life] at the Simferopol airport, as no other newspaper was available. When I opened the paper on the plane, I was amazed to find an article by Mikhail Olshansky, president of the Academy of Agricultural Sciences, attacking me by name.

At a General Assembly of the Academy of Sciences, engineer Sakharov, who has read too many unsigned letters by Medvedev, slandered Soviet Michurinist science and eminent Soviet biologists, disrupting the work of the Assembly.[2]

Evidently I was described as an engineer to conceal my status as an academician and to emphasize my lack of competence as a biologist. The publication of this article heralded a Lysenkoite counterattack, which had powerful backing in Party and government circles, most likely in the Central Committee's department of agriculture and the Ministry of Agriculture itself. The Lysenkoites were rumored to enjoy Khrushchev's favor as well. They probably impressed him (as they had Stalin) with their seductive promises that the application of Michurin's theories would produce quick and easy successes in agriculture.

I decided to write to Khrushchev to "open his eyes" to the truth. I realized, of course, that my knowledge of the subject was limited, but I was acquainted with the general principles and some practical applications of genetics, and also knew something about the molecular theory of heredity. I hoped that my position and my personal contacts with Khrushchev would gain a hearing for my letter. For a week after my return from vacation, my days were taken up with meetings at the Ministry, but I spent from six till eight every morning drafting the letter and then typing it out with one finger. I sent it to Khrushchev on September 10. I included a brief, popular outline of genetics, but I also described the factional behavior of the Lysenko "mafia" (I don't think I used that word, but my meaning was clear) and their domination of many Party and government institutions.

I know of Khrushchev's reaction only from rumor. I gathered from several sources that my speech against Nuzhdin had enraged him to the point that he stamped his feet and ordered Vladimir Semichastny, the KGB chairman,

[1][Zhores Medvedev, *The Rise and Fall of T. D. Lysenko* (Columbia University Press, 1969). See pp. 215–218 for excerpts from Sakharov's and Engelgardt's speeches.]

[2]["Against Misinformation and Slander," *Selskaya zhizn*, August 29, 1964.]

to gather compromising material on me. Khrushchev supposedly said: "First Sakharov tried to stop the hydrogen bomb test, and now he's poking his nose again where it doesn't belong."

He was angry not just with me, but with the Academy's whole stance. I heard he was ready to transfer some of its institutes to other agencies. His stormy reaction suggests that Khrushchev really believed in Lysenko, and there was also some gossip of a family connection. But what annoyed him most of all was that someone was trespassing on "his" domain. The fact that he did not show my letter to other members of the Presidium for some time may also have indicated confusion and doubt.

In any case, my letter was not passed on to other members of the Presidium until just before the October Central Committee plenum, which removed Khrushchev from office. I was told that among the charges leveled at him by Suslov, speaking for the Presidium, was the breakdown of communications with scientists evidenced by his having concealed Sakharov's letter from the Presidium for two weeks.

I heard a few other details about Khrushchev's dismissal from the same source. Khrushchev was vacationing with Mikoyan by the Black Sea when they were summoned to an urgent meeting of the Presidium. No one greeted Khrushchev at the airport. Surprised and alarmed, he rushed to the Kremlin and stalked into the room where the Presidium was in session. To his question "What's going on here?" Suslov replied, "We're discussing Khrushchev's removal from office."

"Are you crazy? I'll have you all arrested right now."

Khrushchev hurried off to the reception room and phoned Malinovsky, the defense minister. "As Commander-in-Chief, I order you to arrest the conspirators at once."

Malinovsky replied that he was a member of the Communist Party and would carry out the decision of the Central Committee. Khrushchev's next move was to phone Semichastny, the KGB chairman, who also refused to help him (soon afterward, the new state leader, Brezhnev, removed Semichastny and replaced him with Andropov).

Khrushchev's fall led to the final rout of Lysenko and his supporters. For the next few years, the previously "disgraced" geneticist Nikolai Dubinin, who was elected to the Academy and made director of the Institute of Genetics in 1966, regularly sent me New Year's cards, recalling how valuable my intervention had been to the geneticists' cause.

IT WAS NOT until after 1964 that I learned of the role allegedly played by Nuzhdin in the persecution of Nikolai Timofeyev-Resovsky, a Russian biologist who worked in Germany after 1925, studying the effects of radiation on heredity and other topics in genetics. (Some of my information, I should note, is secondhand and may not be completely accurate.) Timofeyev-Resovsky was called back to the Soviet Union in 1937, but refused and became a "non-returner." He continued to work in a Berlin laboratory. His wife and his son Foma were with him in Germany; Foma reportedly died in a German concentration camp during the war. Shortly after the end of the war, Nuzhdin visited the laboratory, which was in the Soviet zone, and ordered Timofeyev-Resovsky to turn over his research materials, including the fruit flies and bacterial cultures used in his studies of heredity. When Timofeyev-Resovsky refused, he was arrested, deported to the USSR, and eventually confined in a *sharashka* built especially for him in the Urals. He was held there as a prisoner until the late 1950s and forced to work on research projects assigned by the First Main Directorate. During a game of chess at the test site in either 1949 or 1951, Pavel Meshik (head of the security department at the First Main Directorate) told Zeldovich that Timofeyev-Resovsky had taken part during the war in experiments on prisoners in German camps. This was undoubtedly a barefaced lie.[3]

Sometime around 1960, after Timofeyev-Resovsky's release, I received a letter from his wife, Elena, asking me to put her in touch with the Sakharov brothers, Nikolai in particular. I passed the letter on to my father and discovered that his generation of Sakharovs had been good friends of Elena's family, who were Russified Germans. One of my father's brothers (Yura, it seems) had fallen in love with Elena, but she'd rejected his suit in favor of her future husband. Elena, my father said, had sisters in Tula, one of whom visited us often (I remember her well) at Granatny Lane. During the brief German occupation of Tula, the eldest sister had appealed to a German officer for help in finding her sister in Germany, and had given him a letter for her. When Soviet troops recaptured Tula, the sisters were apparently arrested by SMERSH (army counterintelligence) and most likely were shot. Our family reestablished contact with Elena, and my Aunts Zhenya and Tusya maintained friendly relations with her throughout the 1960s and 1970s until their deaths.

IN 1962, two years before the Nuzhdin affair, another incident foreshadowed my future public activity on behalf of victims of injustice. I happened to read an article (written by the investigator in charge of the case; it appeared in

---

[3][For additional information on Timofeyev-Resovsky, see Zhores Medvedev, *The Medvedev Papers* (Macmillan, 1971), pp. 91–112, and Daniil Granin's documentary novel *The Bison* (Doubleday, 1990).]

Nedelya, the weekly supplement to *Izvestia*) about an old man in a small town who had counterfeited a few coins and hidden them in his yard. He seems to have used one of the coins to buy some milk, and he also dropped mysterious hints about his "buried treasure" to friends, although he never told his wife about it. Word spread, and the old man's house was searched; the counterfeit rubles, wrapped in a handkerchief, were dug up in the garden. The man was arrested, a show trial was held, and he was sentenced to death as a dangerous criminal. The verdict was meant to serve as a deterrent to other would-be counterfeiters; the newspaper story claimed that it had been handed down in response to "numerous demands from working people."

The punishment struck me as completely out of proportion to the gravity of the crime, if you could really call it a crime at all. The old man probably was mentally ill. I stated my opinion in a letter addressed to the editor of *Nedelya,* signed it with all my titles, and asked him to forward it to the Procurator's Office.

The case was typical of Soviet justice in that an extreme sentence was passed on the basis of a new law. Amendments had been incorporated in the RSFSR Criminal Code in July 1962 extending the death penalty to persons convicted of large-scale theft of state property, large-scale currency speculation, and counterfeiting. (The crime of "currency speculation" is a peculiarly Soviet concept; it is rooted in the state's attempt to protect artificial rates of exchange and the profit it derives from them.) This extraordinarily harsh law caused numerous tragedies and monstrous injustices and claimed the lives of some persons innocent of any crime at all by Western standards—the leader of an unregistered team installing electricity on collective farms, and someone manufacturing consumer goods from a state factory's rejects, among others. It is noteworthy that the KGB preempted jurisdiction over such cases from the Ministry of Internal Affairs and the Procurator's Office.

The case of Yan Rokotov and Vladislav Faibishenko, big-time black marketers of jewels, was the immediate spur for the extension of the death penalty. Both had been sentenced to fifteen years in prison, the maximum punishment for their crime, but they began naming their customers among the elite and had to be silenced permanently. They were retried and sentenced to death, despite the fact that they had committed their crimes before enactment of the new decree, and had been duly tried for them under then-existing Soviet law. A number of lawyers in the West voiced their disapproval of this violation of a fundamental legal principle, but the matter ended there.

The old man accused of counterfeiting was swept up by the new broom. Two weeks after sending my letter, I received a reply from the editor-in-chief of *Nedelya,* who had forwarded it to the Procurator's Office. Their reply stated that capital punishment in the USSR was an exceptional measure reserved for especially grave crimes. (In my letter, I had included a few words about the need for particular care in passing a death sentence.) As for the old man, he had been executed. The *Nedelya* editor did apologize for the article's omission of any mention of the defendant's prior conviction, which the court had taken into account when passing the death sentence. The charge had allegedly been armed assault, but the defendant had served a surprisingly short (by Soviet standards) term of two years. In any event, it seemed to me no justification whatsoever for shooting a man who had merely made a feeble attempt at counterfeiting. This was the first criminal case I ever looked into, and it left a bitter taste in my mouth.

18

SCIENTIFIC WORK OF THE 1960S

THE YEARS 1963–1967 were scientifically productive ones for me. One reason was that the special projects work had become less demanding and was occupying my thoughts much less of the time. At home—that is, the cottage at the Installation where I spent much of the year by myself—and during temporary assignments to Moscow and vacations in the Crimea, I now spent most of my time pondering "grand" science. But apparently the most important thing was that the time had come both for me (my father told me that the years after forty are often the most productive) and for problems suited to my abilities, knowledge, and scientific style, ones whose solution lay within my power.

As I noted earlier, my association with Yakov Zeldovich during this period was a vital factor in my scientific career. Early in the 1960s, Zeldovich had begun working on problems in cosmology and astrophysics that were to remain his chief interest. I followed him, and turned my thoughts to "grand" cosmology.

My first paper in cosmology was written in 1963–1964 and titled "The Initial Stage of an Expanding Universe and the Appearance of Inhomogeneity in the Matter Distribution."[1]

Before going into any detail about this effort of mine and those that followed, I must clarify certain concepts and ideas employed in them. (This chapter will differ markedly in style and content from much of the book, and readers who lack interest in the complexities of modern physics may want to

---

[1][Translated as "The Initial Stage of an Expanding Universe and the Appearance of a Nonuniform Distribution of Matter" in Sakharov, Collected Scientific Works, pp. 65–84.]

skip over it or, better, to skim it, and if they find their curiosity piqued, to read it again, more attentively, with additional reference material at hand.)

The cosmological theory of the *expanding universe* is now generally accepted. This theory is based on Alexander Friedmann's nonstatic (time-dependent) solution of the equations of the general theory of relativity and on Hubble and Humanson's discovery of the recession of the galaxies.

As we know, the stars are not distributed uniformly in space, but form aggregations known as galaxies, each of which contains tens and even hundreds of billions of stars. Galaxies are separated from one another by enormous distances—millions of light-years, a light-year being the distance traveled by light in one year. Light propagates at a velocity of three hundred thousand kilometers per second, two hundred thousand times greater than that of a passenger jet, almost forty thousand times greater than that of an artificial earth satellite. The stars visible to us all belong to our galaxy; a few other galaxies can be seen against the sky as minute foggy patches ("nebulae," as they were once known). The nearest large galaxy is the well-known Andromeda Nebula, while a small satellite galaxy called the Magellanic Cloud[2] is practically in our "back yard," only 150,000 light-years away. Hubble and Humanson discovered that all of the galaxies are moving away from ours and that their velocities of recession are proportional to their distances.

The universe is everything that exists: it has no boundaries, and nothing lies outside it. This makes it rather difficult to imagine what could be meant by the "expansion of the universe." An analogy from Misner, Thorne, and Wheeler's excellent *Gravitation*[3] may be helpful here. Let us imagine some two-dimensional beings living on the surface of an inflatable balloon who have no idea that anything but this surface exists; it is their universe (nineteenth-century popularizers used the image of two-dimensional beings on a curved surface to explain concepts of non-Euclidean geometry; Chernyshevsky scoffed at this, for no good reason). Gobs of batter, corresponding to the galaxies of our universe, are stuck to the balloon's surface. Now suppose the balloon is inflated. The "cookies" on its surface will move away from each other, and a two-dimensional inhabitant trudging across one of them would be correct in saying that the other cookie-galaxies are all moving away from his home cookie; and that the farther away a cookie is from him the more rapid its recession. This is precisely the picture observed by astronomers in the case of real three-dimensional galaxies in our three-dimensional universe.

The concept of a nonstatic universe whose geometric properties are time-

---

2[Actually two Magellanic clouds—large and small.]
3[W. H. Freeman, 1973.]

dependent is one of the most sweeping changes wrought in our scientific worldview during the past century. In earlier centuries, science accommodated the mutability of life on earth, changes in the earth's surface and even in the solar system itself, but it was assumed that the universe as a whole was remarkably stable. This was not an easy idea to abandon. Even Einstein, in his attempts to apply his general theory of relativity to the universe as a whole, searched stubbornly for static solutions to his equations. To this end he modified his own original equations, ascribing a "self-repulsion" property to the vacuum (expressed by the so-called cosmological constant, to which I shall return). But not even this stratagem allowed him to escape major, seemingly insurmountable theoretical difficulties.

Friedmann found a simple and ingenious way out of the dilemma in 1922–1924. As the first to consider the possibility of a nonstatic, in fact expanding, universe, he discovered "at the tip of his pen" a phenomenon of a grandeur unequaled by anything else known to us.

Einstein at first believed that Friedmann's work must be mistaken; it was only after several months that he realized that he himself was in error. The special note he published to that effect stands as an additional testimonial to the outstanding personal qualities and scientific rectitude of genius.

Friedmann did not live to see the recession of the galaxies confirmed by observation; he died of typhoid fever in 1925, a year and a half after reading Einstein's note, at the age of thirty-seven. During the First World War, Friedmann acted as a flying observer and was awarded the Cross of St. George. Pyotr Kapitsa once told me that Friedmann was the illegitimate son of a Grand Duke; I don't know if this is true.

The work of Georges Lemaître (whose first paper, from 1927, ties in with Hubble and Humanson's observations) was of great importance along with Friedmann's in forming our views of the expanding universe, and associated cosmological, astrophysical, and general philosophical implications.

If we extrapolate backward in time, the idea of an expanding universe inevitably leads us to an initial state with very high density, and with physical conditions that differ fundamentally from those observable in our everyday life or attainable in the laboratory today, and even from those we can posit as existing in the interiors of stars. How much time has passed since the beginning? Most estimates range from 13 to 20 billion years. The figure has been revised several times since the first estimates by Hubble and Humanson, but for several reasons it remains rather imprecise even today. The qualitative picture of the expanding universe, however, can be regarded as an established fact of great basic importance.

Our picture of the universe, based on observation, is characterized on the one hand by an extremely nonuniform, or inhomogeneous, distribution of matter on relatively small scales: a complex hierarchic structure whose steps are the planets, stars, galaxies, and clusters of galaxies. On the other hand, on scales that exceed the dimensions of galaxy clusters, the distribution of matter is practically uniform, or homogeneous. (According to some recently advanced theories, the universe, on even larger scales than those that are observable, consists of regions with essentially different properties.)

"Grand" cosmology sets out to explain why the galaxies, stars, and planets are precisely as we observe them and not otherwise, and exactly how they formed. Grand cosmology has made increasing use of advances in elementary-particle theory in recent decades; conversely, the large-scale cosmological processes (especially during the instants immediately following the Big Bang) can give us information on elementary-particle physics not yet obtainable by any other means, and so cosmology became a testing ground for new theories in elementary-particle physics. I shall go into some detail about a problem in this area: the baryonic asymmetry of the universe and baryon instability.

The hypothesis that appeared most plausible twenty years ago and is now a basis of cosmological views most popular among physicists boils down to the statement that the initial state of the universe was highly homogeneous: the densities of matter and energy were practically constant in space, and the entire observable structure of the universe appeared afterward due to the effect of "gravitational instability," or clumping .[Many authors believe that, at the initial stage, along with gravitational instability, a major role was played by the instability of the processes of transformation of fields of elementary particles. Some also ascribe a special role to so-called cosmological strings. But in the 1960s none of this was yet on anybody's mind.—A.S. 1987]

Let me refer to a model to clarify what is meant by gravitational instability. Suppose that we have an endless chain of identical heavy spheres spaced at equal distances from one another. As long as the distances are exactly equal, the spheres remain at rest: the forces exerted on each sphere from the left and right cancel one another. But as soon as one of the spheres moves, slightly, say to the right, its attraction to the spheres on its left decreases, while the attraction to the spheres on its right increases (recall that according to Newton's law of gravitation, the force of attraction is inversely proportional to the square of the distance between the spheres). As a result, the displacement of the sphere will increase more and more rapidly, and the other spheres will also be set in motion. This is gravitational instability: the development of large inhomogeneities from small initial ones. The first theory of gravitational instability was derived by James Jeans (the same Jeans whose book *The Universe Around Us* I'd read as a youngster), but his work had a number of weak points.

In 1946, Evgeny Lifshitz published a rigorous and thorough investigation of how gravitational instability might apply to Friedmann's cosmological models. Lifshitz had intended his theory to provide, in particular, an explanation of the formation of galaxies and their subsequent clustering. Ten or eleven years later, William Bonnor found a more elegant way to reproduce some of Lifshitz's results. (Bonnor's surname makes me wonder whether he might not be related to my wife; her kinfolk were scattered all over the world by the events of our century.)

The theory of gravitational instability shows how small initial inhomogeneities grow. But investigation of how these initial inhomogeneities got there in the first place and what determined their size requires additional physical arguments or hypotheses; it constitutes one of the fundamental problems of grand cosmology. I undertook precisely such an investigation in a 1965 paper.

I followed Zeldovich and many other authors of the day and took as my starting point the so-called cold Big Bang model of the universe, in which the initial temperature of the super-dense matter was taken as equal to zero (it was assumed that matter was *heated* afterward by various processes, including nuclear reactions). The cold model, at least in its original form, is now thoroughly discredited. It has in general been replaced by the hot model, in which the initial state is characterized by a very high temperature.

My use of the cold model significantly undercut the value of my first work in cosmology; my results pertaining to the theory of gravitational instability still retain some interest, in particular those pertaining to quantum instabilities and my hypothesis concerning the equation of state of matter at superhigh densities.[4] For the quantum case I examined instabilities with the help of an exact self-similar solution for the wave function of a harmonic oscillator having variable parameters. Here the major difficulties were to account for the effects of pressure, but I overcame them. (For details, I refer the interested reader to my work; I remember the day when I managed to find the solution—April 22, 1964.)

In one of the hypothetical equations of state I examined, the energy density converged to a constant value as the pressure approached infinity. That is, in the limiting case, the energy density does not depend on the density of matter and in this case the pressure is negative. Such an equation of state leads to an exponential expansion of the Universe and the matter is rapidly "diluted" as the volume increases. In the same year Gliner independently wrote on this and with a greater degree of certainty. Recently many researchers, the first among them David Kirzhnitz and Andrei Linde at FIAN, have come to the conclusion

---

[4][The equation of state is the equation that relates the pressure of a fluid to its density. Since density and pressure in the early universe were so high, unusual equations of state have been proposed.]

that a similar situation can arise in modern theories of elementary particles where the internal symmetry of the vacuum is broken. In these theories it is assumed that the vacuum can exist in several states, of which only one (the "true" vacuum) has zero (or very small in absolute terms) energy density. In the other states (the "false" vacuum) the energy density can be colossal.

Alan Guth took the next step, applying these concepts to real cosmological problems. The "young" universe in a false-vacuum state expands exponentially and its dimensions increase an enormous number of times. To distinguish this situation from the more moderate tempo of expansion at later stages in the evolution of the universe, Guth named his scenario "inflation." At the present time the inflationary model of the early universe is the most popular cosmological model and theorists all over the world are working to develop it. Andrei Linde has been very active and successful in this area. Among other Soviet researchers, I should especially mention Andrei Starobinsky, who originated some alternatives that were subsequently incorporated into the general flow of ideas.

The inflationary hypothesis really does explain many astrophysical observations (the absence of magnetic monopoles, the almost "flat" geometry of the Universe and so on). By the way, alternative explanations may yet be found. The basic question about the nature of the field that gives rise to inflation is not clear. It is possible that the existence of various states of the vacuum is here irrelevant—we simply happen to live in that region of the universe where there existed a field with negative pressure that underwent inflation. The existence of similar fields is assumed in several modern theories. On the whole, the situation is far from clear. Inflation should unquestionably be abandoned if it turns out that the geometry of the universe is far from flat (i.e., Euclidean).

The principal value of the 1965 paper was a restoration of confidence in myself as a theoretical physicist. It was a kind of psychological "warmup" that made possible my subsequent papers of the the 1960s.

Evidence of the initial hot state of the universe is found in the so-called microwave background radiation, the thermal radiation arriving from space that was discovered by Penzias and Wilson at about the time I sent my cold-model paper to the publisher. This energy is believed to be the flash left over by the Big Bang. The discovery of the background radiation and acceptance of the hot model in general makes a very dramatic story, but I shall not go into it here, referring the reader instead to the several interesting books on the subject, including Steven Weinberg's *The First Three Minutes*[5] and Zeldovich's notes for the Russian translation he edited, as well as Zeldovich's own

[5](Basic Books, 1976.)

books, written with Igor Novikov. Let me just mention that credit for the original notion of the hot universe belongs to George Gamow.

In my next cosmological paper, I started with the hot model and the highly significant fact that the universe displays "baryon asymmetry" (i.e., as far as we can see, there are only baryons, no antibaryons). Further—and this in particular requires explanation—there are far fewer baryons than background-radiation photons—one one-hundred-millionth or even a billionth as many. Here I am again forced to digress.

Let us recall first of all that "baryon" is a collective term for protons and neutrons that also covers certain unstable particles formed from protons and neutrons in collisions between high-energy particles. Just as there is an "antiparticle" for the electron—a positron carrying a positive electric charge—so are there antiparticles of protons and neutrons—antiprotons and antineutrons or, collectively, antibaryons, which are made from antiquarks. The electric charge of the antiproton is opposite in sign to that of the proton, the sign of the magnetic moment is reversed for both antineutron and antiproton. However, another property common to all antiparticles is more significant: when a particle and an antiparticle meet they "annihilate" each other (annihilation = mutual extinction). The result is formation of photons, pi-mesons, and other particles of small or zero mass. The difference between the number of baryons and the number of antibaryons in any given system is called its "baryon number" (or "baryonic charge"). For example, the mass number of an atomic nucleus (the sum of the numbers of protons and neutrons) is, under this definition, the baryon number of the nucleus.

Until recently it was believed that baryon number was conserved in all natural processes. The laws of conservation of energy and electric charge allow a proton to decay into a positron and various light particles (photons, neutrinos, etc.). However, our daily experience indicates that either this does not occur at all, or occurs only very rarely. The experimental limit for the probability of this process is very low. A ton of matter contains approximately 10^{30} baryons. It is safe to say that less than one baryon decays in one ton in a year! [This limit has by now been lowered a hundredfold.—A.S. 1989] If exactly one baryon per ton has decayed per year, then the fraction of the universe that has decayed over its entire lifetime (10 billion years) is the same fraction that a crumb ¼ millimeter in diameter bears to a cube one kilometer on a side. To explain this staggering stability, physicists have concluded that there is an absolute law of baryon number conservation: in the universe, the total number of baryons minus the total number of antibaryons never changes.

Now let us return to the universe.

As I have mentioned, there now appear to be many more background-radiation photons (about 400 per cubic centimeter) in the universe than there are baryons (10^{-5} to 10^{-6} per cm³ on the average), and (although this is still to an extent hypothetical) no antibaryons at all. But what was the situation at earlier stages in the expansion of the universe? Extrapolating backward for the photons is easiest. The total number of photons is quite stable, but photon density (the number of photons per unit volume) and, very important, their average energy (the temperature of the photon gas) are altered. The change in temperature with a change in volume is the same phenomenon we observe when we inflate an automobile tire; the air heats up when compressed, and cools when it expands. The same is true for the photon gas, and so its temperature was much higher at earlier stages.

The decrease in photon energy during expansion of the universe is known as the cosmological red shift, from the fact that the energy of photons of visible light is highest at the violet end of the spectrum, and lowest at the red end (as expanding photon gas cools, therefore, the spectral lines "shift" toward the red). Hubble and Humanson's 1927 observation of the shift of lines in spectra emitted by galaxies became the observational basis of the theory of the expanding universe. The farther a galaxy from us, the earlier the light now reaching us was emitted, and the stronger, consequently, its red shift.

At the early stages of expansion, when the energy of the photons was greater than the energy required to form baryon-antibaryon pairs, baryons and antibaryons must have been present, and in numbers equal to the number of photons in the same volume. As a result, assuming the conservation of baryon number and the total baryon asymmetry we seem to have today, we have, in a certain volume of the universe (the numbers are arbitrary and given for the sake of illustration):

At present:

Photons	Baryons	Antibaryons
100,000,000	1	0

For the early hot stage, we add 100,000,000 pairs of baryons and antibaryons:

Photons	Baryons	Antibaryons
100,000,000	100,000,001	100,000,000

It is difficult to imagine that the numbers given in the second line were initial conditions "specified by Nature." As such, they offend the eye: "it couldn't have happened that way." It was this fact (which is, as the reader will see, intuitive rather than deductive) that provided the initial stimulus for many studies of baryon asymmetry, including mine.

The hypotheses that have been submitted can be broken down into three groups: the first two assuming conservation of baryon number, and the third assuming that it is violated.

The hypotheses of the first group (Alfvén, Omnes, and others) assume that at present there are regions of the universe in which there are only baryons, and other, equally large regions in which there are only antibaryons; the universe is "patchy." On the average, over the universe there are exactly as many baryons as there are antibaryons. To avoid contradicting observations— the fact that we do not observe antibaryons in our own neighborhood—these regions must be made quite large, say as large as the amount of space per galaxy. For example, our galaxy and the region around it contain baryons, but the Andromeda Nebula might contain antibaryons.

It is assumed further that the universe was composed equally of baryons and antibaryons at an early stage in its expansion; the patchiness appeared later, as a result of spatial-separation processes (which are different according to different authors).

Major difficulties arise in this group of hypotheses ("symmetric with separation"), chief among them the fact that not even a semi-efficient mechanism of spatial separation of baryons from antibaryons has been found.

The macroscopic mechanisms for separation of matter and antimatter that were proposed by various authors before the mid-1970s could function only in extremely rarefied media and were ineffective.

The hypotheses of the second group essentially return us to the cold model. In the initial state, there are only baryons (more precisely, quarks, the constituents of baryons). The temperature is zero, and heating occurs at later but still early stages due to instabilities of some kind that release enormous numbers of photons, on the order of a hundred million per baryon. Excess baryon-antibaryon pairs form and then annihilate, leaving the same baryons with which everything started, and background photons. An interesting variant of this hypothesis is the release of heat and photons due to transformation of vacuum symmetry.

It seems that I am responsible for initiating the third group of hypotheses. In 1966, I advanced the idea that the observed baryon asymmetry of the universe (and the hypothetical lepton asymmetry) appeared early in the cosmological expansion from an initial state that contained equal numbers of particles and antiparticles. This paper was published in 1967.[6]

This would be possible only if:

1) The law of baryon number (and lepton number) conservation is not exact,

and is violated at high temperatures at an early stage in the cosmological expansion (and in such a way that would be consistent with the fact that the baryons observed today obviously have long lifetimes at ordinary temperatures).

2) During the non-equilibrium conditions of the early universe the probabilities of the formation of particles and the formation of antiparticles were different.

I began with a discussion of the *second* premise. By 1966, this was more than a hypothesis, as it was consistent with the sensational experiments on the decay of neutral K-mesons performed two years earlier by Cronin, Cristensen, Fitch, and Turley. The decay of this long-lived particle (called a k-long) into two pi-mesons was evidence of violation of a basic law of conservation called CP invariance. This violation, it turned out, helped explain the unequal formation of particles and antiparticles. A group of Soviet physicists headed by Podgoretsky had previously attempted to observe the k-long-to-two-pi decay, but the beam of k-mesons at their disposal was too weak, and they were able to establish only the upper limit of probability of the decay, which they estimated at about one one-hundredth of the total decay probability (if memory serves). It was later found that the effect that they were looking for amounts to about one five-hundredth. Podgoretsky and his comrades had been that close to the target!

The downfall of CP-invariance completed the reexamination of symmetry under "reflection" that was begun in 1956 by Tsung Dao Lee and Chen Ning Yang (Chinese physicists working in the U.S.). For their 1956 work they received the Nobel Prize. (From the point of view of the psychology of scientific work it is interesting that simultaneously with their paper on "reflection" they carried out an elegant and laborious calculation in statistical physics, on which they lavished no less attention but which is much less known. To Yang, together with Robert Mills, belongs credit for another fundamental work on gauge fields—now known as the Yang-Mills field.)

Before the work of Lee and Yang the existence of three exact, discrete symmetries was considered self-evident and indisputable by particle physicists.[7] The symmetries were:

1) Symmetry with respect to the so-called (spatial) P-reflection, which is equivalent to reflection in a mirror (i.e., it was assumed that any physical process resembles its mirror image).

2) Symmetry with respect to C-reflection, which changes particles into antiparticles. According to this hypothesis, all processes involving antiparticles correspond to processes involving particles.

7[Here, the word "discrete" is used as the antithesis of "continuous." An example of a continuous symmetry is that a sphere "looks" the same when it is rotated around an axis.]

3) Symmetry with respect to time, or T-reflection, which reverses the direction of a process. For example the decay of a particle into two particles is symmetric to the merging of those particles into one.

Lee and Yang's idea was extraordinarily clever and productive. They submitted that all of these symmetries are approximate; in particular, they may be strongly violated in the case of the weak nuclear force, which is involved in radioactive particle decay. On the other hand, there could be no symmetry violations in the strong nuclear force, gravity, and electromagnetism. This idea was of tremendous importance for all of elementary-particle physics and it gave impetus to many experimental and theoretical studies.

Several years earlier, Pauli and Luders had established that the basic principles of quantum field theory imply symmetry under joint CPT-transformation (so-called CPT-symmetry). In other words, a universe made of antimatter would obey the same rules as a universe made of matter—if we took its mirror image and reversed the direction of all processes. This conclusion was later strongly supported by other authors. Physicists therefore have a front line of defense from which they probably will not have to retreat. But there was an initial attempt to "dig in" midway. Several authors, including Landau and Salam, advanced the hypothesis that "combined" CP-symmetry is an exact symmetry. The premise from which Landau worked—zero neutrino mass—is apparently incorrect. The idea itself proved productive, however, and it was soon used as a base for a theory of weak interactions (of the processes that change the charge of particles, e.g., beta decay) that agrees well with experiment.

CP-symmetry (or its synonym, CP-invariance) means that any process taking place in a mirror-reflected antiworld cannot be distinguished from the process in our world. As a consequence, the total probability of any particle-transformation reaction is the same for particles and antiparticles. Therefore, CP-symmetry is no better than C-symmetry as far as the baryonic asymmetry is concerned: both ought to be violated to explain it.

Meanwhile, the seed of doubt planted by Lee and Yang continued to grow. Tests of CP-symmetry were begun. The fate of T-invariance was decided simultaneously; by virtue of the Pauli-Luders CPT theorem, either both the CP- and T-symmetries are simultaneously exact or both of these symmetries are approximate.

Physicists intensified their search for phenomena in which violation of CP- and T-symmetries occurs (the decay of the k-long meson into two pi-mesons is, as I noted, one such phenomenon). A phenomenon in which violation of CP-symmetry and the particle-antiparticle difference are more clearly manifested was discovered a few years later. Among the many modes of decay of the k-long meson, there are two channels (as they say) that are CP- or

C-reflections of each other—while one decays into a pi-plus meson, an electron, and a neutrino, the other yields a pi-minus meson, a positron, and an antineutrino (since we are interested in the total probabilities of each channel, CP- and C-symmetries are equivalent for our purposes).[8]

But it was found that the total probabilities of decay in these two channels differ by 0.6 percent! This is an effect of precisely the kind that I needed to explain the appearance of baryonic asymmetry in the universe from an originally neutral state.

The earliest work known to me that discusses the consequences of conservation of CPT-symmetry and violation of CP- and C-symmetries is that of Susumu Okubo. He submits the following statements (with specific examples):

Let a certain state particle A decay in several channels B_1, B_2, etc., and let the C-reflected state $\overline{A}$ (antiparticle) decay in the C-reflected channels $\overline{B}_1$, $\overline{B}_2$, et cetera. Then:

1) It follows from CPT-symmetry that the mass of A is equal to the mass of $\overline{A}$, and that the total probability of decay of A is equal to the total probability of decay of $\overline{A}$ (the total probability is the sum of the probabilities of decay over all of the possible channels);

2) A result of violation of CP-symmetry is that the channel decay probabilities may be different for particles and antiparticles, e.g., the probability of channel B_1 is not equal to the probability of channel $\overline{B}_1$, and so forth.

It was this insight, together with the violation of baryon number, that formed the basis for my work. On a copy of the paper that I gave to Evgeny Feinberg in 1967, I penned the following epigraph:

> Making use of the effect
> S. Okubo has proposed,
> While the temperature is high,
> The universe is richly clothed
> In a coat made to fit
> Its crooked figure—head to foot.

I now turn to the work's other premise—violation of baryon number.

This hypothesis, as I have noted, ran counter to then established scientific views. Partly for this reason, my effort attracted little attention at the time. As late as 1975, Zeldovich and Novikov's excellent book displays a distinctly

---

[8][If the CP-symmetry held, there should be just as much chance that a K-long meson would break down into the first group of particles as the second group. There would be, in other words, an equal number of electrons (from channel one) and positrons (from channel two).]

skeptical tone in discussing the hypothesis of baryon number violation and any explanation of baryon asymmetry of the universe based on this hypothesis.

I was aware as I wrote my paper (Zeldovich had informed me) of Lee and Yang's suggestion that an attempt be made to detect the existence of a field connected to baryon number. The existence of such a field would confirm baryon number (baryonic charge) conservation, much as the presence of the Coulomb electric field around electrically charged bodies "guarantees" conservation of electric charge. Similarly, the gravitational field that exists in the neighborhood of any system of bodies is uniquely related to the system's conserved mass (or energy, according to Einstein's formula). In general, the very existence of a long-range force (i.e., one that decreases in inverse proportion to the square of distance) is due to some conserved property. The converse—that the absence of a field means the absence of the correspondent conserved quantity—does not follow automatically but is still quite plausible.

The fact that the acceleration of freely falling bodies is independent of their chemical composition, which Galileo verified by dropping various objects from the Tower of Pisa, seems to indicate the absence of a baryonic field. (The historic significance of these experiments is that they marked the beginning of modern science. Moreover, we can now say that Galileo's experiments laid the groundwork for Einstein's theory of gravitation (the equivalence of inertial and gravitational masses), and that, in fact, Galileo was checking whether there exist nonelectrical and nongravitational long-range forces, which bears on the problem of baryon number.) Detection of a difference in the acceleration rates would have had far-reaching consequences. And there is always the danger (or hope) that refinement will yield something new. There have been a number of improvements upon Galileo's experiments: by Newton, who not long afterward made use of pendulums made from various materials; in our century, by Eötvös, Dicke, and then Braginsky and Panov, with steadily increasing accuracy (raised by Braginsky and Panov to 10^{-12}–10^{-13}, still, with a negative result).

I recently learned of Steven Weinberg's conclusion, in 1964 (i.e., before me, like Yang and Lee), that the absence of a baryonic field means that baryon number is not conserved. He also discussed its possible implications for cosmology. Weinberg makes no mention of this hypothesis in his popular 1976 book on cosmology, *The First Three Minutes*, apparently considering it of no particular importance.

I should note that my 1967 paper proposed a specific mechanism of baryon number violation that appears to have no relation to reality. Vladimir Kuzmin published an interesting paper on the genesis of baryonic asymmetry in 1970 (it includes a reference to my work); later Pati and Salam independently published a paper that advanced other hypotheses regarding the proton-instability mechanism. None of these hypotheses appears to correspond to reality. An important fundamental step was taken by Georgi and Glashow in 1974, developing advances made by Glashow, Weinberg, and Salam in combining the weak and electromagnetic interactions of elementary particles into a unified theory. Georgi and Glashow proposed the first (and very interesting) variant of what is now known as the GUT (Grand Unification Theory), which unified the strong, weak, and electromagnetic interactions, leaving out only gravitation.

By this time the idea that baryons are each composed of three quarks (and that antibaryons are composed of three antiquarks) had gained wide acceptance. Theoretically, quarks and leptons (the combined name for electrons and neutrinos) come in on an equal footing and can change into one another. Consequently, reactions are possible that change baryon number. For instance a proton can decay into a positron and two photons. [The former has a baryon number of 1 and the latter are not baryons and so have baryon numbers of 0.] The process of proton decay takes place through intermediate stages with the formation of the so-called X-boson (or other analogous particles; for simplicity I speak only of the X-boson).

Because the proton mass is much smaller than the X-boson mass, the probability of proton decay is extraordinarily small. In fact, in the usual (classical) sense it can't take place at all. There is only a small "swinging" of the vacuum degree of freedom that corresponds to the X-boson. Even the hand of a small child (the proton) can make the clapper of an enormous bell (the X-boson) swing a little, but the larger the mass of the clapper, the smaller will be its swing. According to the theory, the probability of the reaction is inversely proportional to the mass of the X-boson to the fourth power. Georgi and Glashow used certain considerations to estimate the mass of the X-boson and these estimates have since been improved on several occasions. They indicate that the mass of the X-boson is 10^{15} times the mass of the proton (i.e., uncommonly large on the scale of subatomic particles), and, accordingly, that the lifetime of the proton is an enormous 10^{31} years, i.e., ten times the experimental limit of that day. Success in confirming the prediction of proton decay would be a magnificent triumph of the Georgi-Glashow theory and the entire contemporary theory of elementary particles. Large-scale experiments are now being conducted with the object of detecting proton decay in a large mass of pure water with the aid of Cherenkov counters. These experiments are conducted deep underground to eliminate cosmic-ray interference. [The present experimental limit on the proton is 10^{32} years, or even higher. This almost invalidates the initial scenario proposed by Georgi and Glashow, but the contemporary supersymmetric theories suggest much higher values for the proton lifetime.—1989 A.S.]

The X-boson can decay via two channels: into an antiquark and positron, or into two quarks. Correspondingly, the $\overline{X}$ can decay into a quark and an electron or two antiquarks. This is the same situation Okubo described. The total probability of X-decay via the two channels is equal to the total probability of $\overline{X}$ decay via the corresponding two channels. But if CP-symmetry is violated the number of quark pairs formed on decay of X is greater than the number of antiquark pairs yielded by the decay of the same number of $\overline{X}$-particles. And fewer antiquarks and positrons are formed than quarks and electrons in the decay of $\overline{X}$.

It is important that the decay of X is a nonequilibrium, "delayed" process; otherwise, according to the general theory, it would prevent the appearance of baryonic asymmetry. (The best way to demonstrate this is by using the theorem established in the nineteenth century by the American physicist Josiah Gibbs, according to which the probability of any state at equilibrium is uniquely determined by its energy, which is the same for particles and antiparticles by virtue of CPT-symmetry.)

Antiquarks annihilate with quarks in later stages of the cosmological expansion of the universe; the extra quarks then unite to form baryons, and the extra electrons are later incorporated into atoms. This is how matter forms. A majority of physicists did not immediately grasp the cosmological implications of the Grand Unified Theories (GUTs).

I should, of course, have gone right for the GUTs. But unfortunately, I didn't immediately get the sense of these ideas, and lost the chance of participating in their development. I shall return a bit later to an error of mine that in part accounted for this lapse.

In 1976, I attended an international conference on elementary-particle physics at Tbilisi. During a break, one of the foreign scientists came up to me and asked, hadn't I written a paper in which I considered proton decay assuming fractional quark charges? I said that I had written such a paper ten years before, but now tended to favor Pati and Salam's theory in which the quarks have integer charges and are therefore unstable and unobservable. The man excused himself politely and left. The next day I realized that I had disavowed my own work and come out in favor of the theory of integer-charge quarks for no good reason.

Actually one could have been sure even then that the much prettier theory of fractionally charged quarks was correct. Further development confirmed this model, which includes so-called quantum chromodynamics, the dynamic theory of strong interaction. In this theory, quarks are given an additional property known as color; hence "chromo"dynamics. Quantum chromodynamics (QCD) has had major successes in describing the masses and other properties of hadrons [baryons and mesons]. An important feature of QCD is quark confinement: quarks cannot be extracted from baryons or mesons in the same way that an electron can be extracted from an atom. This is due to the formation of a "string" that confines the quark with a force that does not decrease with distance.

I looked around the conference for my questioner, in order to correct my lapse, but I couldn't find him, and I didn't know his name.

In 1978, Motohiko Yoshimura published an important paper in which he accomplished what I might have done, linking GUTs to the baryonic asymmetry of the universe. It should be noted that the question of a relation between GUTs and the baryon-asymmetry problem had been posed before Yoshimura in a paper by Ignatev, Krasnikov, Kuzmin, and Tavkhelidze delivered at an international conference. But Yoshimura's paper is the most widely recognized; it made a powerful impression, and triggered a multitude of new studies that, among other things, clarified the described roles of the X- and Y-particles and other bosons, the so-called Higgs scalars. Among the researchers: Kuzmin, Ignatev, Shaposhnikov, Krasnikov, Weinberg, Nanopoulos, Tamvakis, Susskind, Dimopoulos, Turner, Toussaint, Treiman, Wilczek, Zee, and many others; I am not thoroughly conversant with the literature and may have omitted some authors and important papers.

After these publications, the instability of the proton, once regarded as a probable deficiency of GUTs, has come to be seen as one of its important advantages (and one that I myself had recognized earlier).

Other contributions have pointed out new links between elementary-particle physics and cosmology, a relationship that is, without a doubt, one of the most remarkable features of contemporary science. Did my 1967 paper play any role in the initiation of this scientific process? I have no direct proof that it did, and it appears that Yoshimura was unaware of my paper. But I would like to think that during the ten years that separated my paper from Yoshimura's, it had some influence on the scientific climate.

Finally, I must mention a misconception of mine that was largely responsible for my initial failure to recognize the work of Georgi and Glashow and others on GUTs and baryonic asymmetry and that affected my own work.

The quantum theory of elementary particles offers two ways of describing elementary particles with spin of ½. The first of these methods, developed by Dirac, is the "theory of holes," in which antiparticles are treated as vacancies ("holes") in an unobservable sea of negative-energy particles. The other method, quantum field theory, was developed later, and treats particles and antiparticles on an equal basis. I assumed that it was necessary to consider only those theories in which both methods were applicable and equivalent—a criterion met by most of the theories considered before GUTs. The theory of "holes" implies conservation of the total number of fermions: a process like the decay of an X-boson into two quarks is totally inadmissible. For this reason, I doubted the Georgi-Glashow theory and assumed as my proton-decay mechanism a decay into three leptons (each quark is transformed into a lepton) with conservation of the number of elementary fermions (quarks and leptons).

But now it seems to me that this entire edifice was a misconception. There is no law of fermion-number conservation, since experiments to verify the equivalence principle have failed to detect any field corresponding to fermions. This means that it is unnecessary to require equivalence of the "theory of holes" and the method of quantum field theory. Then the most plausible option are GUTs with the possible decay of the proton into a positron (or into a mu$^+$ meson in some versions of GUTs) and photons (but also without the new exact law of conservation of the difference between the numbers of baryons and leptons, which is posited in certain GUT variants), and the baryon asymmetry of the universe explained in terms of decay of bosons in two competing channels as the principal mechanism.

It is galling that because of these (and other) misconceptions, I was unable to pursue one of my better efforts all the way through.

The basis of my 1967 paper, apart from the desire to explain the observed photon-to-baryon ratio, was the hypothesis of "cosmological CPT-symmetry." I assumed that all processes in the universe are CPT-symmetric about the initial singularity—the state of infinite density that exists at the moment of the Big Bang itself in most cosmological theories. This is one possible answer to the question of what existed before the instant of the "initial" infinitely dense state. A further discussion of CPT-reflection can be found in my 1980 paper.[9] Cosmological CPT-symmetry offers the only possibility of *identical* reversal of time in accordance with the Pauli-Lüders theorem. Whether it is necessary to *require* identical reversal is a separate question, and one I cannot answer.

From cosmological CPT-symmetry it necessarily follows that all conserved numbers have an initial value equal to zero. (The formal proof is in the 1980 article, but the basic idea is clear enough.) In other words, the baryon asymmetry has a dynamic origin. For me the premise of cosmological CPT-symmetry was then, in 1967, the most important one. But not anymore. I remain convinced of the dynamic origin of baryon asymmetry, but now I suspect that the hypothesis of CPT-reflection is incorrect.

Also, I now believe that the violation of CP-symmetry is not contained in the basic equations of the theory, but is a consequence of a certain instability in the CP-symmetric solutions—so-called spontaneous symmetry breaking,

9["Cosmological Models of the Universe with Reversal of Time's Arrow," *Collected Scientific Works*, pp. 131–136.]

which has been proposed by theorists for many types of symmetries. If this is so, then regions with different signs of the violation of CP-asymmetry can arise in the universe and, correspondingly, regions with different signs of baryon asymmetry. To be compatible with observations, the size of the baryon and antibaryon regions must be gigantic—billions of light-years. I want to emphasize that this is an entirely different picture from the one posited in the old hypotheses, which suggested spatial separation of matter and antimatter in the initially charge-neutral plasma.

For a closed model of the universe, the theory of spontaneous symmetry breaking provides that the total volume occupied by baryons and the total volume occupied by antibaryons may be different. For instance, it may be that the region [of baryons] observed by us encompasses the entire universe.

Let me say something here about the further development of the problem of the universe's baryon asymmetry. The inflationary universe scenario requires that the appearance of baryon asymmetry be accompanied by the violation of baryon-number conservation: even if before inflation the density of baryonic charge [number of baryons or antibaryons per volume] is not equal to zero, in the course of inflation, the density is decreased to negligibly small values— much less than observed today. The very fact that baryon asymmetry exists is evidence for the absence of a law of baryon conservation (at the moment, the only evidence).

On the other hand, explanation for the growth of baryon asymmetry in the inflationary theory runs into some difficulties. After all, if a surplus of quarks over antiquarks appeared before inflation, this surplus would also be distributed over a gigantic volume. Therefore, the surplus of quarks over antiquarks should arise after inflation. But it is far from clear whether the temperature after inflation is high enough to create X-bosons (in some inflationary states the final temperature is relatively low). A possible escape from this difficulty is that the baryon asymmetry may survive the dangerous period [the period of inflation] in a "concealed" state; that is, in the form of scalar particles having baryon number, as proposed in the theory of supersymmetry (Afflek and Dine).

In the last few years important work has been done by Ignatiev, Kuzmin, and Shaposhnikov. Basing their work on that of t'Hooft concerning the violation of baryon-number conservation in theories of the unified electroweak interaction, they find that such violation can take place at temperatures much lower than is necessary for the creation of X-bosons. In this case, the transformation of particles [into one another] takes place almost in equilibrium conditions. The baryon asymmetry, arising at earlier stages, therefore decreases with the simultaneous growth of a surplus of antineutrinos.

The title of my popular article "The Symmetry of the Universe," written in 1965 for the collection *The Future of Science,* is a reference to the hypothesis of cosmological CPT-symmetry. Working simultaneously on this and a paper for a scientific journal proved beneficial: all my important ideas occurred to me as I worked on the popular article! But, I'm not certain that my popular-science debut was a success (I suspect even specialists found it difficult to understand; at any rate, it doesn't seem to have prompted any responses from scientists, although it was reprinted in a German popular science journal).

In 1967 or so, on our way back to the Installation from some conference (that is, I was returning to the Installation and Zeldovich was going there on a business trip), Zeldovich asked me which of my theoretical works I was most pleased with. "The baryon asymmetry of the universe," I told him.

He knitted his brow and stiffened. "Do you mean that one where baryon number isn't conserved and time flows backward?"

"Yes, that one."

Zeldovich said nothing, but it was clear that he had his doubts about my ideas. We entered the security zone and the pine woods that surrounded the Installation.

"And which of your works do you like best?" I asked.

"If you're speaking of my old works, then the one with Gershtein on the conservation of the vector current in weak interactions. But in general, I'm always most pleased with my most recent works—but afraid to talk about them. My works too often sink without a trace. . . ."

AMONG THOSE "MOST RECENT" PAPERS of which Zeldovich spoke with such hesitancy was one on the cosmological constant which was among his finest. It was inspired by some sensational astronomical observational results and, in turn, provided the inspiration for my paper on the zero Lagrangian of the gravitational field.

During the first half of the 1960s, so-called quasars, amazing astronomical objects whose immense absolute luminosities make it possible to observe them telescopically at record distances of billions of light-years (much farther away than galaxies), were discovered.

Data that appeared in 1966–1967 concerning the red-shift distribution of the quasars seem to indicate that the expansion of the universe slowed sharply, nearly ceasing, during some period in the past, and then resumed with increasing velocity. This picture would ring true if a cosmological constant were present in the equations of general relativity theory. I mentioned this earlier, and will now go into greater detail. Although observational data were subsequently found to be inadequate, attention had been drawn to the cosmological constant, which has been a point of interest ever since (while previously, for example in the well-known textbook by Landau and Lifshitz, the position was that after Friedmann's work there was no need to consider equations with a cosmological constant).

Introduction of a cosmological constant is equivalent to the assumption that the vacuum possesses a certain energy density and a pressure of the opposite sign that create a gravitational field in accordance with the same laws as "ordinary" matter. Zeldovich's idea was that the cosmological constant represents the energy of the zero-point fluctuations of the quantum fields of the elementary particles and their interactions. At the dawn of quantum field theory, the zero-point oscillation energy was, as I have written, a frightening notion for theoreticians to contemplate. They eventually got used to it and came to regard it as an unseen constant term in the total energy (forgetting that a constant term in the energy must create a gravitational field, as pointed out by Zeldovich). It will be recalled that in quantum mechanics an energy $\hbar\omega\,(\frac{1}{2} + n)$ corresponds to each vibrational degree of freedom of a system (to each "pendulum"), where w is the frequency, $\hbar$ is Planck's constant, and n is a whole number. When n = 0, we have the state of lowest energy, which is nonzero owing to the presence of the $\frac{1}{2}$ in the formula; this is a consequence of the uncertainty principle. The number of degrees of freedom in vacuum is infinite; accordingly, the zero-point oscillation energy of vacuum may also prove to be infinite. A way out is found in the fact that the zero-point energy of fermions—particles with half-integer spins—has the sign opposite to that of the energy of the bosons—particles with integer spin, and cancellation is possible. I believe that the final solution of the problem may come from the use of "supersymmetry" (symmetry between bosons and fermions).

Zeldovich presented his paper on the cosmological constant at a seminar of the theoretical division of FIAN. At the time, I had not yet started to attend the FIAN seminars, and I was not present when the paper was read. The FIAN theoreticians took a sharply negative view of Zeldovich's ideas, which ran counter to the established tradition of ignoring zero-point energy. Zeldovich telephoned me after the seminar and told me the contents of his paper. I found them very attractive, and a few days later, I called him back with an idea of my own that represented a further development of his approach.

I set out to examine the changes that take place in the energy of the zero-point oscillations of elementary-particle fields when making the transition from flat to curved four-dimensional space time and to link these energy changes to the expressions that enter into the equation of Einstein's theory of gravitation. Einstein (and, independently, David Hilbert) postulated these expressions, and the coefficient before them, which is inversely proportional to the gravitational constant, was taken from experiment. My idea was that the functional form of the equations of the theory of gravitation (i.e., of general relativity theory) and the numerical value of the gravitational constant should follow "by themselves" from elementary-particle theory with no special hypotheses.

Zeldovich greeted my idea with delight, and soon afterward wrote up the paper it suggested.

I called my idea the "theory of the zero Lagrangian." This name derives from the fact that theoreticians often find it convenient to deal not with energy and pressure, but with another quantity that is related to them—the so-called Lagrange function (in quantum language, the Lagrangian), which is the difference between the kinetic and potential energies. I had made use of this formalism in some of my papers.

I thought up the descriptive phrase "metric elasticity of the vacuum" as an aid in getting my idea across. When material bodies, which possess a certain energy, are introduced into a vacuum, they tend to "curve" it, i.e., to change its metric (its geometry). But the vacuum "resists" this change, since it possesses "elasticity" owing to the quantum motions taking place within it. Think of a hose with water flowing through it. But in this case, the elasticity is of the opposite sign, and instability arises. The greater the elasticity of the vacuum, the less its geometry is modified by bodies of a given mass, and the smaller the gravitational curvature of the paths. On the subatomic level, the elasticity of vacuum is very high, i.e., for the particles of the microworld, gravitational interactions are weak.

I later became aware that I had predecessors in ideas of this kind (I don't have the references at hand, but I think Leonard Parker was one), and that other authors had arrived independently at similar notions (among them Oskar Klein). In one of his early papers, Weinberg introduces a "zero Lagrangian" for a heavy vector boson. I became aware of this paper no earlier than 1968 (it was my source for the phrase "zero Lagrangian"). The "induced gravitation" idea was further developed by Terazawa and, recently, in the work of Adler and Amati and Veneziano. I also returned to these ideas more than once.

THE FOURTH PAPER that I'd like to discuss here (published in 1966) was written jointly with Zeldovich: "The Quark Structure and Masses of Strongly Interacting Particles."[10] I shall confine myself to the part of the paper that has stood the test of time: the semiempirical formula for the masses of mesons and baryons.

This paper was written when, following the hypothesis of quarks advanced by Gell-Mann and Zweig and the first works on the symmetry of strongly

---

[10][*Collected Scientific Works*, pp. 205–222.]

interacting particles (which we now collectively call hadrons), studies employing symmetry considerations were flooding in at such a rate that scientific journals were forced into a decision to stop printing them. One aspect of the hadron-mass formulas that were then being worked out and published was the different treatment given baryons and mesons. For baryons, the relations were written in such a way that the masses appeared in the first power, or, as we say, linearly, while in the formulas for the mesons they appeared in the second power, or quadratically. This, of course, closed the door to possible comparisons of parameters in these two types of formulas.

We set out to show how to avoid this discrepancy. Our treatment was based on a "naive" quark model in which both baryons and mesons were treated linearly. We took account of the differences in the properties of the two types of quarks—"ordinary" or light quarks, which enter into protons and neutrons, and the so-called strange quark, which is more massive and forms part of certain heavy unstable baryons. No other types of quarks were known at the time, although even heavier quarks are known today.

The point of departure for the entire treatment was the surprising fact of the mass difference between so-called sigma-zero and lambda-zero baryons, which have the same composition, consisting of two different "ordinary" quarks with the electric charges $+2/3$ and $-1/3$ and one "strange" quark with charge $-1/3$. I assumed that the difference between the masses of these baryons was due to different orientations of their quark spins [the vector of their angular momentum] and unequal strengths of the spin interactions between the two ordinary quarks and between the ordinary quarks and the strange quark. Knowing the orientation of the spins in the lambda and sigma, it was possible to calculate the weakening of the spin-spin interaction for the strange quark. The value obtained was 0.61. On the other hand, the same coefficient could be calculated from analysis of the mass difference between two kinds of mesons, those with zero and those with non-zero spin. This gave a value of 0.64 for the weakening.

Agreement was also found for another parameter in the formulas for the mesons and baryons—the mass difference between the strange and ordinary quarks (179 and 177 MeV, respectively). We noted that for baryons it was necessary to use the mass difference between the lambda and the proton, since it is precisely in the lambda that weakening of the spin-spin interaction for the strange quark is not observed. The agreement obtained in the parameters was a major success.

Needless to say, this semiempirical approach is no substitute for the detailed concrete calculations that were subsequently carried out by a number of authors. However, it seems to me that it is useful by virtue of its extreme simplicity and lucidity, and it sheds a great deal of light, like the well-known semiempirical formula of Weizsäcker and Williams for the masses of atomic nuclei, which was also based on very simple and graphical arguments. Further development of the ideas contained in this paper, as well as my other work of the sixties, is described in Chapter 47.

By the end of the fifties, public issues had become a major preoccupation for me, and they became an ever greater part of my world in the 1960s. I felt compelled to speak out, to act, to put everything else aside, to some extent even science (although not always—sometimes science demanded its due). There were also other significant impediments to my scientific work, perhaps equally important, including the natural decrease in the ability to do science that comes with age.

The roots of my involvement with public issues, and the changes in my life—new circumstances, new problems, new people—will be the main subject of the chapters that follow.

II

19

THE TURNING POINT

THE YEARS 1965–1967 were a turning point in my life. I was heavily involved in demanding scientific work, even as I was approaching a decisive break with the establishment.

I still spent most of my time at the Installation, where attention was shifting from the development of nuclear devices to new ventures such as underground "breeder explosions" (which produce radioactive substances when uranium and thorium atoms capture free neutrons and then split) and a nuclear propulsion system for space flight. We spent much of our time developing specialized nuclear charges for nonmilitary applications, including copper mining in Udokan and other strip mining projects, building dams and canals, releasing underground oil reserves from shale, and capping accidental blowoffs of oil and gas wells. The first and second Installations vied with each other in theoretical and experimental research into peaceful uses of nuclear explosions, but the serious risk of contaminating the soil, groundwater, and atmosphere continually thwarted the practical application of our ideas.

Both Installations began to concentrate on problems requiring an "operations research" approach. The first problem of this kind we tackled was an investigation of antiballistic missile (ABM) systems and ways to counter them. In the course of many heated discussions, I, along with the majority of my colleagues, reached two conclusions which, in my view, remain valid today:

1) An effective ABM defense is not possible if the potential adversary can mobilize comparable technical and economic resources for military purposes. A way can always be found to neutralize an ABM defense system—and at considerably less expense than the cost of deploying it.

2) Over and above the burdensome cost, deployment of an ABM system is dangerous since it can upset the strategic balance. If both sides were to possess

powerful ABM defenses, the main result would be to raise the threshold of strategic stability, or in somewhat simplified terms, increase the minimum number of nuclear weapons needed for mutual assured destruction.

These findings, which were apparently shared by American experts, probably helped pave the way for the 1972 Treaty on the Limitation of Antiballistic Missile Systems. I have continued to refine my ideas on ABM systems, and the evolution of my views can be traced in my written comments on the topic, especially *My Country and the World* (1975), my 1983 letter to Sidney Drell ("The Danger of Thermonuclear War"), and my talk on SDI [the Strategic Defense Initiative] delivered at the 1987 Forum for a Nuclear-Free World.

During the second half of the 1960s, I became involved in discussions of a still broader range of problems. I read economic and technical studies concerning the production of radioactive substances, nuclear weapons, and delivery systems, visited several secret military facilities (or "mailboxes" as we called them), and attended one or two conferences on military strategy. Inadvertently, I picked up quite a bit of information (I am thankful that I was not told everything, despite my high-level security clearance). What I learned was more than sufficient to impress upon me the horror, the real danger, and the utter insanity of thermonuclear warfare, which threatens everyone on earth. Our reports, and the conferences where we discussed a strategic thermonuclear strike on a potential enemy, transformed the unthinkable and monstrous into a subject for detailed investigation and calculation. It became a *fact of life*— still hypothetical, but already seen as something possible. I could not stop thinking about this, and I came to realize that the technical, military, and economic problems are secondary; the fundamental issues are political and ethical. Gradually, subconsciously, I was approaching an irrevocable step—a wide-ranging public statement on war and peace and other global issues. I took that step in 1968.

ADDING MY SIGNATURE to a collective letter opposing the rehabilitation of Stalin was one of the significant harbingers of my 1968 essay.

In January 1966, Boris Geilikman, a neighbor formerly associated with FIAN and now at the Institute of Atomic Energy, escorted a short, energetic man to my apartment. He introduced himself as Ernst Henri, a journalist. (I later learned that Geilikman made this introduction at the request of Academician Vitaly Ginzburg.)

After Geilikman left, Henri came straight to the point. There was a real danger, he said, that the forthcoming Twenty-third Party Congress might adopt a resolution rehabilitating Stalin. Influential military and party circles— alarmed by the decay of ideology, the breakdown of values, and the loss of confidence following the failure of Alexei Kosygin's economic reforms—were pushing that idea. But many other Party members understood that Stalin's rehabilitation would have devastating consequences, and prominent representatives of the Soviet intelligentsia should support these "healthy forces."

Henri said he was aware of my stand on genetics, my major role in defense, and my authority. I read his draft letter, found nothing objectionable in it, and added my signature. Pyotr Kapitsa, Mikhail Leontovich, and five or six others had signed before me, but Henri's own name did not appear, because he wanted to limit the list to "celebrities." In total, twenty-five people eventually signed the letter, including the famous ballerina Maya Plisetskaya.

Rereading the letter now, I still agree with its assessment of Stalin's crimes, but I find the line of argument overly influenced by tactical considerations and the tone too deferential. At the time, however, my discussion of the letter with Henri and others greatly advanced my understanding of social issues.

Henri mentioned that foreign correspondents in Moscow would be briefed on the letter, and I made no objection. He asked me to pay a visit to Academician Andrei Kolmogorov, whose authority reached beyond mathematicians to Party and military circles.

Kolmogorov was then engaged in reorganizing the teaching of mathematics, but, in my opinion, his innovations were not constructive. Set theory and mathematical logic are too sophisticated for young students; they complicate the learning of practical mathematical techniques without inculcating a deeper understanding of mathematical principles. I prefer the traditional approach (after all, Euclid served many generations well before the advent of Bourbaki), and would add to it only the study of differential equations and other useful mathematical tools.

Kolmogorov agreed to see me, but made it clear that he was in a hurry. Although he was no longer young and his hair was streaked with gray, he appeared fit, suntanned, and vigorous. He was gentle in manner and speech, pronouncing his "r's" in the old, aristocratic way, and holding himself somewhat aloof. He read the letter, but refused to sign it, because, he said, the soldiers with whom he dealt all idolized Stalin for his wartime leadership. I replied that Stalin's role had been determined by his government post and not the other way around, and that he had committed numerous crimes and had made costly mistakes. Kolmogorov didn't disagree—but he still wouldn't sign. (A few weeks later, however, after foreign broadcasts reported our appeal, Kolmogorov did sign a similar collective letter opposing Stalin's rehabilitation.)

In retrospect, I now realize that Henri's letter was probably inspired by his influential friends in the Party machine or the KGB. Henri became a frequent visitor to my apartment and told me something of his past, leaving (I suspect) much unsaid. His real name is Semyon Rostovsky. In the 1920s he was a

Comintern agent working underground in Germany, and he saw at first hand the absurdity of the Comintern's (that is, Stalin's) policy, which held Hitler's fascism to be a lesser evil than Social Democracy since the popularity of the latter's pluralist philosophy threatened the Communists' monopoly of the working class. Stalin believed he could come to terms with Hitler on spheres of influence (or, if need be, destroy Hitler), but he feared the liberal center: it seemed dangerously beyond his control. Rostovsky wrote a number of articles warning against fascism, and his book *Hitler Over Europe?*[1] brought him fame under the pseudonym Ernst Henri, which he has maintained ever since.

Henri showed me a samizdat article he'd written on Stalin, and some correspondence with Ilya Ehrenburg on the subject. But Henri was never a "dissident."

IN THE FALL of 1966, two men (one of whom, I think, was Geilikman; I don't recall the other) asked me to sign an appeal. Typed out on onionskin paper and addressed to the Supreme Soviet of the Russian Republic (the RSFSR), it opposed the impending enactment of Article 190-1 of the RSFSR Criminal Code [Circulation of Fabrications Known to Be False Which Defame the Soviet State or Social System; maximum sentence: three years labor camp] which would open the way for the prosecution of many more dissidents. Articles 70 [Anti-Soviet Propaganda; adopted in 1960; maximum sentence: ten years labor camp plus five years internal exile] and 190-1 subsequently served as the principal juridical weapons for the suppression of dissent [until they effectively were revoked in 1989].[2]

A prosecution under Article 70 required proof, at least in theory, of the defendant's anti-Soviet intent; Article 190-1 did not. On the other hand, the 1971 *Commentary on the Criminal Code* asserts that "the circulation of fabrications which are not known to be false by the party responsible, as well as the expression of mistaken opinions or suppositions do not constitute crimes under Article 190-1." In practice, however, no attention was paid to this commendable declaration. The courts regularly convicted dissidents for their beliefs, for expressing their opinions, and for reporting information they sincerely believed to be accurate. The statements at issue in such proceedings were based on actual fact (with the exception of a few accidental misunderstandings), and usually exposed human rights abuses such as dissident trials, conditions in labor camps, and the deportation of Crimean Tatars; or—even

---

[1][Simon and Schuster, 1934.]

[2][Harold Berman's *Soviet Criminal Law and Procedure,* 2nd edition (Harvard University Press, 1972), contains English translations of Article 70 (pp. 153–154) and Article 190-1 (pp. 180–181). The translation reflects the imprecise language of the Russian original.]

more telling—the secret additional protocol to the 1939 Soviet-German Non-aggression Pact, the mass executions of Polish officers at Katyn, and so on.[3]

Courts rarely bothered to try to demonstrate that a defendant's allegedly defamatory statements were false; it was enough to show that they were "anti-Soviet." Moreover, no attempt was made to prove that the defendant *deliberately* distorted facts.

Although the above comments are based on my subsequent experience in defending human rights, even in 1966 I realized that the alarm triggered by Article 190-1 was justified, and I signed the letter. In this case, it was clear that its authors were acting on their own initiative and accepted the responsibility for any repercussions. I not only signed the joint letter but, a couple of days later, sent a personal telegram to Mikhail Yasnov, chairman of the RSFSR Supreme Soviet, expressing my concern. There was no reply. (When I told the physicist Boris Ioffe what I had done, he said: "Andrei Dmitrievich, you really are a brave man!")

Since then, I have sent many other letters and telegrams to officials. With a few insignificant exceptions, I have never received a reply, and these efforts have produced little in the way of immediate results. Some people therefore regard them as a form of naïveté, while others condemn them as a dangerous and provocative "game." But I believe that statements on public issues are a useful means of promoting discussion, proposing alternatives to official policy, and focusing attention on specific problems. They educate the public at large, and just might stimulate significant changes, however belated, in the policy and practice of top government officials. Appeals on behalf of specific individuals and groups also attract attention to their cases, occasionally benefit a particular individual, and inhibit future human rights violations through the threat of *glasnost* [public disclosure].

In dealing with civic issues and individual cases, it is most important that appeals be open. Private interventions are sometimes useful as a supplement—not a replacement—for public actions.

IN THIS SAME YEAR, 1966, I made an important new acquaintance—Zhores Medvedev's identical twin, Roy—who helped broaden my understanding of social problems. Roy, a historian by profession, visited me in my Moscow

[3][The Crimean Tatars are a Turkic people who since the early fifteenth century have considered themselves a national entity distinct from other descendants of the Mongols, a fact recognized by the Soviet authorities in 1921, when they created the Crimean Autonomous SSR. It was formally dissolved in 1945. See Alan Fisher, *Crimean Tatars* (Hoover Institution Press, 1978). For the Secret Protocol of the Molotov-Ribbentrop Pact, see *Nazi-Soviet Relations 1939–1941*, Department of State, 1948.]

apartment, and told me about the book on Stalin he'd been working on since the Twentieth Party Congress in 1956.[4]

Roy's father, Alexander, a professor of philosophy, had been a member of a Communist opposition group in the early 1920s. He was arrested during the purges of the 1930s, and died in a labor camp. Roy told me he maintained close relations with many Old Bolsheviks, and their eyewitness accounts and unpublished memoirs provided a wealth of previously unknown details for *Let History Judge*.

Roy left several chapters of his manuscript with me. He was to come back many times, bringing me new chapters in return for the old. He loaned me other samizdat manuscripts, including Eugenia Ginzburg's *Journey into the Whirlwind*,[5] one of the better-known memoirs of Stalin's camps. He also brought me news about dissidents and events of social significance. Some of his reports may have been biased or slanted, but when all is said and done, they did help me escape from my hermetic world. One story he told me (I believe during our first meeting; I can't vouch for its reliability) was about Pyotr Yakir visiting Zeldovich to get his signature on the collective letter protesting Article 190-1. When asked whether he himself had signed, Yakir admitted he hadn't. "After you," he was told. Yakir signed, and Zeldovich followed suit. I'm not at all sure he would have done so later on.

I was fascinated by Medvedev's book on Stalin. I hadn't yet read Robert Conquest's *The Great Terror*, or any other works on the subject, and was largely ignorant of the crimes of the Stalin era. An example of the kind of material Medvedev succeeded in uncovering was the report of the special commission established by Khrushchev to investigate the 1934 murder of Sergei Kirov—a detailed description of the assassination of Stalin's rival and of the subsequent elimination of all eyewitnesses to the crime and to the cover-up.[6] The information contained in *Let History Judge* stimulated the evolution of my views at a crucial time in my life.

Even in 1966, however, I couldn't accept Medvedev's tendency to attribute all the tragic events of the 1920s to the 1950s to the idiosyncrasies of Stalin's personality. Although Medvedev agreed in principle that more fundamental causes were at work, his book failed to explore them. We must still look to the future for a satisfactory analysis of our history, one free from dogmatism, political prejudice, and other forms of bias.

[4][Published in a slightly abridged English translation as: *Let History Judge* (Knopf, 1971) and reissued in a revised version by Columbia University Press in 1989.]

[5][Eugenia Ginzburg, *Journey into the Whirlwind* (Harcourt Brace & World, 1967). A second volume was published posthumously by Harcourt Brace Jovanovich in 1981.]

[6][*Let History Judge* (pp. 157–166) suggests Stalin's complicity in Kirov's murder, the act which triggered the bloody purges of the 1930s.]

Roy Medvedev and I continued to meet for some years, but then our paths, both public and private, diverged, until we broke off relations after 1973.

ON DECEMBER 3 or 4, 1966, I found an envelope in my mailbox containing two sheets of onionskin paper. The first sheet was an anonymous report on the arrest and confinement in a psychiatric hospital of Viktor Kuznetsov, an artist who had helped draft a model constitution for our country—Constitution II—which the authors hoped would spark discussion about the introduction of democracy.

The second sheet announced a silent demonstration on December 5, Constitution Day. It proposed that interested persons arrive at Pushkin Square a few minutes before six P.M., assemble near the monument, and then at the stroke of the hour remove their hats and observe a minute of silence as a sign of respect for the Constitution and support for political prisoners, including Kuznetsov. (I learned much later that Alexander Esenin-Volpin was the author of this Constitution Day appeal, and of several other original and effective ideas to promote respect for human rights.)

I decided to attend. Klava didn't object, though she did say it was an odd thing to do. I took a taxi to Pushkin Square and found a few dozen people standing around the statue. Some were talking quietly; I didn't recognize anyone. At six o'clock, half of those present, myself included, removed our hats and stood in silence. (The other half, I later realized, were KGB.) After a minute or so we put our hats back on, but we did not disperse immediately. I walked over to the monument and read the inscription aloud:

> I shall be loved, and the people will long remember
> that my lyre was tuned to goodness,
> that in this cruel age I celebrated freedom
> and asked mercy for the fallen.[7]

After that, I left the Square with the others.

SOMETIME LATER, Yuri Zhivlyuk—another new acquaintance of 1966—told me that my "escapade" had been filmed by the KGB using infrared film (it had been dusk on the Square) and then shown to high officials. I have never completely understood Zhivlyuk. He was working at FIAN when I met him, and people there told me that in the mid-1960s he had been Komsomol

---

[7][Alexander Pushkin, "Unto myself I reared a monument," 1836.]

secretary in one of the laboratories. A samizdat document, Valery Skurlatov's "A Code of Morals,"[8] was circulating among Komsomol members at the time; I don't know whether this fascist program represented Skurlatov's own views or was a trial balloon launched by some faction using him as a stalking-horse. In any event, Zhivlyuk wrote a bitter complaint to the Komsomol Central Committee, which proceeded to punish both parties—Skurlatov for his essay, and Zhivlyuk for "washing dirty linen in public."

Despite this rebuke, Zhivlyuk maintained some sort of relations with the Komsomol Central Committee, and was sent on a fact-finding mission to Bratsk and the far north in 1969. He told me about the economic and ecological problems of the region and described the deliberate corruption of Siberian trappers. A government procurement official would fly into a settlement in a helicopter loaded with vodka. After a few days the trappers and their parents, wives, and children would all be drunk, and the helicopter would fly off with furs for export.

Zhivlyuk was of Ukrainian descent and had ties to dissidents in the Ukraine. He introduced me to Ivan Svetlichny, a poet and Ukrainian activist. Zhivlyuk also had contacts among Moscow dissidents, Andrei Tverdokhlebov in particular. I suspect Zhivlyuk may have had some sort of link with the KGB (perhaps with its "progressive circles"). In the 1970s he apparently became ensnared in this tangled skein of relationships, and he disappeared from my field of vision.

Early in 1967, Zhivlyuk told me about the case involving Alexander Ginzburg, Yuri Galanskov, Alexei Dobrovolsky, and Vera Lashkova, and the demonstration organized in their defense by Vladimir Bukovsky and Viktor Khaustov. These events, like the February 1966 trial of the writers Andrei Sinyavsky and Yuli Daniel, played a critical role in shaping public consciousness and in forging the human rights movement in our country.[9]

When I heard of the case of Ginzburg and the others, I recalled that in mid-1966 Ernst Henri had shown me Ginzburg's letter of recantation which had appeared in the newspaper *Vechernaya Moskva* [on June 3, 1965]. I still don't know who was behind Henri's attempt to scare me away from Ginzburg, but in February 1967, I decided to ignore his warning. I used Zhivlyuk's

[8][English translation of Skurlatov's "A Code of Morals," in Stephen F. Cohen, ed., *An End to Silence* (Norton, 1982), pp. 171–174. Skurlatov worked in the propaganda department of the Moscow Komsomol.]

[9][For information on the Sinyavsky-Daniel trial see: Max Hayward, editor, *On Trial* (2nd edition, Harper & Row, 1967); on the Ginzburg-Galanskov trial: Pavel Litvinov, ed., *The Trial of the Four* (Viking, 1972); and on the trials resulting from the Bukovsky-Khaustov demonstration: Pavel Litvinov, editor, *The Demonstration in Pushkin Square*, (Harvill Press, 1969). For a general history of the diverse dissident movements, see Ludmilla Alexeyeva, *Soviet Dissent* (Wesleyan University Press, 1985).]

information to write Leonid Brezhnev in defense of Ginzburg, Galanskov, Lashkova, and Dobrovolsky. Although I neither circulated my letter in samizdat nor publicized it in any way, it was a milestone for me in that it was my first intervention on behalf of specific dissidents. (During the Sinyavsky-Daniel trial I was still "out of things," and I paid little attention to Mikhail Sholokhov's speech at the Twenty-third Party Congress recalling that "in the memorable twenties . . . scoundrels and turncoats" like Sinyavsky and Daniel were shot.)

The Ministry learned of my letter. Friends reported that Efim Slavsky had told participants in a Party conference held at the second Installation in March: "Sakharov is a good scientist. He's accomplished a great deal and we've rewarded him well. But as a politician he's muddleheaded, and we'll be taking measures."

Measures were indeed taken. I lost my post as department head, even though I remained deputy scientific director of the Installation. My salary was reduced from 1,000 to 550 rubles a month. (This wasn't the first reduction.) The Chief of Administration, Tsirkov (who had switched from experimental work on magnetic cumulation to administrative work) reportedly said that he didn't understand how anyone could live on so little, even though by ordinary Soviet standards I still enjoyed a high salary.

IN APRIL or May of 1967, Academician Vladimir Kirillin, then chairman of the Committee on Science and Technology and a deputy of Premier Kosygin, invited me to his office. At the appointed time, a dozen or so prominent scientists and engineers, including Vitaly Ginzburg, Yakov Zeldovich, and Ilya Lifshitz, sat down to a table set for tea. Kirillin told us that futurological studies were enjoying a vogue in the United States. Although some of the articles being published were trivial, sophisticated futurology could provide a long-range perspective useful for planning. Kirillin asked us to set down our thoughts on the development of science and technology in the coming decades. We should write without constraint, concentrating on the scientific fields we knew best, but touching on more general questions if we so desired.

I carried out Kirillin's assignment with enthusiasm and managed to include quite a few flights of fancy in a relatively short article. On the plane en route from the Installation to Moscow, I exchanged manuscripts with Zeldovich, and he complimented me on my essay. It was published in 1967 in *The Future of Science,* edited by Kirillin and distributed on a restricted basis.

The work I did on this article had a profound psychological effect on me, and turned my thoughts once again to global issues. Some of my propositions resurfaced later in *Reflections on Progress, Peaceful Coexistence, and Intellectual Freedom* and in the article "The World after Fifty Years."

* * *

THAT SAME YEAR, I tried my my hand at writing once more. Henri suggested that he and I collaborate on an article about the present-day role and responsibility of the intelligentsia: he would ask questions and I would respond. I agreed and we set to work, but my answers were more radical than he had anticipated—I was by now approaching the ideas which were to find expression in *Reflections*.

I took the manuscript to a typist who lived near the Sokol metro station, three bus stops from my Moscow apartment—a woman I had been employing for several years to type up scientific reports. When she handed back the last section of this new article, she was visibly upset. There had been a change in her family situation, she told me, and she could no longer work for me. It was obvious she was hiding something—a visit from the KGB, I suspect. After this experience, I had *Reflections* typed at the Installation.

The editors of *Literaturnaya gazeta* told Henri they needed permission from above to publish the article. Apparently, I'd gone further than they'd expected when they agreed in principle to the project. At Henri's request, I sent the manuscript to Mikhail Suslov via the Ministry. Two or three weeks later I received a letter from his secretary stating that Suslov found the manuscript interesting, but unsuitable for immediate publication since its ideas might be interpreted incorrectly. I returned the manuscript to Henri, visiting his apartment for the first time. It was spacious, evidently a bachelor's establishment, crammed with books and mementos of his years abroad. At that point, I promptly forgot the whole affair.

But that was not the end of the story. Some time later I discovered that the article had been included in a typescript periodical, *Political Diary*, rumored to be a KGB publication, or samizdat for officials. Several years after that, Roy Medvedev announced that he had been its editor. To this day, I wonder how my article ended up in his hands.[10]

IN JUNE or July 1967, at Leontovich's suggestion, I was given Larisa Bogoraz's letter describing the desperate situation of her husband, Yuli Daniel, and an account of her visit to the Mordovian labor camp where he was serving his

---

[10][The Sakharov-Henri article, "Scientists and the Danger of Nuclear War," appears in *An End to Silence*, pp. 228–234. Roy Medvedev claims in his foreword (p. 20) that Sakharov was a regular reader of his monthly bulletin which circulated among a few dozen intellectuals from 1964 to 1971; but he did not recognize the name *Political Diary*, which was used only for foreign consumption.]

sentence. I was about to fly back to the Installation and took the letter with me.

I called Yuri Andropov on the high-frequency telephone from my office at the Installation. Andropov told me he'd already received eighteen requests to look into the Daniel case (even back then, I had some difficulty in believing his statement), and that he would do so. He urged me to send him the original of the letter, and when I asked why, he answered, "For my collection." I pretended I had misunderstood, and mailed him a retyped copy.

Six weeks later, Deputy Procurator General Mikhail Malyarov (the same man who in 1973 would warn me about my conduct) phoned my Moscow apartment. He said that he'd checked on Daniel at Comrade Andropov's request and that both Daniel and Sinyavsky would be released under an amnesty slated for the fiftieth anniversary of the October revolution. I thanked him for this information, which, however, turned out to be false. As usual, the amnesty did not apply to political prisoners. (Roy Medvedev later assured me that the decision to exclude political prisoners had been made at the last moment, but, as always with Medvedev, I don't know where he got his information, and I have some doubts about its accuracy.)

In 1967, I became involved in the effort to save Lake Baikal. The deepest lake in the world, it is an immense reservoir of fresh water. Even more important, the Baikal region is a unique phenomenon of nature, an area of surpassing beauty which has become for many a symbol of our nation. For several years, *Komsomolskaya pravda*, *Literaturnaya gazeta*, and other newspapers had been publishing alarming—and convincing—reports on threats to Baikal from industrial construction along its shores, the felling and rafting of timber, and the discharge of chemical wastes into its waters. Though our efforts to protect Baikal were unsuccessful, I did gain valuable insight into environmental problems, both in general and in the particular context of Soviet society. (Later on, in Gorky, I read Boris Komarov's *The Destruction of Nature*,[11] a comprehensive discussion of environmental problems in the USSR, including Baikal, and a work I recommend highly.)

Let me describe my part in the Baikal campaign. Early in 1967, a student at the Moscow Institute of Energy visited me on behalf of the Komsomol's Committee to Save Baikal. He invited me to attend the committee's meetings, to study the issue, and to join in the defense of Baikal. I took the matter

[11][*The Destruction of Nature in the Soviet Union* (M.E. Sharpe, 1980). Boris Komarov is the pseudonym of Zev Wolfson, an ecologist educated at Moscow University who emigrated to Israel in 1981.]

seriously, and a few days later I visited the Komsomol building on Serov Passage where the meetings were held.

Among the committee's members, I recall Academician Igor Petryanov-Sokolov (the inventor of the Petryanov dust filter); the aircraft designer Oleg Antonov; the journalist Oleg Volkov, a former inmate of Stalin's camps; a member of the RSFSR State Construction Board whose name I have forgotten (he and Volkov were the two best informed and most active members); the limnologist Nikolai Nikolsky; and finally the student who had invited me and who represented the Komsomol on the committee. I was shown a number of startling documents on Baikal and on other ecological problems. Petryanov spoke about his specialty, industrial air pollution, which in some localities was catastrophic. Data on air pollution was classified and, as far as I know, remains so. I also learned about the long-term harm done by the flooding of arable land behind hydroelectric dams built in relatively flat regions.

I conducted some research on my own, meeting with Professor Rogozin, a specialist in the cellulose industry. I learned that in the late 1950s, Orlov, the minister in charge of the paper industry, had ordered construction of a large cellulose complex on the shores of Lake Baikal. This facility was designed to produce a particularly durable viscose rayon cord for airplane tires. It was assumed that polymerization would be facilitated by the pure Baikal water, and the resulting fibers would be stronger, but the plant's actual output showed that this hypothesis was unfounded. More important, the aviation industry switched from rayon cord to metallic cord. Thus, whatever rationale the Baikal complex may once have had—and it never, in any case, offset the potential harm to the lake—vanished. Construction nevertheless went ahead, and whole armies of officials, defending their unfortunate decision and their "regimental honor," continued to insist on the importance of the complex for the defense of the country, the usual clinching argument.

The story goes that Orlov had chosen the site by simply pointing to a place on the shoreline while cruising in a motorboat with his cronies. Building was already under way when Baikal's defenders discovered that this was the precise spot where the famous Verninsky earthquake had caused the lake to swallow up thirty-five acres of shoreline in the last century; it was a seismically active region. Telegrams were duly dispatched to Moscow, but instead of canceling the project, the only reasonable course of action, the authorities transferred responsibility to a new contractor—the Ministry of Medium Machine Building. (Petryanov taunted me: "Do you know who's in charge of the murder of Baikal? Your own Slavsky!") New plans were drawn up for earthquake-resistant multistory aluminum and glass buildings supported by steel piles. It was an engineering miracle, but construction costs had multiplied, and the buildings are still vulnerable to the major earthquakes that have occurred there once or twice a century. As its reward, the Ministry of Medium Machine Building was permitted to cut timber in the Baikal preserve!

The big problem now was treatment of toxic waste. The appropriate institutes worked out a scheme for biological purification, after which the effluents were to flow through a canal into the Angara River, bypassing Baikal. The scientists defending the lake pointed to flaws in the proposal, and their fears proved more than justified when the complex began operating. The Academy of Sciences appointed a commission of experts chaired by Academician Nikolai Zhavoronkov, a chemist with little competence in this particular field but responsive to the wishes of the Academy's president and the State Planning Committee.

Our committee had assembled extensive documentation on the damage to the lake and its surrounding area which could come about through human activity. The pollution caused by floating logs down the rivers which empty into the lake kills the spawn of most fish, including the Baikal *omul*, which a century ago rivaled beef as a source of food for all Russia. The accidental discharge of effluents, deforestation, and fire are other hazards threatening the fragile ecological balance of the Baikal region. We proposed that the lake shores be closed to new industry and that existing enterprises be moved. We calculated the expense of such relocation and showed that it was not excessive—far less than had already been spent on the Baikal project. Our report, signed by us and also by a secretary of the Komsomol Central Committee, was sent to the Party Central Committee together with a sampling of the seven thousand letters on Baikal received by *Literaturnaya gazeta* and *Komsomolskaya pravda*.

For good measure, I decided to telephone Brezhnev personally; it was the last conversation we ever had. He was friendly and courteous, but complained of overwork and suggested that I talk to Kosygin, who was handling the Baikal matter. Unfortunately, I failed to follow up. I had never dealt with Kosygin, did not know him personally, and feared that without preliminary spadework, a call would be useless. I knew nothing about the relations between Brezhnev and Kosygin and didn't realize that Brezhnev was in fact shifting responsibility for an unpleasant task onto someone else. My call to the head of state, I thought, was all that was needed: if Brezhnev and Kosygin were interested (I made no distinction between them), they would take appropriate action. I was wrong.

I soon learned that a final decision had been made at a meeting of the Council of Ministers attended by Mstislav Keldysh, President of the Academy of Sciences and, I think, Zhavoronkov. Kosygin asked Keldysh: "What does the Academy recommend? If the safeguards aren't reliable, we'll stop construction."

Keldysh reported the Zhavoronkov commission's conclusion: the water purification system and the other safeguards for Baikal were completely reliable. He may, of course, have been acting in good faith. Possibly he felt that he was choosing "the lesser evil"; the ecological peril most likely seemed less threatening to him than it did to our committee. Still, my feeling is that his stand and his general outlook were greatly influenced by the Academy's administrative dependence on the bureaucratic machine headed by the Central Committee, the State Planning Committee, the ministries, etc. Keldysh and the Academy's presidium were predisposed to respect the wishes of this machine and to ignore the warnings of whistleblowers, dismissing their arguments *a priori* as demagogic, exaggerated, impractical, and generally nonsensical.

Only a couple of years after these events, a Komsomol expedition brought back photographs showing the massive destruction of Baikal's fish and plankton caused by toxic wastes. But in accordance with standing instructions, no accidental discharges had been logged. As always, everything was fine on paper.

20

1968

The Prague Spring.
Reflections on Progress, Peaceful Coexistence, and Intellectual Freedom.

BY THE BEGINNING of 1968, I felt a growing compulsion to speak out on the fundamental issues of our age. I was influenced by my life experience and a feeling of personal responsibility, reinforced by the part I'd played in the development of the hydrogen bomb, the special knowledge I'd gained about thermonuclear warfare, my bitter struggle to ban nuclear testing, and my familiarity with the Soviet system. My reading and my discussions with Tamm (and others) had acquainted me with the notions of an open society, convergence, and world government (Tamm was skeptical about the last two points). I shared the hopes of Einstein, Bohr, Russell, Szilard, and other Western intellectuals that these notions, which had gained currency after World War II, might ease the tragic crisis of our age. In 1968, I took my decisive step by publishing *Reflections on Progress, Peaceful Coexistence, and Intellectual Freedom.*

My work on *Reflections* happened to coincide with the Prague Spring. A year earlier, I'd finally bought a short-wave receiver, and I listened once in a while to the BBC and Voice of America, especially to programs on the Six Day War. In 1968, I began tuning in regularly to the news from Czechoslovakia, and heard Ludvík Vaculík's stirring manifesto, "2,000 Words"—and much more besides. Zhivlyuk and Roy Medvedev supplied additional details during their increasingly frequent visits.

What so many of us in the socialist countries had been dreaming of seemed to be finally coming to pass in Czechoslovakia: democracy, including freedom of expression and abolition of censorship; reform of the economic and social systems; curbs on the power of the security forces, limiting them to defense against external threats; and full disclosure of the crimes of the Stalin era (the "Gottwald era" in Czechoslovakia). Even from afar, we were caught up in all the excitement and hopes and enthusiasm of the catchwords: "Prague Spring" and "socialism with a human face."

Events in the Soviet Union echoed those in Prague, but on a much reduced scale. In the campaign in defense of Ginzburg, Galanskov, and Lashkova [who were tried in January 1968], more than a thousand signatures—an extraordinary number under Soviet conditions—were collected, mainly from the intelligentsia. A few years earlier, no one would have dreamed of publicly defending such "hostile elements." Later, after 1968, when everyone understood the consequences for himself and his family, even sympathetic people refused to lend their names to such initiatives. The signature campaign and other similar efforts were harbingers of the human rights movement, a sort of Prague Spring in miniature. They frightened the KGB into taking tough countermeasures: firing, blacklisting, public reprimand, expulsion from the Party.

To my shame, I must admit that the signature campaign simply passed me by at the time, just as had the 1964 banishment of Joseph Brodsky from Leningrad and the 1965 arrests of Sinyavsky and Daniel. For some reason, Roy Medvedev and Zhivlyuk delayed telling me about the campaign until it was over.

Sometime around the end of January 1968, Zhivlyuk suggested that I write an article on the role of the intelligentsia in today's world. The idea appealed to me, and I soon set to work. I did most of my writing at the Installation after working hours, from seven to midnight, and brought the draft home with me when I visited Moscow. Klava's attitude toward my project was ambivalent: she knew full well what I was doing and the potential consequences for our family, but she allowed me complete freedom of action. By this time her health was beginning to deteriorate, draining more and more of her physical and emotional energy.

The title I gave my essay, *Reflections on Progress, Peaceful Coexistence, and Intellectual Freedom,* seemed appropriate in tone for a non-specialist inviting his readers to join him in a discussion of public issues. Its scope far exceeded Zhivlyuk's original suggestion, encompassing virtually the entire range of my future public activities and laying a theoretical foundation for them. I wanted to alert my readers to the grave perils threatening the human race—thermonuclear extinction, ecological catastrophe, famine, an uncontrolled population explosion, alienation, and dogmatic distortion of our conception of reality. I argued for *convergence,* for a rapprochement of the socialist and capitalist systems that could eliminate or substantially reduce these dangers, which had been increased many times over by the division of the world into opposing camps. Economic, social, and ideological convergence should bring about a scientifically governed, democratic, pluralistic society free of intolerance and dogmatism, a humanitarian society which would care for the Earth and its future, and would embody the positive features of both systems.

I went into some detail on the threat posed by thermonuclear missiles—their enormous destructive power, their relatively low cost, the difficulty of defending against them. I wrote about the crimes of Stalinism and the need to expose them fully (unlike the Soviet press, I pulled no punches), and about the vital importance of freedom of opinion and democracy. I stressed the value of progress, but warned that it must be scientifically managed and not left to chance. I discussed the need for substantive changes in foreign policy. My essay outlined a positive, global program for mankind's future; I freely acknowledged that my vision was somewhat utopian, but I remain convinced that the exercise was worthwhile.

Later on, life (and Lusia) would teach me to pay more attention to the defense of individual victims of injustice, and a further step followed: recognition that human rights and an *open society* are fundamental to international confidence, security, and progress.

I prefaced *Reflections* with an epigraph taken from Goethe's *Faust*:

> He alone is worthy of life and freedom
> Who each day does battle for them anew!

The heroic romanticism of these lines echoes my own sense of life as both wonderful and tragic, and I still consider them a fitting choice for my essay. Years later I learned that Lusia, who then knew nothing about me, was captivated by the youthful and romantic spirit of this verse, and it established a spiritual bond between us before we ever met.

Another aspect of the truth that I prize and that complements Goethe's metaphor is contained in the following lines by Alexander Mezhirov:

> I lie in a trench under fire.
> A man enters his home, from the cold.

Mezhirov understands that struggle, suffering, and heroic exploits are not ends in themselves, but are worthwhile only insofar as they enable other people to lead normal, peaceful lives. Not everyone need spend time in the trenches. The meaning of life is life itself: that daily routine which demands its own form of unobtrusive heroism. Goethe's lines are often read as an imperative call to revolutionary struggle, but that seems to me unjustified; there is nothing peremptory or fanatical in them once they are stripped of their poetic imagery. *Reflections* rejected all extremes, the intransigence shared by revolutionaries and reactionaries alike. It called for compromise and for progress moderated by enlightened conservatism and caution. Marx notwithstanding, evolution is a better "locomotive of history" than revolution: the "battle" I had in mind was nonviolent.

I rewrote *Reflections* several times, and did, I feel, finally achieve a logical and coherent presentation of my thoughts. But the essay's literary quality leaves a lot to be desired; it suffered from my inexperience and lack of editorial counsel and, in some sections, from a lack of literary taste.

By mid-April, the essay was almost completed. Zhores Medvedev has written that I tried to keep its contents a secret by having several different secretaries type *Reflections*, and Solzhenitsyn has unfortunately repeated this fiction as evidence of my supposed naïveté.[1] The manuscript was in fact typed by a single secretary who had secret clearance. I realized that a copy might well end up in the KGB's ideological department, but I had no wish to lay myself open to allegations of engaging in covert activities. In my situation, any attempts along these lines were bound to be uncovered, and I have always shunned clandestine behavior as a matter of principle.

As far as I know, the KGB did not intervene until *Reflections* began to circulate in Moscow. Before that, it's probable that only the counterintelligence department knew of the manuscript's existence, and they didn't care. At the end of May, however, the KGB was alerted at the Installation, and customs control was reinforced in Moscow. I've been told that two KGB divisions (this may well be an exaggeration) were involved in "Operation Sakharov," the fruitless attempt to prevent the circulation of *Reflections*. But I'm getting ahead of my story.

On the last Friday in April, I flew to Moscow for the holidays, bringing a typed copy of the essay in my briefcase. Roy Medvedev came to see me that evening, and I exchanged *Reflections* for the final chapters of his book on Stalin.

Medvedev claimed that Sergei Trapeznikov, head of the Central Committee's science department, was exerting a negative influence on Brezhnev and through him on domestic and foreign policy in general. I was persuaded to include a reference to Trapeznikov in *Reflections*; I now regret this personal attack, which was entirely out of character for me and alien to the style and spirit of an essay calling for reason, tolerance, and compromise. Moreover, my comments were based on uncorroborated hearsay; ever since meeting Trapeznikov in 1970, I have found it difficult to believe that he could have played a significant political role.

Medvedev came back a few days later. He had shown my essay to friends (which I had given him permission to do); they considered it a historic document, and he passed on some of their written comments. (These were unsigned, but the authors probably included Evgeny Gnedin, Yuri Zhivlyuk, and

[1][*The Oak and the Calf*, pp. 368–369.]

Eugenia Ginzburg, plus a few Old Bolsheviks and writers.) After adding the new paragraphs on Trapeznikov, and making a few other changes and corrections, I gave the manuscript back to Medvedev. He was going to produce a dozen or more carbon copies. Some of these, he warned me, might end up abroad. I replied that I had taken that into account. (We were communicating in writing to foil eavesdroppers.)

On May 18, I paid a call on Khariton at his dacha. In the course of our conversation, I mentioned that I was writing an essay on war and peace, ecology, and freedom of expression. Khariton asked what I intended to do with it. "I'll give it to samizdat," I answered. He became excited and said: "For God's sake, don't do that." "It's too late to stop it now," I confessed. Khariton became even more agitated and changed the subject. Later he pretended that this conversation never took place, which was fine from my point of view.

Early in June (probably on the 6th), I traveled with Khariton to the Installation in his personal railroad car, which contained a spacious compartment for him, a compartment for guests, the conductor's compartment, a kitchenette, and a lounge which could sleep several persons on folding cots (I often slept there myself). After the waitress had cleared the supper dishes and left the lounge, Khariton broached a subject that was plainly difficult for him: "Andropov called me in. His agents have been finding [in the course of clandestine searches] copies of your essay all over the place—it's circulating illegally, and it will cause a lot of harm if it gets abroad. Andropov opened his safe and showed me a copy. [From the way Khariton said this, it was obvious that he hadn't been allowed to examine the copy—hardly the way to treat a three-time Hero of Socialist Labor.] Andropov asked me to talk to you. You ought to withdraw your manuscript from circulation."

"Why don't you take a look at the copy I've got with me?" I suggested.

Khariton retired to his compartment, where he had a desk and a table lamp. I fell right to sleep in the guest compartment, despite the stuffiness of that prerevolutionary railroad car.

In the morning we met again.

"Well, what do you think?" I inquired.

"It's awful."

"The style?"

Khariton grimaced. "No, not the style. It's the *content* that's awful!"

"The contents reflect my beliefs. I accept full responsibility for circulating my essay. It's too late to withdraw it."

For the rest of June, I continued to tinker with the essay, but succeeded only in making it longer, not better. I sent a copy of the slightly revised version to Brezhnev, and showed another copy to Boris Efimov, who preferred the first version. I was unaware that an attempt had already been made to send my essay abroad through a *New York Times* correspondent; he had refused, fearing a provocation.

In mid-June, Andrei Amalrik gave a copy of *Reflections* to Karel van het Reve, a Dutch correspondent.

On July 10, a few days after returning to the Installation and exactly seven years after my clash with Khrushchev, I tuned in the BBC (or VOA?) evening broadcast and heard my name. The announcer reported that on July 6, the Dutch newspaper *Het Parool* had published an article by A. D. Sakharov, a member of the Soviet Academy of Sciences who, according to Western experts, had worked on the Soviet hydrogen bomb. Sakharov called for rapprochement between the USSR and the West, and for disarmament; warned of the dangers of thermonuclear war, ecological catastrophe, and world famine; condemned dogmatism, terror, and Stalin's crimes; and urged democratization, freedom of conscience, and convergence as the way to escape universal destruction. (I don't now recall the broadcast's exact words, but this is the gist of what I hope I heard, and in any case did read later in a number of well-informed reviews of my essay.)

The die was cast. That evening I had the most profound feeling of satisfaction. The following day I was due to fly to Moscow, but stopped at my office at nine in the morning and noticed Khariton at his desk.

"Foreign stations announced yesterday that my article's been published abroad."

"I knew it would happen" was all Khariton could say. He looked crushed.

Two hours later, I left for the airfield. I was never to set foot in my office again.

TOWARD THE END of July, Slavsky summoned me to the Ministry. A translation of *Reflections* from the Dutch newspaper lay on his desk. "Your article?" he asked. I glanced through it and answered in the affirmative.

"Is it the same one you sent to the Central Committee?"

"Not quite, I revised it a bit."

"Give me the new text. Will you protest publication abroad of a preliminary draft without your permission?"

"No, I won't do that. I take full responsibility for the article as published, since it faithfully reflects my opinions."

Slavsky obviously wanted me to make some protest, if only about minor editorial details, but I didn't fall into that trap.

Clearly disappointed, Slavsky made no effort to hide his displeasure: "We won't discuss your opinions today. Party secretaries have been calling from all over the country, demanding firm measures to put a stop to counterrevolutionary propaganda in my ministry. I want you to think about what you've done to us and to yourself. You've got to disown this anti-Soviet publication. I'll read your revised version. Come back three days from now at the same time."

Three days later, Slavsky continued the lecture:

"I've taken a look, and the two versions are practically the same. It's a dangerous muddle. You write about the mistakes of the personality cult as though the Party had never condemned them. You criticize the leaders' privileges—you've enjoyed the same privileges yourself. Individuals who bear immense responsibilities, difficult burdens, deserve *some* advantages. It's all for the good of the cause. You pit the intelligentsia against the leadership, but aren't we, who manage the country, the real intelligentsia of the nation?

"What you wrote about convergence is utopian nonsense. Capitalism can't be made humane. Their social programs and employee stock plans aren't steps toward socialism. And there's no trace of state capitalism in the USSR. We'll never give up the advantages of our system, and capitalists aren't interested in your convergence either.

"The Party has condemned the cult of personality, but without a strong hand, we could never have rebuilt our economy after the war or broken the American atomic monopoly—you yourself helped do that. You have no moral right to judge our generation—Stalin's generation—for its mistakes, for its brutality; you're now enjoying the fruits of our labor and our sacrifices.

"Convergence is a dream. We've got to be strong, stronger than the capitalists—then there'll be peace. If war breaks out and the imperialists use nuclear weapons, we'll retaliate at once with everything we've got and destroy their launch sites and every target necessary to ensure victory."

My understanding then and my recollection now is that Slavsky was speaking only about a *retaliatory* strike, but our response would be an immediate, all-out nuclear attack on enemy cities and industry as well as on military targets. The most alarming thing was that he completely ignored the question of what, other than military force, might prevent war. In a world where contradictions, conflicts, and mistrust are rife, and where each side has an arsenal of awesome weapons at its disposal, brute force alone cannot be relied upon to guarantee the peace. As for my suggestions for an open society and for replacing confrontation with rapprochement, Slavsky evidently considered them too foolish to discuss, and simply skipped over them.

I pointed out to him that *Reflections* warned against exactly the kind of approach he was taking, in which life-and-death decisions are made behind the scenes by people who have usurped power (and privilege) without accepting the checks of free opinion and open debate. Then I raised the issue of Czechoslovakia: was there any guarantee against Soviet intervention there? For that would be a tragedy.

Slavsky said the matter was under discussion in the Central Committee, and that armed intervention had been ruled out, provided there was no overt counterrevolutionary violence such as occurred in Hungary. Words alone would not bother us, he added. (On August 21, this turned out to be untrue, but the decision to invade may have been made after our meeting; in any case, it's unlikely that Slavsky would have been privy to discussions at the very top.)

I've reproduced this conversation in some detail because it's virtually the only serious discussion I've ever had with anyone in authority about *Reflections* or any other statement of mine on public issues.

A couple of weeks after this, Khariton asked me to stop by his home. Slavsky, he told me, opposed my return to the Installation. I asked why.

"Efim Pavlovich [Slavsky] is afraid there might be a provocation against you."

"That's absurd—who would organize it?"

"Those are Efim Pavlovich's orders. You're to remain in Moscow for the time being."

This was tantamount to being fired, and there was nothing I could do about it. I stayed in Moscow, which had been our family's permanent home since 1962. Klava and the children normally joined me at the Installation for the summer, but they were still in Moscow when I was suspended.

ON JULY 22, *Reflections* was published in the *New York Times*. After it was reprinted in August at several American universities, a flood of publications and reactions burst forth. (To my regret, I managed to collect and save only a small fraction of them.) The International Publishers Association released statistics showing that in 1968–1969 more than eighteen million copies of my essay were published around the world, in third place after Mao Zedong and Lenin, and ahead of Georges Simenon and Agatha Christie.

Reflections was well received by liberal intellectuals abroad. The views I had expressed—the threat of thermonuclear war, the value of democracy and intellectual freedom, the need to provide economic assistance to developing countries, the recognition of merit in socialism *and* capitalism, etc.—coincided in large part with theirs. More important, I represented a vindication of their hopes: a kindred voice had reached them from behind the Iron Curtain and, moreover, from a member of a profession which in America was dominated by "hawks." There were even some—mainly journalists—who saw my essay as a trial balloon launched by a Soviet government eager to reduce the risk of war; in this scenario, I was being used as a quasi-official spokesman. On the other hand, my criticism of Soviet society appealed to conservative circles, and everyone seemed pleased by my comments on the environment, my humanitarian concerns, and my scenarios for the future. For all the essay's shortcomings, the publication of *Reflections* was an event, and it had a considerable impact on public opinion in the West.

It circulated widely in the USSR as well—samizdat was flourishing—and the response was enthusiastic. Pyotr Grigorenko's letter has stuck in my mind: he praised my essay as "handy as a spoon at dinnertime." Solzhenitsyn sent me a lengthy critique, anticipating the comments he was to make when we met in person for the first time (see below). I deeply regret that many people were punished for circulating *Reflections*. I know the names of a few: Vladlen Pavlenkov, Sergei Ponomarev, Anatoly Nazarov.[2]

I was particularly gratified by a letter I received from the eminent theoretical physicist Max Born, which was accompanied by a very handsomely inscribed copy of his memoirs in German. Born wrote that he admired my courage and shared most of my ideas, but felt I overrated socialism, which he had always considered a creed for idiots. Nonetheless, he admitted that he had voted Labour while living in England. When Born's memoirs were published posthumously in the USSR, the chapter on his social, ethical, and philosophical views was left out, without any caveat to the Russian reader. Born was criticized for returning to Germany in 1953, but he'd missed the linden trees of his native Rhineland.

I also recall a letter from Georges Pire, the Belgian Dominican priest who won the 1958 Nobel Peace Prize. Vladimir Poremsky sent an interesting letter and Western press clippings about my essay, including his own article.[3]

During the first months following publication of my essay, I received quite a few letters by ordinary mail, although they were probably only a fraction of those that had been sent.

ON AUGUST 21 I went out to buy a newspaper. According to a front-page article, Warsaw Pact troops had entered Czechoslovakia at the request of Party and government officials (unnamed, of course) and were "fulfilling their international duty." The invasion had begun. The hopes inspired by the Prague Spring collapsed. And "real socialism" displayed its true colors, its stagnation, its inability to tolerate pluralistic or democratic tendencies, not just in the

2[Vladlen Pavlenkov, a teacher born in 1929, was sentenced in Gorky to seven years in labor camp for circulating anti-Soviet works and planning to found an anti-Soviet organization. Ponomarev, a writer born in 1945, was sentenced as Pavlenkov's codefendant to five years labor camp. Nazarov, a Dushanbe driver born in 1946, was sentenced to three years labor camp in 1972 for slandering the Soviet system (he mailed Sakharov's essay to a friend).]

3[Poremsky's article appeared in *Posev*, Frankfurt, no. 8, August 1968.]

Soviet Union but even in neighboring countries. Two natural and rational reforms—the abolition of censorship and free elections to a Party Congress—were regarded as too risky and contagious.

The international repercussions of the invasion were enormous. For millions of former supporters, it destroyed their faith in the Soviet system and its potential for reform.

BY COINCIDENCE, Anatoly Marchenko's trial opened the day Czechoslovakia was invaded.

Marchenko had been a young worker in Kazakhstan in 1958 when he was first sentenced to labor camp for a barracks brawl with some Chechens. He wasn't guilty of any crime, but judges aren't overly scrupulous in such cases and ethnic politics may have influenced the verdict. Marchenko escaped from his labor camp and in 1960 was caught trying to cross the Iranian frontier. This time he was sent to a Mordovian camp for political prisoners to serve a six-year sentence. His whole life changed after Yuli Daniel arrived in the camp in 1966; influenced by him, Marchenko chose a new tack of rigorous self-examination, nonconformity, social activism, and struggle, which led to his eventual martyrdom. His distinguishing feature was his absolute honesty, a determination to stick to principle that was often mistaken for sheer obstinacy.

Following his release in November 1966, Marchenko drew on his considerable experience of prison and camp life to write *My Testimony,* a powerful and graphic description of the barbaric penal system that replaced Stalin's Gulag.[4]

He was arrested again in July 1968 and tried for a technical violation of passport regulations: spending more than three days in Moscow without permission. This law was enforced only selectively, but the KGB hated Marchenko's independent attitude and his book, which was popular with human rights activists in the USSR and had been published abroad in many languages. Marchenko received a one-year camp sentence, but that didn't satisfy the KGB. He was tried again while in confinement and sentenced to two additional years for slander; when another prisoner asked him why he was so thin, he allegedly answered: "Because the Communists have drunk my blood."

On the morning of August 21, Marchenko's friends were greeted at the courthouse by Pavel Litvinov, who announced: "Our tanks are in Prague!"[5]

Four days later, at noon on Sunday, August 25, Litvinov and Larisa Bogoraz,

---

[4][*My Testimony* (Dutton, 1969).]

[5]Pavel is the grandson of Maxim Litvinov, an Old Bolshevik who served for many years as Commissar of Foreign Affairs, until he was replaced by Molotov in 1939 to clear the way for rapprochement with Nazi Germany.

along with Konstantin Babitsky, Vadim Delone, Vladimir Dremlyuga, Viktor Fainberg, and Natasha Gorbanevskaya, went out onto Red Square to protest the Soviet invasion of Czechoslovakia. With this bold action—many people were punished just for refusing to attend the innumerable official meetings held in support of the intervention—Litvinov, Bogoraz, and their comrades restored our country's honor. They managed to sit for a minute by Lobnoe Mesto, a traditional place of execution in prerevolutionary Russia, and then KGB agents began beating them and tore up their signs reading "Hands Off Czechoslovakia." All seven were arrested, but their protest had broken a shameful silence. Minutes later, cars carrying Dubček, Smrkovsky, and the other Czechoslovak leaders brought to Moscow by force, shot out of the Kremlin's Spassky Gate and raced across Red Square.

I had no advance notice of the demonstration. One of the participants came to see me on the 24th, but I was out and he didn't tell Klava the reason for his visit. It is possible that my absence was arranged. Zhivlyuk had arrived half an hour earlier and urged: "Andrei Dmitrievich, we have to go see Vuchetich right away. He's waiting for you. He's got access to 'himself' [Brezhnev]; who knows whose idea this meeting is. It could help a lot of people."

I had nothing to lose, so I went. I knew little about artistic circles, and had no clear idea what to expect. (Evgeny Vuchetich had unquestioned talent as a sculptor, but politically he was far to the right.)

On the way, Zhivlyuk told me: "You'll meet Fyodor Shakhmagonov, I gave you his manuscript."

Zhivlyuk had in fact brought me the typescript of a short story by Shakhmagonov about a retired KGB officer, praising it as more courageous and profound than Solzhenitsyn's work, a gross exaggeration.

Vuchetich *was* waiting for us. A man of average height with a loud voice and aggressive manner, he was still suffering from the aftereffects of a recent stroke. Shakhmagonov arrived a few minutes later; he embraced Vuchetich, kissing him three times in Russian fashion.

Vuchetich showed me around his studio, pointing out works he'd done "for the money" and others done "for my soul." An enormous female figure symbolizing the Motherland had been commissioned for the Stalingrad memorial.

"The bosses ask me why her mouth is open; it doesn't look pretty. I tell them: She's shouting 'For the Motherland, you mother-f—ers!' That shuts them up."

The memorial for the Battle of the Kursk Salient captured the charm of youth and, at the same time, the horror of war and death, in the bent head of a dying tank soldier.

"For the soul" Vuchetich had portrayed Lenin in his last years, lost in deep and painful thought.

I never saw Vuchetich again. I've since heard that he carved a bust of me using photographs and his memory of our meeting.

Of Shakhmagonov I was told that he had served as Mikhail Sholokhov's secretary and had written Sholokhov's horrifying address to the Twenty-third Party Congress. Shakhmagonov is rumored to be a KGB general. In 1969, he suggested that I write an essay along the same lines as *Reflections* for the Sovetskaya Rossiya publishing house. The article would have to be "publishable"—i.e., acceptable to the Soviet censors. This may have been an attempt to "tame" me. I left an outline of my proposed article at the publisher's office, and Shakhmagonov phoned a few days later to say that there was no sense in going any further: even the essay's title, which included the word "democratization," seemed "provocative." To whom? To the KGB?

THE DAY AFTER visiting Vuchetich, I had my first meeting with Alexander Solzhenitsyn. Tamara Khachaturova, a widow who worked in FIAN's library and was a friend of Solzhenitsyn's first wife, had passed on his suggestion that we meet. Our rendezvous was postponed several times, but finally took place at the apartment of a friend of mine on August 26. (Solzhenitsyn was the first person to tell me about the demonstration the day before on Red Square.)

In *The Oak and the Calf*, Solzhenitsyn writes about the vivid impression I made on him.[6] I can easily return the compliment. With his lively blue eyes and ruddy beard, his tongue-twistingly fast speech delivered in an unexpected treble, and his deliberate, precise gestures, he seemed an animated concentration of purposeful energy.

Before I arrived, Solzhenitsyn had drawn the curtains. He later wrote that our meeting escaped the notice of the KGB. In this I believe he was mistaken, although I don't pretend to be an expert in detecting surveillance. Since I have nothing to hide, I simply ignore our army of highly paid shadows. On this occasion, however, I noted that the taxi driver who picked me up after the meeting made provocative remarks and seemed unusually intent on engaging me in conversation.

I had read almost everything Solzhenitsyn had written and felt enormous respect for him, which has since been reinforced by publication of his epic work, *The Gulag Archipelago*. Real life is never simple, however, and our relations are now difficult—perhaps unavoidably so, since we are not at all alike and differ markedly on questions of principle.

At our first meeting, I listened attentively as he talked away in his usual

[6][*The Oak and the Calf*, pp. 369-371.]

manner—passionately and with absolute conviction. He began by complimenting me on breaking the conspiracy of silence at the top of the pyramid. Then he voiced his disagreements with me in incisive fashion: Any kind of convergence is out of the question. (Here he repeated Slavsky almost word for word.) The West has no interest in our becoming democratic. The West is caught up in materialism and permissiveness. Socialism may turn out to be its final ruin. Our leaders are soulless robots who have latched onto power and the good life, and won't let go until forced to do so.

Solzhenitsyn claimed that I had understated Stalin's crimes. Furthermore, I was wrong to differentiate him from Lenin: corruption and destruction began the day the Bolsheviks seized power, and have continued ever since. Changes in scale or method are not changes in principle. According to Professor Kurganov, sixty million people had perished as a result of terror, famine, and associated disease. My figure of ten million deaths in labor camps was too low.

It's a mistake, he continued, to seek a multiparty system; what we need is a nonparty system. Every political party betrays its members in order to serve the interests of the party bosses. Scientists and engineers have a major role to play, but in the absence of an underlying spiritual goal any hope that we can use the tools of science to regulate progress is a delusion that will end in our being suffocated by the smoke and cinders of our cities.

Despite the passage of time, I believe I have faithfully reproduced the gist of Solzhenitsyn's critique.[7]

In response, I acknowledged that there was much truth in his comments. Still, my own opinions were expressed in *Reflections* although in an attempt to make constructive recommendations, I had introduced some simplifications into my argument. My primary aim was to point out the dangers we faced and a possible course of action to avert them. I was counting on people's good will. I didn't expect an immediate response to my essay, but I hoped to influence public thinking over the long term. I might revise it at some future date, but first wanted to think things through.

We went on to discuss the punishment facing the demonstrators who had been arrested in Red Square. A few days later, I phoned Andropov on their behalf. Kurchatov had left instructions that I was to be allowed into the Atomic Energy Institute without a pass or other formalities. I went to the office of Anatoly Alexandrov, then the Institute's director, and used his special telephone to call Andropov. I told him:

---

[7]Solzhenitsyn later sent me a written memorandum, entitled "The Agony of Free Speech," repeating and expanding upon his remarks. He published it, with minor revisions and a new title ("As Breathing and Consciousness Return"), in *From Under the Rubble* [Little, Brown, 1975].

"I'm concerned about the people arrested on August 25 on Red Square. Czechoslovakia has become the center of world attention: Communist Parties in the West are following developments, and it will make matters worse if the demonstrators are tried and sentenced."

Andropov said he was preoccupied with Czechoslavakia and had hardly slept all week. The Procurator's Office, not the KGB, was investigating the demonstration. Andropov added, however, that he didn't think the sentences would be severe.[8]

That was my second and last conversation with Andropov.

[8][Dremlyuga was sentenced to three years labor camp; Delone to thirty months labor camp; Litvinov to five years exile; Bogoraz to four years exile; Babitsky to three years exile. Fainberg was sent to a prison psychiatric hospital.]

21

KLAVA'S DEATH

Klava's illness.
The Sakharov-Turchin-Medvedev Letter.
The Seminar at Turchin's.
Grigory Pomerants.

IN 1968, KLAVA'S HEALTH took a sharp turn for the worse. She suffered from constant abdominal pain, and was noticeably losing weight.

As far back as September 1964, she had experienced episodes of severe gastric bleeding, and had twice lost consciousness. The first time I was away and she told me about it over the phone. A few days later, after I'd returned to Moscow from the Installation, she blacked out again—I just managed to catch her as she fell. I rushed her to a nearby clinic, and a nurse gave her an injection to prevent arterial spasms, probably a useless procedure in her case.

After this episode, Klava was admitted to the Kremlin Hospital, where I'd been registered since the 1950s. This hospital for the ultra-privileged boasted excellent equipment but a staff of less reliable quality. Klava was diagnosed as suffering from gastric hemorrhages. In April 1965, she was reexamined at the Petrovsky Clinic after suffering another severe hemorrhage. I'll never understand why neither hospital suggested an operation; it might have saved her life if it had been performed in good time.

IN SEPTEMBER 1968, I traveled to Tbilisi to attend my first international scientific conference in many years. I'd never had leisure for such things while I was working at the Installation, and, besides, I worried that I might not understand the proceedings because of my unsystematic education. As things turned out, I thoroughly enjoyed my first visit to Tbilisi. (Four years later I would return to the attractive Georgian capital with Lusia.)

The 1968 conference, one of a continuing series, was devoted to the theory of gravitation, its application to cosmology, and its relation to the theory of elementary particles. I found the papers informative, and profited to an even greater degree from personal meetings with Soviet and foreign scientists. During the years I was engaged in secret work, my professional contacts outside the Installation had been limited to Zeldovich and a few other scientists.

En route to Tbilisi, during an unscheduled stopover at Mineralnye Vody, I had an opportunity for a good talk with Boris Altshuler, a young theoretical physicist and the son of Lev Altshuler, a colleague at the Installation. Two years earlier, I'd served as the official opponent at Boris's dissertation defense.

At the conference, I delivered a paper on a "zero-Lagrangian" gravitational field [see chapter 18]. I regret now that I didn't talk instead about baryon asymmetry, but Zeldovich, who was a member of the organizing committee, had helped me choose my topic, and at the time he was skeptical about my work in that area. Perhaps I should have been more insistent; but I was also anxious to discuss my latest work, the idea of the zero-Lagrangian, which was directly related to the subject of the conference.

Zeldovich introduced me to John Wheeler, a senior American physicist who had worked with Niels Bohr on nuclear fission in the 1930s and was now a specialist in gravitation. Wheeler and I dined together at the Sakartvelo restaurant, where we spent a memorable two hours absorbed in a discussion of both scientific and social problems.

IN OCTOBER 1968, Klava and I were admitted to the Council of Ministers' sanatorium in Zheleznovodsk after I overrode the objections of the Kremlin Hospital doctors, who'd examined me and found a cardiovascular disorder that supposedly made it inadvisable for me to go south (anyway, it's not that warm in Zheleznovodsk in October). They pronounced Klava in good health, failing to detect her advancing stomach cancer even after taking intestinal X-rays as part of the normal routine.

Our stay in the sanatorium overlapped with our son's. Dmitri had been sent in September to the children's section of the sanatorium to recuperate from infectious hepatitis. A teaching staff was available to help patients keep up with their studies, but we discovered afterward that the atmosphere was ultra-snobbish, and that children who didn't come from elite families were bullied mercilessly.

We would run into Dmitri while we were out walking. On one of our first encounters, he took us aside and whispered to us to please call him "Dima" from then on, instead of Mitya. I never understood his reason, and it bothered me, since it violated a family tradition: all my family, with the exception of my mother, had called my father (another Dmitri) "Mitya."

I suspect that I was admitted to the sanatorium because no one at the Ministry of Medium Machine Building had notified the administrative department of the Council of Ministers of my changed status. I received another pass in 1969, after Klava's death; but in 1970, after protesting Zhores Medvedev's involuntary confinement, I was removed from the register of the Kremlin hospital, clinic, and pharmacy, and also lost my sanatorium privileges, which had been one of my "perks" as a member of the *nomenklatura.*

October 1968 was the last calm month in my life with Klava. She felt better than she had during the summer. We did a lot of walking, just as we had when we were younger. And we rejoiced (naturally, we'd been scared stiff that something might go wrong) when our eldest daughter, Tanya, gave birth safely to our first grandchild, Marina.

Our stay at the sanatorium together with high-ranking officials led to awkward situations. Conversations would be broken off as I approached. Once, on the sanatorium bus, I heard someone behind me saying how wrong it would be to make concessions to the Crimean Tatars, who were "straining at the leash to return to the Crimea. After all, the Crimea's vital to our security." Speaking among themselves, these officials gave voice to the real reason behind the unjust treatment of the Crimean Tatars. I couldn't restrain myself. I turned to them and exclaimed: "But it's their homeland!" They looked away and didn't say another word for the rest of the ride.

Klava overheard a curious conversation between two Central Committee members, who were discussing *July 6,* a recent film about the 1918 uprising of the Left Socialist Revolutionaries. "They shouldn't show films like that," one of them said. "You see Lenin in a moment of doubt, almost weakness. That can't be allowed."

I was fascinated by the sensitivity these ideological *apparatchiks* revealed toward the least display of Lenin's "human face"; it was clear that in their view historical truth should not be allowed to alter the visage of the holy icon of the "founder of the Soviet state." It was no coincidence that just two months earlier Soviet tanks had crushed the "human face" of socialism in Czechoslovakia.

DURING OUR LAST DAYS in Zheleznovodsk, Klava took a turn for the worse. The circulation in her hands became impaired. It was the beginning of the end, though fortunately we didn't realize it. In December, her therapist at the outpatient clinic sent her straight to the Kremlin Hospital. A month later, I was told that she had inoperable cancer. I took her home so she could spend at least a few weeks in familiar surroundings, and she did have some happy moments, especially with our daughters and our son, who, as the youngest child, became very close to her.

Toward the end of February, Klava's pain became unbearable, and could no longer be controlled by opiates. On one of her last days at home, Klava watched a figure-skating competition on television, something she'd always enjoyed. She studied the radiant, excited face of the Hungarian skating champion Zsuzsa Almásy, who'd just won a close contest. As she gazed at this young, vigorous athlete, Klava seemed to be bidding farewell to life. Then she motioned for the television to be switched off. It was never turned on again while she lived.

Klava spent her last week in the hospital, and during those days of grief I was ready to clutch at any straw. I heard that a retired physician had developed a miraculous anti-cancer vaccine. I went to see the woman in Kaluga and found her absolutely convinced of the power of her vaccine, which she had been producing at home for several years (it was being tested in Professor Nikolai Emanuel's laboratory). She gave me a box of ampules, but refused to accept payment.

"My medicine is free. If it helps, then do whatever your conscience dictates. I need a lot of money to buy equipment and to pay my assistants, and your influence with the Academy of Sciences and the Ministry of Health could help. That idiot Blokhin [the Minister of Health] is trying to ban my experiments."

I brought the ampules to Moscow, and Klava was given an injection the day before her death. (I returned the rest of the medicine to the doctor in Kaluga.)

On March 7, Klava gave gifts to the nurses and orderlies for Women's Day (March 8). When I arrived the following morning with the children, we were told that Klava had lost consciousness several hours earlier. But every so often she seemed to come to herself for a few moments and try to speak. Her last words that I could make out were: "Close the window. Dima will catch cold."

Klava died late that afternoon. Her ashes were buried at the Vostryakovsky Cemetery in Moscow, not far from the spot where we'd lived with our daughter Tanya in 1945–1946. Klava's father came for the funeral: he was upset that she'd been cremated. I confess to my shame that because of past quarrels I didn't notify Klava's mother and sister of her death, and so they missed the service.

FOR MONTHS AFTERWARD I remained in a daze, doing nothing in science or in public life, or even around the house, except for routine chores.

In May 1969, Slavsky called me and asked me to come to his office. He wanted to know if I'd object to a transfer back to FIAN, where I'd begun my scientific career in 1945. I assured him that I would be pleased by the appointment.

The director, Academician Dmitri Skobeltsyn, was worried by my assignment to FIAN, but, to the best of my knowledge, he did not protest it. The Ministry quickly sent over my dossier—my personnel file, my work book, and some sort of letter. I became a senior scientist assigned to the department of

LEFT: Andrei Sakharov's great-great-grandfather.
BELOW: Sakharov's paternal great-great-grandmother. 1860s.

LEFT: Ivan Sakharov and Maria Domukhovskaya, Andrei's paternal grandparents, shortly before their wedding. ca. 1885. BELOW: The Sakharov family: Andrei's grandparents Ivan and Maria Sakharov with their children, Sergei, Tatyana, Ivan, Dmitri, Nikolai, and (standing next to Ivan) "baby" Georgy (Yurochka, died ca. 1920). ca. 1917.

ABOVE: Alexei Sofiano, Sakharov's maternal grandfather, at the turn of the twentieth century. LEFT: Zinaida Sofiano, Sakharov's maternal grandmother.

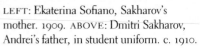

LEFT: Ekaterina Sofiano, Sakharov's mother. 1909. ABOVE: Dmitri Sakharov, Andrei's father, in student uniform. c. 1910.

RIGHT: Andrei Sakharov and his cousin Katya. 1924. BELOW: Alexei and Zinaida Sofiano, Sakharov's maternal grandfather and grandmother, at their dacha. c. 1925.

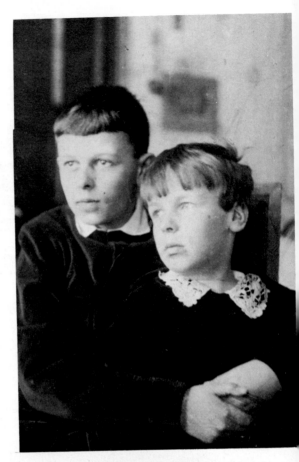

CLOCKWISE FROM LOWER LEFT: Andrei and his younger brother Georgy (Yura). 1927. Andrei and Yura. c. 1930. Andrei and Yura. c. 1932. Andrei and Yura. 1932. Andrei (right) and Yura. 1945.

In the courtyard at No. 3 Granatny Lane. At left are Katya, Andrei, and Yura Sakharov; seated, third from right, is Grisha Umansky; standing in the second row are, at far left, Irina Sakharov and, at far right, Kolya Segal. c. 1928.

Classmates, School 113. *Front row:* far right, Lena Feldman. *Second row:* fourth from left, Misha Shveitser; second from left, Tolya Bashun; far right, Leva Shebtsov. *Back row:* second from right, Yura Orlov; far right, Andrei Sakharov. c. 1937.

ABOVE: Klavdia (née Vikhireva), Sakharov's first
wife. RIGHT: Andrei Sakharov. 1943.

Andrei and Klavdia. July 1943.

Andrei and Klavdia with their daughter Tatyana (Tanya). 1948.

Sakharov and his aunt Tatyana Yakushkin (Aunt Tanya). 1946.

Sakharov's aunts Tatyana (Aunt Tanya) and Eugenia (Aunt Zhenya).

LEFT: Dmitri Sakharov, Andrei's father. c. 1949.
BELOW: Dmitri Sakharov. c. 1950.

Sakharov's daughters, Tanya and Lyuba. 1956.

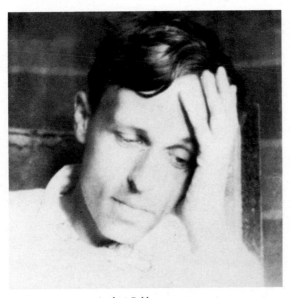

Andrei Sakharov. 1950.

Sakharov and Igor Kurchatov on the grounds of the Atomic Energy Institute. Summer 1957.

ABOVE: Ekaterina and Dmitri Sakharov, Andrei's mother and father. 1959. LEFT: Dmitri Sakharov. c. 1960.

Andrei and his son, Dmitri (Dima). 1970.

theoretical physics. (Tamm was still the formal head of the department, although he was by now too ill to come to work; after his death, it was officially named the Tamm Department in his honor.) I was paid a salary of 350 rubles a month in addition to my 400-ruble stipend as an academician. No one expected me to do any work; they just wanted to separate me from the Installation with as little fuss as possible.

I've tried to continue my scientific work, of course. I'm not very satisfied with my output, but even under normal conditions, most scientists become less productive with the passage of years. What can you do? . . .

In August 1969, I made one last trip to the Installation to collect my belongings and to vacate our half of the cottage that had been my home since 1951.

I also did something I now believe was foolish. During my nineteen years at the Installation, we'd rarely socialized or gone anywhere, so I spent only a small portion of my income. Most of my savings (including my State Prize money) was in a bank account at the Installation. I decided to donate the 139,000 rubles to the building fund of a cancer hospital, the children's fund at the Installation, and the Soviet Red Cross to aid victims of natural disasters and famine. For some reason, the children's fund ended up receiving nothing. Professor Georgy Miterev, chairman of the Red Cross, phoned to thank me and to assure me that the money would be used in strict accordance with my wishes—for "noble purposes," as he put it. I later received a formal letter of appreciation from the Red Cross, but no acknowledgment from the cancer hospital.

This fit of generosity in which I transferred control over my money to the state now seems to me a mistake. A few months later I learned of a fund to assist the families of political prisoners, but could make only modest contributions. I also lost the means of helping our relatives and friends other than my brother and my children; by neglecting to think of this at the time I perhaps betrayed a certain apathy, a "laziness of feeling." And I weakened my position in my approaching struggle with the state.

By 1969, I was already aware of this potential confrontation in the abstract, but I still considered myself part of the establishment. Although I had bluntly criticized many official actions and offered advice concerning future policy, deep down I still felt that the government I criticized was *my* government. After all, I had contributed to the state something of immeasurably greater value than my savings.

* * *

IN OCTOBER 1969, Mikhail Gertsenshtein brought me an article in which he tried to prove that black holes cannot exist. I disagreed with his arguments, but our discussion brought me back to scientific questions and stimulated me to write a paper, "A Many-Sheeted Cosmological Model," which was published by the Institute of Applied Mathematics in 1970 with a dedication to Klava. I was returning to life.

Early in 1970, Yuri Zhivlyuk introduced me to Valentin Turchin, whose name was familiar to me from his book *Jokes Physicists Tell* and from his samizdat essay *The Inertia of Fear*.[1] Turchin, who had been seduced away from nuclear physics into the field of computer languages, was then just beginning to feel the effects of official displeasure.

Turchin had an idea: to write an appeal to the leaders concentrating on a single key issue—the introduction of democracy and intellectual freedom as essential for the advancement of science, and thus for improved economic performance. He understood that the question of democratization was complex, but he believed that a simple, pragmatic approach had the best chance of succeeding with the authorities, and might lead to a more comprehensive dialogue. Turchin suggested that the three of us collaborate in writing such a letter [which was addressed to Brezhnev, Kosygin, and Podgorny; hereafter "the Letter"] and then ask influential persons with liberal sympathies to sign it.

I liked his idea, and soon Turchin, Zhivlyuk, and I were exchanging preliminary drafts. I volunteered to compose the final version, using Turchin's draft as the working document and incorporating ideas from my own draft, and adding an introduction (which I now find unsatisfactory). I left the beginning unchanged, but revised the other sections, working them over several times.

The most difficult part proved to be finding influential liberals brave enough to sign our Letter. The first person I approached was the nuclear physicist Lev Artsimovich. A short while before, I'd run into him on Kurchatov Square, and he'd told me how much he admired *Reflections* and its constructive approach; all the scientists with whom he'd discussed it, in the USSR and abroad (he was just back from America), shared his positive opinion.

After I showed Artsimovich our Letter, he said he thought it was worthwhile, but couldn't sign it: "I'll be frank. I've just remarried and I've got two families to support. It takes a lot of money, and I can't afford to have my income cut. Don't bother to see Leontovich. He'll never sign a position paper he didn't write himself. Try Pyotr Leonidovich [Kapitsa]."

Kapitsa was number one on the list of names Turchin and I had drawn up.

---

[1] [Published in a revised version as *The Inertia of Fear and the Scientific Worldview* (Columbia University Press, 1981).]

Soon I was sitting in a comfortable armchair on the second floor of his palatial home on the grounds of the Institute of Physics. Kapitsa was seventy-six years old, but he was still capable of coming up with original ideas and expressing them with precision, an ability he retained until his death in 1984. Talking with him was sheer pleasure, despite his occasional sermonizing and tendency to condescend toward my "inexperience" and "naïveté" (but that sort of thing doesn't really bother me). Kapitsa began our conversation by praising *Reflections*. He was astonished that a man a whole generation younger and with such a different life experience shared so many of his ideas.

I visited Kapitsa several times. In hopes of securing his signature, I revised parts of the Letter, spoiling it to some extent. But in the end, he refused to sign, and instead promised to write something himself after he'd consulted with Trapeznikov; as he saw it, in order to be effective such an appeal would have to reflect a "better understanding" of the addressees' psychology. So far as I know, however, he never wrote anything.

During my visits, Kapitsa told me something of his life. In 1921, after his first wife and their two children died of Spanish influenza, he left Russia for the West—many promising scientists were sent abroad in the early 1920s. He settled in Cambridge, first working as an assistant to Ernest Rutherford at the Cavendish Laboratory, later conducting his own experiments on superstrong magnetic fields and low-temperature physics. He gained an international reputation, remarried, and apparently had no intention of taking up residence again in the USSR. In the early 1930s Stalin personally ordered Soviet agents to negotiate Kapitsa's return. According to Kirill Khenkin, Willi Fisher (better known by his alias, Rudolph Abel) was one of those sent to lure him back.[2] After bargaining successfully for unprecedented working conditions for himself and the institute that would be created for him, and for his future scientific colleagues, including freedom from the customary Party and police intrusion into personnel matters, Kapitsa returned to the USSR in 1934, and was elected a member of the Academy of Sciences in 1939. It was during those years that he made his most important discovery—the superfluidity of liquid helium— and his principal invention, a turbine to produce liquid oxygen. Such turbines are now used throughout the world.

In the late 1930s, Kapitsa intervened to secure the release of two brilliant physicists, Lev Landau and Vladimir Fock, who had been arrested and charged with counterrevolutionary activity. Kapitsa's initiative demonstrated true civic courage. The success of his intervention depended on his intelligence, his

[2][See Lawrence Badash, *Kapitza, Rutherford, and the Kremlin* (Yale University Press, 1985); Kirill Khenkin, *Okhotnik vverkh nogami* (Posev 1980), pp. 111–112.]

psychological insight, and his exceptional status. He told me the story and showed me his letters to Stalin, an artful blend of diplomacy, honesty, and cunning.

Kapitsa discussed Landau's case with a close associate of Beria, Vsevolod Merkulov, who had shown Kapitsa Landau's investigative file with its "dire accusations."

"I guarantee Landau will not engage in any *further* counterrevolutionary activity," promised Kapitsa.

"He's that important a scientist?"

"Yes! World class!"

(I'm reminded of Himmler's comment when Werner Heisenberg was—incorrectly—denounced as a Jew: "We cannot afford to lose or silence this man.")

Landau was released, as Fock had been earlier.

When Nikolai Ezhov [Beria's predecessor as head of state security] had visited his prison cell, Fock challenged him: "I am Academician Fock. And who are you?" Ezhov, who apparently expected everyone to recognize him and faint dead away at the sight of his green eyes, was dumbfounded.

In 1946, Kapitsa was suspended as director of the Institute of Physics after he refused to participate in the atomic weapons program. (He was replaced by Anatoly Alexandrov.) For several years, Kapitsa lived under a cloud, but in explaining his stand, he stressed his disagreement with the proposed organizational structure and his reluctance to subordinate himself to less capable scientists; by soft-pedaling the moral issues, Kapitsa managed to be charged only with headstrong conduct—"hooliganism," as it was labeled by the security services—instead of sabotage or disloyalty. I believe this was not simply a ruse on Kapitsa's part; his decision probably involved a number of factors, and it's difficult in retrospect to assign relative weights to them.

When I asked for Kapitsa's support in several civic initiatives in 1970–1972, he refused for reasons that seemed to me flimsy and self-serving. His role in the Zhores Medvedev affair and in other such cases has probably been exaggerated.

Is it right to criticize a man who did do so much good? The fact is, Kapitsa's relations with his colleagues, and his stands on academic and publishing matters, unfortunately, were not always beyond reproach. Leontovich called Kapitsa a "centaur"—half-man, half-beast—and yet still had the deepest love for him. And I believe Kapitsa deserved that love.

[Added in March 1988 by A.S.]

In 1987, following my return from Gorky, I learned that Kapitsa had intervened on my behalf on at least two occasions.

On November 11, 1980, he sent a letter to KGB chairman Yuri Andropov, requesting better treatment for Yuri Orlov and myself. Kapitsa began his appeal as follows:

> I am greatly disturbed, as are many other scientists, by the fate of the distinguished physicists Andrei Sakharov and Yuri Orlov. The matter can be put simply: Sakharov's and Orlov's scientific work is of great value, but their dissident activities are deemed harmful. Now they have been placed in conditions which prevent them from engaging in any kind of occupation whatsoever. . . .

Kapitsa went on to describe Lenin's attitude toward the physiologist Ivan Pavlov and the metallurgist Dmitri Chernov, and also his own argument with Tito about the sculptor Ivan Meštrović, using all this as a means of examining the role of heretics in culture and society. He writes:

> Ever since the time of Socrates, active hostility to heretics has been commonplace in the history of culture. . . .
> The source of human creativity is dissatisfaction with the existing state of affairs. . . . Of course, dissatisfaction is not sufficient in and of itself. Talent is also necessary. Since only rare individuals command the talent required to express dissatisfaction in a creative way, we ought to cherish and take good care of the few who do. . . .
> In order to win horse races, thoroughbreds are needed. But there are only a few champions, and they are usually temperamental. An ordinary horse will give you an easier, smoother ride, but you won't win any races. . . .

Kapitsa concluded: "Harsher measures won't lead to anything good. Why not simply reverse course?"[3]

Andropov replied a week later, on November 19. I don't have a copy of his letter, but I've read it and will try to reconstruct its substance. Andropov, clearly pained by Kapitsa's letter, wrote that:

> The philosophical question of dissent cannot be reduced to the specific interpretation you propose. For instance, terrorists may also be dissenters, but we can't tolerate them. As for Sakharov, he long ago commenced subversive activities and has written more than two hundred statements containing the most obnoxious [or some such adjective] slander. He de-

[3]Kapitsa's letter to Andropov was published in *Sovietskaya kultura* on May 21, 1988.

fended the terrorists who exploded a bomb in the Moscow subway, which is objectively the same thing as defending terror. [Could there have been some subconscious psychological reason why the head of the KGB should harp on this slippery subject? Be that as it may, I have never supported terrorism.] Orlov was convicted in court for criminal activity. Sakharov has visited the American Embassy many times, and you know how ardently they pursue our secrets; this too was taken into account when deciding the question of Sakharov's banishment. To "reverse course," as you suggest, is not possible.

On December 4, 1981, while Lusia and I were conducting our hunger strike for Liza's emigration, Kapitsa sent the following letter to Leonid Brezhnev:

> Most esteemed Leonid Ilyich!
> I am an old man, and life has taught me that generous deeds are not forgotten. Save Sakharov. Yes, he has serious faults and a difficult character, but he is one of our country's great scientists.
> Respectfully, Pyotr Kapitsa

I first read the letters addressed to Andropov and Brezhnev in the Kapitsa museum, where I also discovered earlier appeals written by Kapitsa in defense of victims of repression in the 1930s.

IN SEEKING ADDITIONAL signatures for the Letter, I went with Zhivlyuk to meet the film director Mikhail Romm. In the 1930s Romm had directed orthodox films about Lenin, but in the 1960s he made a stunning documentary, *Ordinary Fascism*. In the interim, he directed *Nine Days in a Year*, the film about atomic scientists which I mentioned in Chapter 9.

Ordinary Fascism played only briefly at the time, and has rarely been revived. I saw it first in 1977 with Lusia in a small theatre in Yalta. The film is about the crimes, squalor, and lies of Nazism, but its artistic power turns it into an indictment of all forms of fascism, including the Soviet variety. A lifetime separates the Romm of *Lenin in October* from that of *Ordinary Fascism*. "Alexei Kapler[4] and I were sincere when we produced films about Lenin," Romm told me. "But now times have changed—and so have we."

Romm agonized over the decision, but did not sign the Letter. Scientific

---

[4][Kapler was arrested in March 1943 and banished from Moscow after falling in love with Stalin's daughter, Svetlana Alliluyeva. See her *Twenty Letters to a Friend* (Harper & Row, 1967), pp. 173–183.]

progress was not his main concern. He was working on a major documentary about his generation, which he saw as his masterpiece, an explanation and atonement for his life. I don't know whether he completed the film; perhaps prints or fragments of it are still locked up in the secret archives. [Excerpts from this film were recently broadcast on Soviet television.—A.S. 1988]

At last, compelled to acknowledge the difficulty of enlisting others, Turchin and I decided to release the Letter with just our own signatures. I think it was my idea to bring in Roy Medvedev as a third sponsor—his ideas on democratization seemed close to ours.[5] Turchin readily agreed, so the Letter was issued with three signatures.

Solzhenitsyn has since blamed Roy Medvedev for our non-confrontational approach, but he is wrong.[6] Turchin wanted to build a bridge between the state and society, and I endorsed his idea. Medvedev's sole editorial contribution was to modify—not without argument—my comparison of our country to a driver who steps on the gas and the brakes at the same time, a metaphor borrowed from the Czech writers Jiří Hanzelka and Miroslav Zikmund. Kapitsa had shown me the manuscript of their travel notes on the Soviet Union; publication had been blocked despite the authors' evident sympathy for our country, because they exposed our waste of natural resources and human labor, our swollen and inefficient bureaucracy, and our pervasive censorship.

After signing the Letter, Turchin, Medvedev, and I shook hands. I said, half in jest, that from now on we three would be linked and we'd have to help one another in times of trouble. A couple of months later, I redeemed my pledge when Zhores Medvedev was put into a psychiatric hospital. However, it wasn't long before my relations with the Medvedev brothers cooled, and I developed an antipathy toward them. I remained on good terms with Turchin until his emigration in 1977 cut off contact between us.

TURCHIN WAS HOST to an informal, ongoing seminar which examined ideological, philosophical, and historical issues in the aftermath of the Prague Spring. I occasionally attended these friendly, open discussions in 1970. Turchin's wife, Tanya, would serve tea and sweets, and then sit in the corner, taking notes and paying particular attention when her husband spoke. Turchin, who was determined that at least a few custodians of unofficial thought should survive, directed our attention to Vekhi[7] and other classics from the nine-hundred-year history of Russian ideas. In the late 1970s and early 1980s,

---

[5][See Roy Medvedev, On Socialist Democracy (Knopf, 1975).]

[6][The Oak and the Calf, p. 369.]

[7][A collection of essays by and about the Russian intelligentsia, first published in Moscow in 1909. For an English translation, see Landmarks (Karz Howard, 1977).]

the KGB suppressed such discussion groups, but now they are tolerated once again.

The most stimulating speaker at Turchin's seminar was Grigory Pomerants, a former political prisoner and a specialist in Oriental philosophy. I was astounded by his erudition, his broad perspective, his sardonic humor, and his academic approach (in the best sense of that term). Pomerants's three or four talks paid homage to the civilization created by the interaction of all nations, East and West, over the course of millennia. He praised tolerance and compromise, deploring (as I do) the poverty and sterility of narrow chauvinism, dictatorships, and totalitarian regimes. Pomerants is a man of rare independence, integrity, and intensity who has not let material poverty cramp his rich, if underrated, contribution to our intellectual life.

ONCE AGAIN using Khachaturova as a go-between, Solzhenitsyn suggested a second meeting, this time at Rostropovich's Zhukovka dacha, where he was then living. Turchin accompanied me in the hope of persuading Solzhenitsyn to collaborate on some publication. I'd invited him along in the belief that Solzhenitsyn would be as delighted as I had been when Zhivlyuk first brought Turchin to my house without advance notice. But this belief proved to be mistaken: Solzhenitsyn was clearly annoyed by Turchin's presence and coldly rejected his proposal.

At Solzhenitsyn's request, he and I talked in private for a while before having Turchin join us. Solzhenitsyn was more enthusiastic about our Letter than he'd been about *Reflections*. I was surprised; I didn't yet understand that an appeal to our leaders—if only as a matter of form—was more acceptable to Solzhenitsyn than a call for rapprochement with the "decadent" West. More important, he was elated that I had now entered into clear-cut opposition to the existing system.

I asked if there was anything we could do to help Pyotr Grigorenko and Anatoly Marchenko. Solzhenitsyn cut me short: "Nothing! They attacked the enemy with a battering ram. They chose their own fate and can't be saved. The attempt would only harm them and others."

Solzhenitsyn's remarks—so contrary to normal human feeling—chilled me.

IN THE SPRING of 1970, I was unexpectedly summoned by Sergei Trapeznikov, the head of the Central Committee's science department and an official I had criticized in *Reflections*. But Trapeznikov mentioned neither *Reflections* nor his recent failure to receive the needed votes for election to the Academy of Sciences; our conversation focused on the Letter. Trapeznikov's manner was quite amiable. He immediately called in his secretary and said: "Valya, bring tea for two. We've got an Academician here."

As we sipped our tea, Trapeznikov acknowledged the importance of getting rid of the cult of personality and developing democratic principles. But (in his opinion) the Party had fully exposed Stalin's mistakes. As for democratization, far-reaching proposals had been drafted, but before they could be put into practice, we had to solve our urgent economic problems: after all, a person has to breathe and eat before he can do anything else. Draft legislation on land use, air pollution, and food production would soon be ready for discussion by the nation.

I interjected that all this was interesting, but surely it was the proper concern of the administration's middle echelon. The top leaders ought to be deciding matters of principle; otherwise, the activities of the bureaucracy might turn out to be counterproductive. The personality cult hadn't been entirely eradicated; so far, not one of those rehabilitated had been given a position of authority, and many matters were still being swept under the carpet. I raised the question of continuing political repression in general, and that of Pyotr Grigorenko in particular.

With respect to the personality cult, Trapeznikov responded that we'd already gone further than we should have. Fanning the flames of hatred would only damage state interests and destroy what we'd built. As to current repression, he asserted: "The state has every right to defend itself."

"Even by flouting its own laws?" (I'm not sure I put the question so bluntly.)

The conversation wandered: Trapeznikov frequently digressed into personal reminiscences. He recalled his mobilization in the early 1930s to fight locusts in the Volga region. He was traveling with a Komsomol group when the car door flew open and he was pitched out. Neither the driver—a young man named Leonid Brezhnev—nor his passengers had checked to make sure that the door was securely closed. Trapeznikov's back was injured, and he was hospitalized for several months. After his release, he was appointed secretary of a district Party committee (near Gorky, I think), but his injury flared up again, and he had to return to a hospital, where he suffered through two years of indescribable pain.

This, as matters turned out, saved his life. His predecessor and his two successors were arrested, and most likely perished. Brezhnev did not forget the young man; he apparently held himself partly to blame for Trapeznikov's accident (or else simply felt sorry for him). Every time Brezhnev was promoted, he pulled Trapeznikov along with him, and Trapeznikov not unnaturally repaid him with absolute loyalty. (Such mutually advantageous arrangements are typical of bureaucratic structures, at least in the Soviet Union.)

As our conversation drew to a close, Trapeznikov said: "I agree that your proposals ought to be discussed. I'll call Alexei Rumyantsev and have him organize something at his institute."

"Of course, Turchin and Medvedev should also participate," I replied. To this Trapeznikov made no response.

Academician Rumyantsev was director of the Institute of Applied Sociology. I'd met him twice at the Academy of Sciences, where he was a member of the Presidium. What I didn't know was that his position was becoming shaky: he was regarded as overly sympathetic to reform and democratization. During our conversations he seemed ill at ease, as if I posed a mortal threat to him. And maybe I did.

I still don't understand why Trapeznikov invited me to his office. To have a look at the troublemaker in his diocese? To reeducate me? To neutralize my "malign" role in the Academy's elections? (Incidentally, I never spoke against Trapeznikov's candidacy, although I made no secret of my opinion that he wasn't qualified. When Trapeznikov's first nomination failed, Keldysh telephoned Brezhnev in a panic. Brezhnev is supposed to have answered calmly: "Well, so what? I'm not an Academician, either.") All three motives may have played a role, and there may have been a fourth one at play—to undermine Rumyantsev. That was Zhivlyuk's theory (he referred to confidential sources). In any event, Rumyantsev refused to host a discussion of the Letter at his institute, insisting that he hadn't received any instructions from Trapeznikov.

I saw Trapeznikov once again when Keldysh was running for reelection as president of the Academy. Trapeznikov walked over, shook my hand, and spoke to me in familiar terms as if I were "one of their own." He asked if I intended to vote for Keldysh. I said yes. Satisfied, Trapeznikov walked away.

22

THE DISSIDENTS AND THEIR WORLD

Valery Chalidze. The Grigorenko affair.
Rescuing Zhores Medvedev.

VALERY CHALIDZE phoned me in May 1970, introduced himself, and asked if I knew his name. When I told him I had heard about his samizdat journal *Social Problems* from Roy Medvedev, he said, "That will make things easier."

We agreed to meet, and he asked me if I'd be willing to cosponsor a complaint to the Procurator's Office protesting Pyotr Grigorenko's involuntary confinement in a psychiatric hospital. I was happy to do so, and then delivered the complaint myself to the Procurator's Office.

I had not met Grigorenko, but I had heard a good deal about him, and had been moved by the letter he wrote me in response to *Reflections*. A man of remarkable courage and integrity, he played a leading role in the dissident movement. He has told his story in detail in his fascinating *Memoirs*, [1] so I shall note here only the bare essentials.

Grigorenko fought in the Second World War as a professional army officer and later taught at the Frunze Military Academy, where he was promoted to Major General. After he criticized Khrushchev's mistakes at a Party meeting in 1961, warning that he was planting the seeds of a new personality cult, Grigorenko was demoted and transferred to the Far East. In 1964 he was arrested and confined in a prison psychiatric hospital for circulating leaflets which called for a return to "Leninist principles." He was released in 1965, but reduced to the rank of private, expelled from the Party and left without a job. Grigorenko wrote an informed, persuasive, and widely circulated samizdat article on Stalin's responsibility for the defeats we suffered during the first months of the war. [2] He was an energetic supporter of the Crimean Tatars' efforts to return to their homeland. In May 1969, he was arrested in Tashkent

[1][Pyotr Grigorenko, *Memoirs* (Norton, 1982).]
[2][*The Grigorenko Papers* (C. Hurst, 1976), pp. 12–51.]

when he traveled there to defend arrested Crimean Tatar activists, and he was again confined to a prison psychiatric hospital.

Our complaint, drafted by Chalidze and delivered by me to the Procurator General, pointed out serious procedural violations committed during the preliminary investigation and at Grigorenko's trial.[3]

A young psychiatrist, Semyon Gluzman, studied the available evidence, and affirmed Grigorenko's sanity.[4] After Vladimir Bukovsky collected documents on his case and sent them to the West, a worldwide protest campaign helped to win Grigorenko's release in 1974. He was still energetic, but his health had been undermined. In 1976, he joined the Moscow Helsinki Group. In 1977 he flew to the United States for surgery and to visit his son Andrei, who had emigrated in 1975. While there, Grigorenko was stripped of Soviet citizenship, barring his return to the USSR. He continued to take part in public affairs and, after a long illness, died in New York in February 1987.

My collaboration with Chalidze, which began with the Grigorenko case, soon led to a whole series of joint projects and to friendly personal relations.

ON MAY 29, 1970, Roy Medvedev telephoned. He was extremely agitated; his brother Zhores had been forcibly confined in the Kaluga psychiatric hospital, and diagnosed as suffering from "creeping schizophrenia." Zhores Medvedev's work in two disparate fields—biology and political science—was regarded as evidence of a split personality, and his conduct allegedly exhibited symptoms of social maladjustment. In fact, his detention was the Lysenkoites' revenge for his book attacking them; they were then still capable of mustering significant power inside the establishment.[5]

The Grigorenko affair had sensitized me to the political abuse of psychiatry. I had been battling the Lysenkoites for a long time, and my work with Roy Medvedev on the Memorandum had created a bond between us. I entered the fray even though I was not well. I had sharp pains in my lower abdomen and was running a temperature of 101°; a month later I was operated on for a hernia. (In later years, Lusia and I often faced situations where it was necessary for us to take action despite our poor health.)

On May 30 I went to the Institute of Genetics, where an international

---

[3][According to the Chronicle of Current Events, no. 14, the complaint was signed by Sakharov, Chalidze, Mikhail Leontovich, and Valentin Turchin.]

[4][In 1972, after the Soviet authorities discovered the author of this analysis, which circulated anonymously in samizdat, Gluzman was arrested and sentenced to ten years labor camp and exile.]

[5][The Rise and Fall of T. D. Lysenko (Columbia University Press, 1969). For the story of Zhores's detention, see Zhores and Roy Medvedev, A Question of Madness (Knopf, 1979).]

symposium on biochemistry and genetics was in progress. Many scientists had come from the socialist countries and twenty to thirty from the West. Before the session began, I walked to the blackboard and wrote the following announcement:

> I am collecting signatures in defense of the biologist Zhores Medvedev, who has been forcibly and illegally placed in a psychiatric hospital for his writings. Contact me during the break or reach me at home. *A. D. Sakharov.* (I added my address and telephone number.)

No one stopped me. I went outside and waited in the corridor.

Nikolai Dubinin, director of the Institute and a member of the Academy, was one of the last to notice my announcement. He erased it, and in his opening remarks criticized me sharply for mixing science and politics. Dubinin had been accustomed to sending me holiday greetings in commemoration of our common struggle against the Lysenkoites, but a year or so earlier had ceased to do so.

Two or three scientists signed the appeal during the break, as did two who were working in a laboratory. Others came later to my apartment.

Later, much of the dissident world assembled at Chalidze's room. On this occasion I met for the first time Tanya Velikanova, Grigory Podyapolsky and his wife Masha, Sergei Kovalev, and many others. Everyone there signed the appeal I had drafted, and Kovalev had authorization to sign for Alexander Lavut as well. All those I've named became my friends. Kovalev was distinguished, even among that company, by a deliberate quality of thought. He was tardy, but that was excusable in light of his heavy responsibilities.

The authorities, taken by surprise by my initiative, became alarmed. The poet Alexander Tvardovsky (an acquaintance of Roy Medvedev), the writer Vladimir Dudintsev, and other artists and scientists joined in the protests. I was called in by Keldysh, president of the Academy, and reprimanded for my behavior. I argued with him, and he promised to talk to the Minister of Health, Academician Boris Petrovsky.

On June 12, I was invited to a meeting at the Ministry of Health along with Academicians Boris Astaurov and Pyotr Kapitsa, who had also interceded in behalf of Medvedev. Keldysh was represented by Academician Anatoly Alexandrov. Petrovsky opened the meeting. Georgi Morozov, director of the Institute of Forensic Psychiatry, delivered a carefully worded medical report on Medvedev's condition. Kapitsa spoke, witty and cautious as ever. Then Astaurov and I argued for his release. After I spoke, Alexandrov retorted that my appeals to the West showed that I myself was in need of psychiatric attention. Petrovsky closed the session with a promise to resolve the matter through appropriate channels.

Medvedev was discharged on June 17. The rapidity of his release was unprecedented for a case of involuntary confinement in a psychiatric hospital in such circumstances.

23

THE HUMAN RIGHTS COMMITTEE

The Kiev conference. Pimenov and Vail.
I meet Lusia. The Human Rights Committee.
The Leningrad "skyjacking" affair.

MOST OF JULY 1970 I spent in a hospital, where my hernia was corrected by surgery. Once back on my feet, I decided to attend the international Rochester Conference on elementary particles, which was meeting in Kiev that year.

Before going, I dropped by to see Tamm at his dacha (in 1956 the government had given us adjacent dachas in Zhukovka, not far from Moscow, in a special section of the town reserved for academicians). Tamm spent spring, summer, and fall there, confined to his bed. As mentioned earlier, he had been kept alive on a respirator for several years, but he continued working and managed to stay in touch with a multitude of people. When I entered his room, I saw he had other visitors: Evgeny Feinberg, our colleague from FIAN, and Victor Weisskopf, the author of major contributions to quantum field theory, and for many years director of CERN, the European center for research on elementary particles.

Weisskopf recounted an incident from the 1930s, when he was living in Switzerland. The Swiss police, who worked closely with their German counterparts, accused him of being a Soviet spy. When he asked the basis for their accusation, the response was: "You visit Professor Tamm. He's been given a new apartment in Moscow; with their housing crisis, that's proof enough that he works for the NKVD."

Explanations were unavailing—Weisskopf had to leave Switzerland and was told he could never return. But the ban was revoked after the war, and he was allowed to live there again when he was appointed director of CERN in 1961.

The foreign department of the Academy reprimanded Feinberg after our encounter: "What right did you have to arrange a meeting between Sakharov and Weisskopf?"

"In the first place, I didn't 'arrange' anything. In the second place, what difference does it make? In a week Sakharov and Weisskopf are going to Kiev, where they can talk as much as they like."

"Kiev is the responsibility of the Ukrainian KGB. Here, it's ours!"

In Kiev I spoke freely with foreign scientists, even though I was housed some ten miles from them (presumably to limit our contacts). I remember with particular pleasure a half-hour conversation with Professor Maurice Goldhaber, conducted in an appalling mixture of English and German. We exchanged ideas about the world situation, the USSR and the USA.

BACK IN MOSCOW, I dropped in on Valery Chalidze. He lived in a single, spacious room with a balcony (part of a communal apartment). Chalidze had his own notions of tidiness and order, but he could always lay his hands on notes and other necessary items. Antique sabers and daggers decorated his walls, and he kept a collection of minerals, dried scorpions and other curios under glass. The focus of the room, however, was a king-size sofa, where "the Prince" (Chalidze's nickname) would recline in a casual, aristocratic manner and converse with a continual flow of guests.

Influenced by his friend Esenin-Volpin, he had mastered the criminal and procedural codes, and many people sought his advice. His quick, analytical intelligence was made to order for juridical "games." He was respected by nearly everyone, and loved by many.

At our first meeting, Chalidze told me that his main concern was to keep people out of prison by helping them avoid the deliberate provocations of the authorities and the inadvertent provocations of their friends, and he followed this course without wavering.

When I visited Chalidze after the Kiev conference, he told me about the forthcoming trial of Revolt Pimenov and Boris Vail, who were charged with circulating samizdat. I had met Pimenov, a mathematician employed by the Leningrad branch of the Steklov Mathematics Institute, at the 1968 Tbilisi conference—he had walked over, introduced himself as a former political prisoner, and told me of his interest in *Reflections*. In May 1970 I received a letter from Pimenov describing a search at his apartment. (As I learned subsequently, Lusia brought the letter from Leningrad to Moscow, but instead of delivering it herself, she asked a friend to drop it in my mailbox. Otherwise, we might have met six months earlier!)

Pimenov was arrested in July. Vail was also charged, but was released from custody after giving assurances that he would not leave Kursk, where he worked in a puppet theatre.

Pimenov and Vail had been codefendants once before, when they were tried on political charges in 1957. At that time Khrushchev was boasting that there were no more political prisoners in the USSR, and the Gulag population had in fact sharply declined. But even though most surviving political prisoners were released after Stalin's death through pardon or rehabilitation, many prisoners with twenty-five-year sentences remained in the camps, and sporadic arrests on political charges continued to occur.[1]

Pimenov had been released after serving six years of his ten-year sentence, following the intervention of his colleagues, Academicians Alexander Alexandrov and Mstislav Keldysh. Vail was released in 1965.

The 1970 trial of Pimenov and Vail was the first which I attended. I will describe the proceedings in some detail, since such hypocritical rites were repeated with minor variations in later cases.

The trial was scheduled to begin on October 14 in the old Russian city of Kaluga, a location picked to minimize publicity.

Finding competent counsel for defendants in political cases is difficult. Only a few lawyers deemed "reliable" are granted the clearance required to try political cases, and the KGB, which apparently controls this "privilege," can cancel it at will. If an attorney represents his clients too diligently, he can be disbarred, expelled from the Party, or subjected to other sanctions. In the circumstances, it is no wonder that defense counsel often functions in a purely formal manner, or even worse, works hand in glove with the prosecution.

In the Pimenov-Vail case as in many others, Chalidze helped arrange suitable representation for the defendants. I visited him several times in September and October, and he kept me posted on developments.

Once, when I arrived, Chalidze was reclining on his sofa talking to a beautiful woman; I was impressed by her serious, energetic, and businesslike manner. Chalidze didn't bother to introduce her, and she took no notice of me. After she left, Chalidze announced with a certain pride: "That was Elena Bonner. She's been helping prisoners nearly all her life."

Hoping to find out more about her, I asked whether she worked for the *Chronicle of Current Events.* "I wish she did. Someone as intelligent and firm as she is could make a real difference." Chalidze may have been unfair here to the editors of the *Chronicle,* but I cherish his tribute to Elena (or Lusia, as I call her now, her name when she was a child, which is still used by her family and close friends).[2]

I decided to attend the Pimenov-Vail trial, and following Chalidze's advice, I called Keldysh and asked him to make sure I'd be allowed into the courtroom. "What kind of mess is Pimenov in this time?" Keldysh asked.

---

[1] In 1958, the maximum term of detention was reduced to fifteen years, but the Supreme Soviet, departing from customary legal practice, passed a special law preventing this reduction from applying retroactively.

[2] Chalidze has questioned my recollection of his remark, but my first meeting with my future wife was an unforgettable experience for me and I recall every detail.

I explained that he was accused of circulating samizdat publications. Keldysh didn't give me a direct answer, but his intervention may have been the reason that I was able to observe trials until August 1971.

A few days later, Zeldovich paid me an unexpected visit. "I want to talk seriously. I liked your essay, its constructive tone. Why don't you ask Kirillin to assemble a group of experts under the aegis of the Council of Ministers to reorganize science and technology along progressive lines? Then you'd be doing something useful. By the way, I know you're planning to attend Pimenov's trial. You'll put yourself on the other side of the fence, and you'll lose the opportunity to be effective. Don't go."

I replied that I was already on "the other side." Anyway, plenty of people could give Kirillin advice—the whole Academy. I didn't know how useful I'd be as a trial observer, but I'd already passed the point of no return.

CHALIDZE REFUSED TO let me take a train to Kaluga like any ordinary mortal—he wanted me to appear like some *deus ex machina.* He arranged for a car, and we left for Kaluga at 4 A.M. on October 14. By the time we arrived five hours later, the corridors in the courthouse were packed with the defendants' friends and colleagues, including some familiar faces from the Medvedev case. Policemen were blocking the stairway to the second floor where the trial was about to begin. (How often this scene would be repeated!)

A policeman asked my name. I was a bit disconcerted, but he let me pass when I replied: "Academician Sakharov." A short, slightly stooped woman standing nearby pressed my arm sympathetically, and her simple, impulsive gesture startled me—people didn't do that sort of thing in my former world. (The woman was Natasha Gesse, a friend of Lusia's—and soon of mine—from Leningrad.)

Chalidze wasn't allowed upstairs. Pimenov's wife and his father, Vail and his wife, and the witnesses occupied the front benches. The remaining places were filled by "citizens" imported from Moscow, all wearing identical suits, with their identical gray hats laid in even rows on the windowsills. Packing the courtroom with KGB agents or other goons is a standard ploy at political trials. It ensures that the audience will be hostile to the defendant, since his friends, sympathizers, and sometimes even his relatives can be barred from the courtroom on the grounds that there are no seats for them. The appointed "spectators" read newspapers or doze off, waking up to heckle the defendant and applaud the sentence, even a death sentence.

The trial did not begin that day, because Vail's lawyer failed to appear. A week later, on October 20, I returned to Kaluga, again by car, but this time without Chalidze. Thirty or so friends of the defendants also showed up, including Lusia, who recognized me. She had brought a supply of sandwiches and milk and offered me some, but I prefer hot meals and decided to eat lunch in the second-floor buffet with Vail and his wife (whom I liked very much). (That evening I had tea with Natasha Gesse in a restaurant. She told me about the Leningrad case for the first time, and I found it extremely disturbing.)

The Kaluga trial lasted three days and was a typical samizdat case. In addition to Pimenov and Vail, Pimenov's acquaintance Valentina Zinovieva was also in the dock. Pimenov had given her poetry written in labor camp and other samizdat to read, and she'd copied some of it into a notebook. One day while Zinovieva was out, neighbors entered her apartment when a water pipe in the apartment above hers sprang a leak—or at least that was the excuse. Instead of a leak, they found samizdat. Scared half to death, Zinovieva cooperated with the authorities and quickly implicated Pimenov, and then Vail, to whom Pimenov had dispatched her on some sort of errand. She testified that at Vail's request she had sent a copy of Djilas's *The New Class* to Novosibirsk by registered mail; this incident was the basis for the only charge against Vail. Zinovieva couldn't recall the addressee's name, but she distinctly remembered sending a blouse to someone else on the same occasion. (After the Kaluga trial but before the appeal hearing, Vail's lawyer, Abushakhmin, made a thorough search of the postal registry and found a record of Zinovieva's having mailed a blouse but no trace whatsoever of the package allegedly sent to Novosibirsk. During the Stalin era, evidence was rarely required, and in 1970 the KGB still hadn't gotten the hang of faking it properly. But the KGB's clumsiness didn't really matter; the Appeals Court simply ignored Abushakhmin's argument that his discovery warranted a retrial.)

During a break in the Kaluga trial, the procurator approached me in the corridor and asked: "Well, what do you think? It seems to me that the judge has been thorough and objective."

Most likely he expected me to praise the trial and his summation, since, despite my apparent sympathy for the defendants, he still looked on me as a member of the establishment. I answered curtly: "As far as I'm concerned, the trial is a legal farce." He glowered and walked away.

Pimenov's well-reasoned final plea lasted three hours. Vail confined himself to a single point: "Citizen judges, the verdict decides the defendant's fate and affects his whole life, but it leaves its mark on those who pronounce sentence as well. Be just."

Pimenov and Vail both received sentences of five years in exile—bad enough, but mild by Soviet standards. Perhaps my presence, not yet a matter of course, had helped.

I was about to leave the courtroom when Pimenov's wife came up and nervously thrust a green folder into my hand. "Hide this and take it with you," she whispered. "It can free my husband."

Right under the noses of the guards, Pimenov had managed to pass his wife the file containing the indictment, his notes on the investigation, and his final plea. Such records, of course, shouldn't be kept secret, but in our circumstances, getting hold of them was extraordinary. Pimenov and his wife had exposed themselves and others to great risk, but I was still inviolable. I slipped the file under my jacket and walked downstairs past the policemen and past Lusia. The young doctor who had been assigned by Chalidze as my physician and bodyguard drove with me straight to the railroad station.

The loss of the file was discovered as soon as I'd left the courtroom, and everyone present was detained. Lusia and Sergei Kovalev were followed on their way to the station, but they managed to climb aboard the train just as it was leaving, and the automatic doors slammed shut in the faces of their pursuers. Lusia and Sergei picked up some of Pimenov's documents when they passed through my car.

In order to avoid a potentially damaging commotion, it was decided to return the Pimenov file. Chalidze phoned the day after the trial to tell me that a young woman would come to my apartment. "You'll recognize her. She looks just like her mother." Soon afterward, Lusia's daughter Tanya turned up with a young man. I gave them the file; it was returned to Kaluga that same day and the matter ended there, so far as I know.

A FEW WEEKS before the Pimenov-Vail trial, Chalidze had stopped by without notice, something he rarely did. He had drafted a letter thanking the authorities for dropping charges against Irina Kaplun and Vyacheslav Bakhmin, who had been accused of preparing some samizdat leaflets. I signed it, though I couldn't help feeling that the authorities might well regard such "appreciation" as even more offensive than the usual protests.

Chalidze then proceeded with great enthusiasm to outline on paper his idea for a Human Rights Committee, a voluntary, nongovernmental association that would study and publicize human rights problems in the USSR. He was eager to announce the Committee's formation to the foreign press.

I was intrigued by Chalidze's proposal, despite certain misgivings. An independent association seemed an important and original idea, although it should be noted for the record that in May 1969 fifteen persons had organized the Initiative Group for the Defense of Human Rights and had addressed an appeal to the United Nations concerning human rights violations in the USSR.[3] The publication of the *Chronicle of Current Events* (from April 1968)

---

[3][For more on the Initiative Group and the founding of the *Chronicle of Current Events*, see Peter Reddaway, *Uncensored Russia* (Jonathan Cape, 1972), especially pp. 150–170.]

and the founding of the Initiative Group had marked the emergence of a human rights movement in the USSR in the form which has attracted worldwide attention—respecting the law, relying on public disclosure to achieve its aims, and remaining independent of the authorities.

At the time Chalidze suggested his Human Rights Committee, I knew little of the movement's history, I was uncomfortable with his legalistic approach, despite its merit, and I worried still more that such a grandiloquently named Committee would attract too much attention and arouse too many false hopes. How were we to respond to the letters, petitions, and complaints that would come flooding in? That we were a study circle and not a defense committee? What a mockery that would be!

I expressed my reservations to Chalidze during that first discussion—they would prove justified a hundred times over. Much of the burden, moreover, fell on my shoulders, since people prefer writing to an Academician. Our conversation ended inconclusively, but the seed had been planted.

WHEN I RETURNED to Moscow from Kaluga, Yuli Khariton asked to see me and then passed on an "urgent" request to phone Yuri Andropov, the chairman of the KGB.

"Why didn't he call himself?" I inquired.

"Some people, you know, have their own ideas about status and protocol," Khariton said, giving me Andropov's office number. Before phoning Andropov, I went to see Chalidze, whose advice was: "Don't approach the authorities empty-handed. Think about my idea again: a Human Rights Committee could be very useful."

Chalidze was either mistaken or indulging in irony. [After reading these lines in manuscript, Chalidze stated that he made this remark ironically—A.S. 1987.] After all, Andropov had asked me to call, so it wasn't as if I were making an unsolicited approach. But when all was said and done, the committee seemed like a good idea, and so, suppressing my misgivings, I told Chalidze to go ahead and draft the bylaws, a task he relished.

The Committee's three founding members, Chalidze, his friend Andrei Tverdokhlebov (a young theoretical physicist working at the Institute of Scientific and Technical Information), and myself, signed the bylaws on November 4, 1970.

I tried calling Andropov several times in early November. On each occasion the duty officer would answer: "Comrade Andropov is not in," or "He's busy now. Call back tomorrow." Finally I was told: "Don't call anymore. Comrade Andropov will get in touch with you." He never did, of course: the whole thing had been some sort of game from the start, or perhaps he'd simply changed his mind.

* * *

WE FORMALLY LAUNCHED the Human Rights Committee at an improvised press conference held in Chalidze's apartment on November 11, handing out copies of a news release to foreign correspondents who mingled with a crowd of dissidents. (It was on this occasion that I first met Pyotr Yakir, one of the movement's more celebrated personalities.)

The publicity surpassed anything we'd anticipated. For the next week, a good half of all broadcasts over the Voice of America, the BBC, and Deutsche Welle were about the Committee, stressing its significance as an independent association that would study human rights objectively and then publish its findings.

The Committee met on Thursdays at Chalidze's. Although I didn't always understand the legal technicalities of the problems studied by the Committee, and was at times annoyed when Chalidze and Tverdokhlebov adopted what seemed an overly formalistic and needlessly paradoxical approach, I have never shared Solzhenitsyn's opinion that it was all a waste of time. The main thrust of the work contributed to the safeguarding of important human rights, and that outweighed my irritation with details.

The Thursday sessions turned into friendly get-togethers, which included Alexander Esenin-Volpin, a regular and valuable consultant. Not having been spoiled by an abundance of friends in my life, I prized this opportunity for human contact. Lusia sensed this and jokingly called our meetings "tea parties."

Chalidze introduced the honorific title of "corresponding member" for individuals who had made outstanding contributions to the cause of human rights. The idea, however, had not been properly thought through, and was to cause no end of trouble. Without prior notice, Alexander Galich and Solzhenitsyn were elected corresponding members. Galich was placed in an awkward and even dangerous position when he was informed of his election by telephone. I visited Solzhenitsyn but did a poor job of explaining what was intended, and I'm afraid this led to unwarranted hostility on his part toward Chalidze. To many people, the Committee's premature bestowal of honors seemed largely a device for self-advertisement.

One consequence of my participation in the Committee was the arrival—as I had anticipated—of stacks of letters, and a constant stream of visitors seeking assistance. My inability to help these people troubled my conscience then, and for years afterward.

IN NOVEMBER 1970, Andrei Amalrik, a young historian, and Lev Ubozhko, an engineer, were tried in Sverdlovsk. Amalrik was the author of the controversial essay *Will the Soviet Union Survive Until 1984?*,[4] in which he argued that the stagnation of Soviet society and the centrifugal force of the national minorities would so weaken the Soviet empire that it might fall prey to a Chinese army energized by a still vital ideology and nationalistic fervor. He was not alone in such fears. Solzhenitsyn too was troubled by the threat of Chinese expansion, although he saw the problem in somewhat different terms. I myself expressed concern about China in my 1971 Memorandum, but my worry was fading by the time I added the postscript in June 1972.

In his *Involuntary Journey to Siberia,* Amalrik described his 1965 banishment from Moscow as a "parasite."[5] Article 209 of the RSFSR Criminal Code makes it a criminal offense for individuals to avoid socially useful labor and to engage in "a parasitic way of life." This statute, with its extremely vague language, is a legal monstrosity open to all sorts of abuse; it has been used to coerce dissidents, religious believers, and independent craftsmen, and sometimes to pursue private vendettas.

Ubozhko, Amalrik's codefendant, was charged with showing his landlady a single issue of the *Chronicle of Current Events* and with possessing a copy of Amalrik's *Will the Soviet Union Survive Until 1984?* It seems that Ubozhko, a resident of Sverdlovsk, was indicted to provide a pretext for trying Amalrik in that distant city, which was off limits to foreign correspondents.

I intended to go to Sverdlovsk, but could not get myself organized in time to do so. Amalrik and Ubozhko were each sentenced to three years in labor camp. Ubozhko was sent from the camp to a prison psychiatric hospital in 1972, and remained in confinement until 1987. (He escaped in 1975, but was quickly caught and recommitted.) I shall return to Amalrik's story.

I MET LUSIA again among the crowd at Chalidze's birthday party on November 25; the next time I saw her was in connection with a very different occasion: the Leningrad airplane case.

On June 15, 1970, twelve persons were arrested at Leningrad's Smolny Airport and four more near the town of Priozersk. The twelve had booked a passenger flight from Leningrad; after landing at Priozersk, they had planned to overpower the crew, leave them tied up, pick up their four accomplices, and then fly on to Sweden. From that country, they hoped to reach Israel.

This affair was yet another tragic consequence of the USSR's failure to permit emigration. The original plan had involved a group which included

[4][Harper & Row, 1970.]
[5][Harcourt Brace Jovanovich, 1970.]

Hillel Butman, an engineer, and Mark Dymshits, a professional pilot; they were going to buy up all the seats on a flight from Leningrad to Murmansk and then hijack the plane in flight, but Israel's Ministry of Foreign Affairs categorically opposed the idea, fearing that it would compromise the prospects for legal emigration. Butman and most of his associates dropped out, but Dymshits decided to go ahead with the scheme on a reduced scale.

The revised plan was hazardous and criminal, but not to the extent alleged at the trial. All the passengers were party to the plot, and the danger to the crew was minimal.

At the time, skyjackings were becoming epidemic. Not long after the arrest of Dymshits and his associates, two Lithuanians, Pranas Brazinskas and his son Algirdas, used guns to force the pilot of a Soviet passenger plane to take them to Turkey. They thereby committed a serious crime, and in the fray several members of the Aeroflot crew were wounded, and a young stewardess, Nadya Kurchenko, was killed by a stray shot fired by a Soviet guard.[6] Feelings were running high, and the public could hardly be expected to distinguish the Leningrad case from other, more typical skyjacking incidents.

Lusia's friend Eduard Kuznetsov was among those arrested. (In 1962, he had been tried on trumped-up political charges and sentenced to seven years labor camp. While serving that term, he met Felix Krasavin, who introduced him to Lusia in 1968. Once, when her son Alexei was reading a book on capital punishment, he began to ask questions of Kuznetsov, who replied: "Leave me alone. I'm not interested in the death penalty.")

Immediately after Kuznetsov's arrest, Lusia flew to Leningrad and learned from a baggage handler that Kuznetsov and his co-conspirators had been taken into custody while boarding their plane after KGB agents from Moscow and their Leningrad counterparts had actually come to blows over jurisdiction in the matter. Since Kuznetsov's mother was not physically up to organizing her son's defense, Lusia filed an affidavit claiming to be Kuznetsov's aunt, and the KGB chose to turn a blind eye to this fiction. She then engaged defense counsel for Kuznetsov and his codefendants.

When the trial began in December, Lusia attended it as Kuznetsov's next-of-kin. Every evening she would record the day's proceedings, and then she or a friend would bring the report to Moscow, where it was immediately copied and passed on to foreign correspondents. Lusia's notes were later published as an appendix to Kuznetsov's *Prison Diaries.*[7]

---

[6]Western radio stations should have countered the misleading Soviet propaganda about the incident by reporting the circumstances of Kurchenko's death and the Brazinskases' trial in Turkey, where they served prison sentences before they were permitted to emigrate to the U.S.

[7][Stein and Day, 1975, pp. 217–254.]

Lusia was also in Leningrad for the spring 1971 trial of Butman and others implicated in the original skyjacking plan. Since she could not attend the trial herself, she took down the accounts of relatives and phoned the information to Moscow. Her KGB shadows would gather around the phone booth and peer in through the glass, but they apparently had no warrant for her arrest. Lusia's reports on the two Leningrad trials, in which she managed to convey the naïveté of the defendants and the judicial machine's purposeful, sinister assault, did much to mobilize international public opinion.

On December 25, 1970, Mark Dymshits and Eduard Kuznetsov were sentenced to death. Yuri Fyodorov, who had refused to cooperate during the investigation, got fifteen years as a recidivist; Alexei Murzhenko, also a recidivist, fourteen years; Iosif Mendelevich, twelve years; Silva Zalmanson, Kuznetsov's wife, ten years; and the others, from four to thirteen years.

As the death sentences were announced, the KGB agents and other "spectators" broke into loud applause. Lusia began shouting furiously: "Fascists! Only fascists would applaud a death sentence!" The clapping stopped at once.

Neither Chalidze nor Lusia wanted to involve me in the Leningrad case, since there was some question whether it was properly a human rights matter. (Amnesty International refused to adopt the defendants as "prisoners of conscience" on the grounds that they had been prepared to use violence.) Like people the world over, however, I was shocked by the sentences. I sent a telegram to Brezhnev asking for commutation of the death penalty and reduction of the other sentences. I categorically condemned the defendants' plan, but insisted that there were no grounds for charging them with the capital offenses of treason (which the Criminal Code defines as action detrimental to the state independence, territorial inviolability, or military strength of the USSR) or large-scale theft of state property (since the plane would, of course, have been returned to the USSR).

At this critical moment, I read in the press about a letter from Soviet academicians who were foreign members of the U.S. Academy of Sciences or similar associations asking President Nixon to intercede for the American Communist Angela Davis, who had been indicted for complicity in an armed attempt to free several prisoners while their trial was in progress. No one had approached me for my signature, although I was a member in good standing of the American Academy. I decided to write my own letter to Presidents Nixon and Podgorny, asking clemency for both Davis and the Leningrad defendants, and, in particular, for commutation of the two death sentences. I scribbled out a draft and gave it to Chalidze, who passed it on to Lusia for typing.

The following day, she paid her first visit to my apartment and told me all about the case and the trial. We revised my letter, and that same evening she mailed one copy to Podgorny and gave another copy to her friend Leonid Rigerman, who passed it on to a foreign correspondent for delivery to Nixon. The letter apparently reached him; a few weeks later I received a polite reply stating that Davis was accused of a serious crime, that her trial would be open, and that I would be permitted to attend it if I could get to the United States.

I also made a futile attempt to contact Brezhnev directly. Once again enlisting the cooperation of Alexandrov's secretary, I tried to call Brezhnev on the special Kremlin telephone from the Institute of Atomic Energy. Alexandrov, who was present, asked me what I was calling about. When I told him, he exclaimed: "Skyjackers are pirates. They don't deserve any mercy." He changed his mind, however, after I explained the facts of the Leningrad case, and agreed that the death penalty was excessive.

While waiting for Brezhnev to return my call, I moved to the vacant office of Alexandrov's deputy, Academician Mikhail Millionshchikov, who was absent, performing his "civic duty" as chairman of the RSFSR Supreme Soviet. I'd met him in the 1950s in connection with my professional work. I wrote him a detailed letter, explaining the case and asking him to grant clemency, which was a prerogative of his office, but my appeal had no apparent effect. Brezhnev's secretary called back about nine P.M. to say that Brezhnev was too busy to speak with me at the moment, but would like to see me some other time. Most likely, this was nothing more than a courteous form of refusal, but I decided to turn it to advantage by asking Brezhnev for a meeting at a later date after I had worked out an appropriate agenda. This was the genesis of my 1971 Memorandum.

Lusia saw Kuznetsov immediately after the trial, going alone to this difficult meeting, since Kuznetsov's mother was not well. Kuznetsov even managed a joke or two during the couple of hours they were permitted to spend together in the warden's office, and Lusia gave him some food she'd brought along.

Meanwhile, the international campaign against the death sentences was gaining momentum. A foreign newspaper printed a cartoon of Brezhnev and Franco dancing around a Christmas tree decorated with hanged men. (Basque terrorists had recently been sentenced to death in Spain.) Suddenly, out of the blue, an appeal hearing was scheduled for December 30, catching the defense lawyers off guard—they had to prepare their briefs the night before the hearing, and only two lawyers from Leningrad got to Moscow in time for the proceedings. The sole relatives present were Mendelevich's sister, Fyodorov's mother, and Lusia. When we heard a broadcast on December 30 announcing the commutation of the Basques' death sentences, we took it as a sign that Kuznetsov and Dymshits might also be spared.

Lev Smirnov, later to become chairman of the USSR Supreme Court, presided over the hearing. At first we found his mild, intellectual demeanor pleasing, but after a time, his indifference horrified us, especially when we thought of all those whose fates depended on his decisions.

I had a chance to talk with Lusia while the appeal hearings were in recess, and she spoke to me about her plan to retire at age fifty and live on her pension as a disabled veteran of World War II. She would devote herself to bringing up her prospective grandchildren—her daughter Tanya had just married. Lusia was worried about where the young people would live, a very common problem in the Soviet Union.

On December 31, the court commuted the death sentences to fifteen years in labor camp.

The procurator left the courtroom with us, carrying New Year's gifts for his children. Chalidze, who was in the crowd waiting outside to hear the verdict, exclaimed: "Look, Lusia, *they're* human too!" I was drawn by the anxious eyes of one young man, whose face lit up as I told him the good news. "That's Telnikov," Chalidze explained. "He was in camp with Kuznetsov."

Our group broke up, and I went home alone. Lusia sent a telegram to Kuznetsov, but it was not delivered. Instead, the warden visited his cell and informed him that he would not be executed.

Lusia called me shortly before midnight to wish me a Happy New Year, and I wished her the same.

24

MY 1971 MEMORANDUM

The Memorandum. The Fainberg-Borisov case.
Mikhail Leontovich. Political psychiatry.
The Crimean Tatars.

DURING THE FIRST MONTHS of 1971, I concentrated on writing a "Memorandum"—an aide-mémoire which could serve as an agenda for a meeting with Brezhnev. This seemed a suitable format for putting forward concisely and without literary embellishment my proposals for a program of democratic, pluralistic reforms. In some respects, the Memorandum duplicated *Reflections* and the 1970 Sakharov-Turchin-Medvedev Letter, but it went beyond them. I did not expect the Soviet leaders to take my suggested changes (which touched on economic, cultural, legal, social, and foreign policy matters) seriously, but it seemed worthwhile to formulate a comprehensive, internally consistent alternative to the official Party program. Chalidze compiled and I edited an appendix which described specific instances of political repression; it was based largely on the *Chronicle of Current Events*.

In March, I sent the Memorandum to Leonid Brezhnev through the letters office of the Central Committee. I enclosed a covering note, mentioning the Human Rights Committee and emphasizing the constructive and loyal nature of its activity. I decided to postpone publication of the Memorandum for at least a year in order to allow time for a considered response. I made several telephone calls to the Central Committee, but no one seemed to know anything about the Memorandum. Finally, Andrei Alexandrov-Agentov, Brezhnev's chief aide, told me that it had been received. Since it treated a variety of issues, different sections had been passed on to the appropriate Central Committee departments for study; I could expect a reply in a month or so. But I heard nothing further, and Agentov ceased to return my calls.

I added a postscript to the Memorandum in June 1972 and gave both documents to foreign correspondents and to samizdat.[1] (I left out the appendix on political repression which had been included in my submission to Brezhnev.)

THE HUMAN RIGHTS COMMITTEE met regularly during the winter and spring of 1971, the heyday of its activity.

Igor Shafarevich, a mathematician and corresponding member of the Academy of Sciences, walked over to me during the Academy's spring 1971 General Assembly and volunteered to take part in the Committee's work. He was particularly disturbed by the misuse of psychiatry, by religious persecution, and by other actions which violate the victims' spiritual integrity. After he'd become the fourth member of the Committee, Shafarevich and I tried our best to give priority to the more urgent issues, but Chalidze, Tverdokhlebov, and Volpin had a taste for the paradoxical and the extreme, and their familiarity with the intricacies of the bylaws allowed them to set the agenda. Shafarevich's views are close to Solzhenitsyn's; this cast something of a shadow over our relationship, but I have never lost my great respect for him.

The Committee's report on the rights of mental patients, which denounced the misuse of psychiatry, was adopted in July 1971.[2] But still earlier, I had followed the case of Viktor Fainberg, one of the participants in the Red Square demonstration of August 25, 1968. "Volunteer policemen" (in fact, KGB agents) knocked out some of his teeth in the course of arresting him, which would have made it embarrassing to try him in open court. Fainberg, who had received psychiatric care as a child, was thereupon ruled mentally incompetent and sent to the Leningrad special psychiatric hospital.

Special psychiatric hospitals for insane criminals had been established in the 1930s on the initiative of Andrei Vyshinsky. They are operated by the Ministry of Internal Affairs[3] and they have harsh regimens. Convicts are employed as orderlies. Beatings are frequent. Painful procedures and drugs which have no therapeutic value are used to pacify the inmates and punish them. Sentences are indefinite, with "recovery" and release depending on the findings of special commissions which review cases at six-month intervals. In almost all the instances I've examined, the patient spent more time in the hospital than he would have in a labor camp if he'd received the usual sentence for his alleged crime. In short, these hospitals are psychiatric prisons, and are far more terrible

---

[1][Appendix, p. 641.]
[2][See Valery Chalidze, *To Defend These Rights* (Random House, 1975).]
[3]Control of these hospitals was transferred to the Ministry of Health in 1988.

for their inmates, whether truly insane or healthy persons, than ordinary prisons or hospitals.

Fainberg and his friend Vladimir Borisov smuggled notes out of the Leningrad hospital describing merciless beatings, the wrapping of unruly patients in wet canvas, which causes excruciating pain as it dries and shrinks, and other horrors. When they declared an indefinite hunger strike, they were beaten and subjected to daily forced feeding. One of Fainberg's smuggled letters identified Professor Ruben Nadzharov, deputy director of the Moscow Institute of Psychiatry, as chairman of the commission that examined him on March 17, 1971; it included a transcript of Nadzharov's questions and Fainberg's replies.[4]

I decided to ask Mikhail Leontovich, the only other member of the Academy to show an interest in these matters, to intercede for Fainberg and Borisov. I first met Leontovich in the 1930s, when he came to consult my father about Landsberg's physics textbook. (I remember my father's speaking of him with admiration and warmth.) Leontovich had his eccentricities, but the most striking things about him were the lively, mischievous gleam in his eye and his intelligent, ironic half-smile.

In the early postwar years, I seldom saw him after my abortive attempt to work with him in my second year at university, but I did hear many stories about him. One involved his skirmish with Yakov Terletsky, a theoretical physicist and self-appointed champion of ideological purity. Terletsky had invited Leontovich to join "the battle against the idealist forces of inertia." The question was whether centrifugal force, the Coriolis force, and similar forces are "real," and Terletsky had labeled Semyon Khaikin's explanation of these phenomena "idealist." All this was clearly a matter of semantics and devoid of any real substance, but demagogues thrive on this kind of artificial dispute. Terletsky apparently envied Lysenko's laurels, as did many at the time. Leontovich told me that he threw Terletsky down the stairs, and called him "a practitioner of the oldest female profession" to boot.

Leontovich was elected a member of the Academy in 1946. After I joined that select society in 1953, I was able to observe him at firsthand in his role of Academy gadfly—always on matters of substance, always in defense of honesty. Bold words uttered in private by Soviet scientists traveling abroad sometimes leave foreign colleagues with the impression that our Academy is a den of dissidents. Nothing could be farther from the truth. The Academy's silence about Yuri Orlov, and about myself, should have opened people's eyes: our academicians are habitual conformists. Leontovich was a notable excep-

---

[4][For extracts from this interview, see Sidney Bloch and Peter Reddaway, *Psychiatric Terror* (Basic Books, 1977), pp. 441–447.]

tion. He supported me in 1964 when I opposed Nuzhdin, and he spoke out against other nominees whom he considered unsuitable.

In 1951, Leontovich was appointed director of theoretical work on the magnetic thermonuclear reactor [MTR]. This responsibility obliged him to forego the satisfaction of solving problems himself; instead he assigned them to younger scientists whose work he then had to critique. He told Tamm in 1951: "I'm almost certain that nothing will come of this project, but I'll do everything in my power to investigate its potential, whatever the result may be." He worked on the project for thirty years, until his death in 1981, and his management was crucial for its success.

It was Leontovich who in 1967 passed on to me Larisa Bogoraz's letter about Yuli Daniel's camp experience. He signed, at my request, a 1971 letter urging proper medical care for Yuri Galanskov, and followed up by going to talk with the medical department of the Labor Camp Administration. (Galanskov died on November 4, 1972, in a Mordovian camp hospital, following emergency surgery for a bleeding ulcer. His earlier insistence that the operation be performed only in the Leningrad prison hospital may have contributed to his untimely death—he was just thirty-three.) In several other affairs, Leontovich's intervention clearly mattered. His offer to stand surety for a young woman arrested in Sochi in a samizdat case secured her immediate release. He hired as his secretary Alexander Voronel, a refusenik physicist threatened with arrest as a "parasite."

In the Fainberg-Borisov case, Leontovich set to work with a will. He came with me twice to the Ministry of Health, but our conversations there were a waste of time. We also visited Dr. Nadzharov, who sought to justify the terrible conditions in the special psychiatric hospitals by citing the problems of working with mentally ill criminals. When he lectured us on the danger posed by "creeping schizophrenia," we acknowledged our lack of qualifications to rebut him on medical questions, but we made it clear that we categorically opposed any use of psychiatry for political purposes. Again, Leontovich's intervention seemed to make a difference.[5]

In 1972 he signed my appeals for an amnesty and for abolition of the death penalty, and he always remained willing to sign petitions on behalf of individuals. In time, however, he became more and more skeptical of their utility, and I turned to him less often.

On several occasions I visited Leontovich with Lusia, and our conversations

---

[5][Fainberg was moved to an ordinary psychiatric hospital in February 1973 and released that November. Borisov was moved to an ordinary psychiatric hospital in the summer of 1973, and was released in March 1974. Both now live in Paris.]

were lively and friendly. One story he told us reminded me of my own escapades at the Installation. During the war, a cylinder of liquefied gas was needed at the proving grounds where Leontovich was working. There were KGB men all over the place, and to get a "pass" for the cylinder would have required at least a week of bureaucratic haggling, which might well have reached the ministerial level. Leontovich simply hid the cylinder in one of his trouser legs and smuggled it in. He was lucky, and no one searched him. That's how we saved Soviet power from itself!

Leontovich was one of my heroes, but, sadly, our age difference and other circumstances prevented us from becoming close friends.

THE FAINBERG-BORISOV case brought Lusia back into my life: she introduced me to Borisov's wife, Jemma Kvachevskaya, who had attended the same Leningrad medical institute as Lusia. Jemma had received excellent grades, but was expelled for "actions incompatible with the status of a Soviet student." Notwithstanding the implications of that judgment, she was neither a prostitute nor a thief; she had simply refused to cooperate with the investigation when her brother Lev was arrested on a samizdat charge. The KGB foiled her attempt to enroll in a medical school in Saransk, and Jemma, her second husband, Pavel Babich, and their four children eventually emigrated to escape harassment.

I learned much about punitive psychiatry from the Fainberg-Borisov case, from the cases of Grigorenko, Medvedev, and other victims, and from samizdat, especially the *Chronicle of Current Events*. But I paid a price for my education: one poet I tried to save from forced hospitalization was in fact mentally ill, and she harassed me and my family for years afterward.

The government's use of psychiatry for political purposes is particularly dangerous because it is a direct assault on the victim's mind. Charges of mental illness demoralize, discredit, and humiliate a person, and are exceptionally difficult to rebut. The problem is compounded by the inhuman, illegal conditions of detention in the special psychiatric hospitals, by the conformity and hypocrisy of our closed society, and by the absence of an independent press. I am speaking here about *any* use of psychiatry for political or ideological purposes, and not just those cases when mentally healthy individuals are forcibly confined in psychiatric hospitals. The authorities tend to choose as victims for psychiatric punishment persons who deviate in some way from the norm; the important fact to keep in mind, however, is that their condition almost never requires hospitalization. (In any event, a patient is not going to get proper medical treatment in a special psychiatric hospital.) The diagnosis of mental illness is fuzzy, and this increases the likelihood of mistaken, arbitrary, or criminal actions. The menace is especially grave in a totalitarian society, where a victim's religious or philosophical beliefs can lead to persecution.

The Human Rights Committee and the Working Commission to Investigate the Abuse of Psychiatry (organized in 1977) made valuable contributions to the battle against punitive psychiatry, an issue which has been assigned a high priority by the human rights movement. The authorities are extremely sensitive to the exposure of psychiatric abuse. Bakhmin, Bukovsky, Gluzman, Grivnina, Koryagin, Sergei and Ivan Kovalev, Nekipelov, Osipova, Podrabinek, Ternovsky, and Velikanova were all prosecuted for collecting and publishing information on this subject. They and their allies in the West deserve much of the credit for the March 1988 law which introduces legal safeguards to curb the misuse of psychiatry, but only time will tell how effective these will be, and the assistance of Western psychiatrists is needed to halt psychiatric repression completely.[6]

IN 1971, I became interested in the tragedy of the Crimean Tatar people. On May 18, 1944, Stalin had ordered the deportation of all Tatars living in the Crimea, and since most of the younger men were in the Soviet army, it was mainly women, children, and old people who were jammed into freight cars by special KGB troops under the command of Bogdan Kobulov. Many died on their way to exile in Central Asia (they could not even be buried according to Islamic custom), and tens of thousands died of hunger and disease during the first year of exile. Nearly half the Crimean Tatar population was lost as a result of the deportation—an act of genocide. A massive campaign of slander was mounted against the Crimean Tatars. Russian and Ukrainian place names were substituted for the Tatar ones in the Crimea, and its history was falsified.

The pretext for the deportation was alleged Crimean Tatar collaboration with the German army of occupation. There were some instances of this, but probably to no greater extent than among the Russian and Ukrainian populations; meanwhile, important contributions to our war effort made by Crimean Tatars who fought in the Soviet army and with the partisans have been passed over in silence. Even during wartime—and still less forty years later—an entire nation should not be held accountable for crimes, real or imaginary, committed by individuals.

In 1967, the Presidium of the Supreme Soviet finally passed a decree exonerating the Crimean Tatar nation of the unfounded charge of treason. The

[6][For information on Western efforts to combat Soviet malpractice, see Sidney Bloch and Peter Reddaway, *Soviet Psychiatric Abuse* (Gollancz, 1984).]

decree, however, did not recognize the Tatars' right to return to their homeland, arguing that they had "taken root" in Uzbekistan.

The Crimean Tatars were only one of more than a dozen ethnic groups deported during the war, but most of the other exiled nations were encouraged to move back to their homelands *en masse* in the 1950s and 1960s. Why have the authorities blocked the Tatars' return to the Crimea? I suppose the main reason is its role as a playground for the elite: after all, they don't want to have their victims' offspring living alongside them. Khrushchev compounded the difficulties by giving the Crimea as a "present" to the Ukraine in 1954. And now, foreign tourism has turned the Black Sea coast into an important source of hard currency.

A young Crimean Tatar couple came to see me in 1971 with a typical story. Trusting in the Supreme Soviet's 1967 decree, they returned to the Crimea, from which they'd been deported as infants in 1944. The husband was a tractor driver whose father had been killed at the front. The wife's father, a kolkhoz chairman, had aided the partisans until he was betrayed to the Germans by a Russian collaborator. The couple had been living in a Crimean steppe settlement for several months without a permit. They couldn't find work, they couldn't send their children to school, and they were in danger of losing their home.

The problem of purchasing a house comes up time and again. The authorities have created a vicious circle: a buyer can't acquire clear title to a house without an official residence permit, but having a place to live is a necessary (although not sufficient) condition for obtaining the permit. Local police don't even bother to conceal the patent discrimination against Crimean Tatars in the application of these regulations.

I wrote to Nikolai Shchelokov, the Minister of Internal Affairs, about the Tatar couple's plight. Within a month, I sent off two more letters about similar cases, included some observations on the whole history of the Crimean Tatar problem, and asked for a response on the broader issues. In May or June, I was invited to visit the Ministry, where two officials assured me that they were continually monitoring the situation; they complained, however, that their hands were tied since the Crimea was attached to the Ukraine and the authorities there had their own ideas. The officials trotted out the story of wartime treason, but did not press the point when I reminded them that all peoples— Russians, Ukrainians, and Crimean Tatars alike—had their share of both heroes and traitors. They intimated that particular cases might be resolved "through channels," but a comprehensive solution would have to wait. Patience was needed.

After this meeting, I continued to write Shchelokov regularly about specific Tatar cases, and, up until 1977, my interventions seemed to do some good.

MANY PEOPLE IN our country—not just the Crimean Tatars and other displaced persons—are affected by the restrictions placed on their choice of residence; these are particularly burdensome for collective farm workers and others living in rural areas, and for former political prisoners.

25

FREEDOM OF RELIGION AND FREEDOM OF MOVEMENT

A search at Chalidze's. The trial of
Krasnov-Levitin. Freedom of religion and
freedom of movement.

THE 24TH PARTY CONGRESS opened in Moscow on March 30, 1971. "Preventive measures" such as hospitalizing dissidents and religious believers who have the misfortune to be registered on the psychiatric rosters are routinely taken before holidays and special events. This time, the authorities were even more on edge than usual: early in March, Jews had mounted at least two rallies demanding free emigration to Israel. Spontaneous public demonstrations of any sort are not very common in the USSR, and are frowned upon; many of the participants were sentenced to fifteen days in jail. (Despite this setback, 1971 marked the beginning of a remarkable surge in emigration to Israel.)

On March 29, the eve of the Congress, security officials made two further moves which struck close to home; they arrested Vladimir Bukovsky, and they searched Valery Chalidze's apartment.

Bukovsky was only twenty in 1963 when he was charged with possession of Djilas's *The New Class*; he was confined in the Leningrad special psychiatric hospital and emerged fifteen months later a convinced opponent of psychiatric abuse. In 1967, he was arrested again and sentenced to three years in a labor camp for demonstrating on behalf of Ginzburg and Galanskov. CBS correspondent William Cole interviewed Bukovsky after his release in 1970, and the videotape was broadcast by Western television stations, introducing a new and effective form of publicity. In January 1971, Bukovsky managed to obtain and send abroad official documents (psychiatric reports and other papers) relating to the political misuse of psychiatry.

My first and only meeting with Bukovsky came about ten days before his arrest, when he escorted a Meskhi activist to a session of the Human Rights

Committee.[1] Their appearance was timely; we were then in the process of preparing a report on the resettled peoples. Bukovsky was excited by the committee's potential, and he impressed me as an intelligent, energetic individual.[2] On March 29, he was arrested.

Around eight P.M. on that same day, Boris Efimov (one of the authors of the alternative constitution circulating in samizdat) phoned and told me that Chalidze's apartment was being searched. I alerted Tverdokhlebov by telephone, and then rushed off to Chalidze's place, where I ran into Lusia and her friend Irina Kristi.

This time we were all denied entry, but on other occasions (and I have attended numerous searches over the years), the people who turn up are allowed in and then detained until the operation is over. Visitors frequently are frisked; I myself have been spared this indignity.

Searches are somehow always unexpected and devastating. The warrant usually authorizes the searchers to remove evidence relating to a particular case—but the case may be designated only by a cryptic number, or left completely unidentified. This allows the officers in charge a good deal of latitude. They generally take all typewritten materials having the remotest resemblance to samizdat; all manuscripts, regardless of content; scratch pads, address books, and diaries; printed materials published abroad; Hebrew dictionaries; typewriters (seldom returned), and sometimes even cash, warm apparel, and food, if they suspect that these are destined for prisoners or their families. Tape recorders, cameras, religious literature, and publications in foreign languages are on occasion confiscated, and sometimes not. (During a search of Anatoly Marchenko's home his seven-year-old son Pavel's French readers were taken, along with his sketchbook containing drawings with French captions.)

"Independent" witnesses are supposed to monitor the searches, but they usually collaborate with the authorities or else simply ignore the proceedings, which are used as a form of warning by the KGB: dissidents are only too well aware that interrogation and arrest are likely to follow.

While waiting for Chalidze's search to end, Efimov and I stepped outside for some fresh air. A car filled with KGB agents drove up, and a woman clearly suited to the role of a Nazi camp guard stuck her head out the window. "We'll soon make your whole lot knuckle under!" she yelled at Efimov, following up with a string of obscenities.

Vera Lashkova, a friend of Bukovsky's, was detained on March 29 en route

---

[1][The Meskhi are a Turkic people who were deported during the war from the Georgian-Turkish frontier region. As in the case of the Crimean Tatars, the authorities have hampered the Meskhis' determined attempts to return to their homeland.]

[2][See Bukovsky's autobiography, *To Build a Castle: My Life as a Dissenter* (Viking, 1979).]

to his apartment. She was taken to the nearest police station, where she overheard the dispatcher's chatter absentmindedly divulging the multitude of patrol cars, observation posts, and KGB agents taking part in "Operation Chalidze-Bukovsky."

Around midnight, Chalidze's apartment door swung open, and several KGB agents marched past us, carrying two large sacks filled with their loot. We entered, and Chalidze told us about the search while he brewed tea. They had taken Human Rights Committee documents and a lot more besides. It was three A.M. by the time Lusia and Irina Kristi dropped me off at my house in a taxi. As usual, they were anxious about my safety; I, on the other hand, neglected to ask whether they had enough money with them to pay the fare.

Chalidze was called in for repeated interrogations. His future looked ominous, and a year and a half later he resigned from the Committee and left the country.

NOT LONG after these events the trial of Anatoly Krasnov-Levitin drew my attention to the issue of religious freedom. Krasnov-Levitin, a Russian Orthodox believer and former political prisoner, had been arrested in September 1969 on charges of slandering the Soviet system; he was released from detention in August 1970 without a definitive disposition of his case. He found work as a sexton and continued to write about the persecution of believers and about church and monastic affairs.[3]

Krasnov-Levitin was again taken into custody in May 1971. At Chalidze's request, he had spoken out in defense of some elderly women accused of forgery. They had been collecting signatures on a petition to reopen a church in Naro-Fominsk (a town southwest of Moscow) that in the 1930s had been converted into a warehouse—a common practice, but one deeply offensive to believers. For years there had been sporadic efforts to reconsecrate the church; as far as I know, these still continue. There had been no intention to commit forgery; in their simplicity, the old women were convinced that it was all right to sign the petition on behalf of relatives (and, in one instance, for someone who had died). They had collected more than enough signatures without taking these liberties, but the authorities used their mistake to disrupt the campaign and to take the offensive. Chalidze shouldn't have involved Krasnov-Levitin in public statements on this case while he was still formally under investigation.[4]

Krasnov-Levitin was tried on May 19 in Lublino, a suburb of Moscow

[3][Michael Bourdeaux, *Patriarch and Prophets: Persecution of the Russian Orthodox Church Today* (Macmillan, 1969), contains several articles by Krasnov-Levitin.]

[4][For more on this case, see Chalidze, *To Defend These Rights*, pp. 199–208.]

favored by the authorities for such proceedings, since its remote location discourages the attendance of defendants' family and friends and offers a pretext for barring foreign journalists—there are military installations in the vicinity. (Bukovsky, Tverdokhlebov, Orlov, Osipova, and Velikanova were also tried in Lublino.)

A KGB agent—for some reason I still recall his curly hair—met me outside the courthouse, escorted me to the courtroom, and found me a seat. Later, I realized this courtesy had been designed to prevent me from speaking with any of the dissidents who had gathered in Lublino. I also learned why the KGB goes to great lengths to limit access to such proceedings: not even the most elaborate stage-managing can conceal the fact that the defendants are being tried for their beliefs, and for the public disclosure of information they sincerely believe to be true.

Several incidents at the trial should have given pause to any unprejudiced observer, but despite this, Krasnov-Levitin was sentenced to three years labor camp [for "slandering the Soviet system" and "inciting servants of the church to violate the law on the separation of church and state"]. Just before sentence was pronounced, Vera Lashkova, who had been called as a witness, tossed him a bouquet of red carnations. Krasnov-Levitin rose and bowed with touching, old-fashioned formality. He had made a similar bow when another witness, a young monk, entered the courtroom wearing a black cassock and a pectoral cross. Since his release from labor camp in June 1973 (and his emigration in September 1974), Krasnov-Levitin has continued to champion freedom of conscience in the USSR.

Religious liberty is an important part of the human rights struggle in a totalitarian state. The pervasive, often brutal persecution of churches and religious bodies that characterized the early years of Soviet rule has been replaced by more selective repression directed mainly against those religious institutions of a nonconformist temper, but curbs on worship affect all believers.

Before 1971, I knew little about this subject, but I came to understand the complex and tragic dimensions of religious persecution from Shafarevich's report to the Human Rights Committee on the legal situation of religion in the USSR,[5] from Krasnov-Levitin's studies of church history, from Mikhail Agursky's writing about the antireligious terror of the 1920s, from the *Chronicle of Current Events,* and from personal contact with Baptists, Pentecostals, Seventh Day Adventists, Uniates, and Roman Catholics from the Baltic states.

For me, religious liberty is part of the general issue of freedom of opinion. If I lived in a clerical state, I would speak out in defense of atheists and heretics.

---

[5][Igor Chaferévich, *La législation sur la religion en USSR* (Seuil, 1974).]

* * *

A SECOND CRITICAL problem engaged me at that time—the freedom to choose one's country of residence, with the right both to leave the country and to return. This was, of course, the crux of the Leningrad "skyjacking" case, but it is a mistake to narrow this question to Jewish emigration or even emigration in general.

Early in 1971, a woman who had received permission to leave for Israel came to see me, bringing along her son. She had sold her possessions, but now her ex-husband was objecting to their son's departure, and she refused to go without the boy. She had no money, nowhere to sleep, nothing to eat, and she'd been threatened with having her son removed from her custody. I can't recall what I did to help her, but she did manage to emigrate a few months later.

I have spoken out many times on the subject of the exodus to Israel. It has been fed by Jewish national consciousness, by Zionism (a term I use with no pejorative connotation), by the anti-Semitism that smolders in the Soviet Union and occasionally (as in 1953) bursts into flame, and by a legitimate aspiration to live a life free from discrimination and from the specific constraints peculiar to our country. Jewish emigration won recognition and international support through the efforts of activists such as Shcharansky, Slepak, Nudel, Lerner, and Begun. But the authorities can still open or shut the valve in response to the political situation, since our laws do not guarantee the rights of the individual. Some refuseniks have been waiting for permission to leave since the 1970s. Ironically, exit visas to Israel are sometimes used to rid the country of "undesirables," and many dissidents, both Jews and non-Jews, have left the country by this route. Anatoly Marchenko and others who have refused to play the KGB's game have been cruelly punished.

Would-be emigrants of German descent face even greater obstacles. (Those who want to leave the USSR for reasons not connected with their ethnic ancestry are in the worst situation of all.)

Soon after the founding of the Human Rights Committee in November 1970, Friedrich Ruppel came to see me. The fate of this stocky man of about forty, with a lively, expressive face and curly black hair, was both shocking and typical of hundreds of thousands of Soviet ethnic Germans. In 1941, Ruppel was forcibly deported to Kirghizia. His mother—described by Ruppel as a modest working woman who never opened her mouth in the presence of strangers—was arrested, charged with anti-Soviet agitation, and shot. His father, who was also arrested, returned from the camps after Stalin's death, severely disabled. Some thirty of Ruppel's relatives had been arrested, and most of them died in confinement.

Ruppel himself was arrested in 1941, and thereafter was shunted from one transit prison to another, until two years later he was herded along with a large group of prisoners into a half-ruined church, where they heard their verdicts read out in batches. From the time Ruppel was called up to sign his sentence (ten years), he was a "legal" prisoner—this despite the fact that there had been no investigation, no trial, and no defense. His arrest was evidence enough for the Special Board which convicted him in accordance with the popular maxim: "Show me the man and I'll find the crime."[6]

Ruppel served his term, was released, and became a skilled metalworker. He married. (To my question whether his Russian wife would leave with him, he answered: "The thread follows the needle.") After Ruppel decided to emigrate to West Germany, he set about it with tremendous energy, not only for himself and his family, but for like-minded friends as well. At the same time, he sought posthumous rehabilitation for his mother. Although the case had been an obvious sham, years of effort got him nowhere. Eventually, Ruppel found out that Vorontsov, the judge who had sentenced his mother to death, was now in charge of the review procedure! But his perseverance and courage, together with help from the West German Embassy, German correspondents, and myself, paid off: the matter was taken up by the Western press, pressure was apparently brought to bear on Vorontsov, and Ruppel at long last received a small sheet of paper embellished with Vorontsov's signature and an official seal, rehabilitating his mother and dropping all charges "for lack of any evidence that a crime had been committed." In the 1950s, when the rehabilitation campaign was in full swing, thousands, perhaps hundreds of thousands of these certificates were given to relatives of those who had perished. The fact of the matter is, millions should have been issued, since millions died; Ruppel's certificate, however, was one of the last processed before the campaign ended.

Ruppel finally received permission to emigrate in the spring of 1974, and I accompanied him to the Belorus Station to say farewell and to share in the joy of victory. He popped the cork on the bottle of champagne he had brought along; foam overflowed the cut-glass goblets and spilled onto my best suit. Ruppel, unlike many émigré dissidents, succeeded in finding his bearings abroad. He took courses to improve his skills, and now earns a good living despite the fact that German work culture is light-years ahead of ours. And his children followed his good example.

Many ethnic Germans have struggled for years, even decades, to get exit

---

[6][Beginning in 1934, the Special Board of the Ministry of Internal Affairs was empowered to imprison or exile persons "deemed to be socially dangerous." Hearings were conducted in secret by three Board members, without defense counsel and often in the absence of the accused. The Special Board was abolished in 1953.]

visas. Three generations of one family, the Bergmans, suffered appalling treatment in the course of a fifty-year battle for emigration. Their applications were consistently refused on the grounds that they had no close relatives in Germany. How could they? In the 1970s, Pyotr Bergman was sentenced to three years in labor camp for taking part in a peaceful demonstration, and it wasn't until 1982 that I heard over Deutsche Welle that he'd at last been allowed to go to West Germany.

When Johann Wagner, a worker from Kishinev, applied to emigrate, he was first fired and then brought to trial in the spring of 1978 as a "parasite." He was convicted for "the malicious evasion, by a person leading an anti-social form of life, of an official decision concerning employment and the termination of parasitic existence"—that's the contrived definition in the Criminal Code. (Wagner's thirty-two years as a worker made the charge of parasitism ridiculous on the face of it.) That May, on the eve of Brezhnev's visit to West Germany, I wrote parallel letters to him and to Chancellor Helmut Schmidt, asking them to intercede on Wagner's behalf. This was one of the rare instances when an appeal to higher authority was successful. In August, the Moldavian procurator's office notified me that the case had been reviewed and Wagner released.

Germans who attempt to band together for purposes of mutual aid are severely punished. Dozens have been sentenced to long terms of imprisonment for compiling lists of would-be emigrants, for signing collective petitions, or for taking part in nonviolent demonstrations. Nonetheless, Germans continue to demonstrate in Kazakhstan, in the Baltic states, and in Moscow, and to send their names to the West German Embassy and to foreign correspondents. Ruppel's friends passed on to me lists containing more than 6,000 names. When Senator James Buckley visited me in 1974, I asked him to deliver those precious documents to the West German government, and he did so.

German emigration stems from a natural human desire to return to the land of their forefathers, to share in its culture and language, to enjoy its economic and social achievements. It is understandable that Germans should want to leave a country where they have been victims of appalling injustice—in effect genocide—and where they have been discriminated against in education and employment.

Hundreds of thousands of Soviet citizens of German descent died in labor camps and special resettlement zones, and to this day Germans cannot freely return to their prewar homes in the USSR.[7] A German child is still liable to be branded a Nazi by any classmate who's just been to see a war film!

7[The Volga-German Autonomous Soviet Socialist Republic was established in 1924 and abolished in September 1941, and it has never been restored.]

Why do the Germans' legitimate efforts to emigrate encounter so many difficulties? The main problem is the Soviet authorities' refusal in general to recognize any individual's right to choose his country of residence, whatever his nationality.

Additional factors are also involved. Very few ethnic Germans live in Moscow, and thus their access to foreign correspondents, diplomats, and Soviet agencies is limited. It is a source of satisfaction to me that before my exile to Gorky, I was able to do something about making their plight better known. West German correspondents have always responded favorably to my requests—the majority of them are conscientious journalists, and in contrast to certain of their colleagues from other countries, they do their best to understand matters fully so as not to confuse facts or give a misleading slant to a story. West German diplomats were also sympathetic, but they found it difficult to obtain concessions.

Few ethnic Germans enjoy the benefits of higher education, and this hampers their effort to organize joint actions, to get their stories published, and to cope with shrewd Soviet officials. And then there is the long history of the "German question," carrying, as it does, even more emotional freight than the "Jewish question."

And finally, West German officials and citizens haven't defended the rights of their kinsmen in the USSR with sufficient vigor. I am aware that in saying this I may cause some offense, but I am convinced that Soviet compliance with one of its fundamental obligations under international law should be a prerequisite for détente, trade, and other dealings. All ethnic Germans who want to go to West Germany should be allowed to do so, without invitations from relatives. Few have family there; their relatives live in the Soviet Union, or are buried in the resettlement camps of Kazakhstan, Kirghizia, and the Komi Autonomous Republic. Such lame excuses for delay as "knowledge of state secrets" can scarcely apply to the Germans, who are mostly miners, combine operators, and truck drivers. The regime should put an end to serfdom.

IN AUGUST 1971, I attended the trial of N., a young Russian physicist, and François de Perregaux, a biology teacher and Swiss citizen. At first glance, the defendants looked remarkably alike; on closer examination, however, I realized that de Perregaux might as well have come from another planet.

N., an intriguing fellow who'd been vice-president of an international affairs club at Moscow University, had decided to flee the USSR out of fear of mass repressions in the event of war with China—or at least that's what he told the judge. Following an unsuccessful attempt to cross the Finnish border, he was probably placed under surveillance. He then approached a foreign diplomat involved in his plan, who contacted the Eastern Institute in Switzerland. Sovietologists there came up with de Perregaux, a near-double for N. who was willing to take a risk to save a "dissident" (while enjoying a free trip to the Soviet Union). The plan called for N. to visit de Perregaux's hotel room on some pretext, pour a sleeping powder into his lemonade, steal his identification papers, and use them to fly abroad. The hotel staff would discover the slumbering de Perregaux, the Swiss consul would assist a tourist whose passport had been stolen, and de Perregaux would return safely home. In quest of a nest egg in the West, N. had also tried to send his memoirs ahead through a diplomatic pouch—he anticipated a hefty cash advance from some publisher.

Instead, he was arrested as he went to board his plane, and when de Perregaux awakened, he found himself surrounded by KGB officers instead of hotel staff. N.'s memoirs wound up on the investigator's desk. A plan of such complexity was bound to fail, and the KGB was of course able to outfox the Oriental Institute on what was, after all, its own professional turf. At his trial, N. recanted, explaining that he'd been reading *Pravda* in his prison cell; previously, all his information had come from the BBC. His sentence was reduced from ten to eight years because of his cooperation, and then to six years while he was in labor camp. He emigrated in 1977 and now lives in the U.S.

Why does the West pay more attention to egoistic adventurers than to persons who face danger for the sake of others? I don't understand the Western media's love affair with Soviet citizens who defect while abroad, jeopardizing efforts to establish a firm legal footing for the right to move freely. Some masquerade as conformists in order to get permission to travel abroad; by hoodwinking the Soviet authorities, they only exacerbate official suspicion of others.

I am more kindly disposed toward run-of-the-mill border-crossers who try to leave the country illegally, risking only their own necks. Some of them perform marvels of courage, but the West barely notices them; unfortunately, they lack the glamour of ballet stars and other celebrated defectors.

During a recess, a KGB man walked over to me and asked what I thought of N.'s trial. He added: "You're wasting your time with these drunken dissidents. Riffraff! You can't be sure who's married to whom."

That was the concern of the Civil Registry Office, not of the KGB, I replied, and added that I found the whole trial disgraceful. I had noticed this same KGB man having a word with de Perregaux's father; now, swelling with pride, he told me he'd advised the father that publicly condemning the Eastern Institute could help his son. François de Perregaux was, in fact, released before completing his three-year sentence.

A WHOLE SERIES of events—the complaints of Jewish and German refuse-niks; the Leningrad skyjacking case; Simas Kudirka's abortive attempt to defect at sea, the trial of N.; several tragic incidents at the Berlin Wall—moved me, in October 1971, to send the Supreme Soviet my first comprehensive statement on the freedom to choose one's country of residence.[8] I called for legislation which would deal with this question in the spirit of Article 13 of the Universal Declaration of Human Rights.[9] I received no reply.

As I wrote in my appeal: "The freedom to emigrate, which only a few would in fact use, is an essential condition of spiritual freedom;" it influences the level of protection accorded to other civil and political rights and affects international trust and security. Decisions to leave one's country are not made on a whim; vital interests are almost always at stake: to reunite a family; to seek better economic opportunities; to live in freedom; to escape religious, national, or other forms of discrimination; to live with one's "own kind"; or perhaps simply to see other countries and peoples. But whether the motives for departure appear capricious or not, they are not in any case the state's concern. Nor should a decision to leave be irreversible. Only the combination of freedom to emigrate and freedom to return satisfies the right of free choice of residence proclaimed in the Universal Declaration of Human Rights, and reaffirmed by the Covenant on Civil and Political Rights and by the Helsinki Final Act. This and other rights, including the right to exchange information and ideas, religious liberty, freedom of expression, freedom of the press, freedom of association, and the right to strike, constitute the basis for individual liberty and an open, democratic society.

It is a tragedy that citizens of the USSR are denied the right to freely choose their country of residence, official claims to the contrary notwithstanding. It is a tragedy for the hundreds of thousands who have applied to emigrate and then been refused or harassed. It is a tragedy for those who want to return to the USSR. It is a tragedy for those who want to leave but are deterred by the irrevocability of their action or by the hard lot of the refuseniks. It is a tragedy for the entire country, for all citizens, and for international trust, and it is a threat to peace.

Konstantin Zotov, the former head of the Department of Visas and Registration (OVIR), has written:

There is no social basis for emigration from the Soviet Union. Inasmuch as there is no unemployment, there is no need to leave the country

---

[8][*Sakharov Speaks*, pp. 160–163.]

[9][1. Everyone has the right to freedom of movement and residence within the borders of each state. 2. Everyone has the right to leave any country, including his own, and to return to his country.]

in search of work. Nor do national motivations exist, for all nationalities and ethnic groups in the Soviet Union enjoy full and guaranteed equal rights. Therefore, emigration by Soviet citizens from the Soviet Union is mainly a result of their wish to be reunited with relatives or of marriage to a foreigner.[10]

That's Zotov's pared-down version of the grounds for emigration. And he totally ignores the right to return to one's country. The "competent organs" simply refuse to open a window into our closed society. For decades Soviet citizens have been indoctrinated with the belief that our society, our economic system, our standard of living, our educational and public health systems are superior to anything in the capitalist world. The idea of someone wanting to leave this paradise seems so criminal, so monstrous, that it cannot be uttered aloud. The Soviet authorities will not permit people to travel freely back and forth and make first-hand comparisons of life in different countries. There's also the mystique of power: our masters cannot allow people to escape their control.

If travel restrictions were lifted, democratic social and economic changes might have to be introduced to keep emigration within bounds. That's what makes the right to choose one's country of residence so important, and why Senator Henry Jackson called this right the "first among equals."

Reducing the whole issue to the particular question of family reunification severely cramps the emigration process. Besides the illegitimate requirement that an invitation from a close relative (even sisters and brothers are sometimes excluded as insufficiently close) be submitted, there is the need to produce a written statement from the applicant's parents waiving any financial claims they may have. This in effect grants parents a veto over the departure of their adult offspring, since there is no legal mechanism for compelling them to furnish the necessary affidavit.

What is more, applications are handled in an arbitrary, secretive manner, and the regulations governing the process have not been published. The most common reasons for refusals are: "insufficient motivation for reunification" and "possession of state or military secrets." No further explanation is usually provided, and appeal procedures are rudimentary at best. All this opens the door to the systematic violation of a fundamental human right. Of those who came to me for help in the 1970s, more than half were seeking to emigrate.

10[*Along the Path Blazed in Helsinki* (Progress Publishers, 1980), p. 197.]

MY LETTER TO the Supreme Soviet was typed by Lusia to my dictation. This has become our customary method of working together. Now, however, Lusia often persuades me to amend a statement, usually during a preliminary exchange of opinions or in the course of her typing. Some changes are substantive, others stylistic. We have established a routine: I tell her my idea, then she reads my handwritten draft and comments on it. As she types the final version, our disagreement over certain points may become rather heated; in the end, I adopt some of her suggestions and reject others. She *never* alters a single word without my consent. The sole exception was the acceptance speech she delivered for me at the 1975 Nobel ceremony in Oslo, when the rush of events required changes in my prepared remarks, and she had no opportunity to get in touch with me. (The Nobel lecture itself was entirely my work.)

Lusia made no alterations at all in my statement on emigration. I stress this because some people believe that she instigated my interest in that problem (Solzhenitsyn, in particular, implies this in *The Oak and the Calf*). But it's simply not true. In general, my positions on fundamental questions have been formed over the course of my life. It is important to remember that I wrote and published *Reflections* before I ever met Lusia.

26

LUSIA

In July 1971, I rented a room near Sukhumi and spent two weeks by the Black Sea with my daughter Lyuba and my son Dima. Before leaving on vacation, I met Lusia's mother, Ruth, and her son Alexei when I dropped off our dog, Kid, a dachshund-spaniel mix, at the dacha Lusia had rented in Peredelkino. I also met two close friends of the family—Ignaty Ivich, a writer and literary critic, and Olga Suok, the widow of Yuri Olesha.

Lusia's daughter, Tanya, and her husband, Efrem Yankelevich, stopped by to see me—they too were vacationing in the south. I knew Tanya from the incident with Pimenov's file, but it was the first time I'd met her husband: they'd been married for less than a year. Efrem impressed me. He expected to complete his studies at the Institute of Telecommunications the following spring. Most graduates are assigned to secret work, but Efrem didn't want to become involved in military research; he hoped to go on to graduate school or, if that failed, to find civilian employment. By 1972 he had become "Sakharov's son-in-law"—and Efrem is a Jew as well. He was denied admission to graduate school, with the dean excusing himself: "You understand. . . ."

At our first meeting, I recognized my future son-in-law's uncompromising fidelity to principle, his integrity and sure grasp of situations. There was an immediate rapport and sense of trust between us.

I returned from Sukhumi with a toothache. Lusia phoned: "What's the matter with you?" "An abscessed tooth." "Well, it won't kill you." But she came over and gave me an injection of painkiller. I tell this little story, trivial in itself, because it captures both her dislike of sentimentality and her readiness to help.

I spent August in Moscow, where things had piled up. Lusia was on vacation with Alexei. For months, Lusia and I had been drawing closer, and it was becoming more and more difficult for us to hide our feelings. Finally, after her return, on August 24, we confessed our love. A new life began, and now, as far as we're concerned, each year has to count for three.

The next day, Lusia brought me to her mother's apartment, where Lusia was living with Tanya, Efrem, and Alexei, who was then entering his junior year of high school; for the time being, however, the children were all away in Leningrad visiting their father, Ivan Semyonov. (He had been Lusia's classmate at the Leningrad Medical Institute, and for many years headed the department of forensic medicine there. Lusia and Ivan divorced in the 1960s.) Ruth was ill in bed. Lusia and I went into the kitchen. She put on a record of an Albinoni concerto: the great music and my inner turmoil fused together, and tears came to my eyes in one of the happiest moments of my life.

Since August 1971, Lusia and I have followed a common path and our stories merge. But it is worth recording some of the things Ruth, Lusia, her childhood friend Regina Etinger, and others told me about the history of the Bonner family.

RUTH BONNER was born in 1900 into a family of Siberian Jews who knew their own worth and were confident of their ability to manage their own lives— qualities that set them off markedly from the traditional stereotypes of the Jews of European Russia, particularly those inhabiting the Pale of Settlement.

Ruth's mother, Tatyana Bonner, was widowed early. Left with three small children to support, she went to work and provided them all with an education. Her example was a decisive influence on Lusia.

Ruth took part in the Civil War in the Far East, studied at the Communist University for Peoples of the East, and then worked for the Party in Central Asia, Leningrad, and Moscow. She had two children: Lusia, born in 1923, and her brother Igor, four years younger.

Ruth's husband, Gevork Alikhanov, an Armenian, was born in 1897 in Tbilisi and graduated from a seminary there. Together with his friend and fellow student Anastas Mikoyan, he joined the Dashnaks (the main Armenian nationalist party); later, they joined the Bolsheviks. Alikhanov knew "Kamo"[1] and Lavrenti Beria—in a 1916 incident, he slapped Beria's face for mistreating a young girl. Alikhanov took part in the Baku Commune [the Bolshevik government established in the Caspian port in 1918] and in 1920, was active

---

[1]["Kamo" was the Party nickname for the Armenian Bolshevik Semyon Ter-Petrosian, who organized prerevolutionary robberies—"expropriations"—for the benefit of the Bolshevik treasury.]

in the successful effort to bring Soviet power to Armenia. It was Alikhanov who proclaimed the Bolshevik victory from a balcony in Erevan and then sent an historic telegram to the "Leaders of the World Proletariat—Lenin, Trotsky, Zinoviev"—informing them of the Bolsheviks' success. During a Dashnak uprising, Alikhanov accompanied Red Army units as they defended the Semyonov Pass through several months of bitter winter cold; this led to a lasting friendship with Agasi Khandzhian, First Secretary of the Armenian Communist Party, who would be shot by Beria in 1936. Alikhanov also worked with Sergei Kirov and then became a member of the Comintern Executive Committee, in charge of its personnel department at a time when Georgi Dimitrov was the Comintern's General Secretary and Palmiro Togliatti, Josip Broz Tito, and Dolores Ibarruri ("La Pasionaria") were among the luminaries on the staff.

On May 29, 1937, Alikhanov, together with most of his colleagues, was arrested at his office. A young man whom he'd hired at Ruth's urging (she'd taken pity on the unprepossessing Boris Ponomarev) was one of the few who remained at liberty, an almost sure sign that he was collaborating with the NKVD. Ponomarev later rose to become chief of the Central Committee's International Department.

Few of Alikhanov's associates survived the camps, and those who did had little to say about the Comintern's dramatic and mysterious history during the 1930s, or about the circumstances of his death. In the 1950s, Ruth and Lusia finally received a record of his Party work, a document acknowledging his rehabilitation, and a backdated death certificate which omitted the place of death and gave the cause as pneumonia.

RUTH WAS ARRESTED six months after her husband. She refused to corroborate the charges brought against him despite her inquisitor's promise of a milder sentence. She was labeled "a relative of a traitor to the motherland," a common enough charge in those days, and spent eight years in a hard-labor camp in Kazakhstan, followed by years in exile deprived of all rights.

A story she liked to tell about the camp illustrates Ruth's indomitable spirit. Once, the women were lined up for a morning head count. A bone-chilling wind was blowing; the cold was unbearable. They were suffering from exhaustion and malnutrition and could scarcely stand on their feet. Seeing the first rays of a crimson sunrise, Ruth exclaimed to her neighbor in line: "Look, how beautiful!" The reply: "You've gone mad!"

In 1955 Ruth was rehabilitated, reinstated in the Communist Party, and given a two-room apartment on Chkalov Street in Moscow. Sharing her apartment with her daughter, grandchildren, and later on with her great-grandchildren, she was always considerate and amiable, stoically enduring her chronic ailments.

IN THE 1930S, Lusia had been living with her family in Moscow in a special hotel for Comintern officials. After her parents' arrest, Lusia (then fourteen), and her brother Igor left Moscow to stay with their grandmother, Tatyana Bonner, in Leningrad. Matvei Bonner, Tatyana's son and Lusia's uncle, was soon arrested (he died in the camps), and his wife was sent into exile. Only Tatyana Bonner was left to care for Lusia, Igor, and Natasha, Lusia's two-year-old cousin.

During the school year Lusia had a part-time job as a cleaning woman; in the summers of 1938 and 1939 she worked as a file clerk at a factory that produced printing equipment. But she still found time for gymnastics, running, volleyball, and dance, and she especially enjoyed the courses she took in the children's literary institute founded by the writer Samuil Marshak. Although she was expelled from the Komsomol as the daughter of "enemies of the people," she won reinstatement through sheer persistence. After her graduation in 1940, she took Russian language and literature courses at night school while working days as a Pioneer leader. Life went on, and Lusia proved to be one of those who are strengthened by adversity.

Her mother was forbidden to send or receive mail, but two years after her arrest she recognized Lusia in a photograph of a girls' volleyball team received by another prisoner. In 1938, Lusia went once a month to Moscow, where she would wait in endless lines to hand in parcels for her mother and father until the authorities stopped accepting packages for them.

When the time came for Lusia to get her internal passport, she was able to pick any name she fancied for herself, since her parents had failed to register her and she had no birth certificate. She decided to take her mother's last name, Bonner. (Her brother Igor took his father's name.) She chose "Elena" after Elena Insarova in Turgenev's On the Eve. When war broke out in 1941, Lusia enlisted and was soon on her way to the front. Her childhood sweetheart, Vsevolod Bagritsky, son of the poet Eduard Bagritsky and a poet in his own right, also volunteered; he was killed in combat in February 1942.

At first, Lusia worked as a nurse's aide, carrying the wounded from the battlefield (at night school, she had taken a nursing course to fulfill her military training requirement). After that, she spent most of the war on hospital trains. These were initially made up of heated freight cars, later of converted passenger coaches; they were always packed beyond capacity. Her job—caring for the wounded, washing bandages, chopping wood, battling at every station to make sure the wounded were loaded on—was exhausting, and the train would at times come under enemy fire.

In October 1941, Lusia was wounded, suffering a severe concussion when a bomb exploded next to the railroad car where she was working. She lay covered with earth beside the tracks until some sailors discovered her by pure chance. She remained deaf, dumb, and blind for several days. Her eventual disability was probably a result of this concussion, although she was wounded again later.

A few years ago, the KGB spent hours interrogating the head of Lusia's hospital train (by then, well over eighty) in hopes of collecting "compromising" material, but all he could tell them was "We all loved her very much . . ."

Late in the war, there was a new attempt to expel her from the Komsomol— she'd given a piece of soap and some bread to a German prisoner. But she shouted down her accusers at the meeting which took up her case.

In 1945, she participated in a mine-clearing operation near the Finnish border. She ended the war a lieutenant in the medical corps, and was given a disability discharge: her vision had been impaired by traumatic cataracts and uveitis.

Lusia immediately set off for Kazakhstan, where she spent several days with her mother at the labor camp. Returning to Leningrad as a civilian, she got off the train, walked out of the railroad station, and sat down on the ground, her knapsack beside her; there was no one to tell her where to go or what to do (her grandmother had died in 1942, during the siege). As a veteran, she was given one of the two rooms previously occupied by her grandmother, and this also provided shelter for many of her friends. She sent food packages to political prisoners and exiles, and helped them in other ways as well.

In 1945, she was told she would go completely blind in a few years, and Lusia began to study Braille. After she spent a year in one eye clinic after another undergoing painful treatment, her doctors said that she shouldn't lift anything weighing more than five pounds, have children, enroll in a university, or take a job. None of this deterred her. After kicking up a fuss, she was accepted by the Leningrad Medical Institute.

Lusia married while studying at the institute, and, again violating her doctors' instructions, she gave birth to Tanya in 1950 and to Alexei in 1956.

In January 1953, the Doctors' Plot to kill Stalin rocked the country. Public meetings were organized everywhere to demand the death penalty for the "criminals." A professor in Lusia's institute, Vasily Zakusov, was targeted for denunciation, and Lusia, as a Komsomol member and union activist, drew the assignment to speak against him. To the meeting's amazement, and perhaps her own, she found herself saying instead: "Have you all gone crazy? The death sentence for Vasily Zakusov?!" She was expelled from the institute. But then Stalin died, and Lusia was reinstated.

After graduation, she worked both as a district doctor and as a pediatrician in a maternity home where she specialized in the care of premature babies. She had to moonlight this way, holding down two jobs at once, because salaries for medical personnel were (and are) shamefully low in the USSR. I have no doubt that Lusia was a fine doctor, self-sacrificing, painstaking, and intelligent.

In 1959, she was sent to Iraq to work for a year on a vaccination campaign. (When the World Health Organization announced the eradication of small-pox several years ago, Lusia recalled her own contribution with pride.) That first trip abroad allowed her to see for herself—an experience denied most citizens—that the Soviet system was not the only system possible and was, in some respects, far from the best. She mixed freely with the local population (going beyond the usual bounds placed on Soviet citizens abroad) and made friends with Iraqi communists (many of whom would perish during the next coup), entrepreneurs, and doctors. She happened to be the first doctor to administer aid to Premier Abdul Karim Kassem after an attempt on his life. (In actual fact, helping him had not been entirely a matter of chance. While she was bandaging him, someone from the Soviet-operated hospital called the Soviet consulate to ask whether or not to treat Kassem. "Yes," came the answer, "if you're sure he'll survive.")

Lusia worked for several months in Sulaimaniya, the center of the Kurdish region, where she got to know the Kurdish leader, Mustafa Barzani. Some evenings, she recalls, when she was out walking around the town, he'd send a street urchin to find her and invite her to have a beer with him.

Lusia spent most of her generous salary—or what remained after the state deducted a hefty share for itself—on travel. This included a tour of Babylon and other historical sites, a couple of days in Lebanon, and a visit to Egypt, where she heard Nasser make a speech calling down death and destruction on the heads of Jews and communists alike. After her return to the USSR, Lusia wrote a piece on Iraq which was published in the Leningrad journal *Neva*; even though the editors censored out some of her more incisive observations, the article still reads well today.

In the mid-1960s, Lusia separated from her husband and moved with her children to her mother's Moscow apartment. She began teaching pediatrics in a medical school; this paid a better salary than ordinary medical practice, was convenient to her home, and offered longer vacations (important, because Alexei was ill with rheumatic fever). She enjoyed working with young people: she organized an amateur theatrical group in the medical school and intro-duced the country-bred girls, who were mostly from poor families, to poetry and music.

About this time, she began publishing in the newspaper *The Medical Worker.* One of her articles, "Give Mom a Pass," which urged that mothers be allowed to spend time with their hospitalized children, provoked an enor-mous response.

In 1966, Lusia was sent to Armenia to write a feature story on her father for the fiftieth anniversary of the October revolution. This project had been proposed by the Armenian Central Committee, whose backing assured her VIP treatment and pretty much *carte blanche* to rummage through the archives, including those of the Cheka. Her research gave her a picture of the Revolution and civil war that lacked the customary glamour of horsemen galloping across a movie screen, sabers bared, a bullet-riddled banner waving overhead. Instead, she discovered endless cruelty, filth, treachery, and suffering, although the romantic element did exist as well. In the end, she found herself unable to write about her father: there was too much new and undigested information. At one point she thought of writing about her father's friend Grigory Korganov, a hero of the civil war in the Caucasus, but she abandoned that idea, and went home to Moscow without having written anything at all.

Soon after her return, she joined the Party. Lusia is a doer; she wanted to build a better world, and to reform the Soviet system, and she thought this could be better accomplished from within, as a Party member. In fact, she'd been working to improve the Soviet system for quite a while, but her decision to join the Party came too late—times had changed, the Party had changed, and Lusia herself had changed. People now join the Party in pursuit of promotion and privilege, not for idealistic reasons.

In 1967, Lusia traveled to Poland as the guest of friends there, colleagues of her father who'd survived the camps. Compared to the USSR, Poland is almost a Western country, and Poles, with their strong sense of human and national dignity, have never accepted the unacceptable. Today, things are moving there once again, and the last word remains to be written on that nation's fate.

The next year she visited France and met the French branch of the Bonner family and their friends, including a communist aristocrat who wore ragged jeans while driving a fancy sportscar and a member of the French Central Committee who refused to visit the Soviet Union for fear he'd be disillusioned by the land of "real socialism." She also met émigrés from all walks of life, who had become French and loved their new country, although they continued to follow events in the USSR with interest, and with pain.

Lusia had arrived soon after the events of May 1968, when the frenzied graffiti had not yet been erased by whitewash. But all eyes were now turning toward Czechoslovakia. Then came August 21. Her uncle scolded her: "*Your* tanks have occupied Prague!" Lusia's eleven-year-old cousin refused to say hello: "I won't shake the hand of a Soviet soldier!" French television was broadcasting nonstop about the Czech developments. From the West, the Soviet intervention looked especially frightening and revealing. Whether or not socialism with a human face could exist was clearly irrelevant; the Soviet

Union would not tolerate even a hint of such a thing anywhere in its empire or on its frontiers.

Lusia returned to Moscow, to her courses and to her amateur theatricals. But now she was indifferent to the Party card in her pocket.

And then it was 1970. Eduard Kuznetsov came to visit. He seemed preoccupied. "Edik, are you hiding something from me?" "Don't ask. I can't tell you anything, and I don't want to lie to you." She didn't press the point, which she bitterly regretted when she heard about the Leningrad airplane affair.

IN THE FALL of 1971, Lusia took me to Leningrad to meet Regina Etinger, Natasha Gesse, and Zoya Zadunaiskaya; she wanted to share these particular friends with me, and I am grateful to her for that.

Regina had been her high school classmate, and for forty-three years, until Regina's death in 1980, they loved and sustained each other. Lusia told me that Regina knew more about her than she did herself. In 1963, Regina developed a severe cardiac condition that turned her into an invalid, but her remarkable courage and her friends' devoted care enabled her to lead a meaningful life in the seventeen years that remained to her. The three of them, Regina, Natasha, and Zoya, lived together in an apartment on Pushkin Street: they were not blood relatives, but few families are as close. All three were retired and living on modest pensions. Their home attracted people of all ages for its warm, intellectual atmosphere, its companionship, and its generosity.

Zoya, the eldest, contributed kindness, patience, and practicality. A disciple of Samuil Marshak, she was working on an anthology of fairy tales with Natasha, who was the indispensable third element of the Pushkin Street triangle—decisive, energetic, and intelligent, with a lively interest in people, events, and ideas.

IN OCTOBER 1971 I succeeded in overcoming Lusia's doubts, and we decided to register our marriage. She feared this might precipitate reprisals against her children, while I believed that it would, in fact, make us less vulnerable. It is difficult to say who was right—there can be no "controlled experiments" in such affairs—but first Tanya, and then Alexei, came under attack following our marriage.

The official ceremony took place at a civil registry office on January 7, 1972.

27

POETS AND DISSIDENTS

The poets. A conversation with Tupolev.
The Lupynos case. Bukovsky's trial.
Trips to Kiev. New arrests. The dissidents.

LUSIA HAD MOVED in literary circles when she was young, and in the 1960s she renewed her contacts with poets and writers. In the fall of 1971, she took me to see Bulat Okudzhava. Actually, I had first met him three years earlier, while I was in Tbilisi for the conference on gravitation. During a dinner with colleagues, I'd had too much to drink (practically the only time in my life I've gotten tipsy), so later, when Okudzhava and his wife came to my hotel room, the conversation never really got going. This prior history added to my nervousness at the prospect of visiting someone for whom I had such high regard. I can hear my own life and times and feelings reflected in Okudzhava's songs; like most of our generation, Lusia shares this passion, and for my birthday in 1971, she gave me a marvelous collection of his lyrics, typewritten and bound in a handmade green cover. All his best songs were there, from the haunting "Ella" to the profound and brooding "Mozart."

This time, we got on splendidly, thanks to Lusia. Okudzhava wasn't feeling well when we arrived and had been resting in bed, but he was glad to see us. After this meeting, our lives took us along different paths. Lusia ran into Okudzhava by chance a couple of years later and asked how things were. He answered bitterly: "I'm doing fine. I've got lots of money. I'm going to buy a car."

Shortly before my exile to Gorky, we managed to see him give a brilliant performance of his songs, old and new.

That same fall, Lusia introduced me to David Samoilov, perhaps our finest poet in the classic mold, a direct heir to the nineteenth-century Russian tradition. In their large country house outside Moscow, he and his wife gave us a warm welcome, which clearly reflected their feelings for Lusia. Samoilov read some of his latest poems, but not without first asking me how much I could take. He read beautifully, and his voice sounded even better in that domestic setting than on the stage. Six months earlier, who could have imagined me in such company?

That year I also met Vladimir Maximov, who became a close and loyal friend. Maximov is a man of uncompromising integrity, high-strung, the product of a difficult life. Now he is an émigré and editor of the literary and political journal *Kontinent,* which, for all its shortcomings and occasional lapses, has been a publication of vital importance for us. Maximov was out of sorts at our first meeting. One thing he said then has remained in my mind: "You've got to take this country with you on the soles of your shoes."

Lusia and I visited Alexander Galich after he was expelled from the Writers Union in December 1971. It was the beginning of a new friendship for me and the resumption of an old one for Lusia, who had known him when he was working with Vsevolod Bagritsky on the play *The City at Dawn.* At home, Galich revealed his "hidden" side—he became gentler, simpler, sometimes a bit lost and unhappy. But his aristocratic elegance never deserted him. He and his wife, Angelina, lived alone in a house tastefully furnished with antiques, the fruits of his royalties as a popular filmwriter. Now he was selling his possessions to buy bare necessities. I noticed a beautiful pencil portrait of his wife, which hung beside a bust of Tsar Paul. When I asked Galich about this surprising choice of a partner for Angelina, he said: "You know, history's been unfair to Paul. He had some good ideas."

We became regular visitors to Galich's home, and he often stopped by our apartment on family occasions to entertain us with his wonderful songs. Once, as he paused between numbers, Yuri Shikhanovich asked him to sing "Polezhaev's Picture". Galich strummed his guitar and began: "The three ride, Polezhaev in the middle, a gendarme on either side." Galich's extraordinary voice filled Ruth's small room, and our time-frame shifted backward and forward: the tragic fates of the four Alexanders—Pushkin, Griboedov, Polezhaev and Galich—seemed to merge.[1] Soon after, in September 1972, Shikhanovich was arrested, and then in the summer of 1974, Galich emigrated; three years later he was dead.

The last time I spoke with Galich—October 9, 1975—was the day my Nobel prize was announced. His warm bass cut through the static of the international phone line. "My dear Andrei, we're all at Vladimir Maximov's, drinking your health and Lusia's. We're thrilled. . . ."

In 1975, when Lusia stepped off the train in Paris, the first person she saw

---

[1][Alexander Pushkin (1799–1837), Russia's greatest poet, was killed in a duel. Alexander Griboedov (1795–1829), famous for his comic play *Woe from Wit,* was murdered by an anti-Russian mob while serving as ambassador to Persia. Alexander Polezhaev (1805–1838) was sent by Tsar Nicholas I to serve as a private in the Russian army as punishment for his liberal poem *Sashka.*]

was Galich, elegant, holding a bunch of red roses. In 1977, he traveled to Italy to see Lusia, who was there for eye surgery. Tanya, Efrem, and their children had just emigrated, and were staying with Lusia. She later told me a touching story about Galich's meeting with our four-year-old grandson, Matvei. Galich invited the whole family to dinner at a restaurant, but Matvei refused to go. "You're not the *real* Galich!" he protested. (Matvei had not yet identified the man he saw before him with the recordings he had heard so often.)

"But I *am*!" Galich insisted; he fell to one knee, rested his guitar on the other, and began to sing: "I stand before boundless space . . ."

Matvei listened carefully for a few minutes before declaring: "Grandpa's a good singer *too.*" With that one sentence, Matvei accepted Galich and complimented me. He took Galich's hand and was ready to follow him anywhere.

A few weeks later Galich was dead. The Paris police report stated that he had bought a cheap television set in Italy and was eager to try it out. Returning to his apartment alone, without even taking off his coat, he plugged the antenna into the wrong outlet at the back of the set. The shock felled him, and he was dead by the time Angelina found him. An accident . . . And yet, I'm not entirely convinced that it wasn't murder. A year before his death, Galich's mother received an ominous New Year's greeting in the mail. Upset, she brought it to us. The envelope contained a page from a calendar with a single typewritten line: "The decision has been made to kill your son Alexander." We did what we could to calm her, telling her that they don't issue a warning when they're really serious. But in fact, this is just the sort of trick one can expect from the KGB.

BUT BACK TO 1972. Bukovsky's trial was approaching. (He had been ruled sane, despite our fears that the authorities might again commit him to a psychiatric prison.) I decided to ask the aircraft designer Andrei Tupolev to come with me to the trial. I reasoned that if *two* prominent academicians demonstrated open resistance to illegal repression (and once two did so, the majority might follow), this could have a positive affect not only on the outcome of Bukovsky's trial, but also on the overall situation in the country. I still believe that if Tupolev had agreed, something important might have been accomplished.

Bukovsky's fame in the USSR and abroad as a tireless, selfless human rights spokesman made his case opportune for my purpose. Why did I pick Tupolev? First, his name carried great weight, far more than mine did and almost on a par with Kurchatov's. Second, Tupolev had himself been arrested in 1937 and forced to stand for days on end during exhausting interrogations; his legs would remain swollen for the rest of his life. And I knew that Tupolev had behaved honorably while head of a *sharashka*. He insisted on decent conditions for all the specialists working there—among them Sergei Korolev, whom Tupolev rescued from common labor in a Kolyma camp, and the theoretical physicist Yuri Rumer. After the war, Tupolev became the director of a whole complex of plants and research institutes. He had close ties to the Party *apparat,* especially the departments concerned with defense, since a significant part of his enterprise was devoted to military production. One of his deputies, Vladimir Myasishchev, received a Lenin Prize at the same time I did, and another, Alexander Arkhangelsky, attended the 1955 test.

Igor Tamm, who had known Tupolev since the 1940s, told me that he was extremely wary about speaking out; but I decided it was worth a try.

About December 20, I drove out to Tupolev's dacha in an Academy car. Academicians have the right to request a car and chauffeur in connection with their professional work and dispatchers at the motor pool wink at the use of this privilege for personal errands so long as it isn't abused. From 1970 on I took considerable advantage of this convenience; it's true I may have stretched the rules a bit on this occasion. Tupolev, a widower, lived by himself in a large house surrounded by a high fence which shielded it from view (a groundskeeper opened the gate for me). We talked in his study. There was a model of the supersonic TU-144 on his desk, and the walls were decorated with photographs of planes Tupolev had designed, some taking off or in flight, others in the process of assembly. His bookcases were filled with scientific literature and reference books.

I stated the purpose of my visit as briefly and convincingly as I could. Tupolev listened attentively. He remained silent for a few moments, and then, with a sardonic grin, began asking questions in rapid-fire order, sometimes supplying his own answers. The thrust of his remarks was that he neither knew nor wanted to know Bukovsky—he could tell from what I'd said about him that he was an idler, and nothing in life is more important than work. He refused to attend Bukovsky's trial under any circumstances. Toward the end of our conversation, he suggested that I see a psychiatrist, since my ideas were a chaotic jumble. This was in retort to my observation that Soviet planes piloted by Arabs were committing genocide by bombing refugees in Nigeria. My clear implication was: It's time to think of your soul. He didn't go so far as to claim that Soviet judicial proceedings were the most just in the world; if he had, I could have reminded him that he himself had been falsely convicted for selling blueprints of his bomber to "feudal" Poland for one million zlotys. But that apparently no longer interested him. And so my initiative failed.

As I was leaving, Tupolev remarked fretfully: "You sat on my gloves and wrinkled them."

I could not resist replying that it's far easier to iron out wrinkled gloves than wrinkled souls.

A FEW DAYS after my meeting with Tupolev, I learned that the Ukrainian poet Anatoly Lupynos was about to go on trial in Kiev and might be sent to a psychiatric prison. Lusia and I went to the airport and, with the help of the Hero of Socialist Labor stamp in my passport, had no trouble getting tickets to Kiev. On arrival, Lusia and I were assigned rooms on different floors in the hotel; our marriage had not yet been registered, and Soviet hotel clerks are sticklers for propriety. The man behind us in the check-in line protested: surely an exception could be made for such a distinguished guest. Almost certainly he was our KGB tail and wanted to make it easier to keep track of us.

The next morning, I met Lusia on neutral ground in the hotel lobby, where we were joined by Ivan Svetlichny, a Ukrainian poet and literary critic whom I already knew, and by Leonid Plyushch. Svetlichny explained the situation on our way to court. Lupynos had been convicted in 1956 on charges of engaging in nationalist propaganda and had spent eleven years in a labor camp. He returned with his legs paralyzed; at first, he needed a wheelchair, but later he was able to get around on crutches. In the spring of 1971, he'd taken part in a poetry reading at the Shevchenko monument; one of his poems contained a line about the Ukrainian national flag being used as a cleaning rag. Someone reported this "nationalistic and anti-Soviet statement," and he'd been arrested.

To our amazement, everyone was allowed into the courtroom. But when a clerk finally appeared, it was only to announce that the judge was ill (although he'd been seen that morning) and the trial was postponed. Two weeks later, it opened with no advance notice, even to the defendant's father. Lupynos was sent to the Dnepropetrovsk special psychiatric hospital, one of the worst, where he remained for years—because of a single line of poetry!

RIGHT AFTER New Year's Day 1972, Lusia and I drove out to the dacha in Zhukovka that the government had given me in 1956. I had never spent much time there with Klava, since I was rarely in Moscow and neither of us was up to coping with the housekeeping problems. Now Lusia and I hoped to spend time with my son Dmitri (I wanted to repair our strained relations) and with Alexei, who was a year ahead of Dmitri in school. But a day or two later, our acquaintance Alexei Tumerman arrived with the news that Bukovsky's trial had been scheduled for January 5. We left for Moscow at once.

The trial was conducted in the same Lublino district courthouse where Krasnov-Levitin had been tried. But this time there was no curly-haired KGB escort to greet me; instead, the stairway to the second floor was blocked by "volunteer police" (in fact KGB agents), sporting red armbands and standing shoulder to shoulder. Insolent and sure of their power, they could easily have been taken for the SS men of countless war films. About sixty of "our people" had gathered on the first floor. Every so often I would walk over and ask to see the officer in charge. (We wanted representatives of our group admitted to the courtroom to see for themselves if there were any vacant seats.) "Are you a Soviet man, Academician Sakharov?" the KGB men shouted. This sort of direct challenge was something new.

Later, Bukovsky's relatives told us about the trial. The judge had asked one witness, a customs official who had been Bukovsky's friend: "Did you, as a communist, try to change the defendant's thinking?"

"Yes, of course I did."

"What did you say to him?"

"I told him you can't knock down a wall by banging your head against it."

In his final plea, Bukovsky proudly declared: "I will never renounce my convictions. . . . I will fight for law and justice. I only regret that during the brief period—one year, two months, and two days—when I was at liberty, I managed to accomplish all too little toward that end. But I am proud of what I did do."

He was sentenced to two years in prison, five years in labor camp, and five years internal exile. We were still waiting downstairs, hoping to catch a glimpse of him and wish him well. But suddenly someone shouted that he was already outside in a car. We surged toward the door, but the "volunteers" and regular police barred our way. Lusia gave one policeman a shove and yelled: "Get out of my way, you fascist!" Valery Chalidze later reproached her for behavior unbecoming the wife of an academician. But I did not.

Pyotr Yakir managed to reach Bukovsky's car and shout: "Well done, Vladimir!" A few hours earlier, Yakir had exclaimed with great candor: "Ten, twenty, thirty of these trials. I can't take it anymore! I couldn't face another sentence myself—I haven't the strength." The KGB, no doubt, pricked up its ears.

ON JANUARY 7, Lusia and I were married at our local civil registry office. The witnesses were Natasha Gesse and Andrei Tverdokhlebov. Tanya rushed in, breathless, at the very last moment. I had not informed my own children of the wedding. I'm not proud of the fact—such cowardice only makes life more difficult.

The KGB sent its own witnesses—half a dozen men in identical black suits. Normally, we don't even try to guess the KGB's motives since their values and goals are so different from ours. And anyway, why bother? But in this case, I'd venture a guess that they were demonstrating their disapproval.

THAT SAME EVENING, Lusia and I flew off to Kiev once again, this time to meet with Viktor Nekrasov, author of one of the best books about the war, *Front-line Stalingrad.*[2] We knew he'd corresponded about Bukovsky's case with the director of the Academy of Medicine's Institute of Psychiatry, Professor Andrei Snezhnevsky, who had invented the diagnosis of "creeping schizophrenia"—considered a highly dubious concept by persons better qualified to judge than I am. We were hoping that the letters might be useful in the campaign to defend Bukovsky.

There was perhaps something symbolic about our beginning our official married life in this way. For many years to come, hundreds of similar errands would oblige us to rush off somewhere, to sit up typing until four in the morning, to argue with some official until we became hoarse. But I don't want to make these difficulties sound overly tragic; we managed this part of our life without too much strain.

Nekrasov gave us a warm welcome, and the next morning treated us to a guided tour of his beloved Kiev. Unfortunately, he was unwilling to make public his correspondence with Snezhnevsky, since he considered it to be of a private nature.

That evening, Semyon Gluzman, who had written the anonymous psychiatric report on Grigorenko, saw us off at the station. He impressed us as an exceptionally honest, altruistic person. Although he was still working in a psychiatric clinic, clouds were gathering over his head. In May, he was arrested and sentenced to seven years labor camp and three years internal exile. While in camp, he inevitably got involved in the political prisoners' bitter struggle for their rights and their human dignity—hunger strikes and punishment cells followed one another in quick succession. Gluzman and Bukovsky collaborated on the article "A Dissident's Guide to Psychiatry," which they smuggled out of the camp.[3] In 1979, Lusia visited Gluzman when he was in exile near Tyumen, and later, Alexei's fiancée, Liza, went to see him as well. They reported that he had matured and become stronger, tougher. But the essential goodness remained.

* * *

[2][Harvill Press, 1962.]
[3][In *Survey* (Winter/Spring 1975), pp. 179–198, with an introduction by Nekrasov.]

BACK IN JANUARY 1971 Lusia's status as a disabled war veteran had enabled her to join a building cooperative sponsored by the Moscow military commissariat. With the help of friends, she'd gathered together the money to buy an "inexpensive" apartment. The building was completed quickly by our standards, and in January 1972, Tanya and Efrem moved in. Lusia had been preoccupied with the question of housing since December 1970, and it complicated the problem further when I moved into Ruth's apartment. Tanya and Efrem gave their room to us and slept on a couch in the kitchen; during the day, they had no place they could call their own. Ruth was sharing her room with Alexei.

To help Tanya and Efrem move and to repaint our apartment, Lusia invited over a team of "dissidents." (I've never cared for this term, but it's entered into common usage.) Relations in the dissidents' world were as yet untroubled, or so it seems at least in retrospect. Most still held regular jobs, which provided them with regular though modest incomes. To raise money for the children of political prisoners, they did odd jobs for friends on Saturdays and Sundays. Many donated blood, thereby earning days off, which they spent standing outside courtrooms. It never occurred to them to separate themselves into categories such as "Christians" or "Zionists" or "human rights activists." Those divisions emerged later, and "professional dissidents" had not yet appeared on the scene. I don't use this term as a reproach: it was the authorities who, by firing some dissenters, driving others into emigration, and stripping ex-convicts of all their rights, gave birth to the phenomenon of the "professional dissident."

I remember the dissident world of the early 1970s as young in spirit and pure of heart. Standing outside one courthouse, Tatyana Velikanova said to me with pride: "They must sense our moral force." Eight or nine years later, the same Velikanova exclaimed on the eve of her arrest: "How did all this filth creep in?" This was said in reaction to one particular ugly incident, but the sentiment expressed was plainly more general in tenor.

I don't want to be too critical of the dissident movement as it exists now [1982]; many participants are in detention or have been subjected to serious persecution. The proportion of decent, intelligent, and self-sacrificing dissidents, both veterans and new recruits, is probably no different than it ever was. It's simply that things have become more difficult in a number of ways. And what family doesn't have its black sheep?

By 1972 the fundamental goals, principles, and methods of human rights activity were clearly defined. The *Chronicle of Current Events* had been appearing quite regularly in samizdat since 1968. Its motto was Article 19 of the Universal Declaration of Human Rights: "Everyone has the right to freedom of opinion and expression; this right includes freedom to hold opinions without interference and to seek, receive and impart information and ideas through any media and regardless of frontiers."

The *Chronicle* avoided editorial judgments, concentrating on factual information concerning human rights violations in the USSR. Although the editors were working under exceptionally difficult conditions, they tried to be as accurate and objective as possible; errors were corrected in subsequent issues. It was essential for a journal of this sort to avoid anything that could be regarded as slander or subversion—and the *Chronicle* did in fact avoid such material. Nevertheless, its allegedly libelous character was used as a pretext to mete out exceptionally harsh penalties to anyone even remotely connected with its publication. Nothing frightened our security agencies more than those tattered, typescript bulletins—which only goes to prove the *Chronicle*'s significance and force. It was the clearest and most important expression of our human rights struggle and our only weapon—*glasnost*. The existence of the *Chronicle* for fifteen years was a miracle! The editors were anonymous, but it is now safe to honor the contributions of Natalya Gorbanevskaya, who now lives in Paris; Tatyana Khodorovich, also living in France; Anatoly Yakobson, who died in 1978 after emigrating to Israel; and three who served long terms of imprisonment for their work on the *Chronicle*: Sergei Kovalev, Tatyana Velikanova, and Yuri Shikhanovich.

I've already written about the major roles in the human rights movement played by the Initiative Group for the Defense of Human Rights in the USSR and the Human Rights Committee.

The two days spent refurbishing our apartment in January 1972 effected a reunion of the dissident world. Yuri Shikhanovich was the guiding spirit of the work. Since the cooperative building's elevator wasn't yet in service, Vladimir Gershovich, a refusenik nicknamed "the Jewish Hercules," performed a prodigious feat of strength, carrying a refrigerator up seven flights of stairs on his shoulders. Lusia cooked a roast and boiled potatoes for the weary workmen, who fortified themselves with vodka.

Right after the crew left, we got the alarming news that searches were in progress in Moscow. On January 15, Cronid Lubarsky's home was searched, and on January 17 he was summoned for questioning, and then formally arrested. A new, more trying period was in store for dissidents.

Rumors spread that a high-level decision had been taken in late 1971 to stamp out the *Chronicle* and other expressions of dissent. Whether this was true or not, 1972 certainly did bring a wave of political repression. It was especially harsh in the Ukraine, where Vyacheslav Chornovil, Leonid Plyushch, Daniil Shumuk, Irina Stasiv-Kalynets, and Ivan Svetlichny were arrested in January, Ivan Dzyuba in April, and Semyon Gluzman in May. In Moscow, Pyotr Yakir was arrested in June and Viktor Krasin and Yuri Shikhanovich in September.

28

THE YAKIR-KRASIN CASE

Central Asia and Baku. Appeals on amnesty
and capital punishment. The Memorandum
and Postscript. A meeting with Slavsky. The
Yakir-Krasin case.

TOWARD THE END of March, Lusia and I decided to take a belated honeymoon in Central Asia, where it was already spring. Schools were on vacation, and we asked Dmitri and Alexei to come along. Dmitri, however, refused, owing in part to his sisters' influence.

Lusia, Alexei, and I traveled first to Bukhara. Its squares, bazaars, reflecting pools, alleyways, minarets, and fabulous mosques give it a medieval, Asiatic appearance, and the mausoleum of Ismail the Samanid is one of the architectural wonders of the world. Next we visited Samarkand, a city where several magnificent buildings built by Tamerlane and his successors still stand, and finally we flew over the massive Pamir range to Dushanbe. We spoke there with relatives and the defense counsel of Anatoly Nazarov, who had been sentenced in February 1972 to three years in labor camp for mailing a copy of my *Reflections* to a friend. But our meeting proved counterproductive: very likely because of it, Nazarov was moved from a camp in the vicinity of Dushanbe to one several hundred miles away. After his release, he sent us an invitation to his wedding, but perhaps it was just as well for him that we weren't able to attend.

The area around Dushanbe is known for its spectacular canyons. In the course of our sightseeing, we discovered that some of the most beautiful ones are blocked by fences, with downward-pointing spikes to keep venturesome boys away from the luxurious dachas of the local bigwigs, our modern princelings. Social distinctions are more evident in the various national republics than in Russia proper, where they exist, to be sure, but are better camouflaged.

A month after our return, I was invited to a conference in Baku conducted by the nuclear physics department of the Academy of Sciences. It became almost an extension of our trip to Central Asia. Lusia and I took the traditional excursion to the temple of the fire-worshippers. We also saw recently discovered rock drawings: the dancing figures and animals, realistic and remarkably expressive, probably had magical significance since they were close to the place where in prehistoric times wild beasts had been driven over a precipice to their death. Nearby there was a primitive musical instrument, a stone five yards long supported by three chiseled pillars, which emitted a pleasing tone when struck; stone benches had been arranged in a semicircle to provide seating for the audience. My heart was in my mouth as Lusia climbed up a rock overhang; I cried out for her to stop when she was just inches short of a twenty-yard drop.

On the conference's final day, local science officials arranged an open-air banquet in the botanical gardens for their "honored guests." Fine wine straight from the barrel was accompanied by elaborate Oriental toasts; an outing to the shores of the foam-lashed Caspian Sea followed, along with a taste of the wild local driving.

At the banquet, Lusia unexpectedly caught sight of her foster brother, Andrei Amatuni, whom Ruth had nursed together with Lusia's brother Igor. After Amatuni's father's arrest and death in 1937, the Bonner family had lost touch with Andrei, who had become a theoretical physicist and successful scientific administrator. Later, in Erevan, he invited us to visit him, but he was wary of public contacts with us and didn't dare see us in Moscow.

I HAD BEGUN a new campaign even before our trip to Baku. Tatyana Litvinova (daughter of the former foreign minister, and Chalidze's mother-in-law) suggested an appeal to the Presidium of the Supreme Soviet calling for an amnesty of political prisoners and the abolition of capital punishment on the occasion (December 1972) of the fiftieth anniversary of the USSR's founding. I liked her idea very much, and drafted two separate appeals, since some individuals might be willing to sign one but not the other.

We began a campaign to collect signatures. Sometimes I went by myself, but more often Lusia accompanied me. Dissidents presented very few problems, although Solzhenitsyn turned me down on the grounds that signing might interfere with his responsibilities as an author, a position I considered mistaken. Chalidze unexpectedly balked out of concern that his name would appear alongside those of people he didn't care for. (This was the first of the misunderstandings that periodically put a strain on our relationship.) In the end, however, he signed both appeals. So many prospective emigrants were ready to sign that we felt compelled to limit their number.

I wanted to collect the signatures of prominent scientists, writers, artists, physicians, and other figures whose voices carried weight and who shared the humanitarian goals of the two petitions without being overt dissidents or opponents of the regime. I soon lost any illusions I'd harbored. The days of the 1967 campaign, when more than a thousand persons might sign a petition, were over. Many had lent their names back then because it was fashionable and it cost them nothing. Now, times had changed. I had been turned down by several of my fellow physicists in Baku. One academician went into a panic: "What's the matter with you? Even if the authorities wanted to amnesty political prisoners, they'd be insulted by a collective letter like this and change their minds!"

Pyotr Kapitsa objected: "There are more important things than a few political prisoners. Mankind is facing major challenges. The gravest danger is the demographic explosion, the continuing population increases in the developing countries—*that* threatens millions with death by starvation."

Alexander Imshenetsky was more candid: "Don't try to involve me in anti-Soviet schemes. The Soviet system's been good to me; it's sent me abroad thirty-six times."[1] (This comment may actually have been made on another occasion, but its significance remains the same.)

No one whom I approached would really have been risking arrest or dismissal or even demotion for signing the appeal, but a new psychology was at play, and people were concerned with protecting newly acquired luxuries such as, in Imshenetsky's case, travel abroad. Life is never simple, of course, and many who refused to sign had seemingly persuasive reasons. A journalist didn't want to jeopardize her regular column defending justice and human dignity. An academician was busy preserving relics of the past from the onslaught of the *nouveaux riches*. Another feared that an incautious step might harm his scientific career.

Liza Drabkina, once Yakov Sverdlov's secretary, had spent half her life in the camps, and she feared that signing might affect her chances of passing on the fruits of hard-earned knowledge to the next generation. Her refusal gained her nothing. It was Liza who had declared that Lusia "belongs to us all," and who had given us a photograph with the inscription: "I'm the fool standing next to Lenin." Her husband had cried out on his deathbed: "Give us back our revolution!" What would he have done the second time around? I hesitate to guess.

Once, during a meeting with young people, someone shouted at Drabkina: "You got burned by the fire you lit." Her bitter retort (apt if not entirely accurate): "We lit the fire—but *you* got burned." History plays terrible tricks.

In pursuit of signatures, Lusia and I traveled to Komarovo, a dacha colony for writers and scientists not far from Leningrad. There, the late mathemati-

---

[1][In 1975, Imshenetsky signed the statement of Soviet academicians condemning the award of the Nobel Peace Prize to Sakharov.]

cian Vladimir Smirnov received us warmly, offered us something to eat (he was the only one in Komarovo to do so), and told us stories about the Red terror he had witnessed as a young man in the Crimea. After visiting several more dachas, we took a break, walking through the forest and down to the sea, oblivious to any surveillance. Lusia and I rarely bother to worry whether we're being tailed—if they want to waste public funds, let them. On this occasion, however, we subsequently learned that KGB agents had followed close on our heels, inquiring what Sakharov had been up to in Komarovo.

We submitted our petitions to the Presidium of the Supreme Soviet several weeks before the anniversary celebration. The official reaction was, so far as we could tell, nil. Despite this, and the disappointing number of signatures, I still believe the campaign was worthwhile. I gave copies of the appeals to foreign correspondents, and the reports broadcast by Western radio stations gave people food for thought.[2]

BY JUNE 1972 I felt the time had come to publish my Memorandum. I updated it by adding a postscript, but I failed to make clear that my fears about a possible Chinese threat to our national security had abated. (I was not alone in my earlier concern: Amalrik (in *Will the Soviet Union Survive Until 1984?*) and Solzhenitsyn (in his *Letter to the Soviet Leaders*) expressed similar sentiments.) I had come to believe that it would take several decades before China, handicapped by a backward economy and military technology and preoccupied with domestic difficulties, would be in any condition to attack the USSR.

Sino-Soviet rivalry in the developing countries and Southeast Asia is essentially a by-product of various undesirable aspects of the international scene—in particular, Soviet expansionism and East-West confrontation—and, in my considered opinion, can be peacefully resolved through patience and compromise. Our territorial disputes with China can be settled through negotiations and minor concessions. What should cause the most concern is the potential consequences of Soviet expansionism. Much as I dislike saying so, an irrational move by Soviet hawks might trigger a *preventive* war. (True, this would require substantial changes in both our domestic circumstances and the international situation.) The Chinese threat has been vastly exaggerated by Soviet propaganda. I am convinced that normal relations with China can be established, given a favorable development of the world situation, and this, in turn, very much depends on the actions of the USSR.

---

[2][The texts of the petitions on an amnesty and the abolition of the death penalty are contained in *Sakharov Speaks*, pp. 239–240. Each was signed by more than fifty people.]

In the last few years we have begun to hear reports of a dissident movement in China and its suppression by the regime. I admire our Chinese counterparts, and I have a deep respect for them, and for the Chinese people as a whole. I hope that these comments clarify my views on our relations with China.

PYOTR YAKIR—about whom I'd heard a great deal, although I scarcely knew him personally—was arrested in June 1972. He was the son of Iona Yakir, a famous Civil War commander. In 1937, Iona Yakir was executed and his wife and their son Pyotr, then fourteen, were arrested. After seventeen years spent in various forms of detention, mother and son were released in 1954. Her official rehabilitation seemed to confer some degree of immunity on Pyotr, who managed to evade arrest until after her death.[3]

Pyotr's father had been a close friend of Efim Slavsky, my former boss. They had served together in the First Cavalry during the Civil War, and it was rumored that Yakir had asked Slavsky to look after his son (although Slavsky, in fact, had done nothing to save Pyotr in 1937). In any case, I decided to appeal to Slavsky, who was, after all, a member of the Central Committee and a Minister. I phoned him, and he agreed to see me.

It was an odd experience entering the Ministry's thirteen-story building, where no noticeable changes had been made since my last visit four years before: there were the same people with the same anxious expressions, the same long corridors, even the same carpets. While waiting for my appointment, I examined a model of the town of Navoi in Central Asia, one of many the Ministry had built, first using convict labor and then army construction battalions.

My conversation with Slavsky was brief. I explained the gist of the matter, said something about the general human rights situation, and recalled that Yakir's father had been his friend. Slavsky refused to get involved: "Since you're so concerned about this person I don't know at all, I must presume he's as anti-Soviet as you are."

Despite this rebuff, I raised another matter with Slavsky, involving V. Bogdanov, a worker employed at one of the Ministry's plants near Moscow. Driven to despair by delays in getting an apartment, Bogdanov had burst into Slavsky's office and demanded help. Slavsky had him ejected. (I only learned this part of the story a few years later.) Returning to the plant, Bogdanov stole a secret part and hid it, promising to return it in exchange for an apartment. After a few days, he gave up and handed back the part. (I have been told that

[3][See Pyotr Yakir, *A Childhood in Prison* (Macmillan, 1972).]

the item in question was a cadmium control rod of the type used in nuclear reactors. If so, such rods are on display at the Exhibition of Economic Achievements in Moscow, and no secrets at all were involved in Bogdanov's case.) But the KGB didn't forget the trouble he'd caused. A couple of weeks later, he was asked for a light by some strangers who approached him on the street. He duly obliged—and before he'd reached the end of the block, he was arrested. Bogdanov was tried in 1968 by a "special court" and sentenced to ten years for treason: the prosecution maintained that the people to whom he'd given the light were Argentine intelligence agents (!) to whom he'd been attempting to pass information.

Cases involving security matters are tried by these "special courts," which are separately staffed and sit in closed session. The existence of the special courts is not acknowledged in Soviet legislation or in the press, and there is good reason for this reticence—these tribunals flagrantly violate a defendant's rights to public trial, an effective defense, and equal protection before the law.

Slavsky made a note of Bogdanov's name and promised to check on the case. So far as I know, he did nothing, and Bogdanov served his full term.

This was the last time I met with Slavsky. By the time I returned home—I had been gone for several hours—Lusia was frantic, certain that I'd been arrested at the Ministry.

THE TRIAL OF Pyotr Yakir and his "accomplice" Viktor Krasin opened on August 27, 1973. Late in 1972, we'd heard that they were cooperating with the prosecution, had "repented" of their actions, and were trying to persuade their comrades to give up their "anti-Soviet activity," which they claimed simply made matters worse and created new victims. According to these reports, they insisted that the human rights movement was focusing on petty, secondary issues and urged the immediate suspension of the *Chronicle of Current Events*, warning that each new issue would result in the arrest of additional dissidents, not necessarily those directly linked to the *Chronicle*.

Yakir and Krasin were trotted out on several occasions to confront dissidents under interrogation. It was clear that they were KGB hostages mouthing whatever they were told, but foreign correspondents to whom we tried to explain this either didn't understand or were overcautious; whatever the reason, nothing we told them at the time appeared in print. Soviet citizens who believe that the "capitalist press" hungers after "anti-Soviet sensation" would be surprised if they knew how often Western media ignore the faults of the socialist countries while enthusiastically exposing the shortcomings of their own nations (the latter is not a bad thing in itself, but some sense of proportion is needed).

In early 1973, an embarrassed KGB lieutenant came to my apartment to deliver a letter from Yakir, then in Lefortovo Prison. It was written as if we were old friends, and argued that my actions, far from helping anyone, were causing nothing but harm.

At their trial (family members were admitted, but the general public was barred), Yakir and Krasin condemned themselves as vehemently as did the prosecutor, Assistant Procurator General Pyotr Solonin. On September 5, four days after the trial ended, Yakir and Krasin spoke at a televised press conference, emphasizing their contacts with the notorious NTS.[4] Their sentences were comparatively light: they were sent into exile not very far from Moscow, Yakir to Ryazan and Krasin to Kalinin. A year later, in September 1974, they were pardoned. Yakir returned to Moscow, where he died in November 1982. Krasin emigrated and now lives in America.

During his period of exile in Ryazan, Yakir phoned and asked me to come see him, claiming he had something of importance to tell me. I refused, and that was the end of it.

The KGB's hopes in this case were not fully realized, since the press campaign against Solzhenitsyn and myself and the vigorous response it provoked in the West diverted attention from the Yakir-Krasin trial. Nevertheless, the trial did create an air of gloom, and their "confessions" had a distressing effect on us all.

What happened to Yakir and Krasin? A pretrial investigation is a terrible ordeal for a prisoner. For months on end, he is kept from meeting with anyone, even his family. He is not allowed a lawyer. He talks only to his investigator, usually a skillful professional "inquisitor" who holds all the cards. The prisoner has no independent source of information. He is worried about his own fate and about his family. It should come as no surprise when the investigator successfully exploits a weakness in the defendant's personality or story. The miracle is that so many people do behave with dignity and integrity during their investigation and trial, and in labor camp. We should not condemn those who fail to withstand the pressure.

Yakir and Krasin were both former prisoners. They probably assumed that comrades would understand and forgive their actions as a tactical maneuver in the face of mortal danger. Yakir had become dependent on alcohol, and the investigators must certainly have played on this and tortured him by depriving him of drink. That was probably too much for a man who was already coming apart at the seams. I remembered Yakir's desperate words at Bukovsky's trial, when he admitted his fear of imprisonment.

[4][The acronym for the Popular Labor Alliance, a Russian émigré organization founded in 1930 and now based in Frankfurt.]

While still at liberty, he had given correspondents a statement to be published in the event of his arrest. In it, he declared that any confession or repentance wrung from him while in jail should be dismissed as bogus. It may not have been wise to thus predict his own capitulation, but we should take his testament into account.

29

ARRESTS AND TRIALS

The arrest of Shikhanovich. Demonstration
at the Lebanese embassy. Georgia and
Armenia. Tanya is expelled from Moscow
University. Lubarsky's trial. Lusia leaves the
Party.

LUSIA TRAVELED in September to Eduard Kuznetsov's camp, but she returned without having seen him—permission for the visit had been canceled.
It's always a disastrous moment when this occurs; the prisoner's allotted quota
of visits, small enough already, is reduced regardless of whether the cancellation
was for reasons of punishment or due to administrative necessity (quarantine,
relocation of the visiting area). A visit lost is gone for good. The majority of
cancellations are intended as punitive measures, their causes ranging from the
prisoner's solitary confinement, a hunger strike, or (most common) failure to
fulfill a work quota. Or it may just be official whim.

While Lusia was away, our friend Yuri Shikhanovich was arrested. I'd first
met him at Chalidze's. Someone had remarked that Revolt Pimenov considered himself a mathematician of genius, and in an attempt to cut through the
embarrassing silence that followed, I'd joked that "all mathematicians consider
themselves geniuses"—whereupon Shikhanovich got up and declared in a stage
whisper: "I consider myself a genius—of a teacher." But his opportunities to
apply that genius had been curtailed.

He had been dismissed from Moscow University for signing an appeal in
behalf of his friend and colleague, Alexander Esenin-Volpin, a poet, a specialist
in mathematical logic, and one of the earliest dissidents. Volpin had been
forcibly confined in a psychiatric hospital in February 1968. More than ninety
colleagues signed an appeal asking that he be allowed to resume his scientific
work (they didn't go so far as to ask for his release). Despite its mild tone, the
letter provoked the anxious authorities to reprisals. Mstislav Keldysh, president
of the Academy, spent four hours bullying his brother-in-law, Academician
Pyotr Novikov, head of the Academy's department of logic, into retracting his
signature. Novikov, feeling wretched and humiliated, returned home and suf-

fered a severe heart attack. Volpin was quietly released in May, but by then Shikhanovich had already been dismissed.

Shikhanovich is a shining example of the "classic" dissident. For many years, he has aided political prisoners and their families, writing innumerable letters and traveling to remote settlements with gifts of food and clothing for exiles. In 1971, he traveled to the Tyumen region with Lusia to see Boris Vail, and he helped Lusia when she visited Moscow during the first years of my exile in Gorky.[1]

Shikhanovich intensely dislikes unsubstantiated denunciations. He always demands proof, and if none exists, he insists on a presumption of innocence. He has his eccentricities, albeit very human ones; for example, he's a fanatic about celebrating all dissidents' birthdays. The dissident world relies on his judgments of films—even in Gorky, Lusia and I followed his recommendations and went to see *Don't Shoot the White Swans*, a bitter portrait of a disappearing Russian landscape and, still more, a disappearing people.

The day of Shikhanovich's arrest, I had a call that a search was on at his apartment. Tanya and I and headed straight there by taxi (Efrem was in the hospital) but found our entry barred. The KGB had already toted away sacks of confiscated literature. Soon, a remarkably calm Shikhanovich was led out. Tanya managed to give him a kiss. "Well—so long," he said, as he was bundled into the KGB's black Volga with its unmarked plate (why do they bother with such charades?). His dog, Jean, a white stray he'd acquired off the street a few months earlier, chased the car for several blocks, barking wildly: his instincts told him his master, to whom he'd become terribly attached, was in trouble. Jean returned and curled up woebegone, in a corner. Newspapers around the world carried a shot of Yuri and his dog Jean.

Lusia and I wrote to the procurator's office offering our personal surety for Yuri's appearance in court. (The Soviet Code of Criminal Procedure permits release pending a trial on the assurance of a minimum of two guarantors that the defendant will appear when called.) After six months with no response, a summons came from Shikhanovich's investigator, Galkin. Lusia and I went together, to KGB headquarters, but Galkin held to the letter of the summons, which had been addressed to me, and refused to allow Lusia to participate in our conversation. He took me into his office and stated at once that our offer of surety could not be accepted: we weren't "trustworthy." He backed this up with a copy of the émigré journal *Grani*, which he waved at me, claiming it contained statements and articles I'd written. There was no point in arguing with him. And so ended my first official encounter with the KGB.

I phoned the *New York Times* correspondent Hedrick Smith as soon as I

---

[1] [Shikhanovich was arrested again in November 1983 and subsequently sentenced to five years labor camp and five years exile for editing the *Chronicle*. He was pardoned in 1987.]

returned home. The Western press quickly picked up the case, and French mathematicians in particular were active in their colleague's behalf. All this attention impeded the authorities from exploiting the psychiatric approach any further, and so, as a kind of compromise, Shikhanovich was sent to a regular psychiatric hospital rather than a prison one, where the concern was chiefly to isolate him; he was spared any "treatment." Shikhanovich was freed in July 1974, and it has occurred to me more than once that the photograph with his dog played a role in his relatively prompt release—it provided graphic evidence of his normalcy.

IN 1972, the massacre of Israeli athletes at the Munich Olympics shocked the world. The Palestinian terrorists' aim may have been to publicize their people's tragic plight and punish the Zionists whom they held responsible, but the attack also appeared to act as a springboard for a concerted terrorist campaign to destroy the capitalist world order planned and carried out by certain secret services. (I have no direct proof of this, and only the future will tell if it is true.)

I condemn terrorism on principle. I condemn it as cruel and destructive, regardless of what ends are used to justify it. I decry the 1948 assault on the civilian population of the Palestinian village of Deir Yassin just as I do the Munich massacre.

Following the Munich tragedy, the Israeli government announced that it would retaliate against terrorist acts aimed at its citizens; the bombing of Palestinian camps in southern Lebanon that ensued has claimed many victims, including innocent civilians. But acts of terrorism go on. According to radio reports, 1,300 Israelis were killed in the decade between 1972 and 1982, while an even greater number of Palestinians (who were used as shields by the PLO leaders) perished as a result of retaliatory bombing. As I write this, Israel is embarked on a military offensive to wipe out the PLO's fighting arm in Lebanon. More soldiers and civilians are dying; the death toll in Lebanon alone added more than 100,000 casualties to the toll. And yet, despite everything, I still cling to the hope that a peaceful settlement may come—in time.

Let me say a few words about my attitude toward the Palestinian issue as a whole. I subscribe to the proposition that every people has the right to its own territory—Palestinians, Israelis, and Crimean Tatars as well. Ever since the 1940s, however, the Palestinians have been subject to manipulation and political intrigue by outside forces. The refugees could long since have been resettled in the wealthier Arab countries and given land and equipment, money and education, instead of being left exposed to retaliation for senseless acts of terrorism.

In the future, various means may be found to bring about a peaceful settlement and to secure Palestinian autonomy, but Israel cannot allow an entity dependent on the USSR to exist within or alongside its borders. The only firm foundation for resolution of the Palestinian problem is unconditional recognition of Israel, rejection of terrorism, and guarantees of independence from outside influences.

Israel and the Palestinians should demonstrate their will to negotiate and resolve their differences. They have to stop exchanging insults—"terrorists," "Zionists" (although the latter is not, strictly speaking, an insult)—and military strikes.

[I hope that the current changes in the USSR's domestic and foreign policies will be conducive to peace in the Middle East. In the future, it may well be possible to secure the guarantees of non-interference by the USSR and its allies necessary to alleviate Israel's fears—A.S. 1988.]

When the first reports of the murder of Israeli athletes came through, Jews in Moscow decided to conduct a silent protest in front of the Lebanese Embassy. I decided to go. Lusia was ill, but Tanya, Efrem, Alexei, and I drove there together, only to find that the KGB had rounded up the demonstrators and carted them off to a drunk tank. We were picked up along with them, and arrived at the sobering-up station to find several rooms packed with demonstrators and no drunks in sight. We were processed one by one and within a few hours were released. When my turn came, I omitted any mention of the children in the hope that they'd be spared any special attention. (It had been a mistake to let them come with me.) But the incident gave the KGB grounds to move against them, beginning with Tanya.

I WAS INVITED to an Erevan conference on gravitation theory at the Armenian mountain resort of Tsakhkadzor. Lusia and I stopped en route for several delightful days in Georgia. During the conference, Lusia would go for walks in the wooded hills while I attended the very interesting scientific sessions, and we'd meet up afterward. Lusia introduced me to Armenia's quasi-Biblical landscapes and architecture, to Echmiadzin and Lake Sevan, the ancient ruined temple of Garni, underground stone carvings at Gegmard, and the stunning monument to the victims of the 1915 genocide. She showed me the balcony in Erevan from which her father had proclaimed the Red victory, and the modest reference to him in the Erevan history museum. We met with Karo Kazarian, her father's comrade-in-arms, who shared his recollections of the defense of the Semyonov pass against the Dashnaks, and we saw the pass itself. We also saw a sizable housing development that had been built for Armenians who had returned to their homeland after the Red victory. Many had become disenchanted and departed, leaving their houses vacant.

While in Erevan, we learned that Tanya had been expelled from the Moscow University night school, where she was a journalism student. Her dismissal notice was posted on October 16, a month after the demonstration at the Lebanese Embassy. We immediately flew back to Moscow.

Tanya, who was in her senior year at the university, had completed her course work and had only to write and defend a dissertation. Serious grounds are required to justify the exclusion of a student at that stage. The first reason cited for expulsion, "not employed," was later refined to "not suitably employed": night school students were supposed to hold jobs in their field of specialization, and while Tanya was working as a junior editor on *Quantum*, a first-rate popular physics and mathematics journal for schoolchildren, her name didn't appear on the masthead since she was substituting for an employee on maternity leave. It was obvious that the decision to expel her had been made first and a pretext sought afterward. Tanya had no recourse. She looked for employment elsewhere, and by late October, was working as a salesclerk in a bookstore on the first floor of our building.

We could see that the children—Tanya, Alexei, and Efrem, and, later, Alexei's wife and the grandchildren—had become hostages to my public activity. Their access to education and jobs would be restricted or blocked entirely. Threats of arrest, imprisonment, physical violence, and even murder were a genuine menace, not paranoid delusions, as subsequent events proved. Eventually, after exhausting all the plausible alternatives, we were forced to acknowledge that the children would have to emigrate. It was a difficult and tragic decision.

ON October 26, the trial of Cronid Lubarsky, an astrophysicist charged with distributing the *Chronicle of Current Events*, began.

His fellow astrophysicist Iosif Shklovsky, a corresponding member of the Academy of Sciences whom Lusia and I both knew well, wrote a character reference for Lubarsky, and suffered only a temporary curtailment of his foreign travel. But two or three other scientists whom we approached on Lubarsky's behalf turned us down.

Lubarsky's trial, held in Noginsk, a town near Moscow, was a typical dissident trial, even more crudely staged than Bukovsky's. Only next of kin were allowed into the courtroom and the adjoining corridor. When a dozen of us slipped past the "volunteer police," we found ourselves shoved back outside by a wedge of KGB agents. Arms—including mine—were twisted; some people were trampled. Lusia marched up to the senior KGB officer, who was commanding from the sidelines, and slapped his face, shouting at him. He didn't so much as flinch. During the lunch break the door was padlocked: a fine symbol, indeed, of this travesty of an "open" trial. Lubarsky was sentenced to five years labor camp.

When Lusia and I returned home from the trial, agitated and exhausted, we found *Newsweek* correspondent Jay Axelbank waiting to interview us.[2] I wanted to talk about the trial, but Axelbank had some questions about myself and my views, which I answered. It was the first interview with me published in the Western press, and at the time I was very upset by its failure to give proper emphasis to the Lubarsky case, and by certain inaccuracies. Now, however, having become more accustomed to the workings of the Western press, I realize that Axelbank didn't do all that bad a job. At any rate, we remained on friendly terms with him while he was in Moscow.

On November 9, Lusia was summoned to appear before the Moscow Party Committee. She prepared a statement asking to be removed from the ranks of the Communist Party "because of my beliefs and my numerous violations of Party discipline."

She had resigned from the medical school's staff in March 1972; assignments had been hard to come by after our marriage, and retirement at fifty is an option available to disabled female veterans of World War II. Despite this severance of ties, the medical school's Party secretary was summoned to attend the meeting as well.

The two of them were called in promptly upon arrival and told that the committee had received information that Comrade Bonner had committed acts of "hooliganism" in the vicinity of the Noginsk courthouse and had struck an officer of the state security organs. Could she explain such behavior, which raised doubts about her continued membership in the Party? The threat of expulsion was meant to intimidate her into "recanting" or "promising to behave" in the future; instead, Lusia placed her prepared statement and her Party card on the table. It was an enormously effective stroke. It showed that pressure would not work on her and—even more shocking to them—that she was perfectly prepared to give up membership in the almighty Party.

The medical school Party secretary, who was well disposed toward Lusia, whispered: "What are you doing? Think of your children!"

"Stay out of it," Lusia responded. "What's this got to do with the children?"

The secretary had spoken out of spontaneous and genuine concern, and it was neither the first nor the last time we observed that ordinary people held the Soviet system in even lower regard than most dissidents, who still preserved a few illusions.

Lusia went on the offensive: "You've just confirmed that the KGB was acting illegally—the people at the courthouse didn't identify themselves."

A committee member tried to regain the initiative: "Why are you so hostile to the Soviet system? It's given you everything, an education, interesting work."

2[*Newsweek*, November 8, 1972, p. 13.]

"No one *gave* me anything. I fought in the war, nearly lost my sight, I worked night and day."

A KGB type said: "You don't tell the truth, and it's all because you're so bitter. You keep on saying your father was executed, and it just isn't so."

Was he deliberately lying, or did he know something Lusia didn't? It's not clear. His comment undoubtedly was intended to throw her off balance and confuse her, to draw her into a discussion. Despite inner turmoil, she remained silent.

The KGB man concluded the interview: "We will report your case to the commission."

"Goodbye," Lusia replied and walked out. Her Party card remained on the table. She heard nothing further about the matter, and she never asked. Party rules provide that a member can be expelled only by a general meeting of his or her own primary Party organization, and the expulsion must then be confirmed by the district committee. The individual in question has the right to appeal the decision to a Party control commission. It is unlikely that Lusia's case was discussed at the medical school. One way or another, however, Lusia had broken with the Party for good, and she was no longer concerned as to whether or not they observed their own rules.

30

FAMILY AFFAIRS

Meetings with Petrovsky. Chalidze emigrates.
Chakovsky's article. Interview with Olle
Stenholm. Kornilov's article. Alexei applies
to Moscow University.

IN HOPES OF getting Tanya reinstated, I decided to turn to the rector of
Moscow University, Ivan Petrovsky. This wasn't my first meeting with
Academician Petrovsky; we'd been members of the same department of the
Academy before physics and mathematics were separated in 1961. A distinguished mathematician, Petrovsky had taken on the rectorship in the early
1950s out of a sense of duty. He displayed great courage and determination
in defending the entire academic community, both faculty and students—
protection was sorely needed in those dismal years, when honest, gifted teachers came under fire for "kowtowing to the West," and anti-Semitism ran
rampant. On one occasion shortly before Petrovsky's appointment, a group of
some thirty students failed to appear for class: they'd been arrested, with
sanction from above, the night before. Nothing could be done.

The university became the center of Petrovsky's life. He encountered strong
opposition, even within his own department of mathematics, but he did have
some significant accomplishments to his credit.

I'd met with Petrovsky in 1967 after the tragic death of Sasha Tsukerman,
son of an Installation colleague, following an oral entrance examination
in mathematics conducted by Professor Modenov, a hard-core anti-Semite.
Modenov was actually a member of a different department, but he'd been put
on the admissions committee because of the efficiency and zest with which he
"flunked" Jewish applicants—a skill in great demand. Modenov was up to his
usual tricks with Tsukerman, confronting him with problems not well suited
to oral solution, interrupting and attempting to confuse his victim. When
Tsukerman nevertheless came up with the correct response, Modenov declared
that the exam was over and he had failed.

Tsukerman arrived home with an unbearable headache, had a flareup of his severe mental condition, and died within a week. Although this tragic outcome probably was only triggered by the exam, it caused a storm of indignation, particularly since such unfair practices were a regular feature of the entrance examinations. In my meeting with Petrovsky, I passed on to him Tsukerman's father's suggestion that the oral exam be abolished or replaced by a written one. Petrovsky agreed, and promised to take the matter up with the Ministry of Education and the Central Committee. I believe these promises were sincere, but no change was forthcoming. Petrovsky, who had a heart condition, looked tired and ill.

My 1972 conversations with Petrovsky were difficult for both of us. He was less than honest with me, and never acknowledged that Tanya had been treated unjustly. Had he done so, and admitted that he was powerless to reverse the decision, I would have known how to proceed and matters between us could have rested there. Instead, he kept trying to convince me that Tanya had been given equal treatment—sheer hypocrisy—while hinting that he might be able to "do something." This kept me coming back over and over again with an increasing sense of frustration. At our next-to-last meeting, he called in a reinforcement: Professor Zasursky, dean of the journalism school. Zasursky said that Arab students had demanded Tanya's expulsion—although there were no Arabs in her class, and only one African, who was a friend of hers. But Zasursky's explanation did constitute an admission, albeit an oblique one, that the demonstration was the reason for her ouster.

At our final meeting, Petrovsky called in the university's Party secretary and vice-chancellor. Their hypocrisy and thinly veiled threats were so blatant that I lost my usual self-control and twice pounded on the table with my fist. Petrovsky took little part in the conversation, sitting morose and silent at the head of the table. Later that same day, he dropped dead. He'd gone to the Central Committee to see Trapeznikov, the head of the science department (on the way, he'd been in good spirits, according to the colleague who accompanied him). Trapeznikov criticized a report Petrovsky had written recommending the transfer of certain graduate training from provincial universities to Moscow University. The criticism may have been rather blunt (that wasn't unusual); in any case, Petrovsky was upset. He walked out into the Central Committee courtyard, and suddenly collapsed and died.

It wasn't long before I was accused of responsibility for Petrovsky's death. A letter to that effect came from one of his secretaries, and I heard that Academician Lev Pontryagin, another mathematician, had delivered a speech to the Academy's presidium blaming me (my pounding on the table, etc.), and urging that I be held accountable for the calamity that followed. Academician Pavel Alexandrov, a topologist, wrote me in the same vein. I replied to him, detailing the circumstances of my meetings with Petrovsky. Naturally, I found all this very disagreeable; and I was genuinely sorry about Petrovsky, whom I'd liked despite our differences over Tanya.

Attempts to find Tanya an editorial position, which would have helped her prospects for readmission, proved unsuccessful. In at least one case, the KGB telephoned a potential employer in order to blacklist her. It took two years and the help of Rem Khokhlov, who replaced Petrovsky as rector, to get Tanya reinstated.

In the fall of 1972, I was also upset by Valery Chalidze's impending departure from the USSR. In *The Oak and the Calf*, Solzhenitsyn implies that Chalidze made a deal with the KGB: "The greatest of simpletons will agree that before you get a visa to go and *lecture foreigners on the rights of man in the USSR* you will need to talk things over with the KGB. And this Chalidze did while still a member of the committee!"[1] I can't accept that at all; but Chalidze certainly wasn't entirely frank with me, and it soured our relationship for a time. Officially, his trip came as a result of an invitation to lecture abroad, but it was obvious that permission had been granted because the KGB was eager to get rid of a key figure in the human rights movement. Problems in both his personal and his public life made Chalidze himself eager to leave. He had been blacklisted as a physicist, and he and his wife were in serious financial straits. This can scarcely be read as a direct "deal," and many people depart under similar circumstances.

Chalidze left in November 1972. Three weeks later, he was stripped of his citizenship by a special resolution of the Presidium of the Supreme Soviet. One of the issues dividing us on the eve of his departure had been his refusal to admit that this outcome was practically inevitable.

In January 1973, I criticized him sharply, and when Lusia and I decided my statement had been ignored by the Western media, I passed it on to Solzhenitsyn. (In 1975, in *My Country and the World*, I admitted my mistake.)

Soon after his arrival in the United States, Chalidze founded Khronika Press to fill, insofar as possible, the gap created by the suspension of the *Chronicle of Current Events*. Khronika Press expanded over the next ten years to become one of the most important Russian-language publishers abroad, "independent" in the very best sense of that word. Credit belongs both to Chalidze and to Khronika's co-founder, Edward Kline, an American businessman and human rights advocate. (Fortunately, the *Chronicle* resumed publication in 1974.)

Before leaving, Chalidze resigned from the Human Rights Committee and in December, Andrei Tverdokhlebov followed suit. He did not state his reasons, but apparently one of them was his disapproval of my attitude toward Chalidze's departure.

---

[1][*The Oak and the Calf*, pp. 372–373.]

Grigory Podyapolsky, a geophysicist and a long-time activist in the human rights movement, joined the committee, and during 1973 and 1974, he, Shafarevich, and I met regularly at Chkalov Street. But although we managed to draft and publish several decent reports, we began to feel that the committee had outlived its usefulness. We were issuing typical human rights statements, and gained little by calling them "committee documents." Our meetings turned into information-sharing sessions. Lusia served as hostess, and Podyapolsky's wife, Maria Petrenko-Podyapolskaya, enjoyed helping her. We became friendly with the Podyapolskys and continued to see them, but Shafarevich left our company, and the committee faded out of existence.

LUSIA AND I realized that one way to solve the problem of the children's education was for them to emigrate. But the thought of their departure, with little hope of our ever seeing them again, was difficult to face. Our dream was that they might be allowed to study abroad for a number of years, and that things might change while they were away. We had little faith in such a prospect, but we felt we had to try. Alexei, then fifteen, burst out: "Psychologically, I'm more prepared for a Mordovian labor camp than for emigration!" You have to know Alexei—laconic, precise, a bit of a skeptic, not at all given to poses—to appreciate the full weight of those words. With the help of Evgeny Feinberg, I contacted Professor Victor Weisskopf, the MIT physicist whom I'd met at Tamm's in 1970. In the spring of 1973, Tanya, Efrem, and Alexei received invitations to study at MIT, signed by its president, Jerome Wiesner. The invitations were repeated several times, sometimes notarized by the U.S. State Department, but they failed to secure permission for the children to study in America.

In the spring of 1973, I myself received a phone call which led to a great deal of unexpected publicity. I was invited to visit Princeton University and lecture on theoretical physics during the 1973–1974 academic year. The offer was initiated by Professor John Wheeler, whom I'd met in Tbilisi. I decided that I had nothing to lose by accepting. It would not have been very gracious to turn down Princeton, where Einstein had spent his last years at the nearby Institute for Advanced Study. I realized, of course, that my former position made my chances of receiving permission very small, and so I gave no serious thought to possible lecture topics. I might well have discussed my 1966 work on baryon asymmetry, then practically unknown in the West. My talks might have influenced the course of science. . . .

By this time, some of my Installation colleagues were receiving permission to travel abroad, so there was nothing outlandish about my application, however unlikely its approval. I wasn't worried that the authorities might let me out in order to strip me of Soviet citizenship as they had Chalidze, since they would fear that under such circumstances I might disclose state secrets. The fact of the matter is that I could have violated my security commitments just as easily while remaining in the USSR. But I have never had any intention of doing so, either then or now. My reasoning was similar when I sought permission to attend the Nobel ceremony in 1975, and the AFL-CIO convention in 1977.

In February 1973, *Literaturnaya gazeta* published an article by its editor-in-chief, Alexander Chakovsky, that included an attack on *Reflections* (this, some five years after my essay's publication). While *Literaturnaya gazeta*'s masthead proclaims it to be the voice of the Writers Union, in practice it often serves as the mouthpiece of the Central Committee; Chakovsky himself reportedly enjoyed Brezhnev's confidence. He characterized me as a naïve and conceited person "coquettishly waving an olive branch" and peddling the utopian and therefore harmful idea of convergence. The article's tone was more condescending than critical. It argued that I had become involved in matters outside my competence and had made elementary mistakes. Just why the conspiracy of silence about me should have been broken at that particular moment, I have no idea.[2]

In late June, I had my second interview with a foreign journalist. Olle Stenholm, a Scandinavian radio and television correspondent whom I knew and liked, had given me a list of proposed questions so that I could prepare for the new experience of speaking into a microphone on general topics. After a couple of months, I finally decided to go ahead. Stenholm asked questions about my assessment of the Soviet system, the possibilities for change and the dissidents' potential influence, the authorities' attitude toward dissent, and the general human rights situation.[3]

Foreign radio stations first broadcast the interview on July 2, and it was repeated several times over the next couple of weeks. Then the storm broke—and again in *Literaturnaya gazeta*, which published an article by Yuri Kornilov, a Novosti commentator. (Novosti, which claims to be an independent press agency, was known to be a tool of the KGB.) The article wasn't easy to follow, since it avoided quoting me directly, but it was scathing in its denunciation of my description of Soviet society as state capitalism, with the state and Party exercising an absolute monopoly over the country's economic, ideological, and cultural life. The shrillness of the reaction was proof that I'd scored a direct

[2][Alexander Chakovsky, "And What Next? Reflections on Reading Harrison Salisbury's New Book," *Literaturnaya gazeta*, February 14, 1973. Salisbury had written the introduction and notes for the 1968 Norton edition of *Reflections*.]
[3][Appendix, p. 623.]

hit.[4] Kornilov's article also referred to an earlier piece attacking me in the Austrian Communist newspaper *Volksstimme*. Additional anti-Sakharov articles appeared in *Literaturnaya gazeta, Izvestia,* and other Soviet newspapers. We later discovered that Kornilov himself had been the source of the *Volksstimme* article, and so had started the whole onslaught.

Ruth, remembering the 1930s, was terrified that the press campaign might be followed by something more sinister. And shortly thereafter I did receive a summons to appear before Deputy Procurator Mikhail Malyarov, who'd called me six years earlier about the Daniel case. But before that meeting, we received more bad news—Alexei had been rejected by Moscow University.

He had been enrolled since his sophomore year in Mathematics School No. 2, where he'd done extremely well. He'd enjoyed the school's intellectual atmosphere and freedom, which were in sharp contrast to the situation in most high schools. Even before going there, Alexei had been an excellent student, winning a prize in the math Olympics and receiving invitations from three math schools.

Soviet schools are a subject in themselves. In certain respects, they may be better than public schools elsewhere. But teachers' low salaries, lack of prestige, and excessive class loads are cause for alarm. The official curriculums are too burdensome and impossible to complete. The opposite problem, a lack of intellectual rigor, is also encountered ofter enough, particularly in rural schools. Classrooms are overcrowded, and most schools lack facilities and funds. Alcoholism, cynicism, and other social problems are transmitted to children through their parents and infect the schools. Ethnic discord sometimes reaches the point of racism. Nothing is more likely to cripple a person's development than a bad school or bad family environment.

Mathematics School No. 2, which had first-rate teachers and an exceptional atmosphere, began to deteriorate while Alexei was still there. It has since been shut down, evidently because it didn't fit in with the spirit of the times, and replaced by a school that emphasizes athletics.

During his junior year, Alexei refused to attend the standard "Lenin class," which would have lead to automatic Komsomol membership. I urged him not to jeopardize his future for the sake of a minor formality, since such wholesale enrollment imposed no real moral obligation. Alexei answered: "Andrei Dmitrievich, you allow yourself to be honest. Why do you advise me to behave differently?" (Some years later, Efrem said the same thing to Lusia and me in another connection. Both times I felt ashamed of myself.) A few months before graduation, the school administration stepped up pressure on Alexei to dissoci-

[4][Appendix, p. 631.]

ate himself from me in some way, at least by joining the Komsomol. Given Alexei's straightforward and determined character, the only solution was for him to return to his former school, from which he graduated first in his class.

Alexei applied to Moscow University's mathematics department, along with many of his former classmates from Mathematics School No. 2. The university entrance exams began in July and coincided with the *Literaturnaya gazeta* attack on me. Alexei became the victim of deliberate discrimination. It was a traumatic experience; established procedures were violated and blatantly irregular grading practices were used in order to fail him. We later learned that one examiner had received a direct order to flunk him, or else: "He won't be accepted anyway, and you'd just be fired."

Alexei instead entered the math department of the Teachers Institute, where the caliber of the faculty and students was much lower on average than at Moscow University. As things turned out, he wasn't to have the chance to graduate even from there.

Alexei's story is not unusual for the more prestigious institutions of higher education. Much has been written about discrimination against Jews, a terrible injustice that each year cripples the lives of thousands of gifted young men and women. Religious believers, the children of dissidents, and, in Moscow's institutions of higher education, nonresidents of the city are also subject to discriminatory treatment. Nonresidents actually are required to obtain higher scores on entrance exams. Other forms of unequal treatment are more subtle. Exam papers are identified by number, not by name, but at Moscow University, at least, one key digit of the number alerts the admissions board to "undesirable" candidates, who are routinely assigned to a special group for their oral exams (where arbitrary grading is easier to justify). Members of these special groups are supposed to be flunked—as the story goes, one young Jew, seeing the other members of the group gathering with him for the oral exam, exclaimed: "You mean they're taking us straight from here to Auschwitz?"

Anti-Semitic discrimination in university admissions is not just the work of individual bigots, but part of a deliberate policy of squeezing Jews out of the country's intellectual establishment. The number of Jews elected to the Academy of Sciences has been falling every year. The Central Committee is said to have asked Mstislav Keldysh, then president of the Academy, when its Jewish membership would fall to zero. It would take about twenty years for the "problem" to be solved, he replied. (I must note that Keldysh did *not* reduce the number of Jews in the institutes he directed, and was not himself anti-Semitic.) Anti-Semitism is just one aspect of the widespread anti-intellectualism and the caste prejudices of today's Soviet society. Decent people must be concerned about this cruelly unjust policy. It undermines our future.

31

THE 1973 ANTI-SAKHAROV CAMPAIGN

A summons to Malyarov. The press
conference of August 21, 1973. The
anti-Sakharov press campaign. A statement
in defense of Pablo Neruda. Lusia and the
Kuznetsov prison diary.

ON AUGUST 15, 1973, Mikhail Malyarov, the deputy procurator general, telephoned and asked me to come see him. The next day, we were driven in an Academy car to the Procurator's Office on Pushkin Street. Lusia waited anxiously in the car; when, an hour later, I emerged safe and sound, she urged me to go straight home and write down everything that had been said. (She had done the same during the Leningrad hijackers' trial.) It was good advice. My reconstruction of the conversation [in which Malyarov warned Sakharov that he might be liable to prosecution for his "anti-Soviet statements"] appeared in the New York Times on August 29, accompanied by a drawing of heads being chopped off.

I decided that the time had come to hold a major press conference. There were allegations to refute, and I wanted to make it clear that Malyarov's attempt to intimidate me with the idea that meeting with the foreign press could be regarded as a violation of my obligation not to disclose state secrets was not going to force me to alter my behavior. I was determined to go on speaking out on general issues and in defense of individual victims of persecution.

Some thirty correspondents from Western agencies and newspapers crowded into our apartment on August 21. I began by reading a prepared statement about my meeting with Malyarov, and then handed out copies of the statement. I was surprised by the ease with which I fielded the reporters' many questions; I'm generally not that good at speaking off the cuff.

I was asked about my attitude toward détente, about the prospects for the dissident movement and for democratic change in the USSR, and about violations of human rights. I replied that I supported détente, since it reduced the risk of war, but added that caution, unity, and firmness of purpose were necessary on the part of the West as it embarked on a new and more complex relationship with the USSR. The Soviet Union, I said, is a country "behind a mask," a closed, totalitarian society capable of dangerously unpredictable actions. The West must avoid letting the USSR achieve military superiority, and at the same time do its utmost to promote a more open Soviet society. Only then would détente genuinely promote international security.

To other questions I recall responding (as I would many times over the years with minor variations) with explanations that the dissident movement was a moral and not a pragmatic undertaking, and reminding my listeners that the ingrained conservatism and inertia of the Soviet system militated against any rapid change.

The moment I announced that the conference was over, the correspondents dashed off to file their stories, and within two hours Western radio stations were broadcasting reports. More detailed newspaper and radio coverage followed the next day. Of all my press conferences, this, my first, may have evoked the greatest response.

LUSIA, ALEXEI, and I left Moscow for a nine-day vacation in the South. We wanted to give Alexei a taste of Armenia, relax a bit by the sea, and get back in time for the beginning of the semester at the Teachers Institute. Alexei called his fiancée, Olga Levshin, from the hotel on August 28; she told him the newspapers were carrying a letter denouncing Sakharov, signed by forty academicians. (After Olga hung up, her parents asked her why she'd been going on so to Alexei about this letter—what did he have to do with Sakharov? "He's his stepson," she replied. Her parents were shocked and frightened—but Olga has a mind of her own.

Lusia got the newspaper the next morning, and we read the infamous letter expressing the academicians' indignation at actions "which discredit the good name of Soviet science."[1] Later I was to hear all sorts of stories about the way the signatures had been collected. Some scientists claimed to have been told that their signing such a letter was the only way of saving me from arrest. I heard that Kapitsa had refused to sign, and Zeldovich hadn't even been approached. Keldysh had signed, but his successor as president of the Academy, Alexandrov, avoided doing so. When they called his home, the person who answered said, "Anatoly Petrovich is drunk and can't come to the phone." Whether an excuse or the truth, this had an authentic Russian ring. Some who signed later regretted their act, and several were raked over the coals by their own children.

[1][Appendix, p. 632.]

Although we realized that the situation was serious, we decided not to change our plans. From Erevan we went on to Batumi, where we heard people on the beach discussing "Sakharov, that traitor." We moved to a place outside of Batumi for a few days—that's where Alexei tried to teach me how to swim.

The academicians' letter marked the beginning of a press campaign against me that included letters from scientific research institutes, writers' and artists' unions, and other institutions and enterprises, as well as from individual scientists, authors, physicians, war veterans, steelworkers, miners, and milkmaids. Solzhenitsyn was also included in many of these attacks. The vital truths expressed in his extraordinary literary works and keen polemics had made him the object of virulent Party and KGB hatred for several years; now, there were claims that I alone, or the two of us, were engaged in a slanderous assault on Soviet society and its guarantees of full employment, free medical care, and an unrivaled educational system.

The main charge, and one that has been repeated in all subsequent campaigns against me, was that I was an *enemy of détente* working against the most precious of prizes, peace, whose price was counted in the blood of millions of Soviet citizens. This grave accusation had an insidious plausibility to believers in Soviet foreign policy's pacific aims, the selflessness of our aid to national liberation movements, and the treachery of the imperialists who have surrounded us with their military installations. If we stand for peace, then the more missiles, nuclear warheads, and nerve gas we stockpile, the safer we and everyone else will be. It's not easy to grasp that our Western opponents employ the same line of argument, with absurd results. It's hard for someone whose information is derived entirely from official sources to understand that so long as the socialist sphere of influence keeps expanding, the USSR and its allies must bear much of the responsibility for the perilous international situation. Those who believe in the absolute superiority of our system can't see the dangers in a closed society or the need to struggle for civil rights, freedom of conscience, and the free movement of people and information. Our leaders' peace slogans, even when proclaimed in good faith, are inadequate, but to recognize their defects requires a global and historical perspective that can't be acquired overnight. I like to think that my statements have encouraged a pluralistic approach to these issues and a global perspective, and in so doing have aided rather than hindered the cause of peace.

Some response to the press campaign was obviously vital. On September 5, just after our return to Moscow, I gave foreign correspondents a statement. I met again with them on September 8 and 9, clarifying the points I'd made on September 5 and drawing particular attention to the political abuse of psychiatry. This was the first time I proposed that the International Red Cross request permission to inspect Soviet prisons, camps, and special psychiatric hospitals.

The press campaign against me provoked a strong reaction both in the USSR and abroad. On September 1, Valentin Turchin issued a brilliantly and cogently argued open letter in my support. His defense of me cost him dearly: he was demoted from head of laboratory to senior research assistant, and finally fired. Turchin later became chairman of the first Amnesty International group organized in the USSR and supported himself by tutoring private students until his emigration to the United States in 1977. There, he was instrumental in organizing a boycott by American scientists in support of Yuri Orlov and other victims of injustice.

On September 16, Orlov wrote an open letter to Brezhnev suggesting economic and political reforms and offering a spirited defense of me (like Turchin, he soon found himself out of a job). Orlov, whom I met during this period, impressed me as a man of exceptional courage, industry, and intelligence. In 1956, he'd been dismissed from Moscow's Institute of Theoretical and Experimental Physics after a fiery speech at a Party meeting in which he called for the restoration of "true Leninism." Orlov found a job in Erevan at the Armenian Institute of Physics, where his work on accelerators brought him an international reputation and election as a corresponding member of the Armenian Academy of Sciences. In 1972, he was allowed to return to Moscow, where he worked at the Institute of Terrestrial Magnetism and Radiowave Propagation, until he was fired on January 1, 1974.

Also in September, Lydia Chukovskaya, daughter of the famous author Kornei Chukovsky and herself a well-known and talented writer and editor, wrote "The Wrath of the People," a response to all those phony letters "from the people" attacking me. One day, she warned, popular rage incited and manipulated by the authorities might get out of control and "drown the innocent and the guilty alike in a sea of blood." Her "colleagues" duly took note of the article and expelled her from the Writers Union in January 1974. Chukovskaya may have been overly generous in portraying me as "a man of humane mind and reflective heart who came to hate bombs and all forms of violence," but writing these memoirs has taught me just how difficult it is to find a golden mean between dry mechanical recitation and saccharine sentimentality. Ideological sympathies can further complicate the attempts at an accurate portrait, and there may have been a bit of this in Lydia's article. It's no wonder that an acquaintance of ours was heard to ask: "How can Lydia be fond of both you and Solzhenitsyn at the same time?"

In any event, I owe Lydia Chukovskaya a debt of gratitude for her article, and I prize it. Lusia and I have come to know her well over the years, and despite disagreements on many issues we are bound to her by ties of friendship and respect. Herzen's words—"Work is our prayer"—which she quoted in a letter she sent to us in Gorky, could well serve as a motto for her heroic life, which has been devoted to humane values and cultures. Boris Shragin and Pavel Litvinov jointly, Igor Shafarevich, and Alexander Solzhenitsyn were also among those who responded to the press campaign against me.

On September 5, Solzhenitsyn dispatched his article "Peace and Violence" for publication abroad. Its main thrust was to warn the West about the nature and extent of state violence in the USSR. Just before its publication, however, he added the proposal that I be awarded the Nobel Peace Prize [for: "Sakharov's indefatigable, devoted (and for him personally dangerous) opposition to systematic state violence"]. He told me about the article only after he had authorized its publication, so I couldn't ask him to make any changes. (In any case, I would have found this difficult to do, as I don't like restricting anyone's freedom.) And I doubt that Solzhenitsyn would have paid much attention to my objections, which were based only on a vague feeling that he was exaggerating. Meanwhile, I was delighted by the power of his ideas and the fundamental truths stated in the article.

The press campaign subsided around September 10, but resumed in somewhat muted fashion, focusing on a letter written on September 18 by Galich, Maximov, and myself in defense of Pablo Neruda, the Chilean poet and Communist, and passed on to Western correspondents by Kirill Khenkin, a refusenik. The terminally ill Neruda was under house arrest following General Pinochet's coup d'état. Our letter, addressed to Pinochet, was intended to signal our recognition of the tragic situation in Chile and to express our concern over Neruda's well-being. "The violent death of this great man would darken for a long time what your government has proclaimed as the rebirth and consolidation of Chile," we wrote. The context made it clear that our formal and courteous tone was meant to fortify our request and in no way signaled approval of the new government, but the Soviet and pro-Soviet press twisted our words and claimed to see in them proof of admiration for Pinochet's bloody regime—a canard that still resurfaces periodically.

The West had reacted with unusual attention to my press conference and the academicians' letter denouncing me. I recall an avalanche of statements of support issued by prominent figures ranging from the chancellor of Austria and the Swedish foreign minister to the writer Günter Grass. A telegram sent by Philip Handler, president of the U.S. National Academy of Science, to Mstislav Keldysh, president of the USSR Academy, played a decisive role in bringing the Soviet campaign to a halt. Handler expressed "consternation and a sense of shame" that Soviet scientists had joined in the attacks on me and warned that "were Sakharov to be deprived of his opportunity to serve the Soviet people and humanity, it would be extremely difficult to imagine successful fulfillment of American pledges of binational scientific cooperation, the implementation of which is entirely dependent upon the voluntary effort and goodwill of our individual scientists and scientific institutions."[2]

On October 18, *Literaturnaya gazeta* published Keldysh's reply to Handler (prefaced by a brief summary of Handler's telegram). Keldysh repeated the insinuations contained in the academicians' letter but added assurances that "Sakharov had not been, and is not now, subject to any kind of harassment."

IN SEPTEMBER 1973, Lusia gave a statement to foreign correspondents in which she took full responsibility for transmitting Eduard Kuznetsov's *Prison Diaries*[3] to the West. Here is a brief account of how the manuscript came into her possession.

One day late in December 1972, I was alone at home. I answered the doorbell, and a woman who was a complete stranger to me entered, placed a tiny package sewn carefully into a piece of cloth onto the table, and left without uttering a word. Inside the package was the manuscript of what became known as the *Prison Diaries,* together with a letter from Kuznetsov to Lusia asking her to take charge of it. Like many other materials smuggled out of camp, it was written in minute handwriting on thin cigarette paper and twisted into a tubelike shape. Writing in camp was an extremely dangerous undertaking— and getting it smuggled out was no mean feat either. A number of people were involved, including Pyotr Ruban, a Ukrainian artist against whom the KGB would later exact a cruel revenge.

The handwriting could be deciphered only with a very powerful magnifying glass by someone with better eyes than ours; Lusia asked an acquaintance to do this and then return the manuscript immediately in order to keep the number of those in the know to a bare minimum. This request was not fulfilled, and the consequences were grievous.

Lusia made certain the manuscript reached the West, and in the summer of 1973, the *Diaries* were published first in Italian, then in Russian and a number of other languages. (As mentioned earlier, Lusia's record of the December 1970 Leningrad trial was published as an appendix.) The shocking contents and the author's literary skill generated considerable publicity.

Lusia's statement of September 1973 was an attempt to exonerate Viktor Khaustov (who had previously been convicted for demonstrating on behalf of Ginzburg and Galanskov), and the literary critic Gabriel Superfin, who had

---

[2][*New York Times*, September 11. Sakharov had been elected a foreign associate member of the U.S. National Academy of Science in 1972.]

[3][Stein and Day, 1975.]

been arrested as accomplices in the *Diaries'* dispatch abroad. Evgeny Baraba-nov apparently had another copy of the deciphered version of the *Diaries* that we didn't know about, and had been interrogated several times by the KGB; they were particularly eager to get something on Superfin. The outlook for Barabanov seemed bleak, but in the end, after both he and Lusia had under-gone KGB interrogations, he suffered no more than the loss of his job. In *The Oak and the Calf,* Solzhenitsyn describes Barabanov's bold defense of his role regarding the *Prison Diaries* as a historic step in the "encounter battle"—but he makes no mention of Lusia's statement, and so gives a misleading impres-sion of events.

32

THE THREATS COME HOME

The Yom Kippur War and "Black
September." The Jackson amendment. Lusia
is summoned for questioning at Lefortovo.
The Princeton Invitation. The Academy
Hospital.

IN OCTOBER 1973, Egypt and Syria, seeking to avenge their defeat in the
1967 Six Day War, launched an attack on Israel—the so-called Yom Kippur
War. Soon after the hostilities broke out I made a statement calling for a
peaceful settlement of the Middle East conflict. A few days later, a man arrived
at my door and told me he was a correspondent for a Beirut newspaper and
wanted to ask me about the Middle East situation. Though somewhat dubious
about him, I asked him to come back a bit later, and that evening we recorded
an interview. He managed to slip in some unexpected questions of a rather
provocative nature.

Several days later, on the morning of Sunday, October 18, two men who
looked like Arabs rang our doorbell. There seemed something odd about the
way they stood there, but I let them in (in any case, we had no bolts or chains
on the door). Lusia came in from the kitchen. Ruth had gone to Tanya's to
see her first great-grandchild, then just a few weeks old, and only Alexei was
at home. The taller of the two men sat down next to Lusia on the bed, I was
on a chair opposite, and the shorter one, thickset and wearing a coat, sat on
an armchair between us and a little to the side, facing the telephone.

The taller man did all the talking. His Russian was accented but correct.
When Lusia asked him where he'd learned it, he said at Patrice Lumumba
University, probably the truth. He soon came to the point: "You published a
statement damaging to the Arab cause. We are from the Black September
group, perhaps you've heard of it?" "Yes, I have." "We want an immediate
statement in writing from you admitting your lack of competence in Middle
Eastern affairs and disavowing your statement of October 11."

I didn't answer immediately. Lusia reached for her cigarette lighter, which
was by the phone, but the shorter man sprang like a cat and blocked her. "I

am not about to write or sign anything under duress," I declared. The answer came: "You'll be sorry."

Early in the conversation I'd said (implicitly alluding to the Middle East conflict): "I favor only equitable, compromise solutions. I'm sure you know of my support of the Crimean Tatars' legal and peaceful campaign to return to their homeland."

"We're not interested in your country's internal affairs," retorted the taller man. "Our motherland has been desecrated, you must understand that our mother's honor is at stake!" His voice cracked with emotion. "We are fighting for her honor, *nobody* is going to stand in our way!"

"What can you do to us—kill us?" asked Lusia. "You're not the first to threaten that!"

"We could kill you, of course, but we could do worse: you've got children; a grandchild. . . ."

Matvei was then less than a month old, and we'd said nothing about him to the press. As we were speaking, Alexei came into the room and sat down next to Lusia, who, knowing his hotheaded nature, kept a firm grip on his knee. Alexei told us afterward that there'd been something hidden under the shorter man's coat, perhaps a gun. It was true that the man had kept his right hand under his coat the whole time.

At that moment, the doorbell rang, startling the intruders. They told us to keep quiet and, just in case, to move into the next room, which was farther from the door. The taller man kept up the threats: "Black September acts without warning. We've made an exception with you this time, but there won't be any more!" He told us to stay where we were. A moment later they'd vanished into thin air. We rushed to the telephone, but it was dead; they'd cut the wire.

Within minutes, our apartment was full of people. It was Tanya Khodorovich and the Podyapolskys who had rung the bell; hearing voices but getting no answer, they'd assumed a search was on and had gone to telephone Ruth, Tanya, Efrem, and as many of our friends as they could get hold of. They now returned, and Ruth, Efrem, and Tanya, with little Matvei in her arms, burst in a few minutes later. More people arrived. When he heard what had happened, Tverdokhlebov exclaimed: "And I'd always thought it was *Red October!*"

It was quite unpleasant enough to sit and listen to armed terrorists threatening us, but it was even worse to have to hear an open threat against our children and our grandchild. The intruders may really have been Palestinians—perhaps they even were from Black September; but we never doubted for a moment that they were under strict KGB control. The KGB probably was behind the whole incident, whether or not the intruders knew it (they'd appeared very uneasy the whole time).

I wasted no time informing foreign correspondents about what had happened, and within a few hours I also made a statement to the police—not that I expected anything to come of that. A few days later we were called to the local police station and given a pile of photographs to look through. We couldn't identify any as our terrorists. I suppose the police were going through the motions.

A couple of months later, we received a card from Beirut stating in English: "Thank you for not forgetting the Arab cause. We Palestinians also don't forget our *friends.*" This was unquestionably another threat, and we turned the card over to the police. They did return it to us, but it was stolen in a 1978 search. The death threats against our children and grandchildren (whether they were genuine or not) were to be repeated more than once in years to come.

ON SEPTEMBER 14, 1973, I wrote to the United States Congress in support of the Jackson amendment, one of the few appeals I have ever made to foreign legislative and governmental organs. It is one of the best known and most effective of all my statements, and it is not by chance that in *White House Years,* Kissinger mentions me solely in this connection, and with disapproval: in his view, the Jackson amendment was damaging to détente. But in actual fact, it laid a firmer basis for détente; it just didn't go far enough.

Soviet propagandists never tired of alleging that the letter constituted an appeal to a foreign government to interfere in our internal affairs. In reply to this charge, I must emphasize that the USSR recognizes the right to choose one's country of residence in many of its international obligations, in particular the international Covenants on Human Rights, and the Helsinki Final Act. The Jackson amendment therefore touches upon the USSR's fulfillment of its international commitments on a matter vital to both domestic freedom and international trust. How does insisting that the USSR fulfill its commitments constitute interference in its internal affairs? It is an American trade law that we are discussing, and it seems to me that the Americans' decisions on trading partners, tariffs, and the granting of trade credits are *their* internal affair. I have the right even as a foreigner to apprise Congress of my views, and the Congress, of course, is free to accept or reject them.

On November 13, Lusia was summoned to an interrogation at Lefortovo, where the KGB investigation department and prison (or "isolator," in official terminology) are located. According to the summons, Lusia was to be interrogated as a witness by one Gubinsky. She was seen first by a man named Sokolov, apparently an officer in the department that dealt with our case; and someone we were to encounter a number of times in Gorky. The interrogation itself was conducted not by Gubinsky, but by Lieutenant-Colonel Syshchikov (a most appropriate name[1]), known as a man who could break even the stubbornest suspects. When Lusia asked him where Gubinsky was, he replied: "You must have seen him—he was the young guy who pointed your way to the toilet!" Syshchikov may have been lying; Gubinsky was a well-known "dissident specialist."

Lusia was being interrogated as a witness in the case of Viktor Khaustov and Gabriel Superfin, who were charged with transmitting Eduard Kuznetsov's *Prison Diaries* to the West. Her prior experience alerted her right away that Syshchikov was after any and all evidence; anything she said could be used in court. These trials were just bureaucratic charades; it was better to say nothing at all. The interrogations, of course, were meant to put psychological pressure on us, and we had no way of knowing whether or not Lusia herself might be indicted.

Syshchikov really was a remarkable, even awe-inspiring figure, a brilliant performer who could talk on and on without a break, enveloping one in his deep, penetrating voice: "Trust me, I'll be like a father to you; be honest with me—after all, you're responsible for the fate of these young people [Khaustov and Superfin], you alone can help them!" Nor did he hesitate to turn to shouts and threats in a truly frightening spectacle. Lusia soon realized that she was being drawn willy-nilly into giving answers of substance. After that, she replied to every question: "I decline to answer." At the end of the first interrogation, Syshchikov asked, "Is it true that your friends call you Lusia?" and when Lusia gave her now standard reply. At that, her interrogator blew up, yelling, "I'm getting the guard, I won't have you mocking me!" These tantrums became more and more frequent, a truly impressive one erupting when Lusia asked: "Is Syshchikov your real name, or a pseudonym?"

Over the next two weeks, a summons came just about every day. I would accompany Lusia to Lefortovo and wait in the pass office downstairs, since they wouldn't let me go any further. Each time, Syshchikov piled on more pressure. On her third or fourth visit, he made Lusia sit on the defendant's bench, presumably as a ploy to intimidate her. But Lusia's eyesight was so poor that from the bench she couldn't make out his face, which seemed to expand in a sinister fashion when he shouted—and she actually found sitting there *less* intimidating.

Finally, on November 27, Lusia decided she'd had enough of this bizarre psychological duel and refused the next summons. Messengers began to appear at our home with summonses, but Lusia continued to refuse them. In the end, I intercepted a messenger on the stairway and took the summons myself. I told

---

[1][*Syshchik* means "detective" in Russian.]

him I wouldn't give it to Lusia, that she was ill, and that I accepted responsibility for her failure to appear for any further interrogations. Lusia was furious with me—but the stream of summonses stopped. Even so, the threat had not completely disappeared: we heard that the KGB had testimony implicating her in transmitting Kuznetsov's *Diaries* to the West.

DURING THE PRESS campaign against me, foreign correspondents had driven me mad with questions about emigration and the invitation I had received from Princeton. I well understood the interest: many in the West would have felt easier if I were there. But I couldn't answer one way or the other. I had no idea *how* the authorities would resolve the crisis: just possibly we might all end up going to Princeton and spending six months or a year there, after which Tanya, Efrem, and Alexei could stay in the U.S. to study. A scenario too good to be true, of course; but I didn't want to cut myself off from that chance. Besides, there was always the hope that a public discussion of my possible travel abroad would help the children in some way.

Finally, at the end of November, I decided to provoke a decisive test of the authorities' reaction by instituting the formal steps toward making such a journey. I went to ask the director of FIAN for a character reference, and found myself speaking with his deputy, a former Installation colleague of mine, which, in more propitious times might have stood me in good stead. The whole bureaucratic machine, including the KGB, should have then cranked into action, but instead there was no response. This was a reply in itself. I informed the reporters that I'd been unable to obtain permission for a trip to Princeton, and gave them a statement making it absolutely clear that I had no intention whatever of emigrating. The statement was broadcast—*but without the all-important concluding paragraph* in which I emphasized "my wish to preserve Soviet citizenship and return to my homeland. I scrupulously fulfill the obligations of Soviet citizenship, including the protection of state secrets, and I believe my place—for moral, social, and personal reasons—is in my native land." I was to experience this sort of irresponsibility again and again; at times it made me look like a complete fool. I suspect it wasn't always the media's usual preoccupation with deadlines, or simple incompetence or irresponsibility (although there's quite enough of this) that was to blame for these distortions; a Soviet fifth column may also have been at work. In this instance, I did manage with Maximov's assistance to get my full statement broadcast a few weeks later. But it was the first broadcast that stuck in the public's mind.

IN DECEMBER, Lusia and I were simultaneously admitted to the hospital. Her thyroid complaint required urgent treatment, and I'd long since been advised to have my heart tested. My academician's status entitled us to a private room for just the two of us. It was something of a rest cure, and just what we needed. I got on with the foreword to *Sakharov Speaks*, a collection of my statements which was to be published in the U.S. Lusia went over it, giving sound advice as always, and typed it up.

We had some very welcome visitors. Konstantin Bogatyrev, the poet and translator, and the well-known poet Alexander Mezhirov, both of whom Lusia had known for ages, turned up. Gesticulating and excitable as always, Bogatyrev talked about an incident that had occurred while he was in Stalin's camps, and I entertained them with a "lecture" on quantum mechanics. Mezhirov, with his bent for intricate mental constructions, seemed impressed. Maximov dropped by several times, wearing a brand-new checked suit, his blue eyes sparkling and his grin warm as usual. He always brought some gift—once it was a rare kind of smoked fish—and had stirring news to report. Alexander Galich, Viktor Nekrasov, and Lev Kopelev turned up together, to our delight; we have a photograph of us all, taken in the hospital lobby. Kopelev, a German specialist, writer, critic, and translator who has led a difficult life with many twists and turns, soon became a good friend.

Dropping by as well were Evgeny Feinberg and Vitaly Ginzburg from FIAN. Ginzburg, the director of the theoretical department, said the Academy institutes had all been directed to cut their staffs. "The theoretical department has to get rid of one person," he said. "It's painful, but there's no way around it. We've discussed it among ourselves, and we've decided Yuri Golfand will have to be the one: he's produced hardly anything in the last few years. Besides, he's got a doctorate and it'll be easier for him to find another job." I asked whether it might be possible to fudge the issue, but the response was negative.

Unfortunately, I couldn't think of much to say personally on Golfand's behalf. I didn't know that at a FIAN seminar some months before, he and E. Likhtman had delivered a basic paper on supersymmetry that was to become a classic. It hadn't come out of the blue: Felix Berezin, the brilliant Moscow scientist who met an untimely death in 1980, had already written about supersymmetry transformations. But Golfand and Likhtman were the first to see the value of supersymmetry in constructing a theory of elementary particles. The basic idea was brilliant, and an enormous amount of work would be done on supersymmetry in the following years. It was unquestionably the most natural and practical way to construct a unified field theory that incorporated on an equal basis boson fields (particles with integer spin) and fermion fields (particles with one-half integer spin). Some people maintained that in a unified field theory only fermion fields could be primary fields, but supersymmetry of elementary excitations of fermion "fluid," which can be both fermions and bosons, cannot be ruled out here.

Supersymmetry theories have other features that give hope for further development. One is the natural link between supersymmetry and gravitation; another, no less important, is a possible solution to the problem of ultraviolet divergences, mentioned in Chapter 5. Supersymmetry is also an integral part of string theory.

I later learned that the other departments at FIAN had managed to avoid cutting staff. And Golfand, as it turned out, did not get another job: he may have had a doctorate, but he was also a Jew. When he came to see us in the hospital, Lusia told him: "They're firing you—you ought to emigrate." Some months after that, he applied for a visa to Israel, but was rejected on the baseless grounds that he'd been involved in secret work in Tamm's group twenty years earlier. The work he'd done had been "sanitized"; he had no knowledge of the nuclear devices themselves and had never even been to the Installation. But the bar on his emigration was not lifted, and finally, in the summer of 1980, Golfand was allowed to return to FIAN. For a "refusenik" to get back a job from which he had been dismissed was a rare event indeed.

33

"THIS STRANGE, HUGE, CONSPICUOUS BALLOON..."

In *The Oak and the Calf*, Solzhenitsyn has a lot to say about the events of 1973, about me and my views, and about Lusia (sometimes by innuendo). On some matters he remains silent. I have kept my thoughts about this book to myself for many years, but it's now time to speak my mind. First, a few quotations.[1]

> . . . a miracle occurred when Andrei Dmitrievich Sakharov emerged in the Soviet state, among the swarms of corrupt, venal, unprincipled intelligentsia.
> . . . enjoying the entrée to that narrow circle in which, whatever a man's requirements, the word 'impossible' does not exist . . . he had always felt, all his life, that the abundance that threatened to overwhelm him was dust and ashes, that his soul yearned for truth.
> . . . it became only too evident that [work on thermonuclear weapons] served aggressive purposes.

The grandiose terms in which I am described are wholly inaccurate: I'm no politician, no prophet, and certainly no angel. What I've done and what I am are not the result of any miracle but the natural consequences of what life has made me; I've been influenced, of course, by the people I've known (the so-called "swarms of corrupt, venal, unprincipled intelligentsia") and the books I've read. As for "the abundance that threatened to overwhelm me": it may be a peculiarity of my character, but I've never lived in luxury, and I'm not

---

[1][Solzhenitsyn, *The Oak and the Calf*, pp. 367–368.]

even sure what it is. And if Solzhenitsyn only knew how many things were "impossible" at the Installation! Of the three passages quoted above, the last is the most important, but even here, I reject such a categorical judgment on my weapons work: as I never tire of repeating, life is a complicated thing.

Later on, Solzhenitsyn pours plenty of tar into the barrel of honey. He pays lip service to the importance of human rights, but in practice he treats their defense as a secondary matter which impedes the pursuit of the "primary cause"—it's still not clear to me exactly what that is in his eyes.

I welcome his praise for my 1971 Memorandum and its 1972 Postscript, but he adds:

. . . this document came and went, attracting much less attention than it deserved, probably because the author had used his signature too often and too wastefully.[2]

Solzhenitsyn is making a veiled reference here to my efforts in behalf of a particular Jewish refusenik. As I have tried to make clear in this book, the defense of individuals is for me a matter of principle, and lies at the very heart of my public activity. I don't worry about the amount of attention my "position papers" get: they are meant to be food for thought, a basis for discussion—on occasion I myself review and revise various points.

Solzhenitsyn makes a great deal of my supposed naïveté, my impracticality, my inability to size up a situation, and especially my susceptibility to "pernicious" influences. I'm stranded in Batumi and can't get train tickets. I hand out parts of my manuscript to different typists, not realizing the KGB will get hold of them. . . .

Among those who (in his view) have exerted a pernicious influence on me, hitching themselves "to this strange, huge, conspicuous balloon, which was soaring to the heights without engine or petrol,"[3] Solzhenitsyn names Roy Medvedev and Valery Chalidze. (I've already discussed my relations with these two very different individuals, so I won't repeat myself here.) But Solzhenitsyn's sharpest, if covert, thrusts are aimed at my wife:

Although Sakharov and I continued to meet in Zhukovka in 1972, no joint projects or actions resulted. This was because we were no longer left alone for the space of a single conversation, and I was afraid that anything

[2][Ibid., p. 373.]
[3][Ibid., p. 371.]

we said would be passed around the "democratic movement" in a jumbled version.[4]

He makes it sufficiently clear that it was Lusia who did not leave us alone. But in fact, Solzhenitsyn and I were alone when we spent an hour walking in the woods near Zhukovka (where he was staying at Rostropovich's dacha). He invited me to contribute to the collection of essays *From Under the Rubble*, [5] but I declined out of a vague concern that to do so might compromise my independence. And it's worth recalling that our earlier meetings, in 1968 and 1970, hadn't resulted in any joint actions either.

Neither Lusia nor I was involved in "dissident *salons.*" We have no taste for frenetic social life, for meeting throngs of new people, or for the drinking that so often accompanies such activity.

Solzhenitsyn claims my wife pushed me to go abroad and abandon my public responsibilities, and got me to stress emigration at the expense of more important issues. He describes the events of 1973 as an "encounter battle"[6] and blames me for surrendering prospective gains because Lusia's "deleterious" influence led me to harp on emigration—both the general issue and my personal situation. "Encounter battle" does not seem to me an apt term for describing the course of events during that period. And what kind of serious practical results could we have expected from our public pronouncements, then or later? In my opinion, none whatsoever. I hope the reader will forgive me another lengthy citation (italics mine):

In the *militant* interviews he [Sakharov] gave in August, the damaging emigration motif is never absent. We hear that "it would be *pleasant* to visit Princeton." . . .

The emigration tune will always be played in countries where society is used to losing all its battles. We need not blame anyone for this weakness, and after the vacillations I have described in the last chapter I certainly do not intend to. But there are private persons, all of whose decisions are a private matter. And there are persons who occupy positions in society too important and conspicuous for their decisions to be private except in "quiet" times: while the public is watching them in tense

---

[4][Ibid., p. 373.]

[5][Edited by Solzhenitsyn. Little, Brown and Co., 1975.]

[6][" 'Encounter battle' is the name given by military tacticians to a form of warfare distinct from ordinary offensive and defensive engagements; the two sides, each ignorant of the other's intentions, simultaneously decide to attack and unexpectedly collide." *The Oak and the Calf,* p. 335.]

expectancy, *they forfeit all such rights. This was the law that Andrei Dmitrievich broke,* observed and broke by fits and starts, and what is most vexatious, he broke it not because he himself believed he should (never for one moment was he tempted to evade responsibility, to set at naught the fate of Russia), *but in deference to those close to him, to ideas not his own.*

Such was the inspiration of Sakharov's efforts, prolonged over many months, specifically in support of the right to emigrate, which seemed to take precedence over all other problems. [There is something demonic in this, something reminiscent of the *Protocols of the Elders of Zion.* —A.S.] In the middle of September Sakharov performed just such another erratic maneuver, of which observers of the battle took little notice, but which in fact disrupted our battle line and *robbed us of decisive success.* This was just a day or two after the end of jamming, when our own initial impetus was carrying us forward. A group of some ninety Jews had addressed a written appeal to the U.S. Congress—as usual, on behalf of the Jews: Congress should not accord most-favored-nation status to the USSR unless Jews were permitted to emigrate. The ninety, *who did not feel that Russia was their own country* [familiar words?] and wanted only to break out of it, naturally gave no thought to further consequences. But to lend weight to their appeal they approached Sakharov with a request to sign a similar text in his own name and send it separately. . . . And indeed, following both the tradition and his own inclination in the matter, Sakharov gave them his signature—two or three days after the Mills amendment—without stopping to think that he was making a breach in the front, surrendering positions already in our hands, narrowing down the Mills amendment to the Jackson amendment, and trading the universal rights of man for mere freedom to emigrate.[7] . . . And Congress *returned* to the Jackson amendment. . . . If all we were asking for was emigration, why should the American Senate bother about anything more? . . . I was startled and shocked. On September 16 I wrote to Sakharov about it from out of town.[8]

In point of fact, there'd never been any serious debate about the Mills amendment since the Jackson amendment made substantially more sense from both legal and political perspectives, and had a far better chance for adoption. To have spoken against the Mills amendment would have meant killing both

---

[7][Solzhenitsyn is confused here, and Sakharov's comments which follow are also somewhat misleading. There was no separate Mills amendment; his name was attached as a sponsor to one of the earlier versions of the Jackson-Vanik amendment.]

[8][*The Oak and the Calf,* pp. 375–376.]

it and the Jackson amendment, and I, in contrast to Solzhenitsyn, believe that the Jackson amendment upholds a principle of importance. There was no "front" to "breach." And what about Solzhenitsyn? Did *he* speak out in favor of the Mills amendment if it was so important?

Following my statement endorsing the Jackson amendment, Solzhenitsyn sent me a note and asked me to visit his wife, Natalya Svetlova ("Alya," as he calls her). Lusia and I did so, and Alya asked me (Solzhenitsyn was not present) how I could support the Jackson amendment and attach such importance to the issue of emigration, which, in her view, amounted to a flight from the country and from responsibility. There were far more pressing problems, she argued, citing in particular the situation of millions of collective farmers who were little better than serfs, denied the right to leave their farms and live or work elsewhere. She disparaged our worries about Lusia's children, saying that millions of Russian parents had no chance to give their children any sort of proper education. Outraged by Alya's lecturing tone, Lusia burst out: "Don't give me that 'Russian people' shit! You make breakfast for your own children, not for the whole Russian people!" Lusia's remark about "the Russian people" may have sounded like blasphemy in that home, but she had earned the right to say what she did: all her life she has been one with the Russian people.

In 1973 we visited Solzhenitsyn one more time, our last meeting before his exile. Again I quote from his book:

> On 1 December the Sakharovs arrived at our home together, as always. His wife was ill [Lusia was suffering at the time from a serious thyroid disturbance with a pulse rate of 120], exhausted by interrogation and by *chronic anxiety*: "I shall be put inside in two weeks' time, my son is a candidate for Potma[9], my son-in-law will be banished as a parasite within a month, my daughter is out of a job." "Still, we'd better think about it?" Sakharov cautiously ventured. "No; *you* [Solzhenitsyn's emphasis] think about it." . . .
>
> "I should come straight back. I just want to take them"—his wife's children—"out of the country. . . . I'm not thinking of leaving myself."
>
> "But they won't let you in again, Andrei Dmitrievich!"
>
> "How can they refuse to let me in if I present myself at the frontier?" (He quite genuinely did not see how they could.)[10]

Here Solzhenitsyn gives a thoroughly inaccurate portrait of Lusia as some sort of hysteric suffering from "nerves." I am portrayed as an utter fool and

[9][Reference to the labor camp complex located near Potma, a town in Mordovia.]
[10][*The Oak and the Calf*, p. 377.]

completely under her heel. The fact is, neither she nor I spoke the words he attributes to us. Tanya wasn't "out of work"—she was on maternity leave; Efrem was still employed—he was fired only after Sergei Kovalev's trial in December 1975; and I wasn't as naïve as I'm painted here. As for Alexei's being a "candidate for Potma," this is apparently a distortion of Lusia's description of his reaction to our suggestion that he study abroad: Alexei had replied that he was psychologically better prepared for a labor camp in Mordovia. Solzhenitsyn must have remembered that remark; unfortunately, he managed to twist its meaning.

What actually happened during our meeting? Solzhenitsyn and Alya reproached us for our "harmful" allusions to leaving the country, and reported the reactions of some people to my supposed remarks about emigration. I explained that press reports had distorted my statement and carefully described the true state of affairs: the trip to Princeton would solve the children's problems, but the necessary permission was not likely to be forthcoming; even if I received it, I was absolutely certain that my citizenship would not be revoked.

It's a shame that Solzhenitsyn, driven by his sense of mission, understood so little (perhaps deliberately) about me, my thoughts on emigration, human rights and other matters, and about the real Lusia and her true role in my life.

Toward the end of 1974, a German correspondent brought me a gift from Solzhenitsyn, a copy of *The Oak and the Calf*, with a warm and complimentary inscription from the author. (I had already borrowed a copy from a friend, so I knew what was in it.) When I saw the inscription, I couldn't help exclaiming: "Solzhenitsyn really offended me in this book!"

The correspondent grinned: "Yes, of course, but he doesn't realize it."

34

SOLZHENITSYN'S EXILE

Lusia's operation. Solzhenitsyn's exile.
My answer to his *Letter to the Soviet
Leaders*.

LUSIA AND I were admitted together to the Academy Hospital in December
1973. (Our principal cause for concern was her thyroid disorder: at times her
pulse rate reached 120.) Unfortunately, the doctors seemed quite indifferent
to her condition, and as soon as we were discharged, we traveled to Leningrad
to consult Dr. Alexander Raskin, a professor of endocrinology and Lusia's
long-time acquaintance. After tests, he advised surgery; as it turned out, he and
the consulting ophthalmologist both underestimated the potential adverse
effects of an operation on Lusia's glaucoma, despite doubts she herself expressed on this score. We decided that the surgery should be performed by
Dr. B., a good friend of Natalya Gesse's.

We returned to Moscow, where Lusia began a preoperative course of medication. I visited the Academy's medical services department and the Minister
of Health, Dr. Boris Petrovsky, to get the necessary approvals for Lusia's
treatment in Leningrad, but an unpleasant surprise was in store for us. When
we got to Leningrad, Natalya told us that Dr. B. would not perform the
operation and didn't want to have anything more to do with us: he was about
to defend his dissertation, and feared he might be denied his degree if he
operated on Sakharov's wife.

Lusia had completed her preoperative program, so we had to find another
surgeon quickly. Luckily, Dr. G. Stuchinsky, Lusia's former professor at the
Medical Institute, agreed to take her on as a patient, and he removed her
thyroid gland on February 27, 1974. We returned to Moscow two weeks later,
despite a dangerous increase in her intraocular pressure, a portent of problems
to come.

I spent March 1974 working on my article "On Alexander Solzhenitsyn's
Letter to the Soviet Leaders," beginning it in Leningrad and finishing it in
Moscow.

Some background is needed. Right after New Year's, Alya Svetlova's thirteen-year-old son, Dmitri, paid us an unexpected visit. We were in the kitchen having breakfast, and Lusia offered him a glass of tea, which he refused. I could see that he was bursting to tell us something. He disappeared into the bathroom, then returned with a book that had been concealed under his clothing: it was the first volume of *The Gulag Archipelago*. [1] Ten minutes later Lusia and I were devouring that masterpiece. (During the preceding week, it had been praised in Western broadcasts and attacked viciously in the Soviet press.) Unlike most people in the West and many in our own country, we knew a lot about the Gulag's atrocities and had some idea of their scale, but Solzhenitsyn's book nevertheless was a shattering experience. From the outset, his voice—angry, mournful, sardonic—evokes a somber world of gray camps surrounded by barbed wire, investigators' offices and torture chambers flooded with merciless electric lights, icy mines in Kolyma and Norilsk. This was the fate of millions of our fellow countrymen, the obverse of the enthusiasm and glorious achievements celebrated in official song and story.

A few days later, Maximov, Galich, and I, among others, drafted a letter demanding that Solzhenitsyn be protected from attack or prosecution. I gave several interviews praising Solzhenitsyn and *The Gulag Archipelago*, and a good bit of what I said appeared in print.

ON THE EVENING of February 12, the telephone rang around seven o'clock: we were told that Solzhenitsyn had been taken by force from his home. Lusia and I dashed out, hailed a gypsy cab, and in fifteen minutes were entering the Solzhenitsyns' apartment on Kozitsky Lane. It was already crowded, and I recognized many familiar faces. Alya, looking pale and dejected, would tell each new arrival the details of the raid and then would break off to sort papers, burning some of them, or to attend to some other business. There were two teapots in the kitchen, and people were nervously drinking. We soon learned that Solzhenitsyn hadn't just been taken to the Procurator's Office, but was under arrest. The telephone rang all the time (some parties even managed to get through from abroad), and I took a couple of calls; the shock of events untied my tongue, and I spoke clearly and forcefully.

The following day, a group gathered in the kitchen of our Chkalov Street apartment and drafted the "Moscow Appeal," demanding Solzhenitsyn's release and the organization of an international tribunal to investigate the crimes described in *The Gulag Archipelago*.

[1][Harper and Row, 1974.]

The appeal was passed on to foreign correspondents not long before we learned that Solzhenitsyn had been expelled from the country and flown to the Federal Republic of Germany. We phoned Alya, who'd already heard the news from another source, but refused to believe it. An hour later she called back to say that she'd spoken with Solzhenitsyn himself. The Moscow Appeal was circulated widely. Tens of thousands signed it in West Germany alone.

Lusia and I joined those who gathered at the Solzhenitsyn apartment for a farewell party for Alya, who was leaving with her mother and children to join her husband abroad. Many good people came to this party, and many a fine Russian song was sung.

Before the party, while Lusia was in the hospital in Leningrad, I'd paid a visit to Alya, who'd given me a copy of her husband's *Letter to the Soviet Leaders.* After reading it, I felt obliged to respond publicly, since I disagreed with much of the *Letter's* content and implications. Solzhenitsyn was infuriated by my article—his own rejoinder, among other things, makes that clear—but I could not have done otherwise. Although I've refrained from airing our differences in public since that exchange, I'd like to say a few words here about the nature of my objections to Solzhenitsyn's *Letter,* his 1978 Harvard commencement address, and other public statements by him.[2] But before discussing the issues that divide us, I wish to emphasize once more my profound respect for him, for his gifts as a writer, for his historic achievement in uncovering the crimes of the Soviet state, and for all his years of selfless labor. I admire his passionate refusal to reconcile himself to evil, the sharpness and precision of his mind. And I agree with a great deal of what he writes and says.

But even where I share Solzhenitsyn's general ideas, I often find troubling the peremptory nature of his judgments, the absence of nuance, and his lack of tolerance for the opinions of others. I can understand these shortcomings as perhaps the inescapable counterparts of his virtues of his ardent dedication to his ideals; but they cannot be ignored. For all my admiration of Solzhenitsyn, it's just not possible to avoid an open debate, which is all the more necessary inasmuch as some of his fundamental themes—as expounded in his *Letter to the Soviet Leaders* and elsewhere—seem to me questionable. In my view, he underestimates the need for a global approach to today's most pressing problems, and displays a distinct anti-Western bias. This seems to predicate other facets of his position: isolationism, lack of concern with the problems of

---

[2][For the "Moscow Appeal," see *Solzhenitsyn: A Documentary Record,* 2nd ed. (Penguin, 1974), pp. 383–384. For a slightly revised version of the letter sent to the Soviet leaders in September 1973, see *Letter to the Soviet Leaders* (Harper & Row, 1974). For Solzhenitsyn's rejoinder to Sakharov, see *Kontinent,* pp. 14–23. Solzhenitsyn's 1978 Harvard commencement address was published as *A World Split Apart* (Harper & Row, 1978).]

Soviet nationalities other than Russians and Ukrainians, or with the problems of other nations. His position at times displays elements of Russian nationalism, with idealization of the Russian national character and religion and way of life. It is an attitude not far removed from being slighting or hostile toward other peoples. In my article, I cautioned that the politicians who follow in the footsteps of ideologues tend to be more dogmatic and ruthless than their mentors.

In Solzhenitsyn's view, the West, i.e., the U.S., Europe, and Japan, is losing its battle against totalitarianism, which is on the offensive everywhere. Inconsistent, disunited, lacking firm religious or moral guidelines, the West is wallowing in the pleasures of the consumer society, in permissiveness. It is heedlessly destroying itself amid the smoke and fumes of its cities and the din of hysterical music.

Certainly there is much bitter truth in Solzhenitsyn's complaints. I too have called attention to the West's lack of concerted action, its dangerous illusions, the factional gamesmanship, short-sightedness, selfishness, and cowardice displayed by some of its politicians, its vulnerability to subversion of every sort. And yet, while sounding the alarm, I have not abandoned hope. I believe that Western society is fundamentally healthy and dynamic, capable of meeting the challenges which life continually poses.

The West's lack of unity is the price it pays for the pluralism, freedom, and respect for the individual that constitute the sources of strength and flexibility for any society. It makes no sense to sacrifice them for a mechanical, barracks unity which may have a certain utility if one's goal is aggressive expansion but has otherwise proven to be a failure. Solzhenitsyn's mistrust of the West, of progress in general, of science and democracy, inclines him to romanticize a patriarchal way of life and handicrafts, to expect too much from the Russian Orthodox Church. He regards the unspoiled northeast region of our country as a reservoir for the Russian people where they can cleanse themselves of the moral and physical ravages caused by communism, a diabolic force imported from the West.

Solzhenitsyn suggests that there are already clear signs of a national and religious renaissance, that Russians have always been hostile to the socialist system, and even that they harbored defeatist sentiments during World War II. These ideas, which I may have oversimplified somewhat, are little short of myths. If our people and our leaders ever succumb to such notions (and I have more confidence in the people's resistance than I do in the leaders'), the results could be tragic. Nikolai Nekrasov wrote that the Russian railroads of the nineteenth century were built on Russian bones; an attempt to develop the northeast without modern technology would scatter no fewer bones through its swamps.

I differ with Solzhenitsyn on the role of religion in society. For me, religious belief, or the lack of it, is a purely private matter.

Unlike Solzhenitsyn, I see faults and sound principles in both the socialist and the Western systems. I believe that their convergence is possible, and I welcome that prospect as a chance to save humanity from the confrontation that threatens it with destruction.

I do not share Solzhenitsyn's antipathy toward progress. In my opinion, the ecological and social dangers entailed are more than offset by the better life for everyone that progress brings. It can temper social, racial, and regional conflicts. It can minimize basic inequities and bring relief to millions who suffer from hunger, poverty, and disease. And if mankind is the healthy organism I believe it to be, then progress, science, and the constructive application of intelligence will enable us to cope with the dangers facing us. Having set out on the path of progress several millennia ago, mankind cannot halt now—nor should it.

Solzhenitsyn and I differ most sharply over the defense of civil rights—freedom of conscience, freedom of expression, freedom to choose one's country of residence, the openness of society. For me, these rights constitute the basis for a fully human life and for international security and trust. I have no doubt whatsoever as to the value of defending specific individuals. Solzhenitsyn assigns only a secondary importance to human rights and fears that concentration on them may divert attention from what he sees as more important matters.

The first issue on which I spoke out publicly was the danger of thermonuclear war, and I have repeatedly stressed that this peril must take priority over all other concerns. But Solzhenitsyn has never spelled out his position on this point.

[Of course, I don't consider the danger of thermonuclear war as something opposed to or apart from other global problems: the defense of human rights, the elimination of economic and social backwardness, the eradication of the sickness and famine that plague much of mankind; in fact, I am now inclined to regard the many-faceted ecological threat to our environment as our most serious long-term problem—A.S. 1988]

Letter to the Soviet Leaders made me, at last, fully conscious of my differences with Solzhenitsyn. I felt strongly the need to formulate those differences clearly and make them public. This was the motive for writing my article. I still think that what this article says is important, that it deals with profound and critical issues.

35

THE FIRST HUNGER STRIKE

Vacation in Sukhumi. "The World in Fifty
Years." Lusia's eyes. The first hunger strike.
Silva Zalmanson and Simas Kudirka.

EARLY IN APRIL 1974, Lusia and I left Moscow for a few weeks' vacation in
the South. We managed to find a hotel room in Sukhumi, where we strolled
around the city's outskirts and generally took things easy. A trip to the Amkhel
Gorge remains indelibly etched in memory: mountain air, the sharp contours
of distant peaks, the sound of the slate-blue stream turning to white water as
it rushed through the gorge bed. These were wonderfully carefree days. But
toward the end of our Sukhumi stay my incognito was blown and visitors began
to show up. We moved on to Sochi, thinking, rightly, that it would be quieter.

The *Saturday Review* had asked a number of prominent figures to contribute
articles for a special anniversary issue on "The World in Fifty Years."[1] I gave
my imagination free rein in picturing the world of 2024. Although I drew to
a certain extent on my previous work, this was essentially an original effort
which also reflected some valuable suggestions made by Lusia as she typed it
up. I'd be fascinated to see how my exercise in futurology will appear fifty or
a hundred years from now; at the moment, I'm still quite taken with it.

I worked hard on the article, and I certainly earned my compensation: five
hundred dollars, my first hard-currency earnings. At that time it was still
possible to receive money from abroad in the form of "Beryozka" certificates
accepted at special hard-currency stores that catered principally to Soviet
officials working abroad, and we used my fee to buy canned meat and other
food products to send to prisoners in the camps. The sales people knew
perfectly well who I was and why I was making these purchases; one of them,
apparently unaware that Tanya was with me, said to her: "Look—that's
Academician Sakharov!"

[1]["Tomorrow: The View from Red Square," *Saturday Review/World*, August 24, 1974.]

In mid-May I had to fly back to Moscow, but Lusia and Tanya, who had joined us in Sochi to take a sanatorium cure, stayed on for a couple of weeks. Lusia's eyesight took a sudden turn for the worse: the thyroid operation had aggravated her glaucoma, and the frequency and intensity of the pain from intraocular pressure increased to the point where neither her regular medication nor stronger remedies could do much to relieve it. When I met them at the airport in Moscow, Tanya took me aside: "Mother's going completely blind," she warned.

In June, as Lusia's condition continued to deteriorate, she consulted with a number of specialists, including Zoya Razhivina, a friend from the Leningrad Medical Institute, who was now an ophthalmologist at the Moscow Eye Hospital. In their student days Zoya had, as Lusia put it, "done her eye pathology course on me." Now Lusia couldn't even make out her friend's features from across the office. Zoya was in tears as she finished examining Lusia's eyes. Two days later Lusia entered the Eye Hospital for surgery. But when she left after a month, the operation still had not been performed—the doctors clearly were terrified to do anything. Matters had gone from bad to worse, with an unexplained quarantine being declared and Lusia's attending physician, who was well disposed toward her, being replaced by the assistant chief of staff. Lusia was told in confidence: "We don't know what they're planning to do with you, but you ought to get yourself out of here as fast as you can." The following Sunday, when the senior personnel were off duty, Lusia signed herself out.

Several months of fruitless efforts convinced us that the only answer was for Lusia to ask permission to go abroad for treatment.

MY FIRST hunger strike had taken place during Lusia's stay in the Eye Hospital, timed to coincide with President Nixon's arrival in Moscow on June 27. The aim was to call attention to the plight of political prisoners: Vladimir Bukovsky, Valentin Moroz, Igor Ogurtsov, and Leonid Plyushch; ethnic Germans imprisoned for demonstrating for the right to emigrate; and prisoners in psychiatric hospitals. Newspaper correspondents and television crews traveling with Nixon interviewed me at our apartment, with Tanya acting as interpreter. When a TV journalist tried to transmit an interview with me from the Ostankino relay station, the broadcast was interrupted by the Soviet censor. For several minutes, half the world stared at blank screens instead of the Sakharov interview—leaving a lasting impression, I was told.

I ended my hunger strike after six days. My health had begun to deteriorate, and I felt that my goals had been achieved. The hunger strike, although comparatively brief, had taken a lot out of me, as I'd been busy the whole time, working and giving interviews. While I was fasting, my aunt Zhenya, wife of my father's brother Ivan, passed away; I visited her in the hospital and then attended her funeral.

Lusia, concerned about me, managed almost every day to slip out of the hospital, despite the quarantine; she'd give the watchman a ruble and then take a taxi home. She was there with me when the American physicists Victor Weisskopf and Sidney Drell, in Moscow for an international scientific conference, paid a call.

Joining other patients for a smoke in the hospital stairwell, Lusia was amused to hear them speculate that Sakharov must be sneaking a bit of food on the side, hunger strike or not. They were also certain I was a Jew, and unconvinced by Lusia's statements that they were wrong on both counts—although they'd repeatedly caught glimpses of me through the hospital windows, they didn't realize that Lusia was "the Sakharov woman."

In AUGUST 1974, two prisoners were freed unexpectedly: Silva Zalmanson, Eduard Kuznetsov's wife, who'd been sentenced to ten years in the Leningrad skyjacking case; and the Lithuanian sailor Simas Kudirka, who, like Silva, was serving a ten-year sentence due to expire in 1980. Their early releases were probably the result of backstage diplomacy.

The KGB had promised Silva that Kuznetsov would be released if she left the country immediately. We caught her as she was getting her documents ready for the emigration office and convinced her to sign a demand (we'd already drafted it) for a meeting with her husband before her departure. The authorities agreed with alacrity. Kuznetsov was brought under guard to Moscow by ordinary passenger train. Silva was allowed to see him in the prison warden's office that same day.

Silva blew up at me when I tried to convince her to use the same tactic to achieve a meeting with her two brothers, who'd also been sentenced in the skyjacking case; apparently she'd swallowed the KGB's promises whole. She refused to sign a new statement, and left our apartment, slamming the door behind her.

Understandably, then, I was surprised when the following year I received a four A.M. phone call from a U.S. Jewish organization proposing that Silva, in her capacity as a Soviet dissident, represent me at the Nobel Prize ceremony (it was clear by then that I wouldn't be allowed to attend). I said my wife would be standing in for me.

In 1970 Simas Kudirka had jumped onto the deck of a U.S. Coast Guard cutter anchored alongside his Soviet fish-processing ship in American waters. After the Soviet captain declared falsely that Kudirka had stolen money from the ship's safe, the Americans allowed Soviet sailors to beat him and remove him from their ship by force. Once again, Soviet representatives abroad found Westerners easy prey for their lies.

When Kudirka was summoned to the warden's office and released from Vladimir Prison, he was terrified that it was some sort of trick; he went straight to his mother's home in Lithuania without contacting anyone in Moscow, and they soon left for America together.

Much of the credit for Kudirka's release belongs to Sergei Kovalev, who helped to establish Kudirka's claim to American citizenship (his mother had been born in Brooklyn). It was no mean feat; Kovalev had to enter the American Embassy several times—this in a country where such visits by an ordinary citizen are viewed as near-treason—and on two occasions was stopped and searched after meeting with consular officials.

36

REACHING OUT TO THE WORLD

The Cino del Duco Prize. Activities in
1974–1975. Meeting with Heinrich Böll. Day
of the Political Prisoner. Threats against the
children and grandchildren. Sergei Kovalev.

IN 1974 I received the Cino del Duco prize, an award given in France for
humanitarian service. It was a great honor for me, and the prize money enabled
Lusia to realize her plan for a fund to aid the children of political prisoners.
Additional contributions came in, but the fund gradually faded out of existence
after 1976, when it became impossible to receive Beryozka certificates for
currency transferred from abroad. Some money eventually was sent to Czechoslovakia for the children of Charter 77 activists.

Throughout 1974 and 1975 I continued to speak out in behalf of victims
of injustice in the USSR and abroad: Georgy Vins, a nonconformist Baptist
minister; a group of Jewish war veterans from Minsk who'd been subjected to
harassment after being denied permission to emigrate; Lithuanian prisoners
who had been prevented from returning to their homes in Lithuania after
release (other political prisoners had experienced similar problems); political
prisoners in Indonesia, most of them Chinese, who'd been imprisoned following the abortive 1965 Communist coup; Kurds who were facing persecution
of near-genocidal proportions in Iraq; and many others.

It was in February 1975 that I met Heinrich Böll, whose work had been
published in the USSR since the mid-1950s. Böll's deeply felt commitment to
humanity and his opposition (in common with Remarque, Fallada, and other
German writers) to all forms of fascism had impressed the members of my
generation, who were all too aware that Stalinism, too, had spawned a pervasive
atmosphere of violence. Böll was accompanied on his visit by his wife, Anne-
marie, and two friends, the poet and translator Konstantin Bogatyrev and the
artist Boris Birger, who also did yeoman work as interpreters. We were very
excited about the visit, and Lusia did Böll proud with a spectacular dinner
tailored to his special dietary requirements as a diabetic. (This gives me a

chance to sing Lusia's praises as a cook, something in which she herself takes great pride—she works with pleasure, so rapidly and efficiently you don't realize how much effort she's putting into it.) Also at the table were Efrem's mother, Tomar Feigin, who was staying with us at the time, and little Matvei, good as gold.

My conversation with Böll was substantive and somewhat thorny. Despite our mutual sympathy and Böll's inherent tolerance, our judgments and values often clashed. That's hardly surprising, given the very different worlds we inhabited. On the one hand, the West: pluralistic, changeable, individualistic, in the case of Europe compressed into a small corner of the globe, concerned with spiritual values and, even more, material well-being, (yet sensing their fragility) boasting a broad democratic tradition with a free and influential, if at times irresponsible, press. On the other, the Soviet Union: strictly controlled by the Party-state monopoly, a closed, hypocritical, brutal society, apathetic, degraded by alcoholism and corruption—and yet immense, with a vast variety of human and physical resources; a country where the intelligentsia's inherited humanist values, although eroded, are still pervasive, where anything can happen, and where, as Saltykov-Shchedrin observed, "You'll never be bored." It has become an international hub rivaled only by the United States.

That first encounter (we met once again several years later) found us debating hotly the question of ethnic German emigration. I reproached the West Germans for paying too little attention to the problem, while Böll noted difficulties in assimilating the newcomers and the émigrés' problems in adjusting to a different environment. At the end of our conversation he admitted: "Life in the West is hard—here, it's impossible!"

Boll and I signed a joint appeal on behalf of Vladimir Bukovsky, in particular, and of political and psychiatric prisoners in general. On a personal level, the visit reinforced my admiration for this remarkable man, but I regret that our concentration on topical matters kept us from discussing fundamental issues.

ON OCTOBER 30, 1974, the first Day of the Political Prisoner had been observed, the initiative coming from prisoners themselves. Since then political prisoners in the USSR have developed a tradition of conducting a one-day hunger strike on that day; in Moscow, human rights activists hold a press conference. In 1974 and subsequent years (with few exceptions) those press conferences took place in our apartment.

The 1974 press conference was organized by Sergei Kovalev, Tatyana Khodorovich, Tatyana Velikanova, Malva Landa, and Alexander Lavut, all of whom would eventually do time as political prisoners. I wrote an introductory statement and read my October 24 letter to Brezhnev, which contained detailed information on political prisoners and repeated the call for an amnesty. Sergei Kovalev and others then presented reports and documents, many of which had been smuggled out of prisons and camps at great risk.

According to the official Corrective Labor Code, there are no political prisoners in the USSR. The authorities refuse to admit that anyone is in prison for his beliefs, insisting that people are prosecuted only for criminal offenses, such as slander against the Soviet state. For someone to refer to himself as a political prisoner, whether in an official complaint or a personal letter, is regarded as itself partaking of such slander, and may result in severe retaliative measures.

All convicts in the Soviet Union, including political prisoners, must endure conditions well below the standards of humanitarian treatment of prisoners observed in most democratic countries. The Corrective Labor Code allows such measures as forced labor; severe restrictions on family visits, correspondence, and food parcels; and the use of special punishment cells. And numerous secret regulations serve to make prisoners' lives even more difficult and unpleasant.

The compulsory labor is often dangerous, carried out under conditions hazardous to health. Failure to meet what are in many cases impossibly high quotas may be punished by a cut in already scanty food rations or confinement in a punishment cell. There are strict limitations on the frequency and duration of visits (only relatives are allowed), and arbitrary cancellations occur on the flimsiest of pretexts. Visitors may be turned away because of events (for instance, a hunger strike) that the authorities want to keep secret from the outside world—a calamity for the prisoners and for relatives who may have traveled hundreds of miles to reach the camp. Or visits may be cut short— three days to one, a shorter visit to less than an hour. In extreme cases a prisoner may not be allowed any visitors for a period of years.

The number of letters the prisoners may receive is limited, and the mail is censored and sometimes confiscated for no apparent reason. Cronid Lubarsky, and Sergei Kovalev were among those political prisoners forced into desperate protests when their correspondence was cut off for months at a time.

The special punishment cells and inner camp prisions to all intents and purposes constitute legalized torture by starvation and cold. The "normal" camp diet itself is barely enough to sustain life, deficient in vitamins and protein and scarcely edible. Regulations limiting supplementary food parcels are strict.

Political prisoners who remain true to their beliefs are considered to be refusing to "set foot on the path of reform." Camp and prison authorities employ systematic brutality—which they call "reeducation"—to break them.

This has resulted in countless tragedies, and it is the reason for political prisoners' demands for special status. "It's enough that we're being imprisoned for our beliefs," they say. "At least respect those beliefs once we're here."

Recurring sentences turn political prisoners into eternal convicts. A favorite device is a trial for slandering the Soviet system conducted in the camp or prison with the sole evidence the testimony—often coerced—of other prisoners.

Representatives of the International Red Cross or other impartial international organizations have never been allowed to inspect Soviet camps, prisons, or special psychiatric hospitals. Most of the countries singled out by the Soviet press for human rights violations permit such visits. Still, the Soviet camps of today aren't extermination camps of the type run by Stalin and Hitler. The deaths of Bidia Dandaron, Yuri Galanskov, Juri Kukk, Vladimir Shelkov, Oleksa Tykhy, Vasyl Stus, Anatoly Marchenko, and other political prisoners in the camps were terrible tragedies and in many cases the consequence of the authorities' criminal actions, but these were exceptions.

Many foreign correspondents, most with cameras or tape recorders, attended the October 30 press conference. We had removed the beds and wardrobe in Ruth's room and replaced them with chairs, but some people ended up standing out in the hallway. Western press coverage was extensive, and the KGB took note of the event in its own way, with participation in Political Prisoners Day being recorded in numerous indictments and verdicts.

IN LATE DECEMBER, during the period when the Jackson-Vanik amendment was being debated in the U.S. Congress, we found an envelope in our mailbox containing a clipping of Gromyko's letter to Kissinger denouncing the amendment, together with a typewritten note:

Andrei Dmitrievich!
This debate was provoked by your activities. If you don't cease them, we'll take measures—starting, as you might expect, with the Yankeleviches, senior and junior.
—The Central Committee of the Russian Christian Party

The junior Yankelevich—Lusia's grandson Matvei—was then fifteen months old. We had no doubt that this threat had been inspired by the KGB, and we took it very seriously.

In late 1974 when the senior Yankelevich, Efrem, was visiting his mother near Moscow, two men came up to him as he was emptying the garbage and blocked his way. "Remember, if your father-in-law doesn't cut out his shenanigans, you and your son will wind up in a garbage dump yourself!" one warned.

I reported the threats to the Ministry of Internal Affairs, and in due time I was summoned by a Detective Levchenko. Courteous but elusive, Levchenko suggested that my son-in-law "might be involved with criminal elements who are blackmailing him."

There were other alarming incidents. Alexei was on his way home from school one day when a blind man asked him for help in getting to Sokolniki Park. It was out of Alexei's way, but he wasn't the type to turn down such a request. The blind man vanished suddenly in an out-of-the-way side street and Alexei was attacked by a gang of youths. His glasses were smashed, but he managed to get away. Meanwhile, Lusia and I were nearly out of our minds with worry. When we reported him missing, the police scoffed—"He's probably out drinking with his friends," they told us.

ON DECEMBER 27, 1974, our great friend, the human rights activist Sergei Kovalev, was arrested. When I met Kovalev in 1970, he'd already published more than sixty papers on neural networks and other topics in electrophysiology on the borderline between biology and information science. In the 1960s he was one of the founders of the human rights movement and helped develop its principles: non-violence, *glasnost*, respect for the law, a conscientious attitude toward information. In 1969, after signing protest letters and becoming a founding member of the Initiative Group for Human Rights, Kovalev had been forced out of a senior research scientist position at Moscow University. We didn't see each other all that often, but he became a true friend, close to us in credo and spirit.

Kovalev's hair was fair and wavy and he usually had a tan, even in the winter. His blue-eyed gaze—steady and clear, but often preoccupied—would at times change as he talked and a gentle, boyish smile appeared. Sergei was distinguished by his unfailing sense of right and wrong and a meticulousness which he carried over from his scientific research to everything he did. But this painstaking approach meant that Kovalev was almost always behind schedule and had to drive himself unsparingly to catch up (and later it would prove to be a severe handicap in camp, where it's wiser to fake your way through).

In May 1974, Kovalev, Velikanova, and Khodorovich announced their intention to start publishing the *Chronicle of Current Events* again. This bold move made Kovalev a marked man. In the seven months before his arrest, however, he accomplished a great deal, particularly for Kudirka and in the organizing of Political Prisoners Day.

After his dismissal from Moscow University, Kovalev had worked at the experimental fish hatchery where Vitaly Rekubratsky, who was married to a cousin of mine, directed a research group, and where Efrem later also found work. Kovalev made a strong impression on Efrem, who did well in adopting him as a model.

In the summer of 1974, one of Kovalev's coworkers borrowed his copy of *The Gulag Archipelago* to photocopy. The book was seized, and those involved were called in for questioning. One of them, Valery Maresin, had his salary docked twenty percent for six months for refusing to testify, and others were fired. We heard that an investigator had declared: "We know all about the anti-Soviet organization you've got there, but we're not going after Yankelevich; we don't need the whole world kicking up a fuss about Sakharov's son-in-law!" But we weren't so foolish as to believe that Efrem was "untouchable," and in fact he was eventually dismissed.

In October 1974, Kovalev wrote to Yuri Andropov, then chairman of the KGB, insisting on his right to loan books to anyone he chose and demanding the return of *The Gulag Archipelago*. A few days later, he found the letter, dirty and crumpled, outside his back door. The KGB, which is fond of such pointed gestures, was letting Kovalev know that he'd forfeited his rights as a citizen and become an outlaw.

On December 23, Kovalev's home was searched and he was taken in for a particularly unpleasant interrogation session. His passport was retained, and he was told to return on December 27. He knew he'd probably be arrested. Kovalev spent the evening of December 26 at our apartment, where Alexander Lavut, Tanya Velikanova, and Efrem had gathered to see him. He got there after we'd finished drinking our tea; he was hungry, and asked Lusia:

"Give me one last taste of your cabbage soup."

We sat in the kitchen, Kovalev in his usual spot with his back to the balcony door. We talked about all sorts of things, the mood switching back and forth from half-joking to serious, even philosophical. We all felt that this might be our last conversation with him for a long time. Around midnight, he asked for some paper. He was worried about the threatening letter we'd received a few days earlier from the "Russian Christian Party" (as usual, he was more concerned about others than about himself). He tried to draft a statement; dissatisfied with his first attempts, he kept on making changes. It was after two A.M. when he finally got up and said:

"All right then, I'll be going. I've got some things to do at home."

We saw him to the door and embraced him.

The next morning, Sergei Kovalev was arrested.

THE END OF 1974 was marked by more than arrests and threats. That December, Boris Birger painted a double portrait of Lusia and me. Although it wasn't everyone's cup of tea, in my eyes it captured something of profound importance—the bond between Lusia and me. We were shown sharing a common fate, with all its concerns—and its joys. I seem reflective and pensive in the painting, while Lusia is poised with a cigarette, ready to rush into action to help someone (a romantic at heart, said Birger). Looking now at a reproduction of the portrait, I have the strange, exciting feeling that although the physical, material existence of that moment has faded into the past and will continue to recede farther and farther after our deaths, there is at the same time something deep and lasting there, fixed for all eternity.

The sittings went on through most of December. They had a festive feel; Birger would tell remarkable stories of his experiences in the intelligence service during the war, and the postwar period, when he'd developed a considerable artistic reputation. He'd clashed with Khrushchev at the Manezh exhibition, which did his career no good, and in 1968 had been expelled from the Artists' Union for protesting against the trial of Ginzburg and Galanskov and refusing to recant. It had cost Birger financially, but he'd managed to hold on to his studio, and now he was working harder than ever and improving with every picture. Of course, art is a subjective matter, and there are those who prefer his earlier work, but it's vital that an artist progress and avoid stagnation and repetition. During breaks and after the sittings we would drink strong, boiling-hot tea from thick glasses and polish off Lusia's specialty, cheesecake with raisins, which she'd bring from home, knowing that both Boris and I were fond of it. Our friendship with Birger endured. Every year he would invite us to a private view of his work, and the double portrait was always included.

37

THE NOBEL PRIZE

Lusia's trip abroad. *My Country and the World*. Matvei's illness. The Nobel Prize. Kovalev's trial in Vilnius.

LUSIA'S EYE PROBLEMS stemmed from the concussion she suffered in October 1941, which caused temporary blindness, as well as hemorrhaging within the eye. She was given a disability discharge from the army in 1945; she had also suffered other injuries, but the concussion proved to have the most serious long-term consequences. Following the removal of the lens of her right eye in 1966, she was plagued by glaucoma in addition to chronic uveitis. Then, after her thyroid gland was removed, the glaucoma stopped responding to medication, and surgery became necessary. The uveitis had caused irreversible damage, and her eyesight had become so poor that only her extraordinary adaptability allowed her to lead a normal life.

Our attempts to get the necessary surgery done in the USSR came to naught. Reluctantly, we decided that she would have to go abroad for treatment, and once made, the decision would be irrevocable: there could be no backing down. But with every month's delay representing a further increase in intraocular tension and the irreversible destruction of portions of the retina, Lusia's visual field was shrinking. Glaucoma, if it is not controlled, leads to blindness. Lusia's sight was at stake.

In August 1974 she phoned Italy and asked her friend Nina Harkevich to send an invitation for medical treatment. Nina and Maria Olsufieva, another friend of Lusia's in Italy, went straight to work, and Lusia received an invitation in September and immediately began filling out forms for travel abroad.

She had met Maria Olsufieva in the 1960s through the critic Viktor Shklovsky. In Paris, Maria had discovered a copy of Vsevolod Bagritsky's book *Poems, Letters, Diaries*, edited by Lusia and Bagritsky's mother, and had begun to translate excerpts into Italian. The elderly Russian-born woman on whose night table Maria had spotted the book had told her: "This little book gave me an insight into the differences between the Russian boys who killed Germans during the Second World War and the German boys who were killing the Russians." A few months later Maria visited the USSR, where Shklovsky offered to introduce her to the book's co-editor, Lusia, for whom it had been a labor of love as well as of craft and talent—one of her finest accomplishments. The prewar student milieu of Leningrad comes alive in the pages of this book, which earned a Komsomol prize that no doubt would have ensured a large second edition (the first printing was only 30,000 copies) were it not for the fading of the "thaw."

Maria Olsufieva was born into an aristocratic family that emigrated from Russia into a life that was not always easy. But in Italy she managed to develop a career as a respected and prolific translator of Russian literature and she received the Taormina Prize for her work. She died in 1988.

Through Olsufieva, Lusia had met Nina Harkevich, the granddaughter of a Russian priest sent to Florence at the end of the nineteenth century to preside over the Orthodox parish there. Nina, a physician, declined to retire at seventy and continues to work; she taught anatomy at the Academy of Fine Arts, and she also paints and writes poetry. Lusia introduced me to these two marvelous women in the early 1970s, and they became my friends as well.

Obtaining permission for foreign travel involves an incredible amount of paperwork. In September, Lusia brought the documents to our local Visa and Registration Office (OVIR): her application; Nina's invitation (the official translation bureau had taken two weeks to translate it from Italian into Russian); two copies of a detailed four-page questionnaire; an affidavit that I, as her husband, had no objection to her travel; and six passport photographs. Since she was retired, she did not need a reference from her employer. The clerk at OVIR noticed that her ex-husband's office address was missing, so Lusia had to return home to type it in. (She was not permitted to write it in by hand.) Then the clerk complained that her father's place of death had not been filled in. It took Lusia two days to get a notarized photocopy of Gevork Alikhanov's death certificate—an unusual document issued by a Moscow Civil Registry Office in 1954 that gives his date of death as 1939—fifteen years earlier—but omits the place and cause of death. The young clerk gave us an incredulous look; Lusia had to explain that this was the kind of certificate issued in cases of posthumous rehabilitation.

Months went by. Lusia's eyesight steadily deteriorated. Finally, in April 1975, she was summoned to the central Moscow OVIR. There the deputy director informed her that her application had been turned down: treatment was available in the USSR. We immediately reported this decision to the foreign correspondents who had accompanied us to the office. Our impromptu press conference startled several Soviet bureaucrats who were waiting to pick up travel documents.

A day or two later I went to see Mstislav Keldysh, president of the Academy of Sciences, and asked for his help. He too refused to intervene and cited the availability of Soviet medical treatment. We were down to our last chance: an appeal to world opinion.

On May 3, 1975, we called a press conference and distributed statements explaining Lusia's situation. We appealed to Western politicians and to World War II veterans (citing Lusia's disabled-veteran status) and announced that on May 8, 9, and 10, we would conduct a joint hunger strike during the thirtieth anniversary celebration of the USSR's victory in World War II.

A few hours before the press conference, a messenger from the Ministry of Health showed up with an official letter authorizing treatment for Citizen E. G. Bonner at any of the Ministry's ophthalmological institutes, and indicating the possibility of foreign specialists coming to the USSR to treat her at government expense (this letter disappeared during a 1978 covert search). We had made no appeal to the Ministry of Health; clearly, this was the KGB's latest ploy to deflect us from our goal. I remain convinced that had we taken the bait, nothing would have been done to treat Lusia's eyes.

People all over the world responded to our appeal. I recall a very important letter from the Federation of American Scientists warning Brezhnev that an "inhumane" response to Sakharov's request would have an adverse effect on scientific contacts, and support voiced by Queen Juliana of the Netherlands and West German Chancellor Willy Brandt during visits to the USSR.

Lusia's periodic eye examinations showed that the necrosis was approaching the yellow spot, the retina's most sensitive element. At the end of July 1975, while we were staying at the Zhukovka dacha, Lusia received a call from an OVIR official who told her that permission for a trip to Italy had been categorically denied, but that she would be granted every opportunity for treatment in the USSR (as if medical care were any of their business!). To offer a somewhat softened paraphrase of Lusia's stinging reply: "It's your fault I'm going blind, but I'm not going to any of your doctors." That ended the conversation. Ruth chided Lusia for answering too sharply.

Just twenty-four hours later, the same official phoned to say that Lusia should come to OVIR immediately: she would be granted permission to go abroad. The previous call had evidently been a last-ditch attempt by the KGB to break Lusia. She replied: "It's late. I won't be able to get there before you close." "No problem. We'll wait for you."

When Lusia arrived, an OVIR employee met her in the lobby and steered her by the arm to the second floor. Several people were waiting in the director's office, including the director, Sergei Fadeyev. He repeated that Lusia had been granted permission to travel to Italy for treatment of her eyes and would receive a visa within the next couple of days. During the brief exchange that followed, a man sitting beside Fadeyev suddenly interjected:

"You should understand that your husband will never be able to join you abroad."

I'm not sure what the point of this remark was—maybe just to test Lusia's reaction. "I've had several opportunities to remain abroad in the past," she replied, "but I'm not one of your Soviet bureaucrats; it's medical care I'm going for."

As soon as she got to Chkalov Street, Lusia phoned me at the dacha with the news. Reuters had already called me to check a tip—undoubtedly from the KGB—that a visa would be granted.

I SPENT the first half of 1975 working on *My Country and the World*.

In late 1974, the American senator James Buckley had paid me a visit, one of the first I'd had from an important Western political figure. Despite Buckley's characterization in the Soviet press as an extreme right-wing reactionary, he impressed me as a thoughtful man, concerned with the fundamental problems of our times and free of that common Western weakness, the need to appear "progressive" at any cost. Is that what is meant by "reactionary"? We didn't agree on everything, but our conversation was substantive and ranged over many issues: disarmament and strategic parity, the struggle for an open society, and, in particular, the Jackson-Vanik amendment and the freedom to choose one's country of residence. I handed him the lists of six thousand prospective German emigrants compiled by Friedrich Ruppel and his friends. Buckley agreed to pass them on to the West German government—not a difficult thing for him to do, perhaps, but how many others are willing to undertake such tasks?

After Buckley left, I continued to think about what I'd said and what I failed to say. Around that time, I also received a visit from a group of American scientists, including Wolfgang Panofsky, who were in Moscow to discuss disarmament. They spent a cordial evening with us at our apartment, and the conversation continued as Lusia and I walked our guests back to their hotel. I found much in common between Panofsky's ideas and my own, but again, much was left unsaid.

Lusia suggested that I write an open letter to Buckley delving more deeply into the topics raised at these meetings. She overrode my doubts and convinced me that fundamental issues could not be left unexamined. I set to work, but decided to write an essay rather than an open letter. I worked on it from January through July of 1975. Writing is never an easy task for me (although nothing has ever been so excruciating as these memoirs). I finished the book while confined to bed; in June, alarmed by my EKG and other tests, the doctors had put me on a strict regimen. By mid-July I had more or less recovered, but my heart has never regained its full strength and I still have trouble climbing stairs.

My Country and the World parallels in many respects my *Reflections* of seven years earlier, developing in greater detail such ideas as the need for convergence, disarmament, democracy, and pluralistic reforms. I now placed greater emphasis on strategic parity, and criticized certain aspects of SALT, while welcoming the idea of negotiations. I also stressed the potentially destabilizing effects of antimissile defenses, and of MIRVs. In treating the subjects of human rights and an open society, I paid particular attention to the Jackson-Vanik Amendment. I offered my analysis of the stance and actions of what I would now call the "left-liberal" (I then called it just "liberal," but this is not precise enough) Western intelligentsia.

In *My Country and the World* I included the following list of reforms which I felt were necessary in order "to bring our country out of a constant state of general crisis":

One. Broadening the economic reform of 1965; full autonomy for plants, factories, etc., in matters of economics, production, and personnel policy.

Two. Partial denationalization of all types of economic and social activity, probably excluding heavy industry, major transportation, and communications.

Three. Full amnesty for all political prisoners.

Four. A law granting the freedom to strike.

Five. Laws guaranteeing real freedom of opinion, freedom of conscience, and freedom to circulate information.

Six. Legislation assuring *glasnost* and public oversight with respect to major decisions.

Seven. A law assuring the freedom to choose one's place of residence and of employment within the country.

Eight. Legislation guaranteeing the freedom to leave the country and to return to it.

Nine. Banning all forms of Party and official privileges not directly required by the performance of official duties. Equal rights for all citizens as a basic principle of the state.

Ten. Legislative confirmation of the right of Soviet republics to secede, and the right to discuss the question of secession.

Eleven. A multiparty system.

Twelve. A convertible ruble.

I added:

I feel it necessary to emphasize that I am a confirmed evolutionist and reformist, and an opponent, as a matter of principle, of violent, revolutionary changes of the social order, which always lead to the destruction of the economic and legal systems, as well as to mass suffering, lawlessness, and horrors.[1]

[IT IS VERY INTERESTING to reread these points thirteen years later, in the fourth year of *perestroika,* which in fact has adopted several of them as slogans. Others are still only dreams. I would now amend paragraph 10 to include the idea of a Treaty of Union as put forward by the Popular Fronts of the Baltic Republics.—A.S. 1988]

My Country and the World was published just as my Nobel Peace Prize was announced, and so attracted considerable attention. Lusia also publicized it in her October 2 press conference in Italy.

The Soviet media responded with attacks concentrating their fire on a casual mention of Rudolf Hess—writing about Soviet political prisoners serving twenty-five-year terms, I had mentioned him as an example of a long-term prisoner. Volpin and Chalidze, who had read the manuscript in America before publication, questioned my bracketing Hess with our prisoners. I was reluctant to change my text and cut his name, but I did add a note clarifying my awareness of Hess's role in the creation of the criminal Nazi system. The mention of Hess, along with my alleged support of the military junta in Chile (the appeal Galich, Maximov, and I had made to Pinochet on behalf of Pablo Neruda) became a standard feature of the anti-Sakharov campaign.

LUSIA's glaucoma made her apprehensive about flying, and so, with the help of a French correspondent, she obtained a transit visa from the French consulate and bought a ticket on a train scheduled to leave Moscow for Paris on the evening of August 9. Tanya, Efrem, and their two-year-old son Matvei were staying along with Ruth, Lusia, and myself at the dacha. (Alexei had married his classmate Olga Levshin in November 1974, and they were living elsewhere.) As we were preparing to return to Moscow on the morning of August 9, Tanya noticed that Matvei was running a high fever, and he was uncomfortable and cranky. Still, she didn't think it was anything but an ordinary children's illness, although Lusia was disturbed to note his arms and legs twitching

---

[1][*My Country and the World,* pp. 100–102.]

convulsively. It was Saturday, and I couldn't get a car from the Academy garage, so Lusia phoned Alexei and asked him to get hold of any car he could. An hour and a half later he showed up in an enormous Chaika limousine big enough for all of us: some VIP's chauffeur had jumped at the opportunity to earn a bit on the side.

Back at our apartment, Lusia asked Vera Livchak to come over and take a look at Matvei. When she arrived, they went into the next room to discuss his condition while Tanya stayed with the child. Suddenly, we heard her scream. We ran into the room and saw Matvei lying unconscious and rigid, frothing at the mouth, with his eyes rolled back. Lusia picked him up and carried him over to an open window; Vera pried open his mouth and used a spoon as a depressor to keep him from swallowing his tongue. Tanya called the children's emergency service. An ambulance soon arrived with a doctor who quickly gave Matvei an anticonvulsant injection which, though only partially effective, may well have saved his life. The doctor spent half an hour trying to stop the convulsions and then took the still-unconscious Matvei to the hospital. Tanya and Efrem, who rode along, heard the doctor tell the staff there: "Take care of this little fellow, he's worth it." Lusia, of course, postponed her trip; Vera and I returned the tickets to the station. Throughout that terrible night each of us was wracked by the unuttered fear that Matvei might die.

The next morning, the doctor on duty told us that the Yankelevich child was conscious and out of danger. In a strained voice, Lusia asked: "Doctor, are you certain?" He assured her he was.

We were allowed to bring Matvei his imported pacifier (Soviet pacifiers have a different shape), and the nurse told us he had responded to the sight of the familiar object by whispering "Mama." Lusia exclaimed with relief: "That's what I was waiting for!"—a sign that the child was able to make logical associations, and had not suffered any brain damage.

What had happened? Convulsions are often associated with high fevers in children whose birth was difficult, as Matvei's had been. It's a plausible explanation—but in this case circumstances suggest a less innocent cause. As Matvei was being taken off to the hospital, we suddenly recalled a bizarre incident that had taken place two days before, on the morning of August 7. Matvei, who had been playing in the hallway that led to the courtyard, suddenly screamed and ran into the kitchen, where the adults were sitting and drinking tea. When asked what was wrong, he pointed to his mouth. We thought it might be a bee sting, but there was no sign of any insect bite or swelling. Matvei may simply have had a fright—or he may have been persuaded to swallow some convulsant, less with the aim of harming the child than of delaying Lusia's departure. (In which case it accomplished its purpose.) When Vera used her connections and called the hospital, the doctor on duty irritably asked her to refrain from phoning again: "Someone else just called and said he was a doctor and wanted to know how the Yankelevich child was doing." One can only assume that this was the KGB, perhaps worried they'd overdone it and would have had to face the music.

Another indication that Matvei's illness might have been artificially induced was a call we received at midnight from the intensive care unit, asking if Matvei had access to medicine that might cause convulsions. Lusia said no, but the question disturbed us, especially in light of the Russian Christian Party's threats of a few months before.

Lusia rescheduled her departure for August 16. There was another attempt at intimidation that bore all the earmarks of the KGB. On the morning of August 15, we received an envelope postmarked Norway that contained horrifying photographs, all involving injuries to eyes. They looked like ads for horror movies: there were such sights as eyes gouged out with a dagger, a skull with a knife driven through one eye socket, and a skull reflected in the pupil of an eye. A Norwegian correspondent checked out the return address and discovered that it belonged to a Lithuanian who'd sent me a copy of an appeal he'd written to Brezhnev after his wife had been denied permission to join him; the KGB, it seemed, had removed his letter and substituted the ghastly pictures. This was only one of numerous instances we encountered of such KGB sleight-of-hand. Instead of Christmas cards, we would receive photographs—dozens in the course of a day or so—of automobile accidents or brain surgery or monkeys with electrodes implanted in their brains. Between pages of a scientific journal, I found an article, "The Blind Leading the Blind," written by the émigré (and former refusenik) Tetyonov. It began: "The world Jewish press has raised a heartrending wail over Academician Sakharov's exile."

In the case of Matvei's illness, it was difficult to know for certain whether a crime had been committed, and absolutely impossible to obtain proof that would stand up in court. This is one of the "perks" enjoyed by the organs of state security—until their Nuremberg trial.

At the time of the incident with Matvei, Tanya was in her ninth month of pregnancy. On September 1, she gave birth to her second child, a daughter named Anya. On October 6, Olga and Alexei had a daughter, Katya. Lusia would not see her new grandchildren until the end of December; on August 16, she finally left for Italy.

Professor Frezotti operated in Siena on September 4. This halted the glaucoma, but nothing could be done to restore the vision already lost. Two days after the operation I received false information (ostensibly transmitted by word of mouth from Siena via Paris) that the operation had been a failure. Another KGB "joke."

ON OCTOBER 9, Ruth and I were visiting our friend Yuri Tuvim; foreign correspondents managed to track me down at his home and arrived there with Lev Kopelev. They informed me that I had been awarded the Nobel Peace Prize and persuaded me to say a few words. A videotape of my reaction was rushed onto a plane and broadcast over European television that same day. In my impromptu comments, I stated:

This is a great honor not just for me but for the whole human rights movement. I feel I share this honor with our prisoners of conscience— they have sacrificed their most precious possession, their liberty, in defending others by open and nonviolent means. I hope for an improvement in the lot of political prisoners in the USSR and for a worldwide political amnesty.

Lusia, who was in Italy being fitted with contact lenses that day, later told me that she'd responded almost identically to the news. Soon she was watching me on television and accepting the congratulations that came pouring in from all over the world. Her trip to Italy for medical treatment was interrupted by a multitude of tasks. After all sorts of complications, Lusia traveled to Oslo to represent me at the Nobel ceremonies.

Ruth and I could hear the phone ringing as we climbed the stairs to our apartment. Calls were coming in from friends and strangers, from Moscow and other cities at home and abroad. Many were from foreign journalists, to whom I basically repeated my initial remarks. Sometime between three and four A.M., I received a call from Alexander Galich: Vladimir Maximov was standing beside him, and had just spoken with Lusia, who was elated and feeling fine and sent her congratulations. "It's a joy and a victory for us all, we're all toasting you," Galich said. I hadn't had the pleasure of hearing his voice since his emigration in the summer of 1974, and, although I didn't know it then, this was to be the last time.

A steady stream of calls and visitors continued the next day from morning until late at night. There was a deluge of telegrams, including one from Lusia, whose warmth overcame the constraints of telegraphic style. The first secretary and other officials from the Norwegian Embassy visited, bringing congratulations from the ambassador and a vase of beautiful roses.

After another day of this bedlam, Ruth insisted that we all go out to the dacha. I gave in, although it would have been wiser to refuse—no calls could be received there from abroad; not even Lusia could get through. I should have accepted the responsibilities the prize entailed and not shifted the burden to others. And foreign correspondents still managed to get out to the dacha several times a day; Lusia's first view of her newborn granddaughter, Anya, was in a snapshot taken at the dacha by a French photographer. Another foreign visitor helped forward a letter from Gleb Yakunin and Lev Regelson to the World Council of Churches meeting in Nairobi, where its description of the plight of religious believers in the USSR provoked a considerable response.

I received a very complimentary letter from Roy Medvedev, though I'm afraid I could not help but be reminded of how his brother Zhores declared during the previous year that the Nobel Peace Prize shouldn't go to Sakharov, who'd built the hydrogen bomb. And Lusia discovered during her stay in Italy that Zhores had been sending out bizarre letters: one to Maria Olsufieva claiming that Lusia had exaggerated her grandson's illness because she was scared to travel, and she didn't really need an eye operation; she'd been seen with her husband attending the theatre. In any case, they were entitled to medical treatment at the Kremlin hospital. This privilege had in fact been revoked—after I intervened on Zhores's behalf. And where was Zhores, far away in England, getting his information? From Roy? The KGB? He also warned Maria in another letter to watch out for Lusia's bad character, and to disregard any pleas of financial distress—Sakharov was raking in thousands of dollars from his books. Zhores apparently didn't realize that Lusia's acquaintance with Maria went back further than mine; he thought she'd offered Lusia hospitality solely on my account.

A third letter, to the politician and journalist Nicholas Bethell, claimed that Lusia's statements in her October 2 press conference had been a pack of lies and suggested that Bethell turn to Zhores for the truth.

The official reaction in the USSR to the Nobel award was one of intense irritation and some nervousness. Regina made a collection of Soviet press clippings for me, which unfortunately disappeared during KGB searches. As in 1973, there were many articles ridiculing my activities and writings. The Nobel Committee's decision was termed hostile and provocative. On October 25, *Izvestia* published a letter similar to the one signed by forty academicians two years earlier, this one signed by seventy-two full and corresponding members of the Academy of Sciences. The trade union paper *Trud* printed a sneering and malicious column, "A Chronicle of Life in High Society," by one "Z. Azbel" (the Jewish surname was probably a KGB pseudonym). "We are delighted that Mme Bonner has at last found eye surgeons befitting her social status. . . . And how nice for Mme Bonner to have chosen such a propitious moment to see the world through newly clarified vision, as the wave of her husband's fame was cresting in the West." It was, of course, the KGB who had actually chosen the moment—and they could kick themselves for it.

Sakharov, the column continued, had decided to compensate for his increasing impotence as a scientist by striking out in a new direction; for starters, he "bowed down to Buckley till our intellectual's nose was scraping the floor before the smug businessman." Passages from *My Country and the World* were strung together out of context to demonstrate that I was "several steps ahead of even the most reactionary politicians" and that I'd said that in exchange for détente, "the West shouldn't ask much—just partial denationalization of a wide range of enterprises, partial decollectivization, and immediate secession of the Soviet Union's constituent republics."

Here the author deliberately mingles several fundamentally different notions: the idea that I, and I alone, believe that our country must institute economic reforms (which, I consider internal affairs of the USSR, not subject to external coercion); the need for international defense of human rights, which the USSR itself has acknowledged as legitimate by signing the Helsinki Final Act; and the breaking away of the Soviet Union's constituent republics, which I never described as necessary or expedient. The constitution of the USSR does, however, give citizens the right to discuss and resolve the question of whether to remain part of the Soviet Union, and the prosecution of individuals for supporting secession from the Union is illegal and unconstitutional. The article concludes:

> . . . a bone has been tossed to him in the form of the Nobel Peace Prize. Sakharov has been promised more than $100,000. It's difficult to find an exchange rate to compare that sum to the thirty pieces of silver received by Judas. Mrs. Bonner, who is well versed in such matters, is probably the person best qualified to answer.[2]

This linking of a non-Russian surname and Judas's thirty pieces of silver in traditional anti-Semitic fashion, was calculated to arouse envy, malice, and all the instincts of the pogrom-makers.

From this time on, the KGB, which from the first days of our marriage had made clear its dislike of Luisa, focused its attacks on her.

In November 1975 my daughter Lyuba lost her baby in childbirth. As always with such tragedies, there was the tormenting feeling that there must have been something we could have done. . . .

I was determined to apply for a visa to attend the Nobel award ceremonies. I expected my application to be rejected, but that would allow the Nobel ceremony to go forward, while failure to act would place the Nobel Committee in an awkward position. Certainly there was no real possibility of my being

[2][*Trud*, October 23, 1975.]

forced into permanent exile. I sent my application to OVIR on October 20 and calmly awaited the outcome.

Meanwhile, dramatic events were unfolding in Italy, most likely the result of confusion on the part of the authorities, always dangerous. Early in November, an official from the Soviet embassy turned up unannounced at Nina Harkevich's home in Florence, where Lusia (who was out at the moment) was staying, and demanded Lusia's passport. Despite her lack of experience with Soviet bureaucratic wiles, Nina smelled a rat and refused to surrender the passport.

Lusia was then summoned to the Soviet consulate, where she refused to turn in the passport and submitted a written declaration that she intended to prolong her stay in Italy on medical grounds. She received an extension of her visa a couple of weeks later, in an obvious attempt to defuse the situation created by the decision to refuse me permission to attend the Nobel ceremony. The risk had been genuine that in a fit of pique the authorities might strip Lusia of Soviet citizenship, leaving themselves no avenue of retreat. Lusia and Nina had forestalled the possibility.

On November 14, I was summoned to the Moscow OVIR office. There I found Fadeyev waiting for me in the first-floor room usually occupied by his deputy, who was responsible for rejecting applications. Looking harassed, Fadeyev informed me that permission to go to Norway had been denied me on the grounds that I was "an individual possessing knowledge of state secrets." I told him I would contest the decision.

Interestingly enough, a week earlier Victor Louis, citing anonymous official sources, had published an article in the *London Evening News* stating that I would be refused a visa because of my knowledge of state secrets—obviously a trial balloon to test public reaction. Louis, who maintains an unprecedented dual role as Soviet citizen and correspondent for a British newspaper, often handles such delicate tasks for the regime. On November 7, Italian television reported that I had been given permission to attend the ceremony, an idea whose source still is not clear. Lusia ordered evening clothes for me—which she ended up canceling, of course.

That day or the next, Lusia made use of our restored phone service to call me from Rome, and I asked her to represent me at Oslo. A few days later, however, I came close to making a terrible mistake. I gave way to my fear that she might not be allowed back into the USSR or that the KGB might take some other revenge against her, and suggested that it would be better to find someone else for the job, perhaps Galich.

"I understand," she said, her voice falling in disappointment. "But you're making a mistake."

Ruth had been urging me strongly to keep Lusia from going; and she'd written her daughter to that effect. While it seemed unlikely that the authorities would willingly risk another international scandal, there was always the possibility that they might refuse to allow Lusia back into the country.

Efrem, who had been standing next to the phone in the kitchen doing the dishes when Lusia called, said to me after I hung up: "I don't think you're right, Andrei Dmitrievich." He spoke quietly and with his usual deference, but he was forthright in laying out the reasons why only Lusia could represent me, and after half an hour I was ready to admit my mistake. Luckily, I was able to get a call through to Lusia in Florence within a couple of hours. I shudder to think of what would have happened had it not been for Efrem.

In one of the many interviews I gave during November; this one to a Japanese newspaper, I used the formula: *Peace, progress, and human rights.* These words became the title of my Nobel lecture. The writing came easily; it was a delightful task. The lecture expressed my views on peace, convergence, disarmament, progress, an open society, and human rights, at the same time capturing something of my innermost feelings.

Efrem, who typed out several drafts for me, was my first reader, and an exacting one. Finally, I achieved a version he found satisfactory. Pyotr Kunin, my old university friend, also took a look at it. Lusia was already in Oslo when she received the final text of the Nobel lecture, and she too was pleased with it (as I, for the most part, still am).

The remarks for the award ceremony gave me more trouble. I'd simply run out of steam. Lusia received the draft of my acceptance speech just before leaving Italy for Norway, and did a certain amount of editing to give it some of the clarity, logical continuity, and emotional warmth it lacked. There was no way she could check back with me, and so on this unique occasion she did make changes I hadn't specifically approved. There was one omission, however, that she didn't feel it permissible to rectify, although she was sorely tempted. Of my predecessors as Nobel Peace Prize laureates, I had mentioned only Albert Schweitzer. I have high regard for Schweitzer's life and philosophy, and his opposition to nuclear tests was a spur to my own activity in the 1950s. But I should have paid tribute to others as well—at the very least, I should have recalled Carl von Ossietzky and Martin Luther King, both of whom met tragic deaths in pursuit of their ideals. I hope this belated tribute in some way compensates for my negligence at the time.

Lusia flew to Oslo on the morning of December 9. Alexander Galich, Vladimir Maximov, Nina Harkevich, Maria Olsufieva, Viktor Nekrasov, Professor Renato Frezotti and his wife, and Robert Bernstein and Edward Kline and their wives attended the December 10 ceremony at my invitation. I had also issued invitations to Sergei Kovalev, Andrei Tverdokhlebov, Valentin

Turchin, and Yuri Orlov, knowing, of course, that the Soviet government
would not allow them to attend.

A FEW HOURS before Lusia left for Oslo, on the evening of December 8,
Efrem and I boarded the train for Vilnius. We were on our way to attend
Sergei Kovalev's trial, which was to begin the next day in the chambers of the
Lithuanian Supreme Court. The coincidence of the Nobel ceremony and the
opening of the trial was almost certainly no accident; it seemed a disturbing
portent.

Several individuals en route to the trial were on our train, but Tanya
Velikanova, Malva Landa and others had been detained in Moscow. It is
amazing how many agents the KGB can spare for such petty matters. What
difference can it make to them whether or not Velikanova attends a friend's
trial? Evidently they do care; in fact, the KGB is more attentive to human
rights activists and their activities than are many foreign correspondents.

There was no one waiting to meet us at the station; the Lithuanians who
were supposed to greet us had already been picked up by the police and
detained for several hours. We went to the apartment of our friend Eitan
Finkelshtein, a physicist and long-term refusenik, and left our suitcases there.
More or less unknown in the West, perhaps because he wasn't from Moscow,
Finkelshtein succeeded in emigrating to Israel a few years afterward. We then
made our way to the courthouse, which was swarming with KGB agents and
their hand-picked spectators.

Members of Kovalev's immediate family were allowed into the courtroom,
but, as expected, his friends were not. For the sake of the record, I decided
to ask both the presiding judge and the chief procurator of Lithuania for
permission to attend the trial. I strode past their secretaries and demanded
adherence to the law, while Efrem managed to tape their revealing and flus-
tered responses. We spent the rest of that day, the morning of December 10,
and all of December 11 in the lobby of the Supreme Court building. Lithuanians from all parts of their republic came over and introduced themselves to our
contingent. We sensed their deep sympathy for Kovalev and their outrage that
Vilnius was being used for his trial. KGB agents kept on trying to interrupt
our conversations, and brief scuffles broke out. Efrem became a favorite target;
noticing that Tanya had sewn his gloves to his sleeves so they wouldn't get lost,
the agents taunted him: "Why don't you go shake your mitts in Israel!"

Sergei's wife and son kept us informed about the trial. He was conducting
his own defense, since the lawyers he and his family wanted had not been
allowed to defend him. He was accused of editing issues 28–34 of *A Chronicle
of Current Events*, which included close to seven hundred separate items.

Kovalev acknowledged minor factual errors, none intentional or libelous, in eleven of these items. The court chose to examine only seven items, of which one devoted to conditions in the Dnepropetrovsk Special Psychiatric Hospital was typical. A psychiatrist from that hospital, Doctor Lubarskaya, a frequent state witness in dissident trials, gave an unconvincing rebuttal to the *Chronicle*'s charges; her testimony was confined to incidental matters, and scarcely touched on the overall picture. Leonid Plyushch, who was released from this hospital in 1986, was later to provide detailed evidence of the horrifying conditions there.

Riding the buses in Vilnius taught me how little affection Lithuanians have for Russians; whenever I sat down next to a Lithuanian, he would turn away or change seats. This attitude is understandable in light of the fierce repressions the Baltic republics endured during the 1940s. They haven't forgotten a remark attributed to Suslov in 1949: "We need Lithuania—even without the Lithuanians."

I was unable to get through to Oslo on December 9 or 10—either the line was "not in service" or there was some other excuse. I was linked to Lusia only by the international airwaves—and by an internal elation, born of the day's extraordinary events, that created a spiritual link between us.

Efrem and I did not return to the courthouse after the recess on December 10. We'd been invited to listen to the broadcast from Oslo at the home of Viktoras Petkus, where a number of people had gathered. Petkus, a former political prisoner and a friend of Sergei Kovalev's, was a philologist by profession and an authority on Lithuanian history and culture.

The radio is turned on. A trumpet fanfare. Mrs. Bonner-Sakharov is requested to take her place. Aase Lionaes, president of the Nobel Committee, announces that the Committee has awarded the 1975 Peace Prize to Andrei Sakharov. I can hear Lusia's footsteps as she mounts the rostrum. And then she begins to speak. It takes me a moment to grasp what she is saying, for at first I hear only the timbre of her voice, so close and familiar, and yet seeming to come from another world, solemn and radiant.

After the broadcast we moved to the next room, where a festive table had been set. Fifteen or so Lithuanians I'd seen outside the courtroom were waiting to mark the occasion; there were words of welcome, toasts to me, to Lusia, to Kovalev, and to absent friends. We did full justice to the meal, especially a fantastic Lithuanian cake.

Suddenly, the doorbell rang. Lusia Boitsova, Kovalev's wife, had come directly from the Supreme Court. Her whole body was trembling; she was in a dreadful state. Before even setting foot inside, she cried aloud: "They removed Sergei from the courtroom for calling them a bunch of swine!"

Bit by bit we pieced together what had happened. At the beginning of the session, Kovalev had demanded that the judge admit Andrei Sakharov, Tanya Velikanova, Alexander Lavut, and several other friends to the courtroom. Hoots of laughter and grunting noises erupted from the audience.

The judge said jocularly: "You can see for yourself that I can't grant your request. . . ."

Kovalev blew up. "I refuse to speak in front of this herd of swine! I demand that you remove me from the courtroom!"

Kovalev is normally a model of restraint and courtesy, but, like many mild-mannered people, he can be roused to fury by unethical behavior.

The judge bellowed back: "The defendant is in contempt of court! Guard, remove him!"

Kovalev had time only to cry out: "My love and gratitude to all my friends. My congratulations to Andrei Dmitrievich Sakharov!" Then the guards dragged him away, to the accompaniment of the audience's laughter, hooting, and insults.

The trial continued for about half an hour after Kovalev's removal from the courtroom. The judge then announced a ten-minute recess, adding: "The witnesses are excused." The only witnesses still in the courtroom were friends of Kovalev; the rest had taken off. Fearing (not without reason) that if they left the courtroom they wouldn't be allowed back in, our people decided to stay put. But within a few minutes police rushed in, shouting, "Clear the premises," shoving and dragging people into the hallway. Yuri Orlov, a short man, was lifted up and carried out bodily. Orlov, Mikhail Litvinov, and Turchin were charged with disturbing the peace and detained for several hours at the police station.

That evening I managed to phone Tanya in Moscow and tell her what was happening at the trial. Half an hour later, Lusia called her from Oslo. The first words she heard from Tanya were: "Mama, write this down . . ." There was no time for Lusia to ask about her grandchildren.

And so ended December 10, 1975, the day of Sergei Kovalev, Elena Bonner, and Andrei Sakharov.

THE REMAINDER of Kovalev's trial took place in his absence and in the absence of defense counsel. He wasn't even brought back to hear his sentence pronounced—a serious omission, and grounds for dismissal of the verdict. He later regretted his outburst, as it cost him the chance to deliver the speech he'd spent a full year preparing; he'd intended to expose the investigation's short-comings and to speak out on behalf of the whole human rights movement. It is virtually certain, however, that the KGB-coached judge would have found some means or other of thwarting him. And the manner in which the rest of the trial was conducted—without the defendant or defense counsel—was, if anything, more striking evidence of corruption than any final plea.

On December 12, the day of sentencing, Kovalev's Moscow friends and Lithuanian sympathizers again gathered in the courthouse lobby. There were dozens of KGB agents; the ones standing nearest us indulged in their usual derisive remarks, but we refused to rise to the bait and for the most part succeeded in holding our tongues.

Suddenly, the sound of applause could be heard coming from the courtroom: the verdict had been read, and the "public" was cheering. The room emptied rapidly, the spectators ignoring our questions as they hurried past. Finally Kovalev's family emerged, and his son Ivan announced:

"Seven camp plus three exile."

Efrem was standing beside me. He managed to keep his expression impassive, but the dark shadows under his eyes stood out as his face went pale. Antanas Terleckas, a former political prisoner, was on my other side. I became aware that the KGB officer in charge was addressing me:

"So, you see for yourself that the Lithuanian people have applauded the sentence."

I snapped back: "Hardly; the Lithuanian people were barred from the courtroom."

Grabbing hold of Efrem and Terleckas, I began making my way toward the exit, surrounded by a raucously clowning crowd of KGB agents, some of whom were making monkey faces and hopping around, while others produced squeaking noises; it was a repulsive and frightening display. We forced our way through to the coatroom. There the Lithuanian attendant exclaimed in a voice all could hear: "May God help Dr. Kovalev and his friends!"

Tears filled my eyes. I reached out and took her hand, then quickly left. What repercussions she may have suffered I don't know, but the memory of that scene, and of her drawn face, aging but fine-featured, still haunts me.

A samizdat record of the court proceedings was ready within a few weeks. Kovalev's son Ivan reconstructed the trial from memory, and Efrem took on the mammoth task of editing his report. The Soviet authorities were unable to silence international protests against Kovalev's trial and sentence. He served his term in labor camp and exile with dignity and courage.

Ivan Kovalev and his wife, Tatyana Osipova, were later themselves imprisoned for their human rights activities. When Efrem got back to Moscow he was fired from his job, and he remained unemployed until his forced emigration. For Efrem, to whom Sergei was both friend and mentor, it would have been unthinkable not to attend the trial.

Meanwhile, Lusia was living through an unforgettable few days in Oslo, experiencing everything for both of us. On December 11, she held a press conference at which her ability to think on her feet got her through three hours of impromptu questions. Asked to compare Sakharov and Solzhenitsyn, she came up with the apt analogy—just to both parties, I think—of nineteenth-century Russia's Westernizers and Slavophiles. She delivered my Nobel lecture that same day. There were banquets to attend (not *my* strong point). Lusia was especially moved by a torchlight parade, and was told that this was a spontaneous and quite extraordinary sign of the Norwegian people's approval of the Nobel Committee's selection. She was moved to tears by the words written on a number of posters, translated to her as: "Sakharov is a good man." I, too, was deeply touched when I heard of this.

On December 12, Lusia said farewell to my special guests. Seated in a coffee shop, Galich began stripping off his garments one by one and handing them to Lusia: "This, for my mother; this cardigan for Andrei; this for Efrem . . ." For a minute, she feared he'd end up stark naked! I still have the cardigan. But Galich is gone. . . .

Lusia flew to Paris, where she spent a few days before finally returning to Moscow on December 20. She was met by a crowd of friends, as well as Tanya, Efrem, Matvei (calling loudly to his "Grandma Lyolya" through the barrier); and myself.

Soviet sailors like to sing a little takeoff on a sentimental ditty from some patriotic film which goes like this:

> Home again; how do you know?
> The search they make is head to toe.

Customs inspection is no joking matter even for ordinary Soviet citizens returning from abroad, and Lusia, of course, was a "special case." Customs officials tried to seize a copy of the Italian edition of *My Country and the World,* but Lusia snatched it out of the agent's hands. We had to wait around for several hours, which we whiled away looking through the customs "museum," a display of items confiscated from travelers. We won a partial victory in the war of nerves and succeeded in holding on to the Italian edition, but other books and tapes (which later figured in Lusia's trial) were confiscated.

And so, at last, we were together again.

38

BRUNOV AND YAKOVLEV

ON NOVEMBER 5, 1975, just when it was being decided whether or not I would be going to Oslo, I had a visitor, a strapping young fellow with a look of almost childlike innocence. He gave his name as Evgeny Brunov. He had worked as a legal consultant in Leningrad and gotten into hot water with the authorities—apparently over his religious convictions. (My sources for information about his life were Brunov and his mother.) He had moved with his mother and aunt to Klin, not far from Moscow, but things had gotten worse; he'd been committed several times to a psychiatric hospital, and been beaten up in dark alleys; once he'd even been thrown off a moving train and had sustained a broken leg.

Brunov wanted me to introduce him to foreign correspondents so they could write about the injustices he'd suffered. He had, he said, some interesting material for them. (According to his mother, he'd made a tape of his interrogation by the KGB. I refused. I very rarely arrange such meetings, and I had serious doubts about this case. I was on my way to the dacha, where Ruth and the children were still living, and Brunov offered to accompany me on the subway and help me carry my bags of groceries. There was more than a hint of desperation in his voice as he kept up his efforts to persuade me; he distracted my attention to the point where I missed my stop. But before I got out at the next station, I couldn't help noticing a group of middle-aged men (four of them, I think) listening to us: obviously KGB. One of them addressed me directly: "Hey, Pop," he said, "why bother talking to him—he's had it." "Mind your own business," I retorted, "we don't need your advice." As I got off the train I looked back and through the glass doors saw Brunov's childlike, blue eyes staring fearfully after me.

A month later, early in December, I had a visit from a woman who identified herself as Brunov's mother. She told me that her son had been thrown from a suburban train and killed the very day he'd been to see me. Not everything she said rang true, but I'll report it here to the best of my recollection:

"I knew Zhenya had gone to see you, so I waited all night for him and went to the train to meet him, but he didn't show up. I overheard a couple of men getting off the train talking. One of them said: 'Why did they call him out onto the platform? He wasn't bothering anyone, he was just sitting there quietly. Then there was a horrible scream; I rushed onto the platform but they stopped me: 'It's none of your business!' It didn't occur to me that they were talking about my son, but I remembered the conversation.

"The next morning, there was an unsigned note on a scrap of paper in my mailbox. It said: 'Go to the railroad police station and you'll find out about your son.' But they didn't know anything there. It wasn't until midday that I was told my son's body had been found by the railroad tracks, but they wouldn't let me see the body. On November 11 they gave us the coffin for burial. My son's face was bandaged; his eyes, nose, and cheeks were covered in plaster. We weren't allowed to take it off. But my brother, who was the only person allowed into the morgue, said Zhenya's eyes looked like they'd been gouged out."

The woman refused to give me her brother's name and address; she said they were bitter enemies and that he worked for the Interior Ministry and wouldn't speak to any of us. Tatyana Litvinova took her home. The woman lived in appalling poverty: there wasn't a crust of bread in the house and the place was quite bare. Tatyana was shown the corner of the storeroom where mother and son had listened to foreign radio broadcasts, in constant fear that someone might catch them. Over Zhenya's bed hung an icon, and there were portraits of Solzhenitsyn, Emperor Haile Selassie, and myself. The police had given Brunov's mother a badly crumpled photograph found in her son's pocket. It was of Lusia's sendoff at Belorus Station in August, when she'd left for Italy. There was no mistaking Lusia and me. We'd had this photograph framed and left a few prints of it on our writing desk. Brunov must have asked if he could have it as a memento. I thought I'd refused, but now, looking back on it, I'm not so sure. In January I sent a statement to the Klin police saying I was the last person to see Brunov alive; I asked to be allowed to give evidence in the investigation into his death and to be informed of the results. A month later I was notified that, since the accident had occurred on the railroad, I should contact the Interior Ministry's department attached to the October railway line. I did so, but they refused to speak to me.

Was Brunov's death an accident? Was he (or his mother) mentally deranged? Did he suffer from a persecution complex that had led him to jump out and be hit by a train? Was it a suicide? Or had he been murdered by a

gang of thugs, or by KGB men tired of wasting their time on this troublemaker—weren't they once supposed to have thrown him off a train? Or was
it a murder designed to make it clear to me that my public activities could only
have tragic consequences?

The following facts speak in favor of this last supposition: 1) That all this
took place right after the announcement of the Nobel Prize; 2) the encounter
with the KGB in the subway; 3) a second incident in which a person who
surfaced at my house from nowhere subsequently disappeared.

The following episode took place much later, but I'll describe it here.

IN THE SPRING of 1977, I had a visit from a stranger whose case was nothing
out of the ordinary. He had been a driver at a motor pool in Sverdlovsk and
had, as he put it, "got into a spot of trouble" with the administration, first for
refusing to repair the boss's personal car during working hours, then for speaking out against other, equally widespread abuses. For that, he'd been transferred to a less well paid job. He had quit this job and was now in Moscow,
battling for his rights at the Central Trade Union Council and elsewhere, to
no avail. He wanted my advice on whether he should carry on with his struggle,
get in touch with foreign correspondents, contact the Procurator's Office—or
just forget the whole thing and go off to Kharkov, where his mother lived and
where he figured he'd get a job with no trouble. Lusia was present during the
conversation, and we hadn't the slightest hesitation in advising him to go to
Kharkov rather than get involved in a clearly pointless struggle. With this he
left. A few hours later I had a visit from a woman claiming to be his mother.
She said she had been waiting for him all this time at Kursk Station, which
is ten minutes' walk from us. He'd told her he was coming to see us and had
given her our address just to be on the safe side. But he hadn't come back and
she didn't know what had become of him. We told her whom to get in touch
with. The following day she was back, completely distraught. We gave her
some money, and then Lusia and I called a number of police stations and
morgues, to no avail. A few days after this, the woman called us at the dacha.
She told us her name was Yakovleva; she'd found her son in the morgue at
Balashikha, where she'd been told he had been run down by a car. She was
taking the coffin with her son's body to Kharkov that day.

Lusia and I decided to check out the facts. I asked our local police station
whether there'd been any accidents on the day in question. We were told there
had not, but in any case, the bodies of accident victims on our street were taken
to another morgue; Balashikha was reserved for victims of railroad accidents.
We also questioned some shoeshine boys and newspaper sellers on the stretch
of road between our house and Kursk Station. No one had seen anything.

Several days later, we took an Academy car to Balashikha. We tipped a cleaning woman and found out when the pathologist would be there. We phoned him and he told us that Yakovlev had not been taken there. Six months later, a note reached me in a roundabout fashion saying that Yakovlev's body *had* been in Balashikha, but the pathologist had been told to deny it. Several days after that I had a call from a woman who gave her name as Ivanova, and said she was from the Balashikha morgue. She repeated what the note said.

A year or two after her son's death, Brunov's mother came to see us again. From Yakovlev's mother we heard nothing further, and I don't have her address in Kharkov.

What is one to make of all this? It's possible that Yakovlev really was picked up by the KGB when leaving our apartment and murdered (or killed accidentally while being beaten or attempting to resist), then taken to a morgue some distance away; the KGB people may initially have wanted to hush the whole thing up and then changed their minds. But it's also quite possible that the entire business was a setup, that Yakovlev *wasn't* murdered, and that the woman who came to see us *wasn't* his mother—and that the whole exercise was designed to unnerve me.

39

IN MEMORIAM

Efim Davidovich, Pyotr Kunin, Grigory
Podyapolsky, Konstantin Bogatyrev, Igor
Alikhanov.

LUSIA AND I spent the last days of 1975 and the first two months of 1976 in
the cooperative apartment she'd bought for Tanya and Efrem. During this
period I wrote a brief autobiographical piece for the Nobel collection, and we
played host to my old university friend Pyotr Kunin and the Minsk refusenik
Efim Davidovich. I never saw either of these men again: within a short time
both would suddenly die.

Davidovich told us that his entire family had perished in the Nazi massacre
of the Jewish population of Minsk in 1941–42, while he was serving in the
army. I have no doubt that Davidovich, who ended the war as a colonel, was
an able and courageous commanding officer. He was one of the group of Jewish
officers from Minsk who tried to emigrate to Israel in the early 1970s; they
faced severe harassment after their applications were turned down, but that
did not deter Davidovich, who began a quest to preserve the memory of
Holocaust victims—about whom the official line could be summed up as "The
less said the better"—and to fight present-day anti-Semitism.

Davidovich was determined to publicize the shocking story of the murder
of Grisha Tumansky, a fourteen-year-old Jewish boy, by a group of teenagers.
They had been lying in wait to "teach a lesson" to another young Jew who had
somehow irritated them, and when their intended victim failed to show up,
they decided to go after Grisha, whom they had glimpsed skiing by: "Let's kill
him; after all, he's a Jew, too!" They beat him to death. Grisha was an only
child whose parents had met while fighting as partisans in Byelorussia; both
had lost their entire families to the Nazis. Perhaps the most shocking aspect
of this story was the nonchalance with which the murderers substituted one
Jewish boy for another.

Davidovich had decided to return his war decorations as a protest against rising anti-Semitism and the illegitimate refusal of exit visas for himself and other veterans. We discussed the best means of making certain that this action would not pass unnoticed, and the following day Davidovich met with his Moscow friends. The next day, Tass carried a statement ("A New Anti-Soviet Performance by Mme Bonner") attacking the idea of a Davidovich press conference. The statement was intended for foreign use only and patently based on information that had been obtained from bugging our apartment or Davidovich's friends'. The KGB's hatred of Lusia was manifest: her role in my life and her Oslo triumph were not to be forgotten or forgiven. There was an additional, more sinister purpose behind the attacks, which took us some time to grasp: Lusia was to be cast as the scapegoat for my "fall."

There would be no press conference. Davidovich died without receiving permission to emigrate. His wife and daughter finally obtained visas; they left a few months after his death, taking along his ashes, and Davidovich at last was laid to rest with military honors in Israel. Two years later, his wife, who was not Jewish, decided to return to the USSR.

ON FEBRUARY 25, Pyotr Kunin died. He too may have intended to leave the country, where it was becoming increasingly difficult for him to live and work. His closest friend, Alexander Taksar (with whom I'd been friendly as a student), had emigrated a couple of years earlier. But Kunin never had a chance to tell me his plans.

I'd known Kunin for nearly forty years, but it was only in the last six months of our association that I really began to appreciate him, perhaps as a result of Lusia's influence. Kunin spent so much time sorting out his friends' problems that he often neglected his own affairs. I can't recall for certain, but it's possible he influenced my crucial decision to move to Moscow and enter graduate school in 1945, at least by advising me to do so.

I have fond memories of our warm friendship in hungry wartime Ashkhabad. The difficulty of anyone, especially a Jew, finding a job in the late 1940s forced Kunin and Taksar to move to Riga, where Taksar had contacts. Kunin taught in Riga for some twenty years, so far as I know, successfully. He specialized in the application of the exact sciences and computers to medical diagnosis, and his accomplishments eventually earned him a position in Moscow.

He died suddenly in the midst of a telephone conversation with my colleague at FIAN, Dmitri Chernavsky—Kunin, typically, was in search of some details for a poem he was composing for the occasion of Chernavsky's fiftieth birthday. Suddenly, Chernavsky realized that Kunin's voice had stopped. He was found dead next to the telephone.

On March 8, another friend, Grigory Podyapolsky, died. Our paths had first crossed in 1970, when our signatures appeared side by side on an appeal drawn up by Chalidze in behalf of Pyotr Grigorenko. I was new to public affairs then, while Podyapolsky was one of the founders of the Initiative Group for the Defense of Human Rights.

He joined the Human Rights Committee in 1972, following Chalidze's resignation, and we accomplished a fair amount of useful work in the Committee—and even more on the outside, where we could use more flexible tactics. As I've mentioned, my family became very friendly with the Podyapolskys. He was a brilliant man who often came up with the most unexpected ideas; utterly intolerant of any breach of human rights, he was at the same time unusually patient with people and their weaknesses. This occasionally landed him in trouble, but he always seemed to come through with his honor unsullied. Repeated interrogations and other torments failed utterly to break his will or to frighten, confuse, or deceive him.

By profession, Podyapolsky was a physicist specializing in the application of mathematical techniques to geophysical problems. Fellow specialists spoke highly of his seismological research and work on the physics of underground explosions and tsunamis. He also wrote poetry; it may not have been much to my taste, but it was certainly original. His memoirs, published posthumously in the West, are of genuine interest.

The brain hemorrhage that killed Podyapolsky at the age of forty-nine took place just before the opening of the 25th Party Congress, when a purge of "undesirable elements" sent him out of the capital on some assignment that of course had little relation to his actual work. The funeral was in Moscow; I was afraid that the KGB wouldn't let me speak there, so, as the funeral procession came to a halt outside the crematorium, I said a few words, all the while pressing my hand against the coffin lid in some final bond with Grigory. Podyapolsky's wife, Maria, was to remain a close friend of ours.

A MONTH AND a half later, on the first day of Easter, there was another tragedy, when the poet and translator Konstantin Bogatyrev received a severe head injury in an attack by unknown assailants which took place on the unlit landing outside his apartment door. Bogatyrev died two months later in the hospital. I'd seen a good bit of him, and he'd visited Lusia and me in the hospital. Bogatyrev generally was in a serious mood when he turned up at our apartment, but there were times when he'd be in a state bordering on euphoria, with his turbulent inner life pouring out in cascades of vivid imagery. He'd bring us new versions of the Rilke translations he'd been working on for years. Bogatyrev had been arrested as a youth and had spent years in Stalin's camps, before finally being rehabilitated.

Bogatyrev was buried at Peredelkino on Sunday, June 20. A large crowd was gathered—friends, poets, writers. The occasion for which we were assembled was in poignant contrast to the sunlit skies and the lush summer vegetation and wild flowers that surrounded us as the coffin was borne by hand down a path bordered by tall grass. The grave of Pasternak was nearby.

Many assumed that Bogatyrev was a victim of the KGB, but was there any evidence? any motive? It's hard to say; even Lusia and I don't see eye to eye on it. In the absence of conclusive evidence of KGB involvement, she inclines to the view that Bogatyrev was attacked by one of the irate drinking companions (of whom, in his fast and furious life, he certainly had his share), while I am just about certain that the killers were KGB hit-men. How else to account for all the murders, beatings, and mutilations we'd been experiencing? Are we to believe that the crime rate in the USSR is far higher than, say, in Dallas or the slums of Hong Kong? Why do I think the KGB killed Bogatyrev? He lived in a writers' residence, and there was supposed to be a woman watching the door at the time the attack took place, but she wasn't there and the light was off. The autopsy established that the fatal blow had been administered by a heavy object wrapped in cloth—which suggests the possibility of a professional, premeditated hit. Investigation, moreover, was postponed as long as possible and then carried out perfunctorily; it was clear that no one was anxious to find clues to the identity of the culprits or their accomplices.

Bogatyrev was a conspicuous figure in the literary world, a world that is the object of intense KGB scrutiny in our ideology-bound state. Stalin knew what he was doing when he labeled writers the "engineers of human souls." Bogatyrev indulged himself in unacceptable liberties, associating openly with foreigners—no doubt to the fury of the KGB. He'd been in the habit of meeting practically every day with West German correspondents, drinking with them and discussing life, poetry, love, whatever. This was perfectly natural behavior for a poet with a fluent command of German and with none of the average Soviet citizen's prejudice against consorting with foreigners. But to the KGB this must have seemed a potential danger, a vice to be nipped in the bud before it could spread. And Bogatyrev was a former political prisoner whose rehabilitation meant little to the KGB. Bogatyrev didn't count as a human being; to kill such a person was at most a venal sin. I must note that Bogatyrev was no dissident. His death was the result of conduct unbecoming a Soviet writer, not dissident activities.

Any doubt on this score was eliminated a few days after the attack on Bogatyrev, when a heavy stone was hurled through the window of Lev Kopelev's apartment by "a person or persons unknown." Kopelev, too, was a writer with a habit of associating with West German correspondents in Moscow—many of the same ones as Bogatyrev. The two men were friends. Might that stone not just as easily have struck someone on the head? None of this would stand up as conclusive legal evidence, of course; but then again, nothing is ever 100 percent certain when the KGB is involved.

ANOTHER TRAGEDY, this of a purely personal nature, occurred in 1976. The day before Bogatyrev's funeral, Lusia's younger brother, Igor Alikhanov, a ship's officer and navigator, died of a heart attack at the age of forty-nine. Igor died at sea en route to Bombay; it was several days before his body could be brought back to Moscow.

After their parents' arrest in 1937, Lusia had become responsible for her 10-year-old brother, who had been traumatized by the family's tragedy. Igor had been evacuated from Leningrad in 1942, during the blockade, and sent to Omsk, where he was assigned to factory work. He was on the verge of starvation when Lusia located him and got him a job as an orderly on the hospital train where she was working.

Igor's later life was also filled with difficulties. Still, he did have the satisfaction of fulfilling his dream of becoming a sailor and visiting almost every port in the world. Igor married and had a daughter; in 1987 a grandchild was born.

Ruth, Lusia's mother, had always insisted that there be no contact between Igor and me, and after I moved to Chkalov Street, Igor never again visited the apartment. Ruth was scared—and not without reason—that any association with me might jeopardize his career, the linchpin of his existence. Instead (and these were always special occasions) she'd go and spend a few days with him. Lusia, however, continued to see Igor without Ruth's knowledge. We decided one day to break Ruth's "taboo"; under the pretext of bringing something to Vera, we took an Academy car to their home. The door was opened by a thickset man with Armenian features and a stern expression. The resemblance to Lusia was remarkable, except that she does look a bit more Jewish. "I'd like you to meet Andrei," Lusia said simply. Igor eyed me with curiosity and then warmly shook my hand.

40

1976

Amnesty International. Mustafa Dzhemilev's trial. Andrei Tverdokhlebov. Tbilisi. The Helsinki Group. Attacks on Lusia. The Bukovsky-Cervalan exchange.

IN 1973, Andrei Tverdokhlebov and Valentin Turchin co-founded the first Amnesty International group in the USSR.

Amnesty International works for the release of "prisoners of conscience" throughout the world. As defined by Amnesty, a prisoner of conscience is one who has not used or advocated violence. Amnesty strives to be politically impartial and it adopted more than five thousand prisoners of conscience, detained in countries with every sort of political system. The majority are in the developing countries, Latin America, and South Africa; ten to twenty percent are in the USSR and other socialist countries. Soviet propaganda's claims that Amnesty International is "anti-Soviet" are meant to deflect attention from human rights abuses at home and are patently absurd. Our propaganda is quick to seize upon Amnesty cases from outside the socialist camp, so that the Soviet attitude about this organization is schizophrenic.

Amnesty's desire to remain outside the arena of political struggle is manifest in its refusal to adopt guerrillas and terrorists as prisoners of conscience. I feel that this restriction, which is in accord with both my own dedication to peaceful change and the views of most Soviet dissidents, enhances Amnesty's moral authority. And Amnesty's calls for the abolition of torture and the death penalty have my wholehearted support.

Tverdokhlebov and Turchin managed to contact the Amnesty International Secretariat in London and to register their group [in September 1974]. Each such adoption group is assigned responsibility for specified prisoners of conscience, but it cannot work for prisoners in its own country, a stipulation meant to ensure impartiality. Not all of Amnesty's rules, however, make sense under Soviet conditions; it is difficult or even dangerous to communicate with the London Secretariat, and virtually impossible to get material assistance to prisoners in other countries. Lusia was an active member for about a year, but she and the others could only send postcards to prisoners of conscience in Iran, Pakistan, and elsewhere, and write letters in their defense. I don't mean to imply that the group existed in vain; our human rights activists' entry into the international arena was enough to make it worthwhile. But given Soviet political reality, the USSR Amnesty Group was, sadly, of primarily symbolic importance.

After Tverdokhlebov was arrested and Turchin emigrated in October 1977, Georgi Vladimov, the well-known writer, became the group's chairman. Vladimov, to my mind, is one of our best writers; I admire his novel *Three Minutes of Silence* (published in the USSR in 1969, and *Faithful Ruslan*, whose first publication was in the West.[1] He dedicated the play *The Sixth Soldier* (also first published in the West) to me on the occasion of my sixtieth birthday. As the authorities, disturbed by the Amnesty Group's existence, zeroed in on its members, he and his wife decided to emigrate. They left for West Germany in May 1983, and in August of that year, Vladimov's Soviet citizenship was revoked.

Tverdokhlebov had been arrested at his apartment on April 18, 1975, four months after a search which I, along with other friends, witnessed for several depressing hours. Turchin's apartment was searched the day Tverdokhlebor was arrested, and I was present there as well. Turchin attempted to save his revised version of *The Inertia of Fear* by having his son drop a briefcase with the manuscript out the window; unfortunately, KGB agents waiting in the courtyard below immediately snatched it up.

Two trials—Andrei Tverdokhlebov's in Moscow, and Mustafa Dzhemilev's in Omsk—had been scheduled for the same day, April 6, 1976. This was no coincidence: the KGB wanted to make sure that no one could attend both trials. I decided it was more important for me to go to Omsk, since in Moscow there were plenty of people who would gather outside the building where a well-known dissident was on trial, and foreign correspondents would also be present. Such was not the case in Omsk, and there was reason to fear that little information about that trial would be reported with any speed. I released a statement of my intentions and Lusia and I caught the three-hour flight to Omsk.

The Crimean Tatar activist Mustafa Dzhemilev was only six months old when his family was deported from the Crimea and he obviously had no personal recollection of the horrors of resettlement or the first years in Uzbekistan. But he had grown up hearing about that time and about the beautiful, faraway Crimea, and as soon as he was old enough he plunged himself into the

---

[1][Georgi Vladimov, *Faithful Ruslan* (Simon & Schuster, 1979).]

battle for his people's return to their homeland. He endured several camp terms, and in June 1975, six months before he was scheduled to be released from a camp near Omsk, new charges were brought against him. Dzhemilev, it was claimed, had slandered the Soviet system by claiming that the Crimean Tatars "do not enjoy equal rights in the USSR." It was a statement he had made more than once, and in writing; the KGB, however, felt the need for a witness, and came up with Vladimir Dvoryansky, a fellow prisoner serving a ten-year manslaughter sentence in the death of a man he claimed had insulted his sister. Dvoryansky at first refused to cooperate, and got a note smuggled out of the camp describing the pressure being brought to bear on him. But after a month in an isolation cell, he gave in and agreed to do what the authorities wanted. Dzhemilev, meanwhile, had been on a hunger strike for many months, and we were greatly concerned about his condition.

Dzhemilev's immediate family came to Omsk for the trial, as did a number of Crimean Tatars from Tashkent. His defense counsel was Vladimir Shveisky, a Moscow attorney who had defended Vladimir Bukovsky and Andrei Amalrik and who, we knew, was capable of treading the fine line between professional duty and the exigencies of defending a dissident in a Soviet court.

The trial was postponed on the pretext that a drainpipe had leaked in the prison and a quarantine had been declared; clearly, the authorities wanted to discourage us from attending. We returned to Moscow, and then flew back to Omsk on April 13 even though it was tiring and expensive to make the journey a second time. There was a farcical incident at the hotel when we tried to register: the manager caught sight of my name in my passport, nervously pushed it aside, and exclaimed: "I wouldn't give the likes of you a crust of bread, let alone a hotel room."

The Crimean Tatars had already checked in. They stood behind us, waiting to see how I'd react; they themselves had long since learned to ignore such insults.

We went with the Tatars to their room to talk things over. A half hour passed. Then there was a knock on the door, and the manager said: "Here's the key to your room, Comrade Sakharov. Please come downstairs and register whenever it's convenient."

The KGB, anxious to avoid a scandal, had obviously ordered that I be given a room. The manager's earlier refusal had been the personal initiative of "a true Soviet citizen."

The trial began the next morning. Lusia and I, Alexander Lavut (who'd arrived from Moscow), and several Tatars were forced to remain outside, but Dzhemilev's mother, sister, and brothers were admitted to the courtroom. The atmosphere quickly grew tense. The accused, still on his hunger strike, could barely stand, and the judge interrupted his every word. Dvoryansky retracted the testimony that had been extracted from him with such effort, and the state's case collapsed. The judge used some statement by Dzhemilev's brother as a pretext to expel him from the courtroom. Then his sister was thrown out for letting Dzhemilev know I was in Omsk. On the trial's second day Mustafa's mother was ordered out; barred from reentering after the recess, she put her hands over her face and began to weep.

"Let his mother in; it's her son who's on trial!" I shouted.

Jeering, the KGB agents standing by the door started shoving us back. Lusia slapped the face of the lanky fellow in civilian dress who was running the show, while I went for his assistant—in a flash the police were all over us. The Tatars rushed to our aid and a free-for-all ensued, with several of us being dragged outside to waiting police vans. Lusia was manhandled into a small room in the courthouse with a vigor that left both her arms black and blue.

At the police station I refused to answer questions until I'd seen my wife, and I was released after an hour. I set off on foot to the courthouse. A short while later, Lusia was brought to the station; she asked to see me, and a car was sent to pick me up. Once we were together, Lusia demanded that she be examined by a doctor. Medical personnel showed up but announced that they could only render first aid, and would not sign any certificates. The police advised us that criminal charges might be brought against us. We were released just as sentence was being pronounced on Dzhemilev: two and a half additional years in labor camp, the judge ruling that Dvoryansky's initial testimony had been truthful, and that his retraction was the result of "psychological pressure" exerted by Dzhemilev in the courtroom.

I'd met the judge earlier when I was trying to find out the reason for the April 6 postponement; he seemed an unremarkable family man, a former combat officer who doubtless considered his job necessary, if difficult. According to Dzhemilev's family during the trial the judge had remarked: "Dzhemilev claims the Crimean Tatars aren't allowed to live in the Crimea. So what? I'm not allowed to live in Moscow, and I'm not complaining."

TASS filed a colorful description of the "brawl" started by Academician Sakharov and his wife in a courtroom in Omsk—one we'd never entered! Our friends around the world were alarmed; long-distance phone service to Omsk had been cut off during the trial (the KGB "spares no expense" in attaining its objectives) and there'd been no word of us. But we'd managed anyway to draw attention to the trial.

Dzhemilev's relatives met with him the day after the sentencing. They brought along a letter from me urging him to end his hunger strike, and, to my relief, he agreed.

From our hotel window, we watched two vicious street brawls erupt (the sort of mob violence that can easily turn murderous), and realized that, in stark contrast to the courtroom, not a single policeman was to be seen.

We also went window-shopping. When Lusia caught sight of what looked like butter in one shop, she went in and asked for some, only to be stared at as if she'd gone mad. (It turned out to be blended fat.) We got a similar look when we ordered fish in a restaurant—this in a river city on the banks of the Irtysh. (Not that they had any meat, either.)

ANDREI TVERDOKHLEBOV's trial had also been postponed, the date moved from April 6 to April 14 due to the judge's ostensible illness. By the time we returned to Moscow on April 16, he had been sentenced to five years internal exile. Efrem had been spending his evenings writing up notes on the trial with Tverdokhlebov's sister, working so late we began making jokes about their "affair."

Later that year, in August, Tverdokhlebov's parents showed us photographs he'd sent from exile in the settlement of Nyurbachan in Yakutia. Lusia was disturbed by something in his expression. "We've got to go see him," she said (or rather, *wrote*, on a scrap of paper—we were afraid the KGB would interfere if they knew our plans, and we always assumed that our conversations were bugged).

Without discussing anything aloud, we packed our things and went straight to the airport from the dacha, first on a half-empty commuter train, then by taxi, not stopping by the apartment. On the way to the airport, our taxi was struck from behind by a car with diplomatic plates. Our necks and heads aching from whiplash, we switched to another cab. We secured tickets to Mirny, a city in Yakutia where we could transfer to a smaller plane for the next (375-mile) leg of our journey to Nyurba; from Nyurba, we planned to take a bus for the 15 miles to Nyurbachan.

Apparently thanks to the KGB, we had to wait almost twenty-four hours in Mirny for a plane to Nyurba. Mirny was founded in 1959 after major diamond deposits were discovered in the vicinity, and as we walked around the airport, we caught sight of blue mounds in the distance which we were told were heaps of earth that had been removed to get at the kimberlite below. Diamonds occasionally were found in this discarded earth, and—with the idea that the mounds might be exploited after the richer ore was exhausted—they were guarded and the local population kept away. During our stroll, we met one of the *bichi*, the hoboes, most without permanent residence or family ties, who do heavy and unskilled casual labor in Siberia. Some *bichi* lack papers; they stay a step ahead of the law, living each day with no thought for the morrow: "Feast today, tomorrow famine" seems to be their motto. Existing almost independently of the state, the *bichi* constitute an anomaly in our regimented society, tolerated for the time being because of Siberia's acute manpower shortage.

We spent the night on a bench in the airport waiting room and flew on to Nyurba the next day, where another surprise awaited us—the bus to Nyurba-chan had been cancelled. We had no luck in hitching a ride; a truckdriver told us that a few hundred yards back the police were stopping traffic and warning people not to give us a lift. A police officer eventually picked us up and took us back to the police station we'd walked by two hours earlier. The duty officer was mockingly polite, but when I asked to borrow a car, he replied that they had none available.

"Then take us in one of your motorcycles with sidecars: look how many you've got standing outside."

"But Andrei Dmitrievich, you might catch cold."

We decided to walk.

(We were struck by the great number of police we encountered in Nyurba, a relatively small town. The district police are the main instruments of rule in the provinces, especially those with non-Russian populations.)

It was getting dark by the time we left Nyurba. We walked most of the way by moonlight along a deserted forest road, breathing in the fresh country air, stopping a few times to eat bread and cheese and to drink coffee from a thermos. Presents for Tverdokhlebov were in a bag slung over my shoulder. We felt happy as we walked along, alone together in the night forest, doing something meaningful for the cause we both believed in.

We reached Nyurbachan at five in the morning. People were up and around, but they were afraid to tell us where Tverdokhlebov was living. Lusia recognized his house from the photograph. He was surprised and delighted by our arrival, and kept repeating, "Well, if it isn't . . ."

We spent the day with him, discussing the latest developments and hearing about his trial. But despite some warm moments, Lusia and I were distressed by a certain reserve on his part. Later, after his return from exile, the rift between us deepened until we lost contact with him entirely, something I still don't understand and very much regret.

I had sprained my right leg slightly the previous night. Now, while walking around the lake, I stepped into a deep posthole and twisted my left leg badly. Lusia did what she could to reduce the swelling while Tverdokhlebov went home to get an elastic bandage. He cut me a walking stick, and I hobbled back to his house, every step an agony. The next day the mechanic who shared his place drove us to Nyurba. There were no problems; apparently the authorities were eager to be rid of us.

At the Nyurba airport a sudden pain in my heart forced me to lie down on a bench. Lusia ran for hot water and immediately applied a mustard plaster.

This time there was no delay. On the flight from Nyurba to Mirny we passed over the boundless taiga, its uninhabited marshlands overgrown with scrub forest, and dotted with green ponds. I mused to myself: "So this is the region Solzhenitsyn regards as an untouched reserve for the evolution of the Russian people, the nation's 'saving grace.' We're still a long way from being able to make this swampy soil really productive, unless of course we're prepared to do as Stalin did and send millions of forced laborers to their graves."

We passed over the diamond mines around which Mirny, with its tens of thousands of residents, had developed—a fantastic, unforgettable sight. (My admiration is not inconsistent with my belief that large-scale development of the Northeast is impracticable at present, since diamond mining, which probably yields a greater profit than any other industry, does justify the enormous investment required.)

From the air, the mine was visible as a deep conical cavity, its exposed kimberlite a beautiful shade of gray-blue against the background of green taiga. I estimated the cone's diameter as about a mile in at the surface, tapering to a few hundred yards at the bottom. A spiral ramp about thirty-five yards wide ran down the sides of the crater. Heavy dump trucks, looking like giant beetles, drove up the ramps, loaded with the blue kimberlite clay. We later read that in the processing plants the ore is broken into small pieces, softened with water, and carried along slowly on vibrating belts under powerful X- or ultraviolet rays. This takes place in darkness, and the diamonds, most of them very small, show up as fluorescent sparks.

Industry's use of synthetic diamonds will increase as the supply of natural diamonds declines. The process of producing diamonds from graphite in stationary presses at very high temperatures is well developed; at one time, there was interest in the prospect of using underground nuclear explosions, which could in theory maintain the necessary high temperatures and pressures long enough to form large crystals. But any practical application of this idea is still in the realm of fantasy.

Unable to get a direct flight to Moscow, we flew from Mirny to Irkutsk. We would have been stranded in Irkutsk if Lusia, who was worried about my leg, had not made a scene. Several flights had been cancelled and the airport was packed. The one plane scheduled to leave Irkutsk was en route to Leningrad: it was half empty, but since it was carrying foreign tourists, no one else was allowed aboard. It is standard Soviet practice to isolate foreigners and grant them special privileges; in vacation areas, the best hotels are reserved for them, and Soviet citizens are made to keep their distance. Some restaurants post special hours when only foreigners can be served—and, although this is demeaning to both the foreigners and our own people, everyone accepts it. In Rome or Paris windows would probably be smashed if an attempt were made to impose such restrictions.

Lusia minced no words in demanding that we and the other waiting passengers be given seats on the plane. (A Novosti article later made reference to this "scandal" in Irkutsk: the KGB hears everything—and forgets nothing.) In the end, the airport officials backed down and sold seats on the flight to us and some thirty other passengers. Many of them thanked Lusia and applauded her courage: "We wouldn't have the guts to do that."

Arriving in Leningrad, we spent the night at the Pushkin Street apartment shared by Zoya, Natasha, and Regina. Zoya prepared a foot bath for me which immediately eased the pain. When we reached Moscow, doctors at the Academy clinic confirmed Lusia's diagnosis of a torn ligament and put my leg in a cast.

AMONG THE MEMORABLE events of 1976 was our trip to Tbilisi in July to attend an international conference on elementary particles. Lusia and I were assigned a room at the Hotel Sakartvelo, where I had stayed in 1968. There were a number of interesting talks. The recent discovery of a fourth type of quark—the "charmed" quark—had confirmed a prediction, one of the most successful of recent years, made by Glashow, Iliopoulos, and Maiani, based on Ioffe and Shabalin's research on the anomalously small difference between the masses of "long" and "short" neutral K-mesons.

Some of the theoretical papers were of even more interest than the reports on charmed quarks. In Tbilisi I became a true believer in quantum chromodynamics and Grand Unified Theory. Early in the conference, I'd made an attempt (not entirely successful) to explain my own ideas concerning quarks with fractional charges to one of the foreign participants. And it was here that I was introduced to the use of matrices for numerical calculations in quantum field theory, particularly in relation to the binding of quarks (i.e., to explain why quarks are not observed in a free state).

Personal contact with scientists from America, Europe, and Israel was important and pleasant. Lusia and I renewed our acquaintance with Sidney Drell and Victor Weisskopf and we met many new people, including Francis Lowe and his wife. We entertained Western friends in our hotel room, serving them coffee, fruit, and sweets.

Lusia discovered that some of the Israeli scientists visiting us worked with our friend Yuri Mekler, who had emigrated to Israel in 1972 after serving a five-year sentence for possessing a copy of *Doctor Zhivago*, and then finding himself again under a cloud during the Leningrad skyjacking case. I recall Mekler in our kitchen, weeping bitterly as he bade farewell to us and to the country where he'd spent his whole life. Lusia later saw him in Italy, where he said to her: "What did I lose? What did I leave behind in Russia? The chance to hang around with five or six friends. Evening walks along the banks of the Neva. The Russian language. What did I gain? Freedom, a sense of security, the opportunity to travel where and when I wish. Interesting work. It's just a shame that it came so late, when I was forty."

Lusia spontaneously put together a little gift package—candy and a bottle of Georgian wine—and asked our Israeli guests to deliver it to Mekler and his mother.

There was a government reception on the conference's final day, to which, disgracefully, the Israeli delegation was not invited—something none of the guests, foreign or Soviet, protested. I learned about this only after the reception had already begun, but I might at least have proposed a toast to our colleagues, now absent, in the universal pursuit of science. However, as so often happens, the idea occurred to me too late.

Weisskopf and Drell came to see us shortly before the close of the conference. Shamefacedly, they told us they'd each been given an envelope full of money (under what pretext this obvious attempt at bribery had been made, they didn't say). They asked us to pass on the money to persecuted scientists and their families, which we did. I wonder how many scientists, ordinary tourists, VIP guests, journalists, writers, peace activists, businessmen, politicians, athletes, and musicians receive such "gifts" and are unconsciously influenced by them. Only the KGB knows—but I suspect the practice is widespread.

IN MAY 1976, the Public Group to Promote Observance of the Helsinki Accords in the USSR—the Moscow Helsinki Group—was founded. The Helsinki Group was the brainchild of Yuri Orlov (Andrei Amalrik apparently also played an important role).[2] Orlov had approached me two months earlier and asked me to serve as co-sponsor, but I'd turned him down; I preferred the freedom of speaking out as an individual. It had been a relief to escape the constraints imposed by the Human Rights Committee, and I had no wish to find myself again saddled with such obligations. But I had no objection to endorsing group documents when I approved their content, and did so on many occasions.

Helsinki Groups were formed in the Ukraine, Lithuania, Armenia, and Georgia, and, with some differences in approach, abroad as well.[3] Charter 77 in Czechoslovakia also had much in common with the Helsinki Groups. In

---

[2][See Amalrik, *Notes of a Revolutionary* (Knopf, 1982).]

[3][The Moscow Group was announced on May 12, 1976, the Ukrainian on November 9, the Lithuanian on November 25, the Georgian on January 14, 1977, and the Armenian on April 1.]

Moscow and elsewhere, these groups investigated and publicized human rights violations; they continued the labors of the Initiative Group, the *Chronicle of Current Events*, and individual human rights advocates, and the sanction of the Helsinki Final Act, stressed by Orlov and manifest in their name, lent special weight to their activities.

The concept capitalized on the importance ascribed to the Helsinki Final Act by Soviet leaders, and on the Act's vital "linkage" of international security and human rights. The actions of human rights defenders who "piggybacked" on the Helsinki Act struck a sensitive nerve in the Soviet government and group members, especially in the provinces, were subjected to harsh reprisals. One can't overlook this negative, tragic side of the groups' very existence.

Orlov invited Lusia to join the Group in my stead; she wavered a bit and then agreed, thinking that her presence might offer some protection for the group's members. Lusia stipulated that her membership would be purely formal, with no fixed responsibilities; but she started to assume a significant share of the work, especially after Orlov's arrest.

KGB EFFORTS to blacken Lusia's reputation reached fever pitch in 1976 and 1977, when they invested an amazing amount of time and effort in the Semyon Zlotnik affair.[4]

During this same period, we received from "abroad" a copy of *Russky golos* (Russian Voice), an obscure Russian-language newspaper published in New York. A July 8, 1976, article entitled "Madame Bonner—Sakharov's Evil Genius?" (the question mark was probably a hedge against a libel suit) asserted that Lusia had appropriated donations sent to me (there were no donations). She was depicted standing on the balcony in Oslo "shrieking with delight" and clutching her purse, clearly more interested in the prize money than in the husband she'd left back in the USSR. There were hints that Ginzburg and other young dissidents were her lovers, and other nasty lies—I forget them all. I'm not about to bother refuting this nonsense, but I do feel obliged to note that not even by the most feverish stretch of the imagination could my wife's voice ever be turned into a "shriek."

I thought about suing the editors of *Russky golos* for libel—I regret now that I didn't—but was dissuaded.

---

[4]Described in *Alone Together*, pp. 37–8.

* * *

IN SEPTEMBER 1976 a Soviet pilot, Lieutenant Viktor Belenko, landed his MiG 25 in Japan and asked for political asylum in the United States—his request was granted at once.[5] American experts hurried to examine the latest supersonic Soviet interceptor. In Moscow, there were persistent rumors that Belenko had in fact been sent on an intelligence and disinformation mission and that his plane was an inferior fake designed to diminish the West's vigilance. The rumors may have been circulated by the KGB to confuse American intelligence.

Later that same month another Soviet pilot, Lieutenant Valentin Zosimov, flew a mail plane across the Soviet-Iranian border, surrendered to the Iranian authorities, and requested political asylum. But the plane was of no interest, and Zosimov's application was rejected. Hoping to prevent his extradition to the USSR, Pyotr Grigorenko and I appealed to the United Nations and the Shah on October 26, but, as we later learned, Iran had returned Zosimov and his plane to the USSR the day before.

Lusia and I then wrote a letter to the Shah asking him to intercede with the Soviet government on Zosimov's behalf. We requested an appointment at the Iranian consulate, and on November 3 we met with the consul, another consular official, and an interpreter. A large portrait of Shah Reza Pahlevi in full dress hung on one wall; his uniform was covered with medals, stars, and ribbons and gleamed with diamonds and gold. Similar portraits could be glimpsed in adjoining rooms. The conversation itself seemed an exercise in grandiloquent evasion. We were told that Zosimov had been extradited in order to comply with the convention on the hijacking of civil airplanes which had been ratified by both Iran and the USSR. But Zosimov was a *defector*, not a hijacker, and had escaped in a *military* airplane. We were informed that our letter would be forwarded to the proper authorities.

This was a time when the USSR was flirting with the Shah. The journal *Za rubezhom* (Abroad) printed a sympathetic article about the "White Revolution," the Shah's program to modernize Iran. After the Jackson-Vanik Amendment denied U.S. credits to the USSR, Iran helped fill the gap. There were rumors that the Soviets were turning over Azerbaijani, Kurdish, and Arab refugees to SAVAK, the Shah's secret police.

Whether or not our intervention helped, Zosimov did escape the death penalty; he was sentenced to twelve years labor camp. Over the next two months I received hundreds of letters condemning me for defending a traitor.

[5][The incident is described in John Barron, *MiG Pilot*, McGraw-Hill, 1980.]

Alexei Semyonov with Sakharov and Elena Bonner on the day they registered their marriage. January 7, 1972.

In foreground: Efrem Yankelevich; behind him, left to right: Ruth Bonner, Tanya Semyonov (Yankelevich), Elena Bonner, Sakharov; Alexei Semyonov is in back. December 1972.

THE PUSHKINITES

ABOVE: Zoya Zadunaiskaya and Natalya (Natasha) Gesse.
LEFT: Zoya Zadunaiskaya.
BELOW: Natasha Gesse with unidentified man.

LEFT: Natasha Gesse. ABOVE: Regina (Ina) Etinger.

Sakharov and Bonner in the lobby of the Academy Hospital, where both were then staying. Standing behind them are Viktor Nekrasov (left) and Lev Kopelev. December 1973.

ove: Sakharov and
nner. March 16, 1974.
ght: Sakharov and Bonner.
73.

Ruth Bonner and Sakharov at Yuri Tuvim's on the day the awarding of the Nobel Peace Prize to Sakharov was announced. Moscow, October 9, 1975.

Demonstration in Pushkin Square. December 5, 1975.

Bonner and Aase Lionaes, President of the Nobel Peace Prize Committee, at the Nobel ceremony. December 10, 1975. (Norsk Telegrambyrå A/S, Oslo)

Bonner and Tim Greve, director of the Norwegian Nobel Institute, at a press conference in Oslo. December 11, 1975. (Associated Press, Oslo)

In Vilnius on the day Sergei
Kovalev was sentenced. Third
from left: Yuri Golfand; fourth
from left: Yuri Orlov; second from
right: Eitan Finkelshtein; third
from right: Efrem Yankelevich;
fifth from right: Sakharov;
sixth from right: Mart Niklus.
December 10, 1975.

The Sakharovs with Jewish refusenik leader Vladimir Slepak. c. 1978.

Sakharov outside the Lublino courthouse during the trial of Yuri Orlov. Moscow, May 1978.

Bonner and Sakharov in Gorky. January 1980.

LEFT: Sakharov in Gorky. 1982.
BELOW: View from the Gorky apartment.

LEFT: Bonner, photographed by Sakharov. Gorky, 1984. ABOVE: Sakharov in Gorky. 1985.

Sakharov in Gorky. 1983.

Tanya and Efrem Yankelevich, Alexei and Liza Semyonov, Ruth Bonner. Newton, Massachusetts, summer 1985.

Sakharov returns to Moscow. December 23, 1986. *(Shone/Sijea)*

Sakharov in Canada. February 1989. *(Ottawa Citizen)*

Since the KGB controls my mail, this flood of angry letters reveals that organization's interest in the Zosimov case.

In October 1976, Lusia and I appealed on behalf of Palestinians besieged by Lebanese Christians in the Tel-Zaatar refugee camp. Many women, children, and old people were literally dying of thirst after the attacking forces cut off the camp's water supply.

Notwithstanding our attitude toward the PLO's activities, we sympathized with those who were suffering. I recall vividly Lusia's anguish. Our plea for humane treatment of the women and children in the camp was published and broadcast several times.[6] Given the brutality that reigned, I doubt whether it had any effect, but I nevertheless regard our letter as an important expression of principle.

In 1975, while Lusia was in Italy, Valentin Turchin and Ruth Bonner persuaded me to hire Alexander Ginzburg as a "secretary." The appointment was strictly a formality, since Ginzburg possessed neither the secretarial skills nor the compatibility with my views that it required. But formality or no, it still caused plenty of trouble. Whenever Ginzburg visited the Zhukovka dacha in my absence, he would be picked up, and I'd have to rush to the police station to get him released. And he was involved in matters that had nothing to do with me, as a result of which odd characters started telephoning and dropping by our apartment. All the same, Ginzburg's easygoing ways endeared him to us and to our grandchildren.

In December 1976, I gave a long interview on human rights and our family situation to the Associated Press correspondent George Krimsky, one of the few journalists with whom we developed a personal relationship. Our friendship was probably one reason why Krimsky was attacked in the Soviet press, had his car tires slashed, and suffered other harassment.

Earlier that fall, Krimsky, his wife, and their young child were visiting Tanya and Efrem at our dacha. The police burst in and dragged the Krimskys off to the police station, where they were not allowed to call their consulate, or even feed the child, while a report was prepared. The pretext given was that the dacha was in an area off limits to foreigners, although they'd been to Zhukovka

[6][See Appendix, p. 684.]

several times in the past. Krimsky was expelled from the USSR in early 1977. Such expulsions, far from being tokens of professional failure, were the rewards of exceptional journalistic diligence.

THE EXCHANGE OF Vladimir Bukovsky for Luis Corvalán on December 18 brought to a close one phase of the human rights movement. Bukovsky's release was the result of his own moral authority and an international campaign waged in behalf of this hero of the Soviet human rights movement. There was a simultaneous campaign (in which the Soviet press played a role) for the release of Luis Corvalán, the Secretary of Chile's Communist Party, who had been arrested in 1973 by General Pinochet, and a swap was proposed in the West and accepted by the Soviet Union.

There has been heated debate about the wisdom of this exchange and of exchanges in general. Amnesty International has expressed opposition to exchanges on the grounds that they undercut the principle of general amnesty for all prisoners of conscience. I disagree thoroughly: to me, the release of *anyone* who has suffered for his beliefs is grounds for rejoicing. I simply cannot see how the freeing of one prisoner, in this case Bukovsky, jeopardizes the fate of others. As a human being, I was delighted for Corvalán too, and I find Amnesty International's stance here pedantic to a fault.

Bukovsky's mother had told us of the impending exchange a few days earlier, and on December 18, several dozen Moscow dissidents went to Sheremetevo Airport in hopes of catching a final glimpse of Bukovsky and waving farewell. A number of foreign correspondents also showed up, and the KGB was out in force. Pyotr Grigorenko and I held an impromptu press conference, expressing our hope that this humanitarian act would be followed by the release of other prisoners of conscience, and that someday there would be a universal amnesty. We urged priority for women and seriously ill prisoners and cited specific names. The KGB agents kept their distance as we talked with the correspondents, forming a second, outer ring around us.

After waiting several hours at Sheremetevo, we left without seeing Bukovsky. He had been put on a special flight from a military airfield, along with his mother, sister, and nephew.

A verse celebrating the exchange circulated widely:

> They exchanged a hooligan
> For Luis Corvalán.
> Now where can we find a whore
> To exchange Brezhnev for?

A few hours later, a fire broke out in Malva Landa's room in a communal apartment in the Moscow suburb of Krasnogorsk. She'd just returned home from Sheremetevo.

Landa, a retired geologist, exemplifies all that is finest in the human rights movement. She is wholeheartedly dedicated to the ideas of justice and humanity, full of compassion for those who suffer, and uncompromisingly opposed to official injustice. Few individuals can equal her knowledge of the legal and personal particulars of hundreds of political prisoners, detainees, and suspects, their family backgrounds, personalities, and health problems. Her sympathy and understanding embrace every one of these individuals.

In May 1977, Landa was tried on charges of criminal negligence: the prosecution alleged that the fire in her room had caused serious damage to state property (her apartment) and a neighbor's possessions. The trial served to reinforce my suspicions that this was a case of arson. Malva had gone to the communal kitchen to put on the tea kettle, leaving her door open, and had returned to find the papers on her desk and the floor ablaze. She ran for some water, but found a stranger blocking her way back from the kitchen; she struggled with him for several minutes, to no avail. None of Malva's neighbors knew the man, and the court investigators made no real effort to find him. I am convinced that he was a KGB agent, and probably the arsonist. The investigation failed to establish with certainty whether incendiary substances had been used, but the evidence pointed in that direction. The fire department had been given the wrong address and was delayed in arriving. Something had been done to make it impossible to cut off the electricity. But the judge ignored all these details.

The defense counsel was competent, but he could do nothing for a dissident in Malva's situation. The court exaggerated the extent of the fire damage and in fact it was Malva who was the fire's principal victim; she'd lost all her scanty belongings. (Like most retired persons in the USSR, she lived from one pension check to the next.) She was ordered to pay the inflated damages and was sentenced to two years of internal exile. In March 1978 she was released under the amnesty declared in connection with the sixtieth anniversary of the Revolution, but was not allowed to return to the Moscow region. In March 1980 she was again arrested, this time on a political charge, and sentenced to an additional five years of internal exile.[7]

[7][Malva Landa was released in November 1984.]

41

THE SAKHAROV-CARTER
CORRESPONDENCE

The Moscow subway bomb. Letter to Carter.
Conversation with Gusev. Carter's reply.
Arrests of Ginzburg, Orlov, and Shcharansky.

LATE IN 1976, we learned about the case of Pyotr Ruban. It seemed that the KGB had decided to make Ruban pay for his part in getting Eduard Kuznetsov's *Prison Diaries* smuggled out of a labor camp. After being released from camp in 1973, Ruban, an artist, had found a job in a carpentry shop. From discarded scraps of wood he had collected, he had made an intarsia book cover portraying the Statue of Liberty, which he intended to send as a bicentennial gift to the American people. Instead he had been arrested on an absurd charge of stealing state property—the scraps of wood—and sentenced to eight years labor camp and five years internal exile.[1]

I decided to appeal to Jimmy Carter, the newly elected American President, to intercede in the case. Ruban was suffering for actions committed in the name of Soviet-American friendship, and his defense should have been a point of honor.

In early January 1977, the homes of several Helsinki Group members, including Yuri Orlov, were searched. Money and other property belonging to the Prisoners Aid Fund, documents, typewriters, tape recorders, and radios were confiscated. I addressed an appeal to the heads of state who had signed the Helsinki accords. Reaction on their part might have prompted Soviet authorities to moderate or even forgo altogether a new wave of repression. My appeal went unheeded, however, and the West paid scant attention to the devastating searches.

[1][Ruban was eventually pardoned and now lives in the U.S.]

ON JANUARY 8, a bomb exploded in a Moscow subway car, killing several passengers and injuring many more. The Soviet press remained silent for two days, as foreign stations broadcast contradictory reports about the incident. On January 11, we learned of an article by Victor Louis which stated that Soviet officials blamed dissidents for the crime. Louis is well known as a performer of delicate errands for Soviet authorities as well as a correspondent for British newspapers. He supposedly began his career as a KGB collaborator while a prisoner in a labor camp; he's said to be rewarded with the permission to speculate in paintings, icons, and hard currency.

Louis's article was evidently a trial balloon: if it went unanswered, an all-out attack on the dissident community might follow. I felt compelled to speak out, and did so, issuing a statement that contrasted the regime's illegal actions with the nonviolent, open, and patriotic behavior of human rights advocates. I noted possible KGB involvement in the deaths of Evgeny Brunov and Konstantin Bogatyrev and various other crimes against dissidents, and concluded by saying:

I cannot shake off the deep sense that the explosion in the Moscow subway with its tragic deaths is a new provocation of the agencies of repression—the most dangerous in recent years. It is this feeling, and the accompanying fear that this provocation might lead to a change in the country's domestic climate, that has prompted this article. I would be happy to have my concern proved false.

In any event, I hope that the criminal acts of the repressive organs do not reflect a new policy sanctioned from above, of crushing and discrediting dissenters or fomenting popular rage against them. I would rather believe that these are the criminal adventures of a certain circle seeking to advance its own power and influence and incapable of engaging in an honest struggle of ideas.

I call on world public opinion to demand an open and public investigation, conducted with the assistance of foreign experts and jurists, of the Moscow explosion of January 8. I hope that world public attention, comprehension of the peculiarities of our system, and the solidarity of all honest people the world over will put a stop to this dangerous development of events. I appeal to people to speak out against crime, provocation, and slander, thus in defense not only of dissidents in the USSR and Eastern Europe, but of the policy of détente, international trust, and the future of mankind.[2]

---

[2][The full text of Sakharov's appeal appears in *Alarm and Hope,* pp. 62–63.]

Lusia and I realized that the appeal would provoke KGB retaliation against both ourselves and other members of our family, especially the children. But given the situation, I felt that I had no other choice, and she understood that. The statement was made available to foreign correspondents and attracted significant interest.

ON JANUARY 21 an unexpected visitor arrived as we were having breakfast. He introduced himself as Martin Garbus, an American lawyer, and asked me to draw up for President Carter a list of ten political prisoners on whom efforts should be focused. (At the time, I thought that this request originated with the new American administration, but now I realize that Garbus himself probably initiated it.) A car was waiting downstairs, and his plane for America was leaving in two hours. He gratefully accepted Lusia's offer to make him an omelette; meanwhile, I drafted a letter to Carter in which I named sixteen prisoners—I simply couldn't limit myself to ten—and also mentioned my apprehension that the subway explosion might have been designed as a deliberate provocation or could be used to that end.[3] Lusia and I hurriedly made a copy of the letter (we each did a page) and handed it to our guest, as he rushed off, having spent less than half an hour with us.

Garbus had given me the impression that this was to be a private message to Carter, not intended for publication, and the letter was written accordingly. But this turned out to be a misunderstanding and the letter, slightly abridged, appeared in the New York Times on January 29. There was no harm done; in fact, it helped to attract attention to the plight of our prisoners of conscience.

In his January 20 inaugural address, President Carter stated: "Our moral sense dictates a clear-cut preference for those societies which share with us an abiding respect for individual human rights."

With some allowances for political rhetoric, Carter's commitment to human rights still appears in retrospect to have been serious and sincere, a reflection not only of his personal beliefs but even more important, of a moral and political climate: people around the world were coming to acknowledge the need for international efforts in defense of human rights. True, the Carter administration's human rights policy was marred in practice by a degree of inconsistency that had serious consequences for Soviet dissidents. Especially regrettable was the President's decision, a few months after taking office, to back away from involvement in individual cases. But looking back at Carter's inaugural address, the fact remains striking that for the first time the head of

[3][For the Sakharov–Carter correspondence, see Appendix, p. 686.]

a great power had announced an unambiguous commitment to the international defense of human rights.

ON JANUARY 24, I received a summons to appear at the USSR Procurator's Office. The next day Deputy Procurator General Sergei Gusev warned me that I might be held criminally liable for the statement concerning the Moscow subway explosion and for my other public activities.

Fearing that my family and friends might become the target for new reprisals, I immediately briefed correspondents on my meeting with Gusev. It was widely reported in the foreign media; meanwhile, the TASS international service carried an article by Yuri Kornilov that presented a distorted and misleading account of my views and accused me of deliberate slander.[4]

On January 27, the U.S. State Department issued a brief written statement that ended with the words: "Any attempt by the Soviet authorities to intimidate Mr. Sakharov will not silence legitimate criticism in the Soviet Union and will conflict with accepted standards of human rights." On January 30, members of the press corps caught the President as he was about to board his helicopter, and asked for his reaction. Carter's reported reply was that any comment about Soviet treatment of Sakharov "perhaps should have been said by myself or Secretary Vance." This off-the-cuff remark had serious repercussions; it was seen in both the USSR and the West as a disavowal of the State Department's words. A British newspaper chided Carter for feeding Sakharov peanuts—a tart reference to the President's peanut-farming business.

Carter may have had nothing more in mind than the need to coordinate policy, but it was a mistake to air such differences in public. It's mind-boggling to hear Western statesmen picking each other to pieces, washing their dirty linen for all to see; or, even worse, tailoring their positions on international issues to win points in domestic or party politics. Their adversaries note any sign of discord, inconsistency, naïveté, or cynicism, and capitalize on it. With the world situation as precarious as it is, the West and its politicians cannot afford to behave as though they exist in isolation. Perhaps I am making too much of a chance remark, but this seems as good a place as any to air my very strong feelings on this subject.

The Soviet authorities, who take advantage of any lapse, evidently perceived an opening here. Carter's failure to follow through on such matters as a telegram of support he'd sent the Jewish emigration activist and Moscow

---

[4][For Kornilov's article, "About a Certain Anti-Soviet Uproar," see *Alarm and Hope*, pp. 73–76.]

Helsinki Group member Vladimir Slepak seems to have fed that conviction; when Slepak was subjected to intensified harassment, Carter said not one word more. Most likely, the decision to arrest Orlov and Ginzburg had already been made, but Carter's remark may have affected the timing.

Carter's advisers, or Carter himself, may have sensed a sticky situation developing; this might account for Carter's letter of response, written on February 5 and delivered to me at the U.S. Embassy.[5] This unprecedented step might have had greater impact had it been followed by consistent implementation of the commitment to human rights articulated in the letter: "The American people and our government will continue . . . to promote human rights not only in our country but also abroad" and "to seek the release of prisoners of conscience."

I replied at once, thanking the President, and mentioning some specific cases, in particular the fact that Sergei Kovalev was in urgent need of surgery for a dangerous tumor. This, along with my earlier appeal, may have played a role in Kovalev's transfer from a Perm labor camp to a Leningrad hospital on March 1. I also called Carter's attention to the February arrests of four Helsinki Group members.

My critical remarks should not obscure my appreciation of Jimmy Carter's human rights policy. It may not always have been successful; that, after all, is fate. It's too early to judge the long-term consequences of his actions (and given our imperfect knowledge of the laws of history, we may never know them), but something, I am sure, will remain. As for his personal regard for me, I feel certain it is sincere, and not just politics.

ON FEBRUARY 3, two days before Carter sent his letter, Alexander Ginzburg was seized on the street. He had stayed with us at Chkalov Street for part of January, and then, with Lusia's help, had gotten admitted to a hospital for a checkup, hoping that the authorities' interest in him would blow over. His arrest was particularly worrying because technically he was a repeat offender (he'd been arrested in 1967), and so might be facing time in a special-regimen camp.

Lusia and I went to see Igor Shafarevich the following day. The three of us spent several hours working at the ever-agonizing task of drafting a joint appeal. Lusia and I stopped on our way home for a quick cup of coffee, and then stayed up until three A.M. editing the statement. On February 5, after some hesitation, Shafarevich signed the appeal.[6]

A week later Yuri Orlov was arrested. Orlov's solid scientific reputation (he

[5][Appendix, p. 687.]
[6][See *Alarm and Hope*, pp. 148–150.]

was a corresponding member of the Armenian Academy of Sciences) evoked no leniency from the authorities, and both his sentence and his treatment in detention were notably harsh.

In early February, Tanya ran into trouble. In 1974 her mother-in-law, Tomar Feigin, head of an important pharmaceutical laboratory, had asked for her help. When Tomar needed to pay a lab assistant overtime to wash equipment, she did what Soviet managers usually do; she added a fictitious worker to the payroll—in this case, Tanya. The authorities customarily turn a blind eye to such shortcuts. [I hope that enterprise autonomy—a cornerstone of Gorbachev's *perestroika*—will make such devious methods unnecessary.—A.S. 1987] Tanya knew this was improper, but neither she nor Efrem was prepared to refuse his mother's request. Tanya herself received no money; her "pay" was divided among the assistants who did the extra work.

Lusia and I were unaware of this arrangement until the storm broke. But it soon became obvious that the KGB had known about it from the beginning, and had simply been biding its time, until December 1976, when Tomar Feigin was charged with financial irregularities and fired.

On January 30, 1977, a regional newspaper published an article headlined "The Phantom Lab Assistant," whose author clearly had access to KGB information. There were details about Tanya's stay in the hospital, mention of the fact that Tanya and Efrem owned a car, always a source of envy in the Soviet Union; even a note made of an occasion when they had jumped on a suburban train at the very last moment, too late to pay the fare. A few days later, criminal charges were brought against Tomar. Tanya was summoned repeatedly for questioning, first as a witness and later as a suspect. She and Tomar faced potential sentences of up to seven years on this matter that had been blown up into large-scale "embezzlement of state property." Further developments in this affair will be described later on.

On February 3, the same day Ginzburg was arrested, we suffered a major blow: we learned that our request for an apartment exchange had been turned down. The details of this saga are a telling portrait of the treatment endured by the average Soviet citizen.

Seven of us had been living in Ruth's two-room apartment, moving out to the dacha in the summer. After the threats made against Tanya and Efrem and their children, we were apprehensive about leaving them alone at their cooperative apartment, but Lusia and I couldn't move that far from the center of Moscow. Ruth's 375 square feet of space left us awfully cramped, even by Soviet standards. We decided to see about exchanging the two apartments for a single four-room apartment. For a year or more we studied various possibilities, listing our offering in the monthly apartment-exchange bulletin. We looked at other people's apartments, and they looked at ours. Finally, a complex multistage solution was worked out for an exchange that satisfied both the official regulations and the interests of the seventeen households involved.

Our application, supported by a thick pile of required documents, was duly approved by the District Executive Committee's Housing Commission, ordinarily the final hurdle. But on February 3 we were informed that the committee had reversed the housing commission's decision on the grounds that one of those involved, a single woman who shared a four-room apartment with three families and who was slated to receive a small one-room apartment, had no right to additional living space: her 170-square-foot room exceeded the Moscow norm of 100 square feet. This woman's father had been killed in combat during the war, and the cooperative had approved her proposed purchase and issued the appropriate certificate, which had been attached to our joint application. One would hardly think it was the business of the committee to override the decision of the cooperative whose members paid for the building—but such logic doesn't obtain in our country.

All of us involved in the exchange were crushed. One young fellow, recently widowed, had been counting on moving closer to his parents so they could help look after his two young children. The lawyer we hired advised us that the decision contravened rulings by the USSR Supreme Court. The district court flatly refused to consider our complaint, and when the Moscow regional court heard our appeal in late February, our suit was rejected.

One woman who had long dreamed of escaping from communal apartment living asked the judge in despair: "Why doesn't the court defend citizens' legitimate interests?"

The judge solemnly replied: "In America, it's the court's job to defend citizens' interests. Soviet courts have other responsibilities!"

A Tass statement, "Academician Sakharov's New Provocation," issued on the day of the court ruling, betrayed the KGB's hand in quashing our apartment swap.

ON MARCH 15, another member of the Moscow Helsinki Group, Anatoly Shcharansky, was seized. The authorities hoped his arrest would deal a blow to the Jewish emigration movement and its links with human rights activists. Shcharansky, whom we'd known well even before he joined the Helsinki Group, had, since Alexander Goldfarb's emigration the previous year, served as my interpreter at press conferences. We held Shcharansky in respect and affection for his intelligence and innate honesty, his friendly and energetic nature. His application to emigrate had been rejected on the grounds that while a student at the Moscow Institute of Applied Physics he'd taken courses that were classified as "secret."

On March 5, *Izvestia* published a letter from Alexander Lipavsky, a refusenik who'd once been Shcharansky's roommate, accusing him (along with Professor Alexander Lerner) of espionage. Lipavsky, who had many contacts among Jewish activists, renounced his intention to emigrate, and the tone of his denunciations made it clear that he was a provocateur.

Tanya urged Shcharansky to move to our dacha and wait things out. He said he'd go as soon as he completed some pressing business in Moscow—he had to finish setting up a press conference to report on the release of Dr. Mikhail Stern from a labor camp on March 14. (Stern, an endocrinologist, had been arrested after his sons applied to emigrate; in 1974 he was sentenced to eight years in labor camp for taking bribes from patients. I'd signed an appeal for him, and international pressure had finally forced his release.) On March 15, Shcharansky was arrested on his way to invite correspondents to the press conference.

As the campaign against the Helsinki Groups unfolded, members were arrested in the Ukraine, Lithuania, Georgia, and Armenia. Persecution was especially fierce in the Ukraine; there were numerous arrests, and maximum sentences were the rule. Mykola Rudenko, chairman of the Ukrainian Group, and Alexei Tykhy were seized in February. Miroslav Marinovich and Mykola Matusevich were arrested in April, followed by Lev Lukyanenko, Vasyl Stus, Ivan Kandyba, Olga Geiko (Matusevich's wife), Raisa Rudenko, Oksana Meshko, and others.

I had met Mykola Rudenko prior to the founding of the Helsinki Group, when he brought me the manuscript of his pamphlet, *Farewell, Marx.* Rudenko, who'd been drafted before the beginning of the war, had served in Stalin's personal bodyguard, and then volunteered for front-line service, joined the Party, and suffered a severe spinal injury that left him permanently disabled and in chronic pain. Rudenko turned to writing and became a popular author of poetry and science fiction.

I am far from agreeing with everything in Rudenko's critiques of Marxism, and I never managed to get through *Greetings, Keynes,* his sequel to *Farewell, Marx.* But Rudenko's "physiocratic" perspective offered him an interesting springboard for a theory of political economy that focused on the powers of nature as the basis of national prosperity. Needless to say, there was nothing "anti-Soviet" about this. The KGB tried to break Rudenko by circulating a false rumor that his wife was unfaithful to him while he was in labor camp, but in fact she was later imprisoned because of her efforts in her husband's behalf. (They have both since been released and are now living in the U.S.)

Jimmy Carter's inaugural statement of the need for international efforts in defense of human rights ruffled the Soviet leaders, but his later vacillation may have encouraged them to believe that he was "manageable," and contributed to the difficulties which followed in other aspects of Soviet-American relations.

When Secretary of State Cyrus Vance visited Moscow in the spring of 1977 with far-reaching proposals on disarmament, he was simply shown the door. Andrei Gromyko went on television and demanded that the West respond to Soviet offers instead of introducing counterproposals designed to gain a military advantage. The United States was the moral victor in the exchange, but it led to no concrete results—a fiasco that left its mark on subsequent events.

42

1977

Lusia's second trip abroad. Emigration of the children. A Mordovian labor camp.

IN THE FALL of 1976, Lusia packed Tanya, Efrem, and Matvei off to the south for a few weeks' vacation. Anya, who had just turned one, stayed behind with us at the dacha. I would work at a table in the yard with Anya asleep next to me in her carriage, rocking her gently if she stirred. She'd go right back to sleep. Anya and I became very attached to each other, and I was only half joking when I told people that Anya was the most important woman in my life.

In April 1977, Lusia and I in turn traveled south, taking Matvei with us. We spent three and a half weeks at Sochi's Primorskaya Hotel, where we and Tanya had stayed three years earlier. In the mornings Matvei would crawl into bed with me and we would talk and play; he was especially fond of acting out scenes from such Kipling tales as "The Cat Who Walked by Himself," "The Elephant's Child," "Riki-Tiki-Tavi," and he was a lot better than I was at turning himself into an armadillo and other creatures.

After breakfast, Lusia and Matvei would walk down to the beach, where Matvei would play with pebbles while Lusia swam and sunbathed. Meanwhile, I'd stay up in the hotel room and work—the climb back from the beach was too steep for me. In the evenings we'd go to the park, where there were plenty of attractions for Matvei, or to an open-air cinema where he'd fall asleep in our arms or go wandering off between the rows, making us chase after him.

Lusia and I took turns going to see Mikhail Romm's *Ordinary Fascism* while the other baby-sat. Lusia had already seen the film; I hadn't. For both of us, it was a stunning experience. The images of Hitler and his Party henchmen: repellent, wretched, terrifying. The demagoguery whose poison had infected millions of Germans with incredible ease. Mountains of corpses; war, battles, bombings; Auschwitz and Babi Yar . . . the faces of those who perished in the camps rolling by on the screen . . . the soundtrack abruptly falling silent. (On occasion people in the audience would recognize their own relatives.) Hitler's buffoonery in the Forest of Compiègne. A parade of Hitler Youth, the boys' eyes riveted adoringly on their Führer, one foot already in his grave. Soon, many of these boys would be dead. The Berlin Chancellery. Charred corpses. You're caught in some terrifying, demented nightmare. Other images spring to mind: Kolyma, Vorkuta, Norilsk, and the special trains crammed with deportees half-dead from hunger and thirst.

In Gorky, reading an interesting Soviet book about Hitler, *Criminal Number One*, I was struck anew by the banality of the evil that is fascism—and by the peril it poses—and by the many parallels to events here. I went on to read the writing of Evgeny Gnedin, who had been press chief of the Foreign Ministry under Maxim Litvinov. Gnedin's work on the background of the 1939 Nazi-Soviet Pact makes use of documents published in the West and his own recollections to support the argument that Stalin and Molotov had long been seeking such a rapprochement. Far from being forced by the West's appeasement at Munich, the Pact was the product of a long-term plan that had included covert diplomatic gambits to circumvent the Foreign Ministry. Stalin's terror was an important factor contributing to the Pact and, eventually, to World War II. This is something worth recalling even today, both in a USSR still haunted by Stalin's ghost and in the West.

On May 21 we celebrated my birthday in grand style, dining in a dockside restaurant where we clinked glasses of Pepsi-Cola; we shared Matvei's taste for this fizzy drink, which, thanks, to détente, had recently become available in the USSR.

Back in our hotel room, we were awakened by the phone. Our friend and doctor, Vera Livchak, wanted to let us know that Tanya had become a suspect in the case involving her mother-in-law, and the investigator was about to impound her car, her only valuable possession. We hurried to the airport, exchanged our original tickets, and were home on Chkalov Street by nine that evening.

A few days later, I ordered an Academy car and drove with Tanya and Efrem to the dacha, where her car was parked. The investigator arrived from Krasnogorsk. The process of impounding dragged on, and I finally left before it was over. Lusia was rightly furious with me; I should never have abandoned our kids like that.

BY EARLY SPRING 1977, it was clear that Lusia would need another operation, this time on her right eye. She submitted her application in April, but her visa for Italy didn't arrive until August, just as Tanya and Efrem received their visas to emigrate. A long period of steadily increasing harassment had convinced them to leave; otherwise, the KGB would continue to use them as hostages for my public activities. Tanya and Tomar were already being threatened with criminal prosecution. Efrem was himself in danger of arrest on political charges; he'd been summoned to the Procurator's Office and warned in unmistakable terms. Vague but disturbing (and, needless to say, groundless) accusations were circulating that he was engaged in criminal activity, for instance speculation in books and failure to report an automobile accident. And none of us could put out of our minds the threats against the grandchildren, and Matvei's mysterious 1975 illness. We'd known even that far back that this day would have to come, but the final decision had been postponed repeatedly. Efrem felt he could do more for Kovalev and other friends and their cause here than he could abroad, and there were personal considerations as well—emigration would mean cutting off the family's very lifeblood. In fact the separation has proved considerably more difficult for all of us than we anticipated, and particularly so for Lusia.

The criminal charges looming against Tanya and Tomar were the last straw. The KGB clearly would not let up. They were eager to see Tanya, Efrem, Tomar, and later on, Alexei, go—just why, I'm still not certain. Efrem had made it clear to OVIR that under no circumstances would he leave without his mother, or before Lusia had her visa. "Have your mother apply," he was told. Tomar went straight to OVIR and filled out her application, and the visa was granted quickly, as were visas for her parents, Shmuel, (who had been imprisoned in the 1930s for Zionist activities) and Roza. Efrem's brother and sister-in-law already had their visas. Tanya and Efrem were to travel via Italy to the U.S., where we thought opportunities for employment and study had been set up (as it turned out, this was not exactly the case). All of them, including Tanya and Efrem, had invitations from relatives in Israel.

Lusia, Tanya, Efrem, Matvei, and Anya were all booked on an Alitalia flight to Rome on September 5. On the same day, Tomar and her parents were to fly to Vienna and then on to Israel. More than a hundred people came to a farewell party at the dacha on September 1, Anya's birthday. KGB agents were said to be hiding in the bushes, but we didn't care.

Many friends came to Sheremetevo Airport to see the Yankeleviches off on September 5. Among those present was Vitaly Rekubratsky, my cousin Masha's husband, who had arranged jobs for Sergei Kovalev and Efrem at the experimental fish hatchery; he brought me a letter from the writer Vladimir Korolenko to my grandfather that had been found among my Aunt Tanya's papers. I had no way of knowing then that this was a farewell gift: Rekubratsky committed suicide two weeks later. I saw him for the last time just a few hours before his death, at a birthday party for Sofia Kalistratova on September 19.

He left two sons: Ivan, named for my grandfather, Ivan Sakharov, and Sergei, born a month after Sergei Kovalev's trial and named for him.

DR. FREZOTTI once again operated on Lusia, this time with less success than two years earlier. Her right eye was in worse shape than the left had been, and there was hemorrhaging. Lusia returned to Moscow on November 20, and on December 8 Tanya, Efrem, and the children flew to Boston.

In Italy, Efrem continued his labors on *Alarm and Hope;* he'd been working on it for nearly a year, collecting and editing my statements with the aid of his friend Vladimir Rubtsov. The book appeared in a number of languages and attracted considerable attention. And I love the photograph on the jacket of the American edition, taken by Efrem, which shows Anya snuggling in my arms.

Efrem also helped to organize the second session of the Sakharov Hearings, held in Rome on November 25–28, 1977 (Lusia had already left for home). The first session had been held in Copenhagen on October 17–19, 1975, soon after the announcement of my Nobel Peace Prize. The initial purpose was to provide a forum for reports on the human rights situation in the USSR; later, this was expanded to include East Europe. The Hearings' founders had asked if they might use my name, and I had agreed in the belief that their aim of educating the general public was of great importance. Efrem's logical mind, knowledge and absolute integrity ensured the exclusion of any false, unsubstantiated, or sensational testimony, and a focus on significant issues. The success of the Rome hearings (and of later ones in Washington and London) was due in large part to his efforts.

IN SEPTEMBER 1977, on the eve of the Belgrade Follow-up Meeting, I issued an appeal stressing the Final Act's linkage of international security and civil rights and giving details of human rights violations in the USSR. I listed the names of all arrested members of the Helsinki Group, and urged Western governments to make the convening of the Belgrade Meeting contingent on the release of Orlov and his associates.

I personally delivered copies of this statement to a dozen Western embassies, calling each beforehand and asking that a consular employee meet me on the street to ensure that I would not be denied entry. I used an Academy car to drop off these copies and encountered no difficulties, although KGB agents did make a great show of photographing me at three embassies.

It was at that time, however, that our car, a Zhiguli, was vandalized, with epoxy glue poured into the locks. The car had been parked near a friend's building, and luckily he was able to get a door open before the glue hardened. He drove the car to our place; and while he was telling me what had happened, the vandals struck again, puncturing the radiator in several places so that the antifreeze ran out. We had to buy a new radiator and change the locks. This was obviously the KGB's retaliation for my tour of the consulates. And, I regret to say, Western governments did not heed my request to postpone the Belgrade meeting.

I was happy to accept an invitation to contribute to the Amnesty International Conference on the Abolition of the Death Penalty, held in Stockholm in December 1977.[1] Opposition to the death penalty was something of a family tradition; as I mentioned at the beginning of this book, my grandfather Ivan Sakharov had edited a prerevolutionary work opposing capital punishment. In 1962 I had spoken out against the death penalty imposed on an old man accused of counterfeiting, and in 1972 I had drafted an appeal to the Soviet government to abolish capital punishment. (And in 1979 I voiced my opposition to death sentences in the Moscow subway bombing.)

At the request of František Janouch, a Czech physicist living and working in Sweden, I wrote an article on nuclear energy, advocating the development of nuclear power plants with appropriate safeguards and arguing that nuclear power was less harmful to the environment than coal, and had the political benefit of freeing the West from dependence on oil- and gas-producing countries (including the USSR).[2] These thoughts were repeated in a 1978 exchange of letters with Heinrich Böll, then on a return visit to the USSR. He and his wife were supposed to come to our place, but a last-minute change in plans sent us to the Kopelevs' apartment, with Lusia carrying along some of the food she'd prepared. In our dialogue, Böll and I built on the frank and thoughtful exchange of views we'd begun three years earlier.

SHORTLY BEFORE returning to Moscow from Italy, Lusia gave a major interview to American correspondents on the theme of human rights—the current situation and future prospects. She spoke of the bitter struggle being waged for these rights and the enormous sacrifices it entailed, and of the overriding importance of international awareness of the Soviet situation. The "arithmetic of dissidence"—whether the count of human rights activists was up or down—mattered less than the world's awareness of violations taking place in the USSR. Such knowledge could not be erased by arrests and repression. It was

[1][Appendix, p. 653.]
[2]["Nuclear Energy and the Freedom of the West," *Bulletin of the Atomic Scientists*, June 1978.]

during this interview that Lusia first used the expression "the international ideology of human rights," proposing it as the sole means of uniting people of differing political persuasions, nationalities, religions, educational and social status. I later used this expression, and many other ideas formulated by Lusia in that interview.

By the time the interview was broadcast Lusia was back in Moscow, and we listened to it together. The commentary on it was accurate and detailed, but we were taken aback when the announcer concluded by saying that "a correspondent [unnamed] present during the interview believes Elena Bonner is anxious to leave the USSR." This gratuitous and erroneous comment served to undercut the general thrust of the interview.

A number of countries proclaimed amnesties during 1977. The Soviet amnesty, declared in conjunction with sixtieth anniversary of the Revolution, contained both the usual clause excluding political crimes and a further reservation allowing prison and camp administrators to deny amnesty to prisoners whose behavior they deemed "unsatisfactory"—a loophole that offered wide scope for settling scores.

But we were cheered by the amnesties elsewhere and hailed them as victories in the worldwide battle for human rights. I recall, in particular, the amnesty in Indonesia (unfortunately, only partial), and one in Yugoslavia that prompted us to send a telegram of appreciation to President Tito, an acquaintance of Lusia's from her childhood; he and her father, Gevork Alikhanov, had worked closely together in the Comintern, and Tito had lived in the same Gorky Street building as her family. We gave a copy of our telegram to a journalist from the Yugoslav newspaper Borba, but received no response.

In November 1977, Pyotr Grigorenko left the Soviet Union for surgery and medical treatment in America, where his son Andrei was living. His wife, Zinaida, and invalid stepson Oleg were allowed to accompany him, which, I warned Grigorenko, was a portent that they would be denied reentry. In February 1978, he was indeed stripped of his Soviet citizenship (I protested the action). As Grigorenko had argued persuasively, however, one could hardly expect a mother to forgo the chance to see her son.

Grigorenko and I had quarreled shortly before his departure over proposals to change the date of the annual silent demonstration at the Pushkin monument from December 5 to December 10. I'd never been all that enthusiastic about these demonstrations, which smacked of "revolutionary" party rallies, and I disliked the role of "opposition leader" into which I was thrust. During the 1976 demonstration, in a KGB-engineered scuffle, slushy snow was dumped over my head; I feared the future might bring more serious incidents. I saw no cause to regret a natural end to the Pushkin Square demonstrations. Grigorenko, on the other hand, wanted to keep up the tradition but change the date to December 10, the anniversary of the General Assembly's adoption of the Universal Declaration of Human Rights. I declined to sign the appeal he drafted, and did not attend the 1977, 1978, and 1979 demonstrations.

ALONG WITH several other Soviet dissidents, I was invited by George Meany to attend the annual AFL-CIO convention in Los Angeles in December 1977. What I actually received in the mail was an AFL-CIO envelope containing a drawing of a brontosaurus or some other extinct monster (I'm no expert in paleontology), probably intended as an allusion to the "antediluvian" views of American reactionaries. But as I wrote in my address to the convention: "The real brontosaurus is the repressive system which spawns such illegalities." This was neither the first nor the last occasion on which the KGB switched the contents of my mail.

I went through the motions of formally accepting the invitation, applying to OVIR for a visa, and asking for a character reference from FIAN. Within hours, I received a call reporting that the Presidium of the Academy of Sciences had considered my request and had decided that it would have to be denied owing to my knowledge of state secrets.

AFTER TANYA AND Efrem emigrated in 1977, the role of hostage fell to Alexei. He found work at the Teachers Institute unchallenging, and I asked Academician Rem Khokhlov, the physicist who had replaced Ivan Petrovsky as rector, to help Alexei transfer to Moscow University. (Khokhlov had got Tanya reinstated in the journalism department.) After making inquiries, Khokhlov told me that although Alexei's academic record was satisfactory, his failure to enroll in the Komsomol was considered evidence of my influence and barred his transfer. I was grateful to Khokhlov for his frankness, which kept us from wasting our time and energy.

Alexei remained at the Institute, but did not graduate—he was expelled that fall after he failed his mandatory military training course. Normally, in such instances the student is either permitted to retake the exam after a year, or else must perform army service as a private rather than being commissioned a lieutenant. Officer training in any case was not part of the Institute's official curriculum, and so should not have had any bearing on graduation. Nevertheless, Alexei was expelled, and therefore became subject to immediate induction, which we decided must be avoided at any cost. In our situation, even a labor camp would be safer. However great the horrors of the camps, army brutality (with the KGB operating with a free hand) would have been even worse. We arranged invitations from Israel for Alexei, his wife, Olga, and their two-year-old daughter, Katya.

Now a new drama erupted that had been simmering for some time, unbeknownst to us. In mid-December, Alexei informed Olga that he no longer loved her and was going to leave her; the decision to emigrate had brought the matter to a head. They did submit a joint visa application, but Olga later changed her mind, and Alexei left alone, agreeing to Olga's request that he wait a year before filing for divorce.

A new player appeared on the scene: Liza Alexeyeva, a classmate of Alexei's. Although by now Liza was Alexei's wife in all but name, she could not accompany him, since he was still legally bound to Olga. Liza and Alexei would spend years battling to be reunited, as the KGB made use of their romance, and Liza became a hostage.

ON DECEMBER 15, Lusia, Alexei, and I left by train for Mordovia to visit Eduard Kuznetsov. Lusia hoped that my presence might be the key to obtaining the long-delayed meeting, and Alexei came along, carrying provisions for Kuznetsov. Since 1971 Lusia had made several journeys to the camp, but visits were often cancelled at the last minute. Lusia's acquaintance with the camps had begun back in 1945, with her first visits to Ruth, while I had only observed camp life from a distance, at the Installation. For Alexei, it was the first exposure to this world.

The Mordovian camps (the Dubrovlag complex) are neither the best nor the worst exemplars of the camp world; conditions are more severe where the climate is harsher. There are many accounts available of the journey to Mordovia: passing through Potma, as everyone must en route to Dubrovlag; changing from the Moscow–Tashkent express to a dirty, rackety train on the narrow-gauge Potma–Barashevo line; reaching the end of the line, Barashevo, the site of the Dubrovlag hospital.

The world seems to alter mysteriously as you leave Potma. Colors fade; bright hues give way to grays and browns. People's voices seem—or perhaps they *are*—vicious and grating. The camps ("zones" in camp argot) scattered along both sides of the right-of-way bear a close resemblance to the German concentration camps familiar from war photos and films (Andrzej Wajda's harsh and passionate *Landscape After Battle* comes to mind). Each camp zone comprises a rectangle surrounded by a high gray fence topped with barbed wire. Watchtowers at the corners are manned by guards with submachine guns. Just inside the fence is a "forbidden zone" of plowed earth followed by another fence of barbed wire, and then, at the center, are rows of long, low barracks, single-story gray-plank buildings with darkened windows. The whole scene is illuminated by the lifeless glare of spotlights attached to tall posts. Even by day, there's scarcely a sign of life, although people's presence behind the walls of the barracks can be sensed. From time to time, a German shepherd barks. You realize that the description of the dog as "man's best friend" does not necessarily hold true when the man is dressed in a standard-issue gray quilted jacket or the stripes of a special-regimen prisoner.

Kuznetsov's special-regimen camp was located adjacent to the settlement of Sosnovka, in the heart of Dubrovlag. A large camp for common criminals was located nearby. There are a few dozen houses for married camp personnel and their families in Sosnovka; we stayed in a primitive hotel for visitors which doubled as a dormitory for unmarried camp staff.

The room we were given was cold, the windows could not be opened, and the beds were unmade. It was next to the communal WC. There was no sign of a shower, but there was a heater to boil water for tea. In the morning Lusia and I called on the camp commander to arrange a visit with Kuznetsov. He turned us down categorically: we didn't seem likely to have a "salutary" influence on the prisoner. Nor was Lusia given permission to see Kuznetsov on her own.

We sent telegrams to the Dubrovlag chief at the administrative center in Yavas and to the head of the Main Administration of Corrective Labor Institutions (as the Gulag is known in our civilized age), requesting that a visit be allowed. We settled down to wait, hoping that our presence, which by then was common knowledge in the camp, would embarrass the administration. And so it did—but permission still was not forthcoming. After ten days, we called Kuznetsov's friend Bella Koval, thinking she might be allowed to see him, but to no avail. In the meantime, Kuznetsov, who had learned that we were trying to see him, began a hunger strike. We finally left for Moscow at the end of December, hoping that our departure might ease matters, and Kuznetsov ended his hunger strike a short time later.

For Alexei and me, that first close look at camp life was an unforgettable experience.

Relatives of prisoners came and went in rapid succession, terrified folk who seemed intimidated even by the hotel cleaning women (let alone the camp personnel charged with directing them to the meeting place, who searched them before and after, and could cancel a visit at the slightest whim).

Representatives of industrial enterprises would spend weeks at the hotel on business trips, the camps are a source of what is—at least on paper—cheap labor. Some prisoners work inside the camp compound; others do hard labor outside. Failure to fulfill quotas is punished severely and conditions often are unsafe and dangerous to health. In Mordovia, for example, convicts must cut glass without protective equipment and varnish furniture in unventilated workshops. From what we heard, it seemed clear that camp labor was not only inhumane, but also of dubious value. Prisoners lack skills and motivation. Productivity is abysmal. One man told us that a cooperative of blind workers in his home city of Gorky far surpassed camp laborers in both the quality and the quantity of production: it took six hundred convicts to equal the work of fifty blind workers. It's the eternal problem with slave labor.

Although the economic importance of forced labor has declined since the peak of the Gulag slave-labor empire, it remains a fact of our national life. In Yavas, Lusia and I noticed a poster that declared: *It is our socialist* [!] *duty to increase output by 100% during the next five-year plan.* Since an increase in productivity is virtually impossible, the poster implies an anticipated increase in the number of prisoners. Shameful—but in Yavas, everyone was a member of the club.

Guards and other camp personnel made up the hotel's permanent population. (The higher ranks had separate quarters.) We were constantly running into the residents in the lounge, in the laundry room, and at the water heater. On one occasion, a couple of them introduced themselves and chatted for a while, probably out of curiosity. Both had entered a school run by the Ministry of Internal Affairs after completing their army service, and had been attracted by the high pay, long vacations, and such perks as access to special resorts run by the Ministry. The two were section leaders, but they were very different types. Kolya was thin and nervous, and as he talked about his job, he unwittingly revealed the thrill he derived from his power over other human beings and his malicious, almost sadistic, contempt for those under his control. He told us a story about an old man who had "faked" illness and as punishment was assigned to the most brutal labor, unloading coal in freezing weather. The old man had wept and begged to be spared. Then he actually did fall ill, and collapsed. Whereupon Kolya placed him in a punishment cell for "shirking."

"You know, it was wrong to punish him," the other section leader, Vanya interjected.

No reply from Kolya.

Vanya's tale was quite different. A peasant woman had been caught trying to smuggle ten rubles to her husband. Threatened with losing both that visit and possibly the next one as well, she'd fallen to her knees and begun to weep. "I said to her, I'll let it go this time; here's your money—but don't do it again; I can't let it go twice."

Even in the camps, the differences between people, their behavior and attitudes toward the suffering of others, are obvious.

In the evenings, movies were shown in the lounge, including Eldar Ryazanov's hilarious comedy *The Irony of Fate.* The camp personnel would bring chairs from their rooms and watch, occasionally glancing our way: Sakharov's presence was, after all, something of an event in this out-of-the-way place. Some faces would already be flushed from drink. Later, back in our room, we would hear shouting, swearing, fighting, someone being dragged out into the cold—alcohol taking its daily toll.

Toward the end of our stay, Lusia and I watched David Samoilov giving a spirited recital of his work on a daytime television show, reading one poem after another, including one in which he addressed Pushkin with these words: "Thank God you are free, in Russia, at your estate in Boldino and in quarantine." It occurred to me that this would make an appropriate epigraph for my own memoirs . . .

Vanya, who was off duty that day, was sitting beside me. The realization that we knew Samoilov personally came as a shock to him: the world where people wrote and read poetry seemed infinitely distant from his world of people debasing each other, drinking vodka, cursing and brawling, their days spent bending their backs and their nights seeking oblivion in sleep, a world where the store shelves were empty and the films in the movie theatre had to be spliced over and over. And now, suddenly, our presence bridged that gap and the two worlds met.

Maybe I'm naïve, but when I think of Vanya's face that day, and of similar encounters, I begin to believe that this wretched, downtrodden, corrupt, and drunken people—no longer even a *people* in any real sense of the word—is not yet entirely lost, not yet dead. The grandeur of Russia's history, the Orthodox religious revival, our role in revolutionary internationalism, may all seem unreal illusion when we contemplate today's Russia, but sparks of simple humanity and compassion for others and a thirst for spiritual fulfillment have not yet been utterly extinguished. Will anything come of them? For the nation as a whole, I have no idea, but is that so important? On the personal plane, I am certain that so long as there are people, the sparks will glow.

Back in Moscow, we produced a statement about Kuznetsov and described our impressions of the journey to foreign newsmen. Our comments about our encounter with the two guards gave rise to several Western newspaper articles with comments like: "On their visit to Mordovia, the Sakharovs discovered that a guard's life is just as hard as a prisoner's. . . ."

This, of course, was not what we meant. It would be blasphemy to equate the lives of the prisoners and their guards. The prisoners' lives are virtually unbearable; deprived of every iota of freedom, they must endure the guards' frequently abusive exercises of power. What we were trying to say was that the guards as well as the prisoners were doomed to wretched, gray, and squalid lives, and that this was not only deplorable in itself but also damaging to camp life and morality. Once, when we mentioned the poor quality of the bread given to the prisoners, the mutter came back from a guard: "Well, you should see the rotten bread they sell in our store in Sosnovka."

43

1978

Alexei's emigration. Trials of Orlov, Ginzburg, and Shcharansky. Vacation in Sukhumi. A surreptitious search.

ALEXEI AND OLGA received exit visas three days after submitting their applications. Olga, who remained in Moscow, gave Alexei the financial release required by OVIR, and we reimbursed her as agreed. With Olga's permission, Lusia and I were able to spend some time with our granddaughter. Katya was warm and trusting with me, but more reserved with Lusia, evidently because of some discussions she'd overheard.

Alexei left on March 1, 1978. The night before, he took individual leave of each of us—Ruth; his mother; me; Liza. On the way to the airport, he asked to stop at the Pushkin monument. He got out of the car alone and placed flowers before the poet's statue, bidding farewell to the country he was leaving, not of his own will.

There was a tragicomic episode at the airport. In a fresh show of KGB pettiness, customs officials decided to confiscate a batch of photographs of friends and relatives from Alexei. Lusia and I argued with the officials; they pretended to concede, but as Alexei was undressing for a body search, he saw them taking away the photographs. Infuriated, he rushed at them, pushed one man aside, snatched up the photographs and a bottle of vodka they were also confiscating, and dashed half-dressed to the plane, clutching his trophies. Three hours later he was in Italy. In May he went to the United States.

In the spring of 1978, my daughter Lyuba, who had married in 1973, gave birth to a son, who was named Grigori ("Grisha"). I very much regret that I have seen him only on rare occasions.

TWO TRIALS began on May 15, 1978: Yuri Orlov's in Moscow, and that of Zviad Gamsakhurdia and Merab Kostava, members of the Georgian Helsinki

Group, in Tbilisi. I had planned to divide my time between Moscow and Tbilisi, but when Lusia and I arrived at the Moscow airport on the evening of May 15, we learned that Gamsakhurdia had disavowed his human rights activities, and so we decided to cancel our trip to Georgia.

Evidently that displeased the KGB, and for the next few days I was harassed by phone calls from "Georgians" reproaching me for being there when it was a matter of a meal of Georgian shashlik, but nowhere to be found when Georgians needed help. (They were a bit off the mark with the shashlik—I don't much care for it, and never ate it in Georgia.)

Gamsakhurdia stated at his trial, and again on television, that he regretted his public statements and meetings with foreign diplomats. I'll repeat here what I've often said—I don't think it's right to condemn anyone for recanting. Human strength has its limitations, and there's a tendency to overestimate one's staying power, particularly in the face of the unexpected. And those who break are often their own harshest critics.

All the more reason to admire those who stand firm—like Merab Kostava; left exposed by Gamsakhurdia's capitulation, he refused to yield, and continued to conduct himself with courage and dignity in camps and exile.

Many people, myself included, thought the authorities would hesitate to arrest Yuri Orlov, or that, at worst, he would be sentenced to internal exile. We were mistaken. Orlov was given the maximum sentence for anti-Soviet slander—seven years labor camp and five years exile—and was the victim of extremely harsh treatment while serving his sentence. The Presidium of the Armenian Academy, in flagrant violation of its charter, expelled Orlov from its ranks in a secret session.

Orlov's trial was held on May 15–18 in the Moscow suburb of Lublino. The many friends, foreign correspondents, and diplomats who traveled there were all barred from the courthouse; temporary barriers had been erected, and the police kept everyone at least fifty feet from the building. Orlov's wife and sons were allowed into the courtroom, but twice they were roughed up and their clothes torn in the official zeal to prevent them from taping the "open" trial. During a break, Orlov's lawyer, Evgeny Shalman, was forcibly removed from the courtroom and locked for a time in an office.

On the trial's last day, I argued vehemently that the defendant's friends should be allowed into the courtroom to hear the verdict. As I made my way through the crowd, a scuffle reminiscent of the one in Omsk broke out, first I, then others, were dragged off to police cars parked nearby. I hit one KGB agent; Lusia, receiving a sharp and professional blow to the neck from another one, smacked him back. As she was being shoved into a police car, she accidentally punched the local chief of police. We were released promptly, but were later summoned to appear in court, where we were given fines (fifty rubles for me, forty for Lusia) for "hooliganism"—creating a disturbance during a trial. Reluctant to charge us with assault and battery, they ignored Lusia's statement: "I was right to hit the KGB agent, and don't regret it, but I struck the police chief by mistake, and I'd like to apologize to him." The policemen crowding the courtroom no doubt appreciated that remark.

I felt embarrassed when two persons who had been detained with us were sentenced to fifteen days in jail while we got off with a fine.

Two more trials took place in July: Alexander Ginzburg's in Kaluga, July 10–13, Anatoly Shcharansky's in Moscow, July 10–14. The KGB seemed to have developed a fondness for this tactic of simultaneous trials to divide our depleted forces. Lusia and I attempted to cover both proceedings.

Twice I got a ride to Kaluga with the Vladimovs. A good deal of the testimony against Ginzburg came from rather shady characters, as much criminal as political, who'd been beneficiaries of Solzhenitsyn's Prisoner Aid Fund [Ginzburg had served as its treasurer]. Outside the courthouse, a crowd shouted insults and provocative remarks at us—Lusia believes they were ordinary Soviet citizens; to my mind, though, this demonstration was carefully organized. Alex was sentenced to eight years special-regimen camp.

Anatoly Shcharansky's trial attracted even more attention. It was a Soviet version of the Dreyfus case, with Shcharansky accused of espionage. He and other Jewish activists had interviewed Jews who'd been refused exit visas on the grounds of state security, even though the places where they worked weren't classified as secret. The facts had been passed on to an American correspondent, who duly filed a story. Shcharansky's actions did not violate any law. None of the persons he interviewed were charged with divulging state secrets. President Carter denied publicly that Shcharansky had any connection with American intelligence.

The KGB was not about to relinquish its goal of intimidating potential Jewish emigrants and driving a wedge between them and the dissidents, but it made a mistake in picking on Shcharansky, who stood up to the psychological pressure of a fifteen-month investigation during which he was held in isolation, repeatedly threatened with the death penalty, and offered freedom in exchange for a confession.

Shcharansky also behaved with exceptional courage at his trial. His brother Leonid was allowed to attend most of the sessions; his mother, however, was denied entry to the courtroom on the spurious grounds that she had refused to testify after being called as a witness.

During the trial, I gave an interview to foreign journalists who were standing outside the courthouse; this was broadcast by Voice of America with a gratuitously added comment: "Sakharov expressed the hope that Shcharansky would be exchanged shortly."

I had said nothing of the sort. The remark served to diminish the tragedy of Shcharansky's situation. He was sentenced on July 14 to three years prison and ten years labor camp, and his mother was not allowed into the courtroom even for the reading of the verdict. Leonid emerged from the courthouse after the trial was over and walked to the barricade that was penning Shcharansky's friends in an alley. He'd managed to write down his brother's final plea, and now he read out that powerful statement in a loud, clear voice. We removed our hats, and sang the Israeli national anthem. It began to rain. People continued to sing, their tears mingling with the raindrops. Residents in nearby buildings opened their windows and listened to us. Even the KGB, out in force, did not interfere. For those few moments the handful of people standing behind the barrier were more than a match for the repressive machinery of the state.

Shcharansky's mother and his brother and sister-in-law called on us afterward, making their first visit to our apartment. We stayed in close contact with them during the years Shcharansky spent in prisons and camps.

The trials of Orlov and Shcharansky served to stimulate a more general interest in Soviet human rights violations. New organizations were established abroad to help prisoners of conscience in the USSR; I want to mention, in particular, SOS (Scientists for Orlov and Shcharansky), a committee based in Berkeley, California. This later took up my defense as well, with one "S" now standing for "Sakharov."

IN MID-SEPTEMBER, Lusia and I spent two weeks in Sukhumi. It was still warm, and we swam and went for walks. I got quite a bit of work done, but we also managed to go to the cinema and to accompany the Kopelevs, whom we bumped into on the waterfront, and another friend on a fascinating outing to the Novoafonsky caves. Kopelev's generosity, compassion, tolerance, intellectual breadth, his love of life are all elements of my mental picture of that big, strong, kindly man, with his enormous dark eyes gazing at the world with childlike wonder. Knowing him has enriched our lives.

While swimming in Sukhumi, Lusia suffered a severe hemorrhage in one eye. She had applied that spring for a third visa to Italy: her vision had not stabilized after the second operation, and she needed new glasses and possibly another operation. When we returned to Moscow, I spoke several times on the phone to Boris Shumilin, the Deputy Minister of Internal Affairs responsible for OVIR, in order to expedite Lusia's visa. I wrote to Brezhnev reminding him that the question of Lusia's travel abroad for eye care had been decided in principle in 1975. I sent the letter in mid-November, and left a copy in a large cardboard box on top of my desk along with many other documents and letters, all of which disappeared during a clandestine search of our apartment on November 29.

It was empty for an hour or so, something we normally tried to avoid. When we knew we'd all be out at the same time, we'd usually take the most important papers with us. But that day we neglected to do so. Lusia and I went out to a bookstore around one o'clock; soon after, Ruth and Liza (who was living with us) left for the international telephone office. It was impossible to call Alexei or Tanya and Efrem from our apartment; the KGB agent who monitored our line would immediately terminate the conversation. Not being able to talk is worse than being bugged (after all, unpleasant as bugging is, we had nothing to hide).

Ruth and Liza had managed to place several calls to Alexei from the telephone office, but this time they were cut off. We all returned to the apartment about the same time. A few minutes later, Liza called out from the bathroom: "Where's my robe? I can't find it. . . ."

We discovered a strange assortment of things missing—old clothing, including the pants I liked to wear around the house, a favorite blue jacket which Klava had bought for me, and my eyeglasses, while more valuable possessions in plain sight had not been taken.

When Lydia Chukovskaya came by the next day for a visit and asked to take a look at something I'd written, I discovered that my document box had been rifled. The letter to Brezhnev had disappeared, as had the manuscript representing five months' work on these memoirs. This was the first of many thefts (or "confiscations"—call them what you will) of this Sisyphean labor of mine. (Although, unlike Sisyphus, I always managed to leave atop the hill at least a piece of the rock I was pushing.) To extend the analogy: Sisyphus was condemned for refusing to die when the gods ordained; I was condemned for refusing to fall silent at the behest of our terrestrial powers.

Dozens of appeals for assistance and threatening letters, as well as copies of my published statements, were missing. A pile of less important documents that I'd kept in a desk drawer had been substituted for the stolen papers.

It was obviously the KGB that had gone through the apartment, despite the theft of the clothing. We had locked the apartment door when we left, and it was locked when we returned—but keys are no problem for the KGB's specialists. Four years later, Lusia would undergo an official search aboard the Gorky–Moscow train, but back then the KGB still preferred to use covert, "unofficial" methods.

We reported the theft of the documents, the letter to Brezhnev, and the memoirs, and announced that we would begin an indefinite hunger strike if we failed to receive a reply to Lusia's visa application by January 3, 1979.[1] Boris Altshuler got hold of forty bottles of Borzhomi mineral water—no easy task—and we stored them under the sideboard and bed of our cramped apartment.[2]

Just before New Year's, Konstantin Zotov telephoned from OVIR and told us that Lusia had received permission to go abroad again.

[1][See Appendix, p. 679.]

[2][Drinking mineral water during a hunger strike helps to maintain the body's electrolyte balance.]

44

1979

Lusia's third trip abroad. The Moscow
subway bomb trial. Seventh-Day Adventists
on trial. Arrests of Velikanova and
Nekipelov.

LUSIA FLEW to Italy on January 15, 1979. Dr. Frezotti advised against another operation and instead prescribed non-surgical treatment, a judgment concurred in by Dr. Charles Schepens, the distinguished American ophthalmologist, and Lusia was duly fitted with new glasses. She went to Boston from Italy for her consultation with Dr. Schepens, and thus had a chance to see first-hand how her children and grandchildren were dealing with their new and strange world. [We have never before publicized Lusia's presence in the U.S. at that time. At the clinic, her identity was concealed, and only Dr. Schepens knew who she was. We were aware that the KGB knew about it from the beginning, and since they tipped their hand in a May 1984 *Izvestia* article, I now feel free to tell the whole story.—A.S. 1987] Lusia's impressions of the U.S. and her visit there were vivid and complex, even contradictory.

Following my exile to Gorky, I made Efrem Yankelevich my official representative abroad, but even earlier, from the moment they arrived in the West, he and Tanya were forced to take on the burden of representing my ideas and interests; no one else could match their authority. Being a relative of Sakharov may be less of a problem in Boston than in Moscow, but even in Boston the doors don't automatically swing open. MIT's invitations turned out to have been largely *pro forma,* not to be taken seriously; Alexei was refused admission there. He was, however, accepted as a "walk-in" by Brandeis University: fortunately, they didn't know he was a relative of mine (if they even knew who I was). Brandeis is a very fine school and perhaps it all turned out for the best. Efrem was less fortunate; despite an excellent background and work record, he spent several years without regular employment. To be fair, it should be noted that Efrem and Tanya were constantly having to rush off on business connected with my affairs, to give a talk, or to turn out an article overnight.

Even in a less business-oriented country, this might give pause to potential employers.

These problems, which only came to light toward the end of Lusia's brief visit, left her with some painful impressions. But there'd been much joy, as well: her grandchildren were already thoroughly at home with the language and the life of Newton, the Boston suburb where they lived, and at a delightful family birthday party for Lusia on February 15, the children sang her the traditional American tune, "Happy birthday to you . . ."

WHILE LUSIA was abroad, dramatic events were taking place at home.

In August 1978, the USSR Council of Ministers had adopted Resolution No. 700, granting the Ministry of Internal Affairs broad new authority to deport Tatars from the Crimea, with return forbidden. The resolution was not formally publicized, but Soviet agencies in the Crimea used it to threaten Tatars, and special police units were formed to implement the decree, a task they accomplished using pogrom tactics. Homes were destroyed, and there were occasional outbreaks of violence. Tatars in the Crimea could no longer obtain residence permits, buy houses, or find employment.

I telephoned Albert Ivanov, the Deputy Director of the Central Committee's Department of Administrative Organs, who dealt with travel and residence permits, labor camps, and other functions of the Ministry of Internal Affairs. He confirmed that reports about Resolution No. 700 were true, and when I protested this unjust discrimination against the Crimean Tatars, a nation whose banishment thirty-five years earlier was one of the crimes of Stalinism, he replied:

"Be that as it may, there's nothing for the Tatars in the Crimea. Their place has been taken by the Ukrainians, and we can't deport *them.*"

No one was demanding that the Ukrainians be deported, I responded; the Crimea had as much room as any other region in the USSR, and the only thing needed was an end to this national discrimination. Ivanov said nothing.

Deportations had begun even before the adoption of Resolution No. 700. In June 1978, Musa Mamut, a forty-six-year-old Crimean Tatar who had been refused a residence permit for the Crimean village where he'd settled with his wife and three children, poured gasoline on himself when police showed up to take him in for questioning. They broke down the door, only to be confronted by a human torch. En route to the hospital, where he later died, Mamut, in agonizing pain, had cried out: *"Someone* had to do it!"

In January 1979, just after Lusia's departure, I had several visits from Crimean Tatars, who informed me of new discriminatory actions being carried out on the basis of Resolution No. 700. I drafted an appeal to Brezhnev, but before

I could send it off, another crisis required attention. I wound up submitting two appeals together.

On January 28, 1979, Julia Zaks, Andrei Tverdokhlebov's sister, told me that Stepan Zatikian and two other Armenians, Akop Stepanian and Zaven Bagdasarian, had been sentenced to death for the 1977 subway explosion. No one knew anything about the trial, not even its date or location. On January 26, the defendants' relatives had been rushed to Moscow, where they were informed of the death sentences and told that they would be allowed a final meeting with the condemned prisoners. Julia told me that witnesses and documentary evidence had established that Zatikian had been in Erevan at the time of the Moscow explosion. She and I thought this apparent alibi justified further investigation.

The next morning, I phoned the foreign press agencies, which were used to hearing from me at least once a week, and told them what I'd learned. Kevin Ruane, the BBC correspondent, came to tell me that a source had called him a few days earlier to say that a major trial had begun on January 15, somewhere near Moscow. (Ruane suspected that his informant had KGB connections; correspondents often find such individuals helpful.) As many as a hundred Armenian and Jewish "terrorists" were said to be implicated in the subway bombing. Much of the report seemed confused or erroneous, but the date given for the trial appeared plausible.

On Tuesday evening I wrote an appeal to Brezhnev, asking him to stay the death sentences and order a new investigation. I objected to the secrecy surrounding the proceedings, arguing that "such a trial, in which the principle of openness is totally disregarded, cannot determine the truth." I was about to go to bed when Ruane called. A report had come over the teletype that three Armenians sentenced to death for the Moscow subway explosion had been executed.

Severely shaken, I practically shouted into the telephone: "That's murder! I'll fast·for a day in mourning."

"But, Andrei, they're terrorists," Ruane protested.

"Their guilt hasn't been proved," I answered. "How can you call them terrorists?"

The next morning, I brought my two appeals to the letter window of the Presidium of the Supreme Soviet. On my way there, I stopped to read a newspaper on display with an article entitled "In the USSR Supreme Court." The style was unusual; the site of the trial and the names of the presiding judge and defense counsel were not indicated; it was stated only that the "recidivist S. S. Zatikian" and two unnamed accomplices had been executed for the Moscow subway bombing, following a review of their death sentences by the USSR Supreme Court. This elliptical report did nothing to allay my anxiety.

I alerted foreign correspondents and press agencies about my letter to Brezhnev, and within a few hours our phone started to ring with calls from persons who began by saying they'd attended the trial of the terrorists and then proceeded to express indignation at my defense of murderers. Some callers professed regret at my ignorance and naïveté; others ridiculed me; others threatened me angrily. I attempted to elicit some information about the trial, with little success, although a few of my questions did evoke a response.

"Why weren't the defendants' families present at the trial?"

"For fear of reprisals by the victims' relatives."

"How could Zatikian be guilty when, we know he wasn't in Moscow?"

"He set it up." (Neither Julia nor I had considered the possibility of conspiracy.)

The press carried no further information on the trial, but on February 8 *Izvestia* printed a letter from one D. Tyuzhin, whose brother had been killed by the bomb (Tyuzhin himself had suffered a concussion). Headed "Shame on Those Who Defend Murderers," the letter, which was aimed directly at me, provided a good deal of incidental information. Tyuzhin said he'd been at the trial, along with several hundred representatives of the Soviet public. Zatikian's accomplices (again unnamed) had testified that they had placed an explosive device in a subway car on instructions from Zatikian, whose fingerprints had been found on a second, similar device that had been earmarked for Kursk Station in Moscow. A search at Zatikian's place had turned up a wiring diagram for the device. Malva Landa told me that what had been found was probably a plan for "a doorbell or something," but I thought her explanation was dubious: the wiring of an explosive device really doesn't bear much resemblance to that of a doorbell. Still, the idea that Zatikian would have held on to such a compromising document for a year when he could easily have memorized it was rather surprising. Tyuzhin's letter concluded by saying that Zatikian had behaved disgracefully during the trial, indulging in anti-Semitic outbursts and praising Hitler. "If Sakharov had only heard him!" wrote Tyuzhin.

A few days later, a couple of unexpected visitors showed up at our apartment. They looked as though they'd been crying. "Is something wrong?" I asked.

"Yes, there is: relatives of ours died in the subway explosion. We want you to tell us why you're defending murderers."

The bigger of the two men was flabby and pale, with a pockmarked face and shifty gaze. He kept on dabbing his eyes with a handkerchief he took from his pocket. The other, squat and swarthy, had a malevolent black stare, but he was less menacing than the first one (who apparently was senior in rank). They were obviously KGB agents. I tried to tell them that guilt could be established only in an open hearing. And why hadn't the defendants' families been notified of the trial? I got back what appeared to be the KGB's stock answer: "We would have torn them to pieces—they raised those murderers!"

I kept my voice measured, but they got more and more worked up, and the short man crowded in at me, shouting and waving his fist. I stood my ground and went on trying to reason with them. Liza and Malva heard the commotion and came running.

"This is none of your business, Landa, you'll just be turning out more of your slander!" said one. There was no doubt of his links to the KGB.

Their voices rose and their gestures were menacing; the situation grew increasingly tense. As Liza edged between me and the visitors in order to shield me one of them gave her a sharp and (she later admitted) painful jab in the stomach (I only learned this after the fact). She didn't flinch. The shouting continued as the men retreated toward the door and, finally, left—although not without promising to come back with reinforcements and get even with me once and for all.

I was deluged with letters; there were thirty or forty filled with insults and reproaches, even death threats. One writer vowed to cut off my head and impale it in front of the American Embassy. Many of my correspondents said that they'd done time—and were ready to do more, for the pleasure of disposing of the likes of me.

The KGB, it seems, was genuinely rattled by the subway case. Others also received threatening letters, and propagandists conducting political education lectures at various sites in Moscow in February stated that the bomb had been planted by Armenians motivated by a fierce hatred of the Russian people.

Earlier, soon after the verdict was announced, a pair of young Armenian workers from the Erevan electrical engineering plant where Zatikian had been employed came to see me. They were hoping that prominent Armenians in Moscow would sign a petition to commute or delay the executions. I phoned an Armenian academician on their behalf, but he categorically refused to sign their petition or to meet with them. Two days later, they returned to report that they'd managed to meet with one of the defense lawyers, who had told them: "We had no choice but to surrender; the evidence was overwhelming."

Some dissidents believe the Moscow subway case was a KGB fabrication, or perhaps a provocation originally aimed at dissidents that became an attack on Armenian nationalists. Others believe that Zatikian and his comrades were proved guilty beyond a reasonable doubt; they're not at all surprised that nationalists in the USSR should have turned to terrorism along the lines of the Basque movement or the Irish Republican Army.

I perceive flaws in both scenarios. I stand behind the basic idea expressed in my letter to Brezhnev about this dark and tangled case so strangely interwoven with my own fate; namely, that cases of this sort, especially when there is a question of KGB involvement, can be examined objectively only in a genuinely open court.

In FEBRUARY 1979 I learned that Mustafa Dzhemilev had been rearrested and charged with "violating administrative surveillance." On February 28, Mustafa's brother Asan told me the trial was to begin the following day. It takes about five hours to fly from Moscow to Tashkent; I arrived about one A.M. and made my way to the large apartment building where Asan and his wife lived. The next morning, at the courthouse, we were told that the trial had been postponed.

The trip gave me the chance to meet a number of Crimean Tatar activists living in Tashkent, many of whom had done time in labor camps. They shared a common commitment to returning to the Crimea, and to the use of legal, nonviolent means to achieve that goal. Some were wary that contacts with such people as Alexander Lavut and myself would complicate the simple, straightforward grievances of the Crimean Tatars with a host of unrelated problems. The majority, however, saw the Crimean Tatar cause as an organic part of the broader human rights movement and favored cooperation.

I was back in Moscow when Dzhemilev's trial began without notice on March 6. He was sentenced to four years internal exile.

I FLEW BACK to Tashkent on March 14 to attend the trial of Vladimir Shelkov, the eighty-three-year-old leader of the Church of True and Free Seventh-Day Adventists, and four of his fellow Adventists.

The Adventists had been persecuted under the Tsars, although not so brutally as under the Soviets. They are uncompromising in their independence of temporal rule (for example, although they are willing to serve in the army, they refuse to take the oath or to bear arms), and they pay a stiff price: Shelkov had already spent twenty-five years in confinement, and had been sentenced to death in 1946 for his religious activity (the sentence was later commuted to ten years imprisonment).

Many Adventists live an underground existence, using false names and registering fictitious marriages, in order to remain true to their faith. When the authorities penetrate these disguises, arrests and imprisonments follow. It is a life that breeds strength of character, something we've noticed in all our Adventist acquaintances. Lusia and I had met and liked Rostislav Galetsky, an Adventist who'd visited us in Moscow; now, in Tashkent, I was able to get to know more of these people.

Pondering the fate of the people—or an intelligentsia—in our country, Grigory Pomerants has written:

Perhaps we have to separate in our minds a people's enduring spirit from its physical existence. . . . Which is real? I'm not sure; I only know that I sense a quickening, feel that spirit breaking through to the surface. in petitions to open churches, and among sectarian communities.

I, too, have sensed the existence of this spirit a few times in my life—as I did in Tashkent, where I had the good fortune to come into contact with a still surviving folk community.

My plane arrived in Tashkent before sunrise. I wandered for a few hours along the banks of the Kara-Kum Canal, gazing into its dull green waters: they seemed mysteriously alive, their appearance shifting with every moment as the sun came over the horizon and climbed overhead. I regretted, as I had in the past, that I'm so rarely up and about during this best part of the day.

Finally the workday began, and I managed with some difficulty to find the modest, single-story Tashkent regional courthouse where Vladimir Shelkov and his associates were going on trial. Only two or three persons with documentation of close relationship to the accused were allowed to enter the courtroom. A couple of dozen Adventists remained standing around the porch or sitting on the grass outside the building, and I spent the day with them, talking and listening, sharing the bread and apples they'd brought for lunch. I no longer recall the details of our conversation, but I remember their powerful sense of righteousness, their veneration of "Grandfather" Shelkov, and a kind of spiritual force—all combined with a peasant practicality and common sense.

One elderly woman said to me: "We take our faith seriously. We try to live our whole lives by it: isn't that the whole point of believing?"

They spoke with directness and a surprising lack of bitterness about their persecution, as if discussing a natural phenomenon.

At one point, I wandered away from the courthouse. A man with an Oriental cast of features accosted me in great agitation: "I lost relatives in the Moscow subway, as did a number of us here. We're not about to let a defender of murderers walk the streets of Tashkent."

I opened my mouth to say something about the absence of an open trial, but it was impossible to stem the torrent; he went on shouting in a guttural voice, rolling his eyes wildly (the latter talent must have been decisive in landing him his role). He concluded, in a sinister whisper:

"If you don't leave for Moscow today, I won't be responsible for my actions. I've done time, and I'm willing to do more!"

I was already planning to return to Moscow that day, since I didn't want to miss the weekly FIAN seminar, but I didn't mention that to the KGB goon. One of the Adventists happened to walk over just then; overhearing a snatch of the conversation, he became alarmed. Several Adventists offered to escort me to the airport, but, having heard tales of the treatment regularly meted out to them by the Tashkent KGB, I turned down their offer.

There were no tickets available for the Moscow flight. I searched out a supervisor and showed him my Hero of Socialist Labor card, and he said he'd do what he could. A few minutes later, a message came over the loudspeaker: "Comrade Sakharov, to the ticket counter, please."

A man standing by the counter asked: "Are you Sakharov?"

"Yes."

"Come out on the terrace with me. I have something to tell you."

His face looked familiar, but I couldn't place him right away—was he a former colleague, perhaps? I made the mistake of accompanying him, and immediately regretted it. A second KGB agent was waiting; cutting off my retreat, they began hectoring me for sinking so low as to defend murderers. I offered some rather ineffectual protests, and finally broke away and began to climb the stairs—slowly, as usual, because of my heart condition. The KGB men walked beside me, continuing their harangue. I stopped abruptly. One of the agents asked sarcastically, "Are you trying to give us the slip?"

"On an assignment like this, you should at least remove your Dzerzhinsky badges," I replied.

The two looked at each other: both were wearing the KGB insignia on their lapels. They quickly disappeared up the stairs.

It was remarkable how sensitive the KGB was about my statements on the subway case, considering the lack of response in the West, where I heard only of a one-man demonstration by Jean-Paul Sartre outside the Soviet embassy in Paris.

Shelkov, Lepshin, and Spalin received five-year terms in labor camp, while the other two defendants received shorter sentences.

For Vladimir Shelkov, it proved to be a death sentence; he died in a Siberian labor camp on January 27, 1980. Two Adventists, a mother and her eight-year-old daughter, slipped by the police blockade of our apartment in Gorky to bring me the news of the death. (The policemen on duty hadn't yet learned all the tenants by sight.) The woman was extremely upset, but what could I do? I kissed them and sent them away before the police could show up. I never saw them again.

On April 15, our friend Ari Mizyakin drove me (in our car) to the airport to meet Lusia. I left him with the car while I waited for her to clear customs, but he left his post for a moment to help us with the baggage, and the KGB seized its opportunity. One of the tires was punctured—apparently, displeased by our recent behavior, they wanted to spoil our reunion. A couple of French correspondents helped us change the tire, only to have one of their own tires promptly punctured; the next day, they found all their tires punctured.

Lusia cleared customs quickly, but her delight was short-lived: the customs officials (also employees of the KGB) had stolen quite a few things, worth in total about 500 rubles.

THE APPROACHING 1980 Olympic Games in Moscow had become the topic of heated discussion. Many of our friends abroad were campaigning for a boycott of the Olympics to protest human rights violations in the USSR. Some dissidents agreed with this approach, feeling that even if the boycott failed, the discussion would draw worldwide attention to human rights issues.

I disagreed. It was a mistake, I thought, to call for an Olympic boycott simply as a tactical ploy without any real expectation of success. I didn't want to see the preparatory work disrupted, or millions of innocent people, including the athletes, deprived of the pleasure the games would afford. For me the Olympics were part of the process of détente: the arrival of hundreds of thousands of visitors from the West, even with nothing but sports on their minds, could make a dent in the wall dividing our two worlds. I thought it wiser not to spoil the Olympics, but rather to use the opportunity the Games offered to inform the world about human rights violations and about our situation, and to recruit Western support.

There was a proposal to have Western teams and individual athletes "adopt" victims of Soviet repression—celebrated names such as Orlov and Shcharansky and lesser-known ones, as well. Another idea was to distribute T-shirts with portraits of Soviet prisoners of conscience among Western tourists and athletes. The majority of dissidents in the USSR seemed to favor this type of approach. In June 1978, the Moscow Helsinki Group had addressed an appeal to the International Olympic Committee and its president, Lord Killanin, drawing attention to human rights violations in the USSR, but with no mention of a boycott. I added my name to that appeal as a sign of support. But even within the Helsinki Group, opinions were divided (Naum Meiman, for one, still believes our approach was wrong). Most of the Group's foreign supporters disagreed with our position, and I suspect some had been carried away by the high-powered campaign. Such divisions, agonizing from the beginning, did serious harm later, when the Soviet invasion of Afghanistan made an Olympic boycott a real issue—it was the story of the boy who cried "Wolf" once too often.

EARLY IN 1979, a total stranger turned up; he looked me over carefully before identifying himself as Zbigniew Romaszewski, a member of the Polish Workers Defense Committee (KOR). Romaszewski, a tall, well-built man with angular features and an expressive face, wore an elegantly tailored suit. His Russian was halting but correct, and easy to understand. He displayed real interest in our dissident movement, and knew a great deal more about it than most foreigners (to tell the truth, I found it hard to think of him as a "foreigner"). He gave us a brief and lucid account of the situation in Poland, the country's mood, and KOR's goals. The majority of Polish workers were standing fast, he said; one heard such remarks as: "Now that you intellectuals are with us, we'll show them! We'll straighten things out!"

KOR's members were constantly having to restrain workers from rushing things, going too far. "We're investigating the December 1970 strikes," Romaszewski told us, "and we offer financial and legal assistance to workers who have suffered at the hands of the authorities." But the KOR inquiries were encountering fierce opposition, and there were tales of police brutality and intimidation of witnesses; in one case, the murder of a witness to the fatal beating of a worker. Romaszewski told us that Polish workers respected and took pride in their intellectuals. He recognized that the situation in the Soviet Union was otherwise, and that this made for differences in the goals and prospects of our human rights movements. But, we agreed, they shared a common foundation.

Romaszewski suggested that I write an article for the Paris-based Polish-language journal *Kultura*. I promised to consider the idea, but I never got around to doing anything. Writing doesn't come easily to me, and I didn't want to rehash stale material.

Tatyana Velikanova (who was with me on this occasion) and I were extremely impressed by Romaszewski, who struck us as an informed, reasonable, and thoroughly responsible member of the intelligentsia. I learned much about the roots of Solidarity from our conversations, and I offer sympathy and respect to Romaszewski and his wife, an announcer for the underground Solidarity radio station. I trust that they will bear with fortitude whatever lies in store for them.[1]

VERA LIVCHAK, the doctor who had monitored my health during my 1974 hunger strike and shared our anguish during Matvei's terrible illness, became a good friend of our entire family.

A difficult life has not prevented Vera from remaining a warm-hearted and generous person. After her husband was arrested during the Stalin era, she

---

[1][Romaszewski spent two years in jail after the suppression of Solidarity and the imposition of martial law in Poland. After his release, in September 1984, he wrote a letter to *Kultura* and *Kontinent* protesting the Sakharovs' exile. He is now a leading figure in Poland's new government.]

worked as a camp physician for many years in order to be near him. He died in 1962, and in 1971, Vera's only daughter, who had married a Jew, emigrated to Israel with her husband and their child. Vera, a Russian, did not want to leave the USSR permanently, but she applied in 1972 for permission to visit her daughter and grandchild. Her subsequent experiences offer graphic evidence of how inhumane our system is in matters of foreign travel or emigration. The authorities permit some people to emigrate, but then make it difficult for their relatives to visit them or for the emigrants to visit their former homeland (let alone return for good, in the event that they change their minds).

Vera's attempts to obtain a travel visa came to naught. Before we met her, she'd already received one refusal on the pretext that the USSR didn't have diplomatic relations with Israel. But Vera wanted to go there as a private individual, not as an ambassador. (Let me note here that relatives of people who have left for Israel but later settled elsewhere are refused visas on the grounds that they *should* be in Israel.)

Vera made the rounds of various officials, each appointment costing months of effort, waiting, and aggravation. But no one would lift a finger. The head of OVIR advised: "You'll be refused many times, but don't give up. Keep on fighting and applying again and again."

Deputy Minister of Internal Affairs Boris Shumilin, the highest official with day-to-day responsibility for OVIR, told her: "Try to get a couple of weeks in Austria; it'll be easy for your daughter to meet you there."

Vera took Shumilin seriously and applied; after a year's wait, the request was rejected on the grounds that she had no relatives in Austria! Shumilin, needless to say, had known from the start that this would be the outcome. He then advised Vera to ask that her daughter be allowed to visit the Soviet Union, but this, too, came to nothing.

I tried to help Vera by securing an invitation for her from someone the authorities simply wouldn't be able to refuse—the Queen of England. But I was informed that the British constitution bars the Queen from political actions. That may be true; but helping a seventy-three-year-old woman to see her daughter and granddaughter can hardly be termed "political." I phoned various Soviet officials, the Central Committee, and Shumilin, but to no avail.

In April 1978, after another refusal, Vera suffered a heart attack. Only then did she reluctantly apply to emigrate to Israel.

Among the reasons for her reluctance was Vera's feeling that she could still be of use here. Whenever someone was ill or we needed a baby-sitter, we'd call Vera, and she'd be right over. She and Masha Podyapolsky were in the habit of dropping by on Tuesday evenings. We couldn't imagine the family without them, and we missed Vera very much after she left in August 1978.

THE YEAR 1979 was marked by a new wave of arrests in Moscow, the Ukraine, and the Baltic states.

In the fall, the repressions began to strike people close to us. On November 1, Tatyana Velikanova and the Orthodox priest Gleb Yakunin, a member of the Christian Committee for the Defense of Believers' Rights, were arrested in Moscow. On December 7, Viktor Nekipelov was arrested in Vladimir.

I have known Tanya Velikanova since 1970, and I love and respect her deeply. We first met at Valery Chalidze's apartment during the campaign to win Zhores Medvedev's release from psychiatric detention, and met again at the trial of Pimenov and Vail. Velikanova embodies the moral inspiration of the human rights movement, its purity and force, and its historical significance. A successful mathematician, she has never suffered from feelings of professional or personal inadequacy. She is strong, determined, serious; her human rights activities reflect her profound conviction that the movement is a moral imperative. For more than a decade, from 1968 until her arrest in 1979, Velikanova was at the very center of the movement, under pressure few men or women could withstand for such a length of time. In 1969, she had been a founding member of the Initiative Group for the Defense of Human Rights, and in 1974 she had joined Sergei Kovalev and Tatyana Khodorovich in taking responsibility for reviving the *Chronicle of Current Events*. Later that year, she had helped organize the first Day of the Political Prisoner. Velikanova's arrest and trial were a blow to all who knew her personally, and to all who valued human rights and an open society. Once again, the authorities had displayed their determination to quash the actions of nonviolent dissenters armed only with the word of truth.

Viktor Nekipelov's arrest dealt an equally cruel blow. A gifted poet and a member of the Moscow Helsinki Group, Nekipelov had been arrested in 1973 and sentenced to two years in a labor camp for circulating samizdat materials, including his own poetry. He sought permission to emigrate in 1977, but was turned down: a different fate was being prepared for him.

Nekipelov, who was arrested at the pharmacy where he was employed, is a trained pharmacologist and a family man, simple facts that fail to convey the full tragedy of an honest, talented, emotionally vulnerable, but courageous and compassionate man. It was Nekipelov who publicized the cases of the Belorussian workers Mikhail Kukobaka and Evgeny Buzinnikov; he was active in the Initiative Group to Defend the Rights of the Disabled, and the author of a brilliant work, *Institute of Fools*, about his detention in the notorious Serbsky Psychiatric Institute (as well as an important article exploring psychological and social attitudes toward Stalin.)[2]

[2][*Institute of Fools* (Farrar Straus & Giroux, 1980); "Here a Stalin, There a Stalin, Everywhere a Stalin, Stalin," *New York Times*, Aug. 14, 1979.]

Nekipelov was born in 1928 in Harbin, Manchuria, and moved to the USSR with his parents when he was nine. His parents had been among the hundreds of thousands of people left stranded outside the country by the Civil War. Most of those who returned to Russia suffered tragic fates, which often affected the next generation as well.

45

LETTERS AND VISITORS

OVER THE YEARS I have received a great many letters, some expressing support, others critical or even threatening. The KGB probably intercepted the majority of the sympathetic notes, letting only a small fraction get through. Hostile letters would appear sporadically; after receiving none for a while, I'd find bundles arriving, usually after I'd made some public statement.

The threats were probably the work of the KGB, while criticisms of specific actions of mine may have been culled from spontaneous letters written by aggrieved citizens, and only in exceptional cases manufactured by the KGB.

Here, however, I wish to discuss the letters that asked for my help. These began arriving right after the founding of the Human Rights Committee in November 1970, the same period when strangers began appearing on my doorstep. In the nine years that followed until my exile to Gorky, I received hundreds of letters and visitors, each representing a serious problem that Soviet agencies could not or would not resolve. People would turn to me in desperation; right from the start, however, it was clear to me that I wouldn't be able to help most of them. It's difficult to convey the pain their misdirected expectations caused me; and, unfortunately, uncertain how to respond, disorganized and preoccupied with other urgent matters, I all too often chose the easy way out: I'd put off answering from one day to the next, from one week to another, until the letter was lost or there was no longer any point in replying. Still, my conscience was uneasy.

There would have been an even greater number of unanswered letters had it not been for the invaluable assistance of Sofia Kalistratova—a magnificent person, down-to-earth, just, intelligent, and good—a rare combination of the finest human virtues. For more than twenty years, Sofia, as a trained lawyer, had acted as defense counsel in criminal cases. She put her whole heart into her work, and her thirst for justice, her desire to provide her clients with both tangible results and moral support, never failed to move me. For Sofia, the fate of the individual was always the most important thing.

On one occasion, she acted as defense counsel for a young soldier accused of rape. Sofia was convinced that he was innocent, but despite a lack of incriminating evidence, he was sentenced to death. Sofia took her case to a senior officer, who explained rather openly that discipline had grown slack, that many crimes were committed by soldiers, and that the sentence would bolster authority. He was taken aback by Sofia's fiery response—"So you intend to use that boy's death to teach your subordinates a lesson?!"—and the way she kept on venting her indignation at the top of her lungs; the officer agreed to a review of the sentence.

After an appellate hearing that resulted in reductions of two clients' sentences from fifteen years to ten, Sofia was asked as she collected her papers prior to leaving: "Well, Comrade Lawyer, are you satisfied with the result?"

"Satisfied? With defendants going to prison although there's no evidence they're guilty?"

Rather perplexed by this logic, one juror said: "But if there had been any evidence of guilt, we wouldn't have reduced the sentence, would we?"[1]

Sofia's experiences as a lawyer convinced her that the death penalty was a monstrous and inhumane institution, harmful to society, and that it ought to be abolished. In time, her passion for justice was channeled into the defense of prisoners of conscience, a decision that changed her life. It led her to speak out on public issues and join the Helsinki Group, and eventually subjected her to interrogations, KGB searches, and all sorts of harassment. Appealing on behalf of Kalistratova from Gorky in February 1982, I wrote that "in the Soviet Union, being searched three times is no laughing matter," and called upon members of the legal profession to "speak out in defense of a remarkable woman who has done and is doing so much for others."

The transcripts of Pyotr Grigorenko's and Natalya Gorbanevskaya's trials reveal the intelligence and courage Sofia displayed in court. But also important were the warm interest she displayed when she met with imprisoned clients and the contact she provided with the outside world.

When Sofia agreed to help with my correspondence, I brought her letters by the sackful. She would draft replies, explaining legal points and offering wise counsel. I would discuss the letters with her and then sign them, and she'd mail them. Sofia couldn't perform miracles, of course, and only in rare instances

---

[1][In the Soviet legal system, most cases are decided by a judge together with two lay assistants or jurors.]

were we able to render practical assistance. But at least the letters were answered.

Sofia kept the letters and copies of our replies. The archive was confiscated by the KGB during a search of her home, so I'll have to rely on my memory in describing individual cases.

More than half my visitors were people seeking to leave the Soviet Union. There were two young Romanian sisters, born in what is now the Moldavian Soviet Socialist Republic, who during the war had been taken by their mother to Romania proper, where they grew up and eventually found work as hairdressers. After their mother's death, relatives invited them to come to the Moldavian SSR, and they arrived with all their possessions. For a while things went well, but then their relatives began to change their tune, and the sisters realized that wages and working conditions didn't meet their expectations. They decided to return to Romania. They were refused an exit visa, and so began the ordeal that had brought them to us. They were unemployed; the relatives had kicked them out, keeping most of their belongings, including warm clothing (indeed, they were dressed much too lightly for the time of year).

Leaving the USSR for a socialist country often is more difficult than emigrating to the West or Israel: no one's there to argue your case at the other end. Lusia managed (it wasn't easy) to obtain an Israeli invitation for the sisters, and six months later they left the country, happy and grateful, intending to return to Romania.

And there was Serafim Evsyukov, who had found work as an engineer at Domodedevo Airport after retiring as a civilian aircraft navigator. In 1978 he decided to emigrate with his family. They struck me as honest, intelligent, courageous people who had made their decision fully aware of the consequences they might—and did—suffer. Time and again, Evsyukov was refused a visa. His son, drafted in 1980, refused induction for fear that army service and exposure to military secrets would reduce his chances for emigration; he was sentenced to two and a half years in labor camp.

In the spring of 1986, the father was summoned for a "chat" with the KGB, who told him: "Drop your emigration bid, and your troubles will be over. If you go on with it, you've only yourself to blame for the consequences." The KGB called his wife in for a similar "chat," but Evsyukov refused to take the advice. A month or so later, his son, who had finished serving out his term, was summoned to the recruiting office, where he again refused induction. He was rearrested, beaten up, and delivered to prison in handcuffs. The court sentenced him to three additional years of imprisonment, to be served in one of the worst camps for hardened criminals. The walls in the punishment cells, were perpetually damp, and sadistic guards wearing furlined coats "ventilated" the rooms as half-naked prisoners shivered and, in some cases, died of exposure.

In the fall of 1986, Serafim Evsyukov was put into a psychiatric hospital. The family's fate took a turn for the better in 1987. Evsyukov was discharged from the hospital, and in July his son was freed. Lusia played a key role in publicizing the fate of this family; for years, she used every opportunity and every contact to bring their story to the fore, first with foreign correspondents in the USSR, and later, when she was abroad, with high-ranking politicians and media representatives. In 1987, I joined her in these efforts, and in August of that year the Evsyukovs were permitted to leave the Soviet Union.

THE SECOND-LARGEST group among our visitors were those with grievances related to their jobs—conflicts with management, illegal dismissal, etc. Often, they'd gone all the way to the top in search of justice, with no success. At the USSR Procurator's Office, at the Supreme Soviet, and other government agencies, particularly dogged petitioners are directed to a special room and handed over to orderlies from psychiatric hospitals. In all honesty, however, I must say that some of those who brought their grievances to me were in fact mentally ill.

The stories of the elderly and disabled people who formed the third-largest group revealed to me the hardship, often outright poverty, endured by those who depend on the social welfare system. Pensions in the USSR are for the most part extremely low, the exceptions being retired military personnel and a few other highly paid specialists. The elderly find housing problems particularly daunting. But there was nothing I could do in these cases.

Relatives of persons who had been charged with or convicted of crimes also came to us. (The vast majority of the letters I received were sent by prisoners or their families.) It was terrible to read in their letters or to hear directly from visitors tales of judicial errors caused by debased legal standards, of bias in trials and investigations, especially toward ex-convicts, of beatings and torture during interrogations, of arbitrary brutality in places of detention, of the judiciary's subservience to local party officials and the bureaucracy, and of the futility of appeals to the Procurator's Office or appellate courts, which barricaded themselves behind an endless series of form letters.

Some of my correspondents may have been guilty as charged, but these, I believe, represented only a small minority. The majority of the letters were too grim in content and too naïve in style to have been invented.

I remember some of the cases quite well. Through unofficial channels I received two or three letters from a prisoner in one of the labor camps in the Komi region, notorious for its severe climate; he wrote that he'd been sentenced to several years for an economic crime. After he refused an offer to become a camp informer, he was taken to the guard room, handcuffed, and severely beaten. He was then falsely accused of attempting to attack a guard and sentenced to a new, nine-year term, which he had little hope of surviving.

Another prisoner in a Komi camp wrote that from fear of torture he had confessed to a crime he hadn't committed (this occurred while he was being detained in the prison at Ochamchira, not far from Sukhumi on the Black Sea). He knew that other prisoners had been beaten on the orders of officials investigating their cases. (Gamsakhurdia, before his arrest, had sent me information on numerous cases of torture in Georgian prisons.)

One day, answering my doorbell, I caught a glimpse of a woman hurrying down the stairs. In my mailbox, I found a long letter relating the story of Rafkat Shaimukhamedov, a young Tatar worker convicted in 1974 of murdering a salesgirl while robbing a grocery store along with two accomplices. Shaimukhamedov had been sentenced to death, the others to short terms in labor camp.

In their appeals, defense counsel produced telling evidence of Shaimukhamedov's innocence: eyewitness confirmation of his alibi and expert testimony that the bloodstain found on his jacket did not match the victim's blood type. It was Shaimukhamedov's mother who had written the letter to me; she stated that after her son's arrest, the local procurator had demanded a large bribe, which she'd refused to pay. She and her husband had gone to Moscow to lodge a complaint, but the USSR Procurator's Office refused to intervene, and threatened to have them both sent to a psychiatric hospital. Shaimukhamedov spent more than a year on death row. He went on a hunger strike, demanding a review of his case. The procurator promised to commute the death sentence if he would end his fast, but Rafkat refused. A postscript to the letter stated that Rafkat Shaimukhamedov had been executed in January 1976 with the sanction of Deputy Procurator General Malyarov.

Rafkat's brother was then arrested on a trumped-up charge of assault. Bekbaev, the procurator, called in the mother, informed her of Rafkat's execution, and added: "I'd like to buy your son's home. Sell it to me [it went without saying, at less than its true value]. Remember, I had one of your sons shot, and I can do the same with the other."

A prisoner in a Siberian labor camp wrote that, though innocent, he had been convicted by a judge who was prejudiced against him because he had a criminal record. Many letters told similar tales; unqualified judges severely impair in the administration of justice. This prisoner went on to report that new charges against him were being cooked up in the labor camp, and he feared a long sentence.

A bookkeeper wrote that she was serving an eleven-year sentence for a crime committed by her supervisors.

A woman wrote from Kazakhstan that her son, a Russian, had been beaten to death after his arrest. Savage fights between Russians and Kazakhs during farewell parties for draftees were a tradition in her town. (The letter went on to claim that "Kazakhs hate Russians"—testimony to the state of ethnic relations in the USSR.) Both Kazakh and Russian teenagers involved in one of these melees had been arrested, and the Kazakh investigator in charge of the case had beaten her son to death while trying to obtain a confession.

The wife of a young man convicted of taking part in a drunken brawl wrote me a touchingly naïve letter. She and her husband, Kolya, had both grown up in orphanages; their love for each other was the first happiness either had experienced. Kolya had been talked into a drinking bout; he was guilty of taking part in the subsequent brawl, but he'd received heavier punishment than the others, who were actually more to blame. A disproportionate percentage of my correspondence came from former inhabitants of orphanages, indication of a serious social problem and insensitivity and a lack of understanding of their problems on the part of the courts.

Vodka was the subject of many letters. Drunkenness is our great national tragedy; it makes family life a hell, turns skilled workers into goldbricks, and is at the root of a multitude of crimes. The rise in drunkenness is a reflection of social crisis and evidence of our government's unwillingness and inability to take on the problem of alcoholism. [I wrote this in 1983; today, there is a glimmer of hope that things may change.—A.S. 1987] More recently, cheap fortified wines have become the favored means of turning people into drunkards and siphoning off surplus rubles.

46

AFGHANISTAN, GORKY

THE USSR sent its troops into Afghanistan in December 1979. A special KGB detachment shot President Hafizullah Amin and everyone who witnessed his execution. In a statement broadcast from Tashkent, Babrak Karmal announced the formation of a new government. That was the beginning for the Soviet army of a protracted war against Afghan guerrillas and, in effect, against the Afghan people.

What purpose did the invasion serve and what have been its consequences? According to Soviet propaganda, the legal government of Afghanistan invited our troops into the country in order to defend the April 1978 revolution against bandits infiltrating from Pakistan. But that explanation is untenable; Amin would hardly have asked for the Soviet troops which were sent to assassinate him. The truth is that Amin's determination to pursue an independent course had made him unacceptable to the Soviet leaders. His domestic policies had provoked serious conflict within the country, but he apparently felt he could manage without outside aid. Armed opposition to both Amin and his predecessor, Nur Mohammed Taraki, who had become president after the 1978 revolution, was for the most part local and tribal; only after the Soviet invasion did resistance become nationwide and outside assistance for it begin to come in (and then only in small amounts). For Afghans, the consequences of the Soviet intervention were tragic: it brought war and suffering.

The real motive for the invasion was Soviet expansionism. Our leaders may well have been disturbed when the bloody, KGB-assisted overthrow of President Mohammed Daoud in 1978 made Afghanistan less, not more, manageable; but I am convinced that worry about the local situation served only as a pretext for an invasion with far-reaching geopolitical goals, with Afghanistan being regarded as a strategic springboard to Soviet dominance in the surrounding region.

The seizure of the American embassy in Teheran by "revolutionary students" in November 1979, less than two months before the Soviet move into Afghanistan, fractured American-Iranian relations and paved the way for Soviet penetration, and played so smoothly into Soviet hands that one can't help but wonder whether Soviet agents were involved—as foreign press reports suggested.

The Soviet leaders must have been counting on a quick victory in Afghanistan. But this was a country that had in the past fought off both England and Tsarist Russia, and it did not capitulate. As Karmal's army was crippled by mass desertions and defections to the guerrilla forces, the war became steadily more barbaric. We listened with horror and shame to Western broadcasts reporting the bombing of villages, famine caused by the destruction of crops, and the use of napalm, mines, booby traps, and chemical weapons. Four million Afghans, a quarter of the prewar population, have fled to Pakistan and Iran, where they live in miserable conditions—the largest body of refugees in the world today. Will the Afghans ever forgive the suffering inflicted on them?

During the first months of the war, KGB agents reportedly fired on schoolgirls demonstrating in the streets of Kabul. Crimes like this leave permanent scars. Captured guerrillas are said to have been burned alive, and peasants who aided them executed. The guerrillas themselves are known to have committed atrocities, including savage reprisals against collaborators. One guerrilla spokesman admitted that since they couldn't guard or feed prisoners of war, they shot them. The Soviet forces and their Afghan allies were aware of this practice, but refused to exchange prisoners with the guerrillas; and Soviet helicopters, according to some reports, fired on surrounded Soviet soldiers to prevent their capture.

The invasion of Afghanistan had serious international consequences. It violated that country's nonaligned status, indeed threatened the very concept of nonalignment. It dismayed the Islamic world and placed yet another obstacle in the way of Sino-Soviet rapprochement. The West, the United States and Japan in particular, viewed the invasion as a dangerous display of Soviet expansionism.

Taken together with other events of that period, the invasion cast doubt on the Soviet Union's respect for international obligations and undermined confidence in its policies and its sincerity in preaching peace and security. This psychological shift led indirectly to improved relations between the West and China, the rethinking of the West's arms program and international strategy, and the U.S. Senate's refusal to ratify the SALT II Treaty. An overwhelming majority of the U.N. General Assembly voted to condemn the invasion as a violation of international law, and only a Soviet veto in the Security Council averted the imposition of sanctions.

I am convinced that the invasion was a major blunder, and we don't even know who made the decision or when it was made. Here again, as in Hungary and Czechoslovakia (to say nothing of the 1939 Hitler-Stalin pact), we see the danger posed to the world by a closed, totalitarian society. Westerners ask how Soviet citizens feel about their government's actions in Afghanistan; this question is difficult to answer in the absence of a free press and without public opinion polling on sensitive issues. On the surface, at least, there seems to be astonishing indifference to the true nature of events in Afghanistan, where our sons have become murderers and oppressors—and victims—of a terrible, cruel, dehumanizing war.

As 1980 began, Afghanistan cast a long shadow. Increased latitude was granted to the KGB because of the war, and in anticipation of the forthcoming Olympics; this was evidenced in a series of arrests and in my banishment to Gorky. The expansion of the KGB's role was ominous—one "1937" was enough!

A PHONE CALL I received around January 1 from Dietrich Mummendiel's wife, Zora, is as good place as any to begin an account of the events leading up to my exile. Mummendiel, a correspondent for *Die Welt,* wanted to know if the invasion of Afghanistan had prompted me to change my opinion about a boycott of the Moscow Olympics. I replied that the ancient rules of the Olympics called for suspension of hostilities during the games. "The USSR should withdraw its troops from Afghanistan. If it doesn't, the Olympic Committee should refuse to hold the games in a country that is waging war."

I also agreed to an interview with Anthony Austin, a correspondent for the *New York Times.* He came to our apartment, gave me an update on the news from Afghanistan, and then asked about my reaction to events there. A few hours later, he returned with a draft of his article. Lusia served tea, and I read the article through, checking my answers and his interpretations of them. Because of the importance of the subject matter, I was especially grateful to Austin for allowing me to edit my remarks. Journalists as a rule are reluctant to do this, pleading the exigencies of deadlines; the stories that then appear in print can be enough to drive me wild. Austin's article, which appeared in the January 3 *New York Times,* was broadcast a number of times over Voice of America, and apparently made a strong impression.

On January 7, Ruth received permission to travel to America to see her grandchildren and great-grandchildren; perhaps the KGB wanted to get her out of the way.

The next day, the Presidium of the Supreme Soviet passed a decree depriving me of my government awards, but I did not learn of this until January 22.

On January 14, Charles Bierbauer, an ABC television correspondent, requested an interview and provided me with a list of questions. On January 17, his crew arrived with their equipment and switched on the bright lights. Concerned that they might run into trouble with the KGB, I accompanied them to their car, which they had parked in the small lot next to our building. I was surprised by the number of KGB agents stationed in the area and by something peculiar in the air—a mixture of hostility and gloating. Two KGB cars had the television crew's car boxed in.

I said, "Well, here they are."

"Yes, here we are!" a KGB agent echoed derisively: I suppose they already knew of the decision to deport me. But the Americans were allowed to drive off to the airport without incident.

On the evening of January 21, Georgi Vladimov and his wife, Natasha, came over to discuss the Helsinki Group's statement on Afghanistan, which he and I signed. He reported some rumors circulating in Moscow about Afghanistan and the murder of President Amin and about the suicide of a high official in the Ministry of Internal Affairs. The Vladimovs left around ten o'clock.

Our phone rang at one A.M. Lusia answered. It was Vladimov, very excited: A friend of his had attended a meeting of political propagandists, and the speaker had announced that a decision had been made to deprive Sakharov of his awards and exile him from Moscow. When Lusia relayed this warning to me, I remarked: "A month ago, I wouldn't have taken it seriously, but now, with Afghanistan, anything's possible." Later, Vladimov asked Lusia why we hadn't immediately left town, but I don't think either of us believes that it all would simply have blown over.

JANUARY 22 was a Tuesday, the day the theoretical physics seminar met at FIAN. I followed my customary routine, ordering a car from the Academy's motor pool and leaving home at one-thirty. I intended to stop first at the Academy commissary to pick up some groceries and send the driver back with them, but we never got past the Krasnokholmsky Bridge, where a traffic patrol car overtook us. The policeman signaled us to pull over and stopped in front of us. My driver, surprised, mumbled that he hadn't broken any law. He got out to meet the policeman, who saluted and began examining his papers. From the front seat, I had a good view of what was happening. Hearing the car's rear door open, I glanced around and saw two men get in, flashing red IDs marked "MVD" (of course, they were actually KGB).

They ordered the driver to follow the traffic patrol car to the Procurator's Office on Pushkin Street. He obeyed without a word. We were traveling slowly, and I could see that there were no other cars on the bridge, which apparently had been closed to traffic. We turned into a side street, and as we passed a phone booth, I asked the driver to stop for a moment so that I could call Lusia. The KGB agents reacted instantaneously: one blocked the door handle; the other ordered the driver: "Don't stop, keep moving." Then he turned to me and added: "You can phone from the Procurator's Office."

The car pulled into the Procurator's courtyard. I asked the driver to return the shopping bag to my house, adding that we would be too late to stop at the commissary. I got out of the car and, ringed by KGB agents, was escorted to the fourth floor, where my "chats" with Malyarov in 1973 and Gusev in 1977 had taken place. This time I was told to enter a door marked: "Alexander Rekunkov, Deputy Procurator General."

Rekunkov was seated behind a desk, facing the door. I don't remember what he looked like. Several other persons were seated at a table to my left, but they remained silent. Rekunkov invited me to be seated.

"Why didn't you send a summons instead of shanghaiing me?" I asked. "I've always obeyed the Procurator's summonses."

Rekunkov replied: "I gave orders to have you brought here owing to the extraordinary circumstances and the great urgency involved. I have been instructed to read you a decree passed by the Presidium:

> In view of A. D. Sakharov's systematic actions which discredit him as a recipient of State awards and in response to many suggestions made by the Soviet public, the Presidium of the USSR Supreme Soviet, acting on the basis of Article 40 of the General Regulations on Orders, Medals and Honorary Titles, has decided to deprive Andrei Dmitrievich Sakharov of the title Hero of Socialist Labor and all his State awards.[1]

"It has been decided to banish A. D. Sakharov from Moscow to a place that will put an end to his contacts with foreigners," Rekunkov continued. He looked up and added: "The place that has been selected is Gorky, which is off limits to foreigners. Please sign here to acknowledge that you have been informed of the decree's contents."

He handed me a typewritten sheet of paper on which I saw the last part of the decree and the typed signatures of Brezhnev and Mikhail Georgadze, the Presidium's secretary. It was undated and made no mention of banishment.

As I was studying the paper, Rekunkov said: "The regulations require that

---

[1]The decree (no. 100) on "The Revocation of A. D. Sakharov's State Awards" was dated January 8, 1980, and was published in the *Vedomosti* (Gazette) of the USSR Supreme Soviet, no. 5, January 30, 1980. To the best of my recollection, Rekunkov read me the decree word for word as it was published.

persons deprived of state awards return them to the Presidium." The same instructions were written on the sheet of paper he'd given me. My many questions were deflected for the moment as I wrote that I refused to return my awards since they had been granted in recognition of services rendered.

I asked why the decree was undated and why Brezhnev and Georgadze had not personally signed it. Rekunkov said something about "technicalities," adding: "A representative of the Presidium is present, and can confirm that everything is correct." One of the people sitting at the table rose and bowed in my direction without identifying himself further.

I had inquired whether Gorky really was closed to foreigners, and Rekunkov had answered in the affirmative. But I failed to ask some more important questions: Who had made the decision to banish me? On what authority? I refrained because I considered the entire proceeding completely illegal, and thought it pointless to argue fine points of jurisprudence with those who obviously had no respect for the law. What difference did it make whether the Presidium had acted at the KGB's prompting, or the KGB with the Presidium's acquiescence? By maintaining this attitude all through my first weeks in Gorky, I may have created the inadvertent impression that I accepted their right to proceed in this totally unlawful manner. Even more damaging, my passive attitude may have led me to surrender points which I might have disputed.

Rekunkov raised no objection to my postscript concerning my awards. "Let's get to the practical details. You're to leave for Gorky at once. Your wife may accompany you."

"Can I go home first?"

"No, but you may call your wife."

"Where will we meet?"

"I can't tell you that. She'll be picked up. How much time will she need to pack?"

"I don't know; probably a couple of hours."

"All right. She'll be picked up two hours after you call her."

At this point, I should have questioned Rekunkov about the rules and regulations I'd be subject to in Gorky and whether Lusia would be restricted in any way. But, fearing that I might make matters worse by rushing things, I didn't push for details. The situation would become clear in due time.

In Rekunkov's outer office, where a dozen KGB agents were waiting around, his secretary pointed out the proper telephone to use for a Moscow call. Lusia sounded her usual self; the driver had not been allowed to return to our apartment and warn her of my detention.

"I'm calling from the Procurator's Office. They picked me up on the street."

"Whaaat?"

"Police stopped our car, KGB agents got in and ordered us to drive here. The Deputy Procurator General has told me that I've been stripped of my awards and that I'm being banished to Gorky—it's off limits to foreigners."

"Will you be coming back to the house?"

"No, I'm supposed to leave straight from here, but it's my understanding that you can accompany me." (I tried to indicate by my tone and by stressing the word "can" that Lusia was free to decide whether or not to go, but I don't think the point got across.)

"Where will I see you?"

"They'll be coming for you in two hours."

I could hear Lusia repeating everything I said to Ruth and Liza. When she said that they'd be coming for her in two hours, it came out sounding as if she were about to be arrested. I hung up the phone and mumbled to myself: "So this is it. . . ."

I was asked to return to Rekunkov's office.

"Did you reach her?"

"Yes."

"Do you have any more questions?"

"No." (Here I missed another opportunity to ask about the legal aspects of my situation.)

I said goodbye, he responded, and I turned and walked out. Two of the KGB agents grasped me by the elbows—symbolically, it seemed, for they then released me immediately. One was carrying the grocery bag, which they'd evidently confiscated from the driver. We walked downstairs and out into the courtyard, where we climbed inside a minibus with curtained windows. I sat in the back seat, flanked by KGB agents. We were preceded by a police car with a flashing light and siren and followed by another car, as if in fear that an attempt might be made to rescue me by force. A man seated across from me introduced himself as a doctor; he kept asking if I wanted a sedative (he had a bottle of valerian) or something for a headache, or if I was feeling cold. I said no to all his questions. When we arrived at Domodedevo Airport, I was taken to an office where we waited for more than two hours, until finally one of the KGB agents said: "Let's go. Here comes your wife."

LATER ON, Lusia told me her story. As soon as she hung up, our phone went dead (service wasn't restored until December 1986). Lusia began getting ready to leave; meanwhile, Liza went out to call friends and correspondents. None of the pay phones near our house was working, but Liza ran till she found one in service, and managed to call a reporter and the Podyapolskys' daughter Natalya before that phone went dead. A few minutes later, the Podyapolskys' phone was also disconnected, but by then Natalya had managed to call Irina Kaplun, who alerted several correspondents.

By the time Liza returned, police and KGB had cordoned off our building. The two policemen posted at the apartment door allowed her to pass, but correspondents and friends who arrived just a few minutes later were stopped. A policeman or KGB agent floated the idea I had been taken to Sheremetevo International Airport; this gave rise to rumors that I was being exiled abroad and was expected in Vienna.

Two and a half hours after my call, the police rang the doorbell and asked Lusia: "Are you ready?" They declined her invitation to enter the apartment, but agreed without hesitation to her request that Ruth and Liza be allowed to accompany her. The police led the three of them out the back way and into a minibus with curtained windows similar to the one used to transport me. They too had an escort. Lusia managed to get a glimpse of the route they were taking, and realized they were headed for Domodedevo. What neither she nor the others knew was that the KGB was taking advantage of their absence to search our apartment and grab whatever they wanted: English and Russian copies of scientific articles I'd already submitted for publication, my Nobel diploma (I think this is when it disappeared), and no doubt much else.

Around six o'clock I was brought from the police holding facility to meet the minibus. I kissed Lusia, Ruth, and Liza; five minutes went by, and then an officer announced that our plane was ready. We said goodbye to Ruth and Liza and climbed aboard the TU-154, carrying the bags Lusia had brought from the apartment. Ruth and Liza were driven back to the apartment, where friends and foreign correspondents were waiting to hear the story and broadcast it to the world.

A dozen KGB agents (two of them doctors, or so we were told) accompanied us on our special flight. I later heard that Semyon Tsvigun, deputy chief of the KGB, was flown to Gorky on another plane that same evening—interesting, if true.

We were too relieved at being reunited to worry about where we were headed—we didn't care if it was to the ends of the earth. In some strange fashion, we were actually happy. Normally there's no meal service on short flights, but on this one we were served a first-class dinner—much needed by then, since we'd eaten nothing since breakfast. There was a brief hitch when the landing gear at first refused to drop, but the pilot circled over Gorky until he managed to shake it loose and we were able to land safely.

We were loaded onto another minibus. "Where are we going?" Lusia asked our anonymous escorts. "Home," answered one, grinning.

After a long journey, we were deposited in front of a twelve-story building off what we later learned was Gagarin Avenue and taken to an apartment on the first floor. I was invited into a large room where several people were waiting. (I probably should have insisted on Lusia's presence, but I wanted to get the formalities over with as quickly as possible.)

A man seated behind a desk introduced himself: "I'm Perelygin, Deputy Procurator for the Gorky district. I've been instructed to inform you of your regimen."

Once again I failed to ask who had ordered the regimen and on what authority; I assumed it was the KGB. I didn't even request that Perelygin put his comments in writing. Any interjections on my part, I felt, would be a waste of time.

Perelygin continued: "You are forbidden to go beyond the city limits of Gorky. You'll be kept under surveillance, and you are forbidden to meet with or contact foreigners or criminal elements. The MVD will let you know when you're required to check in with Comrade Glossen at their headquarters on Gornaya Street. They're empowered to have the police bring you in if you fail to answer their summons. If you have any questions, call the KGB, either Major Yuri Chuprov or Captain Nikolai Shuvalov. Take down their phone number."

I made no reply. Perelygin left, along with his associates. Lusia, meanwhile, had been talking with our self-styled "landlady" and had taken a look around the apartment, which had four rooms, plus a kitchen and a bathroom; it reminded us of a hotel suite. The "landlady" told Lusia she was the widow of a KGB officer, and that her husband's colleagues had found her this job. When I appeared, she retired to the room reserved for her use and closed the door. For the next six months she would usually spend a couple of hours at the apartment each day, just sitting there.

At last, Lusia and I were alone together. She immediately launched into a criticism of my behavior, chiding me for not insisting that she be present during my talk with Perelygin. (She had entered the room at one point but had been ordered to leave.) She'd had the foresight to pack our transistor radio, a gift from Alexei, and we tuned in to the evening news: my exile was the lead story, along with Afghanistan. For the next two weeks foreign broadcasts featured excerpts from my articles, along with protests by writers, public personalities, and—of particular weight—scientists, including Sidney Drell, Jeremy Stone, and many others. It's quite possible that the intervention of U.S. National Academy of Sciences president Philip Handler and other prominent scientists forestalled further steps against me. The defense campaign inspired by these statements eventually developed a significance that extended far beyond my personal situation.

My Soviet colleagues, regrettably, kept silent—except for public attacks on me by Academicians Evgeny Fyodorov, Nikolai Blokhin, and others of their ilk, probably acting on instructions. I think that an open statement made by a few—even three might have been sufficient—respected academicians could have turned the situation around for me, and, what is much more important, might have had a positive influence on the country as a whole. By speaking out, they wouldn't have risked arrest, exile, or even loss of their positions; at the very worst, their travel abroad might have been temporarily curtailed—a minimal risk when set against the potential benefits to our country and to science (and to their reputations). But the sad and shameful fact is that top scientists were unwilling to speak out.

In 1911, the physicist Pyotr Lebedev (FIAN is named in his honor) resigned his post after Lev Kasso, then Minister of Education, let gendarmes invade the grounds of Moscow University. Lebedev loved science and the university every bit as much as professors do today. Have our intelligentsia degenerated so greatly since his time? Or have people failed to understand our current crisis and how they can help to overcome it? If it's the latter, then there's still hope for us.

In February 1980, Lusia issued an appeal to Soviet physicists, doing so on her own for fear that discussing it with me might somehow constrain both of us. In March, Anatoly Marchenko addressed an open letter appealing to Pyotr Kapitsa to speak out in my defense.[2] Both these letters deal—from different points of view—with the same subject: the responsibility of scientists today.

Soon after we got to Gorky, we heard Tanya on a broadcast from America, appealing in my behalf. Her voice sounded so close, so warm and vibrant, that our eyes filled with tears. New worries and responsibilities bore down on the children in Boston, further complicating their efforts to begin a new life abroad. This was to me one of the most troubling consequences of my exile.

Izvestia carried a report of my banishment in its evening edition on January 22,[3] and this was followed by articles in many newspapers (including the *Gorky Worker*) condemning my behavior. On television the political commentator Yuri Zhukov denounced me. On January 30, the decree depriving me of my awards was printed in the gazette of the Supreme Soviet. I have heard that it was adopted at a sparsely attended session of the Presidium chaired by future prime minister Nikolai Tikhonov. Semyon Tsvigun delivered the KGB's report. Brezhnev was absent. The KGB may well have seen in this decree—dated January 8—a green light to work out their plan to "take care of Sakharov" by banishing me.

---

[2][For Bonner's appeal, see Appendix, p. 676; Marchenko in *On Sakharov*, pp. 31–37.]

[3][*A Chronicle of Current Events*, no. 56, 1980, contains the text of the *Izvestia* report (pp. 75–76) and excerpts from later articles on the Sakharov case.]

On January 25, three days after our arrival in Gorky, Lusia went to the station to catch a train to Moscow. She had with her a statement in which I described the circumstances of my exile and outlined my thoughts on significant current issues. After Lusia had boarded the train, a police officer came up and asked her to get off.

"Why? Can't I take a trip?"

"You're allowed to travel, but your mother, Natasha Gesse, and Liza are on the way to Gorky by car."

"Whose idea was that?" (She shouldn't have asked that, but the question just popped out.)

"Probably Natasha's" was the sarcastic reply.

Lusia returned to the apartment, irritated by this unexpected complication.

What had happened was that Ruth, Natasha, and Liza, desperate for reliable news of us, had persuaded our friend Emil Shinberg to drive them to Gorky. (We had managed to send a telegram with our address, but when we tried to phone Moscow from the post office, our calls were interrupted.) They arrived on the evening of January 25 after a full day spent on the road in midwinter. It was a heroic journey, especially for Ruth, who was in poor health and nearly eighty years old, but she was always able to find the reserves of strength needed to go to the aid of family and friends.

We greeted them by asking why they'd come—not very fair or polite, perhaps, but they'd thrown a monkey wrench into our plan for Lusia to visit Moscow.

Ruth told us what had been happening in Moscow. We knew that she and Liza had given an impromptu press conference on the evening of January 22. From then on, the apartment had been filled from morning till night with correspondents hungry for fresh information and with friends, acquaintances, and even complete strangers—"a madhouse," as Natasha put it (she herself had responded to the news by racing for the first train leaving Leningrad for Moscow).

The day before, Ruth had gone to a friend's home and called Pyotr Kapitsa. This was an implicit bid for his intervention, but, like our other "celebrities," he did nothing.[4]

---

[4]As I reported in Chapter 21 (p. 303) I have learned that Kapitsa did intervene for me on two occasions. On the other hand, as counterbalance to this positive fact I must note that the widespread impression that the Academy resisted pressure from the authorities to expel me is mistaken, according to my information: while a few particularly "zealous" academicians may have demanded that I be expelled, Alexandrov's reply—that the question of expelling me was not on the Academy's agenda—indicates that no pressure had been put on the Academy by either the science department of the Central Committee or the KGB.—A.S. 1988.

Lusia left with Liza for Moscow on Sunday, January 27. On January 28, at a press conference held in the Chkalov Street apartment, she read my statement. She also visited the Procurator's Office twice in an attempt to determine the official grounds for my exile, and to resolve Liza's visa problem (she still had not received permission to join Alexei in America).

Several Gorky residents visited me during the week Lusia was absent; they'd apparently found out my address from Western radio broadcasts. Felix Krasavin, an old friend of the Bonner family with whom I was also acquainted, paid a call, and the physicist Mark Kovner, whom I'd met in passing at a refusenik seminar in Moscow, stopped by with a couple of friends. I made new acquaintances, among them Sergei Ponomarev, who had served five years in labor camp for "anti-Soviet activity." Each visitor, upon leaving the building, was detained by the police and taken to the nearby "Post for the Maintenance of Public Order" (the sign was later removed). They would be held there for several hours while their papers were checked, and attempts would be made to intimidate them. Many suffered unpleasant repercussions. After a few weeks the authorities changed their tactics, and prevented people from visiting me except those who were sent or approved by the KGB, and could be counted on to say the right things. A few months later, the flow of visitors stopped altogether. Ponomarev and a few others offered their help, but I was afraid that they would get into trouble and replied that it was better to stay away from me. I hope no one felt insulted.

Ruth drove back to Moscow with Emil Shinberg on January 28, but Natasha stayed on with me until Lusia returned. In retrospect, I can see that I committed several blunders in dealing with the authorities that first week. I may have been in a mild state of shock, although I displayed outward calm. My usual lack of assertiveness and my rather slow reaction time in debates may also have caused me to miss out on several opportunities. Lusia was sorely missed; in these respects, as well as many others, she has a definite advantage over me.

A police officer came to the apartment an hour after Ruth left, and ordered me to report to MVD headquarters. Without even asking to see a summons, I drove with Natasha to Gornaya Street, where I was directed to the proper office.

Two men in civilian clothes introduced themselves as Major Chuprov and Captain Shuvalov. They complained that according to information received from foreign radio broadcasts, I had violated the terms of my regimen by phoning Moscow and adding a postscript to a Helsinki Group document.

"They're mistaken," I said.

"Will you put that in writing?"

"Of course."

I took a sheet of paper and wrote that I had not called Moscow; my attempts to telephone had all been illegally cut off. I had added my signature to the document about Afghanistan, but had not made any changes in it, since I was not a member of the Group.[5]

Chuprov had another complaint: "You've also violated your regimen by associating with Krasavin, an ex-convict, with Kovner, who took part in an illegal demonstration, and with Ponomarev, another ex-convict."

I replied: "I've no idea what 'associating with criminal elements' means. I see people who are my friends. We've known Felix Krasavin for a long time; his conviction was wiped off the books long ago, and he works here in Gorky. It's a purely personal association, and I expect it to remain so. I'm well aware that you can make trouble for people who come to see me, and I've warned my visitors, including Ponomarev. [I shouldn't have said that!] Your complaints have no legal basis, and serve no useful purpose."

In retrospect, I regret my failure to take the offensive and assert the right of everyone, not just of Krasavin, to associate with me: another opportunity was missed here to press my claims against the KGB.

I did make several requests, asking Chuprov to write them down and pass them on to officials with sufficient rank to make decisions about my case. I asked that Liza be granted a visa to join Alexei, that young scientists from FIAN be permitted to visit me, that I have access to my regular doctors from the Academy Clinic, and that the telephone be reconnected in Ruth's Moscow apartment (essential because of her age and health), and that phone service be installed in the Gorky apartment—academicians are entitled to a private telephone.

Chuprov agreed to forward my requests. He suggested that I order the telephone myself, and that I make use of clinics in Gorky if I needed medical care.

I said that no one would speak with me at the telephone office since I was not registered in Gorky and was officially still a resident of Moscow.

"You can register as a resident of Gorky."

"Under no circumstances will I do that: I was sent here illegally. And as to medical care, I have no desire to change doctors—and it's my right not to."

I prepared to leave, but Chuprov asked me to stay a minute and sign the register. A man in uniform whom Chuprov introduced as Glossen came in with the registry book. I decided it would be silly not to sign it, since I had shown up; I hadn't yet thought through all my possibilities for resistance.

---

[5][Sakharov signed Helsinki Group Document 119 (January 21, 1980), which condemned the Soviet invasion of Afghanistan and supported the United Nations resolution calling for withdrawal of Soviet troops.]

* * *

THAT SAME EVENING, I answered the doorbell to find two men—drunk or, more likely, pretending to be drunk—who entered, declaring that they wanted to "get a look at this Sakharov guy."

"I'm Sakharov."

"Why do you want an Olympic boycott?"

"Because the USSR is conducting military operations in Afghanistan."

"How come you're defending the bandits who killed that stewardess?"

"I never spoke out for the Brazinskases. They were convicted by a Turkish court of skyjacking, and served their sentences. But they didn't kill Nadezhda Kurchenko—it was a security guard who accidentally shot her."

My deliberate self-control had no effect. Their tempers flared and they began shouting accusations that made less and less sense. Suddenly one pulled a pistol from his pocket; he began playing with it, waving it around and tossing it up in the air—he didn't aim it directly at me, but he came close enough. "A security agent couldn't have shot her by accident," he said. "I've worked as a guard, and I don't miss no matter whether I'm standing, sitting, or lying prone."

The second man pretended to be calming his companion down; at the same time, he kept assuring me that his friend really was a first-class marksman. (I'd earlier asked whether it was a real pistol or just a cigarette lighter; with a forced laugh, one of them had replied: "A cigarette lighter that drills holes in people!")

The man with the gun started to shout: "I'll show you what Afghanistan's really like! I'll turn this apartment into an Afghanistan!" Then they abruptly changed their tune, and one said in a confidential tone: "You won't be here long. They'll take you to a sanatorium where they have medicine that turns people into idiots."

While all this was going on, Natasha and the "landlady" were in the kitchen making tea. Natasha caught sight of the pistol through the open door and decided she had to do something. She whispered to the "landlady": "Pretend you're taking out the garbage and go tell the policeman that drunks are in the apartment and that they've got a pistol."

The "landlady" was gone a good while, but when she returned, she pretended she'd misunderstood Natasha. She had to be sent a second time. At last, several policemen appeared.

"What's going on here?" they asked.

"Nothing out of the ordinary," I replied.

They led the "drunks" away.

That evening I brought my diary up to date. (My diary has been a great help in writing these memoirs; it's a pity that I began keeping it only in January 1977.) I was still writing when Natasha turned out the lights.

GLOSSEN ARRIVED the next morning while Natasha was cooking breakfast. "I need your passport," he told me. Without thinking, I went to get it from the next room. He took it and put it in his briefcase.

"Why do you need my passport?" I asked, beginning to have doubts.

"I was told to get it so that we can transfer your permanent residence from Moscow to Gorky."

That alarmed me, but I was determined to act with the composure befitting an academician. "That's out of the question. You can register me here on a temporary basis if you have to."

Glossen said: "I'll tell my superiors."

I regret not having asked for my passport back, but it would almost certainly have been useless, and I would never have succeeded in regaining it by force. I can't help but wonder why I surrendered it in the first place. I still don't completely understand it, but it seems that several factors were at play: my general instinct to satisfy a request, the fact that I hadn't needed to use my identity papers for a long time and so didn't take them all that seriously; above all, the fact that my situation had changed, but not my habits, and the shock I'd undergone had weakened my usual control over my subconscious impulses. Nor had I worked out an overall strategy to deal with my new circumstances.

The next day, January 30, as I was on my way to do some shopping, a police officer approached me on the street and told me to report to Deputy Procurator Perelygin. As he began to give me the address, I interrupted: "I'll go if I receive a written summons."

During the next hour, several policemen came to the apartment and ordered me to report to Perelygin. I continued to demand a written summons. Finally, one was produced, and I drove to the Procurator's Office with Natasha. Perelygin was waiting in his office alone, which was unusual for such interviews. He said: "Your wife held a press conference in Moscow where she read a statement written by you which contains false and slanderous fabrications. That's a violation of the regimen of which I apprised you on January 22."

"Who established that regimen and on what authority?" I countered. "Show me a written document outlining the grounds for my exile and establishing its terms. I don't feel myself bound by oral statements."

"We'll return to that issue later on," Perelygin said. "Let me finish what I have to say. Measures may be taken to prevent you from violating your regimen unless you comply voluntarily. Your place of exile can be changed. I'm also warning you that anyone helping you maintain contacts with foreigners will be held accountable and appropriate measures taken. For now, I want you to write an explanation of the violations you've committed."

I gave Perelygin the following statement (reconstructed from memory, since I did not keep a copy):

At my request, at a press conference in Moscow, my wife, Elena Bonner, made public a statement I had written on my general views and my current situation. I, and I alone, am responsible for the contents of that statement and for its distribution to the world press. I have every right to comment on public issues and to inform people about my situation. Procurator Perelygin's assertion that such actions violate my regimen is groundless. His threats and accusations made against persons helping to publicize my articles, and in particular against my wife, Elena Bonner, are absolutely illegal and impermissible. Perelygin has called such persons "go-betweens," but from a juridical standpoint that term makes no sense whatsoever in the present context. I make my statements public, relying on my right to freedom of opinion and information. No one else can be held responsible for them.

January 30, 1980   Academician Andrei Sakharov

Perelygin read what I had written, and then grumbled, a wry expression on his face: "Very plainspoken. Please sign this acknowledgment." He handed me a note typed on a half-sheet of paper; it stated that I had been warned that further violations of my regimen, including contacts with foreigners made by others on my behalf, might result in my transfer to a different place of exile or in other penalties.

I signed the paper, remarking: "You said that—and I told you what I thought of it."

Perelygin said: "I see you intend to violate your regimen."

"Of course. I consider it illegal, as I've explained in writing."

I left Perelygin's office and told Natasha what had happened, quite satisfied with myself. It was only several hours later that I realized that the acknowledgment I'd signed might be interpreted as acceding to Perelygin's warning, since it made no reference to my separate statement. Lawyers are masters of such maneuvers. I wrote Perelygin that same evening, making plain that my signature on the note he had prepared confirmed only that I had heard what he'd said. The statement I had written during our meeting explained why I considered his threats illegal and not binding. Two weeks later, I received notification that my letter had been delivered.

I AM PAINFULLY AWARE of the many mistakes I made during the first days of my exile. I cannot help but compare my behavior with the conduct of individuals undergoing the much greater shock and isolation of arrest and imprisonment. Still, my mistakes are not the whole story of my exile. I held to my principles, and, with Lusia's help, I found the strength to go on living and working.

47

LIFE IN GORKY

ALTHOUGH THE first months of 1980 established the basic contours of my existence in Gorky—a paradoxical situation completely outside any rule of law—the KGB never let things settle into a stable pattern; from time to time, they would commit a new outrage that would upset the status quo. My state of mind was seriously affected by the confrontation with the authorities over Liza, an affair I will discuss in detail in the next chapter. So far as circumstances allowed, I continued my public activities and my scientific work.

We were lodged in an apartment on the first floor of a twelve-story building in Shcherbinki, an outlying, newly incorporated district of Gorky. At first, whenever I looked out of the windows, I could see typical plainclothesmen standing on every corner: they augmented the policeman on duty day and night at the entry of our building. Later on, the plainclothesmen became less noticeable except on special occasions such as my birthday, but there was no real slackening in their vigilance, and from time to time they would make their presence known.

Perelygin had forbidden me to associate with foreigners and "criminal elements." It soon became clear that the KGB's interpretation of the latter term was very broad. The only persons ordinarily allowed to visit me were my wife, my children, and three residents of Gorky: Felix and Maya Krasavin (but not their school-age son), and Mark Kovner. [Ruth left for America in May; after that, Liza was forbidden to visit.] The KGB undoubtedly had a purpose in granting the Krasavins and Kovner special status, although we could only speculate as to what it might be. Our visitors were called in for occasional "chats," and it seems the authorities may have appreciated the fact that Maya Krasavin was a physician; Felix usually came to see me alone, but two or three times, when either my heart was giving me trouble or I was suffering from thrombophlebitis, he brought his wife along, and she examined me. Subsequently, when Anatoly Alexandrov, President of the Academy, was asked why I was being deprived of medical care, he exclaimed: "What do you mean? Maya's looking after him." But Maya's sporadic visits were no substitute for serious medical attention, and one wonders how Alexandrov knew about her and her visits. The KGB must have taken pains to inform him.

At first, a few strangers were allowed in to lecture me on my sins, but such visits came to an end after a few months. All other visitors were detained by the police. Beginning in March 1980, there was a policeman stationed in front of our apartment door around the clock. At night, the officer on duty occasionally would doze off, but he was careful to position himself so that no one could reach our door without waking him. Those detained by the police were taken across the street to a special apartment and interrogated on the spot. It's likely that I never found out about many visitors who'd traveled to Gorky to express sympathy or to seek my assistance. Anyone who came to see me was given a hard time, and those from other cities were usually forced to leave Gorky. Some found themselves in serious trouble: later I learned that at least three persons who'd attempted to visit spent several months in psychiatric confinement.

On one occasion, two schoolboys managed to slip into our apartment and talk with us; on their way out they were seized and taken for questioning. For three hours we waited by the window; then they emerged from the building across the street, and gave us a wave which we took as a sign of spirits unbroken. A month later, we received a visit from the boys' parents, workers in a Gorky factory. Unhappily, they told us that the authorities were making life difficult for them, and that the boys' school had been informed of the incident.

On February 15, 1980, Lusia's birthday, Yuri Shikhanovich was detained. He'd accompanied Lusia on the train back from Moscow, helping her carry food and other supplies. The authorities must have had advance notice of their arrival and three policemen were on duty in our lobby. They stopped Shikhanovich and took him away, leaving the packages behind. Lusia rang the bell and shouted to me: "They've got Yuri!"

We rushed across the street to the apartment where visitors were detained. Captain Snezhnitsky, the deputy chief of police in our district and the official responsible for my surveillance, was facing us from behind his desk, dressed in an MVD uniform, as we entered; the KGB was, as usual, keeping a low profile. We demanded to know where Shikhanovich was and what was being done to him. Snezhnitsky, irritated by our intrusion, ordered us removed, and the police obeyed with alacrity: a few professional shoves and we were out the door. I landed flat on the floor; Lusia's glasses protected her eyes when she was struck in the face, but one arm was bruised. As we were pulling ourselves together, Shikhanovich was brought out of the apartment. He managed to toss us his return ticket. Later, he sent us a telegram that he'd been returned to Moscow by plane.

During the first six months the KGB issued at least fifty summonses, trying to get me to register at the police station. I answered them all with a standard refusal, and with a request for a car and driver (a privilege I was entitled to as an academician).

The summonses often contained threats to bring me in by force, and in March 1980 this was tried. First, the lock on our apartment door was broken. The next day two police lieutenants appeared and announced that they had been ordered by Captain Snezhnitsky to bring me to the police station by force if I refused to accompany them voluntarily. I went outside with them; a minibus was waiting on the street for us, but I said that I had to send a telegram and started walking toward the post office. The policemen came running after me, grabbed my arms, and began pulling me toward the minibus. I let my feet drag through the snow and kept shouting about the post office and registration. We began to attract the attention of passers-by. Changing direction, the policemen got me to the entry of our building and suddenly let go. I ran to my apartment, slipped inside, and chained the door.

The next day, a locksmith came to install a new lock. A few minutes later, a police captain arrived and demanded that I appear for registration. When I demurred, he wrote out a complaint that I'd "refused to obey a policeman." The locksmith signed as witness. But that was the end of the matter, and I still don't understand what all the fuss was about.

Whenever I left the building, my KGB tails would shadow me. I came to know many by sight. When I walked in the woods I would occasionally run across a pair pretending to be lovers, and I more than once flushed an observer hiding behind a tree, who would then dash away. In 1981, after Lusia and I began taking drives around Gorky, one or, often, two cars would follow, every so often cutting us off or trying some other stunt meant to intimidate. The KGB doesn't stint on public funds—the agents following us were rotated regularly.

What did they hope to accomplish? For one thing, they prevented us from making long distance calls to Moscow, Leningrad, or other points. When we tried to place a call from a post office, the phones were always "out of order"—our KGB shadows had been there ahead of us. (We weren't allowed to have a telephone in our Gorky apartment, and those in our Moscow apartment and the Zhukovka dacha were disconnected on January 22, 1980.) It was almost impossible to escape the surveillance. Once, however, worried about Natasha's health, I managed to make a call to Leningrad: I carried a trash can out of our building, left it at the collection point, and continued walking right to a post office. From that day until December 16, 1986, we were accompanied by a policeman every time we took out the garbage. Another purpose of the KGB surveillance, probably its main one, was to prevent contacts with people in the street.

Were they afraid I'd sneak off to Moscow? Hardly. They knew their power, and so did I. On the eve of the Academy's March 1980 General Assembly, they put on a show for me. The bylaws require all academicians to attend the annual General Assembly when the president and secretary report on Academy activities, and many organizational matters come up for vote. Absence can be excused only by the Academy's presidium (also the case for Academy elections). I had sent the presidium a telegram requesting an invitation to the meeting (they are normally sent to all academicians, but I didn't receive any during my exile). For a long time there was no reply, so I sent a second inquiry, and I finally received the unprecedented reply: "Your presence at the meeting is not anticipated."

Foreign correspondents may not have appreciated the telegram's curious wording. *Who* wasn't anticipating my presence? The Academy had bowed to the KGB in ignoring its own bylaws, which explicitly required my attendance. The evening before the Assembly, Lusia and I accompanied Ruth and Liza to the station where they were catching the night train to Moscow. As I tried to carry Ruth's suitcase onto the train, several men suddenly appeared and linked arms to block me. One of them even drew a pistol from his holster. I waved goodbye from a distance. (Liza later told me that Ruth—a person who never allowed herself any display of weakness—had tears in her eyes.) This was one way the KGB demonstrated that they took seriously the ban on my leaving Gorky. We later learned that policemen were posted at Ruth's door in Moscow while the Academy was in session, and only a few people were allowed in to see her. I still can't understand what the KGB was afraid of.

Another surprise was in store for us when Lusia and I returned to our apartment after seeing off Ruth and Liza: a personal jamming station had been installed in our immediate vicinity so that all we could hear on our shortwave receiver was a howling noise. In order to listen to the radio, we had to take it 100 yards or more from our building.

In Gorky the KGB did more than supervise my quarantine; it conducted other, more delicate operations as well. From the first days, we detected signs that strangers were entering our apartment. Every so often we would find our tape recorders, radios, and typewriter damaged; we had to have them repaired many times. I took my irreplaceable notes, documents, and books with me whenever I went out. At first, we assumed that some of the policemen who were in cahoots with the KGB let its agents into the apartment.

We discovered, however, that another means of surreptitious entry had been used during the first six months of my exile. I've mentioned that our "landlady" kept the key to one of the rooms in the apartment. She would come almost every day and sit in the room for a few hours with the door ajar, and then, locking the door, would leave. (Occasionally, she'd supply us with clean sheets and towels.) We learned her real function one evening in July when a messenger from the post office came to the apartment at seven P.M. and said a call for us from New York was expected. We left in a hurry for the post office, hoping it might be from the children. (Later, when we examined the notification of the call carefully, we saw that it had been received in Gorky at eleven A.M.; the KGB had delayed its delivery for eight hours. We still don't know who placed it, and we received no more calls from abroad.[1]) Lusia had brought my bag of manuscripts and documents, but as we neared the post office, she realized that she'd left her cigarettes behind. She went back to the apartment for them, and found two KGB agents there, one rummaging through my papers and the other fiddling with my tape recorder (he erased a tape I'd made for the children). Lusia cried out; the KGB agents ran toward the landlady's room, overturned the sofa, and jumped from the window to the ground below. When Lusia showed the policeman on duty the havoc they'd left behind, he seemed genuinely shocked.

We could see now how the "landlady" earned her salary; her main function was to make sure that the window in her room was left unbolted, to allow KGB agents access to the apartment from the street, bypassing the police manning the watch post.

Lusia left for Moscow later that evening. The next morning I sent a telegram to Yuri Andropov, then head of the KGB, protesting the illegal KGB search, a crude violation of the sanctity of the home. Lusia called a press conference in Moscow, where she reported the KGB's actions; she also sent telegrams to Anatoly Alexandrov and the presidents of the American academies of which I am a member. A few days later I was called in by the KGB. I appeared at the appointed time, and spoke with two KGB officers; one introduced himself as the head of the KGB in the Gorky region, and the other one was from Moscow, a Major Ryabinin, whom I would meet again during our 1981 hunger strike. Unfortunately, I was not assertive enough and played down the psychological effects of our situation, and its potential dangers.

After this incident, I no longer allowed the "landlady" into the apartment. She (and the KGB) accepted this, probably because she had lost her value once she was exposed. In retrospect, however, it's clear that the KGB never gave

---

[1][Elena Bonner was able to call Sakharov while she was abroad for medical treatment from December 1985 until June 2, 1986. After she returned to the USSR, her children in Newton were able to speak to her and Sakharov by phone, although portions of their conversations were jammed.]

up its pursuit of my bag of manuscripts and documents. I should, of course, have made copies of the important items. But I was too complacent—and eight months later, the KGB snared its quarry.

That story began in September 1980, when serious dental problems forced me to visit a clinic in Gorky. Quite a lot of work was needed, including several extractions and fitting for dentures, which was done in February. On March 13, I was notified that my dentures were ready and I rushed off to the dentist's office. Lusia was in Moscow at the time, and I was preoccupied with an error I'd just discovered in one of my scientific papers. The dental technician K. met me in the reception area and took me to a first-floor room instead of the usual office on the top floor. This was convenient for me, since my heart condition makes climbing stairs difficult. K. explained that because this was a surgical office, I'd have to leave my bag outside. The filthy floor should have alerted me to the fact that this was utter nonsense—or purposeful deceit. I could have canceled my appointment or insisted that an exception be made to the "rule." Instead, I merely asked a nurse to keep an eye on my bag, or put it in the storeroom.

"Don't worry," she said, "nothing ever gets lost here."

I was confident that my bag would be safe under the eyes of the patients sitting in the hallway and waiting for their appointments. . . . Those whom God would punish, He first deprives of reason.

K. finished working on me, and I went to reclaim my bag—and it was gone. A patient told me that two men had been hanging around and eyeing it; one of them must have picked it up. I never discovered what role the head of the dental clinic played in the theft, but it was she who had issued the instructions that I couldn't keep my bag with me, and there must have a reason for that.

The KGB had struck a powerful blow: I lost notes on scientific matters and current events, personal documents, letters (including copies of Lusia's letters to the children), three thick notebooks containing my diary for the past fourteen months, and three more containing the manuscript of these memoirs. A notebook containing my initial work on the memoirs had disappeared in November 1978 during a surreptitious search of our Moscow apartment. Both these thefts caused me an enormous amount of extra work. On March 17, I issued a statement[2] about the robbery at the dentist's office, which received surprising attention. The KGB had again covered itself with shame. I was compelled to postpone scientific work that I'd been planning to do and to concentrate on my memoirs before the KGB seized them again or found some other means of preventing their completion.

[2][See Appendix, p. 680.]

The loss of my diaries hurt as well. I'd recorded daily events in them, and also ideas, conversations, my impressions of books and movies, abstracts of scientific articles, etc. There were four essays on literary and philosophical themes: two on poems by Pushkin, one on Faulkner's *Absalom, Absalom!*, and a final one on Chingiz Aitmatov's remarkable novel *The Day Lasts Longer Than a Hundred Years*. Later on, I reconstructed the Pushkin articles, combining them into a single essay, but, as is often the case, the second draft was inferior to the original—drier, and somehow mechanical. I tried to show the connection between the "The Three Springs" and "Arion"; the latter poem offers important insight into Pushkin's thought, and also expresses some of my own emotions, cast up on the rock of Gorky as so many of my friends sank into the abyss.[3] I didn't even try to restore the other two articles.

A single item from my bag was returned. When I got home from the dentist, a letter I'd written to the All-Union Institute of Scientific Information requesting reprints of scientific articles was lying on my desk. (I'd taken it with me in the bag, intending to mail it.) The KGB left it as their "calling card" after once again entering my locked apartment. Perhaps they wanted to send the message that they weren't interfering with my scientific work. But they most definitely were!

The theft of my bag was staggering. I was exasperated by my carelessness, and bitterly regretted the loss of documents and manuscripts that would be difficult or impossible to replace. The thought that intimate letters and notes (as well as several items of purely personal value) were in the hands of strangers galled me. When Lusia returned from Moscow that evening, she was stunned by the news, and she says I was in a state of shock, literally trembling. All the same, our spirits weren't broken, and in fact the tempo of my activities actually increased after the theft, although I was forced to set scientific work aside for a time. Looking through my papers, I've found six documents written between March 13 and March 24, when Lusia left again for Moscow: an appeal for Anatoly Marchenko; an autobiographical note for the *Festschrift* compiled by friends for my sixtieth birthday; a chronology of my publications prepared for the *Festschrift*; the article "The Responsibility of Scientists" (which had to be

---

[3][For "The Three Springs" and "Arion," see Walter Arndt, trans. *Pushkin Threefold*, pp. 215, 217. "Arion" ends:

> Both helmsman and sailor perished!—
> I alone, the mysterious singer,
> Swept ashore by the storm,
> I sing the former hymns
> And dry my damp garment
> In the sun at the foot of the cliff.]

completely rewritten since the first draft was in the stolen bag); a letter about Raoul Wallenberg; and my statement about the theft.

We spent the first two days after the theft trying to relax, to free ourselves from the sense of nightmare. We drove the whole length of the city in bone-chilling weather to see the latest Belmondo hit. Life went on. . . .

The story of Raoul Wallenberg [the Swedish diplomat who rescued thousands of Hungarian Jews during World War II and then vanished during the Soviet occupation of Budapest] is well known. In response to inquiries from the Swedish Ministry for Foreign Affairs and other interested parties, the Soviet authorities have maintained that Wallenberg died in Moscow's Lubyanka Prison in 1947 and the file of his case was destroyed. The latter assertion most assuredly is untrue: NKVD and KGB investigation files are stampe 1 "To be preserved forever"; in rare instances specific pages may be removed on instructions from the top leadership, but a file is never completely destroyed. (While working at the Installation, I learned about all this from G., a KGB officer who'd had the job of sorting files from the 1930s and 1940s. In every case, the first page of a file was retained. If a person had been executed, an affidavit that the death sentence had been carried out was included, with a record of the serial number of the pistol used.)

Complete files of cases involving foreign citizens almost certainly were preserved, just to be on the safe side. Diplomats should continue to press the Soviet authorities to clear up the mystery of Wallenberg's fate. If he's still alive, his release would bolster the authority of the USSR's current leaders, who seem to wish to free themselves from the burden of past crimes.[4]

SOON AFTER the theft, I began to reconstruct my diary and the memoirs from memory. Bitter experience had finally convinced me to make a carbon copy of everything, something Lusia had advised me to do. But it's inconvenient to write with a carbon, corrections are a nuisance, and you have to use the right sort of pen. Now, I resigned myself to that. Once or twice a month Lusia would take to Moscow what I'd written and send it on to Efrem and Tanya. How she accomplished this is a story that cannot yet be told. Lusia never parted with the manuscripts, bulky as they often were, for a single minute, on the train or in Moscow. By April 1982, I had finished another draft of this book, and was editing it for publication. Lusia arranged to have it typed in Moscow; there was no way to have it done in Gorky. By August 31, I had revised half the

---

[4][For further information on Sakharov's role in the Wallenberg case, see his article "The Fate of Raoul Wallenberg," *Moscow News*, No. 37, 1989.]

manuscript, and during September I completed the balance—some 900 hand-written pages. On October 11, 1982, the manuscript—the 500 typewritten pages Lusia had brought back from Moscow and the 900 handwritten pages I had recently completed—was again stolen. This time, the theft was staged in more spectacular fashion, employing what can only be called gangster methods.

A few days before Lusia's return from Moscow, a fire broke out in the motor of my Zhiguli car when I started it up one morning. Someone had tampered with the engine by connecting an ignition wire to the fuel pump. The KGB probably expected me to lose my head and leave the manuscript bag behind, but I simply turned off the motor and the fire died of its own accord. (The ignition wires had to be replaced.)

On October 9, Lusia and I drove to town and parked near the market. I walked to the same dental clinic where my bag had been stolen nineteen months earlier, while Lusia remained in the car, sitting in the front seat, with the bag on the floor behind her. A stranger walked over to her and said softly: "Be careful, there's a lot of them around today. I don't know what they're after, but I know them when I see them." Lusia placed the bag under her feet, closed the car windows, and waited to see what would happen next. A man in police uniform came over and asked for her papers. They were in the bag, but Lusia was afraid that it might be taken from her, so she said: "My husband has them. He'll be back soon."

The "policeman" walked away, and no one else approached the car.

On October 11 we again drove into town, parking near the river. Lusia walked to the railroad office, taking her disabled veteran's identification since it allows her to buy tickets at a discount without waiting in line. I stayed in the car, with the bag, as usual, on the floor behind the front seat. It was four o'clock in the afternoon, still light. A man of about thirty-five, with a dark complexion and curly black hair, walked over, looked into the car, and asked through my half-open window: "You've got Moscow plates—are you headed for Moscow?" I told him I was just going to Shcherbinki.

My memory's blank as to what happened then. The next thing I recall is someone pulling the bag through a window (front or back, I don't remember). I tried to get out of the car, but I couldn't find the door handle, something that usually comes automatically. I finally extricated myself, and caught sight of three women standing nearby, one holding what looked like a doctor's kit. "They jumped over the railing; how come you took so long to get out of the car?" one of the women asked me.

"I couldn't find the door handle."

My answer seemed to reassure them. "Did you know they smashed your window?"

The left rear window had been shattered, but *I hadn't heard a thing.* It's my belief that I'd been momentarily stunned by some narcotic; I have no direct evidence to support this hypothesis (there *was* a strange odor, like that of rotting fruit), but it's the only explanation I can think of for the gap in my memory and my failure to hear the window shatter.

The women were still standing there, and one said: "We called the police; they're coming right away."

One of the women must have been a doctor, and the other two were probably nurses assigned to treat me in the event I suffered any ill effects from the narcotic. They'd lied about calling the police. For some reason they didn't want me going straight to the precinct station—maybe they were afraid I'd pass out along the way. In any case, they walked off before I could ask them to serve as witnesses. Lusia showed up then, and even from a distance she could see I was walking strangely, as if drunk, and that there was blood on my hand.

At the train station the cashiers had all been called away to another room, and Lusia had been kept waiting for about ten minutes before they resumed issuing tickets. Apparently, this was the KGB's method of delaying her while they carried out their operation against me.

I went directly to the police and reported the robbery. An investigator drew up a report, examined the scene of the crime, and photographed our car. Everything was done by the book, but, of course, they didn't find anything, not that I'd really expected them to. Again I'd suffered an enormous loss, equal to that of the earlier theft at the dentist's office.

I wrote out another statement, and Lusia took it to Moscow on her next trip.[5] Arriving in Moscow on the morning of October 30, she found a policeman posted at the door of the Chkalov Street apartment. He allowed Lusia to come and go freely, but no one else was permitted to enter. She managed to call a Reuters correspondent from a phone booth and set up a meeting on the street, where she passed on my statement about the theft, and Ida Milgrom relayed the latest news about her son Anatoly Shcharansky, who'd been on a hunger strike in Chistopol Prison for more than a month.

Some hours later Lusia was horrified when she tuned in her radio and heard Voice of America and then Radio Liberty report a completely garbled version of the robbery. Sakharov's daughter had visited him (?!). His wife had gone out (?!). He was left alone, and his bag containing manuscripts and documents had disappeared. (The daughter's role in all this was never made clear.)

An accurate account was broadcast the next day, but nothing was said about the errors in the earlier report, and people tend to remember the first story they

[5][See Appendix, p. 681.]

hear. Millions of Soviet citizens were left with the impression that Lusia was somehow at fault for going out because my daughter had arrived. (In fact, neither of my daughters visited me between March and December 1982.) The KGB was beyond a doubt responsible for circulating the false version of events, in order to cover up its crime and to discredit Lusia. Unfortunately, even in this glaring instance, Western intelligence services displayed their usual lack of interest in finding out who'd planted the disinformation.

Another instance of tampering with information concerning me involved the "Letter to Foreign Colleagues" circulated in my defense in Moscow in January 1983.[6] The letter was anonymous: the authors did not sign their names for fear of jeopardizing their jobs and families. The first Western broadcasts reporting this document mentioned Moscow rumors that Sakharov himself was the author! I'm convinced that the story was KGB-inspired.

In late October, a planned visit by physicists from FIAN was cancelled. I heard in a roundabout way that they'd been advised it was not a propitious time for a visit. The KGB was tipping its hand; I hadn't yet publicly announced the theft of the bag. In any event, it wasn't until mid-January that any physicists showed up—and it was probably no coincidence that they arrived on the eve of my third "anniversary" in Gorky.

I was summoned to the Procurator's Office on November 4, where I was directed again to Perelygin, the regional deputy head. I didn't recognize him at first, and automatically shook his hand. Perelygin took the offensive: "Citizen Sakharov, I've asked you here because of your slanderous statement."

We spent a long time arguing, Perelygin putting words in my mouth and trying to catch me contradicting myself. His main thrust, however, was directed at persuading me to sign a "warning." I categorically refused to sign anything and insisted that the only crime committed had been the work of the KGB. Perelygin finally abandoned his effort; he stood up and announced solemnly that I had once again been warned that I was responsible for having violated the "regimen established for me by the supreme organ of authority."

"The Presidium of the Supreme Soviet?"

"Yes," Perelygin replied, a trifle uncertainly.

I then complained that all my attempts to discover who established my regimen had been fruitless. The only decree that Rekunkov showed me was the one stripping me of my awards. There had been no response to my written inquiries. *Izvestia* had mentioned "competent organs," which everyone assumed to mean the KGB.

Perelygin took a thick volume from the shelf and opened it to a page indicated by a bookmark. "I informed you in 1980 that the Presidium of the

---

6[See *A Chronicle of Human Rights in the USSR*, no. 48, 1983, pp. 27–29.]

Supreme Soviet ordered your regimen, and you signed the appropriate acknowledgment. Here it is."

I said: "You never mentioned the Presidium, and I don't recall signing any acknowledgment to that effect. That's something I wouldn't forget."

The warning that Perelygin had wanted me to sign only fifteen minutes earlier contained no mention of the Presidium. I began to study closely the document he was holding in front of me, but he quickly withdrew it. There was something fishy about it. The size of the paper was different, my handwritten acknowledgment that I'd read the text was missing, and my signature looked like a facsimile instead of the real thing. I'm quite sure that the document Perelygin showed me was a fake. I still don't know the formal basis for my 1980 banishment and the regimen that was imposed.

Decrees of the Presidium of the Supreme Soviet must be published with the signatures of the chairman and secretary. This wasn't done in my case. The most plausible hypothesis remains that the decisions to banish me from Moscow, to send me to Gorky, and especially to impose an unlawful regimen of isolation were made not by the Presidium but at a lower level, by the KGB. (One argument in favor of this assumption was the acquiescence in my refusal to register—they wouldn't have backed down so readily if a Presidium decree had been involved.)

AFTER THE October 1982 robbery, I once again began rewriting these memoirs. I was forced to rely on my unaided memory, since I didn't have the first draft or the two hundred pages of notes I'd used in preparing the edited version. A copy of the first part of the manuscript reached me in April 1983, but the transfer of material was erratic and unreliable: about a third of the material Efrem sent didn't arrive, and I could never be sure that my revisions would get back to him. Adding to my worries, the never-ending complications with the memoirs exposed Lusia to risk. But despite the sword of Damocles suspended over the project, I kept on writing bits and pieces in the hope that they would fit organically into the manuscript which Efrem and Tanya were safeguarding in Newton.

On December 6, Lusia took sections of the memoirs with her on the train to Moscow. A few days before she left, she suffered severe heart pain (this may have been a first infarct), but her trip couldn't be postponed. I went with her to the station. (This time, she had a reserved seat in a compartment for four passengers, but she often had to travel coach and needed her priority as a disabled veteran to get any ticket at all.)

There were no signs of trouble when she left Gorky that evening, but when the train arrived in Moscow at seven the next morning, two detectives entered her compartment. They had come to search Lusia. They ordered a man and a woman to remain, explaining that they were needed as witnesses. The passengers protested, but their objections were brushed aside. I'm convinced this was all staged; when dissidents are to be searched, the authorities make sure the witnesses are tractable, and they'd hardly have allowed an exception in Lusia's case. The address of one witness was 216 Gagarin Street, the building next to mine where my visitors were interrogated and where some of the KGB agents assigned to my case probably lived. Another giveaway was the woman's feigned ignorance of who I was, something everyone in the neighborhood knew.

Lusia immediately handed over my manuscripts, in the belief that they were what the detectives were hunting for. She hoped to cut the matter short, but the proceedings lasted for three hours and included a strip search, a thorough inspection of her luggage, and the time-consuming preparation of a detailed protocol. By this time the train had been shunted onto a siding at the Moscow-3 station, and Lusia had to carry her heavy bags to the suburban train which would take her back to central Moscow. Severe heart pains forced her to sit down several times, but she made herself get up and start moving again. She blacked out briefly as she mounted a bridge over the tracks, but a young man who came along helped her the rest of the way. I'm certain that the deterioration of her health over the next few months was precipitated by this incident. In November, after Lusia's heart pains, Maya Krasavin had taken an electrocardiogram (using a rather primitive portable instrument), and she'd discounted the possibility that Lusia had suffered an attack; this may have reassured the KGB that their planned search-and-seizure operation would not have a fatal outcome. Lusia had another electrocardiogram taken at the Academy clinic in Moscow. The doctors there also failed to detect signs of an infarct, but in March 1984, when Professor Syrkin examined the record, he detected significant irregularities, although Lusia doesn't know his precise diagnosis.

During the search, 250 pages of my manuscript had been confiscated and many other things as well: a valuable 8mm movie camera with films we'd taken; tape recordings I'd made; English-language lessons on tape; *The Correspondence of Boris Pasternak and Olga Freidenberg* (Lusia especially regretted the loss of this book, which, moreover, didn't belong to us); her address book; a letter from Canada informing me that my appeal to the Pugwash Conference couldn't be used (possibly a KGB fabrication); and a copy of my telegram to the Presidium of the Supreme Soviet requesting that prisoners of conscience be included in the amnesty proclaimed for the USSR's sixtieth anniversary.[7]

The official pretext for the search was the case of Sofia Kalistratova, but none

[7][See *A Chronicle of Human Rights in the USSR*, No. 48, 1983, p. 45.]

of the items confiscated bore the slightest relation to Kalistratova (apart from her phone number in Lusia's address book, scarcely a criminal matter). We can only speculate about the KGB's real reason for the search: perhaps to delay my memoirs, perhaps to exert psychological pressure, perhaps to test the waters for an escalation of their campaign against Lusia. Prior to this incident, the KGB had employed only thefts and similar surreptitious acts in their effort to cut my links to the world beyond Gorky, but now they had acted openly and officially, and the stakes had been raised.

A few days later, foreign correspondents asked Roy Medvedev for his thoughts on Lusia's search. He answered: "It was to be expected. I have a right to publish memoirs; Sakharov doesn't, since he was engaged in secret work." Medvedev's unwarranted statement may have inhibited the Western media's coverage of the affair. I've already stated my reasons for committing my memoirs to paper, and I'm convinced that I've every right to do so, excluding, of course, any state or military secrets.

IN ADDITION to working on these memoirs, I managed to publish a number of statements on public issues while in Gorky. My exile was part of a stepped-up campaign against dissent that coincided with the invasion of Afghanistan and preceded the 1981 imposition of martial law in Poland. This disturbing and tragic background dictated the tone and themes of my Gorky writings; the first major article I produced there was entitled "Troubling Times."[8] Before then, I'd given interviews to Kevin Klose of the *Washington Post* and an Italian television correspondent. Lusia brought me their questions in writing and took back my written replies. I've always preferred this type of interview; I don't have a flair for quick response, and I prefer a chance to reflect on my answers. And it was the only form of interview possible from Gorky.

My more important statements written in exile included:

1. My open letter of July 27, 1980, addressed to Leonid Brezhnev and the heads of state of China, France, the U.K., and the U.S., the permanent members of the U.N. Security Council, along with the USSR. This dealt with the tragedy of Afghanistan and the invasion's consequences for the USSR at home and abroad, for international trust and security, and for the fate of peace throughout the world. I wrote that compromise was necessary; that Soviet troops should be withdrawn and replaced by United Nations peacekeeping forces; that free elections should be held with the participation of both the

---

[8][The article was completed on May 4, 1980, and appeared in *The New York Times Magazine*, June 8, 1980, under the title "A Letter from Exile." Reprinted in *On Sakharov*, pp. 223–240.]

guerrillas and Babrak Karmal; that free emigration should be permitted; that Afghanistan should receive economic assistance.[9]

2. "The Responsibility of Scientists" (March 24, 1981) discussed scientists' special responsibilities, with respect both to their profession and to such issues as the opportunities and dangers posed by progress, protection of the environment, war and peace, justice, fundamental human rights, the free flow of information, and the defense of victims of repression. I included a long list of prisoners of conscience who had been prosecuted for nonviolent advocacy of human rights.

3. "What the USA and the USSR Should Do to Preserve World Peace." Here, I developed ideas that had preoccupied me for years, and suggested ways to eliminate threats to international security, trust, and peace, arguing the need for a gradual transition from the dangerous and unstable reliance on nuclear deterrence to a policy based on parity in conventional arms. The article concluded: "Only an equilibrium based on reason—not on fear—is a true guarantee for the future."

4. In "An Appeal to the Pugwash Conference"[10] I warned that the Soviet Union had used détente to tilt the strategic balance in its favor. I again stressed the importance of halting Soviet expansion and restoring strategic parity in conventional weapons so that the West would not have to rely on nuclear weapons for defense. I also called upon the USSR to participate in economic assistance to the developing countries.

5. "The Danger of Thermonuclear War: An Open Letter to Dr. Sidney Drell" (February 2, 1983).[11] Lusia had brought me Drell's articles on the nuclear threat and disarmament, which he had given to her in Moscow in December 1982. "The Danger of Thermonuclear War," written in part in response to his arguments, constituted my most detailed public statement on the suicidal consequences of nuclear conflict. I called for the complete elimination of nuclear weapons, warned that such a major shift in strategy would have to be carried out gradually and carefully in order to prevent a loss of parity in the intermediate phases, and outlined my thoughts on a constructive approach to disarmament negotiations.

6. My speech accepting the Szilard Award (April, 1983).[12] This award, which I prize greatly, was given by the Forum on Physics and Society of the American Physical Society. Lusia made a special effort to get the speech to Tanya in time for the award ceremony on April 19, 1983. I touched briefly on

[9][Appendix, p. 657.]
[10][*The New York Times*, September 10, 1982.]
[11][For an excerpt, see Appendix, p. 664.]
[12][Appendix, p. 660.]

the dangers posed by international terrorism and the Soviet invasion of Afghanistan, and pointed out the importance of eliminating the USSR's gigantic land-based ICBMs and its medium-range missiles, predicting that only after the West had deployed equivalent weapons as bargaining chips would this become possible.

IN ADDITION to my statements on more general topics, I issued numerous appeals to Soviet leaders and to the world at large in behalf of victims of the accelerating campaign against dissenters.

The case of Anatoly Marchenko was especially tragic. I've already described [p. ooo] his remarkable courage and integrity. The KGB could not forgive *My Testimony*'s devastating description of post-Stalin labor camps and prisons or Marchenko's implacable refusal to conform. He was arrested on March 17, 1981—for the sixth time!—and was tried in September on charges of anti-Soviet propaganda. There were no real grounds for criminal proceedings; the principal counts were his letter to Academician Kapitsa[13] in my defense and his essay "Tertium Datum."[14] Marchenko received the maximum sentence as a recidivist: ten years strict-regimen labor camp and five years internal exile—effectively a life sentence for a man who'd spent half his life in confinement and was seriously ill. Before his arrest, Marchenko had been building a house for his family in Karabanovo, about seventy miles northeast of Moscow; he wasn't permitted to live any closer to the capital. After the trial, his son Pavel said he wasn't ready to move to Moscow: "The house has to be finished. That's what Papa would want!" I appealed to Kapitsa to intercede—after all, Marchenko's letter had been addressed to him—but received no reply.

Tatyana Osipova, a member of the Moscow Helsinki Group, was arrested on May 27, 1980, and was sentenced to five years labor camp and five years internal exile. Her husband, Sergei Kovalev's son Ivan, who was also a member of the Helsinki Group, was arrested on August 25, 1981, and received an identical sentence. In 1982–1983, Osipova conducted an extended hunger strike to win the right to see her husband. The Corrective Labor Code does not explicitly permit or prohibit conjugal visits for spouses who are both prisoners, but the authorities choose to treat this omission as mandating a ban. I wrote to then-General Secretary Andropov, asking him to make a meeting of these young persons possible, but I was ignored. The Kovalevs weren't the only ones in this situation; so were the Rudenkos and the Matuseviches, among

---

[13][See *On Sakharov*, pp. 31–37.]
[14][(With M. Tarusevich), *Kontinent* 9 (1976), pp. 81–122.]

others. In the past, Lusia had tried to arrange a visit between Eduard Kuznetsov and his wife, Silva Zalmanson, also without success.

In May 1980, the gifted poet Vasyl Stus was arrested in Kiev, not long after he'd joined the Ukrainian Helsinki Group. Stus died in a Perm labor camp in September 1985.

Merab Kostava was the victim of an outrageous incident of provocation in November 1981, shortly before completing his term of exile. A stranger showed up at Kostava's home in the Siberian village of Kvitok and introduced himself as an exiled artist. The police then appeared, took in the guest on the pretext that he had no papers, and when Kostava went to the police station to find out what was happening, he himself was arrested, charged with malicious hooliganism, and sentenced to five years labor camp.

I drafted a telegram to Eduard Shevardnadze, then First Secretary of the Georgian Central Committee, asking him to intervene: Kostava, I said, had been arrested for fulfilling the Georgian tradition of hospitality. Lusia hadn't yet recovered her full strength after our 1981 hunger strike, but she managed to evade surveillance, put through a call to Moscow, and dictate the telegram to a correspondent. As usual, there was no response.

Yuri Orlov and Anatoly Shcharansky suffered serious and persistent harassment in detention. Malva Landa was rearrested and sentenced to a new term of exile. This mournful roll call went on. . . .

IN MOSCOW in the 1970s, and in Gorky as well, I continued to study physics and cosmology, working on the same themes that attracted my attention in the 1960s, but I wasn't able to come up with any substantially new ideas. This is probably the lot of most scientists when they reach a certain age, although I haven't entirely lost hope that I may yet have a flash of inspiration. In any event, there's a great deal of satisfaction in simply following scientific progress even when you yourself don't actively participate. In this sense, I'm not "greedy."

In 1975, I published results from the previous year during which I developed further the idea of the zero Lagrangian for the gravitational field, as well as the methods of calculation which I had used in my previous papers. (In order to discuss my recent work, I will have to repeat a portion of the material already covered in Chapter 18.) In doing this, it turned out that I arrived at a method that had been introduced many years earlier by Vladimir Fock, and later used by Julian Schwinger. However, my conclusion and the path by which I reached it were entirely different. Unfortunately, I had no chance to send my work to Fock—he died in 1974.

I subsequently discovered several mistakes in my article. The following question remained unclear: does the "induced gravitation" (the modern term for "zero Lagrangian") give the right sign for the gravitational constant in any of the variants I examined?

Also in 1975, I published a paper in which the interpolation formula for the hadron mass, described by Zeldovich and me in our 1966 article, was extended to hadrons containing the "charmed" quark. (The first members of this family had been discovered not long before.) A methodological problem that I had to solve concerned finding the spin-spin interaction for baryons, which contain three different quarks, and I was gratified by my ability to cope with this.

The work was continued in two articles that were published after my banishment to Gorky. Basing them on the ideas of quantum chromodynamics (the dynamical theory of quark interaction; this term is explained in greater detail in the first part of this book), I was able to iron out the wrinkles in the interpolation formula and make it more physical, thereby reducing the number of parameters. In the second paper, I gave a simple method not requiring any complex calculations for estimating the coupling constant between quarks and the gluon field. (The gluon field in quark theory is the analogue of the electromagnetic field. Here the coupling constant is the analogue of the electric charge of an electron.) The method is based on the comparison of two mass increments that are due to the spin-spin strong (gluon) and elctromagnetic interactions, respectively. Unfortunately, because the electromagnetic mass increment is not known exactly, I was able to make only a rough estimate. (Franklin subsequently refined my estimates.) As a by-product of this work, it became possible to define one of the basic parameters of quantum chromodynamics—the number of so-called quark colors (color is a discrete internal quantum number ascribed to the quarks in this theory).

The mass increments known to me then were not in contradiction with the number of quark colors now accepted—three. Refined values for the electromagnetic mass increments now make possible more definite results; I've heard that this has attracted researchers' attention. The exact computation of strong (gluon) quark interaction does, of course, give a more direct answer; but in science it is always important to check the central hypotheses by several independent methods.

Three of my papers—one published before my exile and two while I was in Gorky—are dedicated to cosmological problems. In the first article, I examine the mechanism by which baryon asymmetry arises. The general consideration, in this article, of the dynamics of reactions that lead to the baryon asymmetry of the universe, might be of some interest. However, the specifics of this process were treated on the basis of my old, and now abandoned, hypothesis of a "combined" conservation law (the sum of the quark and lepton numbers is conserved).

Earlier in this book, I explained how I came to this idea and why I now consider it incorrect. On the whole, I consider this part of the work unsuccessful, and I am much more satisfied with that portion of the paper that deals with the "many-sheeted" model of the universe. Here I am speaking of the hypothesis that the universe first expands, then contracts, then expands again, and so on, an infinite number of times. Such models have attracted cosmologists' attention for quite a while: some authors have called them "oscillating" models, but I prefer the term "many-sheeted" [or "mulit-page"], which seems more expressive and more in tune with the emotional and philosophical implications of indefinitely repeated cycles of existence.

While the conservation of baryons was accepted, however, the many-sheeted model encountered an insuperable difficulty that followed from one of the basic laws of nature—the second law of thermodynamics.

Here I must digress. Thermodynamics deals with one characteristic of an object's state known as entropy. I recall my father's once reminiscing about a popular-science book, *The Tsaritsa of the World and Her Shadow,* in which the Tsaritsa is energy, and her shadow—entropy. In contrast to energy, which obeys a conservation law, the second law of thermodynamics demands that entropy must always increase (or, more precisely, never decrease). Processes in which the entropy of a body doesn't change are termed reversible (e.g., mechanical motion without friction). Reversible processes are abstractions; they are the limiting case of *irreversible* processes, which are accompanied by an increase of the system's entropy (from friction, heat exchange, etc.). Mathematically, the change in entropy is equal to the absorbed heat divided by the body's temperature. It is also assumed, or can be derived from general principles, that the entropy at absolute zero is zero, and that the entropy of the vacuum is also zero.)

A numerical example will make this clearer. A certain body which is at a temperature of 200 degrees transfers 400 calories of heat to a second body which is at a temperature of 100 degrees. The entropy of the first body decreases by 400/200; that is, by 2 units. The entropy of the second body increases by 400/100, or 4 units, and therefore the total entropy increases by 2 units, as required by the second law. Note that the result follows from the fact that heat flows from a hotter body to a colder. The growth of entropy in non-equilibrium processes leads to a warming of matter.

Returning to cosmology and to the many-sheeted universe, if we assume the number of baryons is fixed, then the entropy per baryon will increase indefinitely with time. With each cycle of the universe, matter will become hotter, which means that the conditions in the universe will never be repeated!

This difficulty is eliminated if we abandon the assumption that baryon number is conserved and follow my idea of 1966—since developed by many others—that baryon number arises from "entropy" (that is, from neutral hot matter) in the early stages of the expansion of the universe. In this case, the number of baryons formed is proportional to the entropy in each cycle of expansion and contraction, and so the conditions for the evolution of matter and creation of structure might be approximately the same in every cycle.

I first introduced the term "many-sheeted" model in a 1969 article. (In my more recent papers I have used the same term in a somewhat different sense; I mention this to avoid misunderstanding.)

In the first of three articles (1979), I examined a model in which space is considered flat on the average. I also assumed that Einstein's cosmological constant is not zero but very small and negative. In this case, the equations of Einstein's general theory of relativity show that the expansion of the universe will unavoidably turn into a collapse. Then each cycle will duplicate the previous one in terms of its average characteristics. Essentially, this model is spatially flat (Euclidean). The next two articles extend the work to models in which space is Lobachevskian [curved negatively like a saddle] or displays the geometry of a hypersphere (positively curved—the three-dimensional analogue of the familiar two-dimensional sphere).[15] In these cases, however, another problem arises. From one cycle to the next the increase in entropy leads to an increase of the radius of the universe at the corresponding moment in each cycle. Extrapolating to the past, we see that any given cycle can have been preceded by only a finite number of cycles. (I have been informed that a similar model was examined by Richard Tolman in the 1930s.)

In the "standard" cosmology (the "single-sheeted" model) there exists a problem: what existed before the moment of maximal density? The many-sheeted models (that are not flat) also afford no escape from this problem; the question merely becomes "what existed before the first cycle of expansion?" One might take the point of view that the first beginning of expansion[16] (or simply the beginning of expansion in the standard model) was the moment of Creation, and so the question of what was before it lies beyond the limits of scientific research. However, an approach that places no limit on the scientific investigation of the material world and space-time in my opinion is better and more fruitful, even though it leaves no room for an act of Creation: the basic religious concept of the divine meaning of existence does not concern science and lies beyond its limits.

I am aware of two alternative hypotheses concerning what preceded the

---

[15][I.e., the surface of a three-dimensional sphere has two dimensions, and the surface of a four-dimensional sphere has three dimensions.]

[16][Usually called the Big Bang. The author does not use this term, probably because "Big Bang" implies the existence of a singularity.]

beginning. One, I believe, was first advanced by me in 1966 and has been refined in later papers. This is the hypothesis of the "reversal of time's arrow," which is closely linked with the so-called reversibility problem.

As I said earlier, wholly reversible processes do not exist in nature. Friction, heat exchange, the radiation of light, chemical reactions, biological processes are all characterized by irreversibility, a definite distinction between past and future. A film of some irreversible process when run backward on a screen will show something that will never occur in real life (for instance, a freely rotating flywheel increasing its rate of rotation while the bearing cools). Irreversibility finds quantitative expression in the monotonic increase of entropy. On the other hand, the atoms, electrons, atomic nuclei, etc., that make up all objects move according to the laws of mechanics (*quantum* mechanics, though this doesn't affect the argument here), which are entirely time-reversible. (In quantum field theory this requires a simultaneous CP-reflection; see Chapter 18). The asymmetry of the two directions of time (what we call the presence of an "arrow of time") despite the fact that the equations of motion are time-symmetric was noted by the founders of statistical mechanics.

The discussion of this question had begun by the last decade of the nineteenth century, occasionally becoming rather heated. The resolution, which was generally acceptable to everyone, came as part of the hypothesis that the asymmetry arose from the initial conditions—the positions and velocities of all atoms and fields in the "infinitely distant past." These initial conditions should be in some well-defined sense "accidental." At this point the entropy is minimal.

As I suggested in 1966 (and more explicitly in 1980), in cosmological theories having a point that is singled out in time, one ought to relate the accidental initial conditions not to the infinitely distant past $(t = -\infty)$, but to this special point $(t = 0)$.

Then, at this point entropy automatically has a minimum value, and as one moves from this point forward or backward in time, entropy grows. This is what I named "the reversal of time's arrow." Since with the reversal of time's arrow, all physical and informational processes also reverse, no paradoxes arise. Although these ideas of the reversal of time's arrow have not, as far as I know, received recognition in the scientific world, they seem to me to hold some interest.[17]

The reversal of time's arrow restores to the cosmological picture the symmetry of the two directions in time that exists in the equations of motion.

---

[17][The author is not using the term "reversal of time's arrow" in the sense it is often encountered in cosmological literature: that time will reverse when (and if) the universe begins to recollapse.]

In 1966–1967, I proposed that at the point of reversal, CPT-reflection takes place. This assumption was one of the jumping-off points for my work on baryon asymmetry. Here I shall set forth another hypothesis (Kirzhnitz, Linde, Guth, Turner, and others had a hand in it; I am responsible only for the observation that the reversal of time's arrow takes place).

In modern theories of elementary particles it is assumed that the vacuum can exist in different states: "stable," with zero energy density; and "unstable," with a huge, positive energy density (an effective cosmological constant). The latter is sometimes referred to as the "false vacuum." One of the solutions to the equations of general relativity for such theories is as follows. The universe is closed and at every moment it constitutes a "hypersphere" of finite volume. The radius of the universe has a minimum finite value at some moment in time (call it t = o) and increases from that value both forward and backward in time. The entropy is equal to zero for the false vacuum (as in general for any vacuum), and as time moves forward or backward from t = o, the entropy grows as a consequence of the decay of the false vacuum into the true, stable vacuum. In this way there is a reversal of the arrow of time at t = o (but not cosmological CPT-symmetry, which demands infinite density at the point of reflection).

Just as in the case of CPT-symmetry, all conserved numbers are equal to zero (since at t = o a state of vacuum exists). Therefore, in this case it is also necessary to assume that the observed baryon asymmetry arises in a dynamic manner made possible by a violation of CP-invariance.

An alternative hypothesis concerning the prehistory of the universe proposes not just one universe or two, as in the above hypothesis regarding the reversal of time's arrow [one at each side of t = o], but many radically different universes which have originated out of some "primordial" space (or compose its parts—perhaps the same thing). Other universes and the primordial space—if it makes sense to talk about it at all—might differ from our universe in the number of "macroscopic" space and time dimensions. (In our universe, there are three space dimensions and one of time. The reader should not be overly concerned about the adjective "macroscopic," which is connected with the hypothesis of compactification, according to which the majority of dimensions are closed up on themselves on minuscule scales.)

It is assumed that there is no causal connection among the various universes. It is precisely this that justifies their interpretation as separate universes, together making up the grandiose structure I call the "Mega-Universe." Other authors have discussed variations of this hypothesis; for example, Zeldovich defended the hypothesis of the repeated birth of closed universes in one of his articles.

The idea of a Mega-Universe is extremely interesting; perhaps the truth does indeed lie in this direction. But for me, one point remains unclear in some of these models. It is admissible to assume that the conditions in various parts of space are entirely different—but the laws of nature must be identical, everywhere and always. Nature cannot operate like the Queen in *Alice in Wonderland*, changing the rules of the game at will. Existence is not a game. My doubts concern those hypotheses that allow a breakdown of the space-time continuum. Are such processes admissible? Aren't such discontinuities violations of the laws of nature? I repeat that I am not certain that my fears are well founded. It may be that, as in the question of the conservation of fermion number, my perspective is too narrow. And it is entirely possible to come up with hypotheses in which universes are born without a breakdown of the continuum.

The idea that many—or perhaps an infinite number of—universes differing in their parameters are born spontaneously and that our particular universe is distinguished by conditions favorable for the evolution of life and intelligence is known as the "anthropic principle" (AP). Zeldovich notes that the first investigation of the AP in the context of the expanding universe was apparently carried out in 1958 by Idlis.

In the many-sheeted universe the AP can also play a role in singling out one of the successive cycles (we live in the cycle with conditions admitting life). This possibility is examined in my article "The Many-Sheeted Model of the Universe." One of the difficulties in this model is that the formation of black holes and their subsequent merging violate symmetry at the stage of collapse, to such an extent that it is unclear whether the conditions in the next cycle will be favorable for the evolution of highly organized structures.

On the other hand, in sufficiently prolonged cycles both baryon decay and evaporation of black holes will take place, leading to the smoothing out of all inhomogeneities of the density. I have suggested that the combined action of these two mechanisms—the formation of black holes and the smoothing-out of inhomogeneities—results in the alternation of "smooth" cycles with more "turbulent" ones. Our cycle, according to this assumption, was preceded by a "smooth" one in which black holes did not form.

Let's take, for example, a closed universe with a "false" vacuum and the point when the arrow of time reverses. The cosmological constant in this model can be taken to be zero; the collapse takes place simply through the gravitational attraction of matter. The duration of the cycles increases as a consequence of the growth of entropy in each cycle and will eventually exceed any given value (approaching infinity), so that the conditions for the decay of protons and black-hole evaporation are fulfilled.

Many-sheeted models give an answer to the so-called large-numbers mystery (an alternative explanation is the inflationary hypothesis of Guth and others).

Why is the number of photons and protons in the observable universe so large [roughly 10^{87}], but finite? The answer given by the many-sheeted model is very simple. We assume that many cycles have occurred since the moment $t = 0$. During each cycle the entropy (that is, the number of photons) increases, as well as, correspondingly, the baryon surplus. The ratio of photons to baryons in each cycle is a constant, since it is determined by the dynamics of the early stages of the expansion for that cycle. The number of cycles from the moment $t = 0$ can be determined from the observed number of photons and baryons. Since the numbers increase in geometric progression, the number of cycles since $t = 0$ shouldn't be excessively large.

As a by-product of my 1982 work I derived a formula for the probability that black holes merge under mutual gravitation. An estimate based on this formula was used in Zeldovich and Novikov's *Structure and Evolution of the Universe.*

One other intriguing possibility—probably only a fantasy—is linked to the many-sheeted model. A highly developed intellect, having evolved over billions and billions of years, might find a way to encode its most valuable information for its successors in the next cycle, separated by that period of superhigh density. An analogy would be the transmission by living organisms of genetic information from generation to generation, compressed and encoded in the chromosomes of a fertilized cell. This all seemed too fantastic to include in my scientific papers, but in the pages of this book I'm allowing my imagination free rein. And independently of this, the many-sheeted model of the universe has, in my view, important philosophical implications.

Now I would like to return to the spring of 1978. Soon after Alexei's departure, Lusia and I traveled to Leningrad. We took Ruth with us, as we didn't want to leave her alone in Moscow, and we stayed as usual on Pushkin Street. I soon came down with the flu, and they quarantined me in Zoya's room, while Ruth moved in with Regina (unfortunately, these precautions were to no avail, and Ruth became quite seriously ill). As I lay in bed, running a slight fever, I amused myself by thinking up "brainteasers." Here are a few examples:

1. Let us examine the infinite series $a_n = n! + 1$. Prove that the series contains an infinite number of primes. Estimate the number of primes $B(b)$ that are contained in the first b members of the series. For a heuristic examination of the problem (and its variations and generalizations) I used the semi-intuitive idea of the probability $p(i)$ that some number i is a prime. Of course this is far from a rigorous mathematical proof. I don't know whether the answer is true or whether a more strict analysis is known.

1a. Prove that numbers of the form $(n^2)! + 1$ with $n > 1$ are not prime.

2. Show that for the Fibbonacci series ($a_n = a_{n-1} + a_{n-2}$ with $a_1 = 0$ and $a_2 = 1$), the numbers a_n include multiples of any whole number b. Show that if the values of a_1 and a_2 are changed, then the conclusion is not necessarily true.

3. In 1985, on hunger strike and detained in the Gorky hospital, I spent long hours gazing at the clock hanging on the wall of my room. At night, the dim hospital illumination made it at times difficult for me to distinguish the hour hand from the minute hand, and I thought up this brainteaser:

An absent-minded watchmaker accidentally fastens two hands of equal length on a clock with the usual twelve-hour dial. Because of this, there are moments when the time can be read in either of two ways. Find all these ambiguous moments. (I was later told [in 1988] that this problem was published in an American popular-science magazine.)

4. One more brainteaser from an earlier date. Two players are engaged in an "egg war." Each one picks an egg at random from a basket, and then the players strike one egg against the other. The broken egg is thrown away, and the loser takes a new one, while the winner saves his for the next round. (It is assumed that the winning egg remains sound and that the outcome of each round depends only on the relative strength of the eggs.) The question: what is the probability of winning round b + 1 after winning the b preceding rounds?

Now BACK to our life in Gorky. We quickly established a routine, with Lusia traveling every six weeks or so (more frequently during the first year) to Moscow, leaving me alone in the apartment (with a policeman standing guard at the door). She would be gone ten to fifteen days. Each of her trips meant a sleepless night on the train—freezing cold in winter, stifling in summer— quite often in a packed coach when she couldn't get a reservation in first class. This all took a toll, but Lusia's expeditions were vital; they provided our only regular link with the outside world and with the children overseas, and they allowed her to pass on my statements, appeals, and interviews to foreign correspondents, and to send the manuscript of these memoirs out of the country. This all had to be accomplished on the spot without prearrangement, and it placed the utmost demands on Lusia's energy and determination.

She would return laden with supplies—containers of cottage cheese, butter, meat, and other items that were practically unavailable in Gorky, a city with a population of more than a million. To be fair, I should note that this situation improved somewhat in 1983, particularly with regard to vegetables, while in Moscow things got worse. Certain scarce items, like sausages, were sold at factories and other enterprises to employees only, but that didn't help us. The

KGB energetically spread rumors that in Gorky I was receiving deliveries of Finnish salamis and other delicacies available to Party officials. Many people believed this falsehood. On Fridays, I could look out the window and see the special food packages arriving for the KGB agents assigned to my case; the number of packages indicated that there must have been at least thirty-five agents—and these were only the foot soldiers; the chiefs kept their distance.

While Lusia was away, I tried to do as much work as possible, leaving the house only to buy bread and vegetables, always with my bag of documents and manuscripts slung over my shoulder (it weighed twenty-five pounds before the last robbery reduced the load). I was careful never to let the bag out of my hands.

When Lusia returned, we would spend the first day exchanging news. She'd report on people and events—Lusia may be swayed by emotion, but her reactions are to the point and generally on the mark. Sometimes I had letters to read from Ruth, the children, and the grandchildren. The letters were brought into the country *sub rosa,* not because they contained secrets, but because letters sent through the ordinary mail weren't delivered; only some— but not all—of the postcards sent by Ruth reached us that way.

Lusia would bring scientific and other books. The written material she'd collected, together with her comments, would largely determine my priorities. On the second day we would set to to work, with our pace becoming increasingly hectic as the date for her next departure approached. But we did manage to watch television in the evenings and on rare occasions go to the movies. In 1980 and 1981, we would sometimes take a walk to the banks of the Oka River to enjoy the wonderful view, or in autumn wander through the fields, taking care to stay within our prescribed limits. These moments when we left the city and captivity behind us were precious, but by 1982, we had little strength or time for walks, even short ones.

We secured the implicit right to visit the Khainovskys, old friends and distant relatives of Ruth and Lusia. In the 1950s, Ruth, recently released from camp, and forbidden to stay with Lusia in Leningrad, had taken her granddaughter Tanya and moved in with the Khainovskys for a time. She was later banished from Gorky and moved to a village twenty miles away. We were lucky to have the Khainovskys living nearby, and we became close to the entire family. Yuri, a vital, compassionate and sociable man, was its soul. His life had been difficult; childhood in a family of political exiles; being wounded at the front; arrest and imprisonment for speaking too freely; long years on the edge of poverty. Yet the Khainovskys led a normal, happy life, surrounded by friends. They weren't allowed into our apartment, but we weren't prevented from visiting them. The first few times, our KGB agents kept peering nervously in through the windows; then they must have received new instructions, because they later would sit quietly in their cars while they waited for us at the Khainovskys'.

Physicists from FIAN first traveled to Gorky to talk with me in April 1980. After three visits, there was a hiatus (for reasons I will explain later) until 1982, and after the theft of my bag in October 1982, the visits were again interrupted. Although such meetings were important to me, they were no substitute for the normal scientific interchange of seminars and conferences, informal and uninhibited give-and-take with scientists of one's own choosing, or chalk talks where one can ask on the spot for the speaker to explain obscure points in his work. Every scientist knows how essential all this is. My knowledge that the physicists' visits to Gorky were "managed" and designed in part to muffle the campaign in my defense added to the strain of these occasions.

Only one physicist in all of the USSR came to see me (and twice) in Gorky without official permission—my former university classmate, Misha Levin. Levin had been arrested and convicted in a 1940s political case, and after being released, he lived and worked for several years in Gorky. He was finally permitted to return to Moscow after the "thaw." We managed to meet with Levin (and with two other friends, Natasha Gesse and Lusia's classmate Slava Lapin) by showing up at a prearranged time at the main post office or in a café nearby; we would walk around town, talking (and in Natasha's case, dropping in at the Khainovskys'). Through a misunderstanding, Lapin went to Shcherbinki, where he was detained and questioned by the KGB for two hours. We were lucky enough to run into him on the street after we'd given up hope of seeing him.

During my exile in Gorky, whenever foreign scientists came to the USSR and asked about me, Academy officials (Alexandrov, Skriabin, and Velikhov: the president, secretary and vice-president, respectively) would fill them full of moonshine: I was living in a wonderful apartment, I received a minister's salary, I had a secretary and a maid, I was given the finest medical care and special food rations. These were outright lies. Of course, Lusia did do a secretary's work in addition to her regular duties of cleaning the apartment, shopping for groceries, and cooking. When she was away, I took over the household chores. The medical care I received (prior to my extended hunger strikes in 1984 and 1985) boiled down to the dental work that led to the theft of my bag, involuntary hospitalization when Lusia and I conducted our hunger strike (and then I was discharged immediately after I suffered a heart attack), and the presence of medical personnel when I was stunned by a narcotic so that my bag could be stolen from our car.

Before leaving for Moscow, Lusia would prepare a week's food and leave it for me in the refrigerator. I would take her to the station, and a new cycle would begin. . . .

* * *

OUR LIFE in Gorky may not have seemed especially difficult to some people, and certainly it wasn't as terrible as life in a camp or prison. But what I was subjected to was absolutely illegitimate—and very dangerous, for keeping me in unlawful isolation made it easier for the authorities to take arbitrary actions—under cover of law—against all prisoners of conscience. (The situation reminds me a bit of a ploy used by officials during the severe housing shortage that followed the war. They would pacify complainers by saying: "What are you getting excited about? One academician we know is living in a bathtub!" I never believed in the existence of that mythical academician, but in Gorky, through no fault of my own, I played a similar role.)

Our life in Gorky, which to outsiders may have seemed peaceful except for the KGB's occasional excesses, in fact strained our strength and our nerves to the limit. It was particularly hard on Lusia, who, in addition to her constant journeys on overcrowded, uncomfortable trains, in Moscow had to bear the full burden of dealing with reporters, well-wishers from abroad, dissidents (both local and from elsewhere in the USSR), and other visitors. You had to be there to comprehend fully the physical and psychological toll this all took. Natasha Gesse remarked after staying with Lusia in Moscow: "No one can live like this. You're wearing yourself out." These words unfortunately proved prophetic.

Lusia had to cope with a good deal apart from our personal affairs. She had to handle by herself the human rights work we used to share, passing on information about arrests and trials, organizing press conferences, participating in the Moscow Helsinki Group, sending packages to prisoners (perhaps the most time-consuming task), etc., etc. She wasn't a spring chicken and was far from healthy (I wasn't in the best of shape, either). She'd always lived life without sparing herself, and her concussion, her 1974 thyroid surgery, and other medical problems had taken their toll.

The greatest tragedy of her life was the separation from her children and grandchildren. When they were forced to leave the Soviet Union and disappeared into the infinitely distant world beyond our borders, we realized it would be hard on us, but we had no idea how hard. Lusia's parting with her mother in 1980 added to the pain.

People say that a person deprived of connection to the outside world becomes a living corpse. If my surrealistic isolation in Gorky did not turn me into a dead man, that was entirely due to Lusia. From the first day to the last, she helped me set a course that preserved my honor and dignity through all the vicissitudes of fate. She sustained continually my public activity, my science, and my life.

48

LIZA ALEXEYEVA

ALEXEI LEFT the country on March 1, 1978. In May, Liza Alexeyeva began living with us as part of our family. Soon after that, her problems began. On a far-fetched pretext, she was kept from taking her final examinations that spring, and thus lost her chance for a diploma. In July 1979, she was fired from a job as a computer operator—clearly on instructions from above, since she was well regarded at her place of work. After my banishment, the difficulties multiplied. Liza's first attempt to obtain an exit visa failed, and a protracted separation from Alexei ensued: it was nearly four years before she was permitted to join him, and then only after a long campaign to overcome official resistance to her emigration, capped by a 17-day hunger strike conducted by Lusia and myself in November–December 1981.

Liza's connection to me made her situation many times worse, as she became in effect a hostage to my public activities. Her parents' attitude was yet another complication. Decades of isolation from the world, coupled with incessant propaganda, have given Soviet citizens distorted notions of life abroad and prejudiced them against emigration, which is viewed as tantamount to treason. Émigrés, it is assumed, inevitably become agents of the CIA or other foreign intelligence services. Liza's parents were prey to this prejudice, a fact the authorities exploited. In early 1978, Liza's mother, who hadn't yet become aware of the relationship, found a letter from Alexei in Liza's coat pocket. (Letters from abroad were still getting through to us then.) Her mother had a fit: to her, corresponding with an émigré was dangerous nonsense—never mind emigration! Liza's father, a retired military officer who was at the time employed as an engineer in a factory near Moscow, is a sincere and honest man, but a hot-tempered and stubborn one, and it was clear that it would take something extraordinary to reverse her parents' attitude.

Liza was of age—she was twenty-two in 1978—and her parents had no legal right to prevent her departure. In practice, however, it was extremely difficult to submit a visa application without parental consent, since OVIR required an affidavit signed by the applicant's parents stating that they had no financial claims against the would-be emigrant. Lack of the affidavit could bring the whole process to a halt. Some frustrated applicants sent their documents to the Supreme Soviet, which usually passed them on to OVIR despite the missing affidavit; the applicants hoped to overcome their parents' objections while OVIR was reviewing their other documents. Liza tried this, including an invitation sent from Israel by Tomar Feigin, Efrem's mother. No lawful grounds existed for forcing an applicant to submit an invitation, but Liza nonetheless complied even with this arbitrary requirement. Later, she submitted invitations from Alexei, the first one addressed to her as his fiancée and the second as his wife (after their 1981 marriage by proxy).

IN APRIL 1979, soon after Lusia's return from Italy, five of those imprisoned in the Leningrad "airplane" cases—Anatoly Altman, Hillel Butman, Arie Khnokh, Boris Penson, and Wolf Zalmanson—were released fourteen months before the end of their ten-year sentences and issued visas for emigration to Israel. This was probably a goodwill gesture made in anticipation of the June 1979 Brezhnev-Carter meeting in Vienna, where they signed the SALT II treaty. Lusia, who had done so much for the prisoners and thought of them as friends, went to meet them in Riga, where they were released on April 20.[1] She hoped that one of them might claim Liza as his fiancée and ask that she be allowed to leave the country with him. The high-level international stakes involved in the whole affair almost guaranteed success for this plan. She explained her idea on the train from Riga to Moscow, and the discussion with the ex-prisoners continued in our kitchen on April 22. Unfortunately, they hesitated to carry out her request; and then, feeling awkward, they left the country without saying goodbye to us.

I was then suffering severe dizzy spells (apparently the consequence of some sort of circulatory problem) and had to rest in bed. On April 29, we heard the sensational news that five more prisoners—Mark Dymshits, Alexander Ginzburg, Eduard Kuznetsov, Valentin Moroz, and Georgi Vins—had been exchanged at New York's Kennedy Airport for two Soviet spies.

Eight of Pastor Vins's relatives received permission to join him in America,

---

[1][Butman was released in Leningrad, rather than Riga, but all five met in Moscow and left the USSR together on April 27.]

including his son Pyotr, a member of the Ukrainian Helsinki Group, who had recently completed a one-year sentence for "leading a parasitic way of life." I had spoken many times in behalf of both father and son, and I decided to address the same request to Pyotr that we had to the "airmen." Still bedridden, I wrote a letter and asked Malva Landa to deliver it to him in Kiev. When she arrived at the station there, however, she was detained and searched (supposedly in connection with a robbery on the train), my letter was confiscated, and she was forced to take the next train back to Moscow. She wouldn't have been able to reach Pyotr in any case: the Vins home was surrounded by the KGB, and no one was allowed in. Pyotr left without Liza, another setback.

At this point, Liza swallowed a lethal dose of pills. Fortunately, Lusia noticed her peculiar lethargy and called an ambulance, and she was saved. The suicide attempt, which Liza came to regret deeply, was the impulsive act of an inexperienced person caught in a tragic situation. I mention this incident here only because the KGB subsequently made use of it.

Liza was hospitalized for several days. Shortly before she was discharged, Vladimir Fainberg, secretary of the theoretical department's Party organization, approached me after a seminar at FIAN and began to talk about Liza's situation with evident embarrassment; he later came to our apartment to follow up on our conversation. Liza's father had complained to the Party secretary responsible for all of FIAN, and had visited the district Party committee, demanding that Liza be removed from our apartment and from my influence. The district committee was aware of Liza's suicide attempt. I gave Fainberg a brief explanation of the true state of affairs; he replied, looking yet more embarrassed, that the district committee had requested that I not publicize Liza's suicide attempt. He promised that someone would speak to her father and try to calm him. There was even a hint that she would receive help in obtaining a visa. None of these promises was kept.

We honored the district committee's request; we had already decided to spare Liza the pain of having the story disclosed. A month later, however, it became clear that the district committee was serving as a tool of the KGB. *Nedelya, Izvestia*'s Sunday supplement, devoted a full column to Liza and her suicide attempt, painting a grim portrait of an immoral drug addict—but at least shielding her identity by simply identifying her as "N." It was Lusia who was the main target of the slander, and she and I were referred to by name. *Nedelya* had taken advantage of our public silence to get their version into print first. The authors' KGB connections were betrayed when *Nedelya* published a facsimile of my letter to Pyotr Vins which had been taken from Malva Landa.

The article, however, backfired. Readers, especially women readers, wrote *Nedelya*, asking: "If they're that much in love, why can't she go and join him without all the fuss?" Yes—why not?

In late February 1980, Olga Levshin, Alexei's first wife, left for America with their daughter, Katya. Olga's emigration was unexpected, for us and for her friends. The circumstances are obscure, but the KGB probably expedited her visa.

Immediately after her departure, a second article appeared in *Nedelya*. It contradicted the first article in many respects, but who would bother to compare them? Alexei was now said to have strayed (no mention now of Alexei and Liza's love for each other) and then begged pardon at his wife's feet. With the passage of time, Olga had forgiven him, and she was now on her way to join her husband. Lusia (derided as a doting grandmother, as if that were a crime) was trying to arrange an exit visa for Olga and one for Liza, as well, "in order to eliminate a witness to her [Lusia's] crimes." The article, entitled "Beware!" warned "N" [Liza], who supposedly was free to leave the country at any time, that the diabolical Elena Bonner was sending her into a void, since Alexei and Olga had been reconciled. The article thus became the authorities' arcane means of informing Liza that her application had been turned down.

Both *Nedelya* articles were reprinted in the local *Gorky Worker* and, in abridged form, abroad.[2]

It was about this same time that *Sette Giorno*, an Italian newspaper, printed a story on Lusia's "crimes" based on an "interview" with Semyon Zlotnik—the mythical character invented by the KGB who'd cropped up in the "yellow packets" affair. Written in scandal-sheet style, the article slanderously mixed fact and fiction, but demonstrated a detailed knowledge of Lusia's life from the cradle on (collected, no doubt, by an army of KGB sleuths). There was other evidence of an extensive investigation under way; the chief of Lusia's wartime hospital train, now eighty years old, was questioned for several hours by the Leningrad KGB. The *Sette Giorno* article enlarged upon earlier fabrications concerning Lusia's alleged involvement in the deaths of the wives of Moisei Zlotnik and Vsevolod Bagritsky. It concluded with a sinister threat: Elena Bonner had escaped responsibility for two crimes, but if she commits a third, she'll answer for it. That was the point of all this slander. While trying to drive Liza to despair and another suicide attempt, the KGB was laying the groundwork to accuse Lusia of incitement to suicide.

Olga settled in Boston and began working there. Her divorce from Alexei became final in July 1980. She has since remarried and moved to California, but Katya still visits Alexei regularly.

After his divorce, Alexei tried to send an invitation to Liza as his fiancée, but the Soviet consulate in Washington refused to follow its normal practice

---

[2][The first article was printed in *Nedelya*, no. 26, 1979, and the second one in *Nedelya*, no. 11, 1980.]

and attest to Alexei's signature—yet one more proof of the singularity of our situation.

Meanwhile, Liza's situation grew more desperate. For a few months, she was able to visit me freely, but on May 15, 1980, while on the way to Gorky, she left Ruth to buy cigarettes at Moscow's Yaroslavl Station. She was grabbed by plainsclothesmen and dragged off to the office of the railway police. The KGB agents told her: "You know who we are. We don't waste words. You're forbidden to go to Gorky. You shouldn't be living on Chkalov Street. Go home to your parents." (The state of her family relations made this impossible.)

A few days later Liza was summoned to the KGB and officially warned that she would be charged under Article 190-1 (slandering the Soviet system) if she continued her activities. There were other, less formal threats, for instance an incident in Leningrad, when a KGB agent who was following Liza as she accompanied Natalya Gesse to the market warned Liza: "We're going to kill you."

In the summer of 1980, I sent a telegram to Brezhnev asking permission for Liza to join Alexei. I stressed that she was being held hostage as a counter to my public activities.

In August I wrote a more detailed letter to Evgeny Velikhov, a vice president of the Academy of Sciences. It was two months before Velikhov replied to my letter and follow-up telegrams; on October 14, he finally sent me the following telegram (I cite from memory): "Taking steps to explore the possibility of satisfying your request. I will let you know the results." That was the last I heard from Velikhov; he made no reply to my subsequent letters and telegrams.

Lusia and I appealed on Liza's behalf to many persons in the USSR and the West. On November 20 I sent a lengthy open letter to Anatoly Alexandrov, and on February 3, 1981, letters to Yakov Zeldovich and Yuli Khariton. I felt morally justified in appealing to them on Liza's behalf; I'd worked closely with them for more than twenty years, and I counted Zeldovich as a personal friend. As I mentioned earlier, he wrote, pleading his inability to help Liza—his own situation was precarious, he complained; he wasn't allowed to travel any further than Hungary. (I received no written reply at all from Khariton, only indirect word that he shared Zeldovich's sentiments.) Zeldovich was a member of the Academy and a three-time Hero of Socialist Labor. He had never attempted to capitalize on his status, which was every bit as exalted as mine had been years ago. And all I asked him to do was to lobby behind the scenes for Liza!

She had submitted her application to OVIR on November 20, 1979. Eighteen months later, on May 12, 1981, she was summoned to OVIR and informed that her application had been denied. Speaking in the presence of his assistants and two other persons, evidently from the KGB, Colonel Romanenkov, the head of the regional OVIR, told Liza that the basis for the denial was "insufficient grounds for reunification." Liza by this time had an invitation from Alexei, her fiancé, as well as Tomar Feigin's invitation—sufficient to satisfy OVIR's formal requirements. One KGB officer urged Liza to renounce in writing any further attempts to leave the USSR, and then added in a meaningful tone: "That way we'll both have some peace." His proposal, blackmail pure and simple, was testimony to the legal and moral bankruptcy of the authorities' position. Liza flatly refused.

The menace underlying this "peace" offer became evident when Liza was called in for questioning on May 14 and again on May 19, ostensibly in connection with the case of Felix Serebrov.[3] The interrogations were crudely carried out, with shouting that Liza found intolerable, threats of arrest and intimations of physical violence, one investigator swearing he'd throw her out the window.

On May 26 I sent Brezhnev another, more detailed letter about Liza's case, reminding him that we had been personally acquainted for more than two decades and pointing out that the KGB's use of Liza as a hostage or as an outlet for venting their hostility toward me would mar the USSR's reputation abroad. I received no reply.

It was then, in May or June 1981, that I said to Lusia: "It seems to me we've tried everything except a hunger strike." And she agreed.

Meanwhile, on June 9, Alexei was married to Liza by proxy in the district court of Butte, Montana, one of the two American states which allow proxy marriages. The ceremony did not solve the problem of their separation, but it had great significance as an affirmation of their love. At the ceremony, the role of proxy bride was played by Edward Kline, a good friend of our family, who had Liza's power of attorney.[4]

The Soviet authorities and press maintained that the marriage had no legal validity. A foreign correspondent who phoned OVIR and queried whether Liza's marriage might mean a change in her emigration status was told sharply that the marriage was not recognized—and this automatic negative response, once published, acquired a spurious legitimacy (this despite the fact, which we later discovered, that the "Fundamentals of Legislation on Marriage and the Family" obliged the USSR to recognize the marriage, which had been contracted outside the USSR in full compliance with local law). The KGB would hardly have paid attention to the legal niceties in any event, but Liza's parents

---

[3][Felix Serebrov, a member of the Working Commission on the Abuse of Psychiatry and of the Moscow Helsinki Group, was arrested on January 8, 1981, and sentenced on July 21, 1981, to four years labor camp and five years internal exile.]

[4][In *Alone Together* (p. 129), Elena Bonner describes the difficulties she had in convincing American consular officials in Moscow to notarize Liza's signature on this document.]

did change their minds about her emigration after learning of the marriage—
Alexei's act convinced them of his love for Liza. In the summer of 1981, Liza's
father wrote Brezhnev asking that his daughter be allowed to leave. Lusia and
I did not learn of this until later, and the KGB still continued to cite her
parents' objection as an obstacle to Liza's emigration.

In September I once more approached scientists on Liza's behalf, writing
to many of the foreign physicists invited to a major conference on controlled
fusion scheduled that month for Moscow. Most of them chose to adhere to
the ongoing boycott of the USSR, however, and did not attend. I neglected
to write to Professor Falker Engelmann, president of the European Physical
Society, who was to chair the conference together with Velikhov, but I did
write again to Velikhov and to Boris Kadomtsev and Pyotr Kapitsa. I received
no response. I later heard that Engelmann on his own initiative had delayed
the formal opening of the conference for two days, demanding that Sakharov
and the refusenik Yakov Alpert be allowed to attend, and was persuaded to
yield only by some tortuous arguments advanced by Velikhov (who did not
enlighten Engelmann as to Liza's situation).

We were now determined to proceed with a hunger strike. In September,
we learned that Brezhnev would be traveling to Bonn in November for talks
with Helmut Schmidt, and we decided that timing our fast to coincide with
the Brezhnev visit would give it the best chance for success. Our two-year
campaign had made Liza's case widely known, so that we could count on
sympathy and support. Most people would understand that a hunger strike was
not some bizarre extravagance—it was our one remaining option.

At first, Lusia and I exchanged written notes about our plans so that the
KGB couldn't eavesdrop on us. Little discussion was necessary, since we agreed
that the hunger strike was a moral imperative and our only practical course of
action. Our unity, reflected in this common decision, sustained us during our
hunger strike, both when we were together in the apartment and later, during
the final, decisive days, when we were taken by force to different hospitals.

Once we had made our decision, there was no reason to conceal it. On the
contrary, by declaring our intentions, we gave the KGB an opportunity to let
Liza go quietly and save face. It's not our fault they didn't take it.

In October, we sent out many appeals for support, including a message—in
fact, my second—to Chancellor Schmidt, and my "Letter to Foreign Colleagues."

Lusia and I found it difficult to write to Ruth and the children about our
decision. We realized how painful our hunger strike would be for them, more
difficult than it would be for us, but we counted on their understanding,
especially Alexei's, and on the bond that existed among us. Liza would be put
to an equal test. Fortunately, we weren't mistaken. With no direct communica-

tion with us during our hunger strike, the family did more than we believed possible to discourage interference with our plan and to hasten our victory.

I drafted telegrams to Brezhnev and Alexandrov, but at Lusia's request postponed sending them; there could be no retreat after this step was taken. Lusia traveled to Moscow with letters announcing our hunger strike, also taking notebooks containing my diary and the substantial work I had done on my memoirs. I didn't want the KGB to get any of this. A week later I received a telegram from Lusia: "Meet me with porters. Bringing water and a battery." The water was Borzhomi mineral water, which helps to maintain the body's electrolyte balance while fasting. It was impossible to find in Gorky, and not so easy in Moscow either, but Yuri Shikhanovich "collared" (that favorite Soviet term) 100 bottles. (We had a lot left over since we drank only a few bottles before we were hospitalized.) The battery was for our car.

We decided not to delay any longer, and on October 21 I sent the telegrams to Brezhnev and Alexandrov, announcing that our hunger strike would begin on November 22, the day before Brezhnev was scheduled to arrive in West Germany. We had burned our bridges.

The KGB still had a month to work out a peaceful solution, but chose not to do so. Two days after sending the telegrams, we received a different sort of signal: our car was stolen. Everything argues that it was the work of the KGB. The brand-new battery died while we were driving. We locked up the car and left it in the courtyard of a school, where I was assured that it would be safe. When we returned a half hour later, it was gone. Classes were in session, and two employees of the school standing on the street outside said they had seen nothing. A car is a major asset in Soviet life, and in our situation it was a near-necessity. But the KGB was mistaken if they thought the theft would cause us to change our plans.

In November, having waited the stipulated six months after her first application had been turned down, Liza submitted her documents to OVIR for a second time, now adding a copy of her Montana marriage certificate. She was called in on November 16. The inspector asked for affidavits from the management of the building where she was still officially registered in Bronnitsy, and from her parents. After Liza explained that she would not submit an affidavit from her parents, the inspector left the room and was gone a long time. When she returned, she agreed to accept the application anyway. We regarded this as a sign that the KGB might be preparing an avenue of retreat.

On November 15, Lusia traveled to Moscow for a last time before the hunger strike. While she was gone, Alexander Bobylev, Klava's brother-in-law, paid an unexpected visit. He had never come to Gorky before, and we had seen each other only rarely in Moscow. He was there to dissuade me from the hunger strike, and was allowed into our apartment without difficulty. His arguments had a familiar ring. In particular, he thought that Liza's parents had every right to bar their daughter's emigration, even though she was of age. He said a hunger strike was a futile gesture, adding that my children needed their father alive and not dead.

Worried that the KGB might exploit my children's concern, I sent a telegram asking them not to visit; I warned them that I would refuse to see them during the hunger strike unless they brought Liza along. I counted on their understanding that my bluntness here was intended for the KGB, whom I expected to read this message.

While Lusia was in Moscow many friends, dissidents, and acquaintances, made it plain to her that they disapproved of our decision and didn't understand it. Lydia Chukovskaya, for one, said: "I didn't think Andrei Dmitrievich could be so cruel." I am not sure even now just what she meant. The anguish that our family and friends would suffer? In that case, I admit it was a difficult decision, but an inescapable one.

Felix Krasavin was particularly vocal in his objections, assuring us that the KGB would never give in. We would die in vain, he told us. About November 10, when we saw Felix at the Khainovskys', he reported his KGB case officer as telling him that Lusia's wish was going to be fulfilled: she'd be getting rid of her husband and thus be free to go off to America. The case officer also remarked, "The Sakharovs' car has disappeared. Bonner may have hidden it or driven it back to Moscow, but it's bound to turn up by spring." And he warned Felix not to visit us during the hunger strike. This conversation appeared to us to be a KGB threat to kill me and *pin the blame on Lusia.* As it turned out, Felix was able to visit us freely during the hunger strike until we were removed from our apartment, and he kept trying to persuade us to end it.

Pyotr Grigorenko wrote me a letter (which I received only after the hunger strike was over) asserting that because of my value to the human rights movement I had no right to risk my life for such a trivial purpose as my daughter-in-law's happiness. (This was typical of the reasoning offered by opponents of our hunger strike, although for others it was my importance to science, or the cause of peace, or something else equally abstract and "grand.") Grigorenko went into detail about the terrible repression then underway in the Ukraine, concluding his letter with the injunction: "You have made a serious mistake and should correct it. End your hunger strike."

Revolt Pimenov, whose letter also arrived after the event, concentrated on the idea that Alexei and Liza's happiness—"to argue, to make up, to fall into bed," as he wrote—should not be bought at the cost "of a great man's suffering" (that is, mine). Pimenov had a rather odd way of looking at things—he was convinced that you always paid for any victory over the authorities; they'd get their revenge. "In police matters, a special law of conservation is evident," he wrote, citing as evidence the arrests of Orlov and Shcharansky, which followed on the heels of the Bukovsky-Corvalán exchange. If such a law were in fact operative, then opposition to repression would be useless. To me, however, life's causal connections appear so abstruse that pragmatic criteria are often useless; we must rely on our moral code. Later, long after the hunger strike was over, Pimenov admitted that he had been wrong.

It was particularly unfortunate that many dissidents directed their attacks at Liza. Literally and figuratively, they closed their doors to her, holding her responsible for not preventing this hunger strike "on her account." These denunciations were cruel and wholly unwarranted. It should have been obvious to them that Liza had no way of influencing our decision, nor could she have done so. The authorities' refusal to let her rejoin Alexei may have been the immediate cause of our hunger strike, but in a broader sense, it was the consequence of all that had happened to us, including exile in Gorky, and a continuation of my struggle for human rights and the freedom to choose one's country of residence—not in the abstract, but in a situation in which Lusia and I had from the beginning felt a direct responsibility. There had been virtually no objection when I declared a hunger strike in 1974 on behalf of Bukovsky and other political prisoners. This time, I was honoring a more compelling and personal obligation.

In my critics' remarks, I detect something of a "cult of personality" or, to be more precise, a desire to trade on my name. My importance is exaggerated, but at the same time I am regarded as a means to an end rather than a human being. It is also striking that the critics mention only me, seeming to forget Lusia. After all, she and I both took a risk, neither of us is young or healthy; and it is still not clear on whom the fast took the greater toll. We made our decision determined to act as free people. We were both aware of its gravity, and we took full responsibility. In some sense it was a private, family affair. Our fortunes in Gorky had hit bottom. A victory was badly needed. Victories are scarce: we ought to treasure every one of them.

Excerpts from my diary

November 19–20.

I have been slaving away for two days, straightening up the house for Lusia's arrival.

I received a letter (Gorky postmark; no return address) from a stranger named Verigin, probably a KGB attempt to scare me: "I heard on a foreign broadcast that you're getting ready to begin a hunger strike. My friends agree with me that this absurd action will prove fatal. Change your mind. Your nation needs you." A newspaper clipping was enclosed with a detailed description of the death agonies of the hunger strikers in Northern Ireland's Maze Prison.

November 21.

Lusia arrived, wearing a new hat. She gave me a full account of her phone conversation with Ruth and the children, and of Liza's summons to OVIR. On Tuesday Liza traveled to Bronnitsy to obtain an affidavit, but the building manager wasn't there. When she returned on Wednesday, he gave it to her without any problem, and Liza took it to OVIR. On Tuesday, while at Bronnitsy, Liza visited her mother, and this time their conversation was relatively calm. Her mother gave her a jacket as a gift, and asked: "Why are you going there? With the things you're involved in, they'll never let you come back."

"What things?"

"You know what I'm talking about."

The KGB must have spoken with Liza's parents and prepared them for the possibility that she might leave. And the fact that OVIR was willing to make do with just the one affidavit is another hopeful sign. But the KGB is probably working on more than one scenario.

Tomorrow, the first day of our hunger strike, film footage taken of Lusia and Liza on November 16 will be shown on Western television together with the film Lusia shot of me here.

Tonight at midnight, after supper, Lusia and I clinked our glasses of Carlsbad salts [a laxative]. The hunger strike has begun. Our plan is to massage each other's back every day, and to take a five-minute warm bath. Lusia got hold of a notebook to record our weight, blood pressure (she has a sphygmomanometer), pulse, water intake, and urine output.

November 22.

The first day of our hunger strike.

We're settling into a pattern. We watch a lot of television. Beethoven's Fifth Symphony was on last night.

Lusia recounted a story Tanya had told her about when they'd last talked on the phone, on November 16. Tanya said to Anya: "Eat up, or you won't get a husband." Anya: "Oh yes I will, 'cause I'm a good girl." "And what kind of husband do you want?" "A good man." "What does that mean—'a good man'?" Anya thought it over, then said: "A good man is someone like Grandpa Adya."

Felix came and brought us a scale with funny little flowers on the platform. As usual, he initiated a philosophical discussion, trying, as he had in the past, to prove how bad America and its government are. During the ensuing argument, he told Lusia that she was living in an ivory tower. In fact, we don't idealize America and see a lot that is bad or foolish in it, but America is a vital force, a positive factor in our chaotic world. (Of course, the world's a big place, and something new always turns up.)

There is a lot about our hunger strike on the radio.

November 23.
The second day, and we're both slightly dizzy.

Brezhnev's visit to Bonn was covered extensively on television. It's clear that they have not, and could not, come to agreement about medium-range missiles. Schmidt is sticking with NATO's two-track decision. Soviet reports removed his references to SS-20's, to ethnic Germans, and to other sensitive problems. I'm writing this entry on Wednesday (November 25) after Brezhnev's return to Moscow. It's still not clear what the results of the talks were or what the haggling was all about. Brezhnev proposed a moratorium, plus a reduction in the number of SS-20's and other missiles, in exchange for the West's agreement not to deploy Pershings and Tomahawks.

On the evening of the 23rd, Lusia reminded me of Goethe's dictum:

> He alone is worthy of life and freedom
> Who each day does battle for them anew!

Lusia and I feel that we're battling for freedom in general, and not just for Liza's exit visa (although that would suffice—what's more important than the life and love of an individual?). Few people understand this, even among those close to us.

November 24.
The third day.

Mark came. He informed us that Masha has been summoned for questioning on Wednesday and that Brezhnev's visit has been cut short and is ending today. (In fact, it ended on the 25th.)

It seems the KGB is not going to let Liza leave under the cover of Brezhnev's trip. I said to Lusia: "Let's go back to our basic idea. If the KGB doesn't want us to die, sooner or later they'll let Liza go. And if they do want us to die, they have plenty of ways to get rid of us without the hunger strike."

There's been a lot about our hunger strike on the radio every day: 1) Secretary of State Haig's appeal; 2) a Senate resolution; 3) an appeal by twenty American Nobel laureates to scientists and governments; 4) an appeal by French and Norwegian scientists; 5) articles in American, West German, and other European newspapers; 6) sensible programs on Voice of America, BBC, and *Deutsche Welle*; 7) an appeal by the Communist mayor of Florence.

Lusia and I recognized Alexei and Tanya's voices today on a press conference broadcast, but it was difficult to make out what they were saying. (Lusia heard them more clearly when the program was rebroadcast on the 25th.) They're worried about our health, and they have appealed to the Soviet consul in Washington for permission to visit us in the USSR—a good tactic, even though its chances of succeeding are practically nil. Alexei was asked whether he wants to visit the USSR to look after our health or to see Liza and bring her back with him. He replied that if Liza were granted an exit visa, the hunger strike would end.

November 25.

The fourth day of the hunger strike.

Lusia tries to listen to the radio regularly. She succeeds, but it's a real effort. On television we watched the third episode of a Georgian movie about a Party secretary and an excellent concert by the Württemberg Chamber Orchestra. Lusia's legs have started to swell. That worries us. She's losing less weight than I am. Her heart's not good either. I'm worried because it's her first hunger strike. We received an anonymous telegram: "Andrei, have pity on Lusia."

November 26.

Mark came again today. He agreed to send Liza a telegram with our medical data: weight, blood pressure, pulse. On the 24th we received a telegram from Vladimir Kornilov and one on the 25th from Lydia Chukovskaya. We sent replies to both. In France, even the left socialists have come out for Liza.

November 27.

The sixth day of the hunger strike.

Lusia has lost little weight, which doesn't make sense, but there is less swelling. The hunger strike continues to be harder on her. She has a headache. For the second day we walk back and forth on the terrace for about an hour in the afternoon sun. We take measured steps toward each other, pass each other like ships at sea, and then turn at either end. [We didn't leave the house for fear that we might be seized on the street and separated from each other. We thought it less likely that this would happen while we were in the apartment.—A.S. 1987] During the day we sleep or lie down for two hours, bundled up, with the door open. That helps.

Felix came with Maya. She took our blood pressure and our pulse, and listened to our chests. Our lungs are clear. Lusia's blood pressure was 140. That's not good—usually pressure falls during a hunger strike. (The next day it was 130/80.)

In the evening we heard on Voice of America (other stations also picked it up): "According to information received from a scientist with access to Sakharov, his health has taken a turn for the worse." We were infuriated: we feel fine, and we fear the backlash such exaggeration can provoke. The hunger strike is just beginning. The "scientist with access" is going to sound to the West as though my colleagues have been allowed in to see me—an illusion that plays straight into the KGB's hands. It's unclear who's responsible for the report; the KGB? No one seems to understand that the KGB is playing games with us; for instance, first they won't let Felix visit, then they do. We're left to wonder (we didn't have the heart to ask) whether he's shown up on his own initiative or in response to a green light from the KGB.

These games have a purpose, although it's rarely obvious to us. And with their zeal and lack of confidence in our reading of the situation, the dissidents often make things worse.

We received telegrams today from Joel Lebowitz and Jeremy Stone, reporting high-level interest in Liza's case and asking us to end our fast. A little later Felix and Maya arrived. I wrote a reply to Lebowitz and Stone, Lusia copied it onto a telegram blank, and we sent it to Liza with instructions to relay it to Alexei. Most likely it will not reach Liza, but it won't do any harm for the KGB to read it.

Dear Joel Lebowitz and Jeremy Stone,

Thanks for your efforts, concern, attention. For more than two years I've been trying to solve a purely humanitarian problem, which morally and legally is beyond dispute. I have appealed to our head of state, to the USSR Academy of Sciences, to Soviet scientists, and to foreign scientists and statesmen. The only way to halt the hunger strike now is for Liza to go abroad, for the government to cease holding her hostage, for an end to this dangerous and illogical situation, to irresponsible, cruel and illegal acts. I can no longer believe in promises from the authorities not backed by deeds. Please understand this and take it into account.

With esteem and thanks, sincerely, *Andrei Sakharov*

November 28.

The seventh day.

During our walk on the terrace today we're expecting NN. We had arranged with him—a real hero—that he would take the train from Moscow that arrives in Gorky at 11:30 A.M. and then come to our building. I used a magnifying glass to copy over the telegram to Lebowitz and Stone in tiny script, adding a note to Liza, asking her to show the telegram to foreign correspondents.

I also sent a message to Liza and our relatives and friends, assuring them that we were "feeling fine. All signs and symptoms according to the book.

We're determined to stay the course." I warned them to trust only information coming from Liza. I complained that the KGB was trying to gain complete control of our channels of communication and that we had received no telegrams from Liza and no proof that our own telegrams have been delivered.

NN did not appear, but around one o'clock Bella showed up unexpectedly. The KGB had slipped up. Lusia handed her the note intended for NN. Bella remained standing by our terrace for a few minutes, even though Lusia kept pleading with her to leave. The KGB must have caught up with her at the bus stop, because we saw two agents marching her off to their operations center.

At eight P.M., Tamara, our mail carrier, brought us a telegram from Liza and return receipts for three of our telegrams to her. Good news if true, but it contradicts Mark's report (he was here this morning) that Liza had not received any telegrams from us for three days. He also assured us that he would tell Natalya Podyapolsky that we are feeling well, and that he found us improved from his last visit.

I don't like the fact that Lusia's weight has hung at 132 pounds for three days. She didn't feel well today, but it's hard to know just how bad, since she never complains. Maybe the crisis has begun. . . .

November 29.
Lusia asked me if I share her conviction that we have made the right decision. I do. Our whole past existence is fading into the distance. A sense of composure, of the absence of doubt. What the KGB wants is their problem.

A telegram was delivered today from a town near the Installation: "Outraged by your escapade. You're betraying science for your wife's selfish aims. If you haven't forgotten everything, then consider what your wife is destroying in you." The signature meant nothing to me. Is it from the KGB or from a former colleague? Two abusive letters from Gorky were delivered before the telegram. Lusia's weight still hasn't dropped and she doesn't feel at all well. Even her voice has become weak. Maybe she can't do without her thyroid medicine. Mark warned us that people with Basedow's disease must not fast—but she's had her thyroid gland removed.

We read Mihajlo Mihajlov's *Kontinent* article, "The Return of the Grand Inquisitor,"[8] about the danger of Solzhenitsyn-style nationalism and warning against muddling religion, nationalism, the state, and politics all together. A serious article, beautifully written, to the point, thorough, clear. I am 100 percent in agreement with it.

[8][*Kontinent* 28 (1981), pp. 181–211.]

November 30.

Mark came this morning, bringing felt boots for Lusia to wear while walking on the terrace.

A summons was delivered requesting us to meet with detective Rukavishnikov on Gorny Street in order to identify our car. It can wait. Maybe the KGB is trying to lure me out? The car is just a side issue now.

Tonight I finished an eight-page letter to my children that I've been working on for three days. Getting my thoughts down on paper has made me feel better.

December 1.

They've broken the chain on the front door. They probably did it last night. They're letting us know they can enter at will. We hate the thought that they may abduct us and separate us, but we're prepared even for that. This evening Lusia and I attached a new chain that I'd bought some time ago in a hardware store.

Today I drew up a statement explaining that our hunger strike is more than a battle for Liza—"it's also a battle for freedom to leave the country and to return, a battle for freedom in general. And a defense of my dignity and honor in conditions of illegitimate exile and isolation. No deterioration in the state of our health, no unsubstantiated promises, will persuade us to end our hunger strike. Only Liza's departure."

Another summons ordered us to report to Rukavishnikov at the Procurator's Office on Gorny Street. Yesterday Lusia told the girl who brought the summons that I wasn't leaving the house. Today she told her about the hunger strike.

Ten minutes before our customary one o'clock exercise session, something landed on the terrace. We thought it was a snowball. Two policemen ran out from behind the corner of our building, chasing a fleeing man. We'd been expecting a possible visit from MM. Thinking it might be he, Lusia cried out: "You fool! You dissidents don't understand what's happening here!" It wasn't MM, however, and it wasn't a snowball; it was a package containing three apples, white bread and three pieces of meat, still warm. There was a note: "My dears, we're not giving you this to insult you. Voronin." Lusia threw the package away; it's painful for her to see or smell food. This was one of the most trying experiences of our hunger strike. [Lusia tells me she gave the meat and bread to the dogs which prowled beneath our terrace.—A.S. 1987]

Felix came this evening and tried to persuade us to stop, saying that the KGB plainly has decided not to give in and that all protests will be ignored. We explained our position again. Surrendering would destroy me morally. We are prepared to die. It will be murder, not suicide—the KGB began this test of wills two years ago.

I received a letter from my daughter Tanya, dated November 21. I realize that she's worried. She wrote that she's ready to put everything aside and come to Gorky. But the telegram I sent her forbids that, since the authorities would never let her bring Liza.

December 2.

I sent Tanya a telegram this morning: "Thanks for your warm words. I wrote a letter to you, Lyuba, and Dima at Lyuba's address. We're holding up. Kisses. Papa."

Sidney Drell sent a telegram urging us to end our fast and to rely on the efforts of friends. I replied that I appreciated his concern but "we have no alternative. We're not trying to commit suicide. If the result is a tragedy, it will be *murder*, sanctioned by the KGB and by the total silence of my colleagues in the Soviet Academy of Sciences. . . ."

A police lieutenant came to the house and warned us that they will move our car to a public parking lot. It will probably be stripped clean. He insisted that I come to the Procurator's Office. I wrote on the summons: "I cannot appear since I am in the eleventh day of a hunger strike for my daughter-in-law's exit visa. I'm ready to hand over the car keys. We—or our heirs—will pay for the parking lot." Did they really believe that such a shabby trick would lure us out of the apartment? I told the lieutenant that where we may end up, people ride in celestial chariots, not automobiles.

Mark came this evening. N had phoned him. He assured us that everything is all right with Liza. (We have received no telegrams from her since November 28.)

December 3.

The twelfth day.

We're becoming weaker, but overall, we're in pretty good shape. Lusia said, and she's right, that we're doing better because we're *together*. She's disturbed by thoughts of her mother and children, what they're going through now and what they might suffer afterward. But once again we agree that we've made the right decision. The only alternative is complete capitulation.

Receipts were delivered for the telegrams to Tanya and Liza, but not for my replies to Lydia Chukovskaya and Vladimir Kornilov.

We received a telegram from Kiev from someone named Rappoport: "I sympathize with your goals, but urge you to stop and to sacrifice private interest for the general good." What totalitarian thinking!

Felix became alarmed when he rang our doorbell for ten minutes and we didn't answer. We were on the terrace. He circled the building and climbed up onto the terrace. At two o'clock we went inside together.

My DIARY breaks off with the entry for December 3, but in March 1982, I recorded subsequent events while they were still fresh in my mind.

December 4 began with our usual program. It was Tanya and Efrem's anniversary, and we looked forward to clinking glasses with Mark when he stopped by later in the day: mineral water in our glasses, vodka in his.

While we were taking our midday walk on the terrace, the same police lieutenant who visited us on December 2 approached and tried once more to persuade us to come to the Prioksky police station and identify our car. We got rid of him, but as we turned around, we caught sight of a man inside our apartment—a KGB agent whose face was familiar. Lusia hurried in from the terrace, shouting: "How did you get in?" "The door was open," he replied. We saw that eight people had invaded the living room and entry hall. At least some, if not all, were from the KGB. Most were wearing white coats. Lusia said: "They've come to kill us."

The door chain had been ripped off again, and the key was lying on a table. One of the intruders announced that he was from the Municipal Health Department. "We have to hospitalize you. We've received a great many letters from citizens, from your children."

Lusia asked: "Will we be together?" He answered that we would, but he wasn't convincing. We got dressed, realizing that resistance was useless. The KGB agents went outside. We kissed. Tears came to my eyes. Lusia said bitterly: "And on Tanya's anniversary . . ."

When we came out on the street, they began pushing us into two separate ambulances parked outside our building. I tried to call out to passers-by, but I was unable to fight back effectively. The KGB agents got a strong grip on Lusia's arm and pulled her away, but not before she managed to shout: "Breathe deeply." (This was in case they tried force-feeding.)

My carry-all was filled with papers and Lusia's toothbrush and toothpaste; Lusia had my shirts and pants and handkerchiefs in her bag.

When we came to Beketov Street, we turned right and another ambulance turned left. When I asked if Lusia was in the second ambulance, someone reassured me: "Don't be silly. That's a completely different vehicle."

I was taken to Semashko Hospital, the medical center for the Gorky region, while Lusia was taken to Hospital Number 10, a run-down facility located in the Kanavinsky district on the Oka's left bank. But right up until I actually saw Lusia again, I was under the illusion that we were in the same hospital. I was put in a semi-private room. My roommate introduced himself as secretary of a district Party committee. A third bed and patient had been placed in the entry leading into our room—these men, who were acquainted with each other, were both genuinely ill.

A few minutes after I got to the room the attending physician, Dr. Rulev, appeared, and I allowed him to take my pulse and blood pressure. I refused to submit to any other procedures, however, and asked to be reunited with Lusia. I was worried about her, and knew she was worried about me. We each had confidence that the other would not abandon the hunger strike, but separation was difficult to bear—the KGB was apparently counting on that fact to break us.

They were also hoping that the news that the Sakharovs were in the hospital receiving medical care would pacify our friends around the world. A postscript announcing our hospitalization was included in "Another Provocation," a story that appeared in *Izvestia* on December 4, a few hours before the KGB broke into our apartment. But this disinformation didn't achieve the desired results. The rest of the article described Liza's case and our hunger strike in an ugly tone reminiscent of the *Nedelya* articles.

Lusia was shown the article on the day of our hospitalization; she reacted by tearing it up and throwing the pieces at one of the doctors, shouting: "You and your *Izvestia* can go to hell." I became equally upset when the chief physician showed me the article on December 7.

It took a tantrum, but Lusia won permission to walk in the corridor and to take baths. She tore up the "Confined to bed" sign. I didn't have her courage. On the evening of the 4th, after all the patients were in their rooms, Lusia went out into the hallway and had a good cry. She began scribbling notes about our situation on crumpled scraps of paper which she tossed into the courtyard where visitors came and went; she thrust other copies into people's hands as she paced the hallway. Her plea that they be delivered to the Khainovskys went unheeded; they never received even one.

On the first day, I walked out of my room as far as the end of the corridor, hoping for some news of Lusia. I asked a doctor where she was; he said he didn't know, but would inform me if he heard anything. I walked back to the lounge, where a dozen people were watching television, and just as I was about to ask them about Lusia, my doctor, a nurse, and the other two patients from my room appeared and dragged me back to bed, telling me I was supposed to stay there. The patients watching television ignored my appeal.

I spent part of that first night reading Nabokov's *Speak, Memory,* which I had begun at home. In the morning, I wrote a statement addressed to the doctor in charge declaring that my wife and I had been separated by force, that I would refuse all medical procedures until we were reunited, and that I would not end my hunger strike until I was certain that Liza would be granted permission to emigrate.

My socks, shirts, soap, and other articles that had been packed in Lusia's bag were left on my night table, which eased my mind as I concluded mistakenly that she must be nearby. I asked the nurse to give Lusia her toothbrush and the Nabokov book. I wrote a note on the margins of pages 114 and 115: "Lusia, I'm refusing to talk to doctors or to allow any procedures or tests while we're separated. I send kisses. You are always with me. I'm infinitely grateful to you. A." The nurse said she'd deliver the things to Lusia, and, to my surprise, she kept her promise. Lusia discovered my note on the 7th.

The nurses, who were constantly being changed, would bring in meals for me even though I asked them not to. I would leave the untouched trays in the hall. (The other patients were kind enough to eat in the entry, keeping the door to the room closed.) I tried not to spend all my time in bed and went for walks around the ward.

A well-known consultant, Dr. Vagralik, would visit me two or three times a day, accompanied by his assistant, my attending physician, Rulev (who often stopped by alone), and sometimes by a fourth doctor, who was introduced as a neurologist but was, I suspect, a psychiatrist. Vagralik warned me that I was not a young man, that I could slip into a terminal state at any moment, and that he had already noticed irreversible changes whose progress would accelerate. He spoke of his responsibilities as a physician. The neurologist (or psychiatrist) painted an even bleaker picture of my physical condition, and suggested that I was becoming confused and losing my faculties. As he put it, I already had one foot in the grave, and I ought to let the doctors obey the Hippocratic oath and help me.

To all these statements and to Rulev's attempts to take my blood pressure, I responded with a single set phrase: "I refuse to be examined until I'm reunited with my wife." Sometimes I would say: "Put yourself in my place. I have no idea what's happening to my wife!"

Later on, I was shocked to discover that Vagralik and his assistant had been seeing Lusia too, even though they feigned complete ignorance when we asked about each other.

On the morning of December 8, Rulev said: "You have only a few hours to think it over. You *must* end your hunger strike." Earlier, Vagralik had delivered the same ultimatum, but without a specific time limit. When I asked point-blank: "Are you threatening me with forced feeding?" they retreated, saying: "What gives you that idea? Not at all."

A few hours after Rulev's visit, a man entered my room. I realized instantly that he was from the KGB. "We've met before. [It was in 1980, after Lusia surprised the KGB searching our apartment.] My name is Ryabinin. I'm authorized to inform you that your request can now be reconsidered in a positive light, but you must first end your hunger strike." I said that I took the KGB's promises seriously, but that my wife and I had jointly made the decision to begin the hunger strike and we could decide to end it only when we were together. "I'll report your answer. You'll be seeing me again."

That same morning, apparatus for forced feeding was brought into Lusia's room. She warned the doctors that she would resist forced feeding with all her strength, even if she died in the struggle. A few hours after this last attempt to break her will, Ryabinin came to see her and told her much the same as he had me. Lusia asked to see me. Around seven o'clock that evening Lusia was driven to Semashko Hospital. I was told to go to the chief physician's office, where my wife and Ryabinin were waiting. A doctor and nurse pushed me there in a wheelchair (which greatly alarmed Lusia). After four days of painful separation we embraced. We insisted that Ryabinin speak in our presence with Academy President Alexandrov, as an earnest of the KGB's promise; only then would we end our hunger strike.

I returned to my room, and Lusia was taken back to Hospital Number 10. During the ride she asked Ryabinin: "Why did you write such lies about Sakharov in the *Izvestia* article 'A Would-be Caesar'?" Ryabinin answered: "But Elena Georgievna, it wasn't written for you or me." Lusia: "Meaning it was written for the rabble." Then, addressing the doctor who was with them and the driver, she said: "Do you hear? Those lies are all written for you." Ryabinin tried to smooth things over, but it had been a telling comment that revealed a deeply embedded facet of KGB psychology: the state-within-a-state, Orwell's Inner Party, needs accurate and complete information, but the "common herd" can be fed a filtered and sweetened swill. Ryabinin seemed to put us on a par with himself, albeit on the other side of the barricades.

The next morning (Wednesday, December 9) Lusia wrote out a firm demand that we be reunited immediately. By midday, we were together. The other patients in my room were moved out.

By this time we had been fasting for thirteen days in the apartment and four days in the hospital. The campaign in our support had been mounting. Tanya and Efrem were traveling through Europe, Alexei was active in the U.S. and Canada. Generally, in the West, people agreed that we were doing the right thing, although some dissidents and émigrés proved less understanding.

No one can say which was the drop that caused the glass to overflow, which act of support was decisive. I shall mention only a few of all those who deserve credit. In the USSR, Georgy Vladimov, Yuri Shikhanovich, Sergei Khodorovich, and a group of refusenik scientists spoke out in my defense.[9] I particularly wish to note the role played by the French physicists Louis Michel and Jean-Claude Pecker, who traveled to the USSR at the critical moment and succeeded in seeing the president (Alexandrov) and the scientific secretary

[9][The scientists were Yakov Alpert, Boris Altshuler, Yuri Golfand, Irina Brailovsky, Alexander Lerner, Naum Meiman, and Grigori Freiman. For their message, and the statements by Khodorovich and Shikhanovich, see *A Chronicle of Current Events*, no. 63, p. 133.]

(Skriabin) of the Academy. They discussed the meetings at several press conferences, including one in Moscow that garnered major publicity.

During the first days of our hunger strike, Liza had phoned Natasha Gesse
in Leningrad and asked her to come to Moscow, saying: "I'm not in very good
shape." Natasha agreed at once. Her support and advice meant a great deal
to Liza, and she helped stave off pressures from friends and dissidents who
wanted Liza to somehow bring the hunger strike to an end. Some people asked
why Liza herself didn't go on a hunger strike, but that would have been the
undoing of us all. We never could have succeeded without the strength,
wisdom, and energy of this woman of rare courage.

Other people wondered why Ruth remained in America instead of rushing
to her daughter's side. Simply put, it would have been a terrible mistake. Ruth,
Alexei, Tanya, and Efrem maintained their composure in a situation of crisis
and acted with dispatch and intelligence.

LIZA AND NATASHA GESSE traveled to Gorky on December 12. After a delay
during which they discovered that we'd been registered under false names, they
were brought to our room and spent almost three hours with us despite the
doctor's fussing. This was the last time I saw Liza before her departure. She
cried, of course, but I also saw a new expression in her eyes—happiness. It was
worth everything we had been through.

That day I wrote a statement thanking our friends and offering my parting
message to Liza.

We are deeply grateful to everyone who has supported us in this difficult
situation—to the statesmen, the religious leaders and public personalities,
to the scientists and journalists, to our friends, to those whom we know
and to those whom we don't know. There were so many—it is impossible
to name them all.

It was a struggle not only for our children's life and happiness, not only
for my own honor and dignity, but also for every human being's right to
freedom and happiness, for the right to live in accordance with one's
ideals and beliefs, and in the final analysis—it was a struggle for all
prisoners of conscience.

We are relieved that we will not spoil Christmas and the New Year for
our friends throughout the world.

Wishing Liza a happy journey, I hope for the reunion of all who are
separated. And I recall Mihajlo Mihajlov's wonderful words that the
motherland is not a geographical or national concept; freedom is our
motherland.

On December 14, Lusia went to the apartment to pick up some things. It had been sealed, but the police opened it for her. On the way back to the hospital, she first dropped off her police escort at precinct headquarters, and then stopped at the Khainovskys', who were overjoyed to see her and to learn that everything had ended well. Yuri had tried to get through to us, first at the apartment and later at the hospital, but he hadn't been allowed in. After one failed attempt, however, a KGB agent told him: "Don't worry. You'll see them at your home again."

Beaming with joy, Yuri accompanied Lusia to her taxi. It was the last time she saw him—he died six days later. Grief is part of life, as is happiness. Their meeting was at least some slight consolation for Lusia.

Lusia, still weak after the hunger strike, signed herself out of the hospital on December 15 and left for Moscow. She probably shouldn't have done it, but she felt compelled to see Liza off.

With Lusia gone, the original patients were moved back into my hospital room. We had long talks about my ideas and about Poland, where martial law had been declared on December 13. Their views hewed to the orthodox line, but they treated me with respect. The Soviet press was filled at that time with false claims that Solidarity had been preparing an armed counterrevolutionary coup and had drawn up lists of thousands of Party and government officials to be assassinated. My roommates seized on such "irrefutable facts" to try to win me over.

They wrote a few words of thanks to the doctors and nurses in the hospital's "comments and suggestions" book, leaving room for me to sign and in a moment of weakness (and euphoria induced by our victory), I felt unable to refuse. Afterward, however, I was so ashamed of my action that I only told Lusia about it two years later. In 1986, the hospital's chief physician, Dr. Obukhov, used a photocopy of this page as a psychological weapon against me.

Lusia put in long days preparing Liza's departure. On December 19, Liza sent me a telegram from Sheremetevo Airport: "I'm leaving, smiling through tears." She flew to Paris, where Tanya and Efrem were waiting to greet her, and from there to Boston, where she was reunited with Alexei.

WITH LIZA'S DEPARTURE the effects of the hunger strike and the hectic days in Moscow overcame Lusia, and she took to her bed. The most serious problem was her still-inadequate kidney function. Less than a week later, however, still not fully recovered, she returned on December 25 to Gorky.

Lusia and I had agreed with the doctors that I would remain in the hospital until she returned, but it didn't turn out the way we had planned. On December 22, I suffered a heart spasm; a cardiogram was taken on December 23, and

I was abruptly discharged from the hospital the next day—ostensibly because my room was needed. My two roommates were clearly surprised to find themselves also discharged the same day. I was told that Professor Vagralik had approved my release. The day before, while examining me, he had asked how many previous attacks I'd had. When I told him I'd had two microinfarcts, he simply mumbled, "I thought so," and walked out.

My discharge was another example of "manipulated" medicine. The KGB probably didn't want to be held responsible for any further medical problems; and indeed, I did suffer a second heart attack on December 26 from which it took me more than a month to recover.

Despite Dr. Rulev's promise to Lusia that in accordance with customary practice we'd be given our medical records, this wasn't done. In response to our formal request that they be mailed to us, we were told that they had been sent to the clinic in our district.

In mid-January, still suffering from heart pains, I asked Alexandrov to arrange for my admission to an Academy sanitarium. There was no written reply, but Alexandrov's secretary told Lusia: "Anatoly Petrovich asked me to tell you it's out of the question." We received a similar response in 1983 following Lusia's major heart attack.

In Paris and America, Liza was besieged by the press. She gave a series of thoughtful interviews in which she spoke not only of our affairs but of the overall human rights situation. Many problems needed to be aired, and there were those who were surprised by Liza's familiarity with these matters, who didn't realize that she had been a key figure in the human rights movement, responsible for processing and typing many samizdat documents.

Soon after Liza reached the United States, she and Alexei were invited to Montana, the scene of their proxy marriage, for a warm reception and a celebration of "Sakharov Days." For the outside world, that was the "happy ending" of their story. For Liza and Alexei, of course, life continues, with all its complications. But that's a chapter for another book.

One postscript to their story. On February 21, 1983, we received a telegram from Alexei: "Daughter Alexandra born. Healthy, beautiful, weighs 7 pounds 8 ounces. Liza fine. Kisses." Lusia had intended to name her second child Alexandra in honor of an aunt who died fighting with the partisans during the war; now her wish has been fulfilled in the second generation.

I have written at length about Liza's case: For Lusia and me, the hunger strike represents what may have been our finest hour, a proof of our mutual love and commitment.

49

1983

IN FEBRUARY 1983 I finally finished restoring the sections of my memoirs stolen the previous October (more precisely, I rewrote sections that now had to be integrated with the manuscript in Efrem's possession). I recorded the date of completion as February 15, 1983—my wife's sixtieth birthday.

Lusia has brought me happiness and added new meaning to my life. Although these years have been difficult, even tragic for her, she too, I hope, has found in them new purpose.

Not long after we'd begun our life together, Lusia told me a story about the writer Yuri Olesha and his wife Olga. Once, in a restaurant, Olesha addressed their very attractive waitress as "My queen!" As the waitress left their table, Olga asked: "If she's your queen, who am I?" Olesha stared at her a moment, caught off guard. "You?" And then answered solemnly: "You are my self." I am very fond of this story, and I believe that after our shared joys and cares, I too have the right to say to Lusia: "You are my self" (and "my queen" as well).

It is thanks to Lusia that this book, in which she plays such a central role, came to be written and published, and it is to her that I dedicate it with all my love.

I have written of my family; university years in Moscow and Ashkhabad; wartime work in a munitions plant; the research institute where I spent 1945 to 1948; work on thermonuclear weapons; the human rights movement; exile to Gorky. As I have presented my ideas, my doubts, and my accomplishments and failures, I have sought as well to give my impressions of people whom I've known and individuals who have affected my life in some way. The resulting book is a multifaceted work that permits each reader to concentrate on the portions that are of greatest personal interest.

Twenty years of my life, from the age of twenty-seven to forty-seven, were spent in work on thermonuclear weapons. We began our labors convinced that our enterprise was absolutely vital for our national security and the preservation of peace, and we were also exhilarated by its scale. As time passed, however, things began to seem less simple, and I gradually found myself reassessing my views and pursuing new goals.

By the late 1950s I had become profoundly disturbed by the consequences of nuclear testing, and in the early 1960s I helped lay the groundwork for the Moscow Limited Test Ban Treaty.

My work on weapons has led me to think long and hard about the appalling danger of a thermonuclear war—which would be tantamount to collective suicide on the part of mankind—and about ways to avert it. In 1968, I spoke out for the first time on this and other issues of paramount importance in *Reflections on Progress, Peaceful Coexistence, and Intellectual Freedom*. This was followed by *My Country and the World* (1975), "Peace, Progress and Human Rights" (the Nobel Prize lecture, 1975), "What the USA and the USSR Must Do to Preserve Peace" (1981), "The Danger of Thermonuclear War" (1983), my acceptance speech on the award of the 1983 Szilard Prize, my letter to the 1983 Nobel laureates meeting at the Sorbonne, and other articles and books. "The Danger of Thermonuclear War," written in the form of an open letter to Dr. Sidney Drell, is the most comprehensive and incisive record of my views concerning peace and disarmament in the period immediately preceding *perestroika*. [1]

Drell, to whom I have referred several times in these memoirs, is a distinguished American physicist and a friend, who for many years has served as adviser to the U.S. government on nuclear policy and arms control, and has written extensively on these issues. Although I agree with Drell on matters of basic principle, I took issue with him regarding certain specifics of the military and political situation of the early 1980s and some of his suggestions for reducing the danger of thermonuclear war (surely the goal of all reasonable people). [A more recent letter from Drell spelling out the differences between our positions has convinced me that I overestimated them somewhat while writing my article.—A.S.1988]

We agreed that the West's strategic stance ran counter to the paramount principle that nuclear weapons and nuclear deterrence be used only to forestall a *nuclear* threat by a potential adversary. Since 1946, Europe and the United States had been seeking to compensate for their inferiority in conventional arms with superiority in nuclear force. While this strategy may have aided in

[1][See Appendix, p. 664.]

maintaining peace, it is fraught with peril and step by step has led to nuclear stalemate. I am firmly convinced that even an oblique threat to use nuclear force is inadmissible when principle absolutely prohibits the use of such force. The West no longer enjoys nuclear superiority, and, as I have long argued, parity in conventional forces must be restored so that nuclear weapons, which pose a direct threat to the survival of mankind, may be renounced.

The key to international security is trust which depends on a society's openness and respect for human rights. But even if our most optimistic hopes were to be fulfilled, we would still face a protracted and dangerous period of transition. In "The Danger of Thermonuclear War" I broached the idea— hoping to stimulate discussion—that parity (stability) with respect to possible variants of limited nuclear warfare must be preferred until nuclear weapons have been abolished; otherwise an aggressor might be tempted to employ certain kinds of nuclear weapons, hoping to gain an edge while the fear of mutual destruction deterred the defending side from escalation.

It seemed clear to me that the West could expect no real progress in disarmament negotiations unless it had some bargaining chip; therefore it had to be prepared to go ahead with the MX missile as a potential tradeoff for the USSR's powerful silo-based missiles (effectively first-strike weapons since being MIRVed) and to install Pershing and cruise missiles in Europe. But if and when the USSR showed itself ready to make genuine reductions and agree to verifiable destruction of its most powerful weapons, the West should be ready to match these concessions.

Regrettable as it may seem, some continuation of the arms race during this transitional phase appears inevitable—a terrible evil in a world beset by critical problems, but a lesser evil than a slide into all-out nuclear war. I even hazarded a guess as to the duration of this transitional phase—ten to fifteen years—all the while suspecting that it might well be a good deal longer.

[Following the signing of the Intermediate-range Nuclear Forces (INF) Treaty in 1987 and other encouraging events, there are fresh grounds for optimism. I hope full advantage will be taken of the new opportunities for disarmament.—A.S. 1988]

"The Danger of Thermonuclear War" was completed on February 2, 1983, and appeared in the June issue of *Foreign Affairs*. I was well aware that my views might be greeted with some criticism in the West, especially in circles favoring a nuclear freeze, and be used in the Soviet Union to launch new attacks against me. I am satisfied, however, that it had some impact on world public opinion, and perhaps on politicians as well. While making no claim to infallibility in addressing such a complex and critical question, I could not remain silent.

Along with many of my contemporaries, I have come to believe that international security and peace cannot be sustained unless we can ensure openness of society, respect for human rights, and an eventual convergence of the two opposing systems, socialism and capitalism. In my article I placed special emphasis on the need for pluralistic reforms in the socialist world to end the monopoly held by Party and state over the economy, ideology, and culture. We need "freedom of opinion; the free flow of information; control by the people over national life, including decisions affecting war and peace; freedom of religion, freedom of movement; freedom of association; and the unconditional release of all prisoners of conscience from prisons and psychiatric hospitals."

I believe that the majority of our citizens accept the Soviet system and way of life, and not only because most of them lack opportunities for comparison or choice. Without in any way idealizing life in the USSR, one must recognize that the Soviet system has substantial accomplishments to its credit. Convergence and pluralistic reforms are, to my mind, avenues to freedom and prosperity for the people of the socialist nations, and to world peace. I am a convinced reformist, on principle opposed to violent revolution or counterrevolution; even more so to their export. (I often find it difficult to distinguish between them.)

Influenced by Lusia, and by my colleagues and friends, I have devoted more and more attention to individual victims of injustice. I support Amnesty International's call for the release of prisoners of conscience everywhere, as well as its efforts to end the death penalty and the use of torture. I am convinced that only an "ideology of human rights" (the apt expression used by Lusia in one interview) can unite people without regard to nationality, political convictions, religion, or social status.

When speaking in behalf of victims of illegality and brutality, many of whom I know personally, I have tried to convey the full measure of my pain and outrage and the depth of my concern. Many of the names that follow appear elsewhere in the pages of this book: Anatoly Marchenko; Anatoly Shcharansky; Yuri Orlov; Sergei Kovalev; Ivan Kovalev and his wife, Tatyana Osipova; Viktor Nekipelov; Leonard Ternovsky; Merab Kostava; Tatyana Velikanova; Vasyl Stus; Mart Niklus; Viktoras Petkus; Levko Lukyanenko; Ivan Kandyba; Mikhail Kukobaka; Rostislav Galetsky; Malva Landa; Ida Nudel; Alexander Lavut; Vyacheslav Bakhmin; Genrikh Altunian; Gleb Yakunin; Yuri Fyodorov; Alexei Murzhenko; Raisa and Mykola Rudenko; Olga and Nikolai Matusevich; Valery Abramkin; Mustafa Dzhemilev; Reshat Dzhemilev; Alexei Smirnov; Anatoly Koryagin; Sergei Khodorovich; the late Vladimir Shelkov and Bidia Dandaron. . . .

My statements on general issues are often tentative, meant to provoke discussion, and subject to revision. I agree with Leszek Kolakowski when he writes:

Inconsistency is simply a secret awareness of the contradictions of this world . . . a permanent feeling of possible personal error, or if not that, then of the possibility that one's antagonist is right.[2]

My only quarrel is with the word "inconsistency," which I would replace with one that conveys my belief that intellectual growth and social awareness should combine dynamic self-criticism and a set of stable values. I tried to express this in an autobiographical note:

I am not a professional politician. Perhaps that is why I am always burdened by doubt about the usefulness and consequences of my actions. I incline to the belief that a combination of moral criteria and unrestricted inquiry provides the only possible compass.

I respect all labor, be it that of the worker, the peasant, the teacher, the doctor, the writer, or the scientist. I frequently envy those whose work yields tangible results. But my life and my experience have led me to speak out on public issues regardless of my private doubts. This, I hope, comes through clearly in these pages. I have never expected immediate or concrete results from my public statements, but perhaps my ideas will leave some trace in the minds of men. And, most important, I have tried to be true to myself and my destiny.

The twentieth century is the century of science. I have had the privilege of studying quantum mechanics and the elegant geometry of the theory of relativity—products of the human genius of our great contemporaries, they have enabled us to understand and describe an extremely broad range of natural phenomena, and more is yet to come. The great age of quantum field theory and elementary particle theory was well underway when I entered Tamm's theoretical physics department forty-odd years ago, and many felt that full development of these theories would demand the introduction of fundamental new ideas—"crazy ideas," as Niels Bohr once called them. But the "old" theories continue to make extraordinary headway as such innovative concepts as supersymmetry, captive quarks, compact dimensions of spacetime, and "string" theory are introduced into their traditional framework. (To my regret, I speak here only as an interested spectator, not an active player.)

Work on elementary particles has taken us deep into the mysteries of cosmology, into proton decay, and toward an understanding of the laws of gravity. I am happy to have played a role in this research, and my only regret

[2]Leszek Kolakowski, *Toward a Marxist Humanism* (Grove, 1968), p. 24.

is to have accomplished less than I would have liked or than might have been expected of me.

In the 1950s, Tamm and I did pioneering work on controlled thermonuclear reactions, which are a possible future energy source. Our ideas for the design of a magnetic thermonuclear reactor (the Tokamak) have become the basis for a number of major research projects around the world. In the early 1960s, I suggested the possibility of using a laser implosion to create a controlled thermonuclear reaction; that, too, has become the subject of intensive study.

I made brief excursions into futurology in *Reflections* and the article I wrote for *The Future of Science;* and in "The World after Fifty Years," in which I described my vision of the technological, ecological, and social future to come—provided that mankind manages to avoid self-destruction through thermonuclear war, environmental pollution, depletion of natural resources, and overpopulation resulting in destruction of the balance of nature. The fifty years of the title was an arbitrary time frame; it was the notion of "the future" that counted. I envisioned an earth divided into two zones: the Work Territory, where people would live and work, and a large Reserve Territory, where they would spend their leisure amid undisturbed nature. A Universal Information System will bring the wonders of knowledge and culture to everyone, link people everywhere, and make advanced computer technology available for use in everyday life and science and industry. I suggested potential applications of discoveries being made on the cutting edge where biology, chemistry, and physics intersect; for example, the idea that artificial amino acids might serve as a substitute for animal protein, permitting a sharp curtailment of animal husbandry and of land devoted to agriculture. I made other specific predictions, including employment of environment-preserving, battery-powered vehicles on mechanical legs in the Reserve Territory, location of breeder reactors on the moon, extensive exploitation of outer space to service our needs on earth, and exploration of the outer reaches of the solar system. I urged that a serious search be instituted for extraterrestrial civilizations. . . .

My public statements were a constant irritant to the authorities. In 1968 I was cut off from the Installation. After my marriage to Lusia in 1971, the brunt of the authorities' pressure tactics—slander, threats, and various attempts to intimidate—shifted first to her, and soon to the children and grandchildren, who were forced to emigrate in 1977–1978. In 1980 I was stripped of my government awards and illegally exiled to isolation in Gorky.

I WANT NOW to turn to the period after February 15, 1983. On April 25 in Gorky, Lusia had what was apparently her second heart attack. It was a very serious one, and in the weeks that followed, two additional cardiac seizures resulted in further damage to her heart. The mental and physical burden that our life together placed on Lusia, especially after my exile to Gorky, undoubtedly had much to do with her medical difficulties—particularly her separation from her mother, her children, and her grandchildren. Lusia did what was possible in our circumstances to treat her illness.

On May 10 she traveled to Moscow, and on May 14 a cardiogram taken at the Academy of Sciences' clinic confirmed the heart attack. She was offered a bed in the Academy hospital, but she refused to be admitted without me, demanding that we be allowed to share a room in either the Academy hospital or its sanitorium. Once again, Lusia's health was on the line, and I deeply regret that I was less supportive in the ensuing struggle than I should have been. She was, of course, also fighting for a change in my status, but I didn't want to exaggerate my own medical problems and claim that I required immediate hospitalization.

Very few people realized just how serious Lusia's condition was (the Paris-based newspaper *Russkaya mysl,* for instance, published a piece on Elena Bonner's "microinfarct"—as if there were anything "micro" about it). No doubt they found it hard to believe that anyone who had suffered a serious heart attack could be so active.

Lusia strongly felt that she ought to attend the opening of Alexei Smirnov's trial on May 12. Smirnov was the grandson of the celebrated journalist Alexei Kosterin, who had been rehabilitated and restored to Party membership in the 1950s after long years of imprisonment.

Smirnov's interrogation had featured a notable offer by an investigator: "This is the order for your detention. I'm giving you two options: Write down what you know about the *Chronicle of Current Events,* tell us who publishes and distributes it, and I'll tear the order up, Or: refuse, and be locked up." As Smirnov noted at his trial, "I chose the latter." For this, he was sentenced to six years in labor camp and four years internal exile.

As harsh and unlawful sentences continued to be meted out to prisoners of conscience, we inevitably, despite all our attempts to remain optimistic about the future, began to wonder when, if ever, better times would arrive.

After Lusia's heart attack was confirmed, permanent police posts were set up outside our Moscow apartment and in the street below—perhaps six policemen in all, not counting the radio car. One of their duties was to prevent foreign correspondents or other foreigners from visiting Lusia; Soviet visitors were effectively discouraged by the requirement that they register. Doctors from the Academy did examine Lusia, but essentially she was left to fend for herself—without a telephone, ours having been disconnected since 1980. The pay telephone closest to the building had also been disconnected, and when Lusia tried to use a neighbor's phone, it, too, went dead. In case of an emergency, Lusia would have found it almost impossible to summon an ambulance.

The KGB may also have worried that I might try to visit Lusia on the sly if I learned that she was dangerously ill, an unnecessary concern on their part. I was too passive as I tried to pretend nothing had happened (all the while deeply worried for Lusia). I was fatalistic about our being hospitalized together in Moscow, believing that the question would be decided politically. Lusia and I, who had been as one in our battle for Liza's emigration, now found ourselves divided by a lack of communication and understanding.

With the benefit of hindsight, I believe that I should have declared an indefinite hunger strike aimed at obtaining a visa for Lusia's treatment abroad. The argument that hospitalization alone in Moscow (or together with me in Gorky) might have placed Lusia in danger was not made clear, and had something of a "paranoid" ring. The KGB wasted no time in taking advantage of my vacillation. ·

Lusia could not initiate the fight for a visa; her concern, as always, was for me, and her desire for us to be together. It was I who should have made the decision, but I wasn't ready for it. I underestimated the gravity of her illness and postponed the battle, hoping that her condition would stabilize.

On May 20, Lusia held a press conference at which she announced our demand to be hospitalized together. Foreign correspondents, denied entry to the building, clustered by the entrance as the policemen and what must have been a KGB agent in plainclothes attempted in vain to block Lusia from going outside. She bullied her way through, nitroglycerine in one hand and her statement and my letter to Anatoly Alexandrov in the other, perched on a window ledge, and spoke to the press. It was only twenty-five days since her heart attack.

A week later, we sent another telegram to Alexandrov, who sent each of us word that he had instructed a team of specialists to examine me (with regard to the question of my being hospitalized, the telegram to Lusia added). They arrived on June 2, while Lusia was in Moscow, examined me, and took a cardiogram. In response to my persistent questions, Professor Pylayev, the head of the team, acknowledged that hospitalization was advisable in my case, as I had received no treatment for my chronic prostate condition since arriving in Gorky, was plagued by an irregular heartbeat, angina, and borderline hypertension, and apparently had suffered several heart attacks—two minor ones (microinfarcts) in 1970 and 1975, and three attacks in Gorky—as well as a bout of thrombophlebitis. My condition was not nearly so critical as Lusia's, but there was still ample reason for me to be admitted. The doctors returned to Moscow that same day.

I spent several days kidding myself that the authorities were giving my hospitalization serious consideration; I went so far as to clean out my refrigerator and give some food to the Khainovskys so it wouldn't be wasted if I were admitted on short notice. It was foolish of me. Interestingly, a few days later, my contacts with the Khainovskys were invoked at the Academy as proof that I wasn't isolated—just as, on an earlier occasion, Alexandrov had used a visit from Maya Krasavin as evidence that I wasn't being deprived of medical assistance.

I received a reply from the Academy on August 18 (supposedly it had been sent to the wrong address on July 27; this was probably just the KGB up to its usual tricks). The letter was couched in deliberately vague terms, and made no mention of Lusia's heart attack, or of the fact that we had requested to be hospitalized together *in Moscow* and had categorically refused the "manipulated medicine" of the Gorky hospital. But the letter did amount to a tacit acknowledgment of my need for hospital care and made it clear that nonmedical reasons were keeping me from being admitted.

The publication of "The Danger of Thermonuclear War" in *Foreign Affairs* was followed by a letter printed in *Izvestia* on July 3 and signed by four academicians—Anatoly Dorodnitsyn, Alexander Prokhorov, Georgy Skriabin, and Andrei Tikhonov—and headed: "When Honor and Conscience Are Lost."[3] I assume that the letter was actually written by some Novosti or KGB propaganda specialist such as Yuri Kornilov or Yuri Zhukov, and that the academicians simply appended their signatures without even reading it—not that this excuses them.

I later heard that a fifth, unnamed academician had been called to the Central Committee and asked to sign the *Izvestia* letter, but had refused, saying that he'd need to get a look at my article first, and then he'd write something for *Izvestia* in his own name. He was told—presumably it was the KGB speaking here—that there wasn't time for that, and so he escaped with his honor intact. In 1988, Vitaly Goldansky later told me he was the academician in question. I've heard that Prokhorov was genuinely upset over his action; if so, a public retraction on his part would be very welcome, even at this late date.

The *Izvestia* piece was a dishonorable attempt to use yellow journalism to provoke public indignation at my "war-mongering" stance and to brand me a traitor. It's no wonder that *Izvestia* omitted any mention of the fact that my article was entitled "The Danger of Thermonuclear War"—that might make people wonder whether I really did stand on the side of nuclear war and escalation of the arms race and against negotiations, as was being claimed.

[3][Appendix, p. 670.]

Too many of *Izvestia*'s readers seemed to accept the academicians' letter on faith. By the end of October I had received more than 2,400 letters and dozens of telegrams denouncing me as a hatemonger. As many as half of these bore multiple signatures, which meant that the total number of people involved ran into tens of thousands. It's likely that even more letters and telegrams were sent to newspapers and government agencies. And those who wrote probably represented but a small percentage of those who were all too easily duped.

The attack on me, dubious as it was, proved far more effective than any of earlier years. There were low blows aimed at Lusia; while the academicians didn't cite her by name (such crudeness would have belied their "lofty" tone), Soviet propaganda for years had been instilling in impressionable minds the notion that it was Lusia who bore chief responsibility for my "downfall." Along with various gutter insinuations, there was emphasis placed on Lusia's Jewish descent (her Armenian heritage, less useful for these purposes, was ignored), as the stage was set for the suggestion that my article was the product of that "pernicious and insidious" influence. (Few stopped to think that I was the expert on thermonuclear weapons, while Lusia was a pediatrician.)

The third revised edition of Nikolai Yakovlev's book *CIA Target—the USSR* appeared in early 1983, and included a long section about Lusia and myself, no doubt added at the KGB's behest. Yakovlev, trained as an historian, is one of the more shameless apologists for the KGB, and a "dissident" expert. I later got some background on Yakovlev from an acquaintance of mine, who told me that Yakovlev had been arrested as a young man along with his father, a general, and had informed on fellow university students, resulting in numerous arrests. Yakovlev, too, was tried and imprisoned, and apparently began collaborating with the KGB during the investigation or in camp. After he was released, his career immediately took off, an invisible hand supported him through a succession of shady, if not criminal, activities, some conducted on a rather large scale. In private, it was said, he espoused extremely independent-minded, even dissident views. What struck me most, when I met him, was his combination of brashness with an almost tangible obsequiousness, of indisputable literary talent and learning with an utterly unprincipled cynicism and dishonesty.

CIA Target—the USSR devoted considerable space to human rights activists, including Orlov and Velikanova. Like other authors of his ilk, Yakovlev portrayed these dissidents as inconsequential, self-centered, vainglorious nobodies, paid agents of foreign intelligence services, pawns in the game of "human rights," invented by the CIA and played with the assistance of the NTS. According to Yakovlev, Samuel Zivs, and other "specialists," most dissidents hoped to become Western press celebrities so that they could later go abroad and cash in on their fame.

In 1983, the mass-circulation magazine *Smena* published a series of brief but juicy extracts from Yakovlev's book; the final one, "The Way Down," was about Lusia and me. I was now being portrayed as a deranged, psychologically unstable fool, raving about world government and technocracy, consumed by hatred for socialism, manipulated by Western intelligence services assisted by Lusia. She, meanwhile, was depicted as a mercenary adventuress who had been responsible for the deaths of two women. Yakovlev quoted approvingly from the vicious *Russian Voice* article: "It looks like Academician Sakharov has become the hostage of the Zionists, who are dictating terms to him through Bonner, a cantankerous and unstable woman." He then went on:

People have noticed that his emotional state undergoes regular changes. Calm periods when Bonner leaves Gorky for Moscow, alternate with periods of depression when she comes back. Then follows a spell of joint work on some anti-Soviet squib, interspersed with blows, with Sakharov on the receiving end. This is the background against which I view each of the new exposés transmitted by "Western radio voices," purportedly emanating from Sakharov. I cannot shake off the impression that much has been taken down as dictation or written under pressure from someone else.[4]

These lies were not an incidental literary exercise on Yakovlev's part; his hypocritical compassion for me as a victim of my wife's influence portended the KGB's preferred "solution" to the Sakharov problem.

On November 3, the deputy chief of the post office (whether or not on her own initiative, I'm not certain) brought me the October issue of *Chelovek i zakon* [*Man and Law*], an immensely popular journal (circulation at that time 8,700,000) that features items on lawsuits, detective stories, and legal information. This issue contained another article by Nikolai Yakovlev based on material from his book, with a section on "The Firm of Bonner and Children." Yakovlev's language had become more pointed: Lusia was described as "dissolute" rather than merely "undisciplined," and a "sexual brigand"—the "dreadful woman" who "foisted herself on the widower Sakharov"; I was "writing to the dictates of an evil will"; and so on. Of even greater importance, however, was Yakovlev's clear and unambiguous articula-

---

[4][Nikolai Yakovlev, *CIA Target—the USSR* (revised edition), Progress Publishers, 1983, pp. 243–44.]

tion of what previously had been only insinuated or reported in a third party's words:

> In its efforts to undermine the Soviet system from within, the CIA has made widespread use of the services of international Zionism, including its espionage network . . . and the Jewish masonic [!] organ B'nai B'rith, to which it is linked, as well as elements susceptible to Zionist propaganda. Academician Andrei Sakharov has become one of the victims of the CIA's Zionist secret service.

From the context, it is clear that the KGB, speaking through Yakovlev, saw Lusia as the CIA's Zionist agent. Three months earlier he hadn't been that specific. Such was progress. . . . And in what Yakovlev must have realized was a regression to the anti-Semitic slogans of Stalin's last years, Andrei Sinyavsky was described as a "rootless cosmopolitan."

"The Firm of Bonner and Children" concludes:

> A thorough analysis of his articles and other writings (thankfully, not all that voluminous) leaves an inescapable impression of having in large part been written to the dictates of an external—and pernicious—will. But this appraisal of Sakharov's anti-Soviet activities [as not self-initiated —A.S.] does not apply to the general run of renegades, who, aided and spurred on by the CIA, are seeking the demise of socialism and the triumph of bourgeois ideology.

In other words, the KGB pities Sakharov; but all the others, including Lusia, will be punished ruthlessly. Such "compassion" filled me with contempt and anger.

There wasn't a grain of truth in what Yakovlev wrote. To give emotional weight to his lies and blacken Lusia's name, he was prepared to go to any lengths: as they say, the more dirt you fling, the more of it will stick. Lusia was portrayed as a wicked stepmother who had evicted the children of my first marriage "from the parental nest"; in point of fact, they were still living there and Lusia had never even set foot in the place. Lusia was also said to be averse to studying and to have used false papers to get into the medical institute. He described her as:

> a woman who, since her dissolute youth, had developed an almost professional knack for seducing and subsequently sponging off older men. The lady in question began by taking the husband of her sick friend away from her—blackmail and obscene phone calls drove his wife to her death. The

enterprising lady was on the point of marrying Vsevolod Bagritsky, but she was disappointed; he was killed in the war.[5]

"Disappointed" is a slap in the face to all those who lost loved ones in the war; and Vsevolod Bagritsky was no wealthy "older man"—he was twenty when he fell at the front. The nasty-minded insinuations about Bagritsky and his youthful friendship with Lusia were beneath contempt.

Yakovlev's slander extended to Lusia's children, Tanya and Alexei—"children raised in her own image"—and to Efrem and Liza, who were all presented as "loafers and idlers"; Sakharov's "real children," meanwhile, were "trying to protect their own good name." Apparently the KGB felt some need to pit our children against each other. Let me remind the reader that Efrem had successfully completed his higher education in 1972, before the KGB cracked down on him—no idler, he is, on the contrary, exceptionally responsible. Alexei, a top-notch student throughout both secondary school and college, tackles any job he takes on with enthusiasm. Tanya was expelled from Moscow University, not for poor grades or for using "false documents" in 1976, but in 1972 at the KGB's behest.

I can only hope that the truth is clear to my readers by now. And I would like to think that I've succeeded in conveying a sufficient sense of Lusia's determination, selflessness, and generosity to refute Yakovlev's malicious slanders.

On July 14, 1983, while Lusia was in Moscow, Yakovlev actually came to see me. He had been commissioned by *Molodaya gvardia* to interview me about my *Foreign Affairs* article. What did he expect? Perhaps he thought his unannounced visit would unnerve me or that I might grant an interview in order to answer the academicians' attack in *Izvestia*. I wrote down the following account of his visit soon after it happened.

Around 2 P.M., I had two unexpected visitors. One was a flabby-looking man of medium height, fifty to sixty years old; the other, a young woman who chain-smoked throughout the ensuing conversation and never uttered a word. Assuming they were from the KGB (I wasn't far off), I asked them who they were and what they wanted. The man took a nitroglycerin tablet out of his pocket; placing it under his tongue, he said: "I'm Professor Yakovlev, the historian, and this is my associate. We're staying at the Hotel Nizhegorodskaya—we had some trouble getting hold of you. *Molodaya gvardiya* and Novosti have been inundated with letters about your *Foreign Affairs* article, and they don't know how to respond. They've sent me to find out your real views. Might I have a piece of paper? I'm not a specialist in these matters like you, just a historian. I've got my books here"—[he was carrying several volumes under one arm]—"and I'll autograph them for you if you'd like." This was Nikolai Yakovlev, the author of the slanderous *CIA Target—the USSR*.

I told him to forget the autograph: "We're not on that sort of terms. In the nineteenth century, I would have challenged you to a duel." No joke was intended; I wasn't being ironic. Trembling, I went into the next room, took my copy of his book down from the shelf, and grabbed a sheet of paper. The trembling soon passed. I felt no anger, not even indignation, just a mounting revulsion. I'd realized right away that I was going to end up hitting him. I returned to the room where my two visitors were seated. The conversation proceeded as follows:

SAKHAROV: "You tell a lot of lies in your book about my wife, my friends, and myself, and I'm not prepared to discuss anything with you until you publish a written apology. You'll leave me a copy of a letter from you addressed to, let's say, *Literaturnaya gazeta.* Here's a piece of paper."

YAKOVLEV: "Well, I'm prepared to talk about all this. I could see it might be unpleasant and there might even be legal repercussions, but they assured me everything would be taken care of." (I wasn't entirely sure what that was supposed to mean—was it an attempt to intimidate me by suggesting he had influential backing, a "secure rear guard," so to speak?) "My book was written with the greatest respect and affection for you."

SAKHAROV: "I don't need respect or affection from you. Let's not insult me by talking about your feelings or opinions; let's discuss the facts you deliberately distort."

I opened his book and read out some passages. Had I known he was coming, I would have been able to prepare a far more comprehensive list of his lies. I quoted his comment about the stepmother who evicted my children and told him: "My children from my first marriage still live in my old apartment; when I remarried, I moved into the crowded apartment my wife and her mother were sharing."

YAKOVLEV: "Yes, I know."[!]

SAKHAROV: "So why write otherwise? Why say that my wife joined the army to avoid a charge of instigating a murder? She joined the army right at the start of the war, long before Zlotnik's wife was murdered."

YAKOVLEV: "I only learned that after the book was published."

SAKHAROV: "And what was your source for all these lies?"

YAKOVLEV: "I spoke to the procurator in the Zlotnik case, who happens to still be alive."

SAKHAROV: "The procurator must have told you that my wife had nothing to do with the murder. She wasn't even called as a witness at the trial."

YAKOVLEV: "Yes, I know."

SAKHAROV: "You repeat Semyon Zlotnik's lies about this case and about the death of Bagritsky's wife."

YAKOVLEV: "Zlotnik? I don't know him. Where does he live?"

SAKHAROV: "Hard to say, since it's a pseudonym for someone in the KGB. Bagritsky and his wife were married a few weeks before the war. Vsevolod Bagritsky, whom you describe as a rich old man, fell at the front at the age of twenty."

YAKOVLEV (interrupting): "Yes, I know."

SAKHAROV: "And when Bagritsky's wife died several years later, she'd had no contact whatsoever with my wife. And knowing all this, you still go right ahead with your filthy lies." (I was deliberately phrasing this to be as offensive as possible to Yakovlev, but he, pursuing some private agenda, evinced not the slightest reaction.) "And where do you come off sounding like some scandal sheet with this story about my wife's relationships with Kisselman and Semyonov? That was a private matter; the three of them worked it out among themselves and you had no right to write about it."

YAKOVLEV: " 'Scandal sheet' isn't an appropriate term. Now, have you heard the one about . . ."

SAKHAROV (interrupting): "Never mind your jokes."

YAKOVLEV: "Everything I'm writing is for your sake; listen, Yankelevich and Alexei Semyonov have been robbing you of every cent of your Western earnings and you're such a babe in the woods you don't even take any notice."

SAKHAROV: "That's really revolting. I keep track of my earnings . . ." ("and manage my finances as I see fit," I intended to end the sentence, but I got sidetracked. Yakovlev had sold himself body and soul, for substantial pay-offs—in 1983 alone, he published three books—and like the rest of the establishment, he obviously cared a lot for money. These types are generally respectful of anyone who is rich. I couldn't help recalling my conversation with Suslov about Barenblat.) "Calling my son-in-law, who is my representative abroad, lazy is disgraceful; Alexei too: the late Rem Khokhlov called Alexei one of the top students at the Moscow Pedagogical Institute."

YAKOVLEV (interrupting): "I can't understand mountain climbing; Khokhlov's was such a pointless death. What's Alexei Semyonov doing now?"

SAKHAROV: "Finishing his dissertation."

YAKOVLEV (with spurious camaraderie): "*My* son's finishing his dissertation, too."

SAKHAROV: "And what gives you the right to say such things about Tatyana Velikanova?"

YAKOVLEV: "I'm sure Velikanova is a wonderful woman and the soul of honesty, but you can't hang on to all your letters from types like Litvinov if you're planning on staying involved in these affairs—it makes it conspiracy, doesn't it? I had no option once I'd seen those letters."

SAKHAROV: "Why 'conspiracy'? Velikanova wasn't breaking any laws. And why accuse my wife of beating me up and teaching me to swear? Have you seen any bruises on me? Heard any foul language? Although as far as that goes, I have to say I'm tempted to forgo my usual restraint."

YAKOVLEV: "It's not a matter of what *I* say; it's what they told me at the Procurator's Office . . ." (Again, lies about the procurator.) And then, feigning fright: "Elena Georgievna's not here, is she . . . ?"

SAKHAROV: "You know perfectly well she's not—that's why you've shown up . . ."

YAKOVLEV (trying once more to provoke me into giving him an interview): "What do you think of Reagan's plans for . . ."

SAKHAROV (interrupting): "I'm not getting into a discussion with you. If whoever sent you is interested in publishing my views, let them approach me directly, and I'll write them an article."

YAKOVLEV: "You can't go laying down preconditions like that, they're not going to buy a pig in a poke."

SAKHAROV: "I'm not—but I reserve the right to publish if they won't."

YAKOVLEV: "I'll pass it on. But tell me . . ."

SAKHAROV (again interrupting): "You're like that Czech, Řezáč I think was his name, who wanted me to talk about the neutron bomb. And whatever became of that interview?"

YAKOVLEV: "I don't know him."

SAKHAROV: "You serve the same masters."

YAKOVLEV: "I'm a historian, not a Party member."

SAKHAROV: "What difference does that make? Some Party members join out of principle, and so are deserving of respect; but you? Are your history books also filled with lies?"

YAKOVLEV: "Take me to court then; I have witnesses, information from the Procurator's Office. Let the judge decide."

SAKHAROV: "I don't believe I'd get a fair hearing; I'd rather take care of this matter by slapping you."

I dodged around the table. He flinched and avoided the blow, but I surprised him with an unexpected left-handed slap on his flabby cheek. "Now get out of here," I yelled, pushing the door open. He left quickly, followed by his silent companion, who hadn't made a move in his defense when I hit him. I'd obviously had no chance to refute all of Yakovlev's insinuations in a mere twenty minutes, and the slap itself was just symbolic retaliation against a professional liar.

On September 26, 1983, Lusia filed an official complaint against Yakovlev for libel. Legal procedure gave the court a month to either accept or reject the suit, with a written explanation of the grounds for its decision.[6]

UNSURPRISINGLY, MANY OF our Gorky neighbors showed signs of having been affected by the *Izvestia* article and the attacks on Lusia. As far back as July, we'd had some sharp exchanges in the street, and neighbors who'd hitherto been friendly began glancing away when they saw us.

On July 15, a complete stranger approached me as I was getting out of our car, ready to lock up and go into our building. She was livid. Brandishing a copy of the *Izvestia* issue with the academicians' letter, she began shouting at me:

"I've been trying to catch up with you all week, Sakharov. Our women are going to tear you apart limb to limb and hang you by your . . ." (I don't remember her exact expression, but the proprieties were maintained.) "You traitor, what do you mean, supporting the Americans against us, saying they should beef up their arms when they're already armed to the teeth? You've got your nerve appealing to Reagan and this Drell guy. I know what war is, I've seen children die. Those of us who were at the front are going to show you and your Jew-wife Bonner what war means. She's the one behind all this, couldn't you find yourself a Russian woman? If there's a war, we'll all die— there won't be any survivors. At the front, your kind—traitors—were executed; and we'll execute you, *scum*. We'll tear you apart . . ."

She kept on yelling. A dozen or so tenants who were sitting around outside the building and the policeman on duty were all ears. So far, I hadn't been able to get a word in, and I felt pressed to make some effective rejoinder. It's hard for me to give a verbatim account; it wasn't the most coherent of conversations. But here's the gist of it:

SAKHAROV: "The academicians have signed their names to lies that were meant to get people angry. What this doesn't tell you is that my article was entitled: 'The Danger of Thermonuclear War.' "
WOMAN: "Have you got this article?"
SAKHAROV: "Not yet, but I will."
WOMAN: "Here's my telephone number. I want to know if what you're telling is the truth. What does your article say?"
SAKHAROV: "That there must be no nuclear war—it would be suicide. The West must renounce nuclear deterrence; there should be parity in conventional weapons. The greatest danger is posed by powerful multiple-warhead

[6][See Elena Bonner, *Alone Together* (Knopf, 1986), pp. 48–51, for Bonner's account of the court's refusal to accept her suit.]

missiles, which are currently a Soviet monopoly; so long as this remains true, there's no hope that these weapons will be renounced. The arms race is a terrible evil, but it's still less awful than a slide into all-out nuclear war. The article was intended as a means of provoking discussion."

WOMAN (sarcastically): "Ah yes, provoking discussion." (In odd contrast to her gutter-level anti-Semitism, she replied in a manner that told me she'd understood me perfectly and was familiar with the terminology.)

SAKHAROV: "I gave a great deal of thought to this article. I wasn't expecting praise or pay. I'm a nuclear physicist, and I know my subject. My wife had nothing to do with my article."

WOMAN: "Well, just what *is* Elena Bonner's role?"

SAKHAROV: "My faithful wife."

WOMAN: "A Jew can't be a faithful wife."

SAKHAROV: "So, you're an anti-Semite, too."

WOMAN: "Not at all. During the war I helped Jews rescue their children, and they were wonderful people; it's the ones who head for that fascist Begin that I oppose. I know what war is like; you and your Bonner eat our Russian bread and butter, but you've only seen war in the movies. I was born in 1924, I was at the front when I was eighteen."

SAKHAROV: "My wife was at the front right at the start of the war, and *she* was eighteen too, and born in 1924. [It was actually 1923.—A.S.] She was wounded, a severe concussion; she's officially a disabled veteran."

WOMAN: "Which front? What was she? Maybe I know her."

SAKHAROV: "Several: she started out carrying the wounded; then she worked as a nurse on a hospital train. You call her a Jew; in fact, she's half-Jewish, half-Armenian—but does that make any difference?"

WOMAN: "No, it doesn't."

SAKHAROV: "And we've both worked hard for our bread."

WOMAN: "Yes. Of course. What did your wife do after the war?"

SAKHAROV: "Worked as a doctor; she held down two jobs."

WOMAN (skeptical): "She couldn't have graduated from medical school before the war."

SAKHAROV: "She graduated afterward."

WOMAN: "Oh, I see. And how did she get involved in a dirty business like this at her age?"

SAKHAROV: "I'm the one who's involved in what you call 'a dirty business'— because my conscience dictates it, and for humanity's sake." (I used this "lofty" phraseology deliberately.)

WOMAN (aggressive again, as though remembering the reason she was here): "You're a schizo! I've been keeping a close eye on your psychological state for a while now, and your behavior shows clear signs of abnormality."

SAKHAROV: "Many thanks for your diagnosis."

I got out of the car, put my hand on the woman's shoulder, and moved her gently out of my way. "If you write any more," I heard her yell, "we women will find you and your Bonner wherever you are and tear you to bits and your police guards won't be a bit of use to you."

SAKHAROV: "Don't tell me what to do. I'll write if I feel I must."

The tenants were perfectly friendly as I greeted them when I walked by.

ON AUGUST 17, a Gorky newspaper published a selection of letters under the heading, "Come to Your Senses, Mister Sakharov," prefaced as follows:

The furious indignation evinced by the authors of these letters is understandable. Can one really expect simple Soviet folk to remain calm and indifferent while someone defames the holy of holies—our Motherland and people—and makes no secret of his desire to inflict new grief and suffering on his fellow countrymen? Those who have read of Madame Bonner's shady ventures call on the academician to think for himself and not let her do it for him [again, claims of Lusia's alleged pernicious influence on me—A.S.], and urge that measures be taken to stop Bonner's activities as a courier.

Here are excerpts from some of the letters:

". . . Not one family in our village survived the Great Patriotic War unscathed. How one of our Soviet people can call for a nuclear arms race is beyond our ken. . . . The idea that you, the Sakharov who lives on our soil and eats our bread, feel yourself free to slander your Motherland, fills us with indignation. . . . There's no room among us for haters of mankind."

"It's sneaky to attack from behind a corner. Tell us, what turned you into an outcast bent on stirring up international tension?"

". . . How can a Soviet man whose talent blossomed thanks to the zealous concern of our Party and government . . . urge the USA to seek military superiority over the USSR?"

According to the paper, it had published the academicians' letter on July 3 (the same day as *Izvestia,* although the telltale coincidence of dates was hidden and the *Izvestia* article was here said to have been printed on the previous day). The KGB had obviously made a special point of sending the text to Gorky to rouse public resentment against Lusia and me.

On August 19, I came out of the building to find the windows and hood of our car plastered over with cuttings from the Gorky newspaper and handwritten placards. They were badly shredded, and I could make out only a few words here and there: "Sakharov is an *agent provocateur* . . ." "The people's contempt . . ." "Shame on the traitor . . ." Lusia and I spent hours scraping with a sharp knife and wiping away with chemical solvents the special glue that had been used (it was impossible to find it in ordinary stores). I'm convinced that the KGB was responsible, but I don't know whether the local agents were following orders from above or had decided on their own to use this obnoxious means of "debate."

Many people, including some of our neighbors, passed by while we were cleaning the car. Two or three were sympathetic and had harsh words for the vandals, but most looked the other way. Some made it quite clear they thought we'd got what we deserved. One woman, a retiree, told us that "people were talking" about our crimes. Lusia, she kept saying, was "inciting" me and "selling the Motherland at the Jewish church." ("At the synagogue?" asked Lusia. "Yes, yes, at the synagogue.") Lusia's "beating me up" she found an unremarkable family matter—after all, family quarrels are not an unusual occurrence. The next day, when Lusia went out, an elderly woman from the building next door gestured angrily at her. We were disheartened by people's readiness to believe the wildest inventions, especially those with an anti-Semitic twist. The atmosphere of hostility was very painful for Lusia, always sensitive to people and the world around her. And I, although in better physical shape and more of an introvert, didn't find the situation exactly easy.

On September 3, as Lusia and I were about to start our car, a youngish woman came up to us and launched into a hysterical tirade, against me, and especially against "the Jew Lusia." I was supposed to drive her to the station the next day to catch the train for Moscow; when we went out early that morning, we found the car with a flat tire, the valve torn out. I changed the tire and we made it to the station in time. "Let's sit out here in the car for a minute," Lusia said sadly. "It's the only home we've got."

I saw her to the train and then returned to Shcherbinki. For Lusia, the trip turned out to be a terrible ordeal. As the train moved off, the passengers in her compartment began yelling at her, insisting she get off the train at once—honest Soviet people like themselves couldn't possibly travel with a Zionist warmonger traitor. Almost everyone else in the car, including the conductor, joined in. Some of the passengers had read Yakovlev's articles, and agreed with the sentiments expressed; others doubtless were afraid of standing apart from the crowd; others simply relished pogroms. And a pogrom it was—complete with hysterical screams and shouts. Lusia tried at first to respond, but then, realizing that no one was paying the slightest attention, she decided to keep quiet. The confined quarters of the coach offered no escape from the ordeal. In a telegram I received later from her, Lusia said: "It was terrifying, so I stayed perfectly calm."

But at what cost, especially so soon after her recent heart attack? We have our suspicions, though we can't know for sure, that the KGB was behind this incident.

More than an hour passed before the conductor took Lusia to the staff compartment, where she at last found peace. A middle-aged Russian woman with the look of a schoolteacher came by a few minutes later, embraced Lusia, and told her: "Ignore them—they're just the pogrom crowd." Her gesture and words unleashed all Lusia's pent-up tension, and she burst into tears. Our friend Bella Koval, who was meeting Lusia at the Moscow station, took one look at her friend's face and found herself weeping. The usual police guard was at the door of the Chkalov Street apartment. The return journey to Gorky and the following trip to Moscow passed uneventfully. But on Lusia's next return to Gorky there was a rather absurd incident, apparently engineered by the KGB. The porter at the station refused to carry Lusia's bags to the car. I brought the bags out myself on a borrowed luggage cart, helped by a young Jew from Batumi. A porter, apparently acting on KGB orders, suddenly rushed up and tried to wrest the bags away from us and take them back to the platform. There was a skirmish; in the end, the bags made it to the car, but the young man was hauled off to the police station—they apparently assumed he was with us. I followed along to the station and explained: the station chief apologized and let the young man go (after noting down his name and address). As we left the police station, the fellow from Batumi asked me: "Are you *really* Sakharov?"

ON JUNE 20, 1983, the American magazine *Newsweek* published an interview by Robert Cullen with Anatoly Alexandrov.[7] The interview had obviously taken place a week or two earlier, during the critical period when the question of my possible hospitalization was being reviewed. Unfortunately, Cullen didn't raise this issue, but he did ask about my exile, the possibility of my emigrating, and my membership in the Academy. Some interesting remarks by Alexandrov were omitted in the published version: a comparison of President Reagan's proclamation of "International Sakharov Day" with a hypothetical Soviet celebration of a day honoring the assassin of a U.S. president; a hint that I might be expelled from the Academy if there were further actions in the West like Sakharov Day; and a claim that I possessed detailed knowledge of the design of current thermonuclear warheads. In the final sentence of the

[7][*Newsweek* Atlantic edition, June 2, 1983. The questions relating to Sakharov were reprinted in *Alone Together,* pp. 18–20, together with Bonner's letters.]

interview as printed, Alexandrov attributed my behavior to "a rather serious psychic shift."

The Alexandrov interview dealt with more than my personal situation. Alexandrov also told Cullen that the USSR was determined not to be the first to use nuclear weapons, but warned that deployment of American nuclear missiles in Europe would increase the risk of an accidental nuclear exchange—a computer error could send Soviet missiles, which the USSR would be forced to deploy in a launch-on-warning mode, into what would be, effectively, a first strike. Here Alexandrov was speaking to the West in terms at least as threatening as those employed by Ustinov or Gromyko.

In July or August, allegations of my mental instability were repeated by Andropov, the Soviet leader, while speaking with a group of American senators who were in the USSR to explore ways of improving Soviet-American relations and who had asked about my situation. Did these remarks indicate a new KGB strategy for dealing with "the Sakharov problem"? We'll probably never know whether such a plan existed on paper, but many of the actions taken in connection with Lusia and me in later years did seem extremely sinister.

The authorities clearly were reluctant (or, unable for subjective or objective reasons) to banish me from the country, and hesitated to imprison either of us. There is some evidence, including Yakovlev's writings, that suggests that the KGB intended to portray my public activities as a delusion produced by the influence of Lusia, who would be presented as a corrupt, self-serving, loose-living, egotistical, depraved, and immoral Jew prostitute, an agent of international Zionism. I would be transformed back into a distinguished Soviet (*Russian,* of course) scientist who had made invaluable contributions to the Motherland and world science, whose name could be exploited for ideological warfare. This process was to be accomplished either posthumously or while I was alive, by means of forgery, false evidence, or breaking me in some fashion, for example in a special psychiatric hospital (the statements by Alexandrov and Andropov reveal a preference for this tactic), or by using my children—perhaps this was what lay behind Yakovlev's contrasting them with Lusia's children. The main thrust of the KGB's strategy appeared to be to destroy Lusia morally, if not physically as well. The massive campaign of slander against her over the years had been directed at this goal. Lusia did indeed have a great influence on me, but not the kind described by Soviet propagandists. In matters concerning war, peace, and disarmament she had not altered my views in the slightest; they have been shaped over many years and are based on my special knowledge and experience. But it was Lusia's open-hearted and genuine humanity that turned my public activities toward practical humanitarian matters, and she who in word and deed has been my staunch and selfless supporter throughout these difficult years, often at great personal cost. The purpose behind the

slander was to put Lusia's health, even her life, in jeopardy and thus paralyze
my public activities. The pogrom on the train on September 4, and perhaps
even the search that had followed her heart attack the previous year, were
directed to the same ruthless end. But I couldn't rule out the possibility that
other gangster-like methods were being used or would be used: for example,
introduction of dangerous vasoconstrictive medicines into her food and drink.
I had no idea what effect the constant bombardment from "our" jammer was
having on her health. One thing was certain: the KGB was concentrating its
energies on Lusia, and she was by now seriously ill.

SIX MONTHS after Lusia's heart attack on April 25, her condition had not
stabilized. She was still in pain and had to make use of frequent doses of
nitroglycerine and other medication. She had several relapses. The most serious
of these was on October 16. On October 17 she asked me not to leave the
apartment. Around noon she said: "I think it's time we had a talk."

I sat down on the edge of the bed. Lusia spoke of her children and grandchildren, of the happiness they'd brought her. She spoke of her mother and of me.
She talked about my letter to Drell; she understood I had to write it, but I
should understand what it cost her. And then she spoke of the pressure I would
face in the future.

"I'll never betray you, myself, or the children," I declared.

"I know that."

That same day, I called Mark Kovner from a public phone and dictated a
telegram to Ruth, the children, and the grandchildren. We had agreed to
exchange telegrams on October 19, the day of the Lyceum reunion.

> You and I have not changed,
> For us the whole world is a foreign land
> And Tsarskoe Selo our fatherland.

50

LAST YEARS IN GORKY

MANY of the dramatic incidents of our Gorky exile have been described by Lusia in her book, *Alone Together,* but I would like to add a few pages to her story. Lusia's detention at the Gorky airport on May 2, 1984 brought to an end (until late October 1985) her visits to Moscow, our principal means of remaining in contact with the outside world. The investigation of Lusia's case continued from May until August; she was then put on trial, convicted on August 10 of "slandering the Soviet system" (Article 190–1), and sentenced to five years internal exile. In May 1984 and again beginning from April 16, 1985, I conducted hunger strikes demanding that she be allowed to go abroad to visit her mother, children, and grandchildren and to receive medical treatment. I was forcibly confined in Gorky's Semashko Hospital from May until September 1984, and subjected to painful forced feeding. On April 25, 1985, I was again removed against my will to that hospital and force-fed.

After this brief synopsis of intervening events, I take up the story on July 11, 1985, when, no longer able to bear the torture of my isolation from Lusia and the thought that she was ill and alone, I wrote the chief physician of Semashko Hospital, Dr. Oleg Obukhuv, that I was ending my hunger strike. A few hours later, I was signed out and taken home to Gagarin Street and to Lusia.

No doubt, my decision was a gift for the KGB, and they made good use of it. I quickly decided to renew my hunger strike; I wanted to be back in the hospital by August 1, the tenth anniversary of the Helsinki Final Act, and was determined to continue my fast for as long as my strength and will held out.

For two weeks Lusia and I led our usual life—driving within our permitted bounds, hunting for mushrooms, going to the movies and the market, watching

TV at night. We recalled the title of Erich Maria Remarque's book *A Time to Live and a Time to Die*: it was our time to live.[1]

Lusia at first argued against my resuming the hunger strike, but not as fiercely as she had opposed my decision to begin it in April. On July 25, I went out onto the terrace, where Lusia was sitting in the corner behind her flourishing plants, trying to "catch" a Western broadcast through the jamming. She said simply, "I guess you're right." I kissed her and said, "Thank you. I've already begun. I drank the Carlsbad salts."

On July 27, I was taken back to Semashko Hospital by force. Lusia gave me a radio for the hospital, and two or three days later I heard about a KGB film which "proved" that I'd never been on a hunger strike and, in any event, had been living in my apartment with my wife since mid-July.

On or about July 29, I sent letters to Mikhail Gorbachev and Andrei Gromyko (I'd begun them a month earlier) asking permission for Lusia to see her children and her mother after their long years of separation and to receive medical treatment abroad. I wrote about the slander directed against her and about her unjust trial; I recalled her war service, the disability caused by her wounds, and her illness; and I stated her reasons for wanting to go abroad. For her to travel would require the cancellation or suspension of her sentence, or else a pardon (for which she had applied in March 1985). I wrote to Gorbachev that, although I considered my exile and the other measures taken against me to be unjust and illegal, I was willing to be held to account for my actions, but responsibility should not be extended to my wife or to anyone else.

To both Gorbachev and Gromyko, I wrote: "I want to discontinue my public activities apart from exceptional circumstances." I've been criticized for this statement, but I believe it was appropriate for several reasons: 1) I had no desire any longer to speak out on relatively minor civic issues. After years of intense engagement, I felt I'd earned the right to limit my activity and concentrate on science and my private life. 2) I was not surrendering anything of consequence, since my exile and isolation effectively blocked contact with the world at large. 3) I felt obligated to do everything possible to clear the way for Lusia's trip.

I also acknowledged the authorities' competence to regulate my travel abroad because of my past access to classified information and the possibility that I might still know significant secrets.

IN CONTRAST TO 1984, I achieved a degree of peaceful coexistence with the feeding team that allowed me to prolong my hunger strike indefinitely. Usually, I resisted when the feeding began, but swallowed the last spoonfuls voluntarily.

---

[1][For more on this July interlude, see *Alone Together*, pp. 151–157.]

(Those were the moments filmed by the KGB's hidden cameras.) When the feeding team was shorthanded, I would warn them, "You won't get anywhere today." They'd put the tray down on a table, and leave without saying a word. I'd cover it with a napkin so the sight of the food wouldn't bother me. Sometimes, to assert my command of the situation, I would resist with all the force I could muster, spitting out the food and blowing it off the spoon. Then they applied a clamp which scraped the skin off my cheeks and bruised the inside of my mouth. My "solicitous" doctors would smear the wounds with antiseptic.

My normal weight is around 175 pounds, but it dropped to 138 pounds by August 13. That day, they began subcutaneous (into both thighs) and intravenous drips to supplement the forced feedings. In August and September I had fifteen subcutaneous and ten intravenous infusions. Each subcutaneous feeding took several hours, my legs would swell painfully, and I would be unable to walk for the rest of that day, and sometimes the following day as well.

On the morning of September 5, I had a surprise visitor from the KGB: Sergei Sokolov, apparently a high official in the department that "looked after" Lusia and me. In November 1973, before Lusia was interrogated about Eduard Kuznetsov's *Prison Diaries*, Sokolov "scolded" her for her behavior. He had visited Gorky in May, when he talked first with me, and then, separately, with Lusia. He had been blunt with me, apparently hoping to end my hunger strike by painting a picture of its futility, and he almost got me to cave in. That was the time when news of my fast was first beginning to reach the West, and actions in our behalf were picking up steam despite the KGB's disinformation campaign of counterfeit letters, postcards, and telegrams. (I believe that Sokolov was also one of the two "visitors" whom Dr. Obukhov had brought to my room a year earlier, on the night of May 10, 1984. They pretended to be concerned about my health, but I refused to talk to them. The next morning I was force-fed for the first time, and I suffered a slight stroke.)

On this latest visit, Sokolov was polite, almost deferential. Dr. Obukhov was also present. Sokolov said, "Mikhail Sergeyevich [Gorbachev] read your letter, and he's asked some comrades to study your request.[2] They have a number of concerns; one is that your wife might remain abroad and campaign for your emigration on the grounds of 'family reunification.' You should state in writing your agreement to abide by the decision forbidding you to travel outside the country because of your knowledge of secrets."

I replied, "Their fears are ridiculous. My wife would never defect. We're

---

[2] I believe Sokolov mentioned a "commission." He made no reference to Gromyko. I suspect that Lusia's trip had already been approved, but the KGB was stalling for its own reasons. Such tactics are common; they were used to delay Lusia's trip in July 1975 and may have caused Marchenko's death in December 1986.

opposed to such behavior on principle. Besides, my wife understands perfectly well that if she remained abroad, I would never be given permission to leave, no matter how energetic the campaign launched by the West in my behalf. I've already given the assurance you want in my letter to Gorbachev, but I'm willing to write a separate note to that effect."

"The second concern relates to your wife. She should promise in writing not to meet with foreign journalists while abroad and not to hold press conferences."

"Discuss that with her. She included something of that sort in her request for a pardon, which was never answered."

"I can't meet with your wife, but why not talk to her yourself." Sokolov turned to Dr. Obukhov: "You have no medical objection to Andrei Dmitrievich meeting with Elena Georgievna, do you?"

Obukhov quickly replied, "None whatsoever. I'll send a nurse with him and provide a car."

"Fine. The 'comrades' have one more question: you wrote that you'd discontinue your public activities apart from exceptional cases. But your idea of 'exceptional cases' may differ from ours. [Sokolov said this with a tinge of irony.] Or is that caveat just to save face?"

"It's a matter of principle; I have no need to 'save face.' I can't tell you what specific events might force me to repeat Tolstoy's words, 'I cannot remain silent.'"

Sokolov smiled a bit crookedly, but he didn't pursue the matter; he said that he'd be waiting for my acknowledgment that I was subject to security restrictions and Lusia's promise to avoid the foreign press.

Around two o'clock in the afternoon, Dr. Obukhov's black Volga delivered me to our building. I entered our apartment without knocking. (Lusia had the habit of leaving the key in the door so they wouldn't break the lock when they wanted to search the apartment.) She was curled up in an armchair watching TV—it wasn't until later that I noticed how much weight she'd lost. She turned toward me and said softly, "Andrei! I was waiting for you." In a minute we were sitting on the couch with our arms around each other. I quickly told her that I hadn't ended my hunger strike, that I was home for three hours, and about Sokolov's demands.

Lusia said, "Well, I can type the letters for you right away, that's no problem; but what does it all mean?"

"I'm afraid to believe it, I won't let myself believe it, but maybe they've decided to let you go to America."

"I don't dare believe it either."

Lusia told me that Alexei had begun a hunger strike on August 30 to call attention to our plight; during the day he would sit near the Soviet Embassy in Washington. We understood how difficult it must be for him: young people probably suffer more from fasting. Lusia confessed to me, "I keep thinking—if I sent Alexei a telegram asking him to end his hunger strike, he'd almost surely get it, but I'd lose my son." I agreed with her.

Alexei's hunger strike gave renewed impetus to public support for us; the faked KGB films had been holding it in check. Alexei ended his fast in mid-September after the United States Congress passed a resolution protesting our treatment and the State Department pledged renewed efforts in our behalf. Alexei's strike may have tipped the balance—no one can really know . . .

AFTER MY RETURN to the hospital, I gave our statements to Obukhov and asked him to forward them to Sokolov. Another difficult period of waiting began. On October 6, 1985, Lusia sent me a postcard with our agreed signal (a line from Pushkin) that I should end the hunger strike. As she told me later, she intuitively felt we had done everything that depended on us. The postcard was delivered twelve days later (with our signal carefully marked).

Why did the KGB first delay the postcard, and then decide to deliver it? My guess is that they wanted to time things so that Lusia would leave for the U.S. before seeing me, but if that was the case, they still didn't know her.

I asked her to confirm the delayed postcard by telegram (another line from Pushkin), and on October 23, I left Semashko Hospital for good. Lusia greeted me with Goethe's phrase, "He alone is worthy of life and freedom who each day does battle for them anew!"—my epigraph for *Reflections*.

On October 21, Lusia had been called to OVIR and told to fill out her papers. On the 24th, she received permission to travel to Boston, but there was one more battle to fight. Evgenia Guseva, the head of the Gorky OVIR office, told Lusia that she had to leave in two days. Lusia refused. She wouldn't go without first spending a month with me and making sure that I'd recovered from my hunger strike. "Who can tell from the sound of the word 'parting' what kind of bereavements await us"[3]—after all, Lusia was facing a dangerous operation. Harsh words were exchanged. A man from the Ministry of Internal Affairs who was present during this conversation threatened to cancel the trip, but Lusia put her demand in writing. The next day, Guseva informed her that postponement of her departure for one month had been sanctioned. Guseva was clearly stunned by such firmness on the part of an applicant and such acquiescence on the part of the authorities.

---

[3] [From Osip Mandelstam's poem "Tristia." See his *Selected Poems*, trans. by Clarence Brown and W. S. Merwin (Atheneum, 1974), p. 23.]

And so we'd won our three-year struggle for Lusia's trip. I believe this victory helped decide our future, including our return to Moscow a year later. For the first time in many years, I felt at peace with myself, that I had done all that I could do. (Of course, I wasn't completely happy with myself even then: I was concerned for one of my fellow patients, whom I'd asked to take a letter to Moscow, placing him in jeopardy for no good reason. I don't know what problem, if any, this caused the man. I am deeply grateful to him, and still feel guilt on his account. The only thing I can say in my own defense is: "All's fair in love and war.")

My sense of contentment evaporated rather quickly as life moved on. Lusia left Gorky for Moscow on November 25, and on December 2 flew to Italy, where Alexei and Efrem met her plane. Five days later, she was re-united with the rest of her family in Boston. On January 13, 1986, Lusia had open heart surgery. She returned to Moscow on June 2, and to Gorky on June 4. These few sentences summarize an astonishing chapter of our lives.

Tanya telephoned from Newton on January 14 to let me know that Lusia had been operated on by Dr. Cary Akins at Massachusetts General Hospital, and that six bypasses, an exceptionally large number, had been required to repair her heart. It was only later, from Lusia's letters and from what she told me after her return, that I came to realize what a difficult and life-threatening operation it had been.[4]

Lusia's medical program, which included a surgical procedure to improve circulation in one leg and removal of a benign tumor from her lip, was more than sufficient to keep an average person busy for six months, but Lusia managed to accomplish many other things. She wrote a book. (In Russian the title is *Postscript*, since it was intended as an afterword to this book, but the American editor renamed it *Alone Together*; this upset us at first, but we've been assured that it sounds all right in English.) Of course, Lusia is no novice as an author. She writes rapidly, intuitively, and spontaneously. Her first version of a sentence or a story is usually the best. (It's not that way for me.) Lusia's keyed-up emotional state may well have contributed to the book's success; it received favorable reviews abroad and positive comment from readers here.

Lusia visited American universities, met with political and cultural person-alities, and spoke in public on many occasions. Her talks at the National

---

[4]After a preliminary examination in December, Dr. Adolph Hutter, Lusia's attending cardiolo-gist in Boston, treated her with medication for a few weeks before finally deciding on surgery. The press published hasty reports—not without Moscow's prompting, I suspect—that Lusia had exaggerated the severity of her condition in order to get a visa. [See *Alone Together*, pp. 189–192, for a description of the operation.]

Academy of Sciences and to congressional leaders were probably the high points of her public activity and may have contributed to our release from Gorky exile in December 1986. She urged her audiences to concentrate on ending my banishment from Moscow rather than seeking our emigration.

WHILE I WAS in Gorky, high-energy physics did not stand still: a small number of enthusiasts worked on string theory in the hope that it might provide a description of all known interactions and fields, and even of all basic physical laws, which is why it is sometimes referred to as TOE, or Theory of Everything. Of course, string theory (in effect, an extension of the theory of supersymmetry) has not yet been confirmed experimentally. Some physicists consider it a false track, while others are working on parallel theories—membrane theory, generalizations of the Kaluza-Klein theory, superspin theories, etc. I believe that string theory is probably the forerunner to another, more sophisticated theory, but it may, in the interim, be able to account for a very large number of phenomena. As for TOE, I doubt that we will ever know all the laws governing nature (this opinion is based more on intuition than on logic). I believe that every physical theory will continue to have a restricted field of application, and extension beyond this will require the modification of basic concepts and ideas. That has been our experience in the past, which is not, of course, an infallible guide to the future.

I don't intend to write a history of string theory or its authors, even though it's a fascinating subject; but I will try to explain its basic ideas. In contrast to quantum field theory, which treats particles as points, the new theory's fundamental units are "strings," minute, one-dimensional structures, which can be "open" (resembling a worm) or "closed" (resembling a loop). They can change from one form to the other. And they can repel or combine with other strings. Strings can create fields. Space, on the other hand, is considered to lack inherent dynamic qualities and acquires them only through interaction with strings. In other words, string theory is the realization on a new level of my old concept of induced gravity. I can't help feeling proud of myself!

An internally consistent quantum theory of strings requires a space with a greater number of dimensions than the four (three of space and one of time) familiar in everyday life and in traditional experiments. The additional dimensions are curled up within themselves ("compactified"), forming at every point of our familiar three-dimensional space something like a multidimensional spherical (or other closed) surface. In order to visualize this, let's use a "toy" model—a space with one regular dimension and one compact dimension in the form of a loop. This space will have the shape of a long, thin tube. The radii of the loops in string theory are minute—on the order of 10^{-33} or 10^{-32}

centimeters (cm). Compact dimensions will not have an observable effect on phenomena involving measurements of a greater order of magnitude (the diameter of an atom is of the order of 10^{-8} cm, of an atom's nucleus 10^{-12} cm, of a proton 10^{-13} cm; experiments using the most powerful accelerators can study phenomena involving distances of the order of 10^{-15} to 10^{-18} cm).

I set out to learn string theory, the theories associated with it, and the new theoretical developments on the frontier between cosmology and high-energy physics. I don't expect to make original contributions to these fields, but I feel bound to try to understand what may turn out to be the next revolution in physics. From December 1985 until May 1986 I concentrated on science, but the gaps in my knowledge hindered progress. I tried to avoid any distractions, and completely stopped listening to Western broadcasts, which led to the blunder in my initial assessment of the Chernobyl accident which I will describe later in this chapter.

VISITS BY PHYSICISTS from FIAN had been suspended in 1984; they resumed in mid-December 1985 when Evgeny Feinberg and Efim Fradkin came to Gorky and filled me in on Moscow news. Fradkin gave me preprints of some important papers he had written with Arkady Tseitlin on string theory.

In late January 1986, David Kirzhnits and Andrei Linde paid a surprise visit, and we had an interesting scientific discussion. As I was walking them to the bus that evening, Linde took me aside and said, "We were briefed before we came to see you, and I was asked about your intentions if you were allowed to return to Moscow. The briefers stressed that they couldn't make the decision—it will be made higher up—but they have two questions. Would you work on magnetically-confined fusion reactors (MTRs) in Moscow? And second, would your promise not to make public statements [I interrupted: "Apart from special cases!"] remain in force after your return?"

It was clear that the KGB had talked to Linde, and I felt the less said the better. I did answer, "I have no intention of working on fusion reactors. I want to concentrate on field theory and the cosmology of the early universe, and I can't spread myself too thin. I haven't worked on MTRs for more than thirty years, and in that time first-rate experts have created a whole new specialty. As for public statements, the assurances were given with respect to my life in Gorky and in anticipation of my wife's trip. My return to Moscow would create an entirely different situation; it would bring new civic responsibilities, and I'd have to rethink a whole series of questions."

Linde asked if he could repeat all this. I said yes, but added that it would be better to discuss such questions directly, without intermediaries. "Be sure to tell them that."

I don't know whether my frank conversation with Linde—actually with the KGB—expedited our return to Moscow. When Lusia got back from America, she told me that many Western fusion specialists were refusing to cooperate with the USSR so long as I was banished to Gorky and cut off from contacts with them. She had spoken in favor of a boycott while she was in the U.S., but my conversation with Linde had undermined her efforts. I decided to clarify my stand and declare my willingness to participate in discussions on controlled fusion, but not in practical work, for which I had neither the time, nor the strength, nor the requisite knowledge of recent research. In retrospect, I do not regret my conversation with Linde.

IN FEBRUARY 1986, I wrote another letter to Gorbachev—it turned out to be one of my more important initiatives—calling for the release of prisoners of conscience. The immediate occasion was an interview with Gorbachev published on February 8 in *L'Humanité*, the French communist newspaper. Gorbachev spoke about Soviet Jews, about Sakharov, and—of greatest concern to me—about political prisoners. (Naturally, I was interested in what he had to say about Lusia and myself, but no response was required on that account.)

Gorbachev had insisted: "Now, about political prisoners, we don't have any. Likewise, our citizens are not prosecuted for their beliefs. We don't try people for their opinions."[5] In my letter, after quoting these words, I showed that all prosecutions under Articles 70 and 190-1 of the RSFSR Criminal Code are in fact prosecutions for beliefs, and prosecutions under Article 142, which nominally deals with separation of church and state, and Article 227, which deals with the "deleterious effects" of religious rites, are often similarly motivated. I also mentioned persons confined in psychiatric hospitals for political reasons and others imprisoned on trumped-up criminal charges. I gave brief accounts of fourteen whom I knew personally—Anatoly Marchenko headed the list—and called for the unconditional release of all prisoners of conscience.

The letter was mailed on February 19, 1986.[6] I like to think that my letter,

---

[5] [For an English translation of Gorbachev's interview, see his *Selected Speeches and Writings* (Progress Publishers, 1987), pp. 321–340. About Sakharov he said: "It is common knowledge that he committed actions punishable by law. The press reported them more than once. Measures were taken with regard to him according to our legislation. The actual state of affairs is as follows. Sakharov resides in Gorky in normal conditions, is doing scientific work, and remains a member of the USSR Academy of Sciences. He is in normal health as far as I know. His wife has recently left the country for medical treatment abroad. As for Sakharov himself, he is still a bearer of secrets of special importance to the state and for this reason cannot go abroad."]

[6] I received notification that my letter had been delivered on March 3. Six months later, it was published in the West at my request. [For the full text, see the special issue of the *Human*

and my return to Moscow in the era of *glasnost,* may have played some role in the prisoner release program initiated in January 1987.

THE CHERNOBYL catastrophe occurred on April 26, 1986. I learned about it only after several days, from a terse and inaccurate TASS report datelined early May. At the time, I was busy catching up on developments in physics and, as I have mentioned, avoiding all distractions, including Western radio broadcasts and the newspapers. Unfortunately, I missed Velikhov's first televised press conference on Chernobyl; it might have given me a better idea of the true situation.

To my shame, I at first pretended to myself that nothing much had happened. The report printed in early May by the Soviet press that radiation levels in the vicinity of the Chernobyl reactor did not exceed 10–15 milliroentgens an hour led me to adopt far too sanguine an approach to the accident. I discounted any danger of significant radioactive fallout, which might cause ecological harm or nonthreshold biological effects leading to cancer and genetic damage. (One clue that should have alerted me to a possible cover-up was a mid-May report that several firefighters had perished: if the earlier statements had been accurate, what could have caused their deaths?)

I had, in fact, made a serious mistake. The radiation levels published in the Soviet press were one percent or less of the true figure—I still don't know whether this was deliberate deception—and I had no alternative source of information. But there were other, subjective reasons for my complacency: my preconceptions, my mental inertia, and sheer wishful thinking.

On May 21, my sixty-fifth birthday, Vladimir Fainberg and Arkady Tseitlin came to Gorky and told me more about the accident. But in the preceding two weeks, the KGB had capitalized on my ignorance. People pretending to be chance passers-by would stop me on the street to ask about Chernobyl, and I would reassure them, although I always cautioned them that my information was limited. These staged encounters were secretly filmed and sent to the West—with my disclaimers eliminated. The KGB recorded and circulated a stupid remark I made during a phone conversation with Lusia on May 15: "It's an accident, not a catastrophe."

The day before the physicists' visit, a man came up while I was watering our flowers and introduced himself as a reporter for the *Gorky Worker.* Our conversation, at least in its early stages, did not resemble an interview. The

Rights Bulletin published by the International League for Human Rights, New York, December 1986.]

pretext for his visit was an unsigned postcard I'd sent several months earlier, pointing out inaccuracies in the newspaper. Once again, I spoke too lightly about Chernobyl and not carefully enough about disarmament, although I did manage to make a few good points.

Some few days later, realizing what I'd done, I wrote a letter to the editors of the *Gorky Worker* (that is, to the KGB) demanding that they either publish the interview with my corrections or kill it—otherwise, I threatened an immediate appeal to the West. Of course, it was a cry in the wilderness. A week later, Victor Louis sold the German newspaper *Bild* a spliced and edited videotape of the "interview" and pushed a new line in talking with the press: Sakharov is on our side of the barricades (?!). It's his awful wife (you see how she's behaved in the West) who's blocking his return to Moscow: she'd call a press conference the minute they got there!

LUSIA SPENT her last week abroad traveling to England and France, meeting with Prime Minister Margaret Thatcher, President François Mitterrand, and Premier Jacques Chirac, urging them to work for my return to Moscow (*not* for my emigration). She arrived back in the USSR on June 2 and left for Gorky the next day. At the railroad station the KGB agents typically forbade the porters to help Lusia with her things. The trap sprang shut again; she wasn't even allowed to go to Moscow and retrieve her delayed baggage.

She told me a great deal during our first hours together—about the children, the grandchildren, and Ruth; about her bypass operation and her other medical experiences; about the book she'd written; about her meetings in Washington; about all she'd done to help our cause. And also about the KGB films that had been shown in the West; during her phone calls she'd tried to tell me about the hidden cameras which had been filming us for several years (on the street, in doctors' offices, at the Gorky railroad station, at the post office, and elsewhere), but every time she touched on this subject, the connection was broken.

Lusia's information concerning Chernobyl shook me. It had been discussed at the annual convention of the U.S. National Academy of Sciences in late April, before the first Soviet press reports appeared. U.S. television had shown satellite pictures of the burning reactor. Czechoslovakia, Sweden, Poland, and Hungary demanded an explanation from the Soviet authorities for the high levels of radiation registered throughout Europe, but it took quite a while for them to receive a response. Poles were given iodine tablets to speed up the elimination of radioactive iodine from their systems—which raised the question of what was being done in the USSR, where the level of radioactivity was, of course, much greater. In the Ukraine and Belorussia pregnant women were advised to have abortions. It was all horrible, and completely dispelled my initial optimism, which to some degree had persisted even after Fainberg and Tseitlin's visit.

I thought long and hard about how to avoid similar errors of judgment in the future. But it was even more important to decide in my own mind what should be done about nuclear power in general.

THAT JUNE, Dr. Ariadne Obukhova, a cardiologist and Oleg Obukhov's wife, notified me that I was due for a physical. I'd been seen by her three times; and, as I learned from Lusia, the examinations had all been filmed by a hidden camera. I sent Obukhova a telegram: "I refuse to be examined by you. I find repellent the worldwide distribution of illegal films taken by hidden cameras in the offices of yourself and your husband. I have no need of such 'medicine.' *Sakharov.*"

The response was priceless. "I'm sincerely sorry for you, Academician. Naturally, I don't expect any gratitude from you. *Professor Ariadne Obukhova.*"

Neither Lusia nor I had the slightest intention of accepting further medical treatment in Gorky.

LIFE RESUMED its course after Lusia's return. After much fuss and bother, her luggage was delivered to Gorky, and we mailed off a dozen or more packages with gifts for relatives and friends. But we were cut off from all contacts, almost as completely as during our hunger strike. Once we managed to fix a time and place to meet Emil Shinberg, a friend from Moscow, but he was removed from the train halfway to Gorky, and the restaurant where we'd planned our rendezvous was filled with KGB men when we arrived.

The only happy exception to our quarantine was a meeting on August 15 with Misha Levin and his wife, Natasha. They were passing through Gorky, and strolled by our house. I spotted them from the terrace and ran to the street. We spent half the day together, and the KGB did not interfere, but I didn't dare invite the Levins back to our apartment for fear they might suffer unpleasant consequences. I'm enormously grateful to Misha for that meeting, as well as earlier ones.

Lusia and I took frequent drives within the confines permitted us. We had two basic itineraries: the "small loop," and the "big loop" which included a portion of the Kazan highway and a stretch along the Volga. We read books, watched television at night, and sat over coffee and tea in the morning, settling disputed points of history and literature with the help of an encyclopedia. Our isolation from the world was a real test of our psychological compatibility, and we passed it with flying colors. You might even say we were happy with our paradoxical existence—if only Lusia's legs, heart, and overall health had been better!

One change for the better was that we could now speak with the children and Ruth by phone (of course, we had to go to the post office to do this since we still had no telephone in the apartment). On the other hand, once a month Lusia was supposed to register at the district office of the Ministry of Internal Affairs. She had handed in Dr. Hutter's letter forbidding her to go outdoors in cold and windy weather, but we left Gorky before learning whether the authorities would accept this as an excuse for non-appearance.

In early October 1986 I was summoned to the regional Procurator's Office to see USSR Deputy Procurator General Andreyev "in connection with your statement"; I assumed this referred to my letter the previous February about prisoners. After discussion with Lusia, I decided to send a letter through Andreyev (i.e., bypassing the local KGB) to Gorbachev seeking our release from Gorky. I had spent a long time pondering whether to write such a letter or simply to allow the decision to "ripen" on its own. One complication was the assurance I had given Gorbachev a year earlier that I had no personal requests beyond my wife's trip (although the situation had now changed considerably). Besides, I was looking forward to spending the next few months working on physics, and knew I wouldn't be able to concentrate on science in Moscow, where new worries would descend upon us, new responsibilities. But the question of my remaining in Gorky or returning to Moscow was something more than a purely personal matter: it was a yardstick by which the entire human rights situation in the USSR could be measured.

The conversation with Linde the previous January had left me with an uneasy feeling, and I was anxious to clarify my position. In the end, I decided to do everything I could to secure my freedom, to add my own efforts to the efforts of so many other people in the hope that my appeal might somehow influence the unknown balance of forces "at the top." It was only after our actual return to Moscow that I came to appreciate fully the link between my release and the fates of other individuals, human rights, and *glasnost*, not to mention the cares and responsibilities that life in Moscow would force upon us.

On October 3, Lusia drove me to the meeting with Andreyev and then waited for me by the Café Druzhba ("Friendship"). Andreyev had indeed come about my February letter to Gorbachev, but his reply was unsatisfactory and evaded the real issues. He told me that the procurator's office had looked into the facts, and that all the prisoners on my list had been properly sentenced. (He also mentioned a review of medical records, presumably for the prisoners in psychiatric hospitals.) My specific questions received vague or ambiguous replies. Andreyev never did say whether the General Secretary had seen my letter. (My telephone conversation with Gorbachev on December 16 made clear that he had, in fact, read it.) I brought up Marchenko, but Andreyev refused to discuss his case. After we had talked for an hour, I told him that I was disappointed in our meeting and that my letter required a *political* decision to release all prisoners of conscience. Andreyev categorically refused to accept my new letter, declaring that he was not a messenger.

I subsequently revised the letter and mailed it to the General Secretary on October 23. Lusia had advised me not to rush; she wasn't completely happy with it, but I'd made up my mind and saw no reason for delay. I have no way of knowing whether it was this letter that prompted our release, although I suspect it was not. I've heard rumors that our case was under discussion during the summer of 1986 or even earlier; it's just possible, however, that the letter was the imperceptible tremor that touched off the avalanche.

In it, I wrote that I'd been banished illegally, without a court decision. I'd never broken the law or disclosed state secrets. My wife and I were being held in unprecedented isolation. Her sentence, and the slanders printed about her in the press, were actually attempts to shift responsibility for my actions onto her. I mentioned our health problems, and I repeated my promise that I would "make no more public statements, apart from exceptional cases when, in the words of Tolstoy, 'I cannot remain silent.'" In effect, I was reduced to writing what I had told Sokolov in September 1985. (Now that I'm back in Moscow, I can only dream of cutting down on my public activities.) In closing, I mentioned my past services to the country, including my contribution to the Moscow Limited Test Ban Treaty. I again urged the release of all prisoners of conscience. I recalled my work with Tamm on controlled fusion and expressed my readiness to discuss international collaboration in this field (this was to correct my blunder with Linde). The letter concluded: "I hope that you will find it possible to end my isolation and my wife's exile." Once I'd sent off the letter, I forgot about it for the next seven weeks.

I HAD NEVER stopped thinking about nuclear power and how to ensure its safety. Plainly, mankind cannot renounce nuclear power, so we must find technical means to guarantee its absolute safety and exclude the possibility of another Chernobyl. The solution I favor would be to build reactors underground, deep enough so that even a worst-case accident would not discharge radioactive substances into the atmosphere. This would increase the expense of construction, but modern earth-moving technology should hold the cost within acceptable limits. (I have learned since my return to Moscow that specific proposals for building underground reactors have been under discussion in the U.S., in France, and possibly in Switzerland and other countries as well.)

I now believe that international legislation requiring all new nuclear reactors to be sited underground is the best way to ensure against potential catastrophes. (Lusia suggested this approach while helping me prepare my talks for the 1987 Moscow Forum.) After all, fallout does not recognize national frontiers. Existing aboveground reactors should be protected by reliable containment structures. First priority for the installation of safeguards should be given to atomic plants which supply power and heat to large cities (these are usually located near major population centers, e.g., the one under construction in a suburb of Gorky); reactors with graphite moderators like the one that malfunctioned at Chernobyl; and fast neutron breeder reactors.

I also became interested in the possibility of reducing earthquake damage by burying thermonuclear charges deep underground in seismologically active areas and detonating them when strains in the earth's core approach the critical level. Lives are lost because we still cannot predict precisely when an earthquake will occur. A powerful explosion near the potential epicenter of an earthquake might relieve the build-up of tension. If this idea proves feasible, we could control at least the timing of earthquakes: people and property could be evacuated in orderly fashion. Of course, the explosion would have to be deep enough to preclude the escape of any radiation, probably two or more miles beneath the earth's surface.

Seismologists have discussed this idea, but they may lack needed information about the costs and technical features of thermonuclear charges (in 1961, a hundred megaton thermonuclear device was tested in the USSR, and even more powerful devices can be manufactured). A feasibility study should also take into account recent advances in seismology.

In early December 1986 I sent a letter to Guri Marchuk, president of the Academy, outlining my thoughts on nuclear reactor safety and on earthquakes and asking him to foster discussion of these ideas.

ON THE EVENING of December 9, Lusia was twirling the radio dial. The jamming was intense, and it was difficult to get anything even though we were using earphones, as we always did indoors, so as not to attract the attention of our personal jammers. Then, through the crackle, Lusia and I both made out the name "Marchenko." For a few moments we thought he'd been released: ten days earlier, his wife, Larisa Bogoraz, had been asked to fill out an application to leave for Israel. She'd replied that she'd have to talk with her husband before making a decision, and had asked for a meeting with him. We began to hope for movement on the Marchenko case, and Lusia sent Larisa an upbeat postcard.

Since August 4, Marchenko had been on a hunger strike at Chistopol Prison, demanding better conditions for political prisoners and an end to repression.

He hadn't been allowed visitors for two years and eight months, and had spent long periods in punishment cells. In 1981, during his last interlude of freedom, the KGB had suggested several times that Marchenko emigrate to Israel, but he refused, unwilling to play the KGB's game and leave the country where he had become a man in the full sense of that word. Now, when Marchenko was near death, the offer was repeated, this time to Larisa.

We soon realized that the broadcast was not a report of Marchenko's release. Larisa had been notified of her husband's death and had left for Chistopol with her sons Pavel and Sasha. She was not allowed to bring the body back to Moscow; Marchenko was buried in Chistopol. Larisa wasn't told the details of his death or his last days. All she could find out was that he'd been kept in a cell until the evening of the 8th, when he'd asked for a doctor. By the time he was brought to the hospital, his condition was hopeless. During the funeral, the mourners saw black-and-blue marks on the corpse, perhaps from forced feeding. We don't know whether he remained on his hunger strike to the end, or had stopped it a few days earlier. The official report listed a cerebral hemorrhage as the immediate cause of death.

Marchenko was 48 years old. His death was a stunning blow for us, as it was for people everywhere. It was a heroic ending to an astonishing, tragic, and yet happy life. We can see now that it was also the end of an era for the human rights movement, which Marchenko had helped to shape in its early stages through the force of his personality and his powerful book *My Testimony*.

That Sunday, Lusia and I happened to see Eduard Radzinsky's play *Lunin, or The Death of Jacques*, on television. We were astonished by the coincidence of the play's story line with Marchenko's life. In the play, Mikhail Lunin, an army officer exiled to Siberia after the Decembrist rebellion, sits some thirty years later in a prison cell and thinks back over his life as he waits for his executioners. He remembers the tsar's brother Constantine suggesting that he run away to avoid arrest, a proposal he refused, recalling lines from a book about another rebel: "The master thinks a slave will always run away if he can. But there's always at least one man in the Empire who will say: No!" That was Lunin. And that was Marchenko.

An entry from my diary: "My thoughts keep returning to this tragedy, to Tolya's life, to Larisa and Pavel. Constant feelings of guilt (mine and Lusia's)."

December 10, the day after we heard the tragic news, was Human Rights Day. That evening, Lusia placed candles in our windows—a symbolic appeal, suggested by Amnesty International, for the release of prisoners of conscience. They were also a sign of our mourning for Anatoly Marchenko.

DECEMBER 15 was the twenty-fifth anniversary of my father's death. That evening, Lusia was sewing as we watched television. Shortly after ten, the doorbell rang. It was too late for the postman, and no one else ever came to see us. A search? Two electricians escorted by a KGB agent entered the apartment. They had orders to install a phone. (We thought it might be a provocation and that we should refuse, but we said nothing.) The KGB man warned us, "You'll get a call around ten tomorrow morning."

Lusia and I made all sorts of wild guesses. Would someone try to interview me? There had already been two requests: a letter from *Novoye Vremya* (New Times) in September, and a proposal from *Literaturnaya gazeta* in November, passed along by Ginzburg. I'd refused both offers—I had no wish to give an interview "with a noose around my neck."

On December 16, we stayed at home until three in the afternoon, waiting for a call. I was just getting ready to go out for bread when the phone rang, and I answered. (My report of the ensuing conversation is based on my diary, with some comments added.)

A woman's voice: "Mikhail Sergeyevich will speak with you."

"I'm listening."

I told Lusia, "It's Gorbachev." She opened the door to the hallway, where the usual chatter was going on around the policeman on duty, and shouted, "Quiet, Gorbachev's on the phone." There was an immediate silence.

"Hello, this is Gorbachev speaking."

"Hello, I'm listening."

"I received your letter. We've reviewed it and discussed it. [I don't remember his exact words about the other participants in the decision process, but he didn't mention names or positions.] You can return to Moscow. The Decree of the Presidium of the Supreme Soviet will be rescinded. A decision has also been made about Elena Bonnaire."

I broke in sharply: "That's my wife!" It was an emotional reaction, not so much to his mispronunciation of her name as to his tone. I'm glad I interrupted his speech.

Gorbachev continued: "You can return to Moscow together. You have an apartment there. Marchuk is coming to see you. Go back to your patriotic work!"

I said, "Thank you. But I must tell you that a few days ago, my friend Marchenko was killed in prison. He was the first person I mentioned in my letter to you, requesting the release of prisoners of conscience—people prosecuted for their beliefs."

Gorbachev: "Yes, I received your letter early this year. We've released many, and improved the situation of others. But there are all sorts of people on your list."

I said, "Everyone sentenced under those articles has been sentenced illegally, unjustly. They ought to be freed!"

Gorbachev: "I don't agree with you."

I said, "I urge you to look one more time at the question of releasing persons convicted for their beliefs. It's a matter of justice. It's vitally important for our country, for international trust, for peace, and for you and the success of your program."

Gorbachev made a noncommittal reply.

I said, "Thank you again. Goodbye." (Contrary to the demands of protocol, I brought the conversation to a close, not Gorbachev. I must have felt under stress and perhaps subconsciously feared that I might say too much.) Gorbachev had little choice, so he said, "Goodbye."

THREE DAYS LATER, I met with Guri Marchuk at the Gorky Physics Institute. I was driven there in the director's car. The conversation was one-on-one. This was my first meeting with the new president of the Academy of Sciences. He was a solid man, middle-aged, businesslike, quick, a typical science administrator of the new school.

Marchuk said, "Your letter impressed Mikhail Sergeyevich greatly. I have the decrees on your case from the Presidium of the Supreme Soviet." He pulled a cropped and crumpled sheet of paper from his breast pocket and read aloud: "1) End the effect of the Decree of the Presidium of the Supreme Soviet of the USSR of January 8, 1980, banishing Sakharov from Moscow as an administrative measure. 2) Decree of the Presidium of the Supreme Soviet of the USSR pardoning Bonner, E. G., and freeing her from serving the remainder of her sentence." (Those are his words, as I wrote them down at the time.)

Marchuk added that the decrees had been read to him over the phone, and he asked me not to quote him. I replied that in the absence of other sources, I might have to.

In response to my questions, Marchuk said that he knew nothing about the dates of the resolutions or about restoration of my awards. (Their return would have been an oblique admission that the authorities had been wrong when they banished me in 1980, but apparently the new thinking hadn't progressed that far.) I was left in the dark on a number of other points, including the key question—whether I had been banished from Moscow on the basis of an official act or by decision of the KGB. The only decree I have actually seen is the one stripping me of my awards.

Marchuk said he wanted to discuss both my return to scientific work and my public posture. "I'd like to understand your thinking on civic matters. You have great authority; many people listen to your opinions."

I responded at some length, and Marchuk listened attentively, registering disagreement on several points. We differed on the proper approach to "hot spots" (Soviet policies, in my opinion, can sometimes appear provocative to objective observers), and also on Afghanistan and on the "package" principle which linked agreement on intercontinental and Euromissiles to agreement on the Strategic Defense Initiative (SDI).

When I stressed my concern for prisoners of conscience, Marchuk said, "Your question was anticipated, and I was asked to deliver a message from the Presidium of the Supreme Soviet: many prisoners have been released, absolutely or conditionally, or transferred to exile; some have received permission to emigrate. More cases are under review. I was told that a prerequisite for release is a promise to refrain from further antisocial behavior."

I objected sharply: "That's an attack on freedom of thought, an attempt to break people. It's illegal and unfair."

Marchuk replied, "Many academicians feel that if you spend too much time worrying about problems which we're in the process of eliminating anyway, you're likely to find yourself isolated in scientific circles." He went on to tell me about the forthcoming Moscow Forum on disarmament and invited me to participate. I promised to think it over. I spoke about my idea of meeting with Edward Teller so that as independent experts we could discuss disarmament, SDI, and so on. The last part of our conversation centered on my participation in research on MTRs and on the problems of nuclear safety and earthquake control. I mentioned that I'd like FIAN to hire Boris Altshuler.

That same evening, December 19, there was a televised press conference at the Ministry of Foreign Affairs in Moscow dealing with a moratorium on nuclear testing. In response to a planted question, Deputy Minister Vladimir Petrovsky announced, "Academician Andrei Sakharov, currently living in Gorky, addressed the Soviet leadership with a request to move [!?] to Moscow. The relevant organizations, including the Academy of Sciences, have reviewed and approved his request, taking into consideration his long absence from Moscow. At the same time, the USSR Supreme Soviet adopted a decision to pardon Citizen Elena Bonner. Sakharov will have an opportunity to return to academic work, now within the framework of the Moscow facilities of the USSR Academy of Sciences." The style is priceless, and the omissions are significant. I particularly like the reference to the Academy and to my "long absence from Moscow" as the reason for my return. Petrovsky said nothing about a decree.

At the time, Lusia and I had no sense of joy or victory. We were grieving for Anatoly Marchenko. Besides, I was troubled over my October 23 letter to Gorbachev, even though I knew, when I thought about it rationally, that I hadn't demeaned myself in any way and hadn't assumed any legally binding limitations on my freedom of action. Moreover, I hadn't deceived Gorbachev about my intentions: I truly did wish to limit my public statements to important matters. Nevertheless, this experience helped me understand those prisoners of conscience who find it difficult to pledge that they will cease "antisocial behavior" as a condition for their release. Many preferred to remain in confinement rather than sign such statements.

In any case, my introspection was quickly cut short by our new, "free" life which flooded us with demands and responsibilities. And we both now have much less strength to cope with it all than we had in 1980.

On December 22, we hurriedly packed a few bags, leaving most of our possessions behind, and set off for the train station. For the first time in seven years, Lusia and I were going home to Moscow together.

On the morning of the 23rd we stepped off the train at Moscow's Yaroslavl Station onto a platform teeming with reporters from all over the world—and, as I learned later, from the Soviet Union as well. It took me forty minutes to make my way through the crowd. Lusia had been separated from me, hundreds of flashbulbs blinded me, and microphones were continually thrust into my face as I tried to respond to the barrage of questions. This impromptu media event was the prototype of many to follow: the whole scene offered a preview of the hurlyburly life that now awaited us.

IN 1974 I CONCLUDED my futurological article, "The World after Fifty Years" as follows: "I hope that mankind will be able to put an end to the dangers threatening us and to continue its progress while preserving everything that makes us human."

I would like to conclude this book, too, with those words. Today, in the seventh decade of my life, my personal aspirations and my entire existence center on my beloved wife, my children and grandchildren, and all those who are dear to me.

THIS VOLUME of memoirs is dedicated to my beloved Lusia. What matters most is that she and I are together.

EPILOGUE

DURING THE six years which have elapsed since the conclusion of this book, much has happened in my life and Lusia's, and in the world at large. I will mention just a few highlights: the battle for permission for Lusia to travel abroad for a family visit and medical treatment; my hunger strikes in 1984 and 1985; Lusia's trip and her open-heart surgery; our return to Moscow; my participation in the Forum for a Nuclear-Free World, for the Survival and Development of Humanity, where I spoke out against the "package" principle [the USSR's linking of agreements on nuclear weapons reductions to termination of the U.S. Strategic Defense Initiative]; Ruth Bonner's death; creation of the International Foundation for the Survival and Development of Humanity; my article on Nagorno-Karabakh and the Crimean Tatars; my first trip abroad; my visit to Azerbaijan, Nagorno-Karabakh, and Armenia; my election to the Congress of People's Deputies and participation in its work.

Some of these events have been described in Lusia's book *Alone Together;* others will be included in my forthcoming *Gorky–Moscow, and Beyond,* which is a continuation of these *Memoirs.* The main thing is that my dear, beloved Lusia and I are united—I have dedicated this book to her.

Life goes on. We are together.

Moscow
December 13, 1989

ANDREI SAKHAROV

APPENDIXES

APPENDIX

APPENDIX A:
THE 1973 ANTI-SAKHAROV
PRESS CAMPAIGN

The occasion, or more accurately, the pretext, for the campaign initiated by the Soviet press against Andrei Sakharov in 1973 was the following interview which he gave to Scandinavian radio and television correspondent Olle Stenholm in July of that year.

Interview with Olle Stenholm

. . . The most natural thing is for everyone to regard his system as the best, and any deviation from this view involves some kind of a psychological conflict. And when in 1968 I wrote my work [*Reflections*] this process was still in its beginning stages and my own approach was rather abstract. My life has been such that I began by confronting global problems and only later on more concrete, personal, and human ones. Thus, in reading my 1968 essay you must understand this and take into account the route I followed from work on thermonuclear weapons to my concern about the results of nuclear tests—their sometimes fatal effects and their genetic consequences. I was still very far from the basic problems facing the people and the whole country. I was still materially privileged and isolated from the people.

But after that?
After that my life began to change in purely personal terms, psychologically. And the process of development simply went further . . .
Now, what is socialism? I began by thinking that I understood it and that

it was good. Then gradually I ceased to understand a great deal—I didn't even understand its economic [basis]; I couldn't make out whether there was anything to it but mere words and propaganda for internal and international consumption. Actually, what hits you in the eye is the state's extreme concentration—economic, political, and ideological—that is, its extreme monopolization of these fields. One may say, exactly as Lenin did at the beginning of our revolution, that it is simple state capitalism, that the state has simply assumed a monopoly role over all the economy. But in that case this socialism contains nothing new. It is only an extreme form of that capitalist path of development found in the United States and other Western countries but in an extremely monopolized form. Thus, we should not be surprised that we have the same kinds of problems—that is, crime and personal alienation—that are to be found in the capitalist world. But our society represents an extreme case with maximum restraint, maximum ideological restrictions, and so forth. Moreover, and very characteristically, we are also the most pretentious—that is, although we are not the best society we pretend that we are.

What are the major concrete shortcomings you see in today's Soviet society?
The lack of freedom. The lack of freedom, the bureaucratization of government, the extremely irrational and also terribly egoistic—that is, class-egoistic—tendency that actually aims only at preserving the system, maintaining a good appearance to conceal a very unpleasant internal state of affairs. We're a society on the decline. But I've already written about that. And it must be very widely known to attentive observers that for us all social things are more for show than for reality. This relates to education, to its organization, and to medical services. Very often people from the West say: "Well, you have many faults but at least you have free medical service." But actually it is no more free than in many Western countries and often it is even less free, so to speak, because its general quality is so low.

Do you think that Soviet society today is a class society?
Well, that is again a theoretical question—that is a question requiring a theoretical evaluation. But in any case it is a society of great internal inequality. Can we say that it has a class structure? It is in a certain sense a distinctive society. It is hard to say whether it should be called a class society. In a sense this is a matter of definition. It's something like our past arguments as to what kind of society could be called fascist. It is also a question of definition, a question of terminology.

But what about the inequality?
Inequality arises on a very large number of levels. There is inequality between village people and city people; the collective farmers do not have pass-

ports, which means that in practical terms they are bound to their collective farms. And permission is needed (true, it is ordinarily given) for them to leave the collective farm. There is inequality among regions: Moscow and the larger cities are favored in the distribution of food, consumer goods, services, cultural attractions, and so on. And the [internal] passport system accentuates these territorial inequities.

Andrei Dmitrivich, you have yourself said that you are privileged . . .
Yes, I have been privileged, of course, and still am today through inertia. I was privileged in the past, actually hyper-privileged, because I was a worker at the very pinnacle of the arms industry. I had by Soviet standards a colossal salary and bonuses.

And, in your opinion, what privileges do Party officials have in the Soviet Union?
Well, they have great privileges, but these are generally nonmonetary in nature. They enjoy a special system of sanitariums and medical services. Privileges arise from personal connections, personal factors of various kinds. Privileges in work, in one's career. All positions of any importance, like those of factory director, chief engineer, and so on are held only by Party members. Exceptions are very rare. And the shop chief must be a Party member. So everything depends on Party membership, on your situation in the Party structure. These things have enormous influence on your career. And, in addition, there is the traditional Party personnel system that is expressed in the concept of *nomenklatura*. This means that even if a person fails in some kind of work, as long as he is a leading Party worker he will be transferred to some other job not very different in material advantages from the one he gives up.

The whole business of getting a job and promotion is closely tied to personal relationships in this system. Each important bureaucrat has attached to him personally certain people who move with him from place to place as he is transferred. There is something irresistible about this, and it seems to be a kind of law of our state structure.

But if we talk about other material advantages, then they are primarily enjoyed by an isolated but more or less well-defined group that has a special relationship to the administration. The advantages are determined by Party membership but there are also within the Party very large distinctions. It seems as though something like Orwell's concept of an inner party already exists with us in a certain sense.

And if we talk about people in this inner Party, then they have great material advantages. There exists a system of supplemental pay in special envelopes. This system sometimes disappears and then again reappears. I don't know what the situation is at the given moment, but it looks as though the custom has been revived in some places. Then there is the system of closed shops, where not only is the quality of the products better and the assortment wider but also the price differs from the general price structure so that with the same ruble these people can buy a different product at a different price and that means their nominal wage is not really very significant.*

We have talked about shortcomings. Now the question is, what can be done to correct all this?

What can be done and what should be at least attempted are different questions. It seems to me that almost nothing can be done . . .

Why not?

Because the system has a high degree of internal stability. The less free a system, the greater ordinarily its ability to maintain itself.

And outside forces can do nothing?

We have a very poor understanding of what the external world is doing. It seems as if the external world has decided to accept our rules of the game. On the one hand, that is very bad. But there is, of course, another side to the matter. We are now breaking out of our fifty-year isolation and possibly with time this may even exert a beneficial influence. But how this will all come out—it is very difficult to predict. And if we speak of the West, then it is difficult each time to tell whether they want to help us or whether, on the contrary, there is some kind of capitulation, a game involving the domestic interests of the people of the West in which we merely play the role of small change.

Well, those are foreign forces—what about inside the Soviet Union?

Within the Soviet Union certainly some kind of process is going on, but so far it is so imperceptible and hidden that it's not possible to anticipate any positive, general changes, . . . well, it's almost impossible. We understand that such a large state as ours can never be homogeneous but in the absence of information and the absence of contacts among separate groups of people it is almost impossible to understand what is going on. We know that there are very strong nationalistic tendencies on the country's periphery. Whether they are positive or not is very hard to determine in particular cases. In some

---

*In that part of the interview devoted to the privileged position of the members of the Party, I may have given the false impression that Party members and non-Party members in the same job receive different salaries. That is not the case. However, what I said regarding the influence of Party membership on a career, the Party hierarchy, etc. remains in force.

cases—for example, in the Ukraine—they have become very strongly allied with democratic forces. In the Baltic states it is the same—religious and nationalist forces have become interwoven very naturally and easily with the democratic. But in other places it may not be the same. We don't know in detail.

So you are a pessimist in spite of the fact that you yourself . . .

I am skeptical about socialism in general. I don't see that socialism offers some kind of new theoretical plan, so to speak, for the better organization of society. Therefore it seems to me that while we may find some positive elements in our life, on the whole our state has displayed more destructive features than constructive ones. Our society has witnessed such fierce political struggles, such destruction, such bitterness, that now we are reaping the sad fruits of all this in a kind of tiredness, apathy, cynicism, from which we find it most difficult to recover, if recovery is possible at all. What direction our society will take is extremely difficult to predict from within. Perhaps it can be done better from the outside, but for this, one requires the maximum in objectivity.

But, Andrei Dmitrivich, you are doubtful that anything can be done to improve the system of the Soviet Union, yet you yourself go ahead acting, protesting—why?

Well, there is a need to create ideals even when you can't see any way to achieve them, because if there are no ideals then there can be no hope and then one would be left completely in the dark, in a hopeless blind alley.

Moreover, we can't know whether there is some kind of possibility of cooperation between our country and the outside world. If no signals about our unhappy situation are sent out, then there would be no way to make use of any possibility which might exist. We wouldn't know what needs changing or how to change it.

Then there is another consideration—that the history of our country should serve as a warning. It should deter the West and the developing countries from committing mistakes on the scale we have during our historical development. Therefore, if a man speaks out, it does not mean that he hopes necessarily to achieve something. He may hope for nothing but nonetheless speak because he cannot remain silent.

We really have no hopes, and unfortunately, experience shows we are right. Our actions don't lead to positive results.

But what are your goals?
With respect to society?

Yes.

Well, I attempted in my Memorandum to Brezhnev, and especially in the postscript to it, to outline a certain ideal, but in the Memorandum there is much I would like to correct, because it was written a long time ago, in 1971, and it was published a year and a half later without changes. For instance, I wrote then about the Chinese problem in a tone I would not use today, because at that time I simply did not understand our relations with China and what you don't understand, it is better not to write about. For example, I feel that I overemphasized the notion of a Chinese threat, and I would not now accuse China of aggression. As for China itself, it simply represents a more extreme stage of development such as our own society has already passed through, and it is directed more toward revolutionary self-assertion both internally and in the outer world than toward the well-being of its people. China is very similar to Russia in the 1920s and the beginning of the 1930s.

But if you think that socialism in the Soviet Union has not shown its superiority, does that mean you think that in order to remedy the situation you must therefore reconstruct the whole state, or can something be done within the system in order to improve it and eliminate its greatest defects?

That is too difficult a question for me, because to reorganize the state completely—that is unthinkable; there always must be some kind of continuity and some kind of gradualness, otherwise there would again be the terrible destruction through which we have passed several times, and a total collapse. Doing things step by step seems an absolute necessity.

Well, what is to be done first?

What must be done? I think that our present system can do nothing or at least very little by its own internal resources. But still, we have to do something. We must liquidate the ideological monism of our society.

Excuse me—what?

The uniform ideological structure that is anti-democratic in its very essence—it has been very tragic for the state. For example, our isolation from the outside world and the absence of the right to leave the country and to return have a very pernicious effect on our internal life. It is in the first instance a great tragedy for all those who wish to leave for personal or national reasons. But it is also a tragedy for those who remain in the country, because a country from which it is not possible to leave freely, to which it is not possible to return freely is a country that is unsound, a closed system where all processes develop differently from those of an open system.

You know that the right of free exit . . .

It is one of the conditions the country needs for developing along healthier lines.

And what else?

There are things of an economic nature that are very important. Our extreme state socialism has led to the elimination of private initiative in areas in which it would be most effective, not just in large-scale industry and in transport, in which perhaps the state system of administration is more reasonable. Moreover, the suppression of individual initiative leads to strict constraints on personal freedom. This also reflects negatively on the standard of living and simply makes life much more boring and dreary than need be. I am talking about personal enterprise in the field of consumer goods, education, and medicine. All of this no doubt would have a very positive significance in weakening the extreme monopolistic structure of the state. The Party monopoly of administration has reached such unheard-of levels that even the ruling class must realize it can no longer be tolerated.

So—what is needed? We need first of all greater glasnost, openness in the work of the administrative apparatus. A single-party system is excessively rigid. Even under the conditions of a socialist economic system a multiparty system is possible. Actually, on some levels of the people's democracies, the one-party system is not needed. And in some of the people's democracies some elements, of a multiparty system exist, although they are a travesty of the real thing.

We need competitive elections to state organs. In general, we need a series of measures that taken individually might have little effect but that in combination might shake that monolith we have created, which is so fossilized and so oppressive for the life of the whole planet.

The press must change its character. Now it is so standardized that it has lost any significant informational value. And when it does reflect facts, they are expressed in such a way that they are understandable only to the initiated and reflect a distorted picture of real life in the country. As for intellectual life, there is no variety whatsoever.

Intellectual work is badly paid, even in comparison with physical work. And in absolute terms the intelligentsia's living standard is very low in comparison with that in Western countries at a comparable stage of development. The depreciation of the intelligentsia leads to ideological degradation, and an antiintellectual atmosphere in the country, in which the intellectual professions, the professions of teachers, of doctors, do not receive the respect they should have. And the intelligentsia itself has begun to retreat into narrow professionalism, or into a kind of dual intellectual life: conformity at work, but at home, in the narrow circles of their own friends, people begin to think in different ways. This dichotomy leads to more hypocrisy and a further decline in morals and creativity. The effects are particularly pronounced in the humanistic as distinguished from the technical intelligentsia. They feel that they have gotten into a kind of blind alley. As a result, the literature that appears is terribly gray or conventional and generally boring.

Permit me one last question. You personally have never feared for your health and freedom in these years in which you have been so active?

I have never feared for myself, but that is, you might say, in part due to my character and partly because I began from a very high social position, where such fears were completely unjustified and irrelevant. But now I fear pressure, which is not directed against me personally but against members of my family, members of the family of my wife. That is the most painful thing, and it is a very real threat, which is coming closer to us. They picked up the son of Veniamin Levich. This shows how they go about these things.

(The text of this interview was first published in the Swedish newspaper *Dagens Nyheter,* July 4, 1973.)

ATTACKS IN
THE SOVIET PRESS

A Purveyor of Libel

An interview given by Andrei Sakharov to Swedish radio and TV has appeared in several reactionary bourgeois publications. The bourgeois press presents the subject of the interview as "a fighter for civil rights," of which, it is claimed, the Soviet people are deprived. What has Sakharov done to please his Western "clients"?

From beginning to end, his interview deliberately blackens the Soviet Union and Soviet way of life. Sakharov is displeased that the government, not private companies, runs the USSR's national economy; he believes that "stifling of private initiative makes life boring." At a single stroke, he unhesitatingly accuses the entire Soviet intelligensia of being "two-faced" and "preoccupied with narrow professional interests."

In his interview, he alleges that the USSR is "a closed society." "Isolation from the outside world," Sakharov says, "has a ruinous effect on our life." One does not have to be a famous scientist to know that some five million foreigners have visited this "closed society"—the USSR—in the past three years, during which time almost an equal number of Soviet citizens have traveled abroad. In 1972 alone, about 2.5 million foreign visitors from one hundred countries came to the Soviet Union. Intourist is preparing to receive 4.5 million visitors in 1975. But what does Sakharov care about the facts? That's not what is looked for from him . . .

Even the Soviet system's generally recognized social achievements are presented by Sakharov as if in a funhouse mirror. For example, everyone knows that medical services are free in the Soviet Union unlike those in capitalist countries. Sakharov asserts that medical services in the Soviet Union are "no less expensive than in many Western countries, and sometimes cost even more."

Who does not know how much attention is paid to education in the USSR, how many schools are being built, how respected is the profession of teacher? A. Sakharov says unblushingly: "The educational system in the USSR is in shameful condition. . . ."

Yuri Kornilov
Literaturnaya gazeta, July 18, 1973

The Academicians' Letter

We feel it incumbent upon us to bring to public attention our attitude toward the behavior of Academician Sakharov.

In recent years, A. D. Sakharov has withdrawn from active scientific work and has issued a series of statements concerning the government and the domestic and foreign policies of the Soviet Union. Not long ago, in an interview given to foreign correspondents in Moscow and published in the Western press, he went so far as to oppose the Soviet Union's policies aimed at reducing international tension and fostering ongoing positive developments on the international scene.

A. D. Sakharov seeks to justify his statements, which are inimical to the interests of all progressive individuals, through gross distortion of Soviet reality and unsubstantiated criticism of the socialist order. His utterances align him with highly reactionary circles that are working against peaceful coexistence among nations, and against the policies of our Party and state designed to promote scientific and cultural cooperation and world peace. A. D. Sakharov thus makes of himself an instrument of propaganda hostile to the Soviet Union and other socialist nations.

A. D. Sakharov's actions are thoroughly alien to Soviet scientists, and seem particularly repugnant when contrasted with our people's fervent efforts to accomplish the grand tasks of building the USSR's economy and culture and fostering peace and improved international relations.

We greet A. D. Sakharov's statements with indignation, and heartily condemn his actions, which discredit the good name of Soviet science. We can only hope that Academician Sakharov will reflect on his activities.

Academicians: N. G. Basov, N. B. Belov, N. N. Bogolyubov, A. E. Braunshtein, A. P. Vinogradov, S. V. Vonsovsky, B. M. Bul, N. P. Dubinin, N. M. Zhavoronkov, B. M. Kedrov, M. V. Keldysh, V. A. Kotelnikov, G. V. Kurdyumov, A. A. Logunov, M. A. Markov, A. N.

Nesmeyanov, A. M. Obukhov, Yu. A. Ovchinnikov, A. I. Oparin, B. E. Paton, B. N. Petrov, P. N. Pospelov, A. M. Prokhorov, O. A. Reutov, A. M. Rumyantsev, L. I. Sedov, N. N. Semyonov, D. V. Skobeltsyn, S. L. Sobolev, V. I. Spitsyn, V. D. Timakov, A. N. Tikhonov, V. M. Tuchkevich, P. N. Fedoseyev, I. M. Frank, A. N. Frumkin, Yu. B. Khariton, M. B. Khrapchenko, P. A. Cherenkov, V. A. Engelgardt.

—Pravda, August 29, 1973

He Discredits the Title of Citizen

. . . we, Soviet composers and musicologists, express our indignation at A. D. Sakharov's actions directed against the Soviet Union's policy on the relaxation of international tension, as well as his slanderous statement about socialist reality. It is no accident that the reactionary Western press has snatched up his anti-Soviet "revelations."

D. Kabalevsky, K. Karaev, P. Savintsev, G. Sviridov, S. Tulikov,
A. Khachaturian, A. Kholminov, T. Khrennikov, D. Shostakovich,
R. Shchedrin, A. Eshpai, B. Yarustovsky.

Pravda, April 2, 1973

Pleasing the Anti-Soviets

On behalf of the workers of the Leningrad Kirov factory, we feel compelled to declare that we categorically denounce the dishonorable anti-Soviet behavior of Academician Sakharov. While the Soviet people are toiling to fulfill the resolutions of the Twenty-fourth Party Congress for the sake of the triumph of communism, Sakharov libels the Soviet state and the Communist Party.

Many generations of our country's working people have struggled selflessly for the triumph of the socialist system that Sakharov is doing his best to discredit.

Honest people everywhere have welcomed enthusiastically the relaxation of international tension that can be credited to the peace policy being pursued by the USSR's Party Central Committee. Sakharov, who discredits the title of Soviet scientist, makes base and provocative statements pleasing to foreign anti-Soviets, supporters of the cold war.

This renegade deserves the contempt of all, for he has put himself in opposition to the people and has allied himself with our bitter ideological enemies.

E. I. Lebedev (grinders and polishers crew leader, Hero of Socialist

Labor); B. M. Vorobiev (turner, Hero of Socialist Labor); K. V.
Govorushkin (turner, Hero of Socialist Labor); M. V. Gusarov
(metalworkers crew leader, State Prize laureate).

Pravda, April 2, 1973

Letter of the Members of VASKhNIL
(All-Union Lenin Academy of Agriculture)

We fully support the opinion expressed in the letter signed by members of the
USSR Academy of Sciences concerning the behavior of Academician A. D.
Sakharov. We think it our duty to express our deep indignation at the activities
of this individual, who has become a tool of hostile propaganda.

. . . Only one who has lost touch with the life of the people and has betrayed
their interests could so libel our social system, the domestic and foreign policy
of the Soviet Union.

. . . A. D. Sakharov has reached the point where he mercilessly distorts Soviet
reality, and the socialist system, and even demands imperialist interference in
the internal affairs of the USSR and other socialist nations.

. . . A. D. Sakharov's activity is alien to us; his behavior places him outside
the ranks of Soviet scientists.

—Members of the Academy of Agriculture (VASKhNIL): 33 signatures

Izvestia, August 31, 1973

From Antisocial Positions

A. D. Sakharov must be aware that no one has the right to undermine the unity
of the ranks of Soviet scientists through individual apostasy and deviation from
the ideological stance of a Soviet citizen.

It is outrageous that a physicist should oppose the relaxation of international
tension and become an advocate of forces opposed to the relaxation of tension.
A. D. Sakharov is under the thumb of bourgeois propaganda, whose tool he
has become against the Soviet Union.

—Academician V. Glushkov, Vice-President of the Academy of Sciences
of the Ukrainian SSR

Izvestia, August 31, 1973

Impossible to Justify

The scientist's authority is great in our country; our society pays close heed to what he says. False and erroneous notions, expressed by a famous scientist, can be terribly damaging to his homeland. For this reason, a scientist must be scrupulously accurate in his political statements, even more so than in his scientific conclusions and calculations. He must be absolutely objective, and at least as well informed on social issues as in his scientific specialty, particularly if he decides to judge his country's policy with regard to the preservation of peace, as does Academician A. D. Sakharov. Unfortunately, his judgments are hasty and mistaken.

. . . His actions, exploited by forces hostile to our country, are an outrage.

Academician I. Petryanov
Izvestia, August 31, 1973

Letters to *Pravda,* September 5, 1973

A Position Alien to the People

We, Soviet filmmakers, after reading the letter from a group of academicians published by *Pravda,* support fully their opinion of A. D. Sakharov's disgraceful behavior. He tries to discredit the social system and the domestic and foreign policy of the Soviet Union.

. . . He who blackens his country and people and tries to turn history back deserves only contempt and indignation.

—28 signatures

We Are Indignant

Academician A. D. Sakharov's interview published in the Western press evokes only indignation.

. . . What does Academician A. D. Sakharov suggest in his interview? He is opposed to reinforcement of peace. Sakharov forgets that those who take this path foster confrontation, cold war actions, an increase in international tension . . .

It is shameful that this Soviet scientist appeals to the "Western world" to

halt the ongoing relaxation of international tension and to interfere in the
internal affairs of the Soviet Union. . . .

—Academician A. Imshenetsky

Dishonorable Actions

My comrades and I have read the letter about the dishonorable behavior of
Academician Sakharov signed by Soviet academicians. We cannot understand
how someone who has been raised under Soviet rule, whose education and
professional status were provided for by the toil of common laborers, can so
unscrupulously libel our way of life.

—E. Borzenkov, Hero of Socialist Labor

In Concert with Our Enemies

I am profoundly shocked and indignant that among our academicians there is
an individual who cares nothing about the well-being of our people or the
principles of peaceful coexistence. In concert with our bitter enemies, the
imperialists, he is attempting to obstruct those who are doing their utmost to
ensure lives of peace for the people of our planet.

The members of the Academy of Sciences were right to denounce this
renegade. Academician Sakharov deserves general contempt for betraying the
interests of science, of the Soviet people, and of all progressive mankind.

—T. S. Maltsev, agronomist, Hero of Socialist Labor, Honorary Member
of The All-Union Lenin Academy of Agriculture (VASKhNIL)

Letters to *Pravda*, September 9, 1973

Statement of Scientists of the Siberian Branch of the USSR Academy of Sciences.

. . . we have learned from articles in the press that Academician Sakharov, a
member of the USSR Academy of Sciences, has given an interview discrediting
our country's foreign policy.

. . . A. D. Sakharov's interview by no means expresses the aspirations and
views of academicians and the scientific intelligentsia. The interview's contents

link Sakharov ideologically to the most reactionary anti-Soviet and militaristic circles.

Academicians: M. A. Lavrentiev, G. K. Boreskov, V. A. Kuznetsov, G. I. Marchuk, A. V. Nikolaev, A. N. Skrinsky, A. A. Trofimuk. Corresponding members of the Academy of Sciences: O. F. Vasiliev, Yu. L. Ershov, N. A. Zheltukhin, M. F. Zhukov, A. A. Kovalsky, V. A. Koptyug, S. S. Kutateladze, M. M. Lavrentiev, V. P. Mamaev, A. V. Rzhanov, V. N. Saks, R. I. Soloukhin, E. E. Fotiadi.

We Categorically Denounce

We, representatives of the working people of the I. A. Likhachev automobile factory, indignantly and categorically denounce the disgraceful behavior of Sakharov, who libels our state and social system, and discredits the Soviet government's policy aimed at reinforcing peace and détente.

—Hero of Socialist Labor K. Artemova et al. (four signatures)

We Are Indignant

. . . We, farmers, unanimously support the outstanding Soviet scientists who have denounced Sakharov, and express our keen indignation at his actions and words.

. . . We categorically deny his inventions about our socialist system, and wonder why academician A. D. Sakharov has concocted such distortions of Soviet reality. . . .

—A. V. Gitalov, two-time Hero of Socialist Labor and others (12 signatures)

A Letter from the USSR Academy of Pedagogical Sciences
Izvestia, September 4, 1973

Some Western press organs have published a number of anti-Soviet statements made recently by Academician A. D. Sakharov to a group of foreign correspondents in Moscow. In these statements he essentially advances the question of some changes in the essence of the socialist countries' system in the interests of socialism's enemies. . . .

Sakharov's behavior engenders only indignation in us, workers of pedagogical science, and we share the position of the members of the USSR Academy of Sciences. . . .

We are confident that all Soviet teachers and scientific workers of the pedagogical front share our indignation at Sakharov's behavior. This is the behavior of a man who has lost his sense of responsibility toward his people who educated him and gave him every opportunity for scientific creativity. By his statements Sakharov discredits the honor and dignity of Soviet scientists, aligns himself with the reactionaries and champions of war, and forfeits any tie with the Soviet people and his motherland.

We decisively condemn Sakharov's unseemly position.

—23 signatures

Think About It!

We are indignant at Academician Sakharov's utterances against the policy of the Soviet Union in favor of détente. . . .

The actions of Academician Sakharov run counter to the struggle of all Soviet people for peace, happiness, and the bright future of all mankind. We hope that Academician Sakharov will think seriously about his actions and will draw the correct conclusions.

Professors from the Bauman Technical Academy: (29 signatures).

Letter to the Editorial Board of *Izvestia,* September 5, 1973

We, members of the Estonian Academy of Scienses and heads of scientific research institutes, announce our solidarity with the letter denouncing the actions of A. D. Sakharov signed by members of the USSR Academy of Sciences . . .

. . . We, scientists of a republic where socialism was constructed later than in many other Soviet republics, still remember the obstacles that hindered development of human genius in bourgeois nations. The economy, culture, and science of Soviet Estonia have flourished before our eyes, and we know that it is the multinational socialist state which protects us from the horrors of another war. It is for this reason that we are so upset by the statement libelling socialism.

We are indignant and dismayed that Academician A. D. Sakharov has damaged our country, the cause of socialism, and the vital interest of all mankind—peace. We expect Academician A. D. Sakharov to reconsider his position.

—Members of the Academy of Sciences of the Estonian SSR (18 signatures)

To Be a Soviet Scientist Means to Be a Patriot

Pravda, September 8, 1973

Soviet people, familiar with the academicians' letter regarding the actions of the physicist A. D. Sakharov, who has brought discredit to the title of Soviet scientist, have been sending letters and telegrams to newspapers, radio and TV, and TASS, expressing their concern about Sakharov's dishonorable behavior and his attempt to libel our social system and the domestic and foreign policy of the Soviet state.

. . . the Soviet people are deeply indignant about Sakharov's unpatriotic behavior. Workers, farmers, intellectuals: all denounce categorically Sakharov's anti-Soviet activities that have played into the hands of the enemies of peace and socialism.

Members of the Academy of Sciences of all Union Republics have denounced Sakharov's position.

Kiev writer Stepan Oleynik's short telegram is filled with indignation:

"I share all Soviet people's indignation at Sakharov's baseness and his shameless libel of our great and hardworking people, whose bread he eats, and our beloved Soviet state. Shame on Sakharov and his kind."

Here are some lines from a telegram from Platon Voronko, former commander of the Kovpak partisan unit:

"I suffered all the hardships and horrors of war. I was wounded four times in combat against the fascists. I lost my father, brother, and many of my friends during those terrible years. I categorically denounce Sakharov and Solzhenitsyn's positions and actions aimed at undermining and discrediting the noble, humane policy of our Party."

"Sakharov's ideas are alien to the Soviet people and are used by reactionary organs of bourgois propaganda to libel the domestic and foreign policy of our state and to undermine the prestige and authority of our homeland. But their attempts are futile; it is impossible to discredit the cause of peace and the ideas of communism." So reads the statement of the Scientific Council of Moscow University made on behalf of thousands of students and professors of the university. . . .

. . . We agree. To be a Soviet scientist means to be a Soviet patriot. It cannot be otherwise.

—TASS

Letters to *Pravda*, September 6, 1973

Unworthy of a Scientist

. . . Sakharov's interview is, at very least, a shameless libel against the Party, the Soviet government, and our socialist system . . .

Sakharov has in fact joined the camp of those opposed to cooperation among nations, and has become a mouthpiece for anti-Soviet and antisocialist propaganda. He has violated ideals dear to the Soviet people and their beliefs, and has undermined peace on our planet.

. . . We feel compelled to express our indignation at Sakharov's actions. He has attempted to distort Soviet reality, the peaceful course of our state, and of the entire socialist fraternity.

A. Yu. Ishlinsky, academician, Chairman of the All-Union Council
of Scientific-Technical Societies and others (16 signatures in all)

He Plays into the Hands of Reactionary Forces

. . . we, Soviet artists, support the opinion of the authors of the letter [signed by forty academicians], as well as the many representatives of the Soviet public who have denounced Sakharov's attempts to discredit our country in the eyes of peace-loving mankind. . . .

Soviet artists are always loyal to the interests of peace and friendship among nations. We are in close contact with the people, and are fully aware of their contribution to our economic development. We bear witness to the great achievements of our country in this area.

. . . We support enthusiastically the Communist Party's peace initiatives, and denounce categorically the behavior of A. D. Sakharov, who is playing into the hands of reactionary anti-Soviet forces.

—21 signatures

APPENDIX B:
STATEMENTS, LETTERS, AND ARTICLES

MEMORANDUM

I request a discussion of the general questions partially discussed in a previous letter from R. A. Medvedev, V. F. Turchin, and myself, and in my letter of 1968. I also request the consideration of a number of particular questions of a topical nature that I find extremely disturbing.

I have included below, in two general lists, questions that, although differing in degree of importance and self-evidence, have a definite inner connection. A discussion and partial argumentation of these questions will be found in the above-mentioned letters and in the postscript to this memorandum.

I wish also to inform you that in November 1970, I, together with V. N. Chalidze and A. N. Tverdokhlebov, founded a "Human Rights Committee," with the aims of studying safeguards for human rights and promoting knowledge of the law. I enclose some of the committee's documents. We hope to be useful to society, and we seek a dialogue with the country's leadership and a frank and public discussion of problems relating to human rights.

Some Urgent Problems

The problems listed below appear to me to need urgent consideration.
For brevity's sake they have been expressed in the form of proposals. While

recognizing that some of these problems require further study, and conscious that the list is of necessity an incomplete and therefore to a certain extent a subjective one (I have tried to set out several equally important questions in the second half of this memorandum, while several could not be included at all), I nevertheless consider that a discussion of the following proposals by the competent authorities is essential.

1. Concerning political persecution. I feel it is high time to consider the pressing problem of implementing a general amnesty for political prisoners, that is, persons convicted under Articles 70, 72, 190-1, -2 and -3 of the RSFSR Criminal Code and the equivalent articles of the codes of the union republics; persons convicted on religious grounds; persons confined in psychiatric institutions; persons sentenced for attempting to cross the frontier; and political prisoners given an additional sentence for attempting to escape or for disseminating propaganda in their camp.

Measures should be taken to insure real and widespread public access to the hearings of all legal proceedings, especially those of a political character. I consider it important that all judicial verdicts pronounced in violation of the principle of public access should be reviewed.

I hold inadmissible all forms of psychiatric repression, whether based on political, ideological, or religious grounds. I am of the opinion that a law must be passed to protect the rights of persons subjected to compulsory psychiatric hospitalization; resolutions must be passed and the necessary legislative measures introduced to protect the rights of persons presumed to be mentally ill in the course of a prosecution on political charges. In particular, private psychiatric investigation by commissions independent of the authorities should be allowed in both cases.

Independently of the general solution of these problems, I request the examination by the competent organs of a number of pressing individual cases, some of which are listed in an attached note.

2. Concerning glasnost, the free exchange of information, and freedom of opinion. A bill concerning the press and the mass media should be submitted for nationwide discussion.

A resolution should be passed calling for greater freedom in the publication of statistical and sociological data.

3. Concerning nationalities problems and the problem of leaving the country. Resolutions and laws should be passed fully restoring the rights of peoples deported under Stalin.

Laws should be passed to insure that citizens may easily and without hindrance exercise their right to leave the country and freely return to it. Regulations restricting this right and in contravention of the law should be annulled.

4. Concerning international problems. We should show initiative and announce (or affirm, initially on a unilateral basis) our refusal to be the first to use weapons of mass destruction (nuclear, chemical, bacteriological, and incendiary weapons). We should allow inspection teams to visit our territory for effective arms control (assuming that we conclude an agreement on disarmament or partial limitation of certain types of armaments).

In order to consolidate the results of our changed relations with East Germany we should work out a new, more flexible, and realistic position on the question of West Berlin.

We should alter our political position in the Middle East and in Vietnam, and actively seek, through the United Nations and diplomatic channels, a peaceful settlement in the shortest possible time, on the basis of a compromise, with the renunciation by the United States and the USSR of any intervention, military or political, direct or indirect; the promotion of a program of large-scale economic aid on an apolitical, international basis (through the United Nations?); and the proposal that UN troops be widely used to safeguard political and military stability in these areas.

Theses and Proposals with Regard to General Problems

By way of preparation for a discussion of the basic problems of the development and foreign policy of our country, I have attempted to formulate a number of theses. Some of them are set out in the form of discussion points. I have tried to give the fullest possible exposition of my views, although I realize that some of these theses will seem unacceptable and others uninteresting or insignificant.

1. Since 1956 a number of important measures have been taken in our country to eliminate the most dangerous and ugly features of the previous stage of development of Soviet society and state policies. However, at the same time there do occur certain negative phenomena—deviations, inconsistencies, and sluggishness in the implementation of the new line. It is essential to work out a clear-cut and consistent program of further democratization and liberalization, and to take a number of immediate steps as a matter of urgency. This is required in the interests of technical and economic progress, of gradually overcoming our backwardness and isolation from the advanced capitalist countries, and in the interests of the prosperity of large sectors of the population, internal stability, and external security. The development of our country is taking place in the extremely difficult conditions presented by our relations

with China. We are faced with serious internal difficulties in the sphere of the economy and the general standard of living, technical and economic progress, culture and ideology.

One must point out the increasingly acute nationalities problem, the complexities of the interrelationship between the Party-state apparatus and the intelligentsia, and of that between the basic mass of the workers, who find themselves relatively worse off with regard to their standard of living and financial status, their prospects for professional promotion and cultural development, and many of whom feel disillusioned with all the "fine words," and the privileged group of "the bosses," whom the more backward sectors of the workers frequently, and chiefly by virtue of traditional prejudices, identify with the intelligentsia. Our country's foreign policy is not always sufficiently realistic. We need basic decisions in order to prevent possible complications.

2. I venture the opinion that it would be correct to characterize as follows the society toward the creation of which urgent state reforms as well as the efforts of citizens to develop a social conscience should be directed:

a) The basic aim of the state is the protection and safeguarding of the basic rights of its citizens. The defense of human rights is the loftiest of all aims.

b) State institutions always act in complete accordance with laws (which are stable, and known to all citizens, institutions, and organizations). Observance of the law is obligatory for all citizens, agencies, and organizations.

c) The happiness of the people is safeguarded, in particular, by their freedom of work, freedom of consumption, freedom in their private lives, and in their education, their cultural and their social activities, freedom of opinion and of conscience, and freedom of exchange of information, and of movement.

d) Glasnost facilitates the control by society of legality, justice, and the quality of decision-making, contributes to the effectiveness of the entire system, makes for a scientific and democratic system of government, and promotes progress, prosperity, and national security.

e) Competitiveness, glasnost, and the absence of privileges insure a just and equitable distribution of incentives for the labor, skills, and initiative of all citizens.

f) There is a definite stratification of society based on type of occupation, nature of abilities, and [social] relations. . . .

g) The basic energies of the country are directed toward harmonious internal development, with the purposeful deployment of labor and natural resources, and this is the basis of its power and prosperity. The country and its people are always ready to enter into friendly international cooperation and aid within the framework of universal brotherhood, but the society is such that it does not need to use foreign policy as a means of internal political stabilization, or to extend its spheres of influence, or to export its ideas. Messianism, delusions as to the uniqueness of a society and the exclusive merits of its own path, as well as the rejection of the paths of other societies, are alien to society; organically alien to it also are dogmatism, adventurism, and aggression.

In the actual conditions obtaining in our country in particular, we will only overcome our economic difficulties and improve the people's standard of living by a concentration of resources on internal problems, and, given some additional conditions (democratization, the elimination of our people's isolation in terms of access to information from the rest of the world, and economic measures), this alone will give us any hope of gradually narrowing the gap between ourselves and the advanced capitalist countries, safeguard national security in the event of a deterioration in our relations with China, and insure that we have ample opportunity to assist countries in need.

3. *Foreign policy.*

a) Our chief foreign policy problem is our relations with China. While offering the Chinese people the alternative of economic, technical, and cultural aid, and fraternal cooperation and progress together along the road of democracy, and always leaving open the possibility of developing relations in this way, we must at the same time display a special concern for the safeguarding of our national security, avoid all other possible complications in our foreign and domestic policies, and implement our plans for the development of Siberia, keeping the China factor in mind.

b) We must aim at noninterference in the internal affairs of other socialist countries, and mutual economic aid.

c) We must take the initiative in calling for the creation (within the framework of the United Nations?) of a new international consultative organ, an "International Council of Experts on the Problems of Peace, Disarmament, Economic Aid to Needy Countries, the Defense of Human Rights, and the Protection of the Environment," consisting of authoritative and impartial individuals. The council's statutes, and the procedure for the election of its members, must guarantee it maximum independence from the interests of particular states and groups of states. In deciding on the composition and statutes of the council, it is probably essential to take into account the wishes of the main international organizations. An international agreement should be signed obliging legislative and governmental organs to consider the Council of Experts recommendations, which must be well founded and open to scrutiny. The decisions of national organs with regard to these recommendations must be disclosed, irrespective of whether the recommendations are accepted or rejected.

4. *Economic problems, management, personnel.*

a) Extension of the 1965 economic reform: increase in the economic independence of all enterprises; review of a number of regulations which restrict hiring, salaries, and incentives, or hamper the supply system, capital investment, planning, cooperation, product development, and allocation of funds.

b) Management and personnel: resolutions should be passed to make the work of state institutions at all levels more open to public scrutiny, as far as the interests of the state will allow. A review of the "behind-closed-doors" tradition is especially vital. With regard to the problems of personnel policy, there should be increased open and active public control over the selection of personnel and there should be procedures for the election of management personnel at all levels and their replacement if they are found unsuitable. Democracy requires the abolition of the system of holding noncompetitive elections—that is, "elections without choice." At the same time the following are essential: increased availability of information; self-sufficiency; the right to experiment; delegation of responsibility to the enterprise and its employees; improved methods of specialist and management training at all levels; the abolition of special privileges linked to professional and Party rank, since these are very harmful in social and working relations; publication of official salaries; reorganization of personnel departments; abolition of the system of *nomenklatura* and other such survivals of the previous epoch; the creation of scientific councils, composed of scholars with various specialist qualifications, and endowed with the necessary independence, to advise the leadership.

c) Measures to promote the expansion of agricultural production on private plots belonging to collective farmers, workers on state farms, and individual peasants; changes in tax policy; increase in the arable land devoted to this agricultural sector; changes in the system of supplying this sector with modern, specially designed agricultural machinery, fertilizers, etc. Measures to improve the supply of building materials and fuel to the village; the expansion of all forms of cooperative farming in the village, with changes in tax policy, permission to hire and pay laborers in accordance with the requirements of the job, and changes in the system of supplying materials to the village.

d) Increased opportunity for and profitability of private initiative in the service industries, medical care, trade, education, and so on.

5. The gradual abolition of internal passport regulations should be considered, since these are a serious hindrance to the development of the country's productive resources and a violation of civil rights, particularly those of the rural population.

6. *Information exchange, culture, science, and freedom of opinion.*

a) Freedom of opinion, the spirit of inquiry, and creative tension should be encouraged.

b) The jamming of foreign radio broadcasts should be stopped, more foreign literature imported, the international copyright agreement signed, and foreign travel facilitated, in order to overcome the isolation that is having a pernicious effect on our development.

c) The real separation of church and state, and the real (that is, legally, economically, and administratively guaranteed) freedom of conscience and worship, should be ensured.

d) A review should be carried out of those aspects of the interrelations between the Party-state apparatus and art, literature, theater, education, and so on that are harmful to the development of culture in our country, reduce the boldness and variety of creative endeavor, and lead to conformity, grayness, and ritual repetition. In the social sciences and the humanities, which play an ever greater role in modern life (philosophy, history, sociology, jurisprudence, etc.), we must eliminate stagnation, widen the scope of creative endeavor, ensure independence from imposed dogma, and make use of the entire gamut of foreign experience.

7. *Social policies.*

a) Abolition of the death penalty should be explored. Special-regimen imprisonment should be abolished as inhumane. The penitentiary system should be improved, utilizing foreign experience and the recommendations of the UN.

b) A study should be made of the possibility of setting up a public oversight body to eliminate the use of physical coercion (beatings, starvation, cold, etc.) against persons in detention.

c) There must be a radical improvement in the quality of education: increased salaries and independence for schoolteachers and college lecturers; deemphasis of formal diplomas and degrees; a less standardized educational system; a wider curriculum; increased guarantees for freedom of opinion.

d) The struggle against alcoholism should be intensified, and the possibility of public control over all aspects of the problem considered.

e) Stronger measures against noise, air, and water pollution, erosion, salinization and chemical pollution of the soil should be adopted. More should be done to preserve the wilderness and to prevent cruelty to animals.

f) Reform of medical care; expansion of the network of clinics and hospitals; a more important role for doctors, nurses, and aides in private practice; salary increases for health-service employees at all levels; reform of the drug industry; general access to modern medicines and equipment; the introduction of advanced scanning equipment.

8. *Legal policies.*

a) All forms of discrimination, overt and concealed, with regard to beliefs, nationality, etc., should be abolished.

b) There should be real glasnost of legal proceedings, wherever this does not conflict with basic civil rights.

c) The ratification by the USSR Supreme Soviet of the Covenants on Human Rights adopted by the Twenty-first Session of the UN General Assembly, should be reexamined, and also accession to the Optional Protocol of the Covenant on Civil and Political Rights.

9. *The national republics.*

Our country has proclaimed the right of a nation to self-determination, even if this means secession. In the case of Finland, secession was sanctioned by the Soviet government. The right of Union Republics to secede is proclaimed by the USSR Constitution. There is, however, a lack of precision in the guarantees and the procedures for the discussion and implementation of this right. In fact, the mere discussion of such questions frequently leads to prosecution. In my opinion, a juridical settlement of the problem and the passing of a law guaranteeing the right of secession would be of great internal and international significance as a confirmation of the anti-imperialist and anti-chauvinist nature of our policies. The number of republics inclined toward secession is, to all appearances, very small, and these tendencies would doubtless become even weaker with time as a result of increasing democratization of the USSR. On the other hand, there can be no doubt that any republic that secedes from the USSR for one reason or another by peaceful, constitutional means would maintain its ties with the socialist commonwealth of nations. In this event, the economic interests and defense capabilities of the socialist camp would not suffer, since the cooperation of the socialist countries is by nature complete and all-embracing and will doubtless become even more extensive in conditions of mutual noninterference in each other's internal affairs. For these reasons, discussion of the question I have raised does not seem to me to be dangerous.

*   *   *

If this memorandum appears here and there to be excessively peremptory in tone, that must be put down to its abbreviated form. The problems with which our country is confronted are closely connected with the general world crisis of the twentieth century—the crisis of international security, the lack of steady social development, the ideological impasse and disillusionment with the ideals of the recent past, nationalism, and the threat of dehumanization. The constructive, prudent, flexible, and at the same time decisive solution of our problems will, by virtue of our country's special position in the world, be of tremendous significance for the whole of mankind.

March 5, 1971

Postscript To Memorandum

The "Memorandum" was sent to the Secretary General of the CPSU [Leonid Brezhnev] on March 5, 1971. It received no reply. I do not think it would be right for me to delay its publication any longer. This Postscript was written in June 1972. It contains some additions to and partly replaces the note "Concerning political persecution" mentioned in the text.

I began my civic activity approximately ten to twelve years ago, when I realized the criminal character of a possible thermonuclear war and of thermonuclear tests in the atmosphere. Since then I have revised my views to a considerable extent, particularly since the year 1968, which began for me with work on *Progress, Coexistence, and Intellectual Freedom,* and ended, as for everybody else, with the rumbling of tanks in the streets of unyielding Prague.

As before, I cannot fail to appreciate the great and beneficial changes (social, cultural, and economic) that have taken place in our country in the last fifty years, realizing, however, that analogous changes have taken place in many countries and that they are a manifestation of worldwide progress.

As before, I consider that it will be possible to overcome the tragic conflicts and dangers of our time only through the convergence of capitalism and the socialist regime.

In capitalist countries this process must be accompanied by a further improvement in the protection of workers' rights and a reduction in the role of militarism and its influence on political life. In socialist countries it is also essential to reduce the militarization of the economy and the role of a messianic ideology. It is vitally necessary to reduce extreme centralism and dilute the Party-state bureaucratic monopoly in the economic sphere, and also in ideology and culture.

As before, I consider the democratization of society, the development of glasnost in public affairs, the rule of law, and the safeguarding of basic human rights to be of decisive importance.

As before, I hope that society will evolve along these lines under the influence of technological and economic progress, although my prognoses have become more cautious.

It seems to me now, more than ever before, that the only true guarantee for the safeguarding of human values in the chaos of uncontrollable changes and tragic upheavals is man's freedom of conscience and his moral yearning for the good.

Our society is infected by apathy, hypocrisy, petit bourgeois egoism, and hidden cruelty. The majority of representatives of its upper stratum—the Party apparatus of government and the highest, most successful layers of the intelligentsia—cling tenaciously to their open and secret privileges and are profoundly indifferent to violations of human rights, the interests of progress, to the security and future of mankind. Others, though deeply concerned in their hearts, cannot allow themselves any freedom of thought and are condemned to the torture of internal conflict. Drunkenness has assumed the dimensions of a national calamity. It is one of the symptoms of the moral degradation of a society that is sinking ever deeper into a state of chronic alcoholic poisoning.

The country's spiritual regeneration demands the elimination of those conditions that drive people into hypocrisy and time-serving, and that lead to feelings of impotence, discontent, and disillusionment. Everybody must be assured, in deed and not just in word, of equal opportunities for advancement in his work, in education, and cultural growth; and the system of privileges in all spheres of consumption must be abolished. Full intellectual freedom must be assured and all forms of persecution for beliefs must cease. A radical educational reform is essential. These ideas form the basis for many of the proposals in the Memorandum.

In particular, the Memorandum advocates improvement in the material circumstances and independence of two of the most numerous and socially significant groups of the intelligentsia, teachers and medical workers. The sorry state of popular education and of the health service is carefully hidden from the eyes of foreigners, but cannot remain secret from those who wish to see. A free health service and education are no more than an economic illusion in a society in which all surplus value is expropriated and distributed by the state. The hierarchical class structure of our society, with its system of privileges, is reflected in a particularly pernicious way in medical care and education: in the rundown state of public hospitals, in the poverty of the village schools, with their overcrowded classes, the poverty and low standing of the teacher, and the official hypocrisy in teaching, which inculcates in the rising generation a spirit of indifference toward moral, artistic, and scientific values.

An essential prerequisite for the cure of our society is the abandonment of political persecution, in its judicial and psychiatric forms or in any other form of which our bureaucratic and bigoted system, with its totalitarian interference by the state in the lives of the citizens, is capable, such as dismissal from work, expulsion from college, refusal of residence permits, limitation of promotion at work, etc.

The first beginnings of a moral regeneration of the people and the intelligentsia, which resulted from the curbing of the most extreme manifestations of the Stalinist system of blind terror, met with no proper understanding in ruling circles. The basic class, social, and ideological features of the regime did not undergo any essential change. With pain and alarm I have to note that after a period of largely illusory liberalism there is once again an extension of restrictions on ideological freedom, efforts to suppress information not controlled by the state, fresh persecution for political and ideological reasons, and a deliberate aggravation of nationalities problems. The fifteen months since the submission of the memorandum have brought new and disturbing evidence about the development of these tendencies.

The wave of political arrests in the first few months of 1972 is particularly alarming. Numerous arrests took place in the Ukraine. Arrests have also taken place in Moscow, Leningrad, and other regions of the country.

Public attention has also been drawn to the trial of Bukovsky in Moscow and of Strokatova in Odessa, and other trials. The use of psychiatry for political purposes is fraught with extremely dangerous consequences for society and constitutes a completely inadmissible interference with basic human rights. There have been numerous protests and pronouncements on this question. At present Grigorenko, Gershuni, and many others are being kept in prison-type psychiatric hospitals, the fate of Fainberg and Borisov is unknown; there are other instances of psychiatric repression (e.g., the case of the poet Lupynis in the Ukraine).

The persecution and destruction of religion, which has been carried on with perseverance and cruelty for decades, has resulted in what is undoubtedly one of the most serious infringements of human rights in our country. Freedom of religious belief and activity is an integral part of intellectual freedom as a whole. Unfortunately, the last few months have been marked by fresh instances of religious persecution, in particular in the Baltic states.

In this postscript I am passing over a series of important problems that I have already dealt with in the Memorandum and other published statements—in the open letters to the Presidium of the Supreme Soviet, "On freedom to leave the country," and to the Minister of Internal Affairs, "On discrimination against the Crimean Tatars."

I am also passing over the majority of international problems dealt with in the Memorandum. I will single out from their number the question of limiting the arms race. Militarization of the economy seriously affects international and domestic policy; it leads to encroachment on democratic rights, the open conduct of public affairs, and the rule of law; it constitutes a threat to peace. The role of the military-industrial complex in United States policy has been thoroughly studied. The analogous role played by the same factors in the USSR and other socialist countries is less well known. It is, however, necessary to point out that in no country does the military's share of national income reach such proportions as in the USSR (over 40 percent). In an atmosphere of mutual suspicion the problem of verification mentioned in the Memorandum assumes a special role.

I write this postscript a short time after the signing of important agreements limiting ABM defense and strategic missiles. One would like to believe that political leaders and the people who are active in the military-industrial complexes of the United States and the USSR have a sense of responsibility toward humanity.

One would like to believe that these agreements are not merely symbolic, but will lead to a real curtailment of the arms race and to further steps that will improve the political climate in our long-suffering world.

In conclusion, I want to emphasize the importance I attach to the proposal for setting up an international consultative committee, "The International Council of Experts," which would have the right to put forward recommendations to national governments that they would be obliged to consider. I think this proposal is feasible if it receives the wide international support for which I appeal, and I appeal not only to Soviet but also to foreign readers. I hope too that my voice from "inside" the socialist world may contribute in some measure to the understanding of the historical experience of the last decades.

June 1972   A. Sakharov

LETTER TO THE
AMNESTY INTERNATIONAL
SYMPOSIUM ON THE
ABOLITION OF THE
DEATH PENALTY

. . . I regard the death penalty as a savage, immoral institution which under-mines the ethical and legal foundations of a society. The state, in the person of its functionaries (who, like all people, are prone to superficial judgments and may be swayed by prejudice or selfish motives), assumes the right to the most terrible and irreversible act—the taking of human life. Such a state cannot expect an improvement in its moral atmosphere. I reject the notion that the death penalty has any real deterrent effect whatsoever on potential criminals. I am convinced that the contrary is true—that savagery begets only savagery.

I deny that the death penalty is in practice necessary or effective as a means of defending society. The temporary isolation of offenders which may be necessary in some cases must be achieved by more humane and more flexible measures which can be rectified in the event of judicial error and adjusted to take account of changes in society or in the personality of the offender.

I am convinced that society as a whole and each of its members individually, not just the person who comes before the court, bears responsibility for the occurrence of a crime. No simple solutions exist for reducing or eliminating crime, and in any event, the death penalty provides no answer. Only a gradual evolution of society, a growth of humanitarian attitudes which lead people to a deep respect for life and human reason and a greater concern for the difficulties and problems of their neighbors, can reduce crime or eliminate it. Such a society is still no more than a dream. Only by setting an example of humane conduct today can we instill the hope that it may someday be achieved.

I believe that the principle involved in the total abolition of the death penalty justifies disregarding those objections which are based on particular or exceptional cases.

While still a child, I read with horror the remarkable collection of essays *Against the Death Penalty* published in Russia with the participation of my grandfather I. N. Sakharov in 1906–1907 during the wave of executions following the 1905 revolution. I have read the impassioned statements of Tolstoy, Dostoevsky, Hugo, Korolenko, Rozanov, Andreyev, and many others. From the above-mentioned collection I know the arguments of a number of scholars: Soloviev, Bazhenov (the psychology of condemned persons), Gernet, Goldovsky, Davydov, and others. I share their conviction that the psychological horror associated with the death penalty renders it disproportionate to the vast majority of crimes and inappropriate as a just retribution or punishment in every case. And indeed, how can one speak of the punishment of a person who has ceased to exist? I share their conviction that the death penalty lacks any moral or practical justification and represents a survival of barbaric customs of revenge—cold-blooded and calculated revenge, with no personal danger for the executioners, with no passionate personal involvement on the part of the judge, and therefore shameful and disgusting.

I must comment briefly on the widely discussed subject of terrorism. I am of the opinion that the death penalty is completely ineffective in the struggle against terrorism and other political crimes committed by fanatics. In such cases the death penalty serves only as a catalyst for the psychosis of lawlessness, revenge, and savagery. I do not in any way sanction the current phenomenon of political terrorism, which is often accompanied by the death of random persons, by the taking of hostages (including children), and by other dreadful crimes. I am convinced, however, that imprisonment (possibly reinforced by the adoption of a law forbidding release before completion of sentence in cases specified by the court) is a more rational measure for the physical and psychological isolation of terrorists and for the prevention of further acts of terror.

The abolition of the death penalty is especially important in a country like ours with its unrestricted state power, its uncontrolled bureaucracy, and its widespread contempt for law and moral values. You know of the mass executions of innocent people which were carried out during the 1930s and 1940s in a mockery of justice, not to mention the still greater numbers who perished without any legal proceedings at all. We are still living in the moral climate created during that era.

I wish to stress the fact that in the USSR the death penalty is a possible punishment for many crimes which have no relation to crimes threatening human life. You may recall, for example, the case of Rokotov and Faibishenko, who were charged in 1961 with underground traffic in gems and illegal currency operations. After they had been sentenced to imprisonment, the Presidium of the Supreme Soviet passed a law which extended application of the death penalty to large-scale crimes against property. Rokotov and Faibishenko were retried and sentenced to death in violation of the fundamental legal principle barring retroactive application of criminal sanctions. Many other persons have since been executed under analogous laws, essentially for carrying on private business activities. In 1962 an old man was shot for counterfeiting a few coins which he had buried in his yard.

The total number of executions in the USSR is not known; the statistics are a state secret. But there are grounds to believe that several hundred persons are executed annually, a greater number than in most countries where this barbaric institution persists. Other aspects of our life must be taken into account in any discussion of capital punishment in the USSR: the backward and dismal condition of our criminal justice system, its subservience to the state machine, the prevalence of bribery and corruption, and the frequent interventions of local big shots in judicial procedures.

I receive a great many letters from persons convicted of crimes. I cannot check the facts in every case, but taken all together, these letters create an irrefutable and terrible picture of lawlessness and injustice, of superficial and prejudiced investigation, of the impossibility of obtaining review of clearly mistaken or dubious verdicts, of beatings during police questioning.

Some of these cases involve death sentences. Here is one such case. I have before me a copy of the court verdict in the case of Rafkat Shaimukhamedov, documents on his case prepared by lawyers, letters by his mother. On May 31, 1974, in Issyk-Kule, Shaimukhamedov, a worker and by nationality a Tatar, was sentenced to be shot. He had been convicted of murdering a female shop assistant—while intending to commit robbery along with two accomplices. (The latter were sentenced to several years' imprisonment.) Shaimukhamedov denied his guilt, refused to ask for pardon, and declared a hunger strike. He passed twenty months in the death cell expecting either execution or a review of his case. Throughout this time his mother and lawyers submitted dozens of complaints, but all higher authorities sent them back without any examination of the matter. In January 1976 the sentence was carried out with the sanction of Deputy Procurator General of the USSR Malyarov.

The court verdict on Shaimukhamedov is striking for its illiteracy, in both the literal and the juridical sense of the word, given its lack of proofs and its contradictory nature. An even more vivid picture emerges from the complaints of the lawyers and the mother's letters. The convicted person's presence at the scene of the crime was not proved. The court ignored the contradictory versions of the accusation, the testimony of witnesses, and the facts of the expert examination (according to which the victim's blood group did not match that of a spot of blood found on Shaimukhamedov's clothing). The mother's letters state that the reason for this bias lay in the selfish material interest of two procurators (Bekboev and Kleishin). She describes scenes of extortion, bribes received by them from another accused, the fabrication of a criminal case against her second son with the same goal of extortion—even after the shooting of Rafkat. I cannot verify these reports, but to me the main message is clear: with what ease and absence of argument the death penalty was passed, and how easily so terrible a case becomes routine.

I have dwelt on this case in detail because it seems to me that it clearly reflects the complete horror of the death penalty and its destructive effect on society. . . .

September 19, 1977

Andrei Sakharov
Nobel Peace Laureate

OPEN LETTER
ON AFGHANISTAN

To the Presidium of the Supreme Soviet of the USSR and to its Chairman, Leonid Brezhnev

I am sending copies of this letter to the Secretary General of the United Nations and to the heads of state of China, France, the U.K., and the U.S.

I am appealing to you concerning a matter of supreme importance—the situation in Afghanistan. By virtue of my position in the world and as a citizen of the USSR, I feel a responsibility for the tragic events taking place there. I am cognizant of the fact that your point of view is based on information which I am sure is far more comprehensive than that available to me. Nevertheless, the gravity of this question is such that I ask you to give my letter and the opinions expressed in it special attention.

Military operations in Afghanistan have been under way for seven months. Thousands of Soviet and tens of thousands of Afghan citizens have been killed and injured, among them not only Afghan guerrillas, but a great number of civilians in towns and villages—old people, women, and children. More than a million Afghans have become refugees. News of the bombing of villages that assist the guerrillas is extremely ominous, as is the mining of mountain roads, which threatens large regions with starvation. There are reports that napalm, booby traps, and new types of weapons are being used. Reports (unconfirmed) of the use of nerve gas is extremely alarming. Some of this information may be unreliable, but there is no doubt that a terrible situation exists. Escalation of the hostilities and of savagery by both sides continues and no end is in sight.

The events in Afghanistan have also fundamentally altered the international political situation, jeopardizing peace and détente in this region and throughout the world. They have made more difficult, perhaps even impossible, the ratification of the SALT-II Treaty that is so vital to the entire world, in particular as a necessary first step toward disarmament. Not surprisingly, military budgets have been increased and new military-industrial programs have been approved by all the great powers because of the Soviet actions, and these increases will have long-term ramifications by escalating the danger of an arms race. In the U.N. General Assembly, one hundred four countries, including many that have always given unconditional support to the USSR, have denounced the Soviet military operation in Afghanistan.

Supermilitarization of our country, especially disastrous in our difficult economic conditions, is increasing and, as a result, vitally important economic and social reforms are not being implemented. The role of the organs of repression is increasing, and they may easily get out of hand.

I will not analyze in detail the reasons for sending Soviet troops into Afghanistan, whether this was done for legitimate defensive purposes, or as part of some other plan; whether it constituted disinterested assistance for land reform and other social changes, or interference in the internal affairs of a sovereign state. There may be some truth in each of these propositions. I myself believe that the Soviet actions are a clear example of expansionism and are a violation of Afghanistan sovereignty. But it seems to me that even those who hold a contrary view must agree that these actions are a terrible mistake, one that should be corrected with the greatest possible dispatch, especially since that will become more difficult with each passing day. I am convinced that a political settlement is necessary and that it should include the following measures:

—The USSR and the Afghan guerrillas must cease military operations and sign a truce agreement;

—The USSR must declare its readiness to withdraw all its troops, as soon as they can be replaced by U.N. forces. This will be a significant action for the U.N., in accord with the goals proclaimed at its founding, and with the resolution passed by one hundred and four of its members;

—The permanent members of the U.N. Security Council (and the countries neighboring Afghanistan) must guarantee the neutrality, peace, and independence of Afghanistan;

—All member states of the United Nations, including the USSR, should offer political asylum to citizens of Afghanistan who wish to leave their country. Freedom of emigration must be one of the terms of the settlement.

Until elections can be held, the government of Babrak Karmal must transfer its power to a Provisional Council composed of representatives, on a fully equal footing, of both the guerrillas and the Karmal government.

My ideas are meant to serve only as a basis for further discussion. I understand how difficult it may be to implement this program or a similar one, but it is necessary to find a political means to escape from this blind alley. The continuation and, still more, the further escalation of military operations, would, to my mind, lead to disastrous consequences. The world may now be at a crossroads, and the entire course of events in the next few years, even the next few decades, may well depend on the outcome of the Afghan crisis.

July 27, 1980   Andrei Sakharov

ACCEPTANCE SPEECH FOR
THE SZILARD AWARD

I am grateful and proud to accept this award, named for a remarkable man and scientist, Leo Szilard. I know of Szilard's outstanding scientific merits and of his public activity, which sprang from his innate, intense feeling of personal responsibility for the fate of mankind on our planet, and for the possible consequences of science's great victories.

In the years of Szilard's life and activity it became clearer than ever before how great the responsibility of scientists is to the society. And, to a large extent, it is due to Szilard that this awareness began to spread in the scientific community. Unfortunately, today, almost 20 years after Szilard died, the problems that disturbed him are not less acute or tragic.

Today, as then, the world is politically and ideologically divided into two opposing camps. Both sides are threatening each other with missiles and nuclear weaponry. Destructive capacity increases every year and has already reached a level at which its use would cause the deaths of hundreds of millions of people and cause destruction unprecedented in the history of mankind; create chaos, devastation and suffering; and hurl human society back centuries. The total annihilation of mankind and life on Earth is not out of the question—perhaps even with the existing reserves of nuclear arms—and is even more probable with the further quantitative and qualitative development of the means for mass destruction.

Meanwhile, the confrontations are not static. One glance at the map of the world today and in the first postwar years is enough to show that the line separating the areas of prevailing influence has been continuously moving in one direction—to the benefit of the socialist camp. One could call this a manifestation of the laws of history; some might say of historical justice. Others might call this a socialist expansion replacing one sort of social and legal problems with others, no less acute and tragic. The most important thing is the objective result, which is a further aggravation of the international situation and an increasing danger of local conflicts growing into a worldwide clash.

The problems of the underdeveloped countries are as acute as they were earlier. There is no doubt that unevenness of development creates enormous suffering for the greater part of mankind and poses a threat to world stability. Maybe that is the main source of danger. To decrease that unevenness is one of the chief tasks of our times, demanding coordinated action by all countries, developed and developing. Unfortunately, the division of the world produces negative results in this matter as well. At present, the Soviet Union provides the developing countries with only very small amounts of technological and economic assistance—and only to those under its influence. Having practically withdrawn from participation in worldwide joint efforts, the Soviets have, however, become a major supplier of arms.

Since the late 1960s international terrorism, a sort of terrorist international of "left" and "right" groups, has become a serious destabilizing factor. Those states that directly or indirectly encourage these destructive forces are un- doubtedly causing great harm to the entire world, their own people included.

One of the most tragic and dangerous events of recent years was the Soviet invasion of Afghanistan. Many tens of thousands of Afghans have died in the three years of war; according to some estimates, the number of victims exceeds 100,000. Many Soviet soldiers have died. Millions of Afghans have fled the horrors of war and left the country; about one-third of the population have become refugees. The Soviet invasion seriously aggravated the international situation, affected the rate of the arms race and, in particular, the fate of SALT II. If there are no changes for the better in the world, Afghanistan could become the Abyssinia of a new world war!

Today we ask ourselves once again: Does mutual nuclear terror serve as a deterrent against war? For almost 40 years the world has avoided a third world war. And, quite possibly, nuclear deterrence has been, to a considerable extent, the reason for this. But I am convinced that nuclear deterrence is gradually turning into its own antithesis and becoming a dangerous remnant of the past. The equilibrium provided by nuclear deterrence is becoming increasingly un- steady; increasingly real is the danger that mankind will perish if an accident or insanity or uncontrolled escalation draws it into a total thermonuclear war. In light of this it is necessary, gradually and carefully, to shift the functions of deterrence onto conventional armed forces, with all the economic, political and social consequences this entails. It is necessary to strive for nuclear disarmament. Of course, in all the intermediate stages of disarmament and negotiations, international security must be provided for, vis-à-vis any possible move by a potential aggressor. For this in particular one has to be ready to resist, at all the various possible stages in the escalation of a conventional or a nuclear war. No side must feel any temptation to engage in a limited or regional nuclear war.

There are two specific problems. One is that the main part of the Soviet Union's nuclear potential is concentrated in gigantic land-based missiles. Essentially, this is a first-strike weapon. It is necessary to strive to eliminate these weapons or to reduce their number. There is little chance of this happening before the West has analogous missiles and is ready to eliminate them as well as the other means of nuclear war. The second problem is that the Soviet Union is not likely to eliminate its powerful medium-range missiles, which have upset the nuclear equilibrium in Europe and which threaten China and Japan, before the West deploys analogous missiles.

Certainly the ultimate goals are international security, the elimination and demolition of nuclear weaponry, and rapprochement—convergence by countries with different political systems. In the long run, convergence is the only alternative to global destruction. This goal cannot be achieved without profound political and ideological changes—both in the relations between socialist and western countries, and within the countries themselves.

In the postwar years Nils Bohr, as well as Szilard and many other like-minded people, dreamed that open societies would provide an important and indispensable guarantee for international security. Since then, Stalin's tyrannical regime with its monstrous mass crimes has become a thing of the past in the Soviet Union. But the key features of the system formed under Stalin have basically survived. They are: the monopoly of the Party and the state in economics and ideology, which is even harsher in the political and military spheres; and the attendant violation of civil rights, which contradicts the principle of the openness of society—violations of freedom of conscience and the free flow of information; of the right to choose one's country of residence and place of residence within the country; the unfounded persecution of dissidents and prisoners of conscience. Of course, the scale of persecution cannot at all be compared to that of Stalin's times. But to persecute people for their convictions, people who have not resorted to violence or advocated it, is in essence inadmissible. I am certain that the plight of the prisoners of conscience—many of whom are sentenced to seven and even 15 years of deprivation of freedom—cannot help but disturb us. It is very important to fight for each prisoner as an individual. Universal amnesty for prisoners of conscience in the Soviet Union and throughout the world would not only be an act of humanity but an important step on the path of strengthening international trust and security.

I would like once more to remind you of the profound alarm felt by our great predecessors—Einstein, Bohr, Russell, Szilard—for the fate of mankind, and of the ideas they left us. These ideas—about peace, about the danger that threatens mankind, about the importance of mutual understanding and tolerance, about the openness of society, the respect for human rights, the convergence of states with different political systems, the responsibility of scientists—are as important today as when they were expressed for the first time.

April 1983   Andrei Sakharov

THE DANGER OF THERMONUCLEAR WAR

An Open Letter to Sidney Drell

Clearly it is meaningless to speak of victory in a large nuclear war which is collective suicide.

I think that basically my point of view coincides with yours as well as with the opinion of a great many people on earth.

I am also in complete agreement with your other conclusions. I agree that if the "nuclear threshold" is crossed, i.e., if any country uses a nuclear weapon even on a limited scale, the further course of events would be difficult to control and the most probable result would be swift escalation leading from a nuclear war initially limited in scale or by region to an all-out nuclear war, i.e., to general suicide.

It is relatively unimportant how the "nuclear threshold" is crossed—as a result of a preventive nuclear strike or in the course of a war fought with conventional weapons, when a country is threatened with defeat, or simply as a result of an accident (technical or organizational).

In view of the above, I am convinced that the following basic tenet of yours is true: *Nuclear weapons only make sense as a means of deterring nuclear aggression by a potential enemy,* i.e., a nuclear war cannot be planned with the aim of winning it. Nuclear weapons cannot be viewed as a means of restraining aggression carried out by means of conventional weapons.

Of course you realize that this last statement is in contradiction to the

West's actual strategy in the last few decades. For a long time, beginning as far back as the end of the 1940s, the West has not been relying on its "conventional" armed forces as a means sufficient for repelling a potential aggressor and for restraining expansion. There are many reasons for this—the West's lack of political, military, and economic unity; the striving to avoid a peacetime militarization of the economy, society, technology, and science; the low numerical levels of the Western nations' armies. All that at a time when the U.S.S.R. and the other countries of the socialist camp have armies with great numerical strength and are rearming them intensively, sparing no resources. It is possible that for a limited period of time the mutual nuclear terror had a certain restraining effect on the course of world events. But, at the present time, the balance of nuclear terror is a dangerous remnant of the past! In order to avoid aggression with conventional weapons one cannot threaten to use nuclear weapons if their use is inadmissible. One of the conclusions that follows here—and a conclusion you draw—is that it is necessary to restore strategic parity in the field of conventional weapons. This you expressed somewhat differently, and without stressing the point.

Meanwhile this is a very important and non-trivial statement which must be dwelt on in some detail.

The restoration of strategic parity is only possible by investing large resources and by an essential change in the psychological atmosphere in the West. There must be a readiness to make certain limited economic sacrifices and, most important, an understanding of the seriousness of the situation and of the necessity for some restructuring. In the final analysis, this is necessary to prevent nuclear war, and war in general. Will the West's politicians be able to carry out such a restructuring? Will the press, the public, and our fellow scientists help them (and not hinder them as is frequently now the case)? Can they succeed in convincing those who doubt the necessity of such restructuring? A great deal depends on it—the opportunity for the West to conduct a nuclear arms policy that will be conducive to the lessening of the danger of nuclear disaster.

In any case, I am very glad that you (and earlier, in another context, Professor Wolfgang Panofsky) have spoken out in favor of strategic parity in the area of conventional weapons.

In conclusion, I should stress especially that a restructuring of strategy could of course only be carried out gradually and very carefully in order to prevent a loss of parity in some of the intermediate phases.

Is it actually possible when making decisions in the area of nuclear weapons to ignore all the considerations and requirements relevant to the possible scenarios for a nuclear war and simply limit oneself to the criterion of achieving a reliable deterrent—when that criterion is understood to mean an arsenal sufficient to deal a devastating blow in response? Your answer to this question—while perhaps formulating it somewhat differently—is positive and you draw far-reaching conclusions.

There is no doubt that at present the United States already possesses a large number of submarine-based missiles and charges carried by strategic bombers which are not vulnerable to the U.S.S.R. and, in addition, has silo-based missiles though they are smaller than the U.S.S.R.'s—all these in such amounts that, were those charges used against the U.S.S.R., nothing, roughly speaking, would be left of it. You maintain that this has *already* created a reliable deterrent—independently of what the U.S.S.R. and the United States have and what they lack! Therefore, you specifically consider the building of the MX missile unnecessary and similarly consider irrelevant the arguments which are advanced in support of developing it—the U.S.S.R.'s substantial arsenal of intercontinental missiles with large throw-weight which the United States does not have; and the fact that Soviet missiles and MX missiles have multiple warheads so that one missile can destroy several enemy silos during a missile duel. Therefore you consider it acceptable (with certain reservations) for the United States to freeze the nuclear arsenals of the United States and the U.S.S.R. at their current numerical levels.

Your line of reasoning seems to me very strong and convincing. But I think that the concept presented fails to take into account all the complex realities of the opposition that involves two world systems and that there is the necessity (despite your stance) for a more specific and comprehensive unbiased consideration than a simple orientation toward a "reliable deterrent" (in the meaning of the word as formulated above, i.e., the possibility of dealing a devastating retaliatory strike). I will endeavor to explain this statement.

Precisely because an all-out nuclear war means collective suicide, we can imagine that a potential aggressor might count on a lack of resolve on the part of the country under attack to take the step leading to that suicide, i.e., it could count on its victim capitulating for the sake of saving what could be saved. Given that, if the aggressor has a military advantage in some of the variants of conventional warfare or—which is also possible *in principle*—in some of the variants of partial (limited) nuclear war, he would attempt to use the fear of further escalation to force the enemy to fight the war on his (the aggressor's) own terms. There would be little cause for joy if, ultimately, the aggressor's hopes proved false and the aggressor country perished along with the rest of mankind.

You consider it necessary to achieve a restoration of strategic parity in the field of conventional arms. Now take the next logical step—while nuclear weapons exist it is also necessary to have strategic parity in relation to those variants of limited or regional nuclear warfare which a potential enemy could impose, i.e., it is really *necessary* to examine in detail the various scenarios for both conventional and nuclear war and to analyze the various contingencies. It is of course not possible to analyze fully all these possibilities or to ensure security entirely. But I am attempting to warn of the opposite extreme— "closing one's eyes" and relying on one's potential enemy to be perfectly sensible. As always in life's complex problems, some sort of compromise is needed.

Of course I realize that in attempting not to lag behind a potential enemy in any way, we condemn ourselves to an arms race that is tragic in a world with so many critical problems admitting of no delay. But the main danger is slipping into an all-out nuclear war. *If* the probability of such an outcome could be reduced at the cost of another ten or fifteen years of the arms race, then perhaps that price must be paid while, at the same time, diplomatic, economic, ideological, political, cultural, and social efforts are made to prevent a war.

Of course it would be wiser to agree now to reduce nuclear and conventional weapons and to eliminate nuclear weapons entirely. But is that now possible in a world poisoned with fear and mistrust, a world where the West fears aggression from the U.S.S.R., the U.S.S.R. fears aggression from the West and from China, and where China fears it from the U.S.S.R., and no verbal assurances and treaties can eliminate those dangers entirely?

I know that pacifist sentiments are very strong in the West. I deeply sympathize with people's yearning for peace, for a solution to world problems by peaceful means; I share those aspirations fully. But, at the same time, I am certain that it is absolutely necessary to be mindful of the specific political, military, and strategic realities of the present day and to do so objectively without making any sort of allowances for either side; this also means that one should not proceed from an a priori assumption of any special peace-loving nature in the socialist countries due to their supposed progressiveness or the horrors and losses they have experienced in war. Objective reality is much more complicated and far from anything so simple. People both in the socialist and the Western countries have a passionate inward aspiration for peace. This is an extremely important factor, but, I repeat, itself alone does not exclude the possibility of a tragic outcome.

What is necessary now, I believe, is the enormous practical task of education so that specific, exact, and historically and politically meaningful objective information can be made available to all people, information that will enjoy their trust and not be veiled with dogma and propaganda. Here one must take into account that, in the countries of the West, pro-Soviet propaganda has been conducted for quite a long time and is very goal-oriented and clever, and that pro-Soviet elements have penetrated many key positions, particularly in the mass media.

The history of the pacifist campaigns against the deployment of missiles in Europe is telling in many respects. After all, many of those participating in those campaigns entirely ignore the initial cause of NATO's "dual decision"— the change in strategic parity in the 1970s in favor of the U.S.S.R.—and, when protesting NATO's plans, they have not advanced any demands on the U.S.S.R.

A second group of problems in the field of nuclear weapons about which I should make a few supplementary remarks here concerns the talks on nuclear disarmament. For these talks to be successful the West should have something that it can give up! The case of the "Euromissiles" once again demonstrates how difficult it is to negotiate from a position of weakness. Only very recently has the U.S.S.R. apparently ceased to insist on its unsubstantiated thesis that a rough nuclear parity now exists and therefore everything should be left as it is.

Now, the next welcome step would be the reduction of the number of missiles—which must include a fair assessment of the *quality* of missiles and other means of delivery (i.e., the number of charges deliverable by each carrier, its range and accuracy, and its degree of vulnerability—the last being greater for aircraft and less for missiles; most likely, it would be expedient to use your criterion, or analogous ones). And what is absolutely at issue here is not moving the missiles beyond the Urals but *destroying* them. After all, rebasing is too "reversible." Of course, one also must not consider powerful Soviet missiles, with mobile launchers and several warheads, as being equal to the now-existing Pershing I, the British and French missiles, or the bombs on short-range bombers—as the Soviet side sometimes attempts to do for purposes of propaganda.

No less important a problem is that of the powerful silo-based missiles. At present the U.S.S.R. has a great advantage in this area. Perhaps talks about the limitation and reduction of these most destructive missiles could become easier if the United States were to have MX missiles, albeit only potentially (indeed, that would be best of all).

A few words about the military capabilities of powerful missiles: they can be used to deliver the largest thermonuclear charges for destroying cities and other major enemy targets—while for exhausting the enemy's ABM systems there will most likely be a simultaneous use of a "rain" of smaller missiles, false targets, and so on. (Much is written about the possibility of developing ABM systems using super-powerful lasers, accelerated particle beams, and so forth. But the creation of an effective defense against missiles along these lines seems highly doubtful to me.) . . .

A specific danger associated with silo-based missiles is that they can be destroyed relatively easily as a result of enemy attack, as I have just demonstrated. At the same time, they can be used to destroy enemy launch sites in an amount four to five times larger than the number of missiles used for the attack. A country with large numbers of silo-based missiles (at the present time this is primarily the U.S.S.R., but if the United States carries out a major MX program, then it too) could be "tempted" to use such missiles first before the enemy destroys them. In such circumstances the presence of silo-based missiles constitutes a destabilizing factor.

In view of the above, it seems very important to me to strive for the abolition of powerful silo-based missiles at the talks on nuclear disarmament. While the U.S.S.R. is the leader in this field there is very little chance of its easily relinquishing that lead. If it is necessary to spend a few billion dollars on MX missiles to alter this situation, then perhaps this is what the West must do. But, at the same time, if the Soviets, in deed and not just in word, take significant verifiable measures for reducing the number of land-based missiles (more precisely, for destroying them), then the West should not only abolish MX missiles (or not build them!) but carry out other significant disarmament programs as well.

On the whole I am convinced that nuclear disarmament talks are of enormous importance and of the highest priority. They must be conducted continuously—in the brighter periods of international relations but also in the periods when relations are strained—and conducted with persistence, foresight, firmness and, at the same time, with flexibility and initiative. In so doing, political figures should not think of exploiting those talks, and the nuclear problem in general, for their own immediate political gains but only for the long-term interests of their country and the world. And the planning of the talks should be included in one's general nuclear strategy as its most important part—on this point as well I am in agreement with you!

In conclusion, I again stress how important it is that the world realize the absolute inadmissibility of nuclear war, the collective suicide of mankind. It is impossible to win a nuclear war. What is necessary is to strive, systematically though carefully, for complete nuclear disarmament based on strategic parity in conventional weapons. As long as there are nuclear weapons in the world, there must be a strategic parity of nuclear forces so that neither side will venture to embark on a limited or regional nuclear war. Genuine security is possible only when based on a stabilization of international relations, a repudiation of expansionist policies, the strengthening of international trust, openness and pluralization in the socialist societies, the observance of human rights throughout the world, the rapprochement—convergence—of the socialist and capitalist systems, and worldwide coordinated efforts to solve global problems. *February 2, 1983* Andrei Sakharov

When Honor and Conscience Are Lost

A reply by four Soviet academicians to Sakharov's article "The Danger of Thermonuclear War"

On opening an issue of the American magazine *Foreign Affairs* and finding in it a long article by Academician Andrei Sakharov, we began reading it prepared for anything. We know well that Sakharov tries to besmirch all we hold dear, that he slanders his own nation, presenting it to the external world as some sort of gray, completely uncivilized mass.

Sakharov's creation in *Foreign Affairs* amazed us nevertheless. Pretending to enter into a polemic with Sidney Drell, an American professor at Stanford University who supports a freeze of existing Soviet and American nuclear arsenals, Sakharov urges the U.S. and the West under no circumstances to agree to any limitations on the arms race in general and on nuclear weapons in particular. He directly importunes the leaders in Washington to stick to their militarist course, their course toward confrontation with the Soviet Union and toward military supremacy, arguing that the United States and NATO should not slacken the arms race for another ten to fifteen years at least.

This may seem improbable, but what follows turns black into white. Sakharov warns his readers against "relying on the enemy to be perfectly sensible." Who is this "enemy"? The Soviet Union, the country where Sakharov lives. He warns America's bosses: Do not believe in the peace-loving nature of the Socialist countries. Openly, without embarrassment, Sakharov approves U.S. and NATO plans to deploy American Pershing II's and cruise missiles in Western Europe, first-strike weapons which will be targeted on our own and other Socialist countries. Sakharov argues that if Washington possesses MX missiles which are also known to be first-strike weapons, then the "United States will find it easier to conduct talks" with the USSR.

We returned several times to these points in Sakharov's article. We experienced a strange sensation: was it really Sakharov writing all this? We had heard and read it many times before. Secretary of Defense Weinberger makes exactly the same statements. President Reagan speaks like that. It is the language of American generals and political extremists. Sakharov needs only to term the USSR "evil incarnate" and to announce a "crusade" against Communism for them to place him in the Pentagon or the White House.

One other aspect seems unbelievable. Sakharov is a scientist. He knows the facts and is quite well aware of the possible consequences of the actions he urges on the government of a country which has tested weapons of mass destruction on human beings once before. Then the U.S. rained down atomic death on Japanese cities. American leaders wanted to show off their strength to the world and to our country in particular. Sakharov today is really suggesting the use of the monstrous force of nuclear weapons to intimidate the Soviet people again, to compel our country to capitulate before an American ultimatum. And to what country and "civilization" does he belong and what does he want in the end? Can he really not understand that the build-up of weapons which he advocates threatens not just our country which lost 20,000,000 people in the last war, but every nation without exception, and human civilization itself?

And now we begin to think about Sakharov not simply as a scientist. What kind of man is he to fall so low morally, to come to hate his own country and its people? We see in his actions a violation of the norms of humanitarian and decent behavior which we suppose to be obligatory for every civilized person.

We know that Sakharov is very popular with those Americans who would like to wipe our country and socialism off the face of the earth. Such friends are always raising a hullabaloo about "the tragic fate of Sakharov." We do not wish to discuss this boundless hypocrisy right now. No, our government, our people, have been more than tolerant toward this man who is living peacefully in their midst.

Here is what comes to mind. Exactly thirty years ago this summer, one of the most unjust and shameful events of the twentieth century took place in the U.S. The American authorities executed the scientists Ethel and Julius Rosenberg. Their execution was based on absurd and foul charges. The "evidence" was fabricated by the American secret services. And by the way, in contrast to Sakharov, who calls for nuclear blackmail directed against his own country and for making possible a nuclear first strike against us, the Rosenbergs were not simply innocent persons who fell victim to the pitiless mechanism of American "justice." They had spoken out for the destruction of lethal weapons. And they were completely honest, humane people.

To speak of honesty when a man actually calls for a war against his own country is difficult. Several centuries ago Erasmus said that only those few base persons whose own well-being depends on popular misfortune wage war.

Of course, it is not really Erasmus who is at issue. But even in his time decent, thinking people were not blinded by hatred and they did not lose honor and conscience.

Academicians Anatoly Dorodnitsyn, Alexander Prokhorov, Georgy Skriabin, Andrei Tikhonov

Izvestia, July 3, 1983

EXILE TO GORKY

Sakharov's Statement of January 27, 1980

On January 22, I was detained on the street and taken by force to the USSR Procurator's office. A. Rekunkov, First Deputy Procurator General of the USSR, informed me that I was being deprived of my titles of Hero of Socialist Labor, of all decorations and prize awards, by decree of the Presidium of the Supreme Soviet of the USSR. I was asked to return the medals and orders and certificates, but I refused, believing that I was given them for good reason. Rekunkov also informed me of the decision to banish me to the city of Gorky, which is closed to foreigners.

On the same day, with my wife, Elena Bonner, who was allowed to go with me, I was taken by special flight to Gorky, where the city's deputy procurator explained the conditions of the regime decreed for me—overt surveillance, prohibitions against going beyond the city limits and against meeting with foreigners and "criminal elements," against correspondence and telephone conversations with foreigners, including scientific and purely personal contacts, even with my children and grandchildren, Matvei, 6, and Anna, 4. I was instructed to report three times a month to the police, and threatened that I would be taken there by force if I failed to obey.

The authorities are completely isolating me from the outside world. The house is surrounded 24 hours a day by police and the KGB, who keep away all visitors, including our friends. Telephone connections with Moscow and Leningrad are cut off. We have not been able to call even my wife's mother, to tell her how we are. I was unable to call a physicist colleague, a highly respected Soviet scholar. These restrictions also apply to my wife, who is supposedly "free." She sent a telegram to our children in the United States, but there was no answer, so she is deprived of contact with the children.

Even in prison, there is more possibility of communication with the outside world.

No longer youngsters and not in the best of health, we are completely deprived of help from our friends, of medical care from our doctors.

These repressive actions against me were undertaken at a time of general worsening of the international situation and of intensified persecution of dissidents within the country.

The worsening of the international situation was caused by the following actions of the USSR:

1. Launching in Europe a broad and demagogic campaign with the aim of strengthening its military superiority.

2. Seeking to destroy the emerging opportunities for peace in the Middle East and southern Africa.

3. Supporting terrorist regimes in Ethiopia and some other countries.

4. Maintaining military units in Cuba.

5. Supporting the actions of quasi-governmental terrorists in Iran who have violated diplomatic immunity.

6. The culmination of this dangerous policy was the invasion of Afghanistan, where Soviet soldiers are waging merciless war against insurgents, against the Afghan people.

Within the country, the authorities have taken new action against the nucleus of the human rights movement. Velikanova and Nekipelov have been arrested, Landa has been threatened with arrest. The magazine *Poiski* is being broken up. Abramkin, Sokirko, Grimm have been arrested.

The movement for religious freedom is being persecuted and the priests Dudko and Yakunin have been arrested. Regelson has been arrested. Trials and arrests are proceeding in the Ukraine and in the Baltic. Repression has increased against the Crimean Tatars; Reshat Dzhemilev has been convicted.

The actions of the authorities against me in this situation are aimed at making the continuation of my public activities completely impossible. They are aimed at humiliating and discrediting me and at the same time making possible further repressive measures against all dissident groups in the country (with less possibility of the world's finding out about them), and also further international adventures.

On January 24, *Izvestia* published an article containing slander against me and a deliberate distortion of my position. My position remains unchanged. I am for a pluralistic, open society, both democratic and just; for convergence, disarmament, and peace; for the defense of human rights in the whole world—in our country, in the countries of Eastern Europe, in Indonesia, China, Chile, everywhere; for a worldwide amnesty for prisoners of conscience; for doing away with the death penalty. I am for giving priority to the problems of peace, the problem of averting thermonuclear war.

From the article in *Izvestia* it is apparent that the main reason for the repression against me at this particularly anxious time was my position condemning the intervention in Afghanistan, which is a threat to the entire world, and demanding the withdrawal of Soviet troops from that country, perhaps with their replacement by United Nations units, (see my interview with *The New York Times* and with ABC television), as well as my having endorsed a document on the subject issued by the Moscow Helsinki group.

Completely isolated and worried about members of my family, my mother-in-law, and my future daughter-in-law, Liza Alexeyeva—to whom I am no longer able to provide any protection—I demand that they be given an opportunity immediately to leave the USSR. Although my wife is technically free, I will, of course, be afraid not only for her health, but for her life, if she is forced to travel to Moscow to see them (unfortunately, we know that the state security organs are capable of applying Mafia-like techniques).

The actions of the Soviet authorities are a gross violation of my basic right to receive and impart information (Article 19 of the Universal Declaration of Human Rights). Soviet representatives are trying to calm world public opinion by saying that I will be able to continue scientific work and that there is no threat of criminal prosecution against me. But I am prepared to stand public and open trial. I do not need a gilded cage. I need the right to fulfill my public duty as my conscience dictates.

I am grateful to all those who have come to my defense. My fate has been a happy one—I succeeded in being heard. But I ask everyone not to forget those who have selflessly served and are still serving in the defense of human rights, those whom I mentioned in this letter and all those whom I did not mention.

Andrei Sakharov
Gorky, January 27, 1980

Open Letter from Elena Bonner

I write these words out of concern for my husband. This is not easy for me, but the flood of slander directed against him is so horrible, disgusting, and irrational that it is impossible to foresee what might happen, and I am worried about his fate.

In my ten years of life with Andrei Sakharov we have had many guests from the West. I appeal to them: the Germans and Americans, French and English, Norwegians and Swedes, Italians and Spaniards, Dutch and Japanese, who have visited us. Over the years I have begun to feel that we have friends everywhere, those who have shared tea with us in our kitchen or crowded living room; those who have read my husband's books or talked to him about detente, disarmament, SALT, nuclear energy, environmental protection; about the right to choose one's country of residence, to receive and impart information freely; about freedom of conscience; and about those, who under the stifling conditions in our country, have tried to break down the wall of silence by defending the natural right of every person to be free, and have paid for it with years of prison, camp, exile and psychiatric hospitals.

You businessmen and politicians, journalists and scientists, and simply private persons who have come to see Russia and Sakharov: I don't have to tell you what kind of man he is. You have seen him and you have spoken with him. I appeal to you to testify under oath—in the courts, before government and private commissions—on your conversations with Andrei Sakharov, on what he has said and written about today's most pressing problems. My husband's life depends upon your memories of him and your persistence. He is denied a hearing in court, and if you forget him and fall silent, the authorities will finish their planned retaliation, caring little about appearances. I call upon you to become a witness for the defense.

I appeal to scientists. I cannot name my husband's friends in Europe and America because I should then also name Soviet scientists. That is not possible. I know a few of them personally, and they are fine people. Andrei has spoken of so many of you with such love and enthusiasm that his feelings have rubbed off on me as well. We are filled with joy when the radio brings us the voices of Western scientists. We believe that these voices will not fall silent until Andrei Sakharov's right to think, speak and live like a free man is returned. We do believe, but still we are saddened that we no longer hear voices raised in defense of imprisoned scientists including Yuri Orlov and Sergei Kovalev.

Soviet scientists are silent. Even the Presidium of the Academy has lapsed into mute anonymity. Do not interpret this silence as protest. The authorities have not yet issued their order for outright condemnation: they find it expedient to deceive you with silence, for you to meet only the silent.

Of course, the Soviet Union can be a difficult place to live if you don't keep your mouth shut. But silence is not a tactic for defense. Soviet scientists, in calling upon you to defend Andrei Sakharov, I am calling upon you to defend yourselves, your right to be human beings. You all remember earlier times: the cramped communal apartments, the poverty, science devastated, the "doctor's plot," and blind terror stalking the nation with fire and sword, destroying all that the people lived by.

Today it's different. Today a scientist has institutes and laboratories at his disposal, his own apartment, and contacts with the world. Unwittingly, the phrase first uttered by Stalin, then endlessly repeated, comes to mind: "Life's gotten better, comrades, and jollier, too."

Of course, we all have our daily concerns, our families, children, illnesses, old age—such is life, after all, and God grant it always be so! And you, Soviet scientists, are silent for fear of losing these things. But silence can lead you to lose even more. It can return us all to those earlier times. Not a single family in the country was untouched. Many of us remember the footsteps on the stairway at night, and the strained listening: have they come for me this time, or for my neighbor? Don't worry, they haven't come for you yet. They've come for Sakharov and for the others who refuse to be silent.

Sakharov was never concerned about himself. The issues he defended were your science, your right to read, to know, to think, to travel to Pugwash, Cambridge, Stanford, the Sorbonne, Stockholm, even with your family, without the humiliating trembling over whether or not they would let you go. Don't worry, you'll still be able to go to those places, where you will talk about how you care for Sakharov (or cared for him, if they have finished with him) with people there who also say they care for him.

I am not calling for a boycott. That is not my business. But I am asking Sakharov's colleagues in the West to stop having contacts with Soviet scientists who remain silent no matter how personable or gifted they may be. Remember, the Soviet authorities always choose what is expedient. Today they have chosen silence for their scientists.

Soviet scientists, I appeal to you to visit Sakharov. He is not permitted visits by foreigners and "criminal elements." But there is no ban on your visits. Could it be that you fear being labeled a renegade and a criminal for paying a friendly or scientific visit? I offer you hospitality at any time in this one-man "sharashka," which has been so "humanely" designed to finish off this unique man while you remain silent.

Andrei has told me so many good things about Soviet physicists. For him the very word "physicist" is filled with special meaning; to this day, he is sure that a physicist by his nature must possesses a good soul and great courage. You know better than I that Sakharov is good and patient, that he loves his country and he lives science; that he would never lie and never remain silent in the face of untruth or injustice. You all know this better than I.

Today I feel like shouting: Soviet physicists, where are you? Can it be that the "competent authorities" are stronger than your science?

February 9, 1980   Elena Bonner (Sakharov)

P.S. This is the first time I have written such a letter, and I am fearful. I fear that Andrei—who believes it's our business to defend—will view my letter as an accusation. I am not accusing anyone. I am appealing to you to raise your voices in his defense.

STATEMENTS ON
MANUSCRIPT THEFTS

December 2, 1978

On November 29, a covert search and illegal seizure of documents and manuscripts took place at the apartment where I have resided for seven years. On
that day, my mother-in-law (whose apartment it is), my wife, and I all found
it necessary to be absent from the apartment at the same time, and from 12:30
P.M. to 1:50 P.M. the apartment was empty and its door locked. This brief
interlude was, I believe, exploited for the illegal activities of KGB agents
sanctioned at that agency's highest level.

The items stolen included copies of almost all the articles I have published
this year, most of the letters I have received, and copies of my own letters, as
well as several unpublished manuscripts, including an article intended for
publication on "The Human Rights Movement in the USSR and East
Europe—Aims, Significance, Problems," and a large manuscript (68 typed
pages, 170 handwritten) of an autobiographical nature. I had not intended the
latter for publication, but now that it has fallen into outside hands, I may find
myself obliged to publish it. The stolen documents also include copies of
(unpublished) appeals addressed by my wife and myself to L. I. Brezhnev with
regard to her medical treatment. I discovered the theft of the documents on
December 1. Those who carried out the search also took some of my personal
belongings.

Over the years, my family and I and those close to us have been subjected
to various forms of persecution, repression, and threats. For us, the virtually
total blockade of postal and telephone communication with our children and
grandchildren, who were forced to emigrate from the USSR, is particularly

painful. This cutting of communications undoubtedly violates the USSR's international agreements.

The November 29 search and seizure of documents constitutes a new stage in the authorities' actions directed against me (and those close to me), and I feel it imperative to inform the outside world of these events.

Academician Andrei Sakharov

March 17, 1981

KGB agents are again sneaking into the apartment in which I was forcibly placed over a year ago, and where I am held in conditions of illegal isolation. This time they are, apparently, entering with the knowledge of certain policemen on round-the-clock guard duty outside my door, and are again placing me in danger.

I also report that on 13 March 1981 the KGB committed another disgusting crime when they stole a bag containing my manuscripts, my private diary for the past year, copies of letters to my Western and Soviet colleagues, and letters to my children and grandchildren. Three thick exercise books—my diary and purely personal writings, a great many notes made from scientific books and journals, including articles by the 1979 Nobel Prize winners, accounts of new ideas and other materials of scientific research which I need, and my own reflections on physics, literature and many other subjects. Among the stolen items were three thick notebooks containing a manuscript of my autobiography. This compels me to publish it earlier than I had intended. The KGB thieves deliberately left on my table a letter which was in the bag, one I had not yet sent to the Scientific Information Centre (VINITI), possibly to show that they were not interfering in my scientific work. But they did steal my diary, which was to a great extent scientific, as I have written. My Nobel Prize certificate had already been stolen from my Moscow flat. In their latest theft the KGB make it clear that they are determined to deprive me of my memories, records of my ideas, and the possibility of any intellectual life, even in solitude. The responsibility for this theft lies with its perpetrators, the Gorky KGB, and the leaders of the USSR KGB, who authorized it.

October 23, 1982

To: Vitaly Fedorchuk, Chairman of the KGB
Copy to: Anatoly Alexandrov, president of the Academy of Sciences

Once again I have been the target of a criminal act. A bag containing documents and manuscripts was stolen. Similar thefts occurred on March 13, 1981, and during a covert search of my Moscow apartment in 1978. The nature and circumstances of the thefts convince me that they were the work of KGB agents.

The items stolen on October 11 included: 900 handwritten pages and 500 typed pages of memoirs covering 60 years of my life; notebooks and my personal diary; my passport; my driver's license; my will; and important and irreplaceable personal letters and documents.

A camera and a radio which I had left at home were also stolen, as well as my savings bank passbook and sixty rubles. Few of these items would have interested a common thief; he would have thrown away the rest.

The theft took place at 4 P.M. in a square near the river landing in the center of Gorky while my wife was buying a train ticket. I was sitting in the front seat of our car. The bag was on the floor behind the driver's seat. Someone stuck his head in the window and asked me a question. I answered. My memory fails at that point. The glass in a rear window was shattered, and the pieces falling on the pavement must have made a lot of noise, but I can't remember it. I suppose, although I have no legal proof, that I was stunned by some narcotic. I remember only that I saw the bag being dragged out through the window.

I was unable to open the car door for several minutes because of my state. When I did get out of the car, three women were standing there, one carrying a small case which looked like a doctor's kit. They asked me why it had taken me so long to get out of the car. Then one said: "The thieves jumped over the fence with your suitcase. They broke your window. We called the police. They will arrive shortly."

It was a lie that they had notified the police. I believe these individuals were doctors assigned to assist me if necessary and to keep me from going quickly to the police. When my wife arrived, I went to the nearest police station and gave a deposition about the crime. (No one had assisted me at the scene of the crime.)

Please remember that a policeman is stationed at my door around the clock, and during trips and walks around town, KGB agents always follow me by car (sometimes in two cars) or on foot. They take note of everyone who approaches me, and I suspect that they would quickly apprehend a common thief who tried to steal my bag.

I am addressing you as chairman of the KGB. I insist upon the immediate return of all the stolen items and on guarantees that your subordinates will not repeat similar thefts or other criminal acts. I ask you to issue the appropriate orders.

* * *

In a separate note accompanying Dr. Alexandrov's copy, Dr. Sakharov wrote:

I would like to devote the major part of my energy to scientific work. But it is simply impossible to talk of "quiet scientific work" when I am kept isolated in illegal exile and the repeated thefts of my scientific and other manuscripts require me to spend enormous energy simply restoring those works. I wish you and my colleagues in the USSR and abroad to understand this. I will be grateful, Anatoly Petrovich, if you support my request for the return of the items stolen on November 29, 1978, March 13, 1981, and October 11, 1982.

When I began to write my memoirs four and a half years ago, I considered them purely personal and did not plan their publication. Now, after the theft, I feel duty-bound to restore them and publish them as quickly as possible.

Academician Andrei Sakharov

November 10, 1982

On October 11, a bag containing my memoirs and other personal documents was stolen. It was the third such theft. I am convinced that this act was committed not by common criminals but rather by the KGB, which has been assigned responsibility for me. Three weeks after the theft, on November 4, I was summoned by Perelygin, the Deputy Procurator of the Gorky region. Perelygin asserted that my statement which had been distributed to foreign correspondents about the theft was slanderous since it contained unsubstantiated accusations against the KGB. By issuing a statement harmful to the USSR, I had violated the regimen established for me by the Presidium of the Supreme Soviet, the leading body of the State. Perelygin added that it was my second warning and a serious one.

The Deputy Procurator's warning lacked any foundation. My statement which describes what really happened is not slanderous. The persons who drugged me and stole my documents and manuscripts are criminally responsible.

I direct particular attention to Perelygin's assertion that the Presidium of the Supreme Soviet decreed my regimen. I have repeatedly asked the USSR Procurator General Rekunkov and Perelygin to show me a document confirming that assertion and indicating the date and signature on the decree ordering my removal by force to Gorky, my isolation, and my regimen here, but no such document has been produced. The *Vedomosti* (Gazette) of the Supreme Soviet has published only the decree of January 8, 1980, revoking my government awards. A decree ordering my regimen would doubtless be unconstitutional. Perelygin is a lawyer and should know that the use of the term "regimen" with regard to my status is illegitimate. Only a court can impose a regimen, specifying its nature in the verdict pronounced on a defendant. I have not been the subject of a legal procedure. I have not been accused of a crime, and no one has sentenced me.

I have been isolated in Gorky and deprived of my constitutional right to a fair trial (if grounds for a trial exist). I have also been deprived of: the inviolability of my home; my freedom of thought and expression; unhindered correspondence and telephone conversations; treatment by a doctor of my choice; my right to rest; even my right to leave this city. I refuse to believe that the Presidium issued such a decree. I believe that Perelygin is in fact blackmailing me with the implicit threat of harsher repression and new crimes. My banishment from Moscow, my isolation, the simple burglaries followed by the theft involving drugs were all illegal, but they have happened. What is to prevent the use of drugs again and some terrible new crime?

I have been forced to live away from my home and under restraint for almost three years, a period more than sufficient for any investigation and exceeding the terms of punishment specified for many offenses by the Criminal Code. The Soviet press and official Soviet representatives in their contacts with my colleagues abroad and Western statesmen and public personalities portray my illegitimate and arbitrary treatment as originating from humanitarian motives. But humane law cannot be the source of tyrannical acts.

I have reported Perelygin's warning, his vague reference to an unpublished decree of the Presidium of the Supreme Soviet, and his new threats, in the hope that world public opinion will speak out against my illegal exile and isolation. I ask government leaders in States signing the Helsinki Final Act, public personalities, and my scientific colleagues abroad to defend me on legal and humanitarian grounds and to oppose new acts of repression.

THREE STATEMENTS ON
EVENTS ABROAD

To the Secretary General of the United Nations, the Heads of State of member countries of the Security Council, and the President of Lebanon

The tragic situation of the wounded, of children and women in the besieged Palestinian camp of Tel-Zaatar requires immediate and decisive action. Use your great authority and influence to save the dying.

—Elena Bonner
Andrei Sakharov, Nobel Peace Laureate
October 1976

To the Workers' Defense Committee

I support the initiative of the representatives of the Polish intelligentsia, headed by Jerzy Andrzejewski, who created the Workers' Defense Committee to protect workers from reprisals inflicted by the authorities.

In our country, as in Poland, there are many problems which touch the widest strata of the population, including workers. Undoubtedly, the struggle for workers' rights constitutes an important part of the democratic movement for human rights. In the USSR we clearly understand this, although at the present time I am unaware of any concrete actions which compare with the activity of the Polish Workers' Defense Committee in scope and effectiveness.

We know the importance of nonconformity and solidarity under totalitarian conditions, and we also know how difficult they are to maintain. I admire the boldness of our friends in Poland who, in dealing with these real and immediate problems, are expressing the solidarity of intellectuals and workers.

I hope that in time ways will be found for effective cooperation in the struggle for human rights in Poland, the USSR, and the other countries of Eastern Europe.

—Andrei Sakharov,
November 20, 1976

To the Chairman of the State Council of the People's Republic of China, Hua Guofeng

I appeal to you because out of the deep respect I feel for the Chinese people. I ask you to use your influence to reconsider the sentencing of Wei Qin Xen to fifteen years imprisonment for his public speeches in defense of democratic principles. Such an act of justice would increase the authority of the Chinese People's Republic and win it international confidence.

—Andrei Sakharov, Academician and Nobel Peace Laureate
July 27, 1980

THE SAKHAROV-CARTER CORRESPONDENCE

Andrei Sakharov gave the following letter, addressed to President Carter, to Martin Garbus, a New York attorney. It was intended as a private communication, but Garbus released it to the press.

Dear Mr. Carter,

It's very important to defend those who suffer because of their nonviolent struggle for an open society, for justice, for other people whose rights are violated. It is our duty and yours to fight for them. I think that a lot depends on this struggle—trust between peoples, confidence in lofty promises, and, in the final analysis, international security.

Our situation is difficult, almost unbearable—not only in the USSR, but also in all the countries of Eastern Europe. Now, on the eve of the Belgrade Meeting, with the struggle for human rights rising in Eastern Europe and the USSR, the authorities are stepping up their repression and their attempts to discredit dissidents. They are unwilling to make any concessions to the human rights most essential to any society (freedom of belief and information, freedom of conscience, freedom to choose one's country of residence, etc.). They cannot accept the honest competition of ideas. The persecution of the members of the Helsinki Watch Groups in Moscow and the Ukraine, and especially the provocation in the Moscow subway, which we have to compare to the 1933 Reichstag fire and the 1934 murder of Kirov, require emphatic condemnation.

Do you know the truth about the situation of religion in the USSR—the humiliation of official churches and the merciless repression (arrests; fines; religious parents deprived of their children; even murder, as in the case of the Baptist Biblenko) of those sects—Baptists, Uniates, Pentecostals, the True Orthodox Church, and others—who seek independence of the government.

The Vins case is the best-known example. Terror is also used against other groups of dissidents. During the past year we have known of the murders of dissidents—that of the poet and translator Konstantin Bogatyrev is well known—which have not been investigated at all.

It is very important that the President of the United States continue his efforts to obtain the release of those people who are already known to Americans and that those efforts not be in vain. It is very important to continue the struggle for the severely ill and for women political prisoners.

I give you a list of those in need of immediate release, but it is very important to remember that there are many others in equally difficult situations. This is the main list. There are very many others who need the same support, and we haven't got the moral strength to cross out any of the names: Kovalev, Romanyuk, Dzhemilev, Svetlichny, Gluzman, Ruban, Shtern, Fyodorov, Makarenko, Sergienko, Ogurtsov, Pronyuk, Maria Semyonova, Vins, Moroz, Superfin, Fedorenko. (Fedorenko has been on a hunger strike for two years. He is serving a thirteen-year sentence for high treason since he tried to cross the frontier by hanging to the undercarriage of a train.) Detailed information about each of them is available from Khronika Press; its publisher, Edward Kline, knows all the cases . . . .

Andrei Sakharov

January 20, 1977

Andrei Sakharov was invited to the U.S. Embassy in Moscow on February 6, and the text of President Carter's reply was read to him.

Dear Professor Sakharov:

I received your letter of January 21, and I want to express my appreciation to you for bringing your thoughts to my personal attention.

Human rights is a central concern of my administration. In my inaugural address I stated: "Because we are free, we can never be indifferent to the fate of freedom elsewhere." You may rest assured that the American people and our government will continue our firm commitment to promote respect for human rights not only in our country but also abroad.

We shall use our good offices to seek the release of prisoners of conscience, and we will continue our efforts to shape a world responsive to human aspirations in which nations of differing cultures and histories can live side by side in peace and justice.

I am always glad to hear from you, and I wish you well.

Sincerely,

Jimmy Carter

President Carter recalled this correspondence in his memoir *Keeping Faith* (Bantam, 1982), p. 146:

> In mid-February 1977, when Andrei Sakharov, the distinguished scientist and dissident who had been detained by Soviet officials informed me of his plight, I sent him a personal pledge to promote human rights in the Soviet Union. A highly publicized photograph showed him facing the cameraman, holding the letter with my signature.
>
> Brezhnev's tone changed to harshness in his second message on February 25. His primary objection was to my aggressive proposals on nuclear arms limitations—advocating much deeper cuts than had been discussed at Vladivostok in 1975—but he also expressed strong opposition to our human-rights policy. He seemed especially provoked by my corresponding with him and at the same time sending a letter to Sakharov, who was considered by the Soviet leader to be "a renegade who proclaimed himself an enemy of the Soviet state."

It is clear from this brief excerpt that Carter had either forgotten the contents of my letter, which was not concerned at all with my personal situation, or had been mistakenly informed.

—Andrei Sakharov

APPENDIX C:
THE 1984 HUNGER STRIKE

A Letter to the Family

Dear Ruth Grigorievna, Tanya, Alyosha, Liza, and Efrem.

I kiss you all. Two years of such harsh trials and anxiety for Lusia and me and for you are now behind us. And during all this time direct communication has been impossible. But you managed better than anyone to understand what was happening, and your intuition and your wise actions saved us. Here is a short account of some of the things you may still not know.

In 1984 Lusia and I were afraid that during my hunger strike she would fall into the hands of the KGB. I came up with a plan according to which she would ask for temporary asylum at the embassy of the United States of America. Lusia hesitated greatly and put off the start of the action, even when we set the date for March. Finally, we decided to begin on April 13. On April 7 she left Gorky.

But back in March I had cut my leg on a garbage can and developed an abscess on the knee. While Lusia was away they lanced it at the polyclinic, but apparently it did not drain completely. On April 12 doctors came to see me and on April 13 they hospitalized me to lance the abscess again. Lusia flew back on the thirteenth (without her things, without warm clothing) after my telegram of the twelfth, which she received two hours before they came for her from the embassy. . . .

While I was being taken from doctor to doctor at the hospital, I carelessly gave up . . . my bag with documents, which I always carried with me. . . . I had forgotten that I had not destroyed the draft of my letter to the American ambassador. So the KGB learned of my plan. Lusia and I understood that. But we could not retreat. On May 2 when Lusia tried to fly out to Moscow, she was detained at the airport and searched. More documents fell into KGB hands, including her letter to you. Lusia was charged under Article 190-1, you know her case very well (even though the final text of my administrative complaint did not reach you).

Before she got home, I had begun a hunger strike, after taking a laxative. The chief of the Regional KGB came into the house with Lusia. He intoned a "threatening" monologue, in which he called Lusia "Elena Bonner, CIA agent."

The rest you basically know. On May 7 I was forcibly hospitalized. On May 11 I was force-fed (with intravenous injections). That day I had a small stroke (or a spasm). On May 15 Lusia received a telegram:

"Elena Georgievna, we, the children of Andrei Dmitrievich, ask and implore you to do everything you can to save our father from this mad undertaking, which could lead to his death. We know that only one person can save him from death—that is you. You are the mother of children and you should understand us. Otherwise we will be forced to turn to the procurator's office, because you are inciting our father to commit suicide. We see no other way out. Understand us correctly—Tanya, Lyuba, Dima." . . .

This cruel and unfair telegram caused Lusia additional suffering and anxiety in her already horrible and almost unbearable situation. The telegram gave the KGB the "green light" for any action against us. . . . It was the reason that I did not write to my children for the next year and a half, until November 1985.

Lusia will tell you about subsequent events, about our unheard of, unprecedented isolation for that entire year and a half.

In November 1984 I sent a letter (I won't tell you how) to Alexandrov and to the presidium of the Academy of Sciences, in which I asked for help in obtaining permission for Lusia's trip. I described what I experienced during force-feeding. In conclusion I wrote that I was the only academician whose wife has been subjected to shameless slander in the press, illegal sentencing as a criminal for actions she performed at my behest, and for actions which she never performed, and has been deprived of the opportunity to see her family and to have medical care. I wrote that I did not want to participate in a worldwide hoax and asked that my letter be considered as my resignation from the Academy of Sciences if my request was not satisfied (at first I gave them until March 1, and then extended the deadline to May 10).

. . . I started a new hunger strike on April 16, 1985, and was forcibly hospitalized—again taken to the Semashko hospital—on April 21. From that day (April 21) right up to July 11, I was subjected to forcible feeding. During this period and the one that followed, my resistance was sometimes, though not always, of a merely symbolic type.

The feeding was sometimes extremely painful. I was tied up and held down against the bed so violently that my face became badly bruised. A spoon was used to open my mouth and another spoon to pour in the food. My nose was held tight by hand or with a clamp. I resigned myself to eating only when the "feeding team" was present in full strength and only when I was actually in the ward. Twice, they dragged me into the ward with the help of KGB men.

I had no idea whether or not anyone outside Russia knew about my hunger strike.

On July 11, not being able to bear my separation from Elena any longer and not knowing anything about her, I wrote a statement that my hunger strike was at an end. The same day, I was discharged from the hospital. The KGB, clearly, badly wanted me discharged before the Helsinki meeting started.

Lusia and I were together for two weeks. It was a good time to be alive, and it gave us strength to go on. On July 25, I resumed my hunger strike and was hospitalized on July 27. During our short period of freedom, the film known to you was taken by a hidden camera. I ceased my hunger strike and was discharged on October 23. On October 25, the permission for Elena's travel was received.

. . . My weight declined constantly during the period of forcible feeding. My normal weight is 170 to 176 pounds. When I was discharged on July 11, it was 145 pounds. My lowest weight during the second round was 138 pounds on August 13.

Beginning that day, they administered subcutaneous (into both thighs) and intravenous drips containing glucose and protein preparations—15 subcutaneous and 10 intravenous. The sheer quantity of the drip was enormous. My legs blew up like pillows and were painful.

The most cruel measure used against us was a 10-month separation—isolation from each other. It was especially difficult for Elena in her solitude and isolation. In 1985, she did not go on any hunger strike but lost more weight than I did.

These 10 months were as though they had never existed, a period of time deleted from our lives.

In March 1985 Lusia appealed to the Presidium of the Supreme Soviet of the USSR for a pardon and with a request to be allowed to travel. In 1984 and in 1985, I wrote many letters to the leaders of the country and to the KGB, including letters on May 21, 1985, to Chebrikov and on July 29, 1985, to Gorbachev. I stated why Lusia's trip was vitally important, her right to see her mother, children, and grandchildren. I stressed that she was a disabled veteran of the Great Patriotic War, having served four years, and a seriously ill person, I explained the illegality of her conviction. Later I wrote, "My wife has influenced me to place greater stress in my public activity on the fate of specific individuals and on humanitarian concerns, she has not influenced my ideas on general issues. . . . I am prepared to bear the responsibility for my actions—even though I consider the measures directed against me to be unfair and illegal. But a situation in which responsibility for my actions is transferred to my wife is totally intolerable for me." I wrote, "I want to end my public activity and statements (except, of course, for extraordinary situations) and to concentrate on my work. If there is a positive decision on my wife's trip, I am prepared to ask Western scientists, and everyone who acted in my defense, to halt their efforts on my behalf."

Twice (May 31, 1985, and Sept. 5, 1985) I was visited in the hospital by a representative of the KGB of the U.S.S.R., S. I. Sokolov, evidently a big chief. In May, he also talked to Elena.

He conversed with me in a harsh manner. He stressed the reasons why my request for Elena's travel—and also for the children's travel to the U.S.S.R.—could not be granted. He also led me to understand that I must disavow certain previous statements. In particular, my letter to Drell, my statements on the Moscow subway explosion, and my ideas on convergence. I was on a full hunger strike—there was no force feeding. Thus, they "prepared" me for the conversation [with Sokolov in May].

In September, Sokolov informed me that Gorbachev had familiarized himself with my letter and had assigned a group of people to prepare an answer. Sokolov asked me to write a statement on the question of my knowledge of secrets and to convey to my wife a request that she write a statement obliging her not to meet representatives of the mass media while abroad or to take part in any press conference.

I was then allowed 3 hours with Lusia, and we carried out Sokolov's requests. I wrote that I accept the Soviet authorities' right to refuse me permission to travel beyond the country's borders, since I did in the past have access to especially important secret material of a military nature, some of which might still be of significance even now.

(I wish to call attention to the fact that the formulation I used and the similar formulation in my letter to Gorbachev do not justify my deportation to Gorky, which I consider unjust and illegal.)

. . . I have the feeling that I am going with Lusia to visit you, plunging into your colorful, event-filled life. I hope that it will now go into a more peaceful, more "family-like" track. I hope that Lusia has everything necessary done, including her heart, eyes, teeth, and papilloma, and that she will return in better health and less worried about you. I kiss you, be healthy and happy. Kiss the children. . . .

November 24, 1985. Andrei.

P.S. Alexei, in the reprint of my article, "Cosmic Transitions with Changes in the Metrics Signature," the dedication to Lusia was omitted. How did that happen? Can the dedication be reinstated in some of the preprints sent out? It's very important to me.

November, 1985

Administrative Complaint

To the Procurator of the RSFSR From SAKHAROV, Andrei Dmitrievich, Academician; Gorky-137, Gagarin Avenue, 214, apt. 3

In the case of Elena Georgievna BONNER, my wife, sentenced under article 190-1 of the Criminal Code of the RSFSR with the application of article 43 of the Criminal Code of the RSFSR* to five years of exile by the Gorky Regional Court on 10 August 1984, and affirmed without change by the Judicial Collegium on Criminal Cases of the Supreme Court of the RSFSR on 7 September.

On 1 August, 1984, I sent a statement to the investigator and the chairman of the court in the case of my wife, a copy is attached. I stand by the assertions and requests contained in that statement. I received a reply from the investigator, senior assistant of the procurator of Gorky Oblast, G. P. Kolesnikov, according to which my statement was passed on to the Judicial Collegium on Criminal Cases of the Gorky Regional Court. However, my statement was not appended to the case file for E. G. Bonner, and the requests contained therein were not examined by the court. This is a serious procedural violation. I was not called to testify in my wife's trial as a witness, nor was I notified of the date of the trial. Thus, none of my wife's relatives (or friends) had the opportunity to be present in the courtroom, which is a gross violation of the principle of access and openness. Another procedural violation is having the trial and (in my opinion) the investigation in the city of Gorky, because before my wife was charged and not allowed to leave Gorky, she lived in Moscow at Chkalov Street, no. 48B, apt. 68, and because not a single incriminating charge had anything to do with Gorky.

The indictment, the verdict, and the decision of the appeals court are not, in my opinion, well founded, they contain factual and conceptually incorrect

---

*[Article 43 permits the court to set a milder punishment than the minimum specified for a particular crime when mitigating circumstances exist.]

statements and opinions, and are prejudiced and nonobjective. One of the central charges, as I maintain, is based on perjured testimony.

I will begin with a discussion of an episode which was not shown to be a crime either in the indictment or during the trial or during the appeal hearing. There was no discussion of the arguments of the defense attorney and the defendant.

My wife was charged with participating in the writing and distribution of a document by the Moscow Helsinki Group titled "Summary Document for the Belgrade Conference." The indictment, verdict, and decision of the appeals court assert that her participation in the writing and distribution is corroborated by the testimony of Felix Serebrov, and that her participation in writing it is also corroborated by my wife's signature in the text of the document published by Khronika Press in New York. No other proof of my wife's participation in the writing and distribution was produced. The court was not given an original of the document with my wife's signature in her own hand. It was not proved that the document was written before her trip to Italy (the published text does not give the date the document was written, which in itself deprives it of any juridical meaning). At the trial she stated that she learned of the existence of the document when she was in Italy, by telephone, and it was by telephone that she gave permission to sign her name to the document. The verdict and the appeal ruling do not offer any arguments to refute my wife's testimony and do not even mention it except to say that she corroborated her signature.

The flimsiness of the references to Serebrov's testimony is particularly significant, because it is the only attempt to prove Bonner's participation in distributing the document and in general it is the only testimony mentioned in the verdict and the decision of the appeals court in the entire case against my wife. Witness Serebrov maintained in court that P. G. Grigorenko (one of the members of the Moscow Helsinki Group) told him that Bonner brought the documents for the Belgrade conference to Italy and had participated in writing it. But this is *obvious* perjury, in any case, as relates to the distribution. My wife left for Italy for treatment on 5 September 1977. Serebrov was arrested on 16 August 1977, twenty days before my wife left, which is confirmed by documents in the case. After his arrest, Serebrov never saw Grigorenko, who left the USSR in November of that year. This chronological discrepancy was discussed in great detail by the court of the first instance. In direct questioning by defense attorney Elena Reznikova on how he explained this discrepancy, Serebrov could not give an answer and was silent. The attorney's argument at the appeal hearing and the written appeal stressed once again that Grigorenko could not have spoken before August 15 about my wife's bringing out any document on September 5. But this entire discussion (written and oral) was completely ignored in the verdict and the decision of the Judicial Collegium on Criminal Cases of the Supreme Court of the RSFSR. The decision does not even mention that Reznikova disputed Serebrov's testimony dealing with the distribution of the document for the Belgrade conference. I view the above as evidence of the nonobjectivity and prejudice of both courts and as a basis for protesting the sentence.

Article 190-1 of the Criminal Code of the RSFSR deals with "dissemination of deliberately false fabrications slandering the Soviet social and state system." The law does not specify whether the defendant must know that the statements ("fabrications") are false at the time they are disseminated, or whether it is sufficient for their falsehood to be evident only to the members of the court. Since the views and opinions of the members of the court might differ substantially from the views of the defendant by virtue of differing information accessible to them and for ideological reasons, this question is very important for the practical application of article 190-1. If article 190-1 does not envisage criminal prosecution for beliefs, then undoubtedly the first interpretation is correct and the court *must* prove that the accused consciously spread lies, that is, not simply false opinions but statements whose falseness was known to her. This interpretation is reflected in the *Commentary to the Criminal Code of the RSFSR* (Yuridicheskaya Literatura Publishing House, 1971, edited by Professor Anashkin, Professor Karpets, Professor Nikoforov, pp. 403–404, paragraphs 2 and 9a). But the decision of the appeals court, of the second instance in the case of my wife, on the contrary, reads: "Familiarization with the *content* (italics mine—A.S.) of the interviews given by the defendant, and the documents she signed is evidence of the fact that they contain deliberately false opinions slandering the Soviet state and social system." That is, the Judicial Collegium on Criminal Cases of the Supreme Court of the RSFSR (just as the trial court) simply does not consider it necessary to prove that my wife consciously spread lies; thereby these courts are in fact supporting the position of *persecution for beliefs*.

I ask the procurator of the RSFSR to direct particular attention to this circumstance. I feel that such an incorrect interpretation of article 190-1 is a definite basis for reversing the conviction.

The appellate ruling on my wife's case states that "the violation of the human rights of the particular individuals mentioned by Bonner did not take place, the individuals were convicted in conformity with established legal procedures for crimes they had committed." But, according to the beliefs of my wife (and my own beliefs), based on information on the trials of many individuals, they were convicted illegally, that is, for their beliefs, and are prisoners of conscience (they did not use or advocate violence). For my wife, and for myself, the fact of a sentencing does not by itself constitute proof of the rightness of a conviction; a concrete evaluation is necessary, in particular taking into account the fact that the courts systematically use the above-mentioned incorrect interpretation of the concept of deliberate falsehood in charging people under article 190-1 of the Criminal Code of the RSFSR and systematically violate the principle of access and openness in relation to defendants under political articles.

As I indicated in my statement of 1 August 1984, the majority of the statements incriminating my wife were either statements of my own ideas or word-for-word citations (at press conferences in Italy in 1975 and at the Nobel ceremony and the Nobel press conference that same year, and also a press conference in January 1980, after my illegal deportation to Gorky). My wife in accordance with her beliefs appeared on those occasions as my fully empowered representative. She always noted that this was my point of view.

It is perfectly obvious that trying her for these statements without charging me or even calling me as a witness is absolutely illegal. I am prepared to answer for these statements, which correspond with my beliefs. But my wife must be freed of responsibility for them!

The indictment, the verdict of the trial court, and the decision of the appeals court are characterized by inaccurate and prejudiced quotations taken out of context and distortions of my wife's statements. Here is a typical example: My wife is charged with stating that "Soviet newspapers print total lies." But the only evidence given is a citation from an article in the newspaper *Russkaya mysl'* (Russian Thought), which is a free rendition of an interview with my wife in a double translation. And the rest of this long article on my life in Gorky is not mentioned in the summation or by the court. In actual fact my wife never uses such sweeping generalizations "total lies." I call the prosecutor's attention to the illegality of using an unauthorized text as evidence of guilt.

I find particularly outrageous from a moral point of view the use in the summation and sentence of my wife's emotional response during an unexpected meeting with a French correspondent only three days after she had been diagnosed as having had a heart attack. In the indictment, the decision the appeals court, and (apparently) in the verdict, it is maintained that my wife allegedly said that "the Soviet government has created conditions to kill the academician and her." However, if you study the text of the television interview, you will be convinced that those words are not in there. Actually, when asked "What will happen to you then?" my wife replied, "I don't know, I think they're simply killing us." She was not talking about being shot with a gun. But obliquely we are being killed, especially my wife—we are convinced of that—she is being killed with persecution and slander in the press (in the year 1983 alone, she was attacked by publications with a circulation of over ten million),* by the actual deprivation of effective medical care, searches, exhausting interrogations and a trial of a seriously ill person, deprivation of normal contact with her mother, children, and grandchildren. And they are killing me by slowly killing her!

An important basis for protesting the sentence is the incorrect application by the court of article 43 of the Criminal Code of the RSFSR. The sentence does not mention that *my wife is a Group 2 invalid of the Great Patriotic War and that she had a myocardial infarct* (there are affidavits to that effect in her case file), does not mention that she suffers from chronic uveitis and irreversible glaucoma, that she has had three eye operations and major surgery for thyreotoxicosis, and also it does not mention that my wife has an impeccable work record of thirty-two years. All it mentions is my wife's age and the fact that she has no prior convictions. According to the code (article 43 of the Criminal Code of the RSFSR), listing mitigating circumstances in the verdict is mandatory. In using article 43, the court should have given a sentence that was lower than the minimum possible under article 190-1 of the Criminal Code of the RSFSR, that is, a sentence of less than a fine. Exile is not such a sentence.

I summarize: The basis for annulling the verdict of the trial court and protesting the decision of the appeals court is the absence of any crime in the actions of E. G. Bonner, in particular, the absence of *deliberate* falsehood in the statements of Bonner, which were made in accordance with her beliefs. Other important reasons for reversing the sentence are the reliance of the indictment, verdict, and decision on the clearly perjured testimony of F. Serebrov—the only witness mentioned in the verdict, the violation of the principle of access and openness, and the improper application by the court of article 43 of the Criminal Code of the RSFSR.

Based on the above, I ask the procurator of the RSFSR to make use of his right of administrative supervision in order to review this case and annul the verdict of the Gorky Regional Court and the decision of the Judicial Collegium on Criminal Cases of the Supreme Court of the RSFSR.

29 November 1984 A. Sakharov
Gorky

---

*[Yakovlev's book *CIA Target—The USSR* (an edition of 200,000 copies); *Smena,* 1983, no. 14 (circulation 1,170,000); *Man and the Law,* 1983, no. 10 (circulation 8,700,000).]

Letter to Anatoly Alexandrov

Anatoly Alexandrov, President,
U.S.S.R. Academy of Sciences
Members of the Presidium,
U.S.S.R. Academy of Sciences

Dear Anatoly Petrovich:

I appeal to you at the most tragic moment of my life. I ask you to support my wife Elena Bonner's request for permission to travel abroad to visit her mother, her children and her grandchildren and to receive medical treatment for her eyes and her heart. I shall explain why this trip has become an absolute necessity for us. Our unprecedented situation, our isolation, the lies and slander regarding us compel me to write in detail. Please forgive me for the length of this letter.

The authorities have been greatly annoyed by my public activities—my defense of prisoners of conscience and my articles and books on peace, the open society and human rights. (My fundamental ideas are contained in *Reflections on Progress, Peaceful Coexistence, and Intellectual Freedom*, 1968; *My Country and the World*, 1975; and "The Danger of Thermonuclear War," 1983.)

I do not intend to defend or explain my position here. What I wish to make clear is that I alone am responsible for all my actions, which are the result of convictions formed over a lifetime. As soon as Elena Bonner married me in 1971, the KGB adopted a sly and cruel plan to solve the "Sakharov problem." They have tried to shift responsibility for my actions onto her, to destroy her morally and physically. They hope to break and bridle me, while portraying me as the innocent victim of the intrigues of my wife—a "CIA agent," a "Zionist," a "mercenary adventuress," etc. Any remaining doubts about this have been dispelled by the mass campaign of slander mounted against my wife in 1983 (attacks against her were printed in publications with a circulation of 11 million copies); by the two 1984 articles about her in *Izvestia*, and especially by the KGB's treatment of us in 1984, which I describe below.

My wife, Elena Bonner, was born in 1923. Her parents, who were active participants in the Revolution and the civil war, became victims of repression in 1937. Her father, the first secretary of the Armenian Bolshevik Party's central committee and a member of the Comintern's executive committee, perished. Her mother spent many years in labor camps and in exile as a "relative of a traitor to the motherland."

My wife served in the armed forces from the outbreak of World War II until

August, 1945. She began as a first-aid instructor. After she was wounded and suffered a concussion, she became the head nurse on a hospital train. The concussion severely damaged her eyes. My wife is classified as a disabled veteran because of her loss of vision. She has been seriously ill ever since the war, but she has managed to lead a productive life—first studying, then working as a physician and teacher, raising a family, helping friends and strangers in need, sustaining her associates with respect and affection.

Her situation changed drastically after our paths merged. Tatyana and Alexei, my wife's children—whom I consider my own—and our grandchildren were forced to emigrate to the United States in 1977 and 1978 after five years of harassment and death threats. They had in fact become hostages. The pain of this tragic separation has been compounded by the absence of normal mail, cable, and phone communications. My wife's 84-year-old mother has been living in the United States since 1980. It is the inalienable right of all human beings to see their families—and that includes my wife!

As long ago as 1974 many events convinced us that no effective medical treatment was possible for my wife in the U.S.S.R. and, moreover, that such treatment would be *dangerous* because of inevitable KGB interference. Now the organized campaign of slander against her is an added complication. These misgivings relate to my wife's medical treatment and not to my own, but they were reinforced by what physicians under KGB command did to me during my four-month confinement in a Gorky hospital. More about this later.

In 1975, with the support of world public opinion (and I assume on Brezhnev's order), my wife was allowed to travel to Italy to receive treatment for her eyes. My wife visited Italy in 1975, 1977 and 1979 for eye care. In Siena, Dr. Frezzotti twice operated on her for glaucoma, which could not be controlled by medication. Naturally, the same doctor should continue to treat her. Another visit became necessary in 1982. She submitted her application in September, 1982. Such applications are reviewed within five months—and usually within a few weeks. Two years have passed, and my wife is still waiting for a reply.

In April, 1983, my wife Elena Bonner suffered a massive heart attack, as confirmed by a report of the academy's medical department issued in response to an inquiry from the procurator's office. Her condition has not yet returned to normal. She has had recurrent attacks. (Some of these attacks have been confirmed by academy physicians who have examined her; one examination took place in March, 1984.) Her most recent major attack occurred in August, 1984.

In November, 1983, I addressed an appeal to Comrade Yuri Andropov [General Secretary, November, 1982 to February 9, 1984], and I addressed a similar appeal to Comrade Konstantin Chernenko [General Secretary at the time this letter was written] in February, 1984. I asked them to issue instructions permitting my wife to travel. I wrote: "A trip . . . to see her mother, children, and grandchildren and . . . to receive medical treatment has become a matter of life and death for us. The trip has no other purpose. I assure you of that."

By September, 1983, I realized that the question of my wife's trip would be resolved only if I conducted a hunger strike (as in the earlier case of our daughter-in-law Liza Alexeyeva's departure to join Alexei). My wife understood how difficult it was for me to do nothing. Nevertheless, she kept putting off the hunger strike. And, in point of fact, I began the hunger strike only in direct response to actions of the authorities.

On March 30, 1984, I was summoned to the Gorky province visa office. A representative there announced: "On behalf of the visa department of the U.S.S.R., I inform you that your statement is under consideration. The reply will be communicated to you after May 1."

My wife was to fly to Moscow on May 2. I watched through the airport window as she was detained by the aircraft and taken away in a police car. I immediately returned to the apartment and took a laxative, thereby beginning my hunger strike for my wife to be allowed to travel.

Two hours later my wife returned, accompanied by the KGB province chief, who delivered a threatening speech in the course of which he called my wife a CIA agent. My wife had been subjected to a body search at the airport and charged under Article 190-1. They also made her sign a promise not to leave the city. So this was my promised reply to my declaration about my wife's trip abroad.

During the months that followed, my wife was called in for interrogation three or four times a week. She was tried on August 9–10 and sentenced to five years' exile. On September 7 a picked group from the RSFSR Supreme Court made a special trip to Gorky to hear her appeal. They confirmed the sentence. Gorky was designated her place of exile so that she could remain with me, thereby creating a semblance of humanity. In fact, however, it was camouflaged murder.

The KGB managed the whole enterprise—from the charges to the sentence—in order to block my wife's travel abroad. The indictment and the verdict are typical for Article 190-1 cases, although particularly flagrant examples of the arbitrariness and injustice involved. Article 190-1 makes it a crime to disseminate slanderous fabrications known to be false that defame the Soviet state and social system. (Article 190-1 refers to statements that the defendant knows are *false*. In my experience, and that includes my wife's case, the defendants believed their statements to be *true* beyond a doubt. The real issue was their *opinions*.)

Most of the eight counts in my wife's indictment involve her repetition of statements made by me. (To make matters worse, they have been taken out of context.) All the statements concern secondary issues. For example, in *My Country and the World*, I explain what "certificates" are, noting that two or more types of money exist in the U.S.S.R. My wife repeated this indisputable statement at a press conference in Italy in 1975, and she was charged with slander because of it. I—and not my wife—should be charged with statements made by me. My wife acted as my representative in keeping with her own beliefs.

One charge in the indictment exploits an emotional outburst of my wife during the unexpected visit of a French correspondent on May 18, 1983, *three days after her massive myocardial infarct had been diagnosed.* (As you know, in 1983 we requested, without success, that we be admitted together to the academy's hospital.) The correspondent asked, "What will happen to you?" My wife exclaimed: "I don't know. I think they are trying to kill us." She was clearly not referring to being killed by a pistol or knife. But she had more than enough grounds to speak of indirect murder (at least of herself).

My wife's alleged drafting and circulation of a Moscow Helsinki Group document was a key point in the indictment. It was based on patently false testimony and was completely refuted by defense counsel's examination of the chronology of events. A witness testified at the trial that he had been told by a member of the Helsinki Group that my wife had taken one of the group's documents with her when she left the country in 1977. But the witness had been arrested on Aug. 16, 1977, and my wife left for Italy on September 5. Thus he could not have met anyone "from outside" after my wife's departure. Under questioning, the witness replied that he had learned of the document's being carried out of the country in July or August—that is, before my wife's trip.

Moreover, no proof that the document had been written prior to my wife's departure was presented in the indictment or during the trial. (The document was undated. That alone was enough to deprive it of any juridical significance.)

The only "evidence" corroborating the witness's unsubstantiated allegation was the statement of a person who had emigrated in 1977. In defiance of logic this count was included in the verdict and in the decision of the appellate proceeding. If the appellate court had eliminated that count, it would have had to annul the verdict—in part because the only directly incriminating testimony would be lost, in part because of the dated and inconsequential nature of the 1975 episode. Most important of all, none of the charges bore the slightest juridical relation to Article 190-1, which presupposes intentional slander.

In practice my wife's exile has led to restrictions much more severe than those stipulated in the law: The loss of all communication with her mother and children; complete isolation from her friends; still less opportunity for medical care; the virtual confiscation of property left in our Moscow apartment—which is now inaccessible to us—and the potential loss of the apartment itself. (The apartment was given to my wife's mother in 1956 after she was rehabilitated and after her husband was rehabilitated posthumously.)

There was no mention during my wife's trial of the accusations made in the press—her alleged past crimes, her "immoral character," her "links" with foreign intelligence agencies. That is all simply slander for public consumption—for the "sheep" held in such contempt by the KGB directors of the campaign. The most recent article of this sort appeared in *Izvestia* on May 21. The article pushes the idea that my wife has always wanted to leave the U.S.S.R., "even over her husband's dead body." The article claims that as long ago as 1979 she wanted to remain in the United States but had been persuaded to leave. (The context implies that American intelligence agents did the persuading.)

My wife's tragic and heroic life with me, which has brought her so much suffering, refutes this insinuation. Before marrying me, my wife made several trips abroad. She worked for a year in Iraq on a vaccination project. She visited Poland and France. The idea of defecting never entered her mind. It is the KGB that wants my wife to abandon me: It would provide the best demonstration that their slander had been true. But they were hardly hoping for that. They are "psychologists." They carefully hid the May 21 [*Izvestia*] article from me. They did not want to strengthen my resolve to win my goal before seeing my wife. I wanted to protect her from responsibility for my hunger strike.

For four months—from May 7 to September 8—my wife and I were separated from each other and completely isolated from the outside world. My wife was alone in our apartment. Her "guards" were increased. Apart from the usual policeman at the entrance to our apartment, observation posts operated around the clock, and a van with KGB agents on duty was parked beneath our terrace. Outside the house she was followed by two cars of KGB agents who prevented the most innocent contact with anyone. She was not allowed into the regional hospital when I was confined there.

On May 7, while accompanying my wife to the prosecutor's office for her next bout of questioning, I was seized by KGB men disguised in doctors' white coats. They took me by force to Gorky Regional Hospital, kept me there by force and tormented me for four months. My attempts to flee the hospital were always blocked by KGB men, who were on duty round-the-clock to bar all means of escape.

From May 11 to May 27 I was subjected to the excruciating and degrading process of force-feeding. The doctors hypocritically called it "saving my life," but in fact they were acting under orders from the KGB to create conditions in which my demand for my wife to be allowed to travel would not have to be fulfilled. They kept changing the method of force-feeding. They wanted to maximize my distress in order to make me give up the hunger strike.

From May 11 to May 15 intravenous feeding was tried. Orderlies would throw me onto the bed, tie my hands and feet and then hold my shoulders down while the needle was inserted into a vein. On May 11, the first day this was attempted, one of the hospital aides sat on my legs while some substance was injected with a small syringe. I passed out and involuntarily urinated. When I came to, the orderlies had left my bedside. Their bodies seemed strangely distorted as on a television screen affected by strong interference. I found out later that this sort of optical illusion is symptomatic of a cerebral spasm or stroke.

I have retained drafts of the letters I wrote to my wife from the hospital. (Hardly any of the letters, apart from those that were quite empty of information, were actually delivered to my wife. The same is true with respect to the notes and books she sent me.)

In my first letter written (May 20) after force-feeding began and in another draft written at that time, my writing wavers and is noticeably unformed. Letters are repeated two or three times in many words (mainly vowels, as in "haaand"). This is another typical symptom of a cerebral spasm or stroke and can be used as objective, documentary evidence in attempting a diagnosis. The repetition of letters does not occur in later drafts, but the symptoms of trembling persist. My letter of May 10 (the ninth of my hunger strike but prior to force-feeding) is entirely normal. My recollections from the period of force-feeding are confused, in contrast to memory of events from May 2 to May 10. My letter dated May 20 states: "can barely walk. I am trying to learn." The spasm or stroke I suffered on May 11 was not an accident; it was a direct result of the medical measures taken in my case on orders from the KGB.

From May 16 to May 24 a new means of force-feeding was employed: A tube was inserted through my nose. This was discontinued on May 25, supposedly because sores were developing along the nasal passages and esophagus. I believe it was stopped because this method is bearable, if painful. In labor camps it is used for months—even years—at a time.

From May 25 to May 27 the most excruciating, degrading and barbarous method was used. I was again pushed down onto the bed without a pillow and my hands and feet were tied. A tight clamp was placed on my nose so that I could breathe only through my mouth. Whenever I opened my mouth to take a breath, a spoonful of nutriment or a broth containing strained meat would be poured into my mouth. Sometimes my jaws were pried open by a lever. They would hold my mouth shut until I swallowed so that I could not spit out the food. When I managed to do so, it only prolonged the agony. I experienced a continuing feeling of suffocation, aggravated by the position of my body and head. I had to gasp for breath. I could feel the veins bulging on my forehead. They seemed on the verge of bursting.

On May 27 I asked that the clamp be removed. I promised to swallow voluntarily. Unfortunately this meant that my hunger strike was over, although I did not realize it at the time. I intended to resume my hunger strike some time later—in July or August—but kept postponing it. It was psychologically difficult to condemn myself to another indefinite period of torture by suffocation. It is easier to continue the struggle than to resume it.

Much of my strength that summer was dissipated in tedious and futile "discussions" with other patients in the semiprivate room where I was never left alone. This, too, was part of the KGB's elaborate tactics. Different patients occupied the other bed, but each of them tried to convince me what a naïve fool I am—a political ignoramus—although they flattered my scientific ability.

I suffered terrible insomnia from the overstimulation of these conversations, from my realization of our tragic situation, from self-reproach for my mistakes and weakness and from anxiety for my seriously ill wife, who was alone and, by ordinary standards, bedridden or almost bedridden much of the time. In June and July, after the spasm or stroke, I experienced severe headaches.

I could not bring myself to resume the hunger strike, partly from fear that I would be unable to bring it to a victorious conclusion and would only delay seeing my wife again. I never would have believed that our separation would last four months, in any case.

In June I noticed that my hands were trembling severely. A neurologist told me that it was Parkinson's disease. The doctors tried to convince me that if I resumed my hunger strike there would be a rapid and catastrophic development of Parkinson's disease. A doctor gave me a book containing a clinical description of the disease's final stages. This, too, was a method of exerting psychological pressure on me. The head doctor, O. A. Obukhov, explained: "We won't allow you to die. I'll get the women's team out again to feed you with the clamp. We've got another method up our sleeve as well. However, you *will* become a helpless invalid." Another doctor added by way of explanation, "You'll be incapable of putting on your own trousers." Obukhov intimated that this would suit the KGB, since it would escape all blame: Parkinson's disease cannot be artificially induced.

What happened to me in a Gorky hospital in the summer of 1984 is strikingly reminiscent of Orwell's famous anti-Utopian novel, even down to the remarkable coincidence of the book's title—*1984*. In the novel and in real life the torturers sought to make a man betray the woman he loves. The part played by the threat of the cage full of rats in Orwell's book was played for me in real life by Parkinson's disease.

I was able to bring myself to resume the hunger strike only on September 7. On September 8 I was hastily discharged from the hospital. I was faced with a difficult choice: End the hunger strike in order to see my wife after a four-month separation or continue for as long as my strength held out, thereby indefinitely prolonging our separation and our complete ignorance of each other's fate. I could not continue.

Now, however, I am tormented by the thought that I may have lost a chance to save my wife. It was only after our reunion that I first learned about her trial and she learned about my painful force-feeding.

I am very concerned about my wife's health. I believe that a timely trip abroad is the only chance of saving her life. Her death would be mine as well.

I hope for your help, for your appeal to the highest levels seeking permission for my wife's trip. I am asking for help from the presidium of the U.S.S.R. Academy of Sciences and from you personally, as president of the Academy and as a man who has known me for many years.

Since my wife has been sentenced to exile, her trip will probably require a decree of the Supreme Soviet's Presidium suspending her sentence for the period of her travel. (Precedents for this exist both in Poland and, quite recently, in the U.S.S.R.) The Supreme Soviet's Presidium or another body could repeal her sentence altogether on the grounds that my wife is a disabled veteran of World War II, that she recently suffered a massive myocardial infarct, that she has no prior convictions and that she has an irreproachable work record of 32 years. Those arguments should suffice for the Presidium of the Supreme Soviet. I will add, for your information, that my wife was unjustly and illegally convicted even from a purely formal point of view. In reality she was convicted for being my wife and to prevent her from traveling abroad.

I repeat my assurance that her trip has no purpose other than to seek medical treatment and to visit her mother, children and grandchildren; it is not intended to effect any change in my situation. My wife can supply the appropriate pledges herself. She may also pledge not to disclose the details of my confinement in the hospital if that is made a condition for her departure.

I am the only Academician in the history of the Academy of Sciences of the U.S.S.R. and Russia whose wife has been convicted as a criminal, subjected to a malicious, vile campaign of public slander and deprived of all communication with her mother, children and grandchildren. I am the only academician whose responsibility for his actions and opinions has been shifted onto his wife. That is my situation, and it is unbearable for me. I hope you will help.

If you and the Academy's presidium do not find it possible to support me in this tragic matter, which is so vital for me, or if your intervention and other efforts do not lead to resolution of the problem before March 1, 1985, *I ask that this letter be regarded as my resignation from the U.S.S.R. Academy of*

Sciences. I will renounce my title of full member of the Academy—a proud title for me in other circumstances. I will renounce all my rights and privileges connected with that title, including my salary as an academician—a significant step since I have no savings.

If my wife is not allowed to travel abroad, I cannot remain a member of the Academy of Sciences. I will not and should not participate in a great international deceit in which my academy membership would play a part.

I repeat: I am counting on your help.

Respectfully,
A. Sakharov
Oct. 15, 1984
Gorky

P.S. If this letter is intercepted by the KGB, *I will still resign from the Academy* and the KGB will be responsible. I should mention that I sent you four telegrams and a letter during my hunger strike.

P.P.S. This letter is handwritten because my typewriter (together with books, diaries, manuscripts, cameras, a tape recorder, and a radio) was seized during a search.

P.P.P.S. I ask you to confirm receipt of this letter.

Translated by Nicholas Bethell and Richard Lourie

ANDREI SAKHAROV:
A BIBLIOGRAPHY

This bibliography lists almost all of the significant essays, statements, and appeals of Andrei Sakharov. For each entry, an English-language source is given; if none is available, the original Russian-language publication is cited.

The bibliography is divided into six sections: I. Books; II. Articles and Statements; III. Interviews; IV. Appeals; V. Joint Statements; VI. Scientific Works.

Within each section, entries are generally listed in chronological order, according to Sakharov's own dating when known, except for section IV, where the entries are in alphabetical order according to the last name of the principal subject of the appeal.

Many of Sakharov's statements on human rights can be found in the English-language edition of the samizdat journal *A Chronicle of Current Events* (CCE), published by Amnesty International, London, and in *A Chronicle of Human Rights in the USSR* (CHR), published 1973–1983 by Khronika Press, New York. The best Russian-language sources for Sakharov's writings are the books *O strane i mire* (Khronika Press, 1976) and *Trevoga i nadezhda* (Khronika Press, 1978) and the *Arkhiv samizdata,* published by Radio Liberty, Munich. The speeches Sakharov delivered to the Congress of Deputies and the Supreme Soviet have been published in *Izvestia;* many of them can be found in translation in the Foreign Broadcast Information Service's *Daily Reports* on the Soviet Union. The majority of his scientific papers have been translated and published in *A. D. Sakharov: Collected Scientific Works.*

I. *Books*

Progress, Coexistence, and Intellectual Freedom, Norton, 1968. Contains the English translation of the essay referred to in this book as *Reflections.* The 2nd (1970) edition contains the 1970 Sakharov-Turchin-Medvedev "Letter to Brezhnev."

Sakharov Speaks, Alfred A. Knopf, 1974. Contains Sakharov's introduction written in December 1973, *Reflections,* the 1970 "Letter to Brezhnev," the 1971 "Memorandum" with the 1972 "Postscript," and a number of Sakharov's statements of the period 1972–1974.

My Country and the World, Alfred A. Knopf, 1975.

Alarm and Hope, Alfred A. Knopf, 1978. This volume, edited by Efrem Yankelevich and Alfred Friendly, Jr., contains Sakharov's Nobel Peace Prize lecture, and many of Sakharov's statements of the period 1976–1978.

A. D. Sakharov: Collected Scientific Works, Marcel Dekker, 1982. This book, edited by D. ter Haar, David Chudnovsky, and Grigory Chudnovsky, contains 24 of Sakharov's scientific papers from 1947 through 1980, plus commentary by Sakharov himself and by Western physicists.

On Sakharov, Alfred A. Knopf, 1982. This Festschrift, containing articles by and about Sakharov, was edited by Alexander Babyonyshev for Sakharov's 60th birthday.

Andrei Sakharov and Peace, Avon Books, 1985. This anthology of articles by and about Sakharov was edited by Edward Lozansky.

Memoirs, Alfred A. Knopf, 1990.

II. *Articles and Statements*

1. "Nuzhny estestvenno-matematicheskie shkoly" (The Special Science and Math Schools Are Necessary), *Pravda,* November 19, 1958.
2. Article on the danger of nuclear testing, in A. V. Lebedinsky, editor, *Soviet Scientists on the Danger of Nuclear Tests,* Foreign Languages Publishing House, Moscow, 1960.
3. "Igor Tamm: For His 70th Birthday" (with V. L. Ginzburg and E. L. Feinberg) *Uspekhi fizicheski nauk,* 86, no. 2, June 1965.
4. "Ucheny i grazhdanin" (Scientist and Citizen; article about Igor Tamm), *Izvestia,* July 8, 1965.
5. Predictions on the future development of science and technology, Vladimir Kirillin, editor, *The Future of Science,* Moscow, 1967 (Russian-language; restricted distribution).
6. "Scientists and the Danger of Nuclear War" (with Ernst Henri, February 1967), Stephen Cohen, ed., *An End to Silence,* Norton, 1982, pp. 229–234.
7. *Reflections on Progress, Peaceful Coexistence, and Intellectual Freedom* (June 1968), *Sakharov Speaks,* pp. 56–114.
8. "Letter to Brezhnev, Kosygin and Podgorny" (with Valentin Turchin and Roy Medvedev, March 19, 1970), *Sakharov Speaks,* pp. 116–134.
9. "Memorandum" (March 5, 1971; postscript, June 1972), *Sakharov Speaks,* see Appendix B.
10. "In Memory of Igor Tamm" (with V. L. Ginzburg et al.), *Uspekhi fizicheski nauk,* 105, no. 1, September 1971.
11. "Let Soviet Citizens Emigrate" (October 7, 1971), *Sakharov Speaks,* pp. 160–163.
12. On the Problems of Peoples Forcibly Resettled: Letter to the Moscow Human

Rights Committee (March 16, 1972) and Petition to the Presidium of the Supreme Soviet (with Andrei Tverdokhlebov, Valery Chalidze, and Igor Shafarevich; April 21, 1972), *Sakharov Speaks*, pp. 237–239.

13. Letter to Mikhail Millionshchikov on the decree of June 7, 1972, regulating visitors' gifts to prisoners (June 15, 1972), CCE 26, pp. 263–264.
14. "A Talk with Malyarov" (August 16, 1973), *Sakharov Speaks*, pp. 179–192.
15. Statement on the Soviet press campaign against him (September 8, 1973), CHR 4, pp. 21–22.
16. Statement to U.S. Congress in support of the Jackson Amendment (September 14, 1973), *Sakharov Speaks*, pp. 212–215. (Also, a reply to Samuel Pisar's criticism of this statement; *New York Times*, October 8, 1973).
17. Appeal to the Chilean Government on behalf of Pablo Neruda (with Alexander Galich and Vladimir Maximov; September 18, 1973), *Sakharov Speaks*, pp. 243–244.
18. Statement of the Human Rights Committee on the Political Abuse of Psychiatry (with Grigory Podyapolsky and Igor Shafarevich; October 1, 1973), *Sakharov Speaks*, pp. 218–221.
19. Statement criticizing Roy and Zhores Medvedev (November 20, 1973; CHR 5–6, p. 9).
20. Open letter to Andropov on Elena Bonner's interrogations (November 28, 1973), CHR 5–6, p. 15.
21. Statement on an invitation to Princeton (November 30, 1973), CHR 5–6, p. 30.
22. Statement on receiving the Human Rights Award of the International League for Human Rights (December 5, 1973), *Sakharov Speaks*, pp. 228–229.
23. To the International Committee for the Defense of Human Rights (December 29, 1973), *Sakharov Speaks*, pp. 244–245.
24. "Introduction" (December 31, 1973), *Sakharov Speaks*, pp. 29–54.
25. Foreword to Mikhail Agursky's samizdat anthology *Russkie evrei v otsenke svoego proshlogo . . .* (Russian Jews in the Light of Their Past . . .) (March 27, 1974).
26. Open Letter to Academician Vladimir Engelgardt (March 29, 1974).
27. "On Alexander Solzhenitsyn's 'A Letter to the Soviet Leaders' " (April 3, 1974), *Kontinent*, Anchor Books, 1976, pp. 2–14.
28. Appeal to General Suharto for a general political amnesty in Indonesia (April 4, 1974), CCE 32, p. 101.
29. "The World in Fifty Years" (May 17, 1974), published as "Tomorrow: The View from Red Square" in *Saturday Review/World*, August 24, 1974.
30. Letter to Brezhnev and Nixon on prisoners of conscience (June 25, 1974); CCE 32, pp. 95–96.
31. Statement on ending a hunger strike on behalf of Bukovsky and other prisoners of conscience (July 4, 1974), CHR 10, pp. 21–22.
32. Three statements on the emigration of ethnic Germans (August 8, 1974); CHR 10, pp. 11–12.
33. "A Welcome to *Kontinent*" (September 1, 1974), *Kontinent*, Anchor Books, 1976, pp. xvi–xvii.

34. "Open Letter on the Right to Live at Home" (September 11, 1974), CHR 11, p. 32.
35. Letter on the passage of the Jackson-Vanik Amendment (October 17, 1974), CHR 11, pp. 8–10. (On January 18, 1975, Sakharov wrote to the U.S. Congress expressing his regret that the USSR had repudiated the 1972 trade agreement.)
36. Letter to Brezhnev on political prisoners (October 24, 1974), CCE 33, p. 113.
37. Letter to Brezhnev and Ford on prisoners of conscience (November 20, 1974).
38. Letter to Brezhnev and Wilson on prisoners of conscience (February 4, 1975).
39. Statement on emigration (April 22, 1975), CHR 15, pp. 9–11.
40. *My Country and the World* (June 1975), Alfred A. Knopf, 1975.
41. "The Need for an Open World," a letter to the Pugwash Conference in Kyoto (July 10, 1975), *Bulletin of the Atomic Scientists*, November, 1975.
42. Message to foreign readers of *My Country and the World*, October, 1975.
43. Statement on Nobel Prize award (October 9, 1975), CCE 38, p. 70.
44. "Message to the International Sakharov Hearing" (read out on October 17, 1975, at Copenhagen, the opening day of the Hearing), *The International Sakharov Hearing*, Smoloskyp, 1977.
45. Message to the Federation of American Scientists (November 8, 1975), *FAS Public Interest Report*, December, 1975.
46. Nobel acceptance speech, *New York Times*, December 11, 1975.
47. "Peace, Progress, and Human Rights" (the Nobel Peace Prize Lecture, read in Oslo on December 11, 1975 by Elena Bonner), *Alarm and Hope*, pp. 4–18.
48. Message to the International Forum for World Disarmament, *Manchester Guardian*, April 1, 1976.
49. Human rights appeal addressed to the Conference of European Communist Parties (with Valentin Turchin and Yuri Orlov; June 28, 1976), *Alarm and Hope*, pp. 28–31.
50. Message to the International League for Human Rights (September 25, 1976), *Alarm and Hope*, pp. 33–34.
51. "The Siege of Tel-Zaatar: An Appeal to the United Nations" (October 1976), see Appendix B.
52. Message to Gerald Ford and Jimmy Carter (October 11, 1976), *Alarm and Hope*, pp. 43–44.
53. Letter to Amnesty International calling for a general amnesty of political prisoners (October 29, 1976), *Alarm and Hope*, p. 36.
54. Telegram congratulating Jimmy Carter on his election (November 8, 1976), *Alarm and Hope*, pp. 44–45.
55. "Message to KOR (Polish Workers' Defense Committee)" (November 20, 1976), see Appendix B.
56. Message to the Jewish Cultural Symposium (November 29, 1976), CCE 43, p. 60.
57. "The Explosion in the Moscow Subway" (January 12, 1977), *Alarm and Hope*, pp. 59–63; Press conference statement (January 18, 1977); "Statement on Gusev's Warning" (January 25, 1977), *Alarm and Hope*, pp. 69–72; "Reply to Gusev" (March 5, 1977), *Alarm and Hope*, pp. 81–84.

58. Letter to President Carter (January 21, 1977), see Appendix B; Reply to President Carter (February 17, 1977), *Alarm and Hope*, pp. 50–52.
59. "Alarm and Hope" (March 7, 1977), *Alarm and Hope*, pp. 99–111.
60. "Mustafa Dzhemilev's Trial in Omsk" (April 17, 1977), *Alarm and Hope*, pp. 87–89.
61. "The Abolition of the Death Penalty" (September 19, 1977), see Appendix B.
62. Appeal to parliaments on the opening of the Belgrade Follow-up Conference (October 3, 1977), *New York Times*, October 4, 1977, (in an abridged and edited version) and *Alarm and Hope*, pp. 157–159; Letter to the *New York Times* (correcting the translation and editing of his October 3 appeal) (October 10, 1977), *New York Times*, February 4, 1978, and *Alarm and Hope*, pp. 159–162.
63. "Nuclear Energy and the Freedom of the West" (October 11, 1977), *Bulletin of the Atomic Scientists*, June 1978, pp. 12–14, and *Alarm and Hope*, pp. 124–128.
64. Message to the Second Sakharov Hearing (October 30, 1977), *Alarm and Hope*, pp. 129–132.
65. The Third Anniversary of *Kontinent* (November 1, 1977), *Kontinent* 15, appendix pp. 3–4.
66. Message to the Venice Biennale (November 4, 1977), *Alarm and Hope*, p. 113.
67. Statement on the amnesty proclaimed for the 60th anniversary of the October Revolution (November 1977), *Alarm and Hope*, pp. 40–41. An open letter to Ponomarev and Alexandrov on the amnesty (November 15, 1977), CCE 47, pp. 165–166.
68. Congratulating Tito on the Yugoslav amnesty for political prisoners (with Elena Bonner; November 25, 1977), CCE 48, p. 172.
69. Message to the AFL-CIO (November 28, 1977), *Alarm and Hope*, pp. 163–167. (Earlier, Sakharov (with Borisov, Marchenko, and Podrabinek) sent a letter to Meany expressing thanks for their invitations, CCE 47, p. 167.)
70. "A Look at the Past Year" (December 14, 1977), CCE 48, pp. 173–174.
71. The Belgrade Conference (March 9, 1978), CCE 48, pp. 174–175.
72. "Afterword" (May 12, 1978), *Alarm and Hope*, pp. 168–181.
73. "The 1980 Moscow Olympics" (September 14, 1978), CCE 51, pp. 194–195.
74. "The Human Rights Movement in the USSR and Eastern Europe: Its Goals, Significance, and Difficulties" (November 8, 1978), *On Sakharov*, pp. 244–259.
75. Introduction to Evgeny Gnedin's *Vykhod iz labirinta* (A Way Out of the Labyrinth) (November 29, 1978), Chalidze Publications, 1982, pp. 5–9.
76. Statement on clandestine search and theft of documents (December 2, 1978), see Appendix B.
77. Letter to Brezhnev protesting harassment of Crimean Tatars (January 31, 1979), CCE 52, pp. 87–88.
78. Letter to Brezhnev protesting the execution of Zatikian, Stepanian, and Bagdasarian in connection with the Moscow metro bomb (January 31, 1979), CCE 52, pp. 6–7.
79. Letter to Voice of America complaining of inaccuracies (April 5, 1979), CCE 53, pp. 179–180.

80. Statement on the release of Dymshits, Ginzburg, Kuznetsov, Moroz, and Vins (with Elena Bonner) (April 28, 1979), and postscript by Sakharov (May 18, 1979), CHR 34, pp. 5–6.
81. "Examination Questions for Jewish Students in Applied Mathematics" (July 12, 1979), *It Seems I Am a Jew* (Grigori Freiman, Southern Illinois University, 1980), p. 97.
82. Message to the 1979 Sakharov Hearings (September 5, 1979), CHR 35, pp. 49–50.
83. *"Disturbing the Universe* by Freeman Dyson" (book review), *Washington Post Book World*, September 23, 1979.
84. Message to the New York Academy of Sciences accepting its 1979 Presidential Award on December 6, 1979, CHR 36, pp. 25–26.
85. Open letter to *Kontinent* concerning Chalidze's article "Khomeinism and National Communism" (January 21, 1980).
86. *Exile to Gorky*
    Statement on Exile to Gorky (January 27, 1980), see Appendix B.; A Further Statement (February 3), CCE 56, pp. 81–82; "Our Mail" (February 12), CCE 56, pp. 82–83; Telegram to Alexandrov about Academy Elections (February 12), CCE 56, p 84; On the detention of Shikhanovich (February 15), CCE 56, p. 78; Statements to Rekunkov and Andropov (February 23), CCE 56, pp. 83–84; Telegram to Academy Presidium and Statement (March 3), CCE 56, p. 85.
87. "Some Thoughts on the Threshold of the 1980s" (February 22, 1980), *On Sakharov*, pp. 241–243.
88. Statement on the Moscow Olympics (April 26, 1980), CCE 56, pp. 87–88.
89. "A Letter from Exile" (May 4, 1980), *On Sakharov*, pp. 223–240.
90. Open letter to Brezhnev on the war in Afghanistan (July 27, 1980), see Appendix B.
91. "World Security and Human Rights Linked" (August 12, 1980), *Los Angeles Times*, September 9, 1980.
92. "Letter to *Nature*" (October 6, 1980), *Nature*, November 13, 1980, p. 112.
93. "Open Letter to Anatoly Alexandrov" (October 20, 1980), *On Sakharov*, pp. 212–222.
94. Letter to Max Kampelman, U.S. ambassador to the Madrid Follow-up Conference (January 29, 1981).
95. Letter to Sidney Drell (January 30, 1981), CCE 61, pp. 219–220.
96. Statement on KGB thefts (March 17, 1981), see Appendix B.
97. "An Autobiographical Note" (March 24, 1981), *On Sakharov*, pp. xi–xv.
98. "The Reponsibility of Scientists" (written for the International Conference in Honor of Andrei Sakharov, held at Rockefeller University, New York, May 1–2, 1981; March 24, 1981), *On Sakharov*, pp. 205–211.
99. Letter to the Rockefeller University Conference (May 10, 1981), CCE 62, pp. 135–136.
100. "How to Preserve World Peace" (July 1981), *On Sakharov*, pp. 262–269.
101. Political Prisoners Day 1981 (October 28, 1981), CCE 63, p. 169.

102. Letter to Amnesty International seeking a UN resolution on prisoners of conscience (November 14, 1981).

103. *The Case of Liza Alexeyeva*

Letters to: Brezhnev (May 26, 1981), CCE 63, pp. 128–129; Evgeny Velikhov (August 12, 1980), CCE 60, pp. 101–102; Vitaly Ginzburg (September 14, 1980), CCE 60, p 102.

Telegrams to: Brezhnev, Alexandrov, and Velikhov about Liza Alexeyeva (October 21, 1981), CCE 63, p. 129.

Statement on a hunger strike for Alexei and Liza, *On Sakharov*, p. 270–272; Letter to foreign colleagues (November 15, 1981), CCE 63, pp. 131–132; Letter to Joel Lebowitz and Jeremy Stone, (November 27, 1981), *On Sakharov*, p. 272; Messages on the hunger strike (November 28, 1981), CCE 63, p. 133, and (December 1, 1981), CCE 63, p. 134; Telegram to Drell (December 2, 1981) CCE 63, p. 134; Message to friends on ending the hunger strike (December 15, 1981), see chapter 49.

104. "Two years in Gorky" (January 24, 1982), CCE 64, pp. 111–113.

105. Telegram to Dr. Thomas Gehrels (American astronomer) (February 21, 1982), CCE 64, p. 113.

106. Appeal to Soviet scientists on behalf of the Kovalevs and other imprisoned scientists (April 2, 1982), *Nature*, June 3, 1982.

107. Letter to the 32nd Pugwash Conference (May 7, 1982), *New York Times*, September 10, 1982.

108. Letter to Vitaly Fedorchuk, KGB Chairman (October 23, 1982), see Appendix B.

109. Statement on Perelygin's warning (November 10, 1982), see Appendix B.

110. Appeal for an amnesty for prisoners of conscience (December 7, 1982).

111. "The Danger of Thermonuclear War" (February 2, 1983), *Foreign Affairs*, vol. 61, no. 5, pp. 1001–1016, Summer 1983, and see Appendix B.

112. Foreword (April 1983) to Mark Hopkins, *Russia's Underground Press: The Chronicle of Current Events*, Praeger, 1983.

113. "Acceptance Speech for the Szilard Award" (April 1983), see Appendix B.

114. "A Reply to Slander" (about Samuil Zivs's book *The Anatomy of a Lie*), *New York Review of Books*, July 21, 1983.

115. Letter to the Sorbonne Conference of Nobel Laureates (September 23, 1983).

116. Deposition supporting Elena Bonner's complaint against Nikolai Yakovlev (November 19, 1983), *Alone Together*, pp. 43–47.

117. Letter to colleagues on behalf of Elena Bonner (November 1983), *Andrei Sakharov and Peace*, pp. 277–280.

118. Foreword to Mark Popovsky, *The Vavilov Affair*, Archon Books, 1984.

119. Appeal to friends everywhere on the eve of the 1984 hunger strike (April 1984), *Alone Together*, pp. 240–241; Letter to U.S. Ambassador Arthur Hartman (April 6, 1984).

120. Letter to Anatoly Alexandrov (October 15, 1984), see Appendix C.

121. Administrative complaint to the Procurator of the RSFSR about the case of Elena Bonner (November 29, 1984), see Appendix C.

122. Letter to Bonner's family on 1984 hunger strike (November 24, 1985), see Appendix B.

123. Appeal to Gorbachev (February 19, 1986), *Human Rights Bulletin*, The International League for Human Rights, December 1986.

124. Letter on Roy Medvedev's interview (January 13, 1987), *Der Spiegel*, February 2, 1987.

125. Appeal to Vienna Conference (January 1987), *Physics Today*, April 1987, p. 9.

126. Foreword (January 23, 1987) to Anatoly Marchenko, *To Live Like Everyone*, Henry Holt, 1989.

127. "Of Arms and Reforms" (three speeches delivered at the Moscow Forum for a Nuclear-Free World and the Survival of Mankind; February 14–15, 1987), *Time*, March 16, 1987, pp. 40–43.

128. Acceptance Speech on Receiving the Catalan "Golden Minute" Award, *New York Review of Books*, August 13, 1987.

129. " 'It's an Absolute Necessity to Speak the Truth': Impressions of the film 'Risk'," *Moscow News*, No. 45, November 8, 1987.

130. "The Breakthrough Must Be Continued and Widened," *Moscow News*, No. 49, December 13, 1987.

131. "New Political Thinking Is Needed," *Argumenty i fakti*, no. 51, 1989.

132. "Calm and Wisdom," *Moscow News*, No. 14, April 10, 1988.

133. "Neizbezhnost perestroiki" (The Inevitability of Perestroika) (March 25, 1988), *Inogo ne dano* (No Other Way), Progress, Moscow, 1988, pp. 122–134.

134. "A Policy Deserving of Confidence" (June 3, 1988), *New Times*, No. 24, 1988.

135. Remarks at the Woodrow Wilson Center, Washington, D.C. (November 14, 1988), *New York Review of Books* (excerpts), December 22, 1988.

136. Remarks on accepting the Albert Einstein Peace Prize, Washington, D.C., November 15, 1988. *New York Times* (report), November 16, 1988.

137. "You Can Fight Ideas Only with Ideas," *New Times*, supplement: *Perestroika and Human Rights*, December 1988.

138. To the Madrid Conference on East-West Trade and Economic Relations (with Elena Bonner; January 16, 1989).

139. "Pluralism Is Convergence" *XXth Century and Peace*, no. 1, 1989.

140. Election program (January 20, 1989), *Vedomosti "Memorial,"* January 23, 1989, and see *Moscow News*, No. 6, 1989, interview with Gennady Zhavaronkov, and *Knizhnoe obozrenie*, April 7, 1989, interview with I. Filatov and A. Shchuplov.

141. Letter to the editor: "I Actively Support Perestroika" (February 5, 1989); *Izvestia*, February 6, 1989. Reply to a critical editorial in *Izvestia*, "Perestroika and Responsibility."

142. Statement on readiness to serve as a deputy only from Academy of Sciences, *Moscow News*, no. 8, 1989.

143. Statements at the Congress of Peoples' Deputies, May 25–June 9, 1989. A slightly edited transcript of the sessions was published by *Izvestia*; the full text of

Sakharov's interrupted concluding statement (and his proposed Decree on Power) was published in *New York Review of Books,* August 17, 1989.

144. Plea to halt death sentences in China (June 19, 1989), *The Daily Telegraph,* June 20, 1989.

145. Talk at Chatham House, London, (June 20, 1989), *The Observer,* June 25, 1989.

146. "Freedom and Science," speech delivered at Lyons to the Congress of French Physicists (September 27, 1989).

147. "Convergence, Peaceful Coexistence," *50/50: Opyt slovarya novogo myshlenia,* Progress, Moscow, 1989, pp. 13–17.

148. Transcript of a meeting (with Galina Starovoitova) with the people of Chelyabinsk, *Za tyazhelogo mashinostroyeniya,* September 20, 1989.

149. The blockade of Nagorno-Karabakh (October 7, 1989), *Russkaya mysl,* October 20, 1989.

150. Appeal for the Kurds (October 13, 1989), *Russkaya mysl,* October 20, 1989.

151. Remarks at the All-Union Student Forum (November 1989), *Komsomolskaya pravda,* December 16, 1989.

152. 1968 Soviet actions in Czechoslovakia, *New Times,* no. 50, 1989.

153. "Sakharov on Gorbachev and Bush," *Washington Post Outlook,* December 3, 1989; "Sakharov—A Last Memoir," *Washington Post Outlook,* December 17, 1989; and "The Making of an Activist," *Time,* December 25, 1989. Excerpts from the forthcoming *Gorky–Moscow and Beyond.*

154. Sofia Kalistratova (a eulogy) (December 8, 1989), *Russkaya mysl,* December 22, 1989.

155. Draft Constitution, *New Times,* no. 52, 1989.

155a. Speech at the meeting of the Inter-regional Group (December 14, 1989), *Moscow News,* no. 52, 1989.

156. On pretrial detention (December 14, 1989), *Literaturnaya gazeta,* no. 52, 1989.

III. *Interviews*

157. Interview with Jay Axelbank (October 26, 1972), *Newsweek* (international edition) November 8, 1972.

158. Interview with Olle Stenholm (broadcast on TV in Sweden on July 2, 1973), see Appendix A.

159. Interview with Western Correspondents (August 21, 1973; clarification, September 12, 1973), *Sakharov Speaks,* pp. 194–210.

160. Interview with Jan Bezemer (September 6 or 7, 1973), *The Observer* and *A. Sakharov v borbe za mir,* pp. 167–171.

161. Interview with a Lebanese correspondent (October 11, 1973), *Sakharov Speaks,* pp. 224–226.

162. Answers to a French Correspondent (January 8, 1974), Leo Labedz, editor, *Solzhenitsyn: A Documentary Record,* Penguin (2nd edition), 1974, p. 364 (excerpt).

163. *Tribune de Geneve* (January 20, 1974)

164. London *Sunday Times,* February 24, 1974; *Solzhenitsyn: A Documentary Record,* pp. 387–388 (excerpt).

165. BBC (August 22, 1974), CCE 34, pp. 74–75.

166. Interview with Peter Osnos, *Washington Post,* January 13, 1975.

167. Interview with Erno Eszterhas, *Los Angeles Times,* March 19, 1975.

168. Interview with Robert Stephens and Dev Murarka, *The Observer,* June 8, 1975.

169. Interview with James Jackson (October 10, 1975), *Chicago Tribune.*

170. Interview with David Burg (October 10, 1975), London *Sunday Times,* October 12, 1975.

171. *Corriere della Sera* (February 25, 1976), CCE 39, p. 215.

172. Interview with Elizabeth Pond, *Christian Science Monitor,* August 10, 1976.

173. Interview (October 30, 1976), *Alarm and Hope,* pp. 37–40, 98, 113–115, 144–145; CCE 44, pp. 193–196.

174. Interview with George Krimsky (December 6, 1976), *Alarm and Hope,* pp. 84–87 and pp. 90–93.

175. Interview with Albert Axelbank, *The Observer,* January 9, 1977.

176. *Corriere della Sera* (January 26, 1977), *Alarm and Hope,* pp. 139–144.

177. *Newsweek* (February 2, 1977), *Alarm and Hope,* p. 48.

178. CBS (February 10, 1977), *Alarm and Hope,* pp. 48–49, 115–116.

179. *France-Soir* (February 23, 1977), *Alarm and Hope,* pp. 52–53 and 94–95.

180. *Newsweek* (February 24, 1977), *Alarm and Hope,* pp. 134–138.

181. ABC (March 25, 1977), *Alarm and Hope,* pp. 53–54, 98, 116–117.

182. Swedish television (April 14, 1977), *Alarm and Hope,* pp. 117–119.

183. *Grazie* (January 31, 1978), CCE 48, p. 174.

184. Interview with BBC (June 27, 1978).

185. *Le Monde* (August 15, 1978); English translation in *The Guardian* (international edition), August 27, 1978.

186. *Washington Star,* November 12, 1978.

187. Interview (December 25, 1978), *L'Express,* January 27, 1979.

188. *Washington Post* (January 1, 1979); CCE 52, pp. 134–135.

189. Interview with three journalists from college newspapers, *Columbia Daily Spectator,* January 29, 1979.

190. *Le Figaro* (November 26, 1979); Sakharov's protest against inaccuracies (November 30, 1979), CCE 55, p. 65.

191. Interview with Italian journalist (December 21, 1979), CCE 55, pp. 65–67.

192. *New York Times,* January 3, 1980.

193. Interview with ABC correspondent Charles Bierbauer (January 17, 1980), CHR 37, p. 9.

194. *Washington Post* (March 9, 1980), CHR 37, pp. 17–18.

195. Interview with Kevin Klose (June 1, 1981).

196. UPI interview (January 19, 1982), CCE 64, pp. 109–111.

197. *New York Times,* December 25, 1986.

198. *This Week with David Brinkley* (ABC), December 28, 1986.

199. London *Times,* December 29, 1986.
200. Interview with Oleg Moroz and Yuri Rost (December 1986; commissioned but not published by *Literaturnaya gazeta:* see, however, profile by Rost in *Literaturnaya gazeta,* November 16, 1988).
201. *U.S. News and World Report,* January 12, 1987, February 16, 1987 (translation of Italian TV interview), and April 20, 1987.
202. *Der Spiegel,* no. 2, 1987.
203. Interview with Alan McGowan (May 28, 1987); *SIPIscope* June–July 1987.
204. Interview with Gennady Zhavoronkov, *Moscow News,* no. 20, 1988.
205. Interview after the 1988 Pugwash Conference at Dagomys, *New Times,* No. 38, 1988.
206. Interview with Mark Levin for *Youth of Estonia,* October 11, 1988; Jonathan Eisen, *The Glasnost Reader,* New American Library, 1990, pp. 328–341.
207. Roundtable on *perestroika* (November 1988), *Ogonyok* 50, 1988.
208. Interview with Zora Safir of VOA (December 4, 1988).
209. Interview with Morton Zuckerman and Jeff Trimble, *U.S. News and World Report,* January 30, 1989.
210. Interview with Jean-Pierre Barou (January 1989), *Figaro,* January 26, 1989. (Excerpts in Jonathan Eisen, *The Glasnost Reader,* New American Library, 1990, pp. 341–346.) Sakharov questioned the accuracy of the interview as published, and *Izvestia* (February 1, 1989) criticized Sakharov for his alleged remarks.
211. Interview with Antonina Bouis and Jean-Claude Bouis (May 14, 1989); *Life,* July 1989.
212. Interview with Yuri Rost, *Literaturnaya gazeta,* June 21, 1989.
213. Interview with Grigory Tsitrinyak (June 1989), *Ogonyok,* no. 31, 1989.
214. Interview with Ales Adamovich, *Iskusstvo kino,* no. 8, 1989.
215. Interview with Jacques Amalric and Michel Tatu, *Le Monde,* September 1989.

IV. *Appeals*

Boris Altshuler (May 31, 1982; CCE 64, pp. 114–115).
Andrei Amalrik (with Podyapolsky and Shafarevich; May 22, 1973; CHR 2, p. 46); (open letter to Heinrich Böll on Amalrik and Lev Ubozhko; May 27, 1973).
Evgeny Barabanov (with Grigory Podyapolsky; September 20, 1973; CHR 4, pp. 39–40).
Alexander Bolonkin (August 15, 1978; CCE 51, pp. 30–31); (May 3, 1981; CCE 62, p. 113).
Elena Bonner (on refusal of permission to travel abroad for medical treatment; May 7, 1975); (to Alexandrov; May 19, 1983); (to Andropov; November 10, 1983); (to Stockholm Conference; January 12, 1984); (to Chernenko; February 21, 1984).
Vladimir Borisov (and Viktor Fainberg; March 15, 1971); (and Viktor Fainberg; January 1, 1972).
Viktor Brailovsky (December 5, 1980).

Vladimir Bukovsky (January 18, 1972; *Sakharov Speaks*, p. 236); (with Khodorovich and six others; February 27, 1974; CHR 7, pp. 27–28); (with Heinrich Böll, February 18, 1975; CCE 35, pp. 133–134); (with Kopelev; October 18, 1976); (to James Callaghan; October 29, 1976; *Alarm and Hope*, pp. 36–37).

Chudnovsky family (July 23, 1977; *Alarm and Hope*, pp. 154–155).

Lydia Chukovskaya (January 9, 1974; CHR 7, pp. 17–18).

Czech prisoners of conscience (October 24, 1979; CCE 54, p. 141.)

Angela Davis (letter to Richard Nixon; December 27, 1970).

Mustafa Dzhemilev (with Velikanova and four others; July 6, 1975); (June 27, 1975; CHR 16, p. 10); (with Grigorenko; February 19, 1976; CCE 39, p. 200); (April 17, 1976; CHR 20, pp. 15–16); (September 30, 1976).

Fang Lizhi (November 1988; reported in *Washington Post*, December 16, 1988).

Yuri Fyodorov (and Alexei Murzhenko) (June 1, 1981; CCE 62, p. 130).

Balys Gajauskas (April 16, 1978; CCE 49, pp. 13–14).

Alexander Galich (with Bonner and Maximov; January 16, 1974; CHR 7, p. 20).

Zviad Gamsakhurdia (and Kostava, Ginzburg, Orlov, Tykhy, and Rudenko; April 13, 1977; *Alarm and Hope*, p. 152); (and Kostava; with Grigorenko and Kalistratova; April 14, 1977).

Alexander Ginzburg (June 7, 1976; *Alarm and Hope*, pp. 149–150); (with Igor Shafarevich; February 4, 1977; *Alarm and Hope*, pp. 148–149).

Semyon Gluzman (November 15, 1972; CHR 1, p. 48); (November 20, 1974; CHR 11, pp. 28–29).

Sofia Kalistratova (February 24, 1982).

Viktor Khaustov (with Velikanova and four others; March 6, 1974; CHR 8, p. 9).

Mikhail Kheifets (September 15, 1974; CHR 11, p. 15).

Lev Kopelev (February 3, 1980; CHR 37, p. 29).

Merab Kostava (to Eduard Shevardnadze; December 30, 1981; CCE 63, p. 174).

Sergei Kovalev (December 28, 1974; CHR 11, pp. 13–14); (October 6, 1975); (December 9, 1975; CCE 38, p. 89); (December 18, 1975; CCE 38, pp. 90–91); (to King Carl-Gustav XVI of Sweden; June 5, 1978; CCE 51, p. 191); (to Linus Pauling; May 4, 1981; CCE 62, p. 131).

Anatoly Krasnov-Levitin (May 23, 1971).

Mikhail Kukobaka (June 21, 1979; CCE 53, p. 59).

Valery Kukui (with Chalidze; July 16, 1971; CCE 21, pp. 276–278).

Eduard Kuznetsov (and Mark Dymshits; letter to Nikolai Podgorny; December 27, 1970); (with Bonner; December 30, 1977).

Sergei Kuznetsov (November 28, 1989).

Malva Landa (May 12, 1977; CCE 47, p. 1).

Evgeny Levich (open letter to Yuval Ne'eman, rector of Tel Aviv University; May 30, 1973).

Valeria Makaeva (April 13, 1979).

Musa Mamut (July 4, 1978; CCE 51, p. 122).

Anatoly Marchenko (with Bonner; March 22, 1981; CCE 62, p. 4); (October 7, 1981).

Valery Maresin (February 4, 1976; CCE 39, p. 207).

Zhores Medvedev (June 6, 1970; Zhores and Roy Medvedev, *A Question of Madness,* Macmillan, London, 1971, pp. 115–117).

Naum Meiman (and Yuri Goldfarb) (September 9, 1977, *Alarm and Hope,* p. 156).

Valentin Moroz (June 25, 1974; CCE 32, p. 104).

Viktor Nekipelov (and Sergei Pirogov; May 28, 1974; CHR 9, pp. 13–14); (and Vasyl Stus; June 14, 1980; *Index,* vol. 9, no. 6, November 1980).

Viktor Nekrasov (January 19, 1974; CHR 7, pp. 18–19).

Julian Nundy (expelled Reuter correspondent) (August 2, 1974).

Yuri Orlov (with Shafarevich; July 17, 1974; CHR 10, pp. 15–16); (with Shafarevich, Turchin, Meiman, and Yuri Goldfarb; July 11, 1977, *Alarm and Hope,* p. 153); (with Meiman; November 26, 1980); (with Bonner, Golfand, Kalistratova, and Meiman; February 8, 1981; CCE 61, pp. 202–203); (with Meiman; January 10, 1982; CCE 64, p. 101).

Tatyana Osipova (April 3, 1981; CCE 62, pp. 15–16); (February 23, 1983).

Daniil Ostapov (with Shafarevich; March 28, 1974; CHR 8, p. 33).

Revolt Pimenov (and Boris Vail; with Leontovich and eight other scientists; *New York Times,* November 16, 1970).

Leonid Plyushch (with Grigory Podyapolsky; June 25, 1973, *Sakharov Speaks,* pp. 241–243); (with Bonner, Velikanova, Kovalev, Tverdokhlebov, Khodorovich; February 12, 1974; CHR 7, pp. 29–30); (August 2, 1974); (October 1975; CHR 17, p. 18).

Alexander Podrabinek (and Joseph Terelya; with Kalistratova, Meiman, and Grigorenko; October 17, 1977; CCE 47, p. 164).

Zbigniew Romaszewski (October 1982).

Pyotr Ruban (to President-elect James Carter; January 3, 1977; *Alarm and Hope,* p. 42); (January 14, 1977).

Vladimir Rubtsov (January 18, 1977; *Alarm and Hope,* pp. 64–65).

Mykola Rudenko (April 18, 1975).

Friedrich Ruppel (May 18, 1973; *Sakharov Speaks,* p. 241).

Alexei Semyonov (November 10, 1977; *Alarm and Hope,* pp. 96–97).

Anatoly Shcharansky (March 19, 1977; *Alarm and Hope,* pp. 151–152); (to President Mitterrand, January 20, 1982, CCE 64, pp. 103–104).

Vladimir Shelkov (April 16, 1978); (November 27, 1978, CCE 51, p. 192); (March 28, 1979, CCE 53, p. 22).

Yuri Shikhanovich (with Elena Bonner; offer to serve as surety; January 23, 1973, CHR 1, pp. 48–49); (with Bonner and Podyapolsky; July 5, 1973; CHR 3, pp. 49–50); (to Lev Smirnov, chairman of the USSR Supreme Court; with Bonner, Velikanova, Kovalev; October 3, 1973; CHR 4, pp. 35–36).

Alexander Solzhenitsyn (with Galich, Maximov, Voinovich, Shafarevich; January 5, 1974; *Sakharov Speaks,* pp. 232–233); (with Bonner and eight others; February 13, 1974; CHR 7, pp. 12–13).

Martin Sostre (December 7, 1975).

Vasyl Stus (October 19, 1980; CCE 58, pp. 80–81).

Gabriel Superfin (with Tverdokhlebov; May 27, 1974; CCE 32, p. 102).

Valentin Turchin (July 9, 1974).

Andrei Tverdokhlebov (and Mykola Rudenko; April 18, 1975; CHR 14, p. 6); (telegram; April 4, 1976; CCE 40, p. 10); (May 3, 1976; CHR 20, pp. 11–13).

Tatyana Velikanova (with Bonner; November 5, 1979, CCE 54, p. 13), (and Gleb Yakunin; with 56 others; August 29, 1980).

Georgy Vins (September 11, 1974), (with Podyapolsky, Kovalev, and Velikanova: October 22, 1974).

Georgy Vladimov (February 19, 1982).

Wei Quin Xen (July 27, 1980); see Appendix B.

Yankelevich family (open letter to Yuri Andropov; January 6, 1975; CCE 35, pp. 144–145); (June 11, 1976; CHR 22, pp. 17–18); (June 23, 1976).

Valentin Zosimov (with Grigorenko, Orlov, Rudenko, and Bonner; October 26 and November 26, 1976; CCE 43, pp. 65–66); (with Elena Bonner; October 29, 1976; *Alarm and Hope,* pp. 34–35).

V. *Joint Statements*

216. Letter to Brezhnev arguing against the rehabilitation of Stalin (with 24 intellectuals; February 1966), Stephen Cohen, editor, *An End To Silence,* Norton, 1982, pp. 177–179.

217. Letter to RSFSR Supreme Soviet protesting Articles 190-1 and 190-3 of the RSFSR Criminal Code (with 20 intellectuals, September 1966), Pavel Litvinov, *The Demonstration in Pushkin Square,* Gambit, 1969, pp. 14–15.

218. Principles and Bylaws of the Human Rights Committee (November 4, 1970); *Proceedings of the Moscow Human Rights Committee,* The International League for the Rights of Man, New York, 1972, pp. 11–12, 16–18.

219. Petitions to the Supreme Soviet for an amnesty and for abolition of the death penalty (signed by more than 50 Soviet intellectuals; September 1972) *Sakharov Speaks,* pp. 239–240.

220. Statement by members of the Moscow Human Rights Committee (with Shafarevich and Podyapolsky; January 1973), CHR 1, pp. 43–46.

221. Letter to UNESCO on Soviet adherence to the Universal Copyright Convention (with Shafarevich, Podyapolsky, Galich, Maximov, and Voronel; March 22, 1973), CHR 1, pp. 55–56.

222. On international reaction to Soviet psychiatric abuse (with Podyapolsky and Shafarevich; July 9, 1973), CCE 30, pp. 98–99.

223. Statement on the All-Union Copyright Agency (with Galich, Maximov, Voinovich, and Shafarevich; January 5, 1974), CHR 7, pp. 23–24.

224. Letter to Waldheim on Crimean Tatars (with Velikanova, Kovalev, and others; January 1974), CCE 31, p. 160.

225. Call for a General Amnesty (with Sergei Kovalev; December 27, 1974), CCE 34, p. 3.

226. Political Prisoners Day (with Velikanova and seven others; October 31, 1975), CHR 17, pp. 24–28.

227. Appeal for a general amnesty (with Turchin, Orlov, Grigorenko, and Amalrik; February 23, 1976), CCE 39, p. 214.

228. Appeal to European Communist Parties on human rights (with Turchin and Orlov; June 23, 1976), CCE 42, p. 260.

229. Open letter on the rights of scientists (with Orlov, Turchin, and 20 other scientists); CHR 22, pp. 6–10.

230. Statement on Political Prisoners Day (with Bonner, Khodorovich, Lavut, and others; October 30, 1976), CCE 43, pp. 9–11.

231. On the Bukovsky-Corvalán exchange (with Grigorenko and Orlov; December 18, 1976), CCE 43, p. 4.

232. In support of Charter 77 in Czechoslovakia (with about 60 others; February 12, 1977), CHR 25, p. 67.

233. On the hunger strike by political prisoners (with Landa, Bonner, and Khodorovich; April 21, 1977), CCE 45, p. 259.

234. Letter to scientific colleagues opposing repeal of the Jackson-Vanik Amendment (with Meiman; March 10, 1979), CHR 33, p. 29.

235. In support of the Baltic republics' right to self-determination (with Landa, Nekipelov, Velikanova, and Arina Ginzburg; August 23, 1979).

236. Appeal on behalf of imprisoned Czech and Slovak members of Charter 77 (with KOR and the Moscow Helsinki Group; July 31, 1979), CHR 35, p. 34.

237. Moscow Helsinki Group appeal for the withdrawal of foreign troops from Afghanistan (January 20, 1980).

238. Appeal to postpone and change the format of the 19th Party Conference (with Yuri Afanasiev and eight other Soviet intellectuals; April 27, 1988), see the *Wall Street Journal*, May 16, 1988.

239. Open letter about a memorial to the victims of Stalin (with Ales Adamovich, Evgeny Yevtushenko, Yuri Karyakin, Mikhail Shatrov, and Yuri Afanasiev; December 27, 1988), *Vedomosti "Memorial"*, January 28, 1989.

VI. *Scientific Works*

240. "Theory of Nuclear Transitions of the Type O—O" (1947), Candidate of Science thesis, FIAN. A part of this paper was published as "Interaction of the Electron and the Positron in Pair Production" (1948), *Collected Scientific Works*, pp. 255–280.

241. "Generation of the Hard Component of Cosmic Rays" (1947), *Collected Scientific Works*, pp. 239–254.

242. "Excitation Temperature in a Gas-Discharge Plasma" (1948), *Collected Scientific Works*, pp. 43–47.

243. On mu-meson catalysis (1948), FIAN Report.

244. "Theory of a Magnetic Thermonuclear Reactor, Part II" (1951), *Collected Scientific Works*, pp. 11–22.

245. "Reactions Produced by Mu-Mesons in Hydrogen" (with Yakov Zeldovich; 1957), *Collected Scientific Works*, pp. 7–10.

246. "Radioaktivny uglerod yadernykh vzryvov i neporogovye biologicheskie effekty" (Radioactive Carbon from Nuclear Explosions and Nonthreshold Biological Effects), *What Russian Scientists Say About Fallout*, Collier Books, 1962, pp. 45–54.

247. Two chapters ("Optical Quantum Effects" and "The Atomic Nucleus") in a revised edition (1963) of the physics textbook for technical schools written by Dmitri Sakharov (father of Andrei) and M. I. Bludov.

248. "The Initial Stage of an Expanding Universe and the Appearance of a Nonuniform Distribution of Matter" (1965), *Collected Scientific Works*, pp. 65–83.

249. "Magnetic Cumulation" (with R. Z. Lyudaev and seven others; 1965), *Collected Scientific Works*, pp. 23–27.

250. "The Quark Structure and Masses of Strongly Interacting Particles" (with Yakov Zeldovich; 1966), *Collected Scientific Works*, pp. 205–221.

251. "Magnetoimplosive Generators" (1966), *Collected Scientific Works*, pp. 29–41.

252. "Maximum Temperature of Thermal Radiation" (1966), *Collected Scientific Works*, pp. 137–139.

253. "Violation of CP Invariance, C Asymmetry, and Baryon Asymmetry of the Universe" (1967), *Collected Scientific Works*, pp. 85–88.

254. "Quark-Muonic Currents and Violation of CP Invariance" (1967), *Collected Scientific Works*, pp. 89–92.

255. "Vacuum Quantum Fluctuations in Curved Space and the Theory of Gravitation [1]" (1967), *Collected Scientific Works*, pp. 167–169.

256. "Vacuum Quantum Fluctuations in Curved Space and the Theory of Gravitation [2]" (1967), *Collected Scientific Works*, pp. 171–177.

257. "The Symmetry of the Universe," *The Future of Science*, Znanie Publishers, 1967.

258. "Sushchestvuet li elementarnaya dlina?" (Does an Elementary Length Exist?), *Fizika v shkole*, 1968, no. 2, pp. 6–15.

259. "Antiquarks in the Universe" (1969), *Collected Scientific Works*, pp. 93–104.

260. "A Multisheet Cosmological Model" (1970), *Collected Scientific Works*, pp. 105–114.

261. "The Topological Structure of Elementary Charges and CPT Symmetry" (1972), *Collected Scientific Works*, pp. 199–204.

262. "Scalar-Tensor Theory of Gravitation" (1974), *Collected Scientific Works*, pp. 195–197.

263. "Mass Formula for Mesons and Baryons with Allowance for Charm" (1975), *Collected Scientific Works*, pp. 223–226.

264. "Spectral Density of Eigenvalues of the Wave Equation and Vacuum Polarization" (1975), *Collected Scientific Works*, pp. 179–194.

265. "The Baryonnic Asymmetry of the Universe" (1979), *Collected Scientific Works*, pp. 115–130.

266. "Mass Formula for Mesons and Baryons" (1980), *Collected Scientific Works*, pp. 227–232.
267. "An Estimate of the Coupling Constant between Quarks and the Gluon Field" (1980), *Collected Scientific Works*, pp. 233–237.
268. "Cosmological Models of the Universe with Reversal of Time's Arrow" (1980), *Collected Scientific Works*, pp. 131–136.
269. "Multisheet Cosmological Models of the Universe," *Journal of Experimental and Theoretical Physics*, 1982, v. 83, no. 44(10).
270. "Cosmological Transitions with a Change in Metric Signature," SLAC translation, 0211, May 1984.
271. Postscript to Zeldovich's article "Is It Possible to Create the Universe 'From Nothing?'" *Priroda*, no. 4 (April), 1988.

Compiled by Edward Kline

GLOSSARY OF NAMES

Abel, Rudolph [Willi Fischer] (1902–1971). Soviet spy, arrested 1957, exchanged for U-2 pilot Gary Powers in 1962.

Adamsky, V. (c. 1920–). A senior member of the theoretical department at the Installation.

Agrest, Mattes (c. 1920–1989?). Mathematician, a colleague of Sakharov's at the Installation.

Agursky, Mikhail (1933–). Computer scientist, historian. Emigrated 1975.

Aitmatov, Chingiz (1928–). Writer.

Akhmatova, Anna (1889–1966). Poet.

Alexandrov, Alexander (1912–). Mathematician, rector of Leningrad University 1952–1964.

Alexandrov, Anatoly (1903–). Physicist, Academy president 1975–1986.

Alexandrov, Pavel (1896–). Mathematician, academician.

Alexandrov-Agentov, Andrei (1918–). Party official, chief aide to General Secretary Leonid Brezhnev.

Alexeyeva, Elizaveta [Liza] (1955–). Second wife of Elena Bonner's son, Alexei Semyonov. Emigrated 1981.

Alexeyeva, Ludmilla (1925?–) Editor, member of Helsinki Watch Group. Emigrated in 1977.

Alferov, Zhores (1930–). Physicist, academician.

Alikhanian, Artyom (1908–1978). Physicist.

Alikhanov, Gevork (1897–1939?). Elena Bonner's stepfather. Communist official, arrested 1937.

Alikhanov, Igor (1927–1976). Elena Bonner's brother. Merchant marine officer.

Altman, Anatoly (1941–). Leningrad "skyjacker." Emigrated 1979.

Altshuler, Boris (1939–). Physicist.

Altshuler, Lev (1915?–). Physicist at the Installation.

Altunian, Genrikh (1933–). Army officer, human rights activist.

Alvarez, Luis (1911–1988). Physicist. Nobel Laureate in Physics, 1968.

Amalrik, Andrei (1938–1980). Historian, dissident. Emigrated 1976.

Amatuni, Andrei (1927–). Physicist, administrator.

Andronikov, Irakli (1908–). Writer and literary critic.

Andropov, Yuri (1914–1984). Chairman of KGB, 1967–1982; General Secretary, 1982–1984.

Antonov, Oleg (1906–1984). Aircraft designer.

Arbatov, Georgy (1923–   ). Historian, academician, governmental adviser on foreign affairs.

Arkhangelsky, Alexander (1892–1978). Aeronautical engineer.

Artsimovich, Lev (1909–1973). Nuclear physicist, academician.

Astaurov, Boris (1904–1974). Biologist.

Avtorkhanov, Abdurakhman (1908–   ). Chechen Party official, emigrated during World War II.

Babitsky, Konstantin (1929–   ). Dissident.

Badzyo, Yuri (1936–   ). Ukrainian editor and dissident.

Bagdasarian, Zaven (1954?–1979). Armenian nationalist, executed for Moscow subway bombing.

Bagritskaya, Lydia (1898–1969). Widow of Eduard Bagritsky.

Bagritsky, Eduard (1895–1934). Poet.

Bagritsky, Vsevolod (1922–1942). Poet. Son of poet Eduard Bagritsky.

Bakhmin, Vyacheslav (1947–   ). Computer scientist, human rights activist.

Barabanov, Evgeny (1943–   ). Art historian. Russian Orthodox activist.

Barenblat, Grigory (c. 1930–   ). Physicist.

Barenblat, Isaak (c. 1900–1970). Endocrinologist, father of Grigory Barenblat.

Barzani, Mustafa. National leader of the Kurds.

Begun, Iosif (1932–   ). Electronics engineer, Jewish activist. Emigrated to Israel in 1988.

Belenky, Semyon (c. 1925–c. 1960). Physicist.

Berdyaev, Nikolai (1874–1948). Philosopher. Exiled by Lenin in 1922.

Beria, Lavrenti (1899–1953). Secret police chief 1938–1953. Arrested in 1953 and executed.

Bernstein, Robert (1923–   ). U.S. publisher, chairman, Human Rights Watch.

Bethe, Hans (1906–   ). U.S. physicist. Nobel Laureate in Physics, 1967.

Bethell, Nicholas (1938–   ). British journalist, translator, politician.

Birger, Boris (1923–   ). Artist.

Bitter, Francis (1902–1967). Physicist.

Bjorken, James (1904–   ). Physicist.

Blok, Alexander (1880–1921). Poet.

Blokhintsev, Dmitri (1908–1979). Nuclear physicist, academician, administrator.

Boborykin, Pyotr (1836–1921). Novelist, credited with coining the term "intelligentsia."

Bogatyrev, Konstantin (1925–1976). Poet and translator.

Bogolyubov, Nikolai (1900–   ). Mathematician, physicist, academician, administrator.

Bogoraz, Larisa (1929–   ). Human rights activist. Ex-wife of Yuli Daniel, widow of Anatoly Marchenko.

Bohr, Niels (1855–1962). Danish physicist. Nobel Laureate in Physics, 1922.

Boitsova, Lusia (c. 1940–   ). Biologist, wife of Sergei Kovalev.

Böll, Heinrich (1917–1985). West German writer. Nobel Laureate in Literature, 1972.

Bonner, Elena (1923–   ). Pediatrician, human rights activist. Second wife of Andrei Sakharov.

Bonner, Ruth (1900–1987). Former political prisoner, mother of Elena Bonner.

Borisov, Vladimir (1943–). Dissident.

Born, Max (1882–1970). Physicist. Nobel Laureate in Physics, 1954.

Borodin, Alexander (1833–1887). Composer.

Brazinskas, Algirdas. Son and accomplice of Pranas Brazinskas.

Brazinskas, Pranas. Lithuanian hijacker of Soviet plane to Turkey in October 1970.

Brezhnev, Leonid (1906–1982). General Secretary of the Communist Party, 1964–1982.

Brodsky, Joseph (1940–). Poet, emigrated 1972. Nobel Laureate in Literature, 1987.

Bronshtein, Matvei (1906–1938). Physicist.

Buckley, James (1923–). U.S. Senator, 1971–1977.

Bukharin, Nikolai (1887–1938). Bolshevik leader. Executed in purges.

Bukovsky, Vladimir (1942–). Writer and dissident, released from a Soviet prison in 1976 in exchange for Luis Corvalán.

Bulgakov, Mikhail (1891–1940). Novelist and dramatist.

Bulganin, Nikolai (1895–1975). Defense minister, chairman of Council of Ministers 1955–1958.

Butman, Hillel (1932–). Jewish emigration activist, Leningrad "skyjacker." Emigrated 1979.

Cartan, Henri (1904–). French mathematician.

Chakovsky, Alexander (1913–). Writer, editor of Literaturnaya gazeta.

Chalidze, Valery (1938–). Physicist. Human rights activist, writer, publisher. Deprived of citizenship 1972.

Chavchanidze, Vladimir (1921–). Physicist, Sakharov's classmate at FIAN.

Chernyshevsky, Nikolai (1828–1889). Essayist, novelist, political philosopher. Author of What Is to Be Done?

Chornovil, Vyacheslav (1938–). Ukrainian journalist, dissident.

Chukovskaya, Lydia (1910–). Writer, daughter of Kornei Chukovsky.

Chukovsky, Kornei (1882–1969). Writer and literary critic.

Corvalán, Luis (1916–). Chilean Communist freed from imprisonment in 1976 in exchange for the release of Vladimir Bukovsky.

Crick, Francis (1916–). British biologist, Nobel Laureate in Medicine, 1962.

Cronin, James (1931–). U.S. physicist. Nobel Laureate in Physics, 1980.

Dancoff, Sidney (1914–1951). U.S. physicist.

Daniel, Yuli [pseud. Nikolai Arzhak] (1925–1988). Writer, dissident.

Davidovich, Efim (1924–1976). Colonel, Jewish activist, refusenik.

Davis, Angela (1944–). Black activist, feminist, Communist.

Dekanozov, Vladimir (?–1953). Ambassador to Germany, 1940–1941, Deputy Foreign Minister, General in the NKVD.

de Kruif, Paul (1890–1971). U.S. biologist, writer.

Delone, Vadim (1947–1983). Poet, dissident. Emigrated 1975.

Denikin, Anton (1872–1947). General, commander of White Army forces in southern Russia during civil war. Emigrated in 1920.

Dimitrov, Georgi (1882–1949). Leading Comintern official.

Dirac, Paul (1902–1984). British physicist. Nobel Laureate in Physics, 1933.

Djilas, Milovan (1911–   ). Yugoslav political leader, dissident, author of *The New Class*.

Dmitriev, Nikolai (c. 1925–   ). Mathematician, a colleague of Sakharov's at the Installation.

Dobrynin, Anatoly (1919–   ). Diplomat, Soviet ambassador to U.S. 1962–1986.

Dorodnitsyn, Anatoly (1910–   ). Geophysicist, mathematician, academician.

Drell, Sidney (1926–   ). U.S. physicist. Arms control expert.

Dremlyuga, Vladimir (1940–   ). Dissident.

Dubček, Alexander (1921–   ). Communist Party First Secretary of Czechoslovakia during the 1968 Prague Spring.

Dubinin, Nikolai (1907–   ). Geneticist, academician.

Dudintsev, Vladimir (1918–   ). Novelist.

Dymshits, Mark (1927–   ). Jewish emigration activist, pilot in Leningrad "skyjacking." Emigrated in 1979.

Dyson, Freeman (1923–   ). Physicist.

Dzerzhinsky, Felix (1872–1926). First head of Cheka, 1917–1926.

Dzhelepov, Boris (1910–   ). Physicist.

Dzhemilev, Mustafa (1936–   ). Crimean Tatar activist.

Dzyuba, Ivan (1931–   ). Ukrainian literary critic, dissident.

Efimov, Boris (1935–   ). Writer, dissident. Emigrated 1972.

Ehrenburg, Ilya (1891–1967). Poet, critic, novelist.

Eikhe, Robert (1890–1940). Latvian candidate member of Politburo 1935–1938, executed in purges.

Emanuel, Nikolai (1915–   ). Chemist.

Emelyanov, Vasily (1901–   ). Biologist, administrator.

Engelgardt, Vladimir (1894–   ). Biochemist, academician.

Eötvös, Roland (1848–1919). Physicist.

Esenin-Volpin, Alexander (1925–   ). Mathematician, dissident, writer. Emigrated 1972.

Etinger, Regina (1921–1980). High school classmate and lifelong friend of Elena Bonner.

Ezhov, Nikolai (1895–1939). Secret police chief 1936–1938.

Fainberg, Viktor (1931–   ). Dissident. Emigrated 1974.

Farges, Yves (1915–1953). French journalist and politician, Stalin Prize winner.

Feigin, Tomar (1921–   ). Efrem Yankelevich's mother.

Feinberg, Evgeny (1912–   ). Physicist.

Feoktistova, Ekaterina (c. 1920–   ). Physicist, a colleague of Sakharov's at the Installation.

Fermi, Enrico (1901–1954). Physicist. Nobel Laureate in Physics, 1930.

Feynman, Richard (1918–1988). Physicist. Nobel Laureate in Physics, 1965.

Finkelshtein, Eitan (1942–   ). Refusenik. Emigrated 1978.

Fitch, Val (1923–   ). Physicist. Nobel Laureate in Physics, 1980.

Fock, Vladimir (1899–1974). Physicist.

Fradkin, Efim (1924–   ). Physicist, Sakharov's classmate at FIAN.

Frank-Kamenetsky, David (c. 1915–1972?). Physicist, Sakharov's colleague at the Installation.

Freiman, Grigori (1926–   ). Mathematician, Jewish emigration activist, writer. Emigrated 1980.

Frenkel, Yakov (1894–1952). Physicist.

Frezotti, Renato. Italian eye surgeon. Operated on Elena Bonner.

Friedmann, Alexander (1888–1925). Physicist.

Fuchs, Klaus (1911–1989). Nuclear physicist, Soviet atom spy.

Furtseva, Ekaterina (1910–1974). Minister of Culture under Khrushchev.

Fyodorov, Yuri (1943–   ). Dissident, Leningrad "skyjacker."

Gagarin, Yuri (1934–1968). First cosmonaut.

Galanskov, Yuri (1939–1972). Poet, dissident, died in labor camp.

Galetsky, Rostislav (1948–   ). Seventh-Day Adventist, religious activist.

Galich, Alexander (1918–1977). Poet, playwright, balladeer. Emigrated 1974.

Galkin, Alexander (1914–   ). Physicist, academician.

Gamow, George (1904–1968). Russian-American nuclear physicist.

Gamsakhurdia, Zviad (1939–   ). Georgian dissident.

Garbus, Martin (c. 1925–   ). U.S. attorney.

Gauss, Carl Friedrich (1777–1855). Mathematician and astronomer.

Gavrilov, Viktor (c. 1920–early 1970s). Physicist, later molecular biologist, one of Sakharov's colleagues at the Installation.

Geiko, Olga (1953–   ). Philologist. Ukrainian human rights activist.

Gelfand, Izrail (1913–   ). Mathematician, academician.

Gell-Mann, Murray (1927–   ). Physicist. Nobel Laureate in Physics, 1969.

Georgadze, Mikhail (1912–1982), Secre-

tary of the Soviet Presidium, 1957–1982.

Georgi, Howard (1947–   ). Physicist.

Gershtein, Semyon (1929–   ). Physicist.

Gertsenshtein, Mikhail (c. 1950–   ). Physicist.

Gesse, Natalya [Natasha] (1914–   ). Litterateur, friend of Elena Bonner.

Ginzburg, Alexander (1936–   ). Human rights activist. Emigrated 1979.

Ginzburg, Eugenia (1907–1977). Political prisoner, author of *Journey into the Whirlwind.*

Ginzburg, Vitaly (1916–   ). Physicist, academician.

Glashow, Sheldon (1932–   ). Physicist. Nobel Laureate in Physics, 1979.

Gluzman, Semyon (1946–   ). Physiciatrist, human rights activist.

Gnedin, Evgeny (1898–1983). Diplomat, writer, political prisoner.

Goldenveizer, Alexander (1875–1946). Composer and pianist, Sakharov's godfather.

Goldenveizer, Anna [née Sofiano]. (c. 1880–1929). Sakharov's aunt; married to Alexander Goldenveizer.

Goldhaber, Maurice (1911–   ). U.S. physicist.

Golfand, Yuri (c. 1920–   ). Physicist.

Gorbanevskaya, Natalya (1936–   ). Poet, dissident. Emigrated 1975.

Granin, Daniil (1918–   ). Writer.

Griboedov, Alexander (1795–1829). Diplomat, playwright. Author of *Woe from Wit.*

Gribov, Vladimir (1930–   ). Physicist.

Grigorenko, Pyotr [Petro] (1907–1978). General, writer, human rights activist. Emigrated 1977.

Gromyko, Andrei (1901–1989). Soviet foreign minister, 1957–1986.

Gross, David (1941–   ). Physicist.

Gusev, Sergei. Deputy Procurator General of the USSR.

Guth, Alan (1947–   ). Physicist.

Hammer, Armand (1898–   ). U.S. businessman.

Handler, Philip (1917–1981). Biologist, president of U.S. Academy of Sciences.

Hanzelka, Jiří (1920–   ). Czech writer.

Harkevich, Nina (1907–   ). Physician, Italian friend of Elena Bonner.

Heisenberg, Werner (1901–1976). Physicist. Nobel Laureate in Physics, 1932.

Heitler, Walter (1904–1981). Physicist.

Henri, Ernst [pseud. of Semyon Rostovsky] (1904–   ). Journalist.

Hilbert, David (1862–1943). German mathematician.

t'Hooft, Gerardius (1946–   ). Physicist.

Hubble, Edwin (1889–1953). Astronomer.

Ibarruri, Dolores ["La Pasionaria"] (c. 1900–1989). Spanish Communist.

Ignatov, Nikolai (1901–1966). Party official.

Ilf [pseud. of Ilya Faintzilberg] (1897–1937). Satiric writer, collaborator with Petrov.

Ilyushin, Alexander (1911–   ). Physicist.

Imshenetsky, Alexander (1905–   ). Microbiologist, academician.

Iskander, Fazil (1929–   ). Writer.

Izraileva, Revekka (c. 1920–   ). Mathematician, a colleague of Sakharov's at the Installation.

Janouch, Frantisek (1935?–   ). Physicist, head of Charter 77 Foundation in Stockholm.

Jeans, Sir James (1877–1946). Physicist, astronomer, writer.

Juliana (1909–   ). Queen of the Netherlands, 1948–1980 (abdicated).

Kadomtsev, Boris (1928–   ). Physicist, academician.

Kaganovich, Lazar (1893–1989). Politburo member, 1930–1957.

Kalistratova, Sofia (1907–1989). Attorney, human rights activist.

Kaluza, Theodor (1885–1954). Physicist.

Kamenev, Lev (1883–1936). Old Bolshevik, executed in purges.

Kapitsa, Pyotr (1894–1984). Physicist. Nobel Laureate in Physics, 1978.

Kapler, Alexei (1904–1979). Film director and scenarist.

Kaplun, Irina (1950–1980). Dissident.

Karmal, Babrak (1929–   ). Afghan leader, 1979–1986.

Keldysh, Mstislav (1911–1978). Mathematician, Academy president 1961–1975.

Khainovsky, Yuri (1919–1981). Artist, friend of Bonner family in Gorky.

Khandzhian, Agasi (1901–1936). Secretary of the Armenian Central Committee, 1929–1936.

Khariton, Yuli (1904–   ). Physicist, academician, research director of Installation.

Khodorovich, Tatyana (1921–   ). Linguist, human rights activist. Emigrated 1975.

Khokhlov, Rem (1926–1977). Physicist, academician, rector of Moscow University.

Khrushchev, Nikita (1894–1971). General Secretary of the Communist Party, 1953–1964.

Lord Killanin (Michael Morris) (1914–). President of Olympic Committee, 1972–1980.

Kim Il Sung (1912–). Ruler of North Korea since 1948.

Kirillin, Vladimir (1913–). Physicist, chairman, State Committee on Science and Technology.

Kirov, Sergei (1886–1934). Member of politburo 1930–1934.

Kissinger, Henry (1923–). U.S. Secretary of State, 1973–1977.

Klimov, Valentin. Colleague of Sakharov's at the Installation.

Kline, Edward (1932–). U.S. retailer, Russian-language publisher.

Knokh, Arie. (1944–). Jewish emigration activist, Leningrad "skyjacker." Emigrated 1979.

Kobulov, Bogdan (?–1953). General in the NKVD.

Kobzarev, Yuri (1905–). Physicist.

Kolakowski, Leszek (1927–). Polish philosopher, writer. Emigrated 1968.

Kolchak, Alexander (1873–1920). Admiral, leader of White Army in Siberia. Executed in 1920.

Kolmogorov, Alexander (1903–). Mathematician, academician.

Komarov, Boris [pseud. of Zev Wolfson] (1944–). Ecologist, writer. Emigrated 1981.

Kopelev, Lev (1912–). Writer and critic. Stripped of Soviet citizenship 1980.

Kornilov, Vladimir (1928–). Poet, dissident.

Kornilov, Yuri. Journalist.

Korolenko, Vladimir (1853–1920). Populist writer.

Korolev, Sergei (1906–1966). Aeronautical engineer, rocket designer.

Koryagin, Anatoly (1939–). Psychiatrist, human rights activist. Emigrated 1987.

Kostava, Merab (1939–1989). Musicologist, Georgian nationalist.

Kosterin, Alexei (1896–1968). Old Bolshevik, longtime Gulag inmate rehabilitated after Stalin's death, 1960s dissident.

Kosterina, Nina (1921–1941). Daughter of Alexei Kosterin, died in partisan operation.

Kosygin, Alexei (1904–1980). Soviet prime minister, 1964–1980.

Koval, Bella. Moscow friend of Elena Bonner.

Kovalev, Ivan (1954–). Engineer, human rights activist. Emigrated 1987.

Kovalev, Sergei (1930–). Biologist, human rights activist.

Kovner, Mark. Physicist and refusenik.

Kozlov, Frol (1908–1965). Presidium member, 1957–1964.

Krasavin, Felix. (1930?–). Metalworker, a friend of the Sakharovs in Gorky.

Krasin, Viktor (1929–). Economist, dissident. Emigrated 1975.

Krasnov-Levitin, Anatoly (1915–). Writer, religious philosopher, dissident. Emigrated 1974.

Kristi, Irina (1938–). Mathematician, dissident. Emigrated 1985.

Kudirka, Simas (1930–). Lithuanian sailor, attempted to defect in 1970. Emigrated 1974.

Kudryavtsev, Oleg (1921–1956). Historian.

Kukk, Juri (1940–1981). Chemist, Estonian human rights activist.

Kukobaka, Mikhail (1936–). Human rights activist.

Kunin, Pyotr (1921–1976). Physicist, Sakharov's university classmate and his colleague at FIAN.

Kurchatov, Igor (1902–1960). Physicist, academician, director of the Atomic Energy Institute.

Kuznetsov, Eduard (1939–). Writer, dissident, Leningrad "skyjacker." Emigrated 1979.

Kvachevskaya, Dzhemma (1949–). Dissident. Emigrated 1980.

Lakoba, Nestor (1893–1936). Old Bolshevik, Abkhazian official.

Lamb, Willis (1913–). Physicist. Nobel Laureate in Physics, 1955.

Landa, Malva (1918–). Geologist, human rights activist.

Landau, Lev (1908–1968). Physicist, academician. Nobel Laureate in Physics, 1962.

Landsberg, Grigory (1890–1957). Physicist, academician.

Lashkova, Vera (1944–). Human rights activist.

Lattes, Cesare (1924–). Physicist.

Lavrentiev, Mikhail (1900–1980). Mathematician, academician.

Lavut, Alexander (1929–). Mathematician, human rights activist.

Lebedev, Pyotr (1866–1912). Physicist, Moscow University professor.

Lebowitz, Joel (1930–). U.S. physicist.

Lee Tsung-dao (1926–). Chinese physicist. Nobel Laureate in Physics, 1957.

Leontovich, Mikhail (1903–1981). Physicist, academician.

Lerner, Alexander (1914–). Computer scientist, Jewish emigration activist. Emigrated 1987.

Lert, Raisa (1905–1985). Literary critic, human rights activist.

Levshina, Olga (1953–). First wife of Alexei Semyonov. Emigrated 1980.

Linde, Andrei. Physicist at FIAN.

Lipavsky, Alexander (c. 1950–). Refusenik, alleged KGB informer.

Litvinov, Maxim (1876–1951). Revolutionary, foreign minister, 1930–1939; ambassador to U.S., 1941–1943.

Litvinov, Pavel (1940–). Physicist, dissident. Emigrated 1974.

Litvinov, Tatiana (1918–). Translator, human rights activist, emigrated in 1976.

Livchak, Vera (c. 1900–). Physician. Emigrated 1978.

Louis, Victor (1928–). Soviet journalist.

Lubarsky, Cronid (1934–). Physicist, human rights activist, editor. Emigrated 1977.

Ludaev, Robert. Physicist, a colleague of Sakharov's at the Installation.

Luders, Gerhart (1920–). German physicist.

Lukyanenko, Levko (1927–). Ukrainian lawyer, human rights activist.

Lupinos, Anatoly (1937–). Ukrainian poet.

Lysenko, Trofim (1898–1976). Agronomist, opponent of genetic theory of inheritance. President of Agricultural Academy 1938–1956, 1961–62.

Maiman, Theodore (1927–). Physicist, inventor of ruby laser.

Malenkov, Georgy (1902–1988). Soviet prime minister, 1953–1955.

Malot, Hector (1830–1907). French novelist and critic.

Malov, Nikolai. Firearms specialist, chief engineer of Ulyanovsk munitions plant.

Malyarov, Mikhail. Deputy Procurator General of the USSR.

Malyshev, Vyacheslav (1902–1957). Engineer, defense official.

Mamut, Musa (c. 1945–1978). Crimean Tatar activist.

Mandelshtam, Leonid (1879–1944). Physicist, academician.

Marchenko, Anatoly (1938–1986). Writer, dissident.

Marchuk, Guri (1925–   ). Physicist, Academy president (1986–   ).

Markov, Moisei (1908–   ). Physicist, academician.

Marshak, Samuil (1887–1964). Poet, children's writer.

Marinovich, Miroslav (1949–   ). Ukrainian human rights activist.

Matusevich, Mykola (1947–   ). Ukrainian human rights activist.

Maximov, Vladimir (1932–   ). Writer, editor. Emigrated 1974.

McCloy, John (1895–1989). Lawyer, president of World Bank, disarmament negotiator.

Medvedev, Roy (1925–   ). Historian, writer, dissident.

Medvedev, Zhores (1925–   ). Biologist, writer, dissident. Emigrated 1973.

Meiman, Naum (1911–   ). Mathematician, human rights activist. Emigrated 1987.

Mekler, Yuri (1930–   ). Physicist. Emigrated 1978.

Mendelevich, Iosif (1947–   ). Leningrad "skyjacker."

Merkulov, Vsevolod (1900–1953). State security general. Arrested in 1953 and executed.

Meshcheryakov, Mikhail (1910–   ). Physicist.

Meshik, Pavel (c. 1905–1953). Security official, arrested in 1953 and executed.

Meshko, Oksana (1905–   ). Ukrainian human rights activist.

Mestrović, Ivan (1883–1964). Yugoslav sculptor.

Michel, Louis (1923–   ). French physicist.

Michurin, Ivan (1855–1935). Plant breeder, opponent of genetic theory of inheritance.

Migdal, Arkady (1911–   ). Physicist, academician.

Mihajlov, Mihajlo (1934–   ). Yugoslav writer and literary critic.

Mikhalkov, Sergei (1913–   ). Writer, chairman RSFSR Writers Union.

Mikhoels, Solomon (1890–1948). Yiddish actor and director, murdered by secret police on Stalin's orders.

Millionshchikov, Mikhail (1913–1973). Physicist, academician, administrator.

Mills, Robert (1927–   ). Physicist.

Miterev, Georgy (1900–   ). Soviet health minister, 1939–1947.

Mitin, Mark (1901–   ). Philosopher, academician.

Molotov, Vyacheslav [Skriabin] (1890–1986). Foreign Minister 1939–1949 and 1953–1956.

Moroz, Valentin (1936–   ). Historian, Ukrainian dissident. Emigrated in 1970s.

Murzhenko, Alexei (1942–   ). Leningrad "skyjacker."

Muzrukov, Boris (1904–1979). Defense official.

Myasishchev, Vladimir (1902–1978). Aircraft designer.

Nabokov, Vladimir (1899–1977). Writer.

Nazarov, Anatoly (1946–   ). Dissident.

Nedelin, Mitrofan (1902–1960). Marshal. Killed in missile accident.

Nekipelov, Viktor (1928–1989). Writer, human rights activist.

Nekrasov, Viktor (1911–1987). Writer. Emigrated 1974.

Nemirovsky, Pavel (c. 1921–   ). Physicist, Sakharov's classmate at FIAN.

Neruda, Pablo (1904–1973). Chilean poet. Nobel Laureate in Literature, 1971.

Nipkow, Paul (1860–1940). Inventor of early TV scanner.

Noether, Emmy (1882–1935). Mathematician.

Novikov, Igor (1935–   ). Astrophysicist.

Novikov, Pyotr (1901–1975). Mathematician, academician.

Novikov-Priboi, Alexei (1877–1944). Writer.

Nudel, Ida (1931–   ). Jewish emigration activist. Emigrated 1987.

Nuzhdin, Nikolai (1904–   ). Biologist.

Occhialini, Giuseppe (1907–   ). Physicist.

Ogurtsev, Igor (1937–   ). Russian nationalist.

Okubo, Susumu (1930–   ). Physicist.

Okudzhava, Bulat (1924–   ). Poet, novelist, balladeer.

Okun, Lev (1929–   ). Physicist.

Olesha, Yuri (1897–1960). Writer.

Olsufieva, Maria (1907–1988). Translator of Russian works into Italian. Friend of Elena Bonner.

Oparin, Alexander (1894–1980). Biochemist.

Oppenheimer, J. Robert (1904–1967). Physicist. Head of Los Alamos laboratory, later of Princeton Institute for Advanced Study.

Ordzhonikidze, Grigory (1886–1937). Revolutionary, Red Army leader during civil war, minister of heavy industry 1932–1937.

Orlov, Yuri (1924–   ). Physicist, Moscow Helsinki Group chairman. Exiled 1986.

Osinsky, Valerian (1887–1938). Old Bolshevik and supporter of Trotsky, convicted in show trial and executed.

Osipova, Tatyana (1949–   ). Human rights activist, emigrated 1987.

Pasternak, Boris (1890–1960). Poet and novelist. Nobel Laureate in Literature, 1958 (refused the prize).

Pavlenkov, Vladlen (1929–1990). Dissident.

Pavlov, Nikolai (c. 1917–   ). KGB general, defense official.

Penson, Boris (1943–   ). Leningrad "skyjacker." Emigrated 1979.

Penzias, Arno (1933–   ). U.S. Physicist. Nobel Laureate in Physics, 1978.

Perelman, Yakov. Popular-science writer.

Petkus, Viktoras (1929–   ). Lithuanian dissident.

Petlyura, Simon (1879–1926). Ukrainian nationalist leader.

Petrov, Evgeny [pseud. of Evgeny Kataev] (1901–1942). Satirical writer, collaborator with Ilf.

Petrovsky, Boris (1908–   ). Surgeon, academician, health minister.

Petrovsky, Ivan (1901–1973). Mathematician, rector of Moscow University, 1951–1973.

Petryanov-Sokolev, Igor (1907–   ). Physical chemist.

Pimenov, Revolt (1931–   ). Mathematician, writer, dissident.

Pire, Georges (1910–1969). Belgian priest, winner of Nobel Peace Prize in 1958.

Plisetskaya, Maya (1925–). Prima ballerina.

Plyushch, Leonid (1939–). Mathematician, dissident, writer. Emigrated 1976.

Podgorny, Nikolai (1903–1983). Chairman of Presidium of Supreme Soviet, 1965–1977.

Podrabinek, Alexander (1953–). Human rights activist, writer.

Podyapolskaya, Maria (1929–). Human rights activist. Widow of Grigory Podyapolsky, emigrated 1988.

Podyapolsky, Grigory (1926–1976). Geophysicist, human rights activist.

Polezhaev, Alexander (1805–1838). Poet.

Politzer, David (1949–). Physicist.

Pomeranchuk, Isaak (1913–1966). Physicist, academician.

Pomerants, Grigory (1918–). Philosopher, dissident.

Ponomarev, Boris (1905–). Comintern administrator, candidate member of Politburo 1972–1986.

Ponomarev, Sergei (1940–). Writer, dissident.

Powell, Cecil (1903–1969). British physicist. Nobel Laureate in Physics, 1950.

Predvoditelev, Alexander (1891–1973). Physicist, dean of Moscow University in 1940s.

Prokhorov, Alexander (1916–). Physicist. Nobel Laureate in Physics, 1964.

Prokofiev, Sergei (1891–1953). Composer.

Protopopov, Alexei. Leningrad engineer, radiochemist, worked with Sakharov in Ulyanovsk.

Pugachev, Emelian (1726–1775). Leader of peasant rebellion.

Pushkin, Alexander (1799–1837). Russia's national poet.

Rabinovich, Matvei (c. 1920–1982). Physicist, classmate of Sakharov's at FIAN.

Radzinsky, Eduard (1936–). Playwright.

Razzhivina, Zoya (1928–). Ophthalmologist.

Regelson, Lev (1939–). Physicist, religious activist.

Rekubratsky, Vitaly (1935–1977). Biologist.

Rekunkov, Alexander (1920–). Procurator General of the USSR from 1981.

Retherford, Robert (1912–1981). Physicist.

Romanov, Yuri (c. 1920–). Physicist, a colleague of Sakharov's at the Installation.

Romaszewski, Zbigniew (1940–). Polish dissident, KOR member.

Romm, Mikhail (1901–1971). Film director.

Rost, Yuri (1939–). Journalist.

Ruban, Pyotr (1940–). Artist, dissident. Emigrated 1988.

Rudenko, Mykola (1920–). Ukrainian dissident, writer. Emigrated 1987.

Rumyantsev, Alexei (1905–). Economist, official, academician.

Ruppel, Friedrich (1923–). German emigration activist. Emigrated 1974.

Rutherford, Ernest (1871–1937). Physicist. Nobel Laureate in Chemistry, 1908.

Sakata, Shoichi (1911–1980). Physicist.

Sakharov, Dmitri (1889–1961). Physics teacher. Andrei Sakharov's father.

Sakharov, Dmitri [Dima] (1957–). Andrei Sakharov's son.

Sakharov, Ekaterina [née Sofiano] (1893–1963). Andrei Sakharov's mother.

Sakharov, Evgenia [Zhenya] (1890?–1974). Andrei Sakharov's aunt.

Sakharov, Georgy [Yura] (1925–). Chemist. Andrei Sakharov's brother.

Sakharov, Irina (1921–). Andrei Sakharov's cousin, daughter of Nikolai and Valya.

Sakharov, Ivan (1852–1918). Lawyer. Andrei Sakharov's paternal grandfather.

Sakharov, Ivan (1887–1943). Lawyer, banker. Andrei Sakharov's uncle.

Sakharov, Katya (1913–). Andrei Sakharov's cousin, daughter of Ivan and Evgenia.

Sakharov, Lyubov (1949–). Teacher. Andrei Sakharov's daughter.

Sakharov, Maria [née Domukhovskaya] (1862–1941). Andrei Sakharov's paternal grandmother.

Sakharov, Nikolai (1891–1971). Engineer. Andrei Sakharov's uncle.

Sakharov, Tatyana (1945–). Biologist. Andrei Sakharov's daughter.

Sakharov, Valentina [Valya] (?–1965). Andrei Sakharov's aunt.

Salam, Abdus (1926–). Pakistani physicist. Nobel Laureate in Physics, 1979.

Samoilov, Boris (1920–c. 1983). Physicist.

Samoilov, David (1920–1990). Poet.

Sarkisov, Gennady (?–1941). Engineer, husband of Sakharov's Aunt Tusya [née Sofiano].

Schrieffer, John (1931–). Physicist. Nobel Laureate in Physics, 1972.

Schwartz, Laurent (1915–). French mathematician.

Schwinger, Julian (1918–). U.S. physicist. Nobel Laureate in Physics, 1965.

Scriabin, Alexander (1892–1915). Composer.

Sedov, Leonid (1907–). Physicist, academician.

Semichastny, Vladimir (1917–). KGB head, 1961–1967.

Semyonov, Alexei (1956–). Elena Bonner's son. Emigrated 1978.

Semyonov, Ivan (1924–). Physician. First husband of Elena Bonner.

Shafarevich, Igor (1923–). Mathematician, dissident, Russian nationalist.

Shapiro, Fyodor (1915–1973). Physicist.

Shcharansky, Anatoly [now Natan Sharansky]. (1948–). Human rights activist. Deported 1986.

Shchelkin, Kirill (1911–). Physicist, administrator.

Shchelokov, Nikolai (1910–1984). General, state security official, Soviet interior minister, 1968–1982.

Sheinin, Lev (1906–1967). Chief Procuracy Investigator, writer.

Shelkov, Vladimir (1895–1980). Seventh-Day Adventist, religious activist. Died in labor camp.

Shevardnadze, Eduard (1928–). Party and government official, foreign minister since 1985.

Shikhanovich, Yuri (1933–). Mathematician, human rights activist.

Shinberg, Emil. Physician, friend of Elena Bonner.

Shirkov, Dmitri (1928–). Physicist.

Shklovsky, Iosif (1916–1986?). Physicist, administrator.

Shklovsky, Viktor (1893–1985). Literary critic.

Sholokhov, Mikhail (1905–1984). Writer, Nobel Laureate in Literature, 1965.

Shostakovich, Dmitri (1906–1975). Composer.

Shubin, Semyon (c. 1920–1937). Physicist, died in the Gulag.

Shumuk, Daniil (1914–   ). Ukrainian dissident. Emigrated 1987.

Sinyavsky, Andrei [pseud. Abram Tertz] (1925–   ). Writer and literary critic. Emigrated 1973.

Skobelev, Mikhail (1843–1882). Russian general.

Skobelov, Matvei (1885–1938). Onetime Menshevik, then Social Democrat; joined Bolsheviks, died in Gulag.

Skobeltsyn, Dmitri (1892–1977). Physicist, academician.

Skriabin, Georgy (1917–1988?). Biologist, Academy secretary.

Slavsky, Efim (1898–1988?). Engineer, Minister of Medum Machine Building (nuclear weapons).

Slepak, Vladimir (1927–   ). Electronics engineer, long-term refusenik.

Smirnov, Alexei (1951–   ). Dissident.

Smirnov, Leonid (1916–   ). Engineer, defense official.

Smirnov, Lev (1911–   ). Physicist, dissident.

Smirnov, Vladimir (1887–1974). Mathematician, academician.

Smyth, Henry deWolf (1898–1987?). Physicist, government adviser on atomic energy.

Snezhnevsky, Andrei (1904–1987?). Psychiatrist.

Sofiano, Alexei (1845–1929). General. Andrei Sakharov's maternal grandfather.

Sofiano, Ekaterina. *See* Sakharov, Ekaterina.

Sofiano, Konstantin (1890–1936). Engineer. Andrei Sakharov's uncle.

Sofiano, Zinaida [née Mukhanova] (1862–1943). Andrei Sakharov's maternal grandmother.

Solzhenitsyn, Alexander (1918–   ). Nobel Laureate in Literature, 1970.

Solzhenitsyn, Natalya (1940–   ). Mathematician, second wife of Alexander Solzhenitsyn.

Spitzer, Lyman (1914–   ). Physicist.

Stalin, Joseph (1879–1953). General Secretary of the Communist Party, 1922–1953.

Stepanian, Akop (1949–1979). Armenian nationalist. Executed for Moscow subway bombing.

Stone, Jeremy (1935–   ). Mathematician, president of Federation of American Scientists.

Stus, Vasyl (1938–1984). Ukrainian poet.

Sudarshan, Ennackal (1931–   ). Physicist.

Superfin, Gabriel (1944–   ). Literary critic, dissident.

Suslov, Mikhail (1902–1982). Party official. Chief Kremlin ideologist.

Suvorov, Alexander (1730–1800). Russian general.

Svetlichny, Ivan (1929–   ). Ukrainian poet, human rights activist.

Taksar, Alexander [Shura] (c. 1921–   ). Physicist, a classmate of Sakharov's at FIAN. Emigrated in mid-1970s.

Tamm, Igor (1895–1971). Physicist, Nobel Laureate in Physics, 1958.

Taylor, Theodore (1925–   ). Physicist, writer.

Terleckas, Antanas (1928–   ). Lithuanian dissident.

Ternovsky, Leonard (1933–   ). Physician, human rights activist.

Ter-Petrosian, Simon [Kamo] (1882–1922). Revolutionary, ally of Stalin. Instrumental in the Red Army's victory in the Caucasus, 1919–1920.

Tikhonov, Andrei (1906–   ). Mathematician and geophysicist, academician.

Tikhy, Oleksa (1927–1984). Ukrainian dissident, died in labor camp.

Timiryazev, Arkady. Physicist, university professor. Son of Kliment Timiryazev.

Timiryazev, Kliment (1843–1920). Botanist.

Timofeyev-Resovsky, Nikolai (1900–1981). Biologist.

Tito, Josip Broz (1892–1980). Yugoslav leader 1945–1980.

Togliatti, Palmiro (1893–1964). Italian Communist.

Tomonaga, Sin-itiro (1906–1979). Physicist.

Trapeznikov, Sergei (1912–   ). Party science and culture official, 1966–1983.

Treiman, Sam (1925–   ). Physicist.

Trutnev, Yuri (1927–   ). Physicist, academician.

Tsvigun, Semyon (1917–1982). General, state security official.

Tupolev, Andrei (1888–1972). Aircraft designer.

Turchin, Valentin (1931–   ). Mathematician, physicist, writer, human rights activist. Emigrated 1977.

Tvardovsky, Alexander (1920–1971). Poet and editor.

Tverdokhlebov, Andrei (1940–   ). Physicist, dissident. Emigrated 1980.

Ubozhko, Lev (1943–   ). Physicist, dissident.

Ustinov, Dmitri (1908–1989?). Marshal, defense official.

Vail, Boris (1939–   ). Dissident, writer.

Vannikov, Boris (1897–1962). General, defense official.

Vasilevsky, Alexander (1895–1977). Marshal.

Vavilov, Nikolai (1887–1943). Biologist.

Vavilov, Sergei (1891–1951). Physicist, Academy president 1945–1951.

Veksler, Vladimir (1907–1966). Physicist, administrator.

Velikanova, Tatyana (1932–   ). Mathematician, human rights activist.

Velikhov, Evgeny (1935–   ). Physicist, academician, administrator.

Veresaev, Vikenty (1867–1945). Populist writer.

Vikhirev, Alexei (1890–1975). Father of Sakharov's first wife, Klava.

Vikhireva, Klavdia [Klava] (1919–1969). Andrei Sakharov's first wife.

Vikhireva, Matryona [née Snezhkina] (1895–1987). Mother of Sakharov's first wife, Klava.

Vins, Georgy (1928–   ). Baptist preacher. Deported 1979.

Vladimov, Georgy (1931–   ). Writer. Emigrated 1975.

Vlasov, Anatoly. Physicist; one of Sakharov's professors.

Vlasov, Andrei (1900–1946). Soviet general, commanded Russian army units allied with Germans after his capture.

Vlodzimirsky, Lev (c. 1910–1953). State security official, arrested and executed after Beria's fall.

Volkov, Oleg. Ecologist, writer.

Von Neumann, John (1903–1957). Mathematician and information scientist.

Voronel, Alexander (1931–   ). Physicist, Jewish emigration activist. Emigrated in 1970s.

Voroshilov, Kliment (1881–1969). Marshal.

Vuchetich, Evgeny (1908–1974). Sculptor.

Vyshinsky, Andrei (1883–1954). State prosecutor during show trials of 1930s; Procurator General of the USSR; Soviet UN representative, 1953–54.

Wajda, Andrzej (1926–   ). Polish film director.

Wallenberg, Raoul (1912–1947?). Swedish diplomat arrested by the Soviet army in Budapest in 1945.

Watson, James (1928–   ). U.S. biologist, Nobel Laureate in Physiology, 1962.

Weisskopf, Victor (1908–   ). Physicist, director of CERN.

Wheeler, John (1911–1988). U.S. physicist.

Wick, Gian Carlo (1909–   ). Physicist.

Wiesner, Jerome (1915–   ). Physicist, president of MIT.

Wilczek, Frank (1951–   ). Physicist.

Wilson, Robert (1914–   ). Physicist. Nobel Laureate in Physics, 1978.

Yaglom, Akiva (c. 1920–   ). Physicist, twin brother of Isaak.

Yaglom, Isaak (c. 1920–   ). Mathematician, twin brother of Akiva.

Yakir, Pyotr (1923–1982). Historian, dissident.

Yakobson, Anatoly (1935–1978). Editor, literary critic, human rights activist. Emigrated 1973.

Yakovlev, Nikolai (1927–   ). Historian, writer.

Yakunin, Gleb (1934–   ). Russian Orthodox priest and religious activist.

Yakushkin, Nikolai (?–1945). Economist. Andrei Sakharov's uncle.

Yakushkin, Tatyana [née Sakharov] (1883–1977). English teacher. Andrei Sakharov's aunt.

Yang Chen-ning (1922–   ). Physicist. Nobel Laureate in Physics, 1957.

Yankelevich, Efrem (1950–   ). Electronic engineer, son-in-law of Elena Bonner. Emigrated 1977.

Yankelevich, Tatiana [née Semyonov] (1950–   ). Daughter of Elena Bonner. Emigrated 1977.

Zababakhin, Evgeny (1917–   ). Physicist, academician, a colleague of Sakharov's at the Installation.

Zadunaiskaya, Zoya (1903–1983). Litterateur, friend of Elena Bonner.

Zalmanson, Izrail (1949–   ). Leningrad "skyjacker."

Zalmanson, Silva (1943–   ). Engineer, wife of Eduard Kuznetsov. Emigrated 1974.

Zalmanson, Wolf (1942–   ). Leningrad "skyjacker." Emigrated 1979.

Zatikian, Stepan (1946–1979). Armenian nationalist, executed for Moscow subway bombing.

Zavenyagin, Avraami (1901–1956). State security official, minister of Medium Machine-Building in 1950s.

Zeldovich, Yakov (1914–1987). Physicist, Sakharov's friend and colleague.

Zhavoronkov, Nikalai (1907–   ). Chemist, academician.

Zhdanov, Andrei (1896–1948). Stalin's commissar of culture.

Zhivlyuk, Yuri (c. 1930–   ). Physicist, dissident.

Zhukov, Georgy (1896–1974). Marshal, popular World War II commander.

Zikmund, Miroslav (1919–   ). Czech writer.

Zinoviev, Grigory (1883–1936). Associate of Lenin; recanted during show trials.

Zivs, Samuil (1921–   ). Lawyer, member of Soviet anti-Zionist Committee.

Zysin, Yuri (c. 1920–1987). Physicist, a colleague of Sakharov's at the Installation.

INDEX

ACKNOWLEDGMENTS

Grateful acknowledgment is made to the following for
permission to reprint previously published material:

Ardis Publishers and *Walter Arndt:* Excerpt from
Alexander Pushkin: Collected Narrative and Lyrical Poetry,
translated and edited by Walter Arndt (Ardis, 1984).
Copyright © 1984. Reprinted by permission of Ardis
Publishers and Walter Arndt.

Walter Arndt: Copyright © 1972, excerpt from *Pushkin
Threefold,* translated and edited by Walter Arndt. Reprinted
by permission of Walter Arndt. *Atheneum Publishers* and
Oxford University Press: Excerpt from "Tristia" from *Osip
Mandelstam: Selected Poems,* translated by Clarence Brown
and W. S. Merwin. Copyright © 1973 by Clarence Brown
and W. S. Merwin. Reprinted by permission of Atheneum
Publishers, an imprint of Macmillan Publishing Company,
and Oxford University Press, Oxford, England.

Marcel Dekker, Inc.: Excerpt from *Collected Scientific
Works* by Andrei Sakharov (Marcel Dekker, Inc., 1982, p.
iii). Reprinted by permission of Marcel Dekker, Inc.

Foreign Affairs: Excerpts from "The Danger of
Thermonuclear War" by Andrei Sakharov, *Foreign Affairs,*
Summer 1983. Copyright © 1983 by the Council on
Foreign Relations, Inc. Reprinted by permission of *Foreign
Affairs.*

Harper & Row, Publishers, Inc. and *William Collins Sons
& Co., Ltd.:* Excerpt from *The Oak and the Calf* by
Alexander Solzhenitsyn. Copyright © 1975 by Alexander
Solzhenitsyn. English-language translation copyright ©
1979, 1980 by Harper & Row, Publishers, Inc. Rights
outside the U.S. and Canada administered by William
Collins Sons & Co., Ltd. Reprinted by permission of the
publishers.

Alfred A. Knopf, Inc.: Excerpts from *Alarm and Hope* by
Andrei Sakharov. Copyright © 1978 by Alfred A. Knopf,
Inc. Reprinted by permission of Alfred A. Knopf, Inc.

Alfred A. Knopf, Inc. and *William Collins Sons & Co.,
Ltd.:* Excerpts from *Sakharov Speaks* by Andrei Sakharov.

A NOTE ON THE TYPE

The text of this book was set in Electra, a typeface designed by W. A. Dwiggins (1880-1956). This face cannot be classified as either modern or old style. It is not based on any historical model, nor does it echo any particular period or style. It avoids the extreme contrasts between thick and thin elements that mark most modern faces, and attempts to give a feeling of fluidity, power, and speed.

Composed by The Haddon Craftsmen, Inc., Scranton, Pennsylvania.